Trade and Human Health and Safety

This book gathers papers from distinguished experts discussing how health-based, trade-restrictive measures have fared in World Trade Organization (WTO) case law. With an analysis of applicable primary law (General Agreement on Tariffs and Trade [GATT], Technical Barriers to Trade [TBT], and Sanitary and Phytosanitary Measures Agreement [SPS]) and all case law in the area of trade and health, this book offers a comprehensive discussion of the standards established for the regulation of public health and safety issues. Experts in the field answer two important questions – How can a country which is a member of the WTO define its policy on health issues? and What are the WTO constraints on the exercise of health policy, if any? The various contributions in this volume aim to demonstrate how the world trading regime has come of age and accepted that trade liberalization cannot take place at the expense of nationally defined social values.

George A. Bermann is the Walter Gellhorn Professor of Law and Jean Monnet Professor of European Union Law at Columbia Law School. He is also the Director of the European Legal Studies Center at Columbia. He is co-editor-in-chief of *American Journal of Comparative Law* and founder and chair of *Columbia Journal of European Law*.

Petros C. Mavroidis is Edwin B. Parker Professor of Foreign and Comparative Law at Columbia Law School and professor at the University of Neuchatel (Switzerland). He is also a research fellow for the Center for Economic Policy Research (CEPR). He has worked in the WTO's legal division since the 1990s and has written extensively on the organization and its predecessor, GATT. He is also involved with the American Law Institute as a chief co-reporter on the principles of WTO law.

Trade and Human Health and Safety

Edited by

George A. Bermann
Columbia Law School

Petros C. Mavroidis
Columbia Law School

CAMBRIDGE UNIVERSITY PRESS
Cambridge, New York, Melbourne, Madrid, Cape Town,
Singapore, São Paulo, Delhi, Tokyo, Mexico City

Cambridge University Press
32 Avenue of the Americas, New York, NY 10013-2473, USA

www.cambridge.org
Information on this title: www.cambridge.org/9780521384377

© George A. Bermann and Petros C. Mavroidis 2006

This publication is in copyright. Subject to statutory exception
and to the provisions of relevant collective licensing agreements,
no reproduction of any part may take place without the written
permission of Cambridge University Press.

First published 2006
First paperback edition 2011

A catalog record for this publication is available from the British Library

Library of Congress Cataloging in Publication data

Trade and human health and safety / edited by George A. Bermann, Petros C. Mavroidis.
    p.   cm.
Includes bibliographical references and index.
ISBN-13: 978-0-521-85528-0 (hardback)
ISBN-10: 0-521-85528-4 (hardback)
1. Product safety – Law and legislation.   2. Hazardous substances – Law and legislation.
3. Public health laws.   4. Foreign trade regulation.   I. Bermann, George A.
II. Mavroidis, Petros C.   III. Title.
K3663.T68   2005
344.04'7 – dc22   2005018122

ISBN 978-0-521-85528-0 Hardback
ISBN 978-0-521-38437-7 Paperback

Cambridge University Press has no responsibility for the persistence or
accuracy of URLs for external or third-party internet websites referred to in
this publication, and does not guarantee that any content on such websites is,
or will remain, accurate or appropriate.

Contents

Preface to the Series   *page* vii

Introductory Remarks   1
George A. Bermann and Petros C. Mavroidis

1   **A Map of the World Trade Organization Law of Domestic Regulation of Goods**   9
Gabrielle Marceau and Joel P. Trachtman

2   **The WTO Impact on Internal Regulations: A Case Study of the *Canada–EC Asbestos* Dispute**   77
Robert Howse and Elisabeth Türk

3   **Reflections on the Appellate Body Decision in the *Hormones* Case and the Meaning of the SPS Agreement**   118
William J. Davey

4   **The Salmon Case: Evolution of Balancing Mechanisms for Non-Trade Values in WTO**   133
Frank J. Garcia

5   **Lotus Eaters: Reflections on the *Varietals* Dispute, the SPS Agreement and WTO Dispute Resolution**   153
Jeffrey L. Dunoff

6   **Regulatory Purpose and "Like Products" in Article III:4 of the GATT (with Additional Remarks on Article III:2)**   190
Donald H. Regan

7   **The WTO Standard of Review in Health and Safety Disputes**   224
David Palmeter

8   **Expert Advice in WTO Dispute Settlement**   235
Joost Pauwelyn

9   Domestic Regulation, Sovereignty and Scientific Evidence
    Requirements: A Pessimistic View   257
    Alan O. Sykes

10 Time for a United Nations' "Global Compact" for Integrating Human
    Rights into the Law of Worldwide Organizations: Lessons from
    European Integration Law for Global Integration Law   271
    Ernst-Ulrich Petersmann

Index   327

Preface to the Series

This is the first volume of the Columbia Law School series on "The Law and Policy of the World Trade Organization." This series, consisting of biennial thematic volumes, is based upon the papers presented in the Seminar in WTO Law and Policy organized every fall semester at Columbia. Each volume – representing the papers that will have been presented in that seminar over a two-year period – addresses different, but always vital, aspects of the WTO integration process. The contributors are, without exception, outstanding experts in their field of expertise, and they include economists, political scientists, and lawyers, all specializing in the WTO. By the time these volumes appear, each author will have in principle benefited from presentation and discussion of their work in a Columbia Law School seminar composed of a highly select group of WTO students.

WTO law is a dynamic and richly evolving field, and the series will reflect that reality. Upcoming volumes will deal with WTO law and developing countries; intellectual property in the WTO; and the WTO dispute resolution process.

George A. Bermann
Jean Monnet Professor of European Union Law
Walter Gellhorn Professor of Law
Columbia Law School

Petros C. Mavroidis
Edwin B. Parker Professor of Foreign
 and Comparative Law
Columbia Law School

GEORGE A. BERMANN AND PETROS C. MAVROIDIS

Introductory Remarks

I. The Issue

In this volume, we aim to present a comprehensive discussion of the constraints that the WTO agreement imposes on national health policies. The primary WTO texts, to some extent, address this question, and there are by now a number of cases that have dealt with the issue. Health policies are of course domestic policies which may be enforced, either internally or at the border, based on efficiency criteria. There is nothing like a world health policy, that is, some sort of transfer of sovereignty to the world plane to this effect. Cooperation at the world level takes place among governments, usually under the auspices of the WHO (World Health Organization). However, there is evidence, in recent years, of substantial cooperation on this front through non-governmental organizations as well.

Of special interest in this volume is the "conflict" between health policies and trade liberalization. In principle, anything can affect trade flows, health-based measures included. However, it would be unreasonable for governments to enter into contractual arrangements with other governments by which, in the name of trade liberalization, they agree to succumb and expose their populations to health externalities.

The WTO Agreement regulates the interplay between trade and health in various places. The GATS (the General Agreement on Trade in Services) is not immune to such concerns either. Safety regulations in the supply of services can largely affect the supply as such and their trade component as well. This relationship, however, is not the exclusive concern of primary WTO law. The August 2003 decision on pharmaceuticals made the headlines, deservedly so for a series of reasons. TRIPs (the WTO agreement on trade-related intellectual property rights) had been portrayed – mostly rightly so – as a means of transferring wealth from the south to the north. By extending the possibilities of compulsory licensing, the August 2003 decision went some distance toward addressing that concern.

Still, it is no exaggeration to say that the bulk of the discussion of trade and health so far has taken place within the GATT and its annexes.

II. The GATT

The founding fathers of GATT were aware that states may have recourse to "beggar thy neighbour" policies, not only through border measures, but also through internal measures. This is essentially an application of the "equivalence proposition," as explained in economic theory (Lerner theorem). In principle, both border and internal measures can be the subject of a trade contract. The amount of work associated with contracting the latter, however, should not be underestimated. Indeed, negotiators need not only lay out each and every policy which potentially affects trade; they need also to contract specific obligations each and every time the exercise of such policies actually impacts on trade.[1]

The first leg of this exercise is quite demanding: indeed, it is almost impossible to exclude a policy straight off, arguing that it does not affect trade. At least potentially or indirectly, almost all policies (even those most remotely connected to trade) affect trade. On the other hand, policies change, as revealed preferences of societies change over time, and, consequently, there is an unavoidable need to renegotiate the original contract. Besides, contracting social policies might be deemed politically undesirable in some domestic quarters. For all these reasons, and probably others as well, the GATT founding fathers opted for an incomplete contract when designing the disciplines to be applied in shaping domestic policies.[2] They were well aware that various policies, including health, might have an impact on trade, and this is why they decided to discipline the exercise of these policies. They did not, however, proceed to enumerate every one of them, nor did they provide specific disciplines for each. They opted for an incomplete contract in this respect, imposing essentially one obligation on all trading partners: any time a domestic policy has an impact on trade, it must be exercised in a non-discriminatory manner; that is, it must address all products affected in an origin-neutral manner.

There is, of course, a necessary by-product. By opting for an incomplete contract in this respect, and allowing WTO Members to unilaterally define their policies affecting trade, the founding fathers of the GATT, indirectly but clearly, prescribed the legal nature of the GATT. Because domestic policies affecting trade will continue to be unilaterally defined, the GATT is a negative integration type of contract. There is no compulsory adherence to international standards, and there is no pre-defined set of policies to which all WTO Members must subscribe.[3]

The end result is that WTO Members cannot through internal measures afford protection to domestic production. All protection[4] under the GATT regime is a matter of negotiation and must, in light of Article XI of GATT, take the form of tariff protection. In other words, once imported products have paid their ticket of entry (in the form of tariffs) into a particular market, they must be assimilated to domestic products and be subjected to a regulatory regime identical to that applied to domestic products. This means that tariff commitments will not be allowed to become meaningless, as

---

[1] It is also quite onerous to write in payoffs, à la Maskin and Tirole (1999), because, as will become obvious, the nature of the GATT Agreement is such that calculating payoffs is far from a mundane exercise.

[2] See the analysis along these lines in Horn and Mavroidis (2004).

[3] A notable exception is of course TRIPs, adherence to which is compulsory for all WTO Members. Some steps towards positive integration are taken through the incorporation of international standards into the WTO legal regime, by virtue of the TBT and the SPS agreements.

[4] As will be shown *infra*, protection is an elusive notion. Although there are various approaches and suggested definitions in economic theory, we still lack an *operational* definition of this term. On this issue, see Bagwell and Staiger (1995), Bagwell et al. (2002), Grossman and Helpman (2002), Horn (2004), and Neven (2001).

Introductory Remarks

a result of unilaterally defined internal policies. WTO Members, in turn, will have an incentive to continue negotiating and further liberalizing trade, knowing that the end-product of their negotiation will not be undone through subsequent actions that they cannot influence. This is in essence the rationale for the inclusion of the national treatment obligation in the GATT.

This rationale for the inclusion of the national treatment obligation in the GATT has been espoused by the Appellate Body. On page 16 of its report on *Japan – Taxes on Alcoholic Beverages* (WTO Doc. WT/DS 8, 10 and 11/AB/R of 4 October 1996), the Appellate Body pertinently stated:

> ... The broad and fundamental purpose of Article III is to avoid protectionism in the application of internal tax and regulatory measures. More specifically, the purpose of Article III is to ensure that internal measures 'not be applied to imported or domestic products so as to afford protection to domestic production'. Toward this end, Article III obliges Members of the WTO to provide equality of competitive conditions for imported products in relation to domestic products.

The national treatment obligation is therefore a promise given by each WTO Member to its trading partners, but at the same time also a sanction. Policies will be unilaterally defined, and they will eventually have international spill-over (or externalities). Adherence to the national treatment principle guarantees "tolerance" of their international spill-over. From an evidence perspective, because for all practical purposes we are operating here under conditions of informational asymmetry, adherence to the national treatment principle can be also seen as a proxy that the regulation at hand does not operate "so as to afford protection."

We should note at the outset that the national treatment obligation is assumed with respect to laws affecting goods, irrespective whether they are subjected to bound or unbound duties. We quote from page 17 of the Appellate Body report on *Japan – Taxes on Alcoholic Beverages* (WTO Doc. WT/DS 8, 10 and 11/AB/R of 4 October 1996):

> ... The Article III national treatment obligation is a general prohibition on the use of internal taxes and other internal regulatory measures so as to afford protection to domestic production. This obligation clearly extends also to products not bound under Article II.

According to the wording of Article III of GATT, the national treatment obligation extends to regulatory interventions of both a fiscal (Article III:2 GATT) and non-fiscal nature (Article III:4 GATT). However, two measures are explicitly exempted from the national treatment obligation by virtue of Article III:8 of GATT: subsidies and government procurement. Government procurement is not regulated in the context of a multilateral agreement. WTO Members interested in disciplining this activity have entered into a separate contractual arrangement. The agreement on government procurement (GPA) is a plurilateral agreement which, in a nutshell, reintroduces the national treatment obligation for the list of entities (and for purchases above an agreed monetary threshold) as to which each participant has made a commitment.[5]

---

[5] See, on this issue, the various contributions in Hoekman and Mavroidis (1997).

This means that health policies will be unilaterally defined and, to the extent that they affect trade, will have to be exercised in a non-discriminatory manner. Discrimination, however, is a highly elastic notion. The level of disaggregation is crucial in defining whether discrimination has occurred, as is the benchmark (standard of review) that will be adopted by adjudicating bodies to define whether discrimination has occurred, or not. For this, recourse to WTO case law is indispensable.

III. TBT and SPS

The TBT (WTO Agreement on Technical Barriers to Trade) and SPS (WTO Agreement on Sanitary and Phyto-Sanitary Measures) are both relevant to the trade and health discussion. The TBT, in its Article 2.2, explicitly mentions "human health" in the body of an indicative list reflecting the obligations of WTO Members when pursuing their regulatory objectives. The same is true for SPS; the very definition of an SPS measure in the Annex to the Agreement makes it clear that the disciplines imposed concern, *inter alia*, protection of human health.

In contrast to the GATT, the TBT and the SPS agreements fine-tune the non-discrimination obligation. Recourse to proxies, such as scientific evidence, coherence in shaping national health policies, and necessity of the intervention, are employed to facilitate the quest for truth. Assume that country A enacts legislation which is ostensibly based on health concerns but which negatively affects international trade flows. B, a trading partner of A, doubts whether A's policies are health-mandated and introduces a complaint before a WTO adjudicating body. A is the informed, and B the uninformed, party as to what prompted the enactment of the challenged legislation.

The explicit wording of the GATT, TBT, and SPS leaves no room for doubt that trade can be blocked (or reduced), if such a measure is necessary to protect health. So, in principle, health protection may be privileged over trade liberalization. However, in order to ensure that trade has been blocked on genuine health protection grounds, the TBT and the SPS impose, alongside the obligation not to discriminate, additional obligations. In an asymmetry of information context, as in the example of A and B above, intelligent proxies are, in the current state of affairs, an appropriate means of distinguishing wheat from chaff.

IV. The Contributions in This Volume

The various contributions in this volume aim to shed light on all of those issues.

Marceau and Trachtman kick off with a discussion of the relevant legal provisions of the SPS, TBT, and the GATT, and the institutional interplay among them. They note that the three agreements provide norms having subtle but important variations, and that, consequently, it is necessary to evaluate these variations and determine the applicability of these norms. Their analysis provides both a "map" through the highways and byways of the WTO law of domestic regulation of goods and a basis for achieving greater coherence among these agreements. In their view, it is clear that the GATT has concentrated on negative integration, and its negative integration norms remain applicable, while being supplemented in some instances by the SPS and TBT agreements. On the other hand, they note that the SPS and

Introductory Remarks

TBT agreements lend greater support for positive integration, through strengthened incentives for adoption of international standards and promotion of recognition and harmonization. They note too that there are a number of instances of differences in the substantive obligations under these three agreements. Some of the differences, in their view, result in varying room for protectionism and for domestic regulatory autonomy. They would support, in future negotiations, discussions aiming at greater convergence. It is also possible, they note, that the interpretative process of dispute settlement will itself yield a degree of convergence. Already, the jurisprudence seems to read into GATT provisions, and in particular Article XX of GATT, criteria and requirements that are specifically dealt with in the TBT and SPS agreements.

Following analysis of the relevant legal provisions and the interplay among them, we move to the contributions discussing, from a critical perspective, the interpretation of the main provisions in the relevant WTO case law.

Howse and Türk discuss the notorious *Asbestos* litigation. In this case, the WTO adjudicating bodies were called upon to judge whether a French measure banning sales of construction material containing asbestos was consistent with the obligations of the European Community under the WTO. (Asbestos was scientifically proven to be a carcinogenic substance leading to one form of cancer, mesothelioma.) In their view, through this decision, the Appellate Body of the WTO introduced many important refinements in the interpretation and application of key provisions of the GATT that address the relationship of WTO law to internal regulation. Overall, the consequence of this ruling, they argue, is clearer and perhaps more ample assurance to regulators that non-protectionist domestic regulations enacted for important policy purposes will not be significantly constrained by WTO law. This consequence should enhance what another noted scholar, Joseph Weiler, has termed the "external legitimacy" of the WTO. The Appellate Body, they also argue, has at the same time moved in this direction in a manner that is sensitive to what Weiler terms "internal legitimacy." It has framed its interpretations within the evolving GATT/WTO *acquis*, avoiding bold colours and strokes in favour of subtler tones and finishes. In so doing, it has managed to paint a quite different picture from the one that GATT panels had painted in the *Tuna–Dolphin* case law, which, for all practical purposes, condemned unilateral environmental policies for being unilateral.

Davey discusses the famous *Hormones* litigation. The European Community had enacted legislation banning the imports of hormone-treated beef. In doing so, it deviated from an international standard regulating this matter without justifying its deviation. It did not base its measures on scientific evidence, and it did not invoke the precautionary principle. Following a complaint by the United States and Canada, the WTO adjudicating bodies held that the measure at hand was indeed WTO-inconsistent. Davey concludes that the *Hormones* decision of the Appellate Body tends to undermine the SPS Agreement by subverting the obligation to use international standards (although, as the author argues, the decision merely permits justification of lower standards and does not prevent the use of higher standards) and by finding no obligation to conduct a risk assessment prior to adopting SPS measures. The latter decision is perhaps not of great importance because, if challenged, a Member will have to have made a risk assessment and therefore has every incentive to conduct one in any event. Moreover, as Davey notes, at least in advanced democracies, the risk assessment process is mostly well-entrenched legally anyway.

Garcia's chapter is on *Salmon*, a dispute over an Australian measure banning imports of salmon on health grounds, if the fish are not treated in a particular manner. The author takes the view that the SPS "necessity" test has, through the Appellate Body's interpretation in *Salmon*, increased the likelihood that non-trade values will be respectfully considered in traditional Article XX GATT cases. At a minimum, the *Salmon* case, through its influence on cases such as *Korean-Beef* and *Asbestos*, has explicitly left room for consideration of such values in the case law, if not in the text itself. The main shortcoming of the AB's approach, in the author's view, is the possibility it leaves open that the panel will independently weigh the importance of the value pursued. This is disturbing, as this was the main defect identified in traditional Article XX GATT jurisprudence. It seems, the author notes, that for SPS measures, the political decision has been made to favour such measures, by privileging a member's own determination of the appropriate level of protection. Perhaps this is because, for SPS measures, the scientific evidence and risk assessment requirements constitute a check on the potential for protectionist abuse not available in standard Article XX GATT cases. Nevertheless, one can only wonder whether the cure is worse than the disease. Is there no other way, he asks, to address the risk of protectionism, say through the chapeau test, other than to permit a trade panel to independently assess the importance of the values chosen for protection by the Member?

Dunoff deals with the very interesting *Varietals* dispute. In this case Japan invoked *inter alia*, the precautionary principle in order to justify a measure which aimed at the protection of a series of commodities. The burden of Dunoff's chapter is to show that the *Varietals* dispute is less interesting for its specific facts and result than it is for the insights it provides into the structure of the SPS Agreement and the WTO more generally. The author sheds light on the underlying legal structure within which WTO Members find themselves enmeshed, the need to look beyond the agreement's text and WTO dispute resolution reports (at least if we are to understand adequately the effect of the SPS Agreement), and an effective political strategy that panels and the AB might adopt in politically charged areas such as food safety. For these reasons, the *Varietals* dispute, despite its anodyne facts and seemingly technical reports, is worthy of sustained study.

Regan deals with a "horizontal" issue, namely, the standard of review that WTO adjudicating bodies should and do adopt when dealing with non-discrimination cases. Although his chapter focuses on Article III of GATT, its analysis and conclusions are worth reflecting upon even in the TBT and the SPS contexts. Consideration of regulatory purpose, the author argues, is required by the ordinary meaning of "like products" in the context of Article III:4 of GATT. "Like products" must be interpreted in light of the "so as to afford protection" policy of Article III:1 of GATT, and the existence of protectionism depends on regulatory purpose. Ordinary linguistic usage confirms this, as do both the role of Article III in the GATT as a whole and economic theory. (Regulation with a non-protectionist purpose should be presumed by WTO tribunals to optimize local interests, and in the trade context, that is enough to guarantee global efficiency.)

Palmeter's take on the same issue (that is, the standard of review in non-discrimination cases) reflects a different, although not necessarily divergent, perspective. In his view, the Appellate Body's *Asbestos* analysis was not, formally, a standard of review analysis. The issue was not the standard applied by the Panel to the

Introductory Remarks

decision of the French authorities; rather, it was a legal analysis of the national treatment provisions of Article III:4 of GATT, based on the undisputed fact that chrysotile fibres are highly toxic and their substitutes are not. The panel's factual analysis might have been "objective," in the Appellate Body's view, but it was legally incorrect. Still, the author argues, in a broader and perhaps more practical sense, the Appellate Body's *Asbestos* opinion suggests an unspoken sympathy for what it views as well-intentioned health and safety measures. The verbal formulae of standards of review serve the purpose of attempting to draw lines, but verbal formulae are inevitably unclear at some level and open to interpretation. Most complex fact situations can be described in ways that will fit into just about any verbal formula. It really comes down, then, to the facts and how they are viewed by the tribunal. The author cites Robert Hudec, the quintessential trade lawyer, who had observed, in another context, that tribunals frequently "decide the case as best they can by making a 'seat-of-the-pants' judgment about whether the defendant government is behaving correctly or incorrectly – a process of judgment known in some circles as the 'smell test.' " The decisions of panels and the Appellate Body in disputes involving health and safety measures suggest that the "smell test" is alive and well in the WTO.

We then shift gears and turn to one of the most controversial issues in health-related disputes, the implications of the use of expert witnesses. Because at least some of the regulatory interventions will be based on scientific evidence, and because disagreements on this score cannot be *a priori* excluded, WTO judges might find themselves called upon to adjudicate a scientific disagreement. WTO judges, however, more likely than not lack the necessary expertise to opine on such issues. One way out is through court-appointed experts whose testimony can be *ex officio* requested by WTO adjudicating bodies. Court-appointed experts, though, have their own incentive structure and, as a result, the judge might find himself back at square one. Two chapters discuss this issue.

Pauwelyn first performs a reality check. The WTO judiciary makes increasing use of expert advice. This development, in his view, must be applauded, for it helps ensure the quality, transparency, and legitimacy of WTO decisions, in particular those that cut across a number of societal values. The input of expert and other "outside" opinions highlights the complex nature of WTO dispute settlement. It forms, he argues, a process in which a large number of agents interact: the panel, the Appellate Body, the parties and third parties, party-appointed experts and panel experts, standing technical bodies and political WTO organs, *amici curiae*, and other international organisations. As long as the WTO judiciary remains in control of this complex interaction, such dialogue can only be beneficial.

Sykes takes a more general view of this discussion. The battle, he argues, between the proponents of open trade and the proponents of national "sovereignty" has been central to the political fortunes of the WTO since its inception. Defenders of the system regularly insist that the tension is illusory, and that WTO rules do not intrude on proper national prerogatives. Without taking any normative position on the matter, this chapter argues that, in some contexts, a serious tension does indeed arise, and that the goals of open trade and respect for national sovereignty can be irreconcilably at odds, to the point that one of them simply must give way. With particular regard to the scientific evidence requirements of the SPS Agreement, the Appellate Body has embarked on a course that unmistakably elevates the policing of trade-restrictive measures above the ability of national governments to address risk in the face of scientific uncertainty. There is little alternative, he concludes, to such a policy if scientific evidence requirements are to serve as more than window dressing.

Petersmann's chapter is a look into the future. The author places human health among human rights and addresses the more general question as to how the symbiosis between human rights and the world trading regime can evolve in harmony. The author argues that the universal recognition and protection of inalienable human rights at national, regional, and worldwide levels requires a new human rights culture and a citizen-oriented national and international constitutional framework different from prevailing state-centered conceptions and from pure functionalism. The author borrows from the European experience, where the emergence of "multi-level governance" has led to "multi-level constitutionalism" and "divided-power systems" that have succeeded in overcoming Europe's history of periodic wars and of the "constitutional failures" of nation-states to protect human rights and a peaceful division of labour across frontiers. Just as within federal states, "the federal and state Governments are in fact but different agents and trustees of the people, instituted with different powers, and designated for different purposes," international law and international organizations must be understood, the author goes on to claim, as parts of the constitutional apparatus, limiting abuses of foreign policy powers so as to protect human rights more effectively. He concludes that national constitutional law and human rights principles cannot achieve their objectives unless they are supplemented by international constitutional law and by effective protection of human rights – in the economy no less than in the polity.

BIBLIOGRAPHICAL REFERENCES

Bagwell, Kyle, Petros C. Mavroidis, and Robert W. Staiger. 2002. It is all about market access, *American Journal of International Law*, 96: 56–76.

Bagwell, Kyle, and Robert W. Staiger. 1995. Protection and the business cycle, *NBER Discussion Paper 5168*, available at http://ideas.repec.org/s/att/wimass.html.

Grossman, Gene M., and Elhanan Helpman. 2002. *Interest groups and trade policy*, Princeton University Press: Princeton, NJ.

Hoekman, Bernard, and Petros C. Mavroidis. 1997. *Law and policy in public purchasing: The WTO Agreement on Government Procurement*, The University of Michigan Press: Ann Arbor, MI.

Horn, Henrik. 2004. National treatment in trade agreements. *Mimeo, American Economic Review*, 2006.

Horn, Henrik, and Petros C. Mavroidis. 2004. Still hazy after all these years: The interpretation of national treatment in the GATT/WTO case-law on tax discrimination. *European Journal of International Law*, 15: 39–69.

Maskin, Eric, and Jean Tirole. 1999. Unforeseen contingencies, property rights and incomplete contracts, *Review of Economic Studies*, 66: 83–114.

Neven, Damien Jules. 2001. How should protection be evaluated in Article III GATT disputes? *European Journal of Political Economy*, 17: 421–44.

GABRIELLE MARCEAU AND JOEL P. TRACHTMAN[1]

1. A Map of the World Trade Organization Law of Domestic Regulation of Goods

The Technical Barriers to Trade Agreement, the Sanitary and Phytosanitary Measures Agreement and the General Agreement on Tariffs and Trade

I. Introduction

Free trade and regulatory autonomy are often at odds with one another. National measures of an importing state may impose costs on international trade, for example, by regulating goods in ways that vary from home market regulation. National measures may restrict market access of imported goods but may or may not be intended to act as protectionist measures favouring domestic industry to the detriment of imports. At the same time, domestic regulation may protect important values. The distinction between a protectionist measure – condemned for imposing discriminatory or unjustifiable costs – and a non-protectionist measure – restricting trade incidentally (and thus imposing some costs) – is difficult to make.

The search for the right balance between disciplining protectionist measures[2] and allowing Member states to maintain regulatory autonomy has characterized the evolution of the General Agreement on Tariffs and Trade (GATT) rules – namely Articles I, III, XI and XX of GATT; the Technical Barriers to Trade Agreement (TBT)[3] and the Sanitary and Phytosanitary Measures Agreement (SPS).[4] This chapter compares the disciplines on domestic regulation contained in each of these agreements, and provides an analysis of the conditions for application of each agreement and the possibility for overlap and conflict among these agreements.

---

[1] Adapted with permission from Kluwer Law International from Gabrielle Marceau and Joel P. Trachtman, "The Technical Barriers to Trade Agreement, the Sanitary and Phytosanitary Measures Agreement and the General Agreement on Tariffs and Trade: A Map of the World Trade Organization Law of Domestic Regulation of Goods", *Journal of World Trade*, Vol. 36, No. 5 (October 2002), pp. 811–81. The views expressed in this article are personal to the authors and do not bind the WTO Secretariat or its Members. The authors are grateful to George Bermann, Bill Davey, Lothar Ehring, Marisa Goldstein, Merit Janow, Lia Mammiashvili, Petros Mavroidis, Joost Pauwelyn, Lisa Pearlman and Elisabeth Türk for their useful comments on earlier drafts. We are responsible for all opinions and errors herein.

[2] See the first paragraph of the Preamble of the Uruguay Round Ministerial Declaration: "Determined to halt and reverse protectionism and to remove distortions on trade", Ministerial Declaration on the Uruguay Round of 20 September 1986, BISD 33S/19; as well as the first paragraph of the Doha Development Agenda: "... We strongly reaffirm the principles and objectives set out in the Marrakesh Agreement Establishing the WTO and pledge to reject the use of protectionism", WT/MIN(01)/DEC (2001).

[3] Agreement on Technical Barriers to Trade, 15 April 1994, Marrakesh Agreement Establishing the World Trade Organization (hereinafter WTO Agreement), Annex 1A, *Legal Instruments – Results of the Uruguay Round*, Vol. 31, at p. 138 (hereinafter TBT Agreement).

[4] Agreement on the Application of Sanitary and Phytosanitary Measures, 15 April 1994, WTO Agreement, Annex 1A, *Legal Instruments – Results of the Uruguay Round*, at p. 69 (hereinafter SPS Agreement).

Although the Marrakesh Agreement Establishing the World Trade Organization (WTO) and its annexes (WTO Agreement) is today a single treaty, its provisions were originally negotiated through fifteen different working groups,[5] which may not have been sufficiently co-ordinated with one another. It was only towards the end of the negotiation that the creation of a "single undertaking"[6] was agreed on and governments decided to annex the resulting text from each working group to the Marrakesh Agreement Establishing the WTO.[7] Although some efforts of legal co-ordination must have been made, the late action of the Legal Drafting Group,[8] combined with the resistance by the United States to the creation of a formal international organization, must have limited the ability to make changes to the texts already drafted in working groups. In grouping under a framework agreement various negotiated texts, without any extensive discussion of the internal organization and hierarchy of WTO norms, negotiators may have hoped that the flexibility inherent in some of the WTO treaty provisions would suffice to reconcile all tensions among its various provisions. The wording of some WTO provisions does not always support such hope. It becomes very difficult to define clearly and precisely the legal parameters of the relationships among the provisions of different WTO agreements.

This chapter focuses mainly on the relationship between Articles III, XI and XX of GATT; the TBT Agreement and the SPS Agreement, all of which impose different regulatory constraints on government actions relating to standards, technical and sanitary regulations, etc. We have therefore identified disciplines (inherent and common to each set of provisions and often specifically addressed in the TBT or SPS Agreements), compared them, discussed their interaction and suggested some understandings. We have explored the avenues offered by teleological, contextual

---

[5] Ministerial Declaration on the Uruguay Round of 20 September 1986, BISD 33S/19.

[6] During the Uruguay Round negotiations the concept of a single undertaking was widely used. It refers to two different concepts: the "single political undertaking" referred to the method of negotiations ["nothing is agreed until everything is agreed", which was not inconsistent with the possibility of early implementation (early harvest)]; and the "single legal undertaking" which refers to the notion that the results of the negotiations would form a "single package" to be implemented as one single treaty. Both concepts are reflected in the Part I:B(ii) of the Uruguay Round Declaration: "The launching, the *conduct* and the *implementation of the outcome* of the negotiations shall be treated as *parts of a single undertaking*. However, agreements reached at an early stage may be implemented on a provisional or a definitive basis by agreement prior to the formal conclusion of the negotiations. Early agreements shall be taken into account in assessing the overall balance of the negotiations" BISD 33S/19 (emphasis added).

[7] The Marrakesh Agreement Establishing the World Trade Organization together with its annexes form the "WTO Agreement". When reference is made to the Marrakesh Agreement, the intention is to focus on the institutional agreement itself. Although the European Communities, Canada and Mexico put forward a draft for the creation of a multilateral trade organization (MTO) in autumn 1991, it was only in October and November 1993, during the intensive negotiations of the Institutional Group (chaired by Ambassador Lacarte, until recently a member of the Appellate Body), that discussions on the relationship between the various provisions of this "single undertaking" took place. Since its inception, the idea of an MTO was strongly resisted by the United States, which kept a reservation on this chapter until midnight on 14 December 1993. Only then, arguably after sufficient concessions from others, did the United States lift its reservation. See Debra Steger, "WTO: A New Constitution for the Trading System", in M. Bronckers and R. Quick (Eds.), *New Directions in International Economic Law: Essays in Honour of John H. Jackson* (The Hague: Kluwer Law International, 2001), at p. 135.

[8] The Legal Drafting Group was established by Director-General Dunkel, and worked initially from January to May 1992, under the chairmanship of Madan Mathur, a former Deputy Director-General. It reviewed all the agreements. Id.

A Map of the WTO Law of Domestic Regulation of Goods

and objective interpretations, based on the parameters laid out in the Vienna Convention on the Law of Treaties and in international law principles of interpretation. It is interesting to note that some horizontal cross-fertilization has taken place, based on either an "effective" interpretation of the WTO treaty or the jurisprudence's efforts to maintain some WTO coherence. For example, the jurisprudence seems to have read into Article XX of GATT important components of the new more technical provisions of the TBT and SPS Agreements. Some aspects of this jurisprudence are now addressed in decisions of the SPS Committee and may influence the interpretation of other SPS provisions or other WTO agreements. Yet this may not always suffice to rectify inconsistent drafting among those agreements and provisions.

After a brief historical background on the use of separate "codes" in the Kennedy Round and the Tokyo Round, we analyse the separate, and varying, nature of the obligations and rights expressed under GATT, the SPS Agreement and the TBT Agreement, paying attention to the types of rules and standards, their relationship to domestic regulations and the regulatory process, and the way that they incorporate by reference norms from outside the WTO system. Finally, this chapter analyses the bases for invoking these three sources of norms, and evaluates the circumstances under which they overlap, as well as the implications of such overlaps.

II. How the SPS and TBT Agreements Came to Exist

Prior to the Uruguay Round, separate agreements, or "codes," were negotiated and introduced in the Kennedy and Tokyo rounds, in order to address certain types of non-tariff barriers and to extend the coverage of GATT. Contracting parties entered into these agreements on what has come to be known as a "plurilateral" basis, making the agreements binding only on the signatories. It was a GATT of concentric circles, or of multiple speeds. This led to the "fragmentation" of the GATT: all GATT contracting parties were not necessarily bound by the same obligations and the division was often one between developed and developing countries.[9] The desire to avoid this type of fragmentation in the future was one of the basic principles underlying the Uruguay Round negotiations that introduced the concept of a WTO "single undertaking". Arguably, this has had an impact on the relationship between the obligations contained in the TBT and SPS Agreements and those of the GATT 1994, because they now form part of a single treaty, which must be interpreted as a whole.

After the Kennedy Round, contracting parties' concerns over multiple and divergent national standards increased. A first general notification exercise[10] confirmed the broad use of different national standards. The increasing multiplicity of standards was seen as a potential barrier to trade and pointed towards a need to consider harmonization of standards. Disciplines were needed to ensure that

---

[9] At the conclusion of the Tokyo Round, Contracting Parties addressed the issue of the relationship between the provisions of the Tokyo Codes and those of the GATT in a decision which in paragraph 3 stated: "The Contracting Parties also note that existing rights and benefits under GATT of contracting parties not being parties to these agreements, including those derived from Article I, are not affected by these Agreements." Action by the Contracting Parties on the Multilateral Trade Negotiations, BISD 26/201, 28 November 1979.

[10] COM.IND/W/13, 20, 23 and 32, L/3496, L/3756 and Spec (69)51. This compilation was updated in MTN/3B/3, 14 February 1974. See also COM.TD/W/191.

standards are not applied "so as to afford protection to the domestic production".[11] Harmonization of standards and the co-operation of states in the formulation of international standards[12] were viewed as tools to reach such results. Already at that time, Contracting Parties expressed the clear view that the code to be negotiated "in no way interferes with the responsibility of governments for safety, health and welfare of their people or for the protection of the environment in which they live. It merely seeks to minimize the effect of such actions on international trade".[13]

In the context of the conclusion of the Tokyo Round, the Standards Code, which covered mandatory and voluntary technical specifications, mandatory technical regulations and voluntary standards for industrial and agricultural goods, was signed by 43 Contracting Parties. Its main provisions prohibited discrimination and the protection of domestic production through specifications, technical regulations and standards; it also prescribed the preparation, adoption and application of regulations, specifications and standards in a manner more restrictive than necessary; and it urged signatories to base their national measures on international standards and to collaborate and co-operate towards harmonization of such national norms.

In the decade following the 1979 Tokyo Round, a consensus emerged that "the Standards Code had failed to stem disruptions of trade in agricultural products caused by proliferating technical restrictions".[14] Furthermore, of course, one of the great advances of the Uruguay Round was to introduce greater disciplines on other types of agricultural protectionism, including quotas and domestic price supports. In order to protect this advance from potential regulatory defection, it was viewed as necessary to establish the SPS Agreement, and to have it apply universally, not plurilaterally.[15] Of course, enforcement of the original Standards Code was weakened by the existence of a general requirement of consensus to establish a Panel and to adopt a Panel report. The Uruguay Round's Dispute Settlement Understanding remedied this weakness.[16]

The initial Uruguay Round negotiations were merely intended to add stronger disciplines on sanitary and phytosanitary measures to the Standards Code, "but by 1988, a separate Working Party was created to draft an SPS Agreement, as negotiators had concluded that disciplines which elaborated the circumstances under which countries could adopt risk-reducing trade measures which violated the GATT most-favoured-nation (MFN) and national treatment principles could not be conveniently incorporated into the TBT Agreement".[17]

---

[11] Spec (71) 143, 30 September 1971, Section III, Article 1(a).

[12] Spec (71) 143, Section III, Article 1(c).

[13] Spec (71) 143, idem. It is interesting to notice that Article XX of the GATT does not explicitly limit the Contracting Parties' jurisdiction to "their" population and environment. The draft Spec (71) 143 seems to imply that governments' autonomy in protection of the safety, health and welfare of their population and their environment is limited to those situations taking place within their own jurisdiction.

[14] Donna Roberts, "Preliminary Assessment of the Effects of the WTO Agreement on Sanitary and Phytosanitary Trade Regulations", 1 *Journal of International Economic Law* 2 (1998), 377, 380.

[15] Id.

[16] This was true for dispute settlement relating to any alleged GATT violation. However, the Anti-dumping and the Subsidies Tokyo Codes had already put in place a mechanism of automatic establishment of a Panel within 60 days of its request.

[17] Roberts, as note 14 above, at 382 (citation omitted). Roberts explains that SPS measures mitigate risks that vary by source and destination – the incidence or spatial distribution of the hazard in the exporting country, and the possibility for contagion in the importing country, are relevant to the type of measure

A Map of the WTO Law of Domestic Regulation of Goods

The original GATT, with its combination of Articles I, III, XI and XX, and with its consensus-based dispute resolution, was seen as incapable of addressing important disputes over sanitary and phytosanitary measures, including hormones.[18] As a matter of treaty negotiations, it was not possible in the Uruguay Round to amend Article XX of GATT, but it was possible to add "interpretative" agreements[19] or extensions of GATT obligations.[20]

The SPS and TBT Agreements were entered into as part of the "single undertaking", by which states party to the Marrakesh Agreement Establishing the WTO entered into all of the WTO Agreements annexed to it (with the exception of two "plurilateral" agreements)[21] simultaneously. That is, pursuant to Article II:2 of the WTO Agreement, the SPS and TBT Agreements are integral parts of the WTO Agreement, binding on all Members. Therefore, they have the same basic legal status as the General Agreement on Tariffs and Trade 1994: they are co-equal sources of WTO law.[22]

An analysis of the SPS Agreement and the TBT Agreement raises interesting technical issues regarding their relationship with GATT, and with one another. These technical issues overlay important substantive matters regarding the precise disciplines applicable to national regulations. Moreover, the determination of the applicable WTO law (do GATT, SPS or TBT apply?) will affect the status of the WTO's relationship with other treaties. For instance, whether or not there is a conflict between the WTO Agreement and the Biosafety Protocol (of the Biodiversity Convention) may depend on which WTO provisions of the SPS or TBT or GATT Agreements are applicable to a specific set of facts and circumstances. The applicable WTO law is itself determined by the specific aspects of the measure challenged, the nature of the disciplines imposed by each provision and the relationship among these provisions.

III. Comparing the Disciplines of the SPS Agreement, the TBT Agreement and the GATT

The SPS, TBT and GATT Agreements all contain a number of different disciplines on national regulation. This section discusses selected disciplines under the following categories:

(1) Non-discrimination: national treatment and most-favoured-nation
(2) Necessity and proportionality tests
(3) Appropriate level/scientific basis
(4) Harmonization; conformity with international standards
(5) (Mutual) recognition and equivalence

---

that is required. Thus, SPS measures may legitimately vary depending on the geographical source or destination, making them more likely to violate national treatment or MFN.

[18] See Theofanis Christoforou, "Settlement of Science-Based Trade Disputes in the WTO: A Critical Review of the Developing Case Law in the Face of Scientific Uncertainty", 8 *New York University Environmental Law Journal* 3 (2000), 624–5.

[19] See, for instance, the GATT 1994 Understandings.

[20] See, for instance, the Multilateral Trade Agreements of Annex 1A.

[21] Initially there were four plurilateral agreements. The International Dairy Agreement and the International Bovine Meat Agreement were terminated in September 1997; see documents IMA/8 and IDA/8, 30 September 1997.

[22] We discuss further below the conflict rule of Annex 1A, which gives priority to the provisions of the TBT or SPS over those of the GATT 1994, in case of conflicts.

(6) Internal consistency

(7) Permission for precautionary action

(8) Balancing

(9) Product/process issues and the territorial–extraterritorial divide[23]

To some extent these disciplines relate to each other. Often they are specifically addressed in the TBT or SPS Agreements and the GATT jurisprudence has had to deal with them. They represent different aspects of the WTO disciplines on the domestic normative autonomy of Members. These disciplines work in varying combinations within each of these three sources of WTO law. They also work together from the broader perspective of general WTO law. To a great extent, the TBT and SPS Agreements can be seen as an evolution of GATT provisions.

In this section, we simply describe the tests under these three agreements. The effective interpretation of the WTO Agreement calls for a coherent and harmonious reading of all its provisions (including the SPS Agreement, the TBT Agreement and the GATT).[24] However, in grouping various treaty provisions under the umbrella of a single WTO Agreement, negotiators may not have envisaged all possible situations of overlap.

A. Non-Discrimination: National Treatment and Most-Favoured-Nation

Obligations of non-discrimination in internal regulation, including the application of internal regulation at the border,[25] occupy a primary position in the GATT, and in the SPS and TBT Agreements. Discrimination between products and between situations is condemned. In this section we examine mainly the obligation of non-discrimination as between domestic and imported products: national treatment.

1. GATT

(a) GATT Article III:4 – National Treatment Obligation

It is appropriate to begin with Articles III:1 and 4 of the GATT, which provide:

1. The contracting parties recognize that internal taxes and other internal charges, and laws, regulations and requirements affecting the *internal* sale, offering for sale, purchase, transportation, distribution or use of products, and internal quantitative regulations requiring the mixture, processing or use of products in specified amounts or proportions, should not be applied to imported or domestic products so as to afford protection to domestic production. (emphasis added)

---

[23] This last parameter is addressed in both section C and section D, relating to the scope of application of these agreements.

[24] See Appellate Body Report, *Korea – Definitive Safeguard Measure on Imports of Certain Dairy Products* ("*Korea – Dairy*"), WT/DS98/AB/R, adopted 12 January 2000, at para. 81: "In light of the interpretive principle of effectiveness, it is the *duty* of any treaty interpreter to 'read all applicable provisions of a treaty in a way that gives meaning to *all* of them, harmoniously'. An important corollary of this principle is that a treaty should be interpreted as a whole, and, in particular, its sections and parts should be read as a whole" (footnotes deleted).

[25] See Article III, General Agreement on Tariffs and Trade, 30 October 1947, 55 UNTS 194 (hereinafter GATT).

A Map of the WTO Law of Domestic Regulation of Goods

4. The products of the territory of any contracting party imported into the territory of any other contracting party shall be accorded treatment no less favourable than that accorded to like products of national origin in respect of all laws, regulations and requirements affecting their internal sale, offering for sale, purchase, transportation, distribution or use.

This language has been interpreted in several GATT and WTO cases. In its first report, *Japan – Alcoholic Beverages*, the WTO Appellate Body declared that the broad purpose of Article III is to prohibit "protectionism",[26] a concept that it did not define. It also rejected the "aims-and-effects" approach to the obligation of national treatment, at least as a search for subjective intent.[27] It refused to see any issue of the subjective intent of the Member state in Article III determination:

It does not matter that there may not have been any desire to engage in protectionism in the minds of the legislators or the regulators who imposed the measure. It is irrelevant that protectionism was not an intended objective if the particular tax measure in question is nevertheless, to echo Article III:1, applied to imported or domestic products so as to afford protection to domestic production. *This is an issue of how the measure in question is applied.*[28] (emphasis added)

---

[26] "The broad and fundamental purpose of Article III is to avoid protectionism in the application of internal tax and regulatory measures". More specifically, the purpose of Article III "is to ensure that internal measures not be applied to imported and domestic products so as to afford protection to domestic production". Toward this end, Article III obliges Members of the WTO to provide equality of competitive conditions for imported products in relation to domestic products . . . Article III protects expectations not of any particular trade volume but rather of the equal competitive relationship between imported and domestic products", *Japan – Taxes on Alcoholic Beverages* ("*Japan – Alcoholic Beverages II*"), WT/DS8/AB/R, WT/DS10/AB/R, WT/DS11/AB/R, adopted 1 November 1996, at p. 16.

[27] See Appellate Body Report, *Japan – Alcoholic Beverages II*, WT/DS8/AB/R, WT/DS10/AB/R, WT/DS11/AB/R, at p. 27: "This third inquiry under Article III:2, second sentence, must determine whether 'directly competitive or substitutable products' are 'not similarly taxed' in a way that affords protection. This is not an issue of intent. It is not necessary for a Panel to sort through the many reasons legislators and regulators often have for what they do and weigh the relative significance of those reasons to establish legislative or regulatory intent"; and at p. 29: "Although it is true that the aim of a measure may not be easily ascertained, nevertheless its protective application can most often be discerned from the design, the architecture, and the revealing structure of a measure." See Robert E. Hudec, "GATT/WTO Constraints on National Regulation: Requiem for an Aims and Effects Test", 32 *International Lawyer* (1998), 619.

[28] See Appellate Body Report, *Japan – Alcoholic Beverages II*, WT/DS8/AB/R, WT/DS10/AB/R, WT/DS11/AB/R, at p. 28. A WTO Member's measure can be challenged under GATT/WTO dispute settlement procedures, if it is binding and not discretionary, even if it is not yet in force. Three recent panel reports stated that although it was possible to conceive that the laws would be applied in a manner incompatible with WTO rules, the competent authorities had the discretion to apply them consistently with such rules. Therefore the laws did not necessarily violate the SCM provision (because there was no evidence of specific violations, the claims of SCM violations were rejected). See Panel Report, *United States – Measures Treating Export Restraints as Subsidies* ("*US – Export Restraints*"), WT/DS194/R, adopted 23 August 2001, at paras. 8.126–8.132; Panel Report, *Brazil – Export Financing Programme for Aircraft – Second Recourse by Canada to Article 21.5 of the DSU* ("*Brazil – Aircraft (Article 21.5 II – Canada*")], WT/DS46/RW/2, adopted 23 August 2001, at paras. 5.11–5.13, 5.43, 5.48, 5.5, 5.55, 5.126, and 5.142; and Panel Report, *Canada – Export Credits and Loan Guarantees for Regional Aircraft* ("*Canada – Aircraft Credits and Guarantees*"), WT/DS222/R, adopted 19 February 2002, at paras. 7.56–7.62. The requirements of Article III:4, calling for market assessments (even potential), and those on SPS measures "applied" to protect a Member's territory, will in most cases necessitate that the measure be actually enforced (applied) before they can be challenged.

The Appellate Body stated that "it is possible to examine objectively the underlying criteria used in a particular tax measure, its structure, and its overall application, to ascertain whether it is applied in a way that affords protection to domestic products".[29] The *EC – Asbestos* Appellate Body report reiterated that the text of Article III:4 reflected the general principle of paragraph 1 of Article III in seeking "to prevent Members from applying internal taxes and regulations in a manner which affects the competitive relationship, in the marketplace, between the domestic and imported products involved, so as to afford protection to domestic production".[30]

For a violation of Article III:4 to be established, the complaining Member must prove that the measure at issue is a "law, regulation, or requirement affecting their internal sale, offering for sale, purchase, transportation, distribution, or use";[31] that the imported and domestic products at issue are "like products"; and that the imported products are accorded "less favourable" treatment than that accorded to like domestic products.[32]

(i) *Imported and Domestic Like Products*

The prohibition against discrimination in the national treatment obligation can apply only when imported and domestic products are "like". The majority of the Appellate Body in *EC – Asbestos* found that "likeness" under Article III:4 is, "fundamentally, a determination about the nature and extent of a competitive relationship between and among products".[33] To perform such an assessment the Appellate Body recalled that the four classic, and basic, criteria, derived from the *Border Tax Adjustment* report – (i) the physical properties of the products in question; (ii) their end-uses; (iii) consumer tastes and habits *vis-à-vis* those products; and (iv) tariff classification[34] – are to be used as tools in the determination of this competitive relationship between products. These criteria do not exhaust inquiry.[35]

The competitive relationship between imports and domestic goods is the determinant of likeness. "If there is – or could be – no competitive relationship between products, a Member cannot intervene, through internal taxation or regulation, to protect domestic production".[36]

This competitive relationship is to be determined using the classic criteria of the *Border Tax Adjustment* report. The balancing of the criteria identified in the *Border*

---

[29] See Appellate Body Report, *Japan – Alcoholic Beverages II*, WT/DS8/AB/R, WT/DS10/AB/R, WT/DS11/AB/R, at p. 29.

[30] Appellate Body Report, *European Communities – Measures Affecting Asbestos and Asbestos-Containing Products ("EC – Asbestos")*, WT/DS135/AB/R, adopted 5 April 2001, at para. 98.

[31] The Appellate Body clarified that the word 'affecting' assists in defining the types of measures that must conform to the obligation not to accord 'less favourable treatment' to imported 'like products' and "...it is, therefore, only those [regulations] which 'affect' the specific transactions, activities and uses mentioned in that provision that are covered by Article III:4 of GATT." Appellate Body Report, *United States – Tax Treatment for Foreign Sales Corporations – Recourse to Article 21.5 of the DSU by the European Communities, ["US – FSC (Article 21.5, EC)"]*, WT/DS108/AB/RW, at para. 208.

[32] Appellate Body Report, *Korea – Measures Affecting Imports of Fresh, Chilled and Frozen Beef ("Korea – Various Measures on Beef")*, WT/DS161/AB/R and WT/DS169/AB/R, adopted 10 January 2001, at para. 133.

[33] Appellate Body Report, *EC – Asbestos*, WT/DS135/AB/R, at para. 99. Note the different opinion with regard to the very specific aspects mentioned in para. 154.

[34] Working Party Report, *Border Tax Adjustments*, adopted 2 December 1970, BISD 18S/97.

[35] Appellate Body Report, *EC – Asbestos*, WT/DS135/AB/R, at para. 101.

[36] Id., at para. 117.

A Map of the WTO Law of Domestic Regulation of Goods

Tax Adjustment report is intended to approximate the competitive relationship between the relevant goods. A more precise and refined measure of whether a competitive relationship exists is the economic concept of cross-elasticity of demand.[37] If the price of one good rises, to what extent do consumers shift consumption to the other good being tested? Although not as accurate or refined as testing cross-elasticity of demand to determine a competitive relationship, the qualitative *Border Tax Adjustment* factors may be used to assess a competitive relationship between products.

The more important critique of the *Border Tax Adjustment* test is that it is relatively ignorant of factors that motivate regulation. The economic theory of regulation suggests that regulation is necessary precisely where consumers cannot adequately distinguish relevant goods – where, but for the regulation, they are in close competitive relation. Thus, a competitive relationship test for likeness could often result in a finding that goods that differ by the parameter addressed by regulation are indeed like, and should be treated the same.[38] Hence, many domestic regulations would *prima facie* violate Article III – as like products would be treated differently by the said regulation and often in reducing market access to imported like products; they would need the justification of Article XX to be WTO-compatible. This is why the Appellate Body's two-step analysis, used first in *Korea – Various Measures on Beef*[39] and described more precisely in paragraph 100 of the *EC – Asbestos* decision, discussed hereafter, is important.

(ii) *Less Favourable Treatment*

The less favourable treatment criterion involves an "effects test". In *Korea – Various Measures on Beef*, the Appellate Body reversed the Panel, which had concluded that a regulatory distinction based exclusively on the origin of the product necessarily violated Article III. The Appellate Body emphasized the fact that "differential treatment" may be acceptable, so long as it is "no less favourable". Article III only prohibits discriminatory treatment, which "modifies the conditions of competition in the relevant market to the detriment of imported products".[40]

Is this "modification of the conditions of competition to the detriment of imported products" the benchmark to assess the existence of "protectionism" condemned by Article III? In *EC – Asbestos*, the Appellate Body reiterated that the "broad and fundamental purpose" of the obligation of national treatment of Article III of GATT is "to avoid" the application of "protectionist" internal measures; this determination is based on whether such internal measures are applied in a manner which

---

[37] See, for instance, the criteria of cross-elasticity of demand to determine whether imported and domestic products are directly competitive or substitutable in the Appellate Body Report in *Japan – Alcoholic Beverages II*, at p. 26, or in Appellate Body Report, *Korea – Taxes on Alcoholic Beverages* ("*Korea – Alcoholic Beverages*"), WT/DS75/AB/R, WT/DS84/AB/R, adopted 17 February 1999, at paras. 108–24, or in the Appellate Body Report, *United States – Transitional Safeguard Measure on Combed Cotton Yarn from Pakistan* ("*US – Cotton Yarn*"), WT/DS192/AB/R, adopted 5 November 2001, paras. 89–102.

[38] Moreover, if it is true that consumers would not consider them interchangeable, then some may say that the regulation was not necessary.

[39] Appellate Body Report, *Korea – Various Measures on Beef*, WT/DS161/AB/R and WT/DS169/AB/R, at paras. 133–49.

[40] Appellate Body Report, *Korea – Various Measures on Beef*, WT/DS161/AB/R and WT/DS169/AB/R, at para. 137.

affects the competitive relationship, in the marketplace, between the domestic and imported products involved, "so as to afford protection to like domestic production".[41] This decision established a two-step analysis, wherein the first step requires a determination whether like products are treated differently, and the second step determines whether this differential treatment amounts to "less favourable treatment".

In *EC – Asbestos*, the Appellate Body made the following statement:

> A complaining Member must still establish that the measure accords to the group of 'like' imported products 'less favourable treatment' than it accords to the group of 'like' domestic products. The term 'less favourable treatment' expresses the general principle, in Article III:1, that internal regulations 'should not be applied . . . so as to afford protection to domestic production'.[42]

And as it had stated in *Korea – Various Measures on Beef,* "a formal difference in treatment between imported and like domestic products is thus neither necessary, nor sufficient, to show a violation of Article III:4". Whether or not imported products are treated less favourably than like domestic products should be assessed instead by examining whether a measure modifies the conditions of competition in the relevant market to the detriment of imported products. Different treatment is neither sufficient nor necessary to prove less favourable treatment. Thus, it is not enough to find a single foreign like product that is treated differently from a domestic like product. The class of foreign like products must be treated less favourably than the class of domestic like products. In order for this to occur, it would seem necessary that the differential regulatory treatment be predicated, either intentionally or unintentionally, on the foreign character of the product. However, in *Korea – Various Measures on Beef,* the Appellate Body made clear that differential treatment based on nationality, alone, would not necessarily amount to "less favourable" treatment.[43] Thus a violation would only occur if after respecting the legitimate categories, the measure is still found less favourably treated.

As the Appellate Body applies this principle in future cases, we may be able to determine whether a regulation allowing for distinctions (different treatment) based on non-protectionist goals and considerations is captured by the less favourable treatment provision and therefore condemned by the application of Article III just because it affects negatively market opportunities for imports. It may be that the less favourable treatment criterion only condemns protectionist or other illegitimate regulatory distinctions. It is worth noting that a similar consideration motivated the aims-and-effects test.[44] It is also possible that "less favourable treatment" could

---

[41] Appellate Body Report, *EC – Asbestos,* WT/DS135/AB/R, at paras. 96 and 98: ". . . in endeavouring to ensure 'equality of competitive conditions', the 'general principle' in Article III seeks to prevent Members from applying internal taxes and regulations in a manner which affects the competitive relationship, in the marketplace, between the domestic and imported products involved, 'so as to afford protection to domestic production.' "

[42] Appellate Body Report, *EC – Asbestos,* WT/DS135/AB/R, at para. 100.

[43] Appellate Body Report, *Korea – Various Measures on Beef,* WT/DS161/AB/R and WT/DS169/AB/R, at para. 134.

[44] See Hudec, as note 27, above; and Frieder Roessler, "Diverging Domestic Policies and Multilateral Trade Integration", in Robert E. Hudec and Jagdish Bhagwati (Eds.), *Fair Trade and Harmonization, Pre-requisite for Free-Trade,* Vol. II (Cambridge, MA: MIT Press, 1996).

A Map of the WTO Law of Domestic Regulation of Goods

19

be interpreted broadly so as to include any market distortion favouring domestic products, even if the goal, object and purpose of the measure are not protectionist. In such case reliance on Article XX to justify such measure would remain possible.

(b) Most-Favoured-Nation Principle

Article I of GATT provides that for all matters referred to in paragraph 4 of Article III, any advantage, favour, privilege or immunity granted by any Member to any product originating in or destined for any other country shall be accorded immediately and unconditionally to the like product originating in or destined for the territories of all other Members.

Mutual Recognition Agreement

Article 2.3 of the SPS Agreement and Article 2.1 of the TBT Agreement provide similar MFN obligations. Interestingly, both Article 4 of the SPS Agreement and Article 6.3 of the TBT Agreement encourage "mutual recognition" agreements. Mutual recognition agreements (MRAs), of course, reduce barriers to imports of goods from beneficiary states, but they may provide inferior treatment to imports of goods from non-beneficiary states. This could arguably violate the MFN obligation.[45] This will depend on the "architecture" and functioning of the specific MRA. These MRAs are part of the positive integration exercise, along with harmonization discussed in Section D below.

2. TBT Agreement

Article 2.1 of the TBT Agreement, following closely Articles III and I of GATT, requires: "treatment no less favourable than that accorded to like products of national origin and to like products originating in any other country". However, it is worth noting that the TBT Agreement has no equivalent of Article XX, providing an exemption under certain circumstances.

Problems may occur if the scope of the term "like products" is the same as that under Article III:4, while justifications under Article XX are not available to violations of Article 2.1 of TBT. It is conceivable that the "accordion" of like products[46] may

---

[45] See William J. Davey and Joost Pauwelyn, "MFN Unconditionality: A Legal Analysis of the Concept in View of Its Evolution in the GATT/WTO Jurisprudence with Particular Reference to the Issue of 'Like Product'", in Thomas Cottier, Petros C. Mavroidis and Patrick Blatter (Eds.), *Regulatory Barriers and the Principle of Non-Discrimination in World Trade Law* (Ann Arbor, MI: University of Michigan Press, 2000), pp. 23–4, evaluating mutual recognition agreements under the MFN principle: "On the one hand, such agreements offer an effective means of facilitating trade. On the other hand, they also have an impact on the competitive strength of non-participating countries. This is why two WTO agreements (TBT and SPS) encourage Members to negotiate MRAs but at the same time require that they do so in a transparent and open way." See also Petros C. Mavroidis, "Transatlantic Regulatory Cooperation: Exclusive Club or 'Open Regionalism'", in George A. Bermann, Matthias Herdegan and Peter L. Lindseth (Eds.), *Transatlantic Regulatory Cooperation: Legal Problems and Political Prospects* (Oxford: Oxford University Press, 2001), pp. 263, 266: "Any interpretation of the WTO agreements that the MFN principle precludes MRAs must be rejected, because it runs counter to the principle of 'effective interpretation' of the treaties as laid down in the Vienna Convention on the Law of treaties."

[46] In *Japan – Alcoholic Beverages II*, the Appellate Body stated that "The concept of 'likeness' is a relative one that evokes the image of an accordion. The accordion of 'likeness' stretches and squeezes in different places as different provisions of the WTO Agreement are applied. The width of the accordion in any one

allow a distinction between "like" products of GATT Article III (or I) and that of 2.1 of TBT. The sixth preambular paragraph of the TBT Agreement,[47] combined with the necessity requirement of Article 2.2, may suggest that a narrow interpretation of "like products" is appropriate in the context of Article 2.1. The emphasis of the Appellate Body on the "no less favourable" language may serve as a less strained defence for non-protectionist domestic regulation and therefore reduce the need to invoke Article XX to justify measures based on listed non-protectionist policy goals. Otherwise we would be faced with an incongruous situation where, for instance, many of the environment-based technical regulations could be inconsistent with Article 2.1 while the same regulations would be authorized by Article XX (after a prior determination that it was *prima facie* inconsistent with Article III:4 of GATT).

The negotiators of the Tokyo Round Standards Code seem to have wanted to maintain states' rights to take measures for the protection of health and the environment and for security reasons; these concerns are reflected in the preamble of the Uruguay Round TBT Agreement. Because Article 2.2 of the Uruguay Round TBT Agreement allows Members to base their TBT regulations on any "legitimate" policy, Members do not need to invoke Article XX of the GATT to justify action based on the policy considerations listed there. Therefore (and adding to this the fact that Article XX of GATT is contained in a different agreement), it is doubtful whether Article XX (or Article XXI) was expected to be available to be invoked as a defence to a claim of violation of Article 2.2.

3. SPS Agreement

Two provisions of the SPS Agreement concern discrimination directly: Articles 2.3 and 5.5. The SPS Agreement should be understood, to some extent, as an expansion of Article XX of GATT, and its drafters were concerned with the need to (1) expand the scientific and procedural requirements for a Member to impose an SPS measure and (2) encourage reliance on and participation in international standard-setting bodies. Yet the obligations of the SPS Agreement stand alone, and the panel in *EC – Hormones* stated that because the SPS Agreement adds to Articles III, XI and XX of GATT, there is no obligation to prove a violation of Articles III or XI before the SPS Agreement can be invoked.[48]

---

of those places must be determined by the particular provision in which the term 'like' is encountered as well as by the context and the circumstances that prevail in any given case to which that provision may apply". Appellate Body Report, *Japan – Alcoholic Beverages II*, WT/DS8/AB/R, WT/DS10/AB/R, WT/DS11/AB/R, at p. 23.

[47] "Recognizing that no country should be prevented from taking measures necessary to ensure the quality of its exports, or for the protection of human, animal or plant life or health, of the environment, or for the prevention of deceptive practices, at the levels it considers appropriate, subject to the requirement that they are not applied in a manner which would constitute a means of arbitrary or unjustifiable discrimination between countries where the same conditions prevail or a disguised restriction on international trade, and are otherwise in accordance with the provisions of this Agreement."

[48] In *EC – Hormones (US)*, the European Communities submitted that "the 'substantive' provisions of the SPS Agreement can only be addressed if recourse is made to GATT Article XX(b), i.e., if, and only if, a violation of another provision of GATT is first established". The panels rejected this argument, indicating as follows: "The SPS Agreement contains, in particular, no explicit requirement of a prior violation of a provision of GATT which would govern the applicability of the SPS Agreement, as asserted by the

A Map of the WTO Law of Domestic Regulation of Goods

The discrimination condemned in Articles 2.3 and 5.5 appears parallel to the type of discrimination referenced in the chapeau of Article XX, discussed in sub-section 3. Article 2.3 of the SPS Agreement provides as follows:

Members shall ensure that their sanitary and phytosanitary measures do not arbitrarily or unjustifiably discriminate between Members where identical or similar conditions prevail, including between their own territory and that of other members. Sanitary and phytosanitary measures shall not be applied in a manner which would constitute a disguised restriction on international trade.

Article 5.5 restricts "arbitrary or unjustifiable distinctions" between "different situations, if such distinctions result in discrimination or a disguised restriction on international trade".

Although both these provisions seem to have adapted their operative language from the chapeau of Article XX of GATT,[49] the panel in *Australia – Salmon Article 21.5 DSU*, was of the view that Article 2.3 prohibits discrimination between both similar and different products.[50] The scope of Article 2.3 would thus be much broader than that of Article 5.5 of SPS which was said to be "but a complex and indirect route"[51] to proving the discrimination prohibited by Article 2.3. Article 5.5, which

European Communities" (para. 8.36). The panels added: "... on this basis alone we cannot conclude that the SPS Agreement only applies, as Article XX(b) of GATT does, if, and only if, a prior violation of a GATT provision has been established. Many provisions of the SPS Agreement impose 'substantive' obligations which go significantly beyond and are additional to the requirements for invocation of Article XX(b). These obligations are, *inter alia*, imposed to 'further the use of harmonized sanitary and phytosanitary measures between Members' and to 'improve the human health, animal health and phytosanitary situation in all Members'. They are not imposed, as is the case of the obligations imposed by Article XX(b) of GATT, to justify a violation of another GATT obligation (such as a violation of the non-discrimination obligations of Articles I or III)" (para. 8.38). Panel Report, *EC Measures Concerning Meat and Meat Products (Hormones) – Complaint by the United States* ["*EC-Hormones (US)*"] WT/DS26/R/USA, adopted 13 February 1998 as modified by the Appellate Body Report, WT/DS26/AB/R, DSR 1998:III, p. 699.

[49] The chapeau requires that measures exempted under Article XX must not be applied in a manner that would constitute "a means of arbitrary or unjustifiable discrimination between countries where the same conditions prevail, or a disguised restriction on international trade...".

[50] Panel Report, *Australia – Measures Affecting Importation of Salmon – Recourse to Article 21.5 of the DSU by Canada* ["*Australia – Salmon (Article 21.5 DSU)*"], WT/DS18/RW, adopted 20 March 2000, at para. 7.112: "We are of the view that discrimination in the sense of Article 2.3, first sentence, may also include discrimination between different products, e.g. not only discrimination between Canadian salmon and New Zealand salmon, or Canadian salmon and Australian salmon; but also discrimination between Canadian salmon and Australian fish including non-salmonids."

[51] On the relationship between 2.3 and 5.5 of the SPS Agreement, see the Appellate Body statement in *Australia – Salmon*: "We recall that the third – and decisive – element of Article 5.5, discussed above, requires a finding that the SPS measure which embodies arbitrary or unjustifiable restrictions in levels of protection results in 'discrimination or a disguised restriction on international trade'. Therefore, a finding of violation of Article 5.5 will necessarily imply a violation of Article 2.3, first sentence, or Article 2.3, second sentence. Discrimination 'between Members, including their own territory and that of others Members' within the meaning of Article 2.3, first sentence, can be established by following the complex and indirect route worked out and elaborated by Article 5.5. However, it is clear that this route is not the only route leading to a finding that an SPS measure constitutes arbitrary or unjustifiable discrimination according to Article 2.3, first sentence. Arbitrary or unjustifiable discrimination in the sense of Article 2.3, first sentence, can be found to exist without any examination under Article 5.5." Appellate Body Report, *Australia – Measures Affecting Importation of Salmon* ("*Australia – Salmon*"), WT/DS18/AB/R, adopted 6 November 1998, DSR 1998:VIII, 3327, at para. 252.

imposes a form of internal consistency requirement, and the guidelines on Article 5.5 adopted by the SPS Committee, are further discussed in sub-section F on "Internal Consistency".

The test under the SPS is different from that of Articles III, XI and XX of GATT; there is no like products analysis or product–process distinction per se (as with Article III of GATT) in the SPS Agreement. The focus of the analysis is the justification for discrimination between situations under the SPS prohibition itself.

B. Necessity and Proportionality Tests

One important general discipline on domestic regulation in WTO law is the necessity test, which, until the recent *EC – Asbestos* and *Korea – Various Measures on Beef* decisions of the Appellate Body, was generally interpreted as requiring the domestic regulation to be the least trade restrictive method of achieving the desired goal. The TBT and SPS Agreements have made it a "positive requirement" on all relevant regulations while the GATT keeps it, under Article XX, as a "justification" for restrictions found to violate other provisions, including basic market access rights.

A broader "proportionality" requirement may include least-trade-restrictive-alternative analysis. While proportionality is a general concept of international law,[52] as it relates to retorsion and other international legal remedies, it has already emerged as a principle of EC law.[53] In the EC context, proportionality *stricto sensu*[54] inquires as to whether the means are "proportionate" to the ends: whether the costs are excessive in relation to the benefits. It might be viewed as cost–benefit analysis with a margin of appreciation, as it does not require that the costs be less than the benefits. A wider definition of proportionality developed in the European legal context includes three tests: (i) a simple suitability, or means–ends rationality, test, (ii) a least-trade-restrictive-alternative test, and (iii) proportionality *stricto sensu*.[55] A means–ends rationality test, or suitability test, simply inquires as to whether the measure is a rational or suitable means, among many others, to achieve the purported goal. It is a weak test that is generally easy to satisfy. Thus, we focus on two components of proportionality: proportionality *stricto sensu*, which is similar to a balancing test, and a least-trade-restrictive-alternative test.

1. The Necessity Test in the GATT

Since its inception, the GATT has always recognized that legitimate government policies may justify measures contrary to basic GATT market access rules. Traditionally in GATT, the exceptional provisions of Article XX(b) and (d) are available

---

[52] See J. Delbruck, "Proportionality", in R. Bernhardt (Ed.), *Encyclopedia of Public International Law*, Vol. 3 (Amsterdam: Elsevier Science, 1997), p. 1140.

[53] Case 11/70, Internationale Handelsgesellschaft, [1970] E.C.R. 1125, 1135.

[54] Nicholas Emiliou, *The Principle of Proportionality in European Law: A Comparative Study* 6 (London: Kluwer Law International, 1996). See also Joel Trachtman, "Trade and . . . Problems", 9 *European Journal of International Law* 1 (1998), 32, 74–6.

[55] For an explication of these tests as they have been developed in the EC context, see Jan Neumann and Elisabeth Türk, "Necessity Revisited – Proportionality in WTO Law After EC – Asbestos", 37 *Journal of World Trade* 1 (2003).

A Map of the WTO Law of Domestic Regulation of Goods 23

to justify measures – otherwise incompatible with other GATT provisions – if they are "necessary". This has been interpreted to require that the country invoking these exceptions demonstrate that no other WTO-compatible or less-restrictive alternative was reasonably available to pursue the desired policy goal.

> It was clear to the Panel that a contracting party cannot justify a measure inconsistent with another GATT provision as 'necessary' in terms of Article XX(d) if an alternative measure which it could reasonably be expected to employ and which is not inconsistent with other GATT provisions is available to it. By the same token, in cases where a measure consistent with other GATT provisions is not reasonably available, a contracting party is bound to use, among the measures reasonably available to it, that which entails the least degree of inconsistency with other GATT provisions.[56]

The "necessity" qualifications contained in Articles XX(b) and (d) of GATT have been interpreted to require the national measure to be the least-trade-restrictive alternative reasonably available. A fundamental question arises from the inclusion of the "reasonably available" qualification in the necessity test: what is reasonable?[57] If the reasonableness test amounts to a requirement that the least-trade-restrictive alternative not be so costly as to countervail the benefits of the regulatory measure, then it bears some resemblance to cost–benefit analysis. This necessity test thus would truncate cost–benefit analysis by not examining the benefits of the regulatory measure, or compare those benefits with the trade restriction.[58]

The WTO jurisprudence has changed the traditional GATT reading of Article XX, including the parameters of the so-called "necessity test". First, in *US – Gasoline*, the Appellate Body determined that compliance with Article XX is now to be demonstrated in a two-prong test: first, whether the challenged measure is covered by one of the sub-paragraphs of Article XX; and second, whether or not the measure is "applied" in a manner that constitutes arbitrary or unjustifiable discrimination or a disguised restriction on trade. While Members have a right to invoke the exceptions, the exceptions should not be applied so as unjustifiably to frustrate the legal obligations owed to other Member states under the GATT.[59]

(a) The Necessity Test Under Article XX(b) and (d)

The Article XX necessity test was addressed in *Korea – Various Measures on Beef*, where Korea attempted to justify its dual retail system for beef by arguing the need for

---

[56] See GATT Panel Report, *United States – Section 337 of the Tariff Act of 1930* ("*US – Section 337*"), adopted 7 November 1989, BISD 36S/345, at para. 5.26; GATT Panel Report, *United States – Measures Affecting Alcoholic and Malt Beverages* (*US – Malt Beverages*), adopted 19 June 1992, BISD 39S/206), at para. 5.52; and GATT Panel Report, *Thailand – Restrictions on Importation of and Internal Taxes on Cigarettes* ("*Thailand – Cigarettes*"), adopted 7 November 1990, BISD 37S/200, at para. 223.

[57] The SPS Agreement specifically (although not unambiguously) adds a reasonableness qualification. These provisions leave some ambiguity in light of Article 2.2 of the SPS Agreement, which provides a necessity test in respect of the application of sanitary and phytosanitary measures, but lacks a reasonableness qualifier.

[58] Thus, if cost–benefit analysis would analyse the regulatory benefits net of regulatory costs, and the trade costs, this test examines the trade costs, and the regulatory costs (under the "reasonably available" heading), but does not evaluate the regulatory benefits.

[59] Appellate Body Report, *United States – Standards for Reformulated and Conventional Gasoline* ("*US – Gasoline*"), WT/DS2/AB/R, adopted 20 May 1996, at p. 22.

compliance with a domestic regulation against fraud. The Appellate Body interpreted the necessity test of Article XX(d) to imply a requirement for balancing among at least three variables:

> In sum, determination of whether a measure, which is not 'indispensable', may nevertheless be 'necessary' within the contemplation of Article XX(d), involves in every case a process of weighing and balancing a series of factors which prominently include the contribution made by the compliance measure to the enforcement of the law or regulation at issue, the importance of the common interests or values protected by that law or regulation, and the accompanying impact of the law or regulation on imports or exports.[60]

After reiterating that WTO Members have the right to determine for themselves the level of enforcement of their domestic laws[61] (a concept close to the "appropriate level of protection" referred to in the SPS Agreement), the Appellate Body called for an authentic balancing and weighing of (at least) these variables: "The more vital or important those common interests or values are, the easier it would be to accept as 'necessary' a measure designed as an enforcement instrument";[62] "The greater the contribution [to the realization of the end pursued], the more easily a measure might be considered to be 'necessary'";[63] or "A measure with a relatively slight impact upon imported products might more easily be considered as 'necessary' than a measure with intense or broader restrictive effects".[64]

It is not clear how these variables affect each other, nor is it clear how their balancing would affect the final determination that a measure qualifies under Article XX and how this new test relates to the traditional "least-trade-restrictive alternative reasonably available" test. Yet in *EC – Asbestos*, the Appellate Body tried to reconcile its new balancing test with the traditional least-trade-restrictive-alternative test. For the Appellate Body, the balancing referred to in *Korea – Various Measures on Beef* is part of the determination of whether a WTO-compatible or less-trade-restrictive alternative exists to obtain the end pursued [as called for by the traditional necessity test of Article XX(b)].[65] In light of France's chosen level of protection, and noting that the protection of human life is vital and important to the highest degree,[66] the *EC – Asbestos* Appellate Body report concluded that "the remaining question, then,

---

[60] Appellate Body Report, *Korea – Various Measures on Beef,* WT/DS161/AB/R and WT/DS169/AB/R, at para. 164.

[61] Id., at para. 177.

[62] Id., at para. 162.

[63] Id., at para. 163.

[64] Id.

[65] Appellate Body Report, *EC – Asbestos,* WT/DS135/AB/R, at para. 172: "We indicated in *Korea – Beef* that one aspect of the 'weighing and balancing process ... comprehended in the determination of whether a WTO-consistent alternative measure' is reasonably available is the extent to which the alternative measure 'contributes to the realization of the end pursued'. In addition, we observed, in that case, that '[t]he more vital or important [the] common interests or values' pursued, the easier it would be to accept as 'necessary' measures designed to achieve those ends. In this case, the objective pursued by the measure is the preservation of human life and health through the elimination, or reduction, of the well-known, and life-threatening, health risks posed by asbestos fibres. The value pursued is both vital and important in the highest degree. The remaining question, then, is whether there is an alternative measure that would achieve the same end and that is less restrictive of trade than a prohibition."

[66] Id.

A Map of the WTO Law of Domestic Regulation of Goods

is whether there is an alternative measure that would achieve the same end and that is less restrictive of trade than a prohibition".[67]

It is not yet clear what the impact of such a policy of the highest importance has had on the rest of the determination. But it seems that panels and the Appellate Body are asked to assess the reasonableness and importance of the values at the basis of the challenged measure ("The more vital or important those common interests or values are, the easier it would be to accept as 'necessary' "[68]). In *Korea – Various Measures on Beef* the possibility of an unreasonable or inauthentic policy goal was raised:

> ... The application of such measures for the control of the same illegal behaviour for like, or at least similar, products raises doubts with respect to the *objective necessity* of a different, much stricter, and WTO-inconsistent enforcement measure.[69]
>
> *We think it unlikely that Korea intended to* establish a level of protection that totally eliminates fraud with respect to the origin of beef (domestic or foreign) sold by retailers. The total elimination of fraud would probably require a total ban of imports. Consequently, *we assume that in effect Korea intended to reduce considerably* the number of cases of fraud occurring with respect to the origin of beef sold by retailers.[70] (emphasis added)

To some extent, the *EC – Asbestos* and *Korea – Various Measures on Beef* cases have introduced a form of balancing test or proportionality test into Article XX of GATT.[71] We discuss this development in Section H.

It is important at this stage to note the similarity between the wording of the necessity tests under Article XX, that of Article 2.2 of the TBT Agreement and that of Article 5.6 of the SPS Agreement and its footnote, although of course Article XX operates as a defence. We discuss the possibility for common interpretation below.

(b) The Test Under Article XX(g)

The invocation of Article XX(g) against claims of GATT violations can also raise issues in the context of the relationship between the SPS Agreement and the TBT Agreement, and GATT, for instance with respect to some of the so-called "green" labelling requirements. In its *US – Gasoline* report, although parties had both relied on the GATT "primarily aimed at" test, the Appellate Body noted that the threshold of Article XX(g) did not contain a requirement that the measure be "primarily aimed at", but only a requirement that the measure be "related to".[72] The Appellate Body examined whether "the means (the challenged regulations) are, in principle, reasonably related to the ends" and whether "such measures are made effective in conjunction

---

[67] Id.

[68] Appellate Body Report, *Korea – Various Measures on Beef*, WT/DS161/AB/R and WT/DS169/AB/R, at para. 162.

[69] Id., at para. 172.

[70] Appellate Body Report, *Korea – Various Measures on Beef*, WT/DS161/AB/R and WT/DS169/AB/R, at para. 178.

[71] See Neumann and Türk, as note 55, above.

[72] Appellate Body Report, *US – Gasoline*, WT/DS2/AB/R, at pp. 17–22 in particular: "... participants and third parties agree ... accordingly we see no need to examine this point further, *save, perhaps, to note that the phrase primarily aimed at is not itself treaty language and was not designed as a simple litmus test for inclusion or exclusion from XX*" (emphasis added). Id., at pp. 21–2.

with restrictions on domestic production or consumption" ("... a requirement of even-handedness in the imposition of restrictions"[73]).

In *US – Shrimp*, the Appellate Body appears to have abandoned the "primarily aimed at" test and focused on the means–ends relationship[74] between the measure and the goal pursued: "We must examine the relationship between the general structure and design of the measure here at stake, Section 609, and the policy goal it purports to serve, that is, the conservation of sea turtles".[75]

(c) The Chapeau of Article XX

In *US – Shrimp* the Appellate Body stressed the fact that the chapeau of Article XX is a recognition of the need to maintain a balance between the right of a Member to invoke one of the exceptions in Article XX and the substantive rights of other Members under GATT rules. It noted that the task of applying the chapeau is a delicate one of finding and marking out a "line of equilibrium"[76] between these two sets of rights in such a way that neither will cancel out the other. The various balancing tests arising under different provisions of GATT are discussed in Section H.

The chapeau of Article XX establishes three standards regarding the application of measures for which justification under Article XX may be sought: first, there must be no "arbitrary" discrimination between countries where the same conditions prevail; second, there must be no "unjustifiable" discrimination between countries where the same conditions prevail; and, third, there must be no "disguised restriction on international trade".[77] These concepts impart meaning to one another:

> "Arbitrary discrimination", "unjustifiable discrimination" and "disguised restriction" on international trade may, accordingly, be read side-by-side; they impart meaning to one another. It is clear to us that "disguised restriction" includes disguised discrimination in international trade. It is equally clear that concealed or unannounced restriction or discrimination in international trade does not exhaust the meaning of "disguised restriction". We consider that "disguised restriction", whatever else it covers, may properly be read as embracing restrictions amounting to arbitrary or unjustifiable discrimination in international trade taken under the guise of a measure formally within the terms of an exception listed in Article XX. Put in a somewhat different manner, the kinds of considerations pertinent in deciding whether the application of a particular measure amounts to "arbitrary or unjustifiable discrimination",

---

[73] Id., at pp. 20–2.

[74] See Appellate Body Report, *US – Shrimp*, WT/DS58/AB/R, paras. 156–60.

[75] See id., at para. 141: "In its general design and structure, therefore, Section 609.... Focusing on the design of the measure here at stake, it appears to us that Section 609, cum implementing guidelines, is not disproportionately wide in its scope and reach in relation to the policy objective of protection and conservation of sea turtle species. The means are, in principle, reasonably related to the ends. The means and ends relationship between Section 609 and the legitimate policy of conserving an exhaustible, and, in fact, endangered species, is observably a close and real one, a relationship that is every bit as substantial as that which we found in *United States – Gasoline* between the EPA baseline establishment rules and the conservation of clean air in the United States."

[76] Appellate Body Report, *US – Shrimp*, WT/DS58/AB/R, at paras. 156–60.

[77] See the Appellate Body Report, *US – Gasoline*, WT/DS2/AB/R, at pp. 21–2; Appellate Body Report, *United States – Import Prohibition of Certain Shrimp and Shrimp Products – Recourse to Article 21.5 of the DSU by Malaysia* [" *US – Shrimp (Article 21.5-Malaysia)*"], WT/DS58/AB/RW, at para. 118; and Appellate Body Report, *US – Shrimp*, WT/DS58/AB/R, at para. 150.

A Map of the WTO Law of Domestic Regulation of Goods

may also be taken into account in determining the presence of a "disguised restriction" on international trade. The fundamental theme is to be found in the purpose and object of avoiding abuse or illegitimate use of the exceptions to substantive rules available in Article XX.[78]

Therefore a violation of either of these concepts would suffice to disqualify the measure under Article XX.[79] Yet the standards embodied in the language of the chapeau of Article XX are not only different from the requirements of Article XX(g) but are also different from the standards used for the substantive violations of GATT.[80]

When the analysis of the chapeau of Article XX took place in the context of the invocation of sub-paragraph (g) thereof, the Appellate Body [faced with a measure benefiting from a provisional justification under Article XX(g)] examined, under the chapeau of XX, whether less-trade-restrictive alternatives were reasonably available to the United States and whether the restrictiveness of the measure was somehow disproportionate because similar costs were not at all imposed on domestic producers. In other words, even after Article XX(g) itself is satisfied, some form of a necessity test (least-trade-restrictive-alternative analysis) seems to be performed under the chapeau of Article XX.

In sum, Article XX offers justifications that can lead to rebuttal of the *prima facie* conclusion of inconsistency with any provision of GATT,[81] in situations where the

---

[78] See the Appellate Body Report, *US – Gasoline*, WT/DS2/AB/R, at p. 25. See also the Appellate Body Report, *US – Shrimp*, WT/DS58/AB/R, at para. 184, where after finding that the measure at issue was a means of unjustifiable and arbitrary discrimination the Appellate Body decided that it was not necessary to examine also whether the measure was applied in a manner that constituted a disguised restriction on international trade.

[79] See the Appellate Body Report, *US – Shrimp*, WT/DS58/AB/R, at para. 184, where after finding that the measure at issue was a means of unjustifiable and arbitrary discrimination the Appellate Body decided that it was not necessary to examine also whether the measure was applied in a manner that constituted a disguised restriction on international trade.

[80] Appellate Body Report, *US – Shrimp*, WT/DS58/AB/R, at para. 150 (citations omitted). It is worth noting the following excerpts on the relationship between Articles III and XX from two reports, first in *US – Gasoline* and then in *EC – Asbestos*, where the Appellate Body seems to have changed position. In *US – Gasoline*, the Appellate Body also stated: "The provisions of the chapeau cannot logically refer to the same standard(s) by which a violation of a substantive rule has been determined to have occurred" (p. 23), and "The context of Article XX(g) includes the provisions of the rest of the General Agreement, including in particular Articles I, III and XI; conversely, the context of Articles I and III and XI includes Article XX. Accordingly, the phrase 'relating to the conservation of exhaustible natural resources' may not be read so expansively as seriously to subvert the purpose and object of Article III:4. Nor may Article III:4 be given so broad a reach as effectively to emasculate Article XX(g) and the policies and interests it embodies"; Appellate Body Report, *US – Gasoline*, WT/DS2/AB/R, at p. 23; and in *EC – Asbestos*: "Article III:4 and Article XX(b) are distinct and independent provisions of the GATT 1994 each to be interpreted on its own. The scope and meaning of Article III:4 should not be broadened or restricted beyond what is required by the normal customary international law rules of treaty interpretation, simply because Article XX(b) exists and may be available to justify measures inconsistent with Article III:4. The fact that an interpretation of Article III:4, under those rules, implies a less frequent recourse to Article XX(b) does not deprive the exception in Article XX(b) of *effet utile*. Article XX(b) would only be deprived of *effet utile* if that provision could *not* serve to allow a Member to "adopt and enforce" measures "necessary to protect human . . . life or health"; Appellate Body Report, *EC–Asbestos*, WT/DS135/AB/R, at para. 115.

[81] See Appellate Body Report, *US – Gasoline*, WT/DS2/AB/R, at p. 24: "The exceptions listed in Article XX thus relate to all of the obligations under the General Agreement: the national treatment obligation and

trade restriction or discrimination is viewed as necessary, or otherwise appropriately and proportionally related, to the implementation of the policies listed in Article XX. The Appellate Body in *US – Gasoline* concluded when discussing the application of the chapeau of Article XX that "The resulting discrimination must have been foreseen, and was not merely inadvertent or unavoidable".[82] Indeed, the reference to "unjustifiable discrimination" in the chapeau of Article XX indicates that some discrimination may otherwise result from measures authorized under Article XX. This necessity discipline on possible justification for inconsistencies has been made into a positive requirement for all TBT and SPS measures.

2. TBT Agreement

The exceptional provisions of GATT Article XX only become relevant after a violation of another provision of GATT is found. This is a significant distinction from both the SPS Agreement and the TBT Agreement, which apply requirements of least-trade restrictiveness independently. Under GATT, of course, the least-trade-restrictive alternative requirement of Articles XX(b) and (d) is an affirmative defence, with both the burdens of persuasion and proof on the defendant. Under the SPS and TBT Agreements, on the other hand, the same standard is framed as an obligation of the defendant, with the complainant required to make out an affirmative case. Thus, whether a specific measure is an SPS measure or technical regulation under the TBT Agreement, or rather another type of measure under Article XX (say a measure adopted for environmental purposes) will determine which Member bears the burden of proof in case of a challenge.[83]

Article 2.2 of the TBT Agreement adds a curious phrase to the necessity test: it provides that "technical regulations shall *not be more trade-restrictive than necessary* to fulfill a legitimate objective, taking account of the risks non-fulfilment would create".[84] On its face, the italicized language above of Article 2.2 appears non-sequacious: what part of the necessity test – as a search for the least-trade-restrictive alternative – would consider the risks of non-fulfilment of the regulatory goals?

If one refers to the new balancing test developed in *Korea – Various Measures on Beef,* "the risk of non-fulfilment" can also be viewed as part of the analysis of two of the criteria: the importance of the values and policies protected by the measure and the extent to which a specific measure contributes to the end pursued. If the necessity test is thought of as more of a balancing or cost–benefit analysis test, as suggested by *Korea – Various Measures on Beef* and *EC – Asbestos,* considering the potential costs of regulatory failure as part of its calculus, then this language may make sense. In other words, taking account of the risk of non-fulfilment is part of a balancing test,

---

the most-favoured-nation obligation, of course, but others as well. Effect is more easily given to the words "nothing in this Agreement", and Article XX as a whole including its chapeau more easily integrated into the remainder of the General Agreement, if the chapeau is taken to mean that the standards it sets forth are applicable to all of the situations in which an allegation of a violation of a substantive obligation has been made and one of the exceptions contained in Article XX has in turn been claimed."

[82] Id., at p. 27.

[83] See Robert Howse and Petros C. Mavroidis, "Europe's Evolving Regulatory Strategy for GMO – The Issue of Consistency with WTO Law: Of Kine and Brine", 24 *Fordham International Law Journal* (*2000*) 317, 324.

[84] TBT Agreement, Article 2.2 (emphasis added).

A Map of the WTO Law of Domestic Regulation of Goods

or cost–benefit analysis. Cost–benefit analysis would ordinarily discount a risk by its probability in order to calculate its "cost". In addition, if the necessity test under this provision is thought of as proportionality testing, in the strict sense, which would evaluate whether the costs are disproportionate to the benefits, the magnitude and probability of risk become relevant.

We note that, towards the end of the negotiation of the Uruguay Round, there was a footnote included after the additional sentence in draft Article 2.2 that reads, "This provision is intended to ensure proportionality between regulations and the risks non-fulfilment of legitimate objectives would create".[85] This footnote and the reference to proportionality have since disappeared, but the conclusion of a 1993 Note from the Secretariat is interesting:

> Its use [least-trade-restrictive alternative test] in the context of standards has evolved to mean that those standards which have the least degree of trade restrictiveness should be used. Consideration of the degree of restrictiveness should be proportional to the risk of non-fulfilment of the legitimate objectives in the case of TBT. In the SPS case, because the assessment of risks to health are already reflected in the determination of the appropriate level of protection, contracting parties should use the least restrictive means to achieve this level of protection.[86]

An important distinction between Article 2.2 of the TBT Agreement and Article XX of GATT is that the former does not contain a closed list of policies. Rather, any "legitimate" policy that may be the basis for a TBT regulation. We discuss this issue further in Section IV.C.

3. SPS Agreement

The SPS Agreement also contains a necessity test, subject to a "reasonable availability" qualification, requiring that sanitary and phytosanitary measures be "not more trade restrictive than required to achieve their appropriate level of protection, taking into account technical and economic feasibility".[87] The related footnote indicates that this standard disciplines two of the three components of regulatory cost and benefit. First, it asks whether there is a regulatory alternative that is significantly less restrictive to trade. Second, it asks whether that regulatory alternative is reasonably available.

On its face it declines to discipline the extent to which the measure maintains its ability to meet the appropriate level of protection; that is, it does not require any reductions in protection, no matter how costly in trade terms. At the same time, Article 5.4 of the SPS Agreement exhorts (but does not require) WTO Members, "when determining the appropriate level of sanitary or phytosanitary protection, [to] take

---

[85] See Document TER/W/16 and corr. 1.

[86] Id.

[87] SPS Agreement, Article 5.6. Footnote 3 thereto states as follows: "For purposes of paragraph 6 of Article 5, a measure is not more trade-restrictive than required unless there is another measure, reasonably available taking into account technical and economic feasibility, that achieves the appropriate level of sanitary or phytosanitary protection and is significantly less restrictive to trade". This is necessity testing subject to a "reasonably available" qualification. See also Article 2.2: "Members shall ensure that any sanitary or phytosanitary measure is applied only to the extent necessary to protect human, animal or plant life or health . . . ".

into account the objective of minimizing negative trade effects". Arguably this is similar to (or even less stringent than) the third variable (impact on trade) of the balancing test developed in *Korea – Various Measures on Beef*.

A Member must first determine its appropriate level of protection (see Section C); then it must ensure that its appropriate level of protection is consistently applied to the extent required by Article 5.5 of the SPS Agreement. The jurisprudence has confirmed that "the level of protection deemed appropriate by the Member establishing a sanitary . . . measure, is a prerogative of the Member concerned",[88] and that a distinction must be drawn between the appropriate level of protection and the subsequent choice of a specific measure to pursue that appropriate level.[89]

In *Australia – Salmon*, the Appellate Body stated that Article 5.6 clearly provides a three-pronged test to establish a violation. The complaining party must prove that there is a measure that (1) is reasonably available taking into account technical and economic feasibility; (2) achieves the Member's appropriate level of sanitary or phytosanitary protection; and (3) is significantly less restrictive to trade than the SPS measure contested.

> These three elements are cumulative in the sense that, to establish inconsistency with Article 5.6, all of them have to be met. If any of the elements is not fulfilled, the measure in dispute would be consistent with Article 5.6. Thus, if there is no alternative measure available, taking into account technical and economic feasibility, or if the alternative measure does not achieve the Member's appropriate level of sanitary or phytosanitary protection, or if it is not significantly less trade-restrictive, the measure in dispute would be consistent with Article 5.6.[90]

Does this assessment differ from the balancing test under Article XX(b) established in *Korea – Various Measures on Beef*? Does it shed light on how the elements of the necessity test under Article XX should be performed? Recall the findings in *EC – Asbestos* where after noting the chosen level of protection by France (a concept parallel to that of "an appropriate level of protection"), and the importance of the value at stake, the Appellate Body asked itself "the remaining question, then, is whether there is an alternative measure that would achieve the same end and that is less restrictive of trade than a prohibition". These are the same three questions that the *Australia – Salmon* report had identified, with the difference that under Article XX, the Appellate Body insisted on the obligation for Panels to assess the degree of effectiveness of the measure, where in *Australia – Salmon*, it is as if the declared degree of performance of the measure was unchallengeable. Under Article XX(b) the defending Member would have to be able to answer any one of these three questions in the negative, while under the SPS the complaining party would have to be able to answer each of those three questions in the affirmative.

The impact and reference to the GATT "importance of the value at stake" – absent in the SPS Agreement balancing under Article 5.6 – is not clear. Perhaps the SPS Agreement assumes that there is no compromising of authentic health values under the SPS Agreement.

---

[88] Appellate Body Report, *Australia – Salmon*, WT/DS18/AB/R, at para. 199.
[89] This distinction is discussed below.
[90] Appellate Body Report, *Australia – Salmon*, WT/DS18/AB/R, at para. 194.

A Map of the WTO Law of Domestic Regulation of Goods

C. Appropriate Level/Scientific Basis

1. SPS Agreement

Article 2.2 of the SPS Agreement provides that sanitary and phytosanitary measures must be based on scientific principles and may not be maintained without sufficient scientific evidence, except as permitted under Article 5.7.

Article 2.2 of the SPS Agreement requires Members to ensure that any measure is applied only to the extent necessary to protect human, animal or plant life or health. The interpretive question here relates to the significance of the term "applied". This term appears here, and also in the chapeau of Article XX of GATT. In the *US – Shrimp* and *US – Gasoline* cases,[91] the Appellate Body suggested that the chapeau's requirements relate, not to the substance of the measure itself, but to the way in which it is applied, e.g., whether it is applied in a way that constitutes arbitrary or unjustifiable discrimination.[92] Article 5.6, also imposing a "least trade restrictive alternative" requirement, does not limit itself to the manner in which the measure is applied, but addresses measures themselves. The operation of this distinction – between a measure and its application – is unclear, and its relation to jurisprudence, as in the *US – Section 301*[93] and *US – 1916 Act*[94] cases, holding that measures may violate WTO law even if they are not yet applied in a way that violates a specific provision of WTO law, is also unclear.

The sixth preambular paragraph of the SPS Agreement confirms that Members should not be forced to "change their appropriate level of protection of human, animal or plant life or health". Annex A defines the appropriate level of protection as the level deemed appropriate by a Member. The SPS jurisprudence has determined that usually Members must, first, determine their "appropriate" level of protection for each specific case.

> The 'appropriate level of protection' established by a Member and the 'SPS measure' have to be clearly distinguished. They are not one and the same thing. The first is an objective, the second is an instrument chosen to attain or implement that objective.
>
> It can be deduced from the provisions of the SPS Agreement that the determination by a Member of the 'appropriate level of protection' logically precedes the establishment or decision on maintenance of an SPS measure.[95]

---

[91] Appellate Body Report, *US – Shrimp*, WT/DS58/AB/R, at para. 115; Appellate Body Report, *US – Gasoline*, WT/DS2/AB/R, at p. 22.

[92] See Robert Howse, "Democracy, Science and Free Trade: Risk Regulation on Trial at the World Trade Organization", 98 *Michigan Law Review 7* (June 2000), 2329, 2354, citing John T. Barcelo, "Product Standards to Protect the Local Environment – The GATT and the Uruguay Round Sanitary and Phytosanitary Agreement", 27 *Cornell International Law Journal* 3 (1994), 755.

[93] See Panel Report, *United States – Sections 301–310 of the Trade Act of 1974* ("*US – Section 301 Trade Act*"), WT/DS152/R, adopted 27 January 2000.

[94] Appellate Body Report, *United States – Anti-dumping Act of 1916* ("*US – 1916 Act*"), WT/DS136/AB/R, WT/DS162/AB/R, adopted 26 September 2000, at para. 89.

[95] Appellate Body Report, *Australia – Salmon*, WT/DS18/AB/R, at paras. 200–20. Id., at paras. 203: "...The words of Article 5.6, in particular the terms 'when establishing or maintaining sanitary...protection', demonstrate that the determination of the level of protection is an element in the decision-making process which logically precedes and is separate from the establishment or maintenance of the SPS measure. It is the appropriate level of protection which determines the SPS measure to be introduced or maintained, not the SPS measure introduced or maintained which determines the appropriate level

The SPS "Guidelines to Further the Practical Implementation of Article 5.5" recognize that determination of the appropriate level of protection is an element in the decision-making process that logically precedes the selection and use of one or more sanitary or phytosanitary measures. The guidelines encourage Members to express the appropriate level of protection with the use of quantitative terms when feasible and to publish it.[96]

Article 3.3 of the SPS Agreement permits Members to introduce measures that result in a higher level of protection than international standards, if (a) there is scientific justification,[97] or (b) as a consequence of the Member's appropriate level of protection.

> Under Article 3.3 of the SPS Agreement, a Member may decide to set for itself a level of protection different from that implicit in the international standard, and to implement or embody that level of protection in a measure not 'based on' the international standard. The Member's appropriate level of protection may be higher than that implied in the international standard. The right of a Member to determine its own appropriate level of sanitary protection is an important right.[98]

In all cases where a standard other than an international standard is used, the Member imposing an SPS measure must be able to rely on a relevant risk assessment pursuant to Article 5.1 to 5.4 of the SPS Agreement. These requirements[99] were interpreted in each of the three cases under the SPS Agreement: *EC – Hormones*,[100] *Australia – Salmon*[101] and *Japan – Agricultural Products*.[102] In addition

---

of protection. To imply the appropriate level of protection from the existing SPS measure would be to assume that the measure always achieves the appropriate level of protection determined by the Member. That clearly cannot be the case."

[96] See Section B in the Guidelines: "The SPS Agreement does not contain explicit provisions, which oblige a Member to determine its appropriate level of protection, although there is an implicit obligation to do so. In practice, and for various reasons, Members are not always able to indicate precisely their appropriate level of protection. In such cases, the appropriate level of protection may be determined on the basis of the level of protection reflected in the sanitary or phytosanitary measures in place". In *Korea – Various Measures on Beef*, while examining the application of Article XX, the Appellate Body had to presume of the level of protection chosen by Korea, see Appellate Body Report, *Korea – Various Measures on Beef*, WT/DS161/AB/R and WT/DS169/AB/R, para. 178.

[97] Note 2 to Article 3.3 explains that a scientific justification exists if, on the basis of scientific evidence, the regulating state determines that international standards are insufficient to achieve appropriate level of protection.

[98] Appellate Body Report, *EC – Measures Concerning Meat and Meat Products (Hormones)* ("*EC – Hormones*"), WT/DS26/AB/R, WT/DS48/AB/R, adopted 13 February 1998, DSR 1998:I, 135, at para. 172.

[99] In *Australia – Salmon*, the Appellate Body stated: "On the basis of [the] definition [prescribed in the first part of paragraph 4 of Annex A], we consider that, in this case, a risk assessment within the meaning of Article 5.1 must: (1) identify the diseases whose entry, establishment or spread a Member wants to prevent within its territory, as well as the potential biological and economic consequences associated with the entry, establishment or spread of these diseases; (2) evaluate the likelihood of entry, establishment or spread of these diseases, as well as the associated potential biological and economic consequences; and (3) evaluate the likelihood of entry, establishment or spread of these diseases according to the SPS measures which might be applied." Appellate Body Report, *Australia – Salmon*, WT/DS18/AB/R, at para. 121.

[100] Appellate Body Report, *EC – Hormones*, WT/DS26/AB/R, WT/DS48/AB/R.

[101] Appellate Body Report, *Australia – Salmon*, WT/DS18/AB/R.

[102] Appellate Body Report, *Japan – Measures Affecting Agricultural Products* ("*Japan – Agricultural Products II*"), WT/DS76/AB/R, adopted 19 March 1999.

A Map of the WTO Law of Domestic Regulation of Goods

to the interpretations provided by the Appellate Body, Paragraph 4 of Annex A of the SPS Agreement defines two types of "risk assessment".[103]

2. TBT Agreement

The Preamble of the TBT Agreement also makes clear that each Member may determine the level of protection it considers appropriate. The SPS "appropriate level of protection" described earlier can be viewed as parallel to the chosen level of protection (*EC – Asbestos*) and the right of Members to adopt the level of protection they consider appropriate under the TBT Agreement. This "appropriate" level will be reflected in the choice of a specific measure which itself is subject to Article 2.2 of the TBT Agreement, concerned with less-trade-restrictive measures reasonably available to attain the end pursued. The importance of the value and common interest at stake is not explicitly referred to in the balancing of Article 2.2, but the right of Members to pursue any legitimate objective may call for an indirect examination of the degree of "legitimacy" of such objective (how serious is the matter at issue?, the value at stake?), not in theoretical terms but when "taking into account the risks non-fulfilment would create".

The TBT Agreement does not explicitly regulate risk assessments or require scientific bases for regulation. While necessity or proportionality or other standards applicable under the TBT Agreement or GATT may implicitly require some scientific basis, this implicit requirement can be expected to be significantly less rigorous than the explicit requirements of the SPS Agreement.

3. The GATT

In *Korea – Various Measures on Beef*, the Appellate Body stated that "...it is not open to doubt that Members of the WTO have the right to determine for themselves the level of enforcement of their WTO-consistent laws and regulations".[104] A similar general statement was made in *EC – Asbestos*: "We note that it is undisputed that WTK Members have the right to determine the level of protection of health that they consider appropriate in a given situation".[105] "A Member is not obliged, in setting health policy, automatically to follow what, at a given time, may constitute a majority

---

[103] "We note that the first type of risk assessment in paragraph 4 of Annex A is substantially different from the second type of risk assessment contained in the same paragraph. While the second requires only the evaluation of the potential for adverse effects on human or animal health, the first type of risk assessment demands an evaluation of the likelihood of entry, establishment or spread of a disease, and of the associated potential biological and economic consequences. In view of the very different language used in para. 4 of Annex A for the two types of risk assessment, we do not believe that it is correct to diminish the substantial differences between these two types of risk assessments, as the European Communities seems to suggest when it argues that 'the object, purpose and context of the SPS Agreement indicate that no greater level of probability can have been intended for the first type of risk assessment than for the second type, [as b]oth types can apply both to human life or health and to animal or plant life or health'. (Third participant's submission of the European Communities, para. 7)." Appellate Body Report, *Australia – Salmon*, WT/DS18/AB/R, at footnote 67 to para. 120.

[104] Appellate Body Report, *Korea – Various Measures on Beef*, WT/DS161/AB/R and WT/DS169/AB/R, at para. 176.

[105] Appellate Body Report, *EC – Hormones*, WT/DS26/AB/R, WT/DS48/AB/R, at para. 186.

scientific opinion."[106] Relevant to this regulatory autonomy is the Appellate Body's conclusion in *US – Shrimp*, which affirms that a Member may unilaterally determine its policy within the parameters of Article XX:

> It appears to us…that conditioning access to a Member's domestic market on whether exporting Members comply with, or adopt, a policy or policies unilaterally prescribed by the importing Member may, to some degree, be a common aspect of measures falling within the scope of one or another of the exceptions (a) to (j) of Article XX.[107]

Although this right to determine an (appropriate) level of protection is absolute, pursuant to Article XX, the "measure chosen" to implement the policy (end) pursued and the appropriate level of protection can be challenged and set aside by WTO adjudicating bodies.[108] Moreover, because the specific level of protection is not always clearly stated by a Member, the Appellate Body seems to reserve to the panel or itself the right to identify the "authentic" level of protection desired by the concerned Member.

> *We think it unlikely that Korea intended* to establish a level of protection that *totally eliminates* fraud with respect to the origin of beef (domestic or foreign) sold by retailers. The total elimination of fraud would probably require a total ban of imports. Consequently, *we assume that in effect Korea intended to reduce considerably* the number of cases of fraud occurring with respect to the origin of beef sold by retailers.[109] (emphasis added)

Without stating it, the Appellate Body is subjecting to scrutiny the value and common interest at stake, which formed the declared policy basis for Korea's chosen (appropriate) level of protection.

D. Harmonization; Conformity with International Standards

One of the core problems facing the WTO is the imbalance between its new (since 1994) dispute settlement authority on one hand, and its extremely limited legislative capacity on the other hand. The legislative capacity of the WTO is limited by virtue of both legal constraints and a network of informal expectations and attitudes. Moreover, there are substantial questions about the subject matter competence of the WTO – the extent to which the WTO can or should address areas outside of its "core competency" of international trade. Increasingly, the core of international trade is intertwined with a penumbra of traditionally domestic regulatory prerogatives, such as the environment, health, labour, culture, tax, etc.

Although this chapter points to certain negative integration powers (the power of the WTO to strike down domestic regulations) available in WTO dispute settlement, to be exercised through the application of general standards, the WTO has much more limited powers of positive integration (the power of the WTO to "re-regulate" at a multilateral level) available to be exercised through the legislation of specific rules.

---

[106] Appellate Body Report, *Korea – Various Measures on Beef*, as note 104, above, at para. 178.

[107] Id., at para. 121.

[108] Id., at paras. 161–4.

[109] Id., at para. 178.

A Map of the WTO Law of Domestic Regulation of Goods

Yet the law making in the areas covered by the SPS and TBT Agreements is quite unique. Positive integration has two main potential components: harmonization (international legislation or standardization) and recognition. While these agreements contain no requirements of harmonization, they provide some incentives for states to formulate and conform to international standards developed in other fora.

1. SPS Agreement

Interestingly, in the Uruguay Round, in the area of sanitary and phytosanitary measures, certain quasi-legislative authority was referred to certain other functional organizations. That is, the definition of "international standards" contained in Annex A to the SPS Agreement appoints the Codex Alimentarius Commission (Codex), International Office of Epizootics (OIE) and International Plant Protection Convention (IPPC) as "quasi-legislators" of these standards in relevant areas. What do we mean by "quasi-legislators"?[110]

First, the standards developed by Codex, OIE and IPPC for human, animal and plant health, respectively, are, under the terms of their own constitutive documents, non-binding. However, Article 3.1 of the SPS Agreement provides that "Members shall base their sanitary or phytosanitary measures on international standards, guidelines or recommendations, where they exist, except as otherwise provided for in this Agreement, and in particular in paragraph 3". Moreover, Article 3.2 states that SPS measures of WTO Members that are in conformity with international standards, guidelines or recommendations shall be "presumed to be consistent with the relevant provisions of this Agreement". In its *EC – Hormones* decision, the Appellate Body found that the terms "based on" in Article 3.1 and "in conformity with" in Article 3.2 have different meanings. "Based on" means simply derived from, and provides greater flexibility to Members.[111] However, reversing the panel, the Appellate Body found that while Article 3.2 was a safe harbour, it did not establish the converse presumption: the panel erred in presuming that measures that did not conform to international standards were inconsistent with the SPS Agreement. Members can always adopt norms above international standards as long as they comply with the SPS Agreement, including Article 5 on risk assessments.[112] This is true also for Article 2.5 of the TBT Agreement.

This is a refined system of applied subsidiarity,[113] subtly allowing national autonomy subject to certain constraints. Prior to the advent of the SPS Agreement, Codex

---

[110] Note the difference with the TRIPS Agreement where pre-existing norms developed in WIPO treaties are explicitly cross-referenced and made WTO law.

[111] In the *EC – Hormones* decision, the Appellate Body rejected the Panel's finding that "based on" and "conform to" have the same meaning. See Appellate Body Report, *EC – Hormones*, WT/DS26/AB/R, WT/DS48/AB/R, at para. 165.

[112] Therefore, Article 3.3 permits states to introduce measures, which result in a higher level of protection than international standards, if (a) there is scientific justification, or (b) as a consequence of Member's appropriate level of protection. Members can always adopt norms above international standards as long as they comply with the SPS Agreement including Article 5 on risk assessments.

[113] Subsidiarity is the principle that action should not be taken at a higher vertical level of organization if the goal can be accomplished satisfactorily at a lower level. The complex constraints of the SPS Agreement, combined with the international standards to which it refers, set up a system for scrutinizing certain types of state actions and supporting certain types of standard-setting at the international level.

standards had no particular binding force unless accepted for application by national legislation.[114] Given the quasi-legislative character of standards set by Codex, OIE and IPPC (and other organizations), it is worthwhile to examine how these organizations adopt standards.[115] It may be that the SPS Agreement will give rise to modified legislative procedures.[116]

The Codex Commission makes "every effort to reach agreement on the adoption of standards by consensus".[117] However, in instances in which "efforts to reach a consensus have failed",[118] voting does occur, and decisions of the Commission are "taken by a majority of the votes cast".[119]

So, while Codex, OIE and IPPC do not by any means legislate in the normal, or full, sense, the norms that they produce have certain force in creating a presumption of WTO/SPS compatibility when such international standards are respected. The SPS Agreement provisions mentioned earlier provide important incentives for states to base their national standards on, or conform their national standards to, the Codex, OIE and IPPC standards (although compliance with international standards is not required by the SPS or the TBT Agreements). Another important systemic issue is that the WTO Panels and Appellate Body may be obliged to interpret the Codex, OIE and IPPC standards to the extent necessary to interpret the WTO provisions and or a Member's compliance with the WTO provisions.

The fact that the "legislative" act in connection with sanitary and phytosanitary standards takes place outside of the WTO provides some interesting features. First, it may provide the WTO with a degree of insulation from criticism. Second, it provides a legislative device that may evade the need for unanimity, or at least consensus, within the WTO. Amendments and decisions within the WTO have varying formal requirements, up to and including effective unanimity for states to be

---

[114] See Matthias Herdegen, "Biotechnology and Regulatory Risk Assessment", in G. A. Bermann, M. Herdegen and P. L. Lindseth (eds), *Transatlantic Regulatory Cooperation: Legal Problems and Political Prospects* (Oxford: Oxford University Press, 2001) and *The Procedures for the Elaboration of Codex Standards and Related Texts*, available at http://www.fao.org. See also the summary of procedures for adoption of certain types of standards in David G. Victor, "The Sanitary and Phytosanitary Agreement of the World Trade Organization: An Assessment After Five Years", 32 *New York University Journal of International Law and Politics* 4 (2000), 865, 885–95.

[115] See Terence P. Stewart and David S. Johanson, "The SPS Agreement of the World Trade Organization and International Organizations: The Roles of the Codex Alimentarius Commission, the International Plant Protection Convention, and the International Office of Epizootics", 26 *Syracuse Journal of International Law and Commerce* (1998), 27.

[116] Codex standards are generally adopted by consensus. Although the Codex Rules of Procedure provide for voting, it is generally not used. In the event of a vote, decision is by majority of states present at the particular session. Compliance with Codex standards is voluntary. E-mail from Ellen Y. Matten, Staff Officer, US Codex Office, to Joel P. Trachtman (8 August 2001) (on file with author). Furthermore, under the Statements of Principle Concerning the Role of Science in the Codex Decision-Making Process and the Extent to which Other Factors are Taken Into Account, "When the situation arises that members of Codex agree on the necessary level of protection of public health but hold differing views about other considerations, members may abstain from acceptance of the relevant standard without necessarily preventing the decision by Codex".

[117] *CODEX Alimentarius and CODEX Commission*, Ontario Ministry of Agriculture, Food and Rural Affairs, at http://www.gov.on.ca/OMAFRA/english/food/inspection/codex.htm.

[118] Id.

[119] Food and Agriculture Organization and World Health Organization, *Rules of Procedure of the Codex Alimentarius Commission*: Procedural Manual Rule VI.2, 11th ed. (Geneva: WHO, 2000).

A Map of the WTO Law of Domestic Regulation of Goods

bound by amendments, but these formal requirements form the background for informal consensus-based practices. Codex and other standard-setters may provide opportunities for less rigorous adoption of measures. Third, there is the possibility, subject to the difficulty of changing WTO law, to legislatively override Codex or other outside sources of standards. Fourth, this structure provides an opportunity for subject matter specialists, as opposed to trade specialists, to take a leading role in formulating the standards.

Article 3.5 of the SPS Agreement requires the WTO Committee on Sanitary and Phytosanitary Measures (SPS Committee) to monitor international harmonization activities and to co-ordinate with the "relevant international organizations". In October 1997, the SPS Committee adopted provisional procedures to monitor the use of international standards.[120] These procedures were reviewed and continued in July 1999 and in 2001.[121] This SPS decision is only a commitment to "monitor" identified international standards.

The July 2000 decision by the TBT Committee on "Principles for the Development of International Standards Guides, Recommendations with Relation to Articles 2, 5 and Annex 3 of the TBT"[122] differs and seems to go one step further in identifying criteria to be used in the determination of whether an international standard can be used for TBT compliance purposes: transparency, openness, impartiality and consensus, effectiveness and relevance, coherence, and the concerns of developing countries. The purpose of the decision was not to dictate to other international organizations how they should proceed but rather to encourage the participation of Members in the law-making (standard-setting) bodies to which the TBT seems to have lent certain quasi-legislative authority.

In different legal systems, and in different historical moments, it may be better for legislators or treaty makers to engage in more specific negotiations toward more specific rules, or to engage in more general negotiations toward more general "standards", for subsequent interpretation by a court.[123] It is possible for a "legislative" act to provide either a broad or a narrow mandate to a court. A narrow mandate will call for less discretion to be exercised by the court, whereas a broad mandate implicitly delegates greater authority to the court.

Not only do treaty writers delegate authority to dispute resolution tribunals, they also maintain complex relationships with the dispute resolution process, both formal and informal. First, of course, is the possibility of legislative reversal: if the authors of the treaty become discontented with the manner of its application, they may amend the treaty. Furthermore, they may restrain dispute settlement. Second, and relatively unusual in general international law, is a formal "political filter" device, allowing a political body to prevent a more formal legal decision from being taken. This political filter was much more important prior to the adoption of the WTO Understanding on Rules and Procedures for the Settlement of Disputes (DSU), but still exists in an attenuated form.

---

[120] See Document G/SPS/11. At its meeting of 8 July 1999, the Committee adopted the First Annual Report on the monitoring procedure; see document G/SPS/13.

[121] G/SPS/R/9/Rev. 1, para. 21; G/SPS/R/15, Section II; G/SPS/18. The procedures can be found in G/SPS/11.

[122] G/TBT/9, Annex 4.

[123]

Finally, we may consider standard-setting, or positive integration and its relationship to "adjudicative" scrutiny of national measures, or negative integration. Negative integration provides some incentives for states, including the direct incentive arising from the fact that an international standard may be viewed as the least-trade-restrictive alternative, or may be privileged under the SPS or TBT Agreement. We have seen this type of effect in connection with the EU's so-called "new approach to harmonization". In that context, the EU relied on substantial judicial scrutiny, including judicially required recognition under *Cassis de Dijon* and other precedents,[124] while engaging in "essential" harmonization to establish further prerequisites for mutual recognition. Of course, in the trade area, recognition is consistent with complete regulatory market access. Recognition means that the foreign producer has access to the import market on the basis simply of the foreign producer's home country regulation: no additional regulatory requirements are imposed.

2. TBT Agreement

Article 2.4 of the TBT Agreement requires Members to use international standards as a basis for their technical regulations, unless the international standards are an inappropriate or ineffective means to achieve legitimate objectives; so deviations from international standards is discouraged.

This provision was interpreted in *EC – Sardines*.[125] This case addressed a European Communities regulation establishing common marketing standards for preserved sardines (the "EC Regulation"). The EC Regulation provided that only *Sardina pilchardus Walbaum* may be marketed under the name "sardines". Peru produced and exported products of the species *Sardinops sagax*. These species are different, but have certain similarities. The former is mostly found in the Eastern North Atlantic and Mediterranean, whereas the latter is found in the Eastern Pacific. A Codex Alimentarius standard, Codex Stan 94, reserves the name "sardines", used alone, for *Sardina pilchardus Walbaum*, but allows other species, such as *Sardinops sagax*, to be referred to, *inter alia*, as "X sardines" of a country, "in a manner not to mislead the customer".

The EC Regulation, and the Codex Stan 94 standard on which it was allegedly based, both predated the 1995 TBT Agreement. Here, the European Communities did not argue that the TBT Agreement does not apply to continuing measures. Rather, the European Communities argued that there is no ongoing obligation to reassess pre-existing measures in the light of the adoption or modification of international standards. Indeed, one might imagine that the negotiators of the TBT Agreement and SPS Agreement did not expect the procedural requirements of those agreements would apply to pre-existing technical standards. Thus, according to the European Communities, Article 2.4 addresses the preparation and adoption of technical standards, which "measures" in this case were completed and, in effect, ceased to exist, prior to the coming into force of the TBT Agreement. There was little explicit textual

---

[124] Case C-120/78, *Rewe v. Bundesmonopolverwaltung für Branntwein* ("*Cassis de Dijon*"), 1979 ECR 649, para. 8; Case C-302/86, *Commission v. Denmark* ("*Danish Bottles*"), 1988 ECR I-4607, para. 9.

[125] Appellate Body Report, *European Communities – Trade Description of Sardines (EC – Sardines)*, (WT/DS231/AB/R), adopted 26 September 2002.

A Map of the WTO Law of Domestic Regulation of Goods

basis for the EC argument. The Appellate Body referred to its statements in the *EC – Hormones* decision to the effect that continuing measures cannot be assumed to be excepted without greater textual support.[126]

The panel had determined that Codex Stan 94 was a "relevant international standard" within the meaning of Article 2.4. The European Communities argued that only standards adopted by *consensus* may qualify as "relevant international standards", and that the panel failed to determine whether Codex Stan 94 was indeed adopted by consensus. This argument related to the interpretation of the definition of "standard" contained in Annex 1.2 of the TBT Agreement. This definition simply refers to documents "approved by a recognized body", without specifying "consensus". In addition, an "explanatory note" to this definition adds the following two sentences: "Standards prepared by the international standardization community are based on consensus. This TBT Agreement covers also documents that are not based on consensus." The Appellate Body accepted the panel's interpretation to the effect that the latter sentence serves to include within "standard" documents that do not achieve consensus.[127] Neither the panel nor the Appellate Body dealt with the logical absurdity of the quoted language of this explanatory note: if these standards are indeed based on consensus, then anything not based on consensus is not a standard. However, in order to give effect to the second sentence – to allow it *effet utile* – it seems appropriate to reach the conclusion reached by the panel and Appellate Body.

It is worth noting that this conclusion has ramifications for international governance and democratic accountability. That is, states may find that standards that they did not accept – that they in fact rejected – are required to be taken into account and have other legal significance under Article 2.4 of the TBT Agreement.

Article 2.4 requires that Members use "relevant international standards" "as a basis for" their technical regulations. In *EC – Sardines*, the European Communities argued that the EC regulation at issue was based on Codex Stan 94 because it adopted the portion of Codex Stan 94 that reserves the term "sardines" exclusively for *sardina pilchardus*.[128] It argued that this relationship satisfies the requirement, in the European Communities' view, for a "rational relationship" between the international standard and the technical regulation.

The Appellate Body rejected the European Communities' arguments. It recalled its decision in *EC – Hormones*, addressing the meaning of "based on" in Article 3.1 of the SPS Agreement. The Appellate Body here agreed with the panel's use of the *EC – Hormones* decision, finding that in order for a standard to be used "as a basis for" a technical regulation, it must be "used as the principal constituent or fundamental principle for the purpose of enacting the technical regulation".[129] Furthermore, one thing cannot be the "basis" for another if the two are contradictory.[130] Article 2.4 requires that Members use relevant international standards, "or the relevant parts of them, as a basis for their technical regulations". The Appellate Body determined

---

[126] Id., para. 208.

[127] Id., para. 222.

[128] Id., para 241 *quoting* European Communities Appellant's Submission, para. 150.

[129] Id., para. 243.

[130] Id., para. 248.

that the relevant parts of Codex Stan 94 are those relating to the use of the term "sardines" to identify fish products, and not only those portions that reserve the term "sardines" alone for *sardina pilchardus*.[131] The Appellate Body narrowed the scope of its examination to evaluate the relationship between only the portion of the EC Regulation challenged by Peru, and the portions of Codex Stan 94 that address these issues. The Appellate Body found that the EC Regulation contradicts the portion of Codex Stan 94 that *permits* the use of the term "sardines" in combination with, *inter alia*, the name of the country of origin.[132]

The Appellate Body then turned to the question of whether the EC could take advantage of the exceptional language of Article 2.4 of the TBT Agreement. The first question is which state would have the burden of proof as to the matters comprising the basis for this exception. The Appellate Body recalled its statement in *EC – Hormones* that merely characterizing a provision as an "exception" does not alone result in allocation of the burden of proof to the respondent, and criticized the panel's conclusion that this logic is irrelevant in connection with Article 2.4 of the TBT Agreement.[133] The Appellate Body's concept is founded in legal realism: there is no general rule–exception relation, but rather a more refined, or more limited, rule. Under this reasoning, it is for the complainant to show the violation of the more limited rule, including the unavailability of the exception.

Accordingly, the Appellate Body found no general rule–exception relationship between the first and second parts of Article 2.4. Therefore, it was for Peru to bear the burden of proving violation of Article 2.4 *as a whole*. This burden includes establishing that Codex Stan 94 has not been used "as a basis for" the EC Regulation, as well as establishing that Codex Stan 94 is effective and appropriate to fulfil the "legitimate objectives pursued by the European Communities through the EC Regulation."[134] For those concerned about restrictions on domestic regulatory prerogatives pursuant to the TBT Agreement, this allocation of the burden of proof will provide some comfort.

3. The GATT

The GATT does not specifically require the use of international standards at all, although the least-trade-restrictive-alternative requirements under Article XX and or the good faith requirement under the chapeau of Article XX may include a requirement to attempt to create an international or regional standard before applying a unilateral one.

> Clearly, and 'as far as possible', a multilateral approach is strongly preferred. Yet it is one thing to *prefer* a multilateral approach in the application of a measure that is provisionally justified under one of the subparagraphs of Article XX of the GATT 1994; it is another to require the *conclusion* of a multilateral agreement as a condition of avoiding 'arbitrary or unjustifiable discrimination' under the chapeau of Article XX. We see, in this case, no such requirement.[135] (emphasis added)

---

[131] Id., para. 251.
[132] Id., para. 257.
[133] Id., para. 274.
[134] Id., para. 275.
[135] See Appellate Body Report, *US – Shrimp (Article 21.5 DSU)*, at para. 124.

A Map of the WTO Law of Domestic Regulation of Goods

Reliance on international or even regional standards may provide a *de facto* presumption of good faith as required by Article XX.[136]

E. (Mutual) Recognition and Equivalence

1. SPS Agreement

Article 4.1 of the SPS Agreement requires recognition of other states' regulations: "Members shall accept the sanitary or phytosanitary measures of other Members as equivalent, even if these measures differ from their own or from those used by other Members trading in the same product, if the exporting Member objectively demonstrates to the importing Member that its measures achieve the importing Member's appropriate level of sanitary or phytosanitary protection."

On 25 October 2001, the SPS Committee adopted a decision on the implementation of Article 4 on equivalence to "make operational the provisions of Article 4 of the Agreement on the Application of Sanitary and Phytosanitary Measures".[137] It sets up the possibility for other states to serve as "regulatory laboratories" to come up with alternate means to achieve the same regulatory goals. It imposes an obligation on an importing Member, upon the request of the exporting Member, to explain the objective and rationale of the SPS measure, to identify clearly the risks that the relevant measure is intended to address, and to indicate the appropriate level of protection, which its SPS measure is designed to achieve.[138] In addition, the exporting Member must provide reasonable access, upon request, to the importing Member for inspection, testing and other relevant procedures for the recognition of equivalence. Such requests should proceed rapidly, especially with traditional imports, and should not in themselves disrupt or suspend ongoing imports.[139]

---

[136] See id., at paras. 130–1. For an elaboration of this suggestion that compliance with an MEA may provide, in certain circumstances, a *de jure* or *de facto* presumption of compatibility with Article XX, see Gabrielle Marceau, "A Call for Coherence in International Law", 33 *Journal of World Trade* 5 (October 1999), 128–134. See also the panel and Appellate Body Report in *US – Shrimp (21.5 DSU)*.

[137] See document G/SPS/19.

[138] It adds that in doing so, Members should take into account the *Guidelines to Further the Practical Implementation of Article 5.5* adopted by the Committee on Sanitary and Phytosanitary Measures at its meeting of 21–2 June 2000 (document G/SPS/15, dated 18 July 2000).

[139] An interesting issue concerns the legal value of this SPS Decision: If this decision is considered "secondary legislation" (*droit dérivé*), its violation may be invoked in WTO dispute settlement as being part of the "WTO applicable law" binding on all Members. Arguably, the fact that the SPS Committee was given, in Article 12.1, the power to adopt decisions by consensus for the "implementation" of the provisions of the agreement renders it secondary legislation in this sense. Therefore, it is arguable that the SPS Committee may adopt decisions which cannot conflict with or contradict the SPS treaty provisions but which may "implement" them. Many WTO Members believe that the only binding WTO obligations (i.e., those which can be the basis of a claim before WTO courts) are those that are listed in the WTO treaty itself and which they have accepted. For this latter group, the decisions adopted by Members are nothing but gentlemen's agreements. In dispute settlement, the question would arise whether this secondary legislation is a binding part of WTO law. Panels and the Appellate Body may have to decide the WTO nature of such a decision and its compatibility with WTO law. This is a form of indirect judicial control. Most experts would agree that such a decision could also be viewed as "any subsequent agreement between the parties regarding the interpretation of the treaty or the application of its provisions" pursuant to Article 31.3(b) of the Vienna Convention, or at least a rule of international law applicable to the relations between

2. TBT Agreement

The requirement of the SPS Agreement is stronger than the more hortatory obligation of Article 2.7 of the TBT Agreement, which simply requires Members to give positive consideration to accepting foreign regulation as equivalent, if the foreign regulation fulfils the importing state's objectives. In the Second Triennial Review, the TBT Committee considered that "Members may find it useful to further explore equivalency of standards as an interim measure to facilitate trade in the absence of relevant international standards".[140]

Since Article XX requires that Members maintain an appropriate level of flexibility in the administration of their regulatory distinctions,[141] it is probable that Article 2.7 (or Article 2.2 in a manner parallel to Article XX) will be interpreted as requiring sufficient flexibility in normative determinations and good faith consideration of the alternative and equivalent standards suggested by the exporting country.

3. The GATT

GATT contains no explicit equivalency requirement or facility of recognition. However, it is possible that necessity requirements under Article XX(b) or (d) could require recognition. In addition, the Appellate Body in *US – Shrimp (Article 21.5)* seems to have identified such an embryonic requirement in the chapeau of Article XX. "An approach based on whether a measure requires "essentially the same regulatory programme . . . as that adopted by the importing Member . . . [does] not meet the requirements of the chapeau of Article XX". A measure requiring United States and foreign regulatory programmes to be "comparable in effectiveness", as opposed to being "essentially the same" would comply with the prohibition against a disguised restriction on trade.[142] This appears to function as a "soft" equivalency requirement.

---

the parties pursuant to Article 31.3(c), which therefore shall be taken into account in the interpretation of the SPS Agreement. Finally decisions by WTO bodies build on "practice" of the organization and/or state practice, relevant in the interpretation of the WTO treaty, must also be taken into account in the interpretation of WTO provisions. On the issue of secondary legislation, see K. C. Wellens, "Diversity in Secondary Rules and the Unity of International Law: Some Reflections on Current Trends", 25 *Netherlands Yearbook of International Law* (1994), p. 3.

[140] Taking into account the obligation of Members under Article 2.6, the committee emphasized that the possible use of this approach must not hinder the process of development of international standards, guides and recommendations. *TBT Triennial Review*, para. 23, G/TBT/9.

[141] Appellate Body Report, *US – Shrimp*, WT/DS58/AB/R, at para. 165; and Appellate Body Report, *US – Shrimp (Article 21.5)*, WT/DS58/AB/RW, at paras. 135–52.

[142] Appellate Body Report *US – Shrimp*, WT/DS58/AB/R, at para. 144: "In our view, there is an important difference between conditioning market access on the adoption of essentially the same programme, and conditioning market access on the adoption of a programme comparable in effectiveness. Authorizing an importing Member to condition market access on exporting Members putting in place regulatory programmes comparable in effectiveness to that of the importing Member gives sufficient latitude to the exporting Member with respect to the programme it may adopt to achieve the level of effectiveness required. It allows the exporting Member to adopt a regulatory programme that is suitable to the specific conditions prevailing in its territory. As we see it, the Panel correctly reasoned and concluded that conditioning market access on the adoption of a programme comparable in effectiveness, allows for sufficient flexibility in the application of the measure so as to avoid 'arbitrary or unjustifiable discrimination'."

A Map of the WTO Law of Domestic Regulation of Goods

F. Internal Consistency

1. SPS Agreement

Article 5.5 of the SPS Agreement addresses an interesting theoretical issue: Why do people accept greater risk in some circumstances than in others? Article 5.5 requires a regulating state to "avoid arbitrary or unjustifiable distinctions in the levels it considers to be appropriate in different situations, if such distinctions result in discrimination or a disguised restriction on international trade". This provision adds a specific route to be followed to demonstrate discrimination generally prohibited by Article 2.3 SPS.

In *EC – Hormones*, the Appellate Body stated that:

> ... the goal set [by Article 5.5] is not absolute or perfect consistency, since governments establish their appropriate levels of protection frequently on an *ad hoc* basis and over time, as different risks present themselves at different times. It is only arbitrary or unjustifiable inconsistencies that are to be avoided.[143]

It identified three elements which cumulatively must be demonstrated for a violation of Article 5.5 and pointed to "warning signals".

> 214. The first element is that the Member imposing the measure complained of has adopted its own appropriate levels of sanitary protection against risks to human life or health in several different situations. The second element to be shown is that those levels of protection exhibit arbitrary or unjustifiable differences ('distinctions' in the language of Article 5.5) in their treatment of different situations. The last element requires that the arbitrary or unjustifiable differences result in discrimination or a disguised restriction of international trade. We understand the last element to be referring to the measure embodying or implementing a particular level of protection as resulting, in its application, in discrimination or a disguised restriction on international trade....

> 215. We consider the above three elements of Article 5.5 to be cumulative in nature; all of them must be demonstrated to be present if violation of Article 5.5 is to be found. In particular, both the second and third elements must be found. The second element alone would not suffice. The third element must also be demonstrably present: the implementing measure must be shown to be applied in such a manner as to result in discrimination or a disguised restriction on international trade. The presence of the second element – the arbitrary or unjustifiable character of differences in levels of protection considered by a Member as appropriate in differing situations – may in practical effect operate as a 'warning' signal that the implementing measure in its application might be a discriminatory measure or might be a restriction on international trade disguised as an SPS measure for the protection of human life or health.[144]

The Appellate Body report in the *Australia – Salmon* decision[145] found that an unexplained distinction in the levels of protection imposed by Australia ("internal

---

[143] Appellate Body Report, *EC – Hormones*, WT/DS26/AB/R, WT/DS48/AB/R, at para. 213.

[144] Id., paras. 214–15.

[145] Appellate Body Report in *Australia – Salmon*, WT/DS18/AB/R, at para. 240. See also Joost Pauwelyn, "The WTO Agreement on Sanitary and Phytosanitary (SPS) Measures as Applied in the First Three SPS Disputes", 2 *Journal of International Economic Law* 4 (December 1999), 641.

inconsistency") resulted in a disguised restriction on international trade, in violation of Article 5.5 of the SPS Agreement, and by implication, Article 2.3. Interestingly, in that report, the Appellate Body did not adopt the kind of balancing test it had used in the *US – Shrimp* decision[146] to determine whether the US measure in that case constituted arbitrary or unjustifiable discrimination pursuant to the chapeau of Article XX. In that context, in *EC – Hormones*, the Appellate Body also refused the automatic incorporation into Article 5.5 of the SPS Agreement of the legal test developed in *US – Gasoline* for the chapeau of Article XX.[147]

With a view to clarifying the practical implications of the requirements of Article 5.5, Members adopted on 18 July 2000 "Guidelines to Further the Practical Implementation of Article 5.5".[148] The decision on guidelines has to some extent built on the SPS jurisprudence and the practice of Members and has added variables to be used for the operationalization of Article 5.5, keeping in mind the different type of risk assessment for the protection of human life or health.[149] They then identify "warning signals" along the lines of those identified by the Appellate Body in the *EC– Hormones* decision.

With regard to a SPS measure dealing with human, animal or plant life or health, qualitative and quantitative assessments are encouraged and quantification is favoured.[150]

---

[146] See Sections III B.1. and III.H of this chapter.

[147] "However, we disagree with the Panel on two points. First, in view of the structural differences between the standards of the chapeau of Article XX of the GATT 1994 and the elements of Article 5.5 of the SPS Agreement, the reasoning in our Report in *US – Gasoline*, quoted by Panel, cannot be casually imported into a case involving Article 5.5 of the SPS Agreement. Second, in our view, it is similarly unjustified to assume applicability of the reasoning of the Appellate Body in *Japan – Alcoholic Beverages* about the inference that may be drawn from the sheer size of a tax differential for the application of Article III:2, second sentence, of the GATT 1994, to the quite different question of whether arbitrary or unjustifiable differences in levels of protection against risks for human life or health "result in discrimination or a disguised restriction on international trade". Appellate Body Report, *EC – Hormones*, WT/DS26/AB/R, WT/DS48/AB/R, at para. 239.

[148] See Doc. G/SPS/15, adopted on 18 July 2000.

[149] "In the case of protection of plant or animal life or health from pests or disease, situations might be compared if they involve either the risk of entry, establishment or spread of the same or a similar disease, or the risk of the same or similar associated potential biological and economic consequences. In the case of protection of human life or health from specific risks, i.e. food-borne risks, or of animal life or health from risks arising from feedstuffs, situations involving the same type of substance or pathogen, and/or the same type of adverse health effect, could be compared to one another." See Doc. G/SPS/15, adopted on 18 July 2000.

[150] Donna Roberts argues that the SPS Agreement does not permit consideration of the benefits of imports. The SPS authorizes Member states to set the approximate level of protection (ALOP), based on the Member state determination, which may or may not include benefits of the relevant goods. Roberts is right in her (implicit) assertion that Member states would not necessarily include in their calculus the benefits of imported, as opposed to domestic, goods. Part of the problem is the relationship between risk assessment and the appropriate level of protection. Risk assessment, by definition, considers only risks. The appropriate level of protection might consider benefits. Risk assessment determines the level of risk; appropriate level of protection determines how much risk is acceptable, presumably taking benefits into account. Roberts makes an extremely interesting point that Article 5.5 seems potentially inconsistent with this kind of cost–benefits analysis, where differential benefits of imports result in different appropriate levels of protection. However, since the purpose of the SPS is to promote imports, it is quite probable that Article 5.5 would not be interpreted as a prohibition against considering the benefits of imports. Donna Roberts, "The Integration of Economics into SPS Risk Management Policies: Issue and Challenges", in

A Map of the WTO Law of Domestic Regulation of Goods

Risk in the context of the SPS Agreement refers to the likelihood that an adverse event (pest or disease) will occur and the magnitude of the associated potential consequences on plant or animal life or health of the adverse event, or to the potential for adverse effects on human or animal life or health from food-borne risks. Accordingly, categorizing risks as 'similar' must include a comparison of both the relevant likelihood and the corresponding consequences.

Faced with differences noted in this comparison, Members are explicitly invited to review their appropriate level of protection: "the proposed level may need to be modified, or the level of protection previously determined may need to be revised in light of the Member's current views on its appropriate level of protection, or a combination of the two". The guidelines also call on Member states to develop common risk assessment and evaluation procedures, especially with respect to risks affecting human life or health, a common approach for consideration of risks to animal life or health, and a common approach for risks to plant life or health.

The test under Article 5.5 of the SPS is definitely more sophisticated than that under the chapeau of Article XX. Members have a right to take SPS measures, but it is a conditional right and the conditions are stringent. Under Article XX, Members have an exceptional right to take measures based on policies therein listed. The conditions attached are less stringent but this right has to be balanced against the market access rights of other WTO Members.

2. TBT Agreement

The TBT Agreement does not contain any explicit consistency requirement but, as discussed hereafter, the GATT Article XX necessity test appears to contain a soft consistency requirement. A similar requirement could thus exist in the operationalization of the Article 2.2 necessity test.

3. The GATT

Although there is no formal consistency requirement in Article XX(d),[151] the Appellate Body in *Korea – Various Measures on Beef* seems to have read some soft consistency requirement into it, or at least considered that the absence of consistency may be evidence of the lack of objective necessity of the measure:

> The application by a Member of WTO-compatible enforcement measures to the same kind of illegal behaviour – the passing off of one product for another – for like or at least similar products, provides a suggestive indication that an alternative measure which could 'reasonably be expected' to be employed may well be available. The application of such measures for the control of the same illegal behaviour for like,

---

K. Anderson, C. McRae and D. Wilson (Eds.), *Economics of Quarantine and SPS Agreement* (Adelaide: CIES, 2001), p. 9.

[151] See Appellate Body Report *Korea – Various Measures on Beef*, WT/DS161/AB/R and WT/DS169/AB/R, at para. 170: "Examining enforcement measures applicable to the same illegal behaviour relating to like, or at least similar, products does not necessarily imply the introduction of a 'consistency' requirement into the 'necessary' concept of Article XX(d). Examining such enforcement measures may provide useful input in the course of determining whether an alternative measure which could 'reasonably be expected' to be utilized, is available or not."

46 Gabrielle Marceau and Joel P. Trachtman

or at least similar, products raises doubts with respect to the objective necessity of a different, much stricter, and WTO-inconsistent enforcement measure.[152]

G. Permission for Precautionary Action

1. SPS Agreement

The precautionary principle, of course, has been the subject of extensive debate, which cannot be replicated here.[153] However, it is worth pointing out that the precautionary principle is stated in a very specific, and limited, form in Article 5.7 of the SPS Agreement.[154] It is available to allow provisional measures where scientific evidence is insufficient, where the Member acts on the basis of available information, and where the Member seeks to obtain the additional information needed for a more objective assessment of risk within a reasonable period of time. In *EC – Hormones*, the Appellate Body did not reach any conclusion whether the "precautionary principle" had indeed crystallized to become a general principle of law.[155] For the Appellate Body, various elements, including the right of Members to determine the level of protection they want, confirmed that aspects of the precautionary principle were already reflected in different provisions of the SPS Agreement:

> 124. It appears to us important, nevertheless, to note some aspects of the relationship of the precautionary principle to the SPS Agreement. First, the principle has not been written into the SPS Agreement as a ground for justifying SPS measures that are otherwise inconsistent with the obligations of Members set out in particular provisions of that Agreement. Secondly, *the precautionary principle indeed finds reflection in Article 5.7 of the SPS Agreement.* We agree, at the same time, with the European Communities, that there is no need to assume that Article 5.7 exhausts the relevance of a precautionary principle. *It is reflected also in the sixth paragraph of the preamble and in Article 3.3. These explicitly recognize the right of Members to establish their own appropriate level of sanitary protection, which level may be higher (i.e., more cautious) than that implied in existing international standards, guidelines and recommendations.* Thirdly, a panel charged with determining, for instance, whether 'sufficient scientific evidence' exists to warrant the maintenance by a Member of a particular SPS measure may, of course, and should, bear in mind that responsible, representative governments commonly act from *perspectives of*

---

[152] Appellate Body Report, *Korea – Various Measures on Beef*, WT/DS161/AB/R and WT/DS169/AB/R, at para. 172.

[153] On the state of the precautionary principle see, for instance, T. O'Riordan, J. Cameron and A. Jordan (Eds.), *Reinterpreting the Precautionary Principle* (London: Cameron & May, 2001); Mark Geistfeld, "Reconciling Cost-Benefit Analysis with the Principle That Safety Matters More Than Money", 76 *New York University Law Review* (2000), 114; Gabrielle Marceau, "Le principe de précaution et les règles de l'Organisation mondiale du commerce" dans *Le principe de précaution et le droit international*, under the direction of Charles Leben and Joe Verhoeven (Paris: Editions Panthéon-Assas, 2001), p. 131.

[154] It is reported that Article 5.7 of the SPS Agreement was initially drafted to be used in emergency situations where, for example, the spread of a disease had to be stopped urgently before it may be feasible to complete a risk assessment. Discussion with Gretchen Stanton, Secretary of the SPS Committee.

[155] The Appellate Body in *EC – Hormones* stated, "The status of the precautionary principle in international law continues to be the subject of debate among academics, law practitioners, regulators and judges. . . . We consider, however, that it is unnecessary, and probably imprudent, for the Appellate Body in this appeal to take a position on this important, but abstract, question." Appellate Body Report, *EC – Hormones*, WT/DS26/AB/R, WT/DS48/AB/R, at para. 123.

A Map of the WTO Law of Domestic Regulation of Goods

prudence and precaution where risks of irreversible, e.g. life-terminating, damage to human health are concerned. (emphasis added)

125. We accordingly agree with the finding of the Panel that the precautionary principle does not override the provisions of Articles 5.1 and 5.2 of the SPS Agreement.

The WTO adjudicating bodies do not have the capacity to enforce non-WTO rules that would add to or diminish WTO obligations and rights.[156] The crystallization of the precautionary principle into an authentic general principle of law could not add to or diminish the rights and obligations under the covered agreements and thus, could not set aside the WTO treaty provisions. However, such a general principle of law would be taken into account in the interpretation of the relevant WTO provisions [pursuant to Article 31.3(c) of the Vienna Convention]. Having recognized the limited jurisdiction of WTO adjudicating bodies,[157] it should also be noted that WTO Members are bound to respect all their obligations simultaneously ("the" or "a" precautionary principle would be of equal hierarchical value to the treaty provisions of the WTO). Under international law, WTO Members would be under an obligation to comply with both their WTO obligations and any general principle of law regarding the precautionary principle, although such a general principle could not be given direct effect by WTO adjudicating bodies but they could recognize its existence and appreciate its impact on WTO law. Most often it will be possible for states to respect both their WTO rights and obligations and the rights and obligations entailed by the precautionary principle.

If the right of Members to determine their appropriate level of protection is an indication or a component of the precautionary principle, one may say that similar "expressions" of the precautionary principle exist in the TBT Agreement and in Article XX of GATT. Indeed, the rights of Members to determine the level of protection they want[158] and to act with prudence on the basis of minority opinion[159] were recognized by the Appellate Body in its interpretation of Article XX.

---

[156] On this issue, see Joel Trachtman, "The Domain of WTO Dispute Resolution", 40 *Harvard International Law Journal* (1999), 333; Marceau, as note 126; Gabrielle Marceau, "Conflicts of Norms and Conflicts of Jurisdictions", 35 *Journal of World Trade* 6 (December 2001), 1081. For a contrary view see Joost Pauwelyn, "The Role of Public International Law in the WTO: How Far Can We Go?", 95 *American Journal of International Law* (July 2001), 595; Lorand Bartels, "Applicable Law in WTO Dispute Settlement Proceedings", 35 *Journal of World Trade* 3 (June 2001), 499; Thomas J. Schoenbaum, "WTO Dispute Settlement: Praise and Suggestions for Reform", 47 *International and Comparative Law Quarterly* (2000), 647; David Palmeter and Petros Mavroidis, "The WTO Legal System: Sources of Law", 92 *American Journal of International Law* 3 (July 1998), 398.

[157] See Trachtman, ibid.; Marceau, as note 126, above; and Marceau, *Conflicts of Norms*, as note 156, above.

[158] "... we note that it is undisputed that WTO Members have the right to determine the level of protection of health that they consider appropriate in a given situation." Appellate Body Report, *EC – Asbestos*, WT/DS135/AB/R, at para. 168.

[159] See Appellate Body Report, *EC – Asbestos*, WT/DS135/AB/R, at para. 178: "In addition, in the context of the *SPS Agreement*, we have said previously, in *European Communities – Hormones*, that "responsible and representative governments may act in good faith on the basis of what, at a given time, may be a *divergent* opinion coming from qualified and respected sources" (emphasis added). In justifying a measure under Article XX(b) of the GATT 1994, a Member may also rely, in good faith, on scientific sources which, at that time, may represent a divergent, but qualified and respected, opinion. A Member is not obliged, in setting health policy, automatically to follow what, at a given time, may constitute a majority scientific opinion."

In *Japan – Agricultural Products II*,[160] the Appellate Body found that Article 5.7 is available subject to the satisfaction of four cumulative requirements: (i) relevant scientific evidence is insufficient, (ii) the measure is adopted on the basis of available pertinent information, (iii) the Member seeks to obtain the additional information necessary for a more objective assessment of risk, and (iv) the Member reviews the measure accordingly within a reasonable period of time. In the instant case, the panel made a finding only as to the insufficiency of relevant scientific evidence, determining that there was indeed sufficient scientific evidence on the issues at hand.

In *Japan – Apples II*, the Appellate Body found that the standard of sufficiency under the first prong of this test refers to the measure of information necessary to perform an adequate assessment of risks as required under Art. 5.1.[161] The Appellate Body insisted that the application of Article 5.7 is triggered "*not by the existence of scientific uncertainty*, but rather by the insufficiency of scientific evidence" and "the two concepts are not interchangeable".[162]

2. TBT Agreement

Under the TBT Agreement, there is no requirement of any form of specific evidence and no provision for situations where scientific evidence would be insufficient to justify a norm. Yet Article 2.2, in requiring that measures be no more restrictive than necessary, will call for some demonstration that some objective necessity exists. Scientific evidence may be called for.

Situations where the scientific evidence is insufficient or not available may thus occur, and in these situations, the analysis would be similar to that described earlier with respect to the SPS Agreement.

3. The GATT

If Members' rights to determine the level of protection they want, to be prudent and to rely on minority opinion, are expressions or indications of the precautionary principle (as the Appellate Body seems to have established), one may argue that the interpretation of Article XX has already taken into account aspects of a precautionary principle. As with the SPS Agreement, the crystallization of the precautionary principle would not reduce the requirements contained in Article XX nor could it be enforced autonomously before a WTO adjudicating body. However, it could be used in the interpretation of WTO provisions.

For the Appellate Body, Article XX (and 11 of the DSU) had to be interpreted in light of this right of democratic government to be responsible and prudent:

> In the context of the SPS Agreement, we have said previously, in *European Communities – Hormones*, that responsible and representative governments may act in good faith on the basis of what, at a given time, may be a divergent opinion coming from

---

[160] Appellate Body Report on *Japan – Agricultural Products II*, WT/DS76/AB/R, para. 89.

[161] Appellate Body Report on *Japan – Measures Affecting the Importation of Apples*, WT/DS245/AB/R, adopted 10 December, para. 179.

[162] Appellate Body Report on *Japan – Measures Affecting the Importation of Apples*, para. 184 (emphasis added).

A Map of the WTO Law of Domestic Regulation of Goods

qualified and respected sources. In justifying a measure under Article XX(b) of the GATT 1994, a Member may also rely, in good faith, on scientific sources which, at that time, may represent a divergent, but qualified and respected, opinion. A Member is not obliged, in setting health policy, automatically to follow what, at a given time, may constitute a majority scientific opinion.[163]

The *EC – Asbestos* Panel had also stated: "... to make the adoption of health measures concerning a definite risk depend upon establishing *with certainty* a risk ... would have the effect of preventing any possibility of legislating in the field of public health" (emphasis added).[164]

H. Balancing

To many commentators, the idea of balancing tests in contexts where domestic regulation is subject to international scrutiny has been an anathema to judicial restraint and national sovereignty, as expressed in the following sentences. There are two likely reasons. First, balancing tests seem to some to accord too much power to courts. However, it is not unusual for courts to be assigned the task of balancing, explicitly or implicitly, under specified circumstances. Under the Appellate Body's opinion in *EC – Asbestos*, even the determination of violation of national treatment obligations under Article III may be understood as requiring a type of balancing, to determine whether imports are subject to "less favourable treatment". Second, balancing tests seem to intervene too greatly in national regulatory autonomy.[165] This intervention is not considered excessive because it might strike down domestic regulation, but because it might involve an international tribunal in too extensive an inquiry into the costs and benefits of domestic regulation. In other words, it is not the intervention of a court under this second concern that is troubling, but the intervention of an international court.

1. The GATT

The GATT has no specific language authorizing a balancing test. The SPS Agreement and the TBT Agreement, while providing for least-trade-restrictive-alternative analysis, also avoid specific reference to balancing tests. Note that a least-trade-restrictive-alternative test, at least as earlier conceived, avoids evaluation of the value of the goal sought to be achieved by the relevant domestic regulation, as well as a comparison between that value and the detriment to international trade caused by the domestic regulation.[166] As further discussed later, the Appellate Body in *Korea – Various Measures on Beef* has added an additional element to the search for a less-trade-restrictive alternative: the importance of the value or interest at stake.

---

[163] Appellate Body Report, *Korea – Various Measures on Beef*, WT/DS161/AB/R and WT/DS169/AB/R, at para. 178 (footnote omitted).

[164] Panel Report, *European Communities – Measures Affecting Asbestos and Asbestos-Containing Products* ("*EC – Asbestos*"), WT/DS135/R and Add. 1, adopted 5 April 2001, as modified by the Appellate Body Report, WT/DS135/AB/R, at para. 8.221.

[165] For a more extensive analysis of the objections to balancing tests, see Trachtman, *Trade and ... Problems, supra* note 54.

[166] See Trachtman, as note 54, above. See also Axel Desmedt, "Proportionality in WTO Law", 4 *Journal of International Economic Law* (2001), 441.

(a) Balancing Under the Necessity Test [Article XX(b) and (d)]

The classic "least-trade-restrictive-alternative" test has been challenged by the Appellate Body's recent decisions in *Korea – Various Measures on Beef* and *EC – Asbestos*. In *Korea – Various Measures on Beef*, the Appellate Body first examined the definition of "necessity" under Article XX(d) of GATT, finding that it could comprise something less than absolute indispensability. Interestingly, the Appellate Body stated that "a treaty interpreter assessing a measure claimed to be necessary to secure compliance of a WTO-consistent law or regulation may, in appropriate cases, take into account the relative importance of the common interests or values that the law or regulation to be enforced is intended to protect".[167] This statement would involve the Appellate Body in assessing the importance of national goals to a degree not seen, at least explicitly, before.[168]

It is interesting that the Appellate Body refers to "common interests or values". Does this require, or prefer, a degree of homogeneity of purpose? Must the interest be common to all people, or only the Member state imposing the measure? In practice it may be difficult to reconcile the right of Members to determine their appropriate level of protection (even in abstract terms) and the balancing of the importance of the value at stake in the necessity assessment of Article XX. In other words, a Member has a right to choose any appropriate level of protection, but if it chooses a silly one relative to the value at stake as evidence of its chosen measure, its relative importance will be discounted in the balancing test.[169]

Indeed, the Appellate Body sets up, rather explicitly, a balancing test. It considers the degree to which the measure contributes to the realization of the end pursued: "the greater the contribution, the more easily a measure might be considered to be 'necessary'."[170] It would also consider the "extent to which the compliance measure produces restrictive effects on international commerce".[171] The Appellate Body's statement will be breathtaking to some:

> In sum, determination of whether a measure, which is not 'indispensable', may nevertheless be 'necessary' within the contemplation of Article XX(d), involves in every case a process of weighing and balancing a series of factors which prominently include the contribution made by the compliance measure to the enforcement of the law or regulation at issue, the importance of the common interests or values protected by that law or regulation, and the accompanying impact of the law or regulation on imports or exports.[172]

This statement constitutes a significant shift toward a greater role of the WTO adjudicating bodies in weighing regulatory values against trade values. It appears to be intended to speak beyond the Article XX(d) context to all necessity testing,

---

[167] Appellate Body Report, *Korea – Various Measures on Beef*, WT/DS161/AB/R and WT/DS169/AB/R, at paras. 162, 163.

[168] See Trachtman, as note 54, above.

[169] Under the SPS Guidelines on 5.5, the conclusion by a Member (after the comparison called for under Article 5.5 SPS) should lead to a change of appropriate level of protection.

[170] Appellate Body Report, *Korea – Various Measures on Beef*, WT/DS161/AB/R and WT/DS169/AB/R, at para. 163.

[171] Id. (citation omitted).

[172] Id., at para. 164.

A Map of the WTO Law of Domestic Regulation of Goods

including that under Article XX(b), and presumably, the SPS Agreement and TBT Agreement.

The Appellate Body found that the panel was justified in examining enforcement measures in similar circumstances, without, as Korea complained, imposing a formal "consistency" requirement. "Examining such enforcement measures may provide useful input in the course of determining whether an alternative measure which could 'reasonably be expected' to be utilized, is available or not."[173] The application of WTO-compatible measures to the same kind of behaviour suggested to the Appellate Body that a reasonably available alternative measure might exist.[174] The Appellate Body confirmed the panel's conclusion that Korea failed to demonstrate that alternative measures were not reasonably available.

Interestingly, in its decision regarding *EC – Asbestos*, the Appellate Body referred to its decision in *Korea – Various Measures on Beef* to the effect that in determining whether another alternative method is reasonably available, it is appropriate to consider the extent to which the alternative measure "contributes to the realization of the end pursued".[175] This discussion suggests an incursion on the degree to which a state may expect to achieve its appropriate level of protection. This is a significant departure from the conventional understanding of "reasonably available", which would consider the costs of the alternative regulation but not the degree of its contribution to the end (as the test under Article 5.6 of the SPS seems to announce). In fact, the degree of contribution to the end seemed before to be inviolable. This is not the ordinarily understood meaning of necessity as a search for the least-trade-restrictive alternative reasonably available: that formulation would not ordinarily involve an evaluation, or any compromise, of the end pursued.[176] Furthermore, the Appellate Body referred to *Korea – Various Measures on Beef* for the proposition that the more important the common interests or values pursued, the easier it would be to accept the national measure as necessary.[177]

The balancing test for determining "necessity" under Article XX(b) and (d) developed in these reports will stimulate much discussion and controversy. It is less deferential to national regulatory goals than a test that would simply seek to confirm whether those goals are met, rather than assessing the degree to which they are met. It actually purports to examine the importance of those national goals. These are to be balanced against the impact on trade.

(b) Balancing Under the Chapeau of Article XX

When Article XX(g) has been satisfied, a form of "necessity" test (thus a balancing) is still performed under the chapeau of Article XX.[178] However, there is also a

---

[173] Id., at para. 170.

[174] Id., at para. 172.

[175] See Appellate Body Report, *EC – Asbestos*, WT/DS135/AB/R, at para. 172 (citing its report in *Korea – Various Measures on Beef*, WT/DS161/AB/R and WT/DS169/AB/R, at paras. 161–4).

[176] See Trachtman, as note 54, above.

[177] Appellate Body Report, *EC – Asbestos*, WT/DS135/AB/R, at para. 172.

[178] The operation of the chapeau of Article XX seems to vary whether it follows the invocation of subparagraphs (g) or (b) and (d). On four occasions the Appellate Body had to examine the application of the chapeau of Article XX. Three times [in *US – Gasoline*, *US – Shrimp* and *US – Shrimp (21.5 DSU)*], it was done in the context of a measure that was considered to have "passed" (provisional justification) under

broader balancing of rights and obligations, which is called for by the chapeau of Article XX.[179] In *US – Shrimp*, the Appellate Body stated that the chapeau of Article XX "embodies the recognition of the . . . need to maintain a balance of rights and obligations" between the right of a Member to invoke the exceptions of Article XX on the one hand and the rights of the other Members under the GATT 1994, on the other hand. This interpretation and application of Article XX requires "locating and marking out a line of equilibrium between the right of a Member to invoke an exception under Article XX and the rights of the other Members under varying substantive provisions". "The location of the line of equilibrium is not fixed and unchanging; the line moves as the kind and the shape of the measures at stake vary and as the facts making up specific cases differ."[180]

This line of equilibrium must find expression in the respective scope of application of Articles III:4 and XX. In *US – Gasoline*, the Appellate Body stated that Article XX(g) cannot "be read so expansively as seriously to subvert the purpose and object of Article III:4. Nor may Article III:4 be given so broad a reach as effectively to emasculate Article XX(g) and the policies and interests it embodies." However, in *EC – Asbestos*, the Appellate Body also said – in justifying its decision that health risks ought to be taken into account in assessing the competitive relationship between imports and domestic like goods – "The scope and meaning of Article III:4 should not be broadened or restricted beyond what is required by the normal customary international law rules of treaty interpretation, simply because Article XX(b) exists and may be available to justify measures inconsistent with Article III:4. The fact that an interpretation of Article III:4 under those rules implies a less frequent recourse to Article XX(b) does not deprive the exception in Article XX(b) of *effet utile*. Article XX(b) would only be deprived of *effet utile* if that provision could not serve to allow a Member to "adopt and enforce" measures "necessary to protect human . . . life or health".[181]

(c) Balancing Under Article III

In its *EC – Asbestos* decision, the Appellate Body may have recognized that its competition-based interpretation of "like products" would result in a relatively broad scope of application of Article III:4. In order to avoid a commensurately broad scope of invalidation of national law, the Appellate Body emphasized the second element required under Article III:4:

> A complaining Member must still establish that the measure accords to the group of 'like' imported products 'less favourable treatment' than it accords to the group of

subparagraph (g) of Article XX, which contains fairly lenient requirements. In *EC – Asbestos*, although the Panel had reached conclusions on the application of the chapeau of Article XX, and even if both the application of sub-paragraph (b) and the chapeau of XX was appealed, the Appellate Body did not mention the chapeau of Article XX and simply concluded that the measure was necessary pursuant to Article XX(b) without any reference to the appeal of the findings on the chapeau of XX. With the components of the necessity test developed by the Appellate Body (with soft consistency and flexibility and non-discrimination requirements), it is difficult to conceive what additional analysis could be performed under the chapeau of Article XX.

[179] The chapeau requires that measures exempted under Article XX must not be applied in a manner which would constitute "a means of arbitrary or unjustifiable discrimination between countries where the same conditions prevail, or a disguised restriction on international trade . . . ".

[180] See Appellate Body Report, *US – Shrimp*, WT/DS58/AB/R, at para. 158.

[181] Appellate Body Report, *EC – Asbestos*, WT/DS135/AB/R, at para. 115.

A Map of the WTO Law of Domestic Regulation of Goods

'like' domestic products. The term 'less favourable treatment' expresses the general principle, in Article III:1, that internal regulations 'should not be applied . . . so as to afford protection to domestic production'.[182]

In *Korea – Various Measures on Beef*, the Appellate Body had already insisted that "A formal difference in treatment between like imported and domestic products is thus neither necessary, nor sufficient, to show a violation of Article III:4. Whether or not imported products are treated "less favourably" than like domestic products should be assessed instead by examining whether a measure modifies the conditions of competition in the relevant market to the detriment of imported products". In *EC – Asbestos*, it clarified that foreign like products as a class must be treated differently from, and less favourably than, domestic like products. Thus, it may be argued that it is not enough to find a single foreign like product that is treated differently from a single domestic like product. Rather, the class of foreign like products must be treated less favourably than the class of domestic like products. The area left for panel or Appellate Body discretion is in determining, in cases of *de facto* and unintentional disparate regulatory treatment, whether there is a violation of the national treatment requirement.[183]

Although the exercise of this discretion is not balancing per se, it is worthwhile to speculate as to how panels or the Appellate Body would exercise this discretion. They would presumably examine, explicitly or implicitly, whether the less favourable treatment is justified by an appropriate regulatory goal. This exercise would be done either under Articles III or XX. The examination would presumably involve a degree of balancing.

2. TBT Agreement

It seems reasonable to expect that the interpretation of the positive requirements of Article 2.2 for a measure not more trade restrictive than necessary will be parallel to that developed under the necessity test of Article XX. There has been an important cross-fertilization between the SPS jurisprudence and the interpretation of Article XX. For instance, when the Appellate Body was discussing Article XX, it was making use of systemic considerations, such as the balance between market access obligations and the right of Members to pursue policies other than trade. This balance of rights and obligation finds explicit expression in the TBT and SPS agreements, which, however, articulate and operate them differently. Ultimately similar variables are balanced for a search to capture protectionist measures not otherwise justified by what WTO Members consider legitimate policies.

---

[182] Appellate Body Report, *EC – Asbestos*, WT/DS135/AB/R, at para. 100 (emphasis in original).

[183] See Joel P. Trachtman, "Decision of the Appellate Body of the World Trade Organization: European Communities – Measures Affecting Asbestos and Asbestos-Containing Products", 12 *European Journal of International Law* (2001), 793, available at http://www.ejil.org/journal/curdevs/sr13.html; Lothar Ehring, *De Facto Discrimination in WTO Law: National and Most-Favoured-Nation Treatment – or Equal Treatment?*, Jean Monnet Working Paper No.12/01, available at http://www.jeanmonnetprogram.org/papers/01/013201.html, last visited 1 June 2002. See our prior discussion. It is also possible that "less favourable treatment" be interpreted broadly so as to include any market distortion favouring domestic products, even if the goal, object and purpose of the measure are not protectionist. In such case, reliance on Article XX to justify such measure would remain possible.

3. SPS Agreement

The criteria identified by the SPS jurisprudence seem to call for a necessity/balancing test under Article 5.6 of the SPS Agreement fairly similar to that developed in *Korea – Various Measures on Beef* and *EC – Asbestos*, discussed earlier. Yet, contrary to Article XX, the test under Article 5.6 SPS does not appear to call for an assessment of the degree of the measure's contribution to the end. As with the classic least-trade-restrictive alternative "reasonably available", the degree of contribution to the end seemed before to be inviolable: states were entitled to complete accomplishment of the end reflected in their regulation.

I. Product/Process Issues and the Territorial–Extraterritoriality Divide

Finally, an area of great importance is the territorial scope of application of the national measures: that is, to what extent can a state take action under its domestic law to protect health or other "domestic" regulatory values outside its own territory? This issue has arisen explicitly in connection with the application of Article XX(b) and (g), but has also arisen implicitly, in the form of the product–process distinction, the PPM issue.[184]

1. The GATT

The legal issue relating to PPM is whether GATT/WTO law authorizes Members to maintain regulatory distinctions based on process and production methods (PPMs) of imported products. In particular the debate has focused on whether products that comply with specified PPM criteria and those that do not are "like" for the purpose of the national treatment obligations of Article III.

GATT case law did not seem to accept any PPM's consideration as a *prima facie* basis for regulatory distinctions. For example, in *US – Measures Affecting Alcoholic and Malt Beverages*,[185] a Minnesota tax credit for micro-breweries was invalidated, even though it was available to foreign as well as domestic brewers, because the beer, though produced by a different method, was deemed like, and the discriminatory tax treatment was therefore an Art. III violation. The *Tuna* panel took the following line: Under a GATT Article III analysis, regulation of production processes, which processes implicitly take place in the exporting state, is not "subject to" Article III, fails the strict scrutiny test of Article XI and is therefore an illegal quantitative restriction, unless an exception applies under Article XX. Under the WTO Agreement, the *US – Shrimp* dispute presented similar facts and was analysed at the panel level in a similar manner, but the Article XI violation found by the panel was not challenged

---

[184] For discussions of the product/process distinction, see Robert E. Hudec, "The Product-Process Doctrine in GATT/WTO Jurisprudence", in Marco Bronckers and Reinhard Quick (Eds.), *New Directions in International Economic Law: Essays in Honour of John H. Jackson* (The Hague: Kluwer Law International, 2000); Robert Howse and Donald Regan, "The Product/Process Distinction – An Illusory Basis for Disciplining "Unilateralism" in Trade Policy", 11 *European Journal of International Law* (2000), 249, and the cogent response to the Howse/Regan article from John Jackson at 11 *European Journal of International Law* (2000), 303.

[185] GATT Panel Report, *US – Malt Beverages*, adopted 19 June 1992, BISD 39S/206.

A Map of the WTO Law of Domestic Regulation of Goods

by the United States and therefore the Appellate Body did not have an opportunity to consider whether PPMs should be analysed under Article III.

Various elements support the view that Article III does not "apply" to regulatory distinctions based on extra-territorial policy considerations not affecting the products. Article III refers to measures affecting "internal sales"; Article III's concern is the internal market of the importing Member. The wording of Articles I, II, III and XI of GATT only refer to "products". Annex 1A covers rules applicable to trade in goods. Moreover the Appellate Body has recognized that when determining whether two products are directly competitive or substitutable for the purpose of Article III GATT, Article 4 of the Agreement on Safeguards or Article 6.1 of the Agreement on Textiles and Clothing, it is looking at the "product characteristics":[186]

> A plain reading of the phrase 'domestic industry producing like and/or directly competitive products' shows clearly that the terms 'like' and 'directly competitive' are characteristics attached to the domestic products that are to be compared with the imported product. We are, therefore, of the view that the definition of the domestic industry must be product-oriented and not producer-oriented, and that the definition must be based on the products[187] produced by the domestic industry which are to be compared with the imported product in terms of their being like or directly competitive.[188]
>
> ... a careful reading of our Report [in *Korea – Alcoholic Beverages*] would show we used the terms 'directly competitive' and 'directly substitutable' without implying any distinction between them in assessing the competitive relationship between products.[189] We do not consider that the mere absence of the word 'substitutable' in Article 6.2 of the ATC renders our interpretation of the term 'directly competitive' under Article III:2 of the GATT 1994 irrelevant in terms of its contextual significance for the interpretation of that term under Article 6.2 of the ATC.[190]
>
> The criteria of 'like' and 'directly competitive' are characteristics attached to the domestic product in order to ensure that the domestic industry is the appropriate industry in relation to the imported product.[191]
>
> 'Competitive' is a characteristic attached to a product and denotes the capacity of a product to compete both in a current or a future situation.[192]

The advantage of this approach is that the product–process distinction serves as a clear and simple rule on territorial–extraterritorial regulatory distinctions in the main GATT market access rules: production processes occur in the exporting Member. Policies effected in the other Members are not under the jurisdiction of the

---

[186] Note that if the competitive behaviour of a product is considered to be a characteristic of the product, then the product characteristic referred to in the definition of the TBT Agreement may not be limited to the physical characteristics of the product.

[187] [Original footnote] "In *United States – Lamb Safeguard*, we also found that the *product* defines the scope of the definition of the domestic industry under the Agreement on Safeguards. In that case, the 'like' product at issue was lamb meat (Appellate Body Report, as note 41, above, paras. 84, 86–8 and 95)."

[188] Appellate Body Report, *United States – Transitional Safeguard Measure on Combed Cotton Yarn from Pakistan* (*US – Cotton Yarn*), (WT/DS192/AB/R), adopted 5 November 2001, at para. 86.

[189] Original footnote referring to *Korea – Alcoholic Beverages* at paras. 114–16.

[190] See Appellate Body in *US – Cotton Yarn*, para. 94

[191] Id., at para. 95

[192] Id., at paras. 92 and 96.

importing Member. Products coming into the territory of the importing state are. This way, a certain territorial vision of the regulatory autonomy of both the importing and exporting Members would be maintained. Physical characteristics of products can be regulated by the importing Member but not non-product-related policies. Some extra-territorial policy considerations may be available under the exceptional provisions of Article XX.[193]

Others may argue that Article III covers all internal regulations, even when based on extra-territorial considerations not reflected in the physical characteristics of the products as such. GATT, one of the agreements of Annex 1A of the WTO Agreement, is concerned with disciplines on products and thus disciplines on regulations broadly affecting trade in goods. For them, the issue would rather be whether – based on the criteria established by the jurisprudence – the products complying with the PPM requirements are competing with those that do not, and whether the challenged regulation affects the latter group negatively (if they are imported). According to this view, Article III applies to PPM regulations but the operationalization of Article III will generally lead to the conclusion that PPM and non-PPM-based products are like products[194] and should not be *prima facie* the target of regulatory distinctions restricting market access.

Some have suggested that Members should be authorized to use PPM-type regulations in order to make distinctions between two otherwise similar goods and consider them "unlike" for the purpose of Article III. For some of them,[195] in *EC – Asbestos*, the Appellate Body has opened up the likeness test to insist on the need to consider consumers' preferences relating to PPMs. The determination of likeness requires consideration of any evidence that indicates whether the products are in a competitive relationship in the marketplace.[196] For the Appellate Body, evidence

---

[193] See also Lorand Bartels, "Article XX of GATT and the rules of Public International Law on Extraterritorial Jurisdiction: The Case of Trade Measures for the Protection of Human Rights", 36 *Journal of World Trade* 2 (June 2002).

[194] It is, however, conceivable that faced with a PPM distinction referring to human rights violations or other very serious concerns, consumers' preferences will be so strong as to reverse the *prima facie* evidence that goods that are physically similar be nonetheless considered unlike, pursuant to the Appellate Body statement in para. 118 of its *EC – Asbestos* Report. This type of situation may also constitute a justification under Article XX. The point is that if consumer preferences are strong enough to make them unlike, there is little need for regulation. This argument holds if the persons protected by the regulation are the consumers, rather than third parties.

[195] For instance Howse and Regan, however, argue that analysing PPMs under Article XI does not make sense, because PPMs which are enforced internally, even as against foreign products, will not be caught by quota restrictions or border measure disciplines (Articles II or XI of GATT) and will therefore be undisciplined. Robert Howse and Donald Regan, "The Product/Process Distinction – An Illusory Basis for Disciplining "Unilateralism" in Trade Policy", 11 *European Journal of International Law* 2 (2000), 249. If, as Howse and Regan suggest, PPMs ought to be evaluated under Art. III, then the like products test comes into play. They argue that the likeness test should be interpreted as looking for the existence of differences between products that justify different regulation. Recently Howse and Türk have elsewhere suggested that the *EC – Asbestos* decision opens the door to consider distinctions based on PPMs in the context of the like products test. Robert Howse and Elizabeth Türk, "The WTO Impact on Internal Regulations – A Case Study of the Canada–EC Asbestos Dispute", in Gráinne de Búrca and Joanne Scott (Eds.), *The EU and the WTO: Legal and Constitutional Aspects* (London: Hart Publishing, 2001).

[196] Appellate Body Report, *EC – Asbestos*, WT/DS135/AB/R, at paras. 97–9.

A Map of the WTO Law of Domestic Regulation of Goods

relating to health risks[197] (carcinogenicity, or toxicity) associated with the product can be examined under the existing *Border Tax Adjustment* report categories of physical properties and consumer tastes and habits and products' end-use;[198] this fuelled the argument that consumer preference could legitimate PPM distinctions under the Article III like-product test.

In determining whether this competitive relationship actually exists, the Appellate Body[199] seems to have focused a good deal on the physical characteristics of the products, namely their carcinogenicity or toxicity. Although it stated that all of four criteria must each time be examined,[200] and that these four criteria are not a closed set, despite the possibility of conflicting evidence from those criteria,[201] it arguably gave a heavier weight to physical characteristics, or at least differences in physical characteristics, when it wrote:

> In such cases, in order to overcome this indication that products are not 'like', a higher burden is placed on complaining Members to establish that, despite the pronounced physical differences, there is a competitive relationship between the products such that all of the evidence, taken together, demonstrates that the products are 'like' under Article III:4 of the GATT 1994.[202]

A contrario, if goods are physically similar, it will not be easy to prove that they are not otherwise competing with each other.[203] Although consumers may at times distinguish based on production processes, and some competitive effect is quite possible, it is difficult to envision a circumstance where the effect would be great enough to render physically similar products "un-like".

To summarize, the WTO jurisprudence has not yet clarified whether Article III "applies" to or covers PPM-type regulatory distinctions. If Article III does not cover PPM-type regulations, then, under **ad** Article III, PPM regulations will be viewed as border import restrictions (a ban of products not respecting the PPM prescriptions) controlled by Article XI. If Article III covers PPM-type regulations, the Appellate Body's application of a competition-based test in *EC – Asbestos* suggests that in most cases, different PPMs would be insufficient to make products "un-like". The test under Article III would then prohibit treating like products differently on the basis of PPM considerations. In this sense the product–process distinction may often serve as a proxy to control the extra-territorial application of national measures which extra-territorial application is perhaps exceptionally permitted under the circumstances set forth in Article XX.

---

[197] Note the inconsistency between this perspective and the economic theory of regulation, which assumes that the reason for regulatory intervention is because the health risks are not sufficiently reflected in the market place.

[198] Appellate Body Report, *EC – Asbestos*, WT/DS135/AB/R, at para. 117.

[199] And even more so the dissenting member of the Appellate Body for whom the particularly different physical characteristics – toxicity – of the products at issue was irrebuttable evidence against their "likeness"; id., at paras. 151–3.

[200] Id., at paras. 102, 109, 111, 113, 139 and 140.

[201] Appellate Body Report, *EC – Asbestos*, WT/DS135/AB/R, at para. 120.

[202] It also added, "Furthermore, in a case such as this, where the fibres are physically very different, a panel cannot conclude that they are 'like products' if it does not examine evidence relating to consumers' tastes and habits". Id., at para. 121.

[203] Id., at paras. 117 and 118.

However, it is possible that the Appellate Body's focus on whether the difference in treatment is "less favourable" could provide a basis for finding that a particular PPM regulation does not violate Article III, if the treatment offered to the non-PPM product were to be considered "different" but *not* less favourable (or protectionist). Furthermore, the Appellate Body has left open the possibility that Article XX of GATT can authorize exceptional extraterritorial policy or PPM considerations if they comply with the requirements of the relevant sub-paragraph as well as those of the chapeau of Article XX.

2. TBT Agreement

Annex 1 of the TBT Agreement defines "technical regulation" as a "document which lays down product characteristics or their related processes and production methods, including the applicable administrative provisions with which compliance is mandatory". In the early draft of the first Standards Code, regulations based on process rather than products were explicitly excluded from the coverage of the TBT Agreement.[204] Article 14.25 of the Tokyo Standards Code[205] seemed to allow explicitly dispute settlement proceedings under the TBT for allegations that process methods were used in technical regulations as a means to circumvent the obligations of the code. This is curious. If dispute settlement against PPMs is expressly authorized, then the TBT Agreement covers or applies to PPMs, even if it is only to invalidate them. Early debates during the Uruguay Round about the definition of technical barriers to trade were motivated by a desire to include processes and production methods within the disciplines of the TBT Agreement, in order to prevent them from becoming barriers to trade.[206]

Many developing countries have argued that the TBT Agreement does not "cover" PPM regulations and have politically challenged notifications of labelling requirements based on social considerations[207] and timber process[208] not having any physical impact on the product traded. It is important to note that the

---

[204] The first drafts stated that "Standards includes, where applicable, testing, packaging, marking or labelling specifications and codes of practice, to the extent that they should have affected *products rather than process*" (emphasis added) [see, for instance, Spec (72)3, 20 January 1972]. In June 1976 the United States proposed to add "For the purpose of this Code 'technical specifications' include processes and productions methods in so far as they are necessary to achieve the final product" (MTN/NTM/W/50, p. 2). In the draft of May 1977 (Draft Document MTN/NTM/W/94, 20 May 1977), the reference to product rather than process was deleted from the definition of a technical regulation.

[205] Article 14.25 reads as follows: "The dispute settlement procedures set out above can be invoked in cases where a Party considers that obligations under this Agreement are being 'circumvented' by the drafting of requirements in terms of processes and production methods rather than in terms of characteristics of products".

[206] See Note by WTO Secretariat, *Negotiating History of the Coverage of the Agreement on Technical Barriers to Trade with Regard to Labeling Requirements, Voluntary Standards, and Processes and Production Methods Unrelated to Product Characteristics*, WT/CTE/W/10; G/TBT/W/11 (29 August 1995).

[207] See the notification by Belgium on "socially responsible products", G/TBT/N/BEL/2 and the discussions of Members in G/TBT/M/23 of 8 May 2001 and G/TBT/M/24 of 14 August 2001.

[208] See the Netherlands notification G/TBT/Notif.98.448 and the discussions of Members in G/TBT/M/13 of 15 September 1998, G/TBT/M/14 of 20 November 1998, G/TBT/M/23 of 30 March 2001 and G/TBT/M/24 of 29 June 2001.

A Map of the WTO Law of Domestic Regulation of Goods

non-application of the TBT Agreement to PPM-type regulations would not make such PPM regulations incompatible with WTO law. If the TBT Agreement does not cover or apply to PPM regulations, such regulations will be examined under Articles III/XI of GATT and may find justification under Article XX. To remove PPM-type regulations from the coverage of the TBT Agreement would exempt them from the other requirements of the same TBT Agreement, including those on notification, harmonization and mutual recognition. Furthermore, as noted below, unlike the case of the SPS Agreement, the TBT Agreement contains no presumption of compliance with GATT. It would be curious if non-PPM technical regulations were subject to the more stringent requirements of the TBT Agreement, while the less transparent PPM-type technical regulations, possibly justified under Article XX of GATT, were not. It would be even more curious because PPM labels appear to be covered by the TBT Agreement.

Under the TBT Agreement, technical regulations include "packaging, marking, or labelling requirements as they apply to a product, process or production method". Note that there is no reference to "their related" PPMs. It seems that the TBT Agreement would cover PPM labels, with less or no risk of contradictory analysis under Articles III/XI and XX of GATT.[209] Yet some Members are of the view that only product-related PPM labels are covered by the definition of technical regulation. It may be in that context that Members called for a notification of all technical regulations independently of the kind of information contained in the label:

> In conformity with Article 2.9 of the Agreement, Members are obliged to notify all mandatory labelling requirements that are not based substantially on a relevant international standard and that may have a significant effect on the trade of other Members. That obligation is not dependent upon the kind of information which is provided on the label, whether it is in the nature of a technical specification or not.[210]

Whether PPMs regulations generally are included in the definition of technical regulations depends on how one reads "characteristics" of the products and "their related process and production methods". Are characteristics of a product only those reflected physically in that product? As mentioned before, on three occasions[211] the Appellate Body stated that the competitive nature and capacity of products constituted characteristics of the same products. On the other hand, the Tokyo Standards Code made an explicit distinction in Article 14.25 in allowing challenges against "drafting requirements in terms of processes and production rather than in terms of characteristics of products". Is the prescription for "their related" process and production methods a reference to PPMs that have a physical relation to the products? If so, do only the PPM regulations that have a physical impact on the product constitute technical regulations covered by the TBT Agreement? Or does this definition refer to PPMs that relate to the production of the said product (even without any physical impact on the product), as opposed to policy considerations that are general and that are not concerned specifically with the production or the process of any specific

---

[209] Yet it is still possible that a measure that is incompatible with the TBT will be compatible with GATT.

[210] G/TBT/1/Rev.7, Section III:10.

[211] See Appellate Body Report, *US – Cotton Yarn*, WT/DS192/AB/R, at paras. 86, 92, 96.

products, such as a distinction between imports that come from Members that have family allowances programmes and those who do not?

If the TBT Agreement does not cover PPMs, then PPM regulation will be examined under Articles III/XI and XX of GATT which will remain the only WTO applicable law.

3. SPS Agreement

Annex A to the SPS Agreement contains a definition of "sanitary and phytosanitary measures" that includes only measures that protect health within the territory of the regulating Member. It therefore excludes from its coverage measures addressing health outside the regulating Member's territory. This leaves importing state regulation seeking to regulate processes and production methods in the exporting state, with the goal of protecting health outside the territory of the importing state, outside the coverage of the SPS Agreement, but potentially subject to GATT or the TBT Agreement. Importantly, it includes measures of importing states regulating PPMs outside of their territory, where the goal is to protect health within the territory; for example, regulation of foreign slaughterhouse practices may be considered SPS measures. Most SPS PPMs will be product-related because they focus on the health risk of imported food products. Yet it is worth noting that Annex A includes in the definition of "SPS measures" regulations concerned with "relevant requirements associated with transport of animals and plants".

J. Conclusion

The purpose of this section has been to outline certain critical rules applicable under GATT, the SPS Agreement and the TBT Agreement, in order to motivate the following analysis of the relative coverage of these agreements, and the norms contained therein. This section has already raised several of the issues of scope of application.

This section has shown that GATT is more *laissez-régler* than the SPS Agreement and TBT Agreement, at least for most purposes. Its primary discipline in connection with domestic regulation is non-discrimination. Article XX is only invoked after a finding of violation of, for example, Article III or Article XI. Furthermore, the TBT Agreement is generally less strict in its scrutiny of domestic regulation than the SPS Agreement. For example, the TBT Agreement lacks an explicit requirement of a risk assessment. Yet the jurisprudence seems to have read into Article XX of GATT, albeit in softer terms, some of the more explicit norms of the TBT and SPS agreements.

Now, how would these different provisions work together?

IV. Invoking the Disciplines of SPS, TBT and the GATT

It has been necessary to describe the disciplines provided by the SPS Agreement, TBT Agreement and GATT, prior to describing the way in which these sources of norms interact with one another. Now we may proceed to analyse the relationships among these disciplines. The scope of application of these agreements may determine their effect on Members' behaviour. We begin with the general principle that each of these treaty norms hold equal binding force, and, of course, were entered into at the same time, so among them there are no issues relating to *jus cogens* or *lex posterior*.

A Map of the WTO Law of Domestic Regulation of Goods

There are two junctures at which to consider the invocation of the disciplines of the SPS Agreement, the TBT Agreement and GATT.[212] First is the question of the conditions of application of each agreement individually.

Second is the question of what happens when more than one agreement on its face applies to a particular national measure: Does the application of one discipline result in deference by another, and under what circumstances? The Uruguay Round brought a number of new subjects within the GATT/WTO legal system. It may not have been completely anticipated that the treatment of some of these new subjects in one agreement would overlap with another agreement. For example, where there are alleged barriers to the distribution of goods, issues may arise under both the GATT, relating to goods, and the General Agreement on Trade in Services, relating to services. Indeed, this occurred in the *EC – Bananas III* litigation.[213] In its decision on *EC – Bananas III*, the Appellate Body made clear that the scope of application of each of the GATT and the GATS are independent, and may well overlap.[214]

A. Conditions of Application: Applicable Law

1. The GATT

GATT generally applies to all trade in goods. We discussed earlier the PPM issue, but it is important to note that the PPM issue does not influence the scope of application of GATT, but only the relative scope of application among Articles I, III, XI, XIII and XX thereof. The issue is whether the PPM measure is an internal regulation (imposed at the border) subject to Article III or a border import restriction subject to Article XI? Does Article III impose disciplines on PPM-type regulation and thus "apply" to them or are PPMs "not covered", and therefore "not regulated" by Article III, leaving them to the application of Article XI? In any event, it appears that Article XX would justify some PPMs.

2. TBT Agreement

The TBT Agreement applies both to voluntary standards and to mandatory technical regulations relating to all products, including industrial and agricultural products.[215]

In the *EC–Asbestos* case, the panel and Appellate Body had occasion to consider the scope of application of the TBT Agreement. The panel found that the TBT Agreement did not apply to the part of France's measure setting out the prohibition on goods containing asbestos. According to the panel, as a blanket prohibition, the measure did not "lay down product characteristics" within the meaning of Annex 1 of the TBT Agreement. The panel separated this prohibition from the decree's exceptions for purposes of analysis.

---

[212] On the issue of the relationship between GATT 1994 and other WTO multilateral trade agreements, see Elisabetta Montaguti and Maurits Lugard, "The GATT 1994 and Other Annex 1A Agreements: Four Different Relationships?", 3 *Journal of International Economic Law* 3 (September 2000), 473.

[213] See Appellate Body Report, *European Communities – Regime for the Importation, Sale and Distribution of Bananas* ("*EC – Bananas III*"), WT/DS27/AB/R, adopted 25 September 1997.

[214] Id., at paras. 221–2.

[215] Article 1.3 of the TBT Agreement.

Canada appealed this separation, and the finding that the TBT Agreement did not apply. Furthermore, Canada argued that a "general prohibition" qualifies as a technical regulation under Annex 1.1 of the TBT Agreement. The Appellate Body found that the measure must be examined as a whole.[216] When examined as a whole, the French measure was not a total prohibition, but if this measure consisted only of a prohibition on asbestos fibres, it might not constitute a "technical regulation".[217] The Appellate Body found that the core of the definition of "technical regulation" is the laying down of one or more product characteristics, in either positive or negative form: that is, as a requirement or as a prohibition. The Appellate Body found that the ban on asbestos fibres under the decree must be understood as a ban on products containing asbestos fibres. The Appellate Body concluded that the decree, viewed as an integrated whole, lays down "characteristics" for certain products (those that might otherwise contain asbestos), and is accordingly a "technical regulation" under the TBT Agreement.[218] The Appellate Body emphasized, however, that this does not mean that all internal measures covered by Article III:4 of GATT are necessarily "technical regulations". Would all technical regulations be covered by Article III:4? Probably, so long as they "affect" internal sales.

In *EC – Sardines*, the Appellate Body revised the definition of "technical standard". The European Communities argued that the EC Regulation was not a technical regulation in respect of *Sardina pilchardus Walbaum* and not in respect of *Sardinops sagax*. Here, the Appellate Body agreed with the panel[219] to the effect that, under the *EC – Asbestos* jurisprudence, the products covered need only be identified, and may be addressed in either a positive or negative way, to be included within a technical regulation. The Appellate Body rejected the European Communities' argument that the EC Regulation did not identify *Sardinops sagax* as irrelevant to the question of whether the EC Regulation *negatively* regulated *Sardinops sagax* by prohibiting its labelling as sardines.

3. SPS Agreement

As noted earlier in connection with our discussion of PPMs, the SPS Agreement's scope of application is limited to sanitary and phytosanitary measures that may affect international trade.[220] Sanitary or phytosanitary measures are defined by reference to their purpose,[221] and include measures applied:

> (a) to protect animal or plant life or health within the territory of the Member from risks arising from the entry, establishment or spread of pests, diseases, disease-carrying organisms or disease-causing organisms;

---

[216] Appellate Body Report, *EC – Asbestos*, WT/DS135/AB/R, at para. 64. See a similar conclusion by the Appellate Body under Article XX of GATT in *US – Gasoline*, WT/DS2/AB/R, at pp. 13–14.

[217] Appellate Body Report, *EC – Asbestos*, WT/DS135/AB/R, at para. 71.

[218] Id., at para. 75.

[219] *European Communities – Trade Description of Sardines*, WT/DS231/R, 29 May 2002, WT/DS231/R/Corr.1, adopted on 10 June 2002, as amended by the Appellate Body.

[220] Article 1.1 of the SPS Agreement.

[221] Contrary to TBT regulation defined by reference to, arguably, more objective criteria based on products' characteristics.

A Map of the WTO Law of Domestic Regulation of Goods

(b) to protect human or animal life or health within the territory of the Member from risks arising from additives, contaminants, toxins or disease-causing organisms in foods, beverages or feedstuffs;

(c) to protect human life or health within the territory of the Member from risks arising from diseases carried by animals, plants or products thereof, or from the entry, establishment or spread of pests; or

(d) to prevent or limit other damage within the territory of the Member from the entry, establishment or spread of pests.[222]

We can summarize these parameters as including measures designed to protect against pests and diseases, as well as food-borne dangers. As noted above, although PPMs may be included as sanitary or phytosanitary measures, they are only covered to the extent that they are "applied" or "have effects" to protect animal, plant or human life within the territory of the Member taking the measure. Therefore, the SPS Agreement would not cover extraterritorially motivated PPMs.[223] Another issue relates to circumstances where pests, diseases and food-borne dangers are not the only purpose of a measure. If a measure is only partially motivated by sanitary or phytosanitary purposes, is it still covered by the SPS Agreement?[224] As yet, there is no jurisprudence on this issue. However, based on the concept of cumulative obligations under the WTO agreements, a measure might be only partially motivated by health concerns, and still be subject to the SPS Agreement. So, a measure might be partly an SPS measure and partly a TBT measure, and subject to both agreements.

Finally, in the *EC – Hormones* case, it was decided that the SPS Agreement applies to all measures in force, including measures initially taken prior to the time the SPS Agreement entered into force (1 January 1995).[225]

B. Cumulative Application and the Interpretative Principle of Effectiveness

The *EC – Bananas III* and *Canada – Periodicals*[226] decisions of the Appellate Body in connection with the relationship between the GATT and the GATS suggest that the rights and obligations under these agreements are cumulative. This conclusion is supported, in the context of the relationship between GATT Article III, the TRIMS

---

[222] SPS Agreement, Annex A.

[223] It is possible that a PPM would have a mixed territorial and extraterritorial motivation, for example, where the goal is to comply with an international effort to eradicate a particular disease that might not yet pose a threat in the state implementing the measure at issue. Under these circumstances, there would be a factual question whether the measure is sufficiently intended to protect life or health within the territory of the relevant state.

[224] See Pauwelyn, as note 156, above, at pp. 643–4.

[225] Appellate Body Report, *EC – Hormones*, WT/DS26/AB/R, WT/DS48/AB/R, at para. 128. The interpretation of the relevant provision of the SPS Agreement on measures "applied" was supported by an additional reference to Article 28 of the Vienna Convention. The parallel provision of the TBT on measures prepared, adopted and applied would also be interpreted along similar lines.

[226] Appellate Body Report, *Canada – Certain Measures Concerning Periodicals* ("*Canada-Periodicals*"), WT/DS31/AB/R, adopted 30 July 1997, DSR 1997:I, 449.

Agreement and the SCM Agreement (*Indonesia – Automobiles*[227]), GATT Article XIII and the Agreement on Agriculture (*EC – Bananas III*), GATT Article XIII and the Safeguards Agreement (*US – Line Pipe*[228]) and the Agreement on Safeguards and GATT Article XIX (*Korea – Dairy Safeguards*).

> We agree with the statement of the Panel that: It is now well established that the WTO Agreement is a 'Single Undertaking' and therefore all WTO obligations are generally cumulative and Members must comply with all of them simultaneously.[229] . . .
>
> In light of the interpretive principle of effectiveness, it is the duty of any treaty interpreter to 'read all applicable provisions of a treaty in a way that gives meaning to all of them, harmoniously'.[230] An important corollary of this principle is that a treaty should be interpreted as a whole, and, in particular, its sections and parts should be read as a whole.[231, 232]

This was a simple application of the principle of effective interpretation. This fact that all provisions of a treaty must have an effective meaning and must be interpreted so as to ensure that no other provisions is made a 'nullity' is expressed in the principle for 'effective interpretation'.

It is suggested that the principle of effective interpretation calls for the harmonious interpretation and application of both rights and obligations. In *US – Gasoline*, the Appellate Body insisted that Article XX provides rights and other provisions of the GATT that should not be interpreted and applied so as to nullify the exercise of such rights.[233] In *Brazil – Desiccated Coconut*, the Appellate Body upheld the panel

---

[227] Panel Report, *Indonesia – Certain Measures Affecting the Automobile Industry* ("*Indonesia – Autos*"), WT/DS54/R and Corr.1,2,3,4, WT/DS55/R and Corr.1,2,3,4, WT/DS59/R and Corr.1,2,3,4, WT/DS64/R and Corr.1,2,3,4, adopted 23 July 1998, DSR 1998:VI, 2201.

[228] Panel Report, *United States – Definitive Safeguard Measures on Imports of Circular Welded Carbon Quality Line Pipe from Korea* ("*US – Line Pipe*"), WT/DS202/R, adopted 8 March 2002.

[229] Appellate Body Report, *Korea – Definitive Safeguard Measures on Imports of Some Dairy Products Dairy* ("*Korea – Dairy*"), WT/DS98/AB/R, adopted 12 January 2000, para. 74.

[230] [Original Footnote] We have emphasized this in Appellate Body Report, *Argentina – Safeguard Measures on Imports of Footwear* ("*Argentina – Footwear (EC)*"), WT/DS121/AB/R, adopted 12 January 2000, at para. 81. See also Appellate Body Report, *United States – Gasoline*, WT/DS2/AB/R, at p. 23; Appellate Body Report, *Japan – Alcoholic Beverages II*, WT/DS8/AB/R, WT/DS10/AB/R, WT/DS11/AB/R, at p. 12; and Appellate Body Report, *India – Patents*, para. 45.

[231] [Original Footnote] The duty to interpret a treaty as a whole has been clarified by the Permanent Court of International Justice in *Competence of the I.L.O. to Regulate Agricultural Labour* (1922), PCIJ, Series B, Nos. 2 and 3, p. 23. This approach has been followed by the International Court of Justice in *Ambatielos (Greece v. United Kingdom)* 1953 *International Court of Justice Reports* 10 (19 May); *Reservations to the Convention on the Prevention and Punishment of the Crime of Genocide* 1951 *International Court of Justice Reports* 15 (28 May); and *Rights of Nationals of the United States of America in Morocco (France v. United States)* 1952 *International Court of Justice Reports* 196, 196–9 (27 August). See also I. Brownlie, *Principles of Public International Law*, 5th ed. (Oxford: Clarendon Press, 1998), p. 634; G. Fitzmaurice, *The Law and Procedure of the International Court of Justice 1951–1954: Treaty Interpretation and Other Treaty Points*, 33 *British Year Book of International Law* (1957), 211, 220; A. McNair, *The Law of Treaties* (Oxford: Clarendon Press, 1961), pp. 381–2; I. Sinclair, *The Vienna Convention on the Law of Treaties* (Manchester: Manchester University Press, 1984), pp. 127–9; M. O. Hudson, *La Cour Permanente de Justice Internationale* (1936), pp. 654–9; and L. A. Podesta Costa and J. M. Ruda, *Derecho Internacional Público*, Vol. 2 (Buenos Aires: Editora Argentina, 1985), p. 105.

[232] Appellate Body Report, *Korea – Dairy*, WT/DS98/AB/R, para. 81.

[233] Appellate Body Report, *US – Gasoline*, WT/DS2/AB/R, at pp. 22–3.

A Map of the WTO Law of Domestic Regulation of Goods

that the transitional rights given in the SCM Agreement could not be nullified by an interpretation of Article VI of GATT 1994.[234] The Panel in *Turkey – Textiles* suggested that because the WTO Members have a right under Article XXIV to form regional trade agreements, the interpretation of the other WTO provisions should be such as to ensure that this right does not become a "redundancy or a nullity".[235]

In case of inconsistencies within a treaty between two obligations or between obligations and rights, rules have been developed to identify how to deal with such situations and include the presumption against conflicts, the *lex posterior* principle, the *lex specialis* principle and the inviolability of *jus cogens*. Because there is no issue of *jus cogens* here, and all WTO provisions were adopted at the same time, the WTO's obligations and rights must apply cumulatively and harmoniously unless set aside because of a conflict with another provision, or because another provision is *lex specialis*[236].

1. Possibility of Conflicts

(a) General Interpretative Note to Annex 1A

The General Interpretative Note to Annex 1A to the WTO Charter (the "General Interpretative Note") provides that

> [i]n the event of conflict between a provision of the General Agreement on Tariffs and Trade 1994 and a provision of another agreement in Annex 1A to the Agreement establishing the World Trade Organization (referred to in the agreements in Annex 1A as the 'WTO Agreement'), the provision of the other agreement shall prevail to the extent of the conflict.

The other agreements in Annex 1A include, *inter alia*, the SPS Agreement and the TBT Agreement. Thus, the latter prevail over GATT in the event of conflict. The note is irrelevant in the case of conflicts between the TBT and the SPS agreements.

(b) Definition of a Conflict in WTO Law

In international law a conflict[237] is a rather specific and narrow concept:

> ... [T]echnically speaking, there is a conflict when two (or more) treaty instruments contain obligations which cannot be complied with simultaneously.... Not every

---

[234] Appellate Body Report on *Brazil – Measures Affecting Desiccated Coconut* (*"Brazil – Desiccated Coconut"*), WT/DS22/AB/R, adopted 20 March 1997, at p. 17.

[235] Panel Report, *Turkey – Restrictions on Imports of Textiles and Clothing Products* (*"Turkey-Textiles"*), WT/DS33/R, adopted 19 November 1999, at paras. 9.96 and 9.103, recalling the Appellate Body's wording in *US – Gasoline*.

[236] See, for instance, the statement of the Appellate Body in *EC – Bananas III*: "Therefore the provisions of the GATT 1994, including Article XIII, apply to market-access commitments concerning agriculture products, except to the extent that the Agreement on Agriculture contains specific provisions dealing specifically with the same matter". Appellate Body Report, *EC – Bananas III*, WT/DS27/AB/R, at para. 155. On this issue, see Marceau, *Conflicts of Norms*, as note 156, above.

[237] For a thorough discussion on the concept of conflict, see Joost Pauwelyn, *The Issue of Conflict in WTO Law*, PhD thesis, University of Neufchatel (2001).

such divergence constitutes a conflict, however. . . . Incompatibility of contents is an essential condition of conflict.[238]

The presumption against conflict is especially reinforced in cases where separate agreements are concluded between the same parties, since it can be presumed that they are meant to be consistent with themselves, failing any evidence to the contrary.[239]

In the WTO context, this narrow definition of a conflict was confirmed in *Guatemala – Cement*,[240] when the Appellate Body stated that "a special or additional provision should only be found to prevail over a provision of the DSU in a situation where adherence to the one provision will lead to a violation of the other provision, that is, in the case of a conflict between them". Recently, in *US – Hot Rolled Steel from Japan*, the Appellate Body supported again a narrow definition of "conflict" and stated that "there is no conflict between Article 17.6(i) of the Antidumping Agreement and Article 11 of the DSU"[241] and ". . . we see Article 17.6(ii) as supplementing, rather than replacing, the DSU, and Article 11 in particular"[242]. The strict conflict approach was also followed by the *Indonesia – Autos* Panel, requiring, as a matter of general public international law, outside the context of the General Interpretative Note, "mutually exclusive obligations".[243]

(c) Conflicts Between the GATT, TBT and SPS Agreements?

In the context of the question of the relationship between GATT, on the one hand, and the TBT and SPS agreements on the other hand, strict conflict is unlikely – it is difficult to imagine circumstances where one requires what the other forbids.

---

[238] *Encyclopedia of Public International Law* (Amsterdam: Elsevier Science, 1984), p. 468. See also Wilfred Jenks, "The Conflict of Law-Making Treaties", 29 *British Year Book of International Law* (1953), p. 425ff. For in such a case, it is possible for a state which is a signatory of both treaties to comply with both treaties at the same time. The presumption against conflict is especially reinforced in cases where separate agreements are concluded between the same parties, since it can be presumed that they are meant to be consistent with each other, failing any evidence to the contrary. See also E. W. Vierdag, "The Time of the 'Conclusion' of a Multilateral Treaty: Article 30 of the Vienna Convention on the Law of Treaties and Related Provisions", 64 *British Year Book of International Law* (1988), p. 100; Sir Robert Jennings and Sir Arthur Watts (eds), *Oppenheim's International* Law, 9th ed. (London: Longman, 1992), Vol. 1, Parts 2–4, p. 1280; Fitzmaurice, as note 231, above, at 237; and Sinclair, as note 231, above, at 97.

[239] Jenks, ibid.

[240] Appellate Body Report, *Guatemala – Anti-Dumping Investigation Regarding Portland Cement from Mexico* ("*Guatemala – Cement*"), WT/DS60/AB/R, adopted 25 November 1998, at para. 65. The same narrow definition was also used in Panel Report, *Indonesia – Autos* WT/DS54/R and Corr.1,2,3,4, WT/DS55/R and Corr.1,2,3,4, WT/DS59/R and Corr.1,2,3,4, WT/DS64/R and Corr.1,2,3,4, at paras. 14.29–14.36 and 14.97–14.99.

[241] Appellate Body Report, *United States – Antidumping Measures on Certain Hot-Rolled Steel Products from Japan* ("*US – Hot-Rolled Steel*"), WT/DS 184/AB/R, adopted 23 August 2001, at para. 55

[242] Ibid., at para. 62.

[243] Panel Report, *Indonesia – Autos*, WT/DS54/R and Corr.1,2,3,4, WT/DS55/R and Corr.1,2,3,4, WT/DS59/R and Corr.1,2,3,4, WT/DS64/R and Corr.1,2,3,4, at footnote 649. For further discussion on the conflicts within the WTO and conflicts between WTO provisions and provisions of treaties or customs, see Gabrielle Marceau, "The WTO Dispute Settlement and Human Rights", *European Journal of International Law* 13/4 (2002) and Joost Pauwelyn, *Conflict of Norms in Public International Law, The Example of the WTO: Internal Hierarchy and How WTO Relates to Other Rules of International Law*, unpublished PhD thesis, University of Neuchâtel (2001) (on file with author).

A Map of the WTO Law of Domestic Regulation of Goods

2. Lex Specialis

Another relevant principle in the context of overlapping treaty provisions is that of *lex specialis derogat generali*: the special law derogates from the general law. Although this principle does not appear in the Vienna Convention, it has been recognized and applied in a number of cases by the International Court of Justice and is recognized by a number of learned commentators.[244]

The object of such a rule is that when a subject matter is dealt with in specific terms by a (set of) provision(s), the general rule, if it cannot be read harmoniously with the specific one, is set aside and the matter is governed by the specific one(s).[245] For some, the *lex specialis* is an exception to the *lex posterior* rule, which cancels out, supersedes or abrogates the general clause if it provides for a special regime of rules.[246] For others, the *lex specialis* is only a principle of interpretation according to which a matter governed by a specific provision is thereby taken out of the scope of a general provision – the *lex specialis* and the *lex generalis* do not deal with the same subject matter, and therefore do not conflict.[247] When a specific right or an exception is provided for against a general prohibition, the *lex specialis* rule may find application.

In WTO dispute settlement, it is clear that the customary rules of interpretation of general international law are applicable.[248] One of these customary rules of interpretation is *lex specialis*.[249] This principle of interpretation would lead to identifying the more specific WTO obligation(s). The Appellate Body report in *EC – Bananas III* did not go so far as to say that the specific controls the general: it stated that whenever GATT and another agreement in Annex 1A to the WTO Agreement appear to apply

---

[244] For instance, see *Encyclopedia of Public International Law* 468 (Amsterdam: Elsevier, 1984). V. Lowe refers to B. Cheng, *General Principles of International Law*, 25–6 (1987); Fitzmaurice, *supra* note 231. A. McNair, *The Law of Treaties* 219 (Oxford: Clarendon Press, 1961); Sir R. Jennings and Sir A. Watts, *Oppenheim's International Law*, 9th ed. (London: Longman, 1992), p. 1280; D. P. O'Connell, *International Law*, 2nd ed. (1970), 12–13.

[245] For a recent example of a *lex specialis* regime that was allowed to govern a dispute to the detriment of the general system, see *Southern Bluefin Tuna Cases (New Zealand v. Japan; Australia v. Japan), Provisional Measures* (2000) *International Tribunal for the Law of Sea Case* Nos. 3 and 4 (4 August), available at http://www.itlos.org.

[246] H. Aufricht, "Supersession of Treaties in International Law", 37 *Cornell Law Quarterly* (1952), 655, 698.

[247] The *lex specialis derogat generali* principle "which [is] inseparably linked with the question of conflict". See the discussion by Gaetan Verhoosel on the Gabcikovo–Nagymaros Case, *Gabcikovo–Nagymaros: The Evidentiary Regime on Environmental Degradation and the World Court, European Environmental Law Review* (1997), 252. See also Jenks, as note 238, above, at p. 469; *Encyclopedia of Public International Law* 468 (1984), and Fitzmaurice, as note 231, above.

[248] See Article 3(2) of the *Understanding on Rules and Procedures Governing the Settlement of Disputes of the World Trade Organization*.

[249] Panel Report, *United States – Anti-Dumping Act of 1916 – Complaint by Japan* ["*US – 1916 Act (Japan)*"], WT/DS162/R and Add. 1, adopted 26 September 2000, as upheld by Appellate Body Report, WT/DS162/AB/R, at para. 675, citing the Appellate Body Report, *EC – Bananas III*, WT/DS27/AB/R, at para. 204, and the PCIJ decision in *Serbian Loans* (1929), where the PCIJ stated that "the special words, according to elementary principles of interpretation, control the general expression" (PCIJ, Series A, No. 20/21, at p. 30). But see Robert Howse and Petros C. Mavroidis, "Europe's Evolving Regulatory Strategy for GMOs – The Issue of Consistency with WTO Law: of Kine and Brine", 24 *Fordham International Law Journal* (2000), 317, 322–3 (suggesting that *lex specialis* is not part of customary international law).

to a measure, this measure should be examined on the basis of the agreement that "deals specifically, and in detail" with measures of this kind.[250]

Assuming a *lex specialis* rule, it would appear likely that the TBT and SPS Agreements would generally be *lex specialis* relative to the GATT, with the consequence that the TBT and SPS Agreements that are more specific should/could control the parallel provisions of GATT that are more general. However, so far the wording of Article 2.4 of the SPS Agreement seems to exclude the possibility of a strict *lex specialis* that would exclude the application of GATT 1994 and the jurisprudence has not considered the TBT *lex specialis* to GATT. In *EC – Asbestos*, the Appellate Body, after noting the application of the TBT Agreement, continued its analysis under Articles III and XX. Indeed the Appellate Body clearly stated that the TBT Agreement "added" to the GATT obligations. Therefore the TBT and GATT obligations were both applicable to the French measure (in addition to the provisions of the TBT Agreement).[251] In *US – Gasoline* as well, notwithstanding the claims of TBT violations, the Panel and the Appellate Body concentrated exclusively on the claims and defences based on GATT.

So far in the WTO context, the term *lex specialis* has been used as a principle of interpretation, to help in the identification of the set of provisions that are more specific and must be examined first, even if the other general rules continue to apply but may be examined after the completion of the analysis under the more specific rules, when need be. Yet it has happened that the adjudication proceeded only on the basis of the general provisions.

C. General Application of the Agreements

1. The GATT Versus SPS

Article 2.4 of the SPS Agreement provides that

> Sanitary or phytosanitary measures which conform to the relevant provisions of this Agreement shall be presumed to be in accordance with the obligations of the Members under the provisions of GATT 1994 which relate to the use of sanitary or phytosanitary measures, in particular the provisions of Article XX(b).

This provision has two conditions: first, it addresses sanitary or phytosanitary measures, and second, those measures must not violate the SPS Agreement.[252] If these conditions are met, this provision establishes a presumption that the relevant measures comply with GATT.

---

[250] Appellate Body Report on *EC – Bananas III*, WT/DS27/AB/R, at paras. 155 and 204.

[251] Appellate Body Report, *EC – Asbestos*, WT/DS135/AB/R, at para. 76.

[252] There may certainly be circumstances governed by Article XX(b) of GATT that are not covered by the SPS Agreement. For example, the French measure that comprised the subject matter of the Asbestos decision was not a sanitary or phytosanitary measure, as it did not relate to pests or disease or food, but was certainly subject to Article XX(b). See Hans-Joachim Priess and Christian Pitschas, "Protection of Public Health and the Role of the Precautionary Principle under WTO Law: A Trojan Horse Before Geneva's Walls?", 24 *Fordham International Law Journal* (2000), 519.

A Map of the WTO Law of Domestic Regulation of Goods

This presumption is probably best understood as rebuttable.[253] As a presumption, it would operate in the same way as Article 3.2 of the SPS Agreement, as interpreted by the Appellate Body in the *EC – Hormones* case, shifting the burden of proof to the complaining party, but not providing any substantive support to the defending party. It is possible to imagine circumstances where a difficult question arises. For example, the SPS Agreement would apply to PPM regulations that are intended to safeguard health in the importing state. If a panel or the Appellate Body were to hold that such measures conform to the SPS Agreement, this provision would raise a presumption that they also conform to GATT. If the analysis is continued under Article XX, the challenged Member would carry the benefits of this presumption in its GATT Article XX analysis (as a factual matter) and its measure would be presumed to be justified under Article XX. It would be for the challenging Member to reverse this presumption and demonstrate that less-trade-restrictive alternatives were reasonably available to the importing country to ensure the same reasonable level of protection. It is doubtful that a Member that did not succeed in demonstrating the existence of such less-trade-restrictive alternatives in its SPS claim would manage to do so to rebut the application of Article XX GATT.

So long as the necessity tests in Article 5.6 SPS and Article XX GATT are similar (or at least so long as Article XX is not more stringent), and the two disputing parties have exactly the same evidence for both legal analyses, a Member who managed to avoid a violation under the SPS Agreement should not be caught under Article XX.[254] It may, however, be concluded that the new test under Article XX calls for an actual balancing of the degree to which the challenged measure contributes to the end pursued, whereas Article 5.6 of the SPS Agreement does not. If this were the case, it would be possible that an SPS measure that passes Article 5.6 could be found inconsistent with Article XX. Of course, a measure would only be required to comply with Article XX if it violates another provision of GATT.

What about the reverse presumption: would sanitary or phytosanitary measures that violate the SPS Agreement necessarily also violate the GATT? In the *EC – Hormones* case, again dealing with the presumption under Article 3.2 of the SPS Agreement, the Appellate Body found that a presumption that "if x then presume y" (where x is conformity with international standards and y is consistency with the SPS Agreement and GATT) cannot be interpreted as indicating also the converse: "if not x then presume not y".[255] If similar reasoning applies to the presumption under

---

[253] If the intent were to deem such measures to comply with GATT, the treaty could have said so, or could have stated that the presumption is irrebuttable. In any event, the plain language of "presumption" will likely be taken to mean nothing more. See Appellate Body Report, *EC – Hormones*, WT/DS26/AB/R, WT/DS48/AB/R, at para. 170 (terming the unqualified presumption in Article 3.2 of the SPS Agreement "rebuttable"). However, see Article 3.8 of the Dispute Settlement Understanding, clearly stating that the presumption it is rebuttable. On the parallel application of the TBT Agreement and GATT, see Robert Howse and Elizabeth Türk, "The WTO Impact on Internal Regulations – a Case Study of the Canada – EC Asbestos dispute", in Gráinne de Búrca and Joanne Scott (Eds.), *The EU and the WTO: Legal and Constitutional Aspects* (London: Hart Publishing, 2001).

[254] Recall however that Articles III/XX have a broader coverage than the SPS so a single regulation may be the object of a partial overlap between the SPS and GATT.

[255] Appellate Body Report, *EC – Hormones*, WT/DS26/AB/R, WT/DS48/AB/R, at paras. 101–2.

Article 2.4, then non-compliance with the SPS Agreement cannot serve as a basis for a presumption of non-compliance with GATT.

At the same time, according to the eighth preambular paragraph of the SPS Agreement, that Agreement is intended to "elaborate rules for the application of the provisions of GATT 1994 which relate to the use of sanitary or phytosanitary measures, in particular the provisions of Article XX(b)".[256] Under Article 31(2) of the Vienna Convention, this preambular language would be "taken into account" in interpreting the SPS Agreement, and so a panel or the Appellate Body might interpret ambiguous provisions of the SPS Agreement to accord with GATT. This appears to presume that the SPS Agreement is more stringent than Article XX.

(a) Which Provisions of Which Agreements Should Be Examined First?

Given an understanding that the obligations reflected in the SPS Agreement are cumulative in relation to the obligations in GATT, it is necessary to decide the order in which these claims must be evaluated. The decision on order is made on the basis of logic and judicial economy. The *Australia – Salmon* Panel and *EC – Hormones* Panel each found it appropriate to examine the SPS Agreement first, and the GATT subsequently.[257] This is because the SPS Agreement is more specific, and, because of the operation of Article 3.2 of the SPS Agreement, it might not be necessary to examine the GATT if the measure were found to comply with the SPS Agreement. Moreover, the Article 3.2 presumption does not run the other way, so even if the measure were found to comply with GATT, it would still be necessary to examine it under the SPS Agreement.

(b) Would a Panel or the Appellate Body Continue Its Analysis Under the GATT If It Found a Violation of the SPS Agreement?

Would a Panel or the Appellate Body examine the claim of violation of Articles III/XI (and XX) if it had reached the conclusion that the measure violated the SPS Agreement? The answer is probably no. Panels are requested to address

> those claims on which a finding is necessary in order to enable the DSB to make sufficiently precise recommendations and rulings so as to allow for prompt compliance by a Member with those recommendations and rulings 'in order to ensure effective resolution of disputes to the benefit of all Members'.[258]

It is doubtful that the application of the general provision of Article XX may bring additional indications for an effective implementation of the Panel's SPS recommendations. Yet, as suggested before, if the necessity test under Article 5.6 appears somehow less stringent than that of for example Article III combined with Article XX of GATT (i.e., Article 5.6 calling for less incursion into the degree of effectiveness

---

[256] (Footnote omitted).

[257] Panel Report, *Australia – Measures Affecting Importation of Salmon* ("*Australia – Salmon*"), WT/DS18/R and Corr. 1, adopted 6 November 1998, as modified by Appellate Body Report, WT/DS18/AB/R, at para. 8.39; see also Panel Report, *EC – Measures Concerning Meat and Meat Products (Hormones) – Complaint by Canada* ["*EC – Hormones (Canada)*"], WT/DS48/R/CAN, at para. 8.45; and Panel Report, *EC – Hormones (US)*, WT/DS26/R/USA, at para. 8.42.

[258] Appellate Body Report, *Australia – Salmon*, WT/DS18/AB/R, at para. 223.

A Map of the WTO Law of Domestic Regulation of Goods

of the challenged measure for instance), one may conceive of incongruous results under SPS and GATT. The difficulty of comparing the two is increased by the fact that the test under Article 5.5 is necessarily more stringent and more sophisticated than that of the chapeau of Article XX. How the addition of those variables would actually work (an Article 5.5 more stringent and an Article 5.6 less stringent than Article XX of GATT) is difficult to say in the abstract.

There is at least one important question left open. If a measure violates Article III of GATT, but is permitted under Article XX(b), or under the SPS Agreement, is an action for non-violation nullification or impairment available to the complainant? The *EC – Asbestos* decision of the Appellate Body suggests that it may be.[259]

2. The GATT Versus TBT

The TBT Agreement lacks an explicit provision relating it to the GATT. The TBT provisions often add to those of Article III:

> We observe that, although the TBT Agreement is intended to 'further the objectives of GATT 1994', it does so through a specialized legal regime that applies solely to a limited class of measures. For these measures, the TBT Agreement imposes obligations on Members that seem to be different from, and additional to, the obligations imposed on Members under the GATT 1994.[260]

The Appellate Body, while seemingly announcing the TBT as a *lex specialis* regime (as a specialized legal regime for a limited class of measures) and stating that it was "applicable law",[261] did not take the next step to implement this view (since it declined to pursue its analysis under the TBT Agreement) and went on to apply Articles III and XX of GATT to the French measure.

Any reading of the TBT Agreement and GATT must not be such as to discourage compliance or reduce incentives to comply with the more stringent requirements of the TBT Agreement. As with the SPS Agreement, it would be best if compliance with the TBT Agreement gave rise to a presumption of compliance with GATT. In addition, compliance with an international standard (Articles 2.4 and 2.5 TBT) should lead to a presumption of compliance with Article 2.2 of the TBT Agreement, and not simply the presumption of necessity provided by Article 2.5. The use of such international standards should also *de facto* lead to the conclusion that the domestic TBT measure is necessary for the purpose of Article XX. The same should generally be true for any measure that complies with Article 2.2 of the TBT Agreement. Because the TBT Agreement adds different obligations to those of the GATT, does it mean that a single measure may be in violation of the TBT while compatible with GATT? Possibly. Nevertheless, the reverse is less probable: a technical regulation that complies with Article 2.1 and 2.2 of the TBT Agreement is likely to be compatible with Articles III and XX. However, if the necessity test under Article 2.2 TBT is somehow less stringent than that of, for example, Article III combined with Article XX of GATT (i.e., if Article 2.2 TBT

---

[259] Appellate Body Report, *EC – Asbestos*, WT/DS135/AB/R, at para. 187.

[260] Id., at para. 80 (emphasis added).

[261] Id., at paras. 77 and 78.

is interpreted like 5.6 SPS, calling for less incursion into the degree of effectiveness of the challenged measure for instance than the XX jurisprudence), one may conceive of incongruent results under TBT and GATT.

Another interesting issue is the coverage of Article 2.1 of the TBT Agreement and its relationship with Articles I, III and XX of GATT. If the scope and meaning of Article 2.1 is similar to that of Articles III and I, a single technical regulation could be a *prima facie* violation of Article III but be justified under Article XX of GATT, while also in violation of Article 2.1 of the TBT Agreement without any possibility of justification – even if the same regulation were found not to be in violation of Article 2.2 of the TBT Agreement. One may argue that Article XX of GATT 1994 could be invoked as a defence to a violation of Article 2.1 and this seems to have been accepted by the Appellate Body in *EC – Asbestos* when it concluded that the TBT Agreement was applicable to the measure at issue but decided not to complete the analysis under that agreement (for various reasons including judicial economy). Its findings were that the measure could in any case be justified under Article XX of GATT. However, Canada had made a claim under Article 2.1 of the TBT Agreement. If there was a possibility that the French measure violated TBT Article 2.1 without any acceptable defence – in the TBT Ageement or in the GATT 1994 – the Appellate Body would have committed a denial of justice against Canada in refusing to address its claim under Article 2.1 of the TBT Agreement.

Three potential solutions to this incongruous result may be available. The first two require a rather heroic approach to interpretation. First, Article 2.1 could read using the "accordion" approach of the Appellate Body to defining "like products" – a definition of "like product" under the substantive disciplines of the TBT Agreement recognizing that non-compliance with the characteristic mentioned in a legitimate TBT regulation made products "un-like". A second alternative solution would consider that, all WTO provisions being cumulative and simultaneously applicable, Article XX (as well as Articles XXI or XXIV of GATT) could be invoked to justify a violation under another agreement of Annex 1A.[262] Under this view, the effective interpretation principle would dictate that rights (in addition to obligations) under the WTO agreements are cumulative. As noted earlier, this effective interpretation principle would depend on an interpretation of the specific provisions at issue.

A third approach to this problem is to emphasize the 'right' of Members to maintain TBT regulation for 'legitimate objectives' is recognized in the sixth paragraph of the TBT Preamble and in Article 2.2 of the TBT Agreement. Article 2.1 cannot be interpreted and applied so as to nullify the rights and obligations contained in Article 2.2. Therefore, the words "less favourable" contained in Article 2.1 could be interpreted as the Appellate Body has done in the Article III context in paragraph 100 of its *EC – Asbestos* decision and paragraph 137 of its *Korea – Various Measures on Beef* decision. Under this approach, a violation would only occur if, after respecting 'legitimate' regulatory categories, the measure is still found to be "less favourable".

---

[262] Note for instance that Article XIV of GATS can be invoked to justify a violation of Article VI of GATS which contains in its paragraph 4 a necessity test parallel to that of GATT Article XX and that of Article 2.2 of the TBT Agreement.

A Map of the WTO Law of Domestic Regulation of Goods

Another interesting issue is the fact that the TBT Agreement allows Members to base their TBT regulations on "any legitimate governmental policies" whereas Article XX contains a closed list of policies. Therefore it is conceivable that a measure based on a policy not listed in Article XX (say the protection of the French language) could be considered not more restrictive than necessary pursuant to Article 2.2 TBT, while not being able to find any provisional justification under any of the sub-paragraphs of Article XX of GATT. Unless the TBT Agreement is understood as *lex specialis* to the exclusion of GATT, the GATT provisions continue to apply while the TBT Agreement may also be applicable.

(a) Which Provisions of Which Agreement Should Be Examined First?

The TBT Agreement does not have any provision similar to Article 2.4 of the SPS Agreement, explicitly setting forth its relationship with GATT. A Member could therefore not benefit from a presumption of compatibility with GATT if it were to be considered to have complied with the TBT requirements. Also, to the extent that the TBT Agreement contains different and additional obligations to those of the GATT, a prior examination of the GATT may not exhaust the need to examine claims under the TBT Agreement. A panel may therefore decide that as a matter of efficiency, it will examine claims under the TBT Agreement first. Recall, however, that in both *US – Gasoline* and *EC – Asbestos* the claims under GATT were addressed first and the identification of GATT rights and obligations was considered sufficient to settle the dispute (TBT claims were never examined).

(b) Would a Panel Continue Its Examination Under the GATT If It Found a Violation Under the TBT Agreement?

As with the SPS Agreement, judicial economy does not reduce the need to provide the losing Member with sufficient remedial information so as to ensure efficient compliance. It is difficult to foresee – albeit possible – circumstances in which a finding under Articles III or XX would add to findings under Articles 2.1 and 2.2 of the TBT Agreement, unless the terms "like products", "less favourable treatment" and the "necessity tests" have different meanings and applications under each of these agreements and are more stringent under the GATT.

3. SPS Versus TBT

Article 1.5 of the TBT Agreement provides that the TBT Agreement does not apply to sanitary or phytosanitary measures, as defined in the SPS Agreement. The TBT Agreement covers all technical regulations, other than those that are sanitary or phytosanitary measures as defined in the SPS Agreement. This means that the purpose of a measure – whether or not it is applied to protect against pests and diseases, as well as food-borne dangers[263] – is central to the division of jurisdiction between the TBT Agreement and the SPS Agreement.

However, there are measures, such as some extraterritorial measures, that would not be included as sanitary or phytosanitary measures by virtue of their

---

[263] See the definition of "sanitary or phytosanitary measure" in Annex A to the SPS Agreement.

extraterritorial protective purpose, but which are intended to protect health. If the TBT covers PPMs or extraterritorial considerations, some of these measures may be covered by the TBT Agreement even if the SPS does not apply to them. The possibility depends on whether "technical regulations" include measures intended to protect extra-territorial human, animal or plant life that specify "product characteristics or their related processes and production methods". This of course depends on how these words are interpreted.

The same reasoning applies to "labelling" requirements. The SPS Agreement defines SPS measures as including "packaging and labelling requirements directly relating to food safety". To the extent that the object of the PPM label was the protection of people, animals or plants in the territory of the importing country, such label would be covered by the SPS Agreement. If such label is not directly related to food or its object is the protection of the environment generally (say the planet's biodiversity) the label may not be covered by the SPS Agreement and may call possibly for the application of the TBT Agreement or the GATT. Under the TBT Agreement, technical regulations include "packaging marking or labelling requirements as they apply to a product, process or production method". Note that there is no reference to "their related" process and production methods, so non-product-related PPM labelling requirements would be covered by the TBT Agreement. It seems that the TBT Agreement would cover PPM labels, with less or no risk of contradictory analysis under GATT Articles III/XI and XX.

Article 1.4 of the SPS Agreement provides that nothing in the SPS Agreement affects rights under the TBT Agreement, with respect to measures not covered by SPS. Article 1.5 of the TBT Agreement provides that the TBT Agreement does not apply to SPS measures. Thus, where the SPS Agreement applies by its terms, the TBT Agreement would be inapplicable and vice versa. It is however possible that aspects or components of a specific measure could be covered by the SPS Agreement while others would be covered by the TBT or GATT, depending on how one defines the measure.

D. Application to Specific Types of Overlap

1. If a Measure Violates the SPS Agreement, but Is Consistent with the GATT, Is It WTO-consistent?

It is possible for a measure to violate the SPS Agreement, but to be consistent with the GATT. For example, a measure may violate the requirement in Article 5.1 of the SPS Agreement for a risk assessment, but may be a non-discriminatory regulation of a product as such within the terms of Articles I or III of GATT. The best interpretation of the SPS Agreement and the GATT is that their provisions are cumulative, and therefore, the violation of the SPS Agreement would not be "cured" by GATT legality.[264]

---

[264] See Panel Report, *EC – Hormones (US)*, WT/DS26/R/USA, at para. 8.42; Panel Report, *Australia – Salmon*, WT/DS18/R and Corr. 1, at para. 8.39.

A Map of the WTO Law of Domestic Regulation of Goods

2. If a Measure Violates TBT, but Is Consistent with the GATT, Is It WTO-consistent?

Here, again, the better reading is that these obligations are cumulative, and therefore that a violation of the TBT Agreement cannot be cured by GATT legality. There remains the issue of the proper reading of Article 2.1 of the TBT Agreement and its relationship with Article XX.

3. If a Measure Violates the GATT, but Is Consistent with SPS, Is It WTO-consistent?

This situation is difficult to conceive. Article 2.4 of the SPS Agreement sets up what is likely to be interpreted as a *rebuttable* presumption that conformity with the SPS Agreement entails compliance with the GATT. However, if the measure is clearly a violation of the GATT, so that the presumption is rebutted, compliance with the SPS Agreement is no defence.

4. If a Measure Violates the GATT, but Is Consistent with TBT, Is It WTO-consistent?

The TBT Agreement contains no explicit substantive provision establishing the relationship between its norms and those of the GATT. Therefore, the obligations under these two agreements are best understood as cumulative. The TBT Agreement would therefore provide no defence in the case of a violation of the GATT, and no presumption similar to that under Article 2.4 of the SPS Agreement. The presumption provided under Article 2.5 of the TBT Agreement might be interpreted to assist with the establishment of necessity under GATT Article XX. For legitimate policies other than those listed in Article XX, incongruent results between the TBT and the GATT may be possible.

V. Conclusion

As the SPS Agreement, TBT Agreement and the GATT provide norms with subtle but important variations, it is necessary to evaluate these variations, and to determine the applicability of these norms. This chapter has attempted to do so. This analysis provides both a "map" through the highways and byways of the WTO law of domestic regulation of goods, and a basis for considering greater harmonization or unification among these agreements.

It is clear that the GATT has concentrated on negative integration (the power of the GATT Panels to find domestic regulations inconsistent with the prohibition against discrimination, etc.), and its negative integration norms remain applicable, and are supplemented in some cases by the SPS Agreement and the TBT Agreement. However, the SPS Agreement and TBT Agreement add greater support for positive integration, through strengthened incentives for adoption of international standards and promotion of recognition and harmonization.

There are several instances of difference in the substantive obligations under these three agreements. Some of the differences result in varying concerns for protectionism, and for domestic regulatory autonomy. Perhaps in future negotiations, there will be discussion of greater convergence. It is also possible that the interpretative process of dispute settlement will yield a degree of convergence. Already, the jurisprudence seems to read into GATT provisions, and in particular Article XX, criteria, behaviour and requirements that are specifically dealt with in the TBT and SPS agreements.

ROBERT HOWSE AND ELISABETH TÜRK

2. The WTO Impact on Internal Regulations

A Case Study of the *Canada–EC Asbestos* Dispute

Introduction[1]

The WTO[2] is facing increasing criticism. This was highlighted during the third ministerial meeting in Seattle, where massive street protests disrupted the conduct of the conference. Apart from demonstrations, a series of groups used the Seattle ministerial meeting to articulate a range of views on the future of the trading system, in most cases far more subtle than a blanket or dogmatic rejection of globalisation or even the WTO. Non-governmental organisations and public policy-makers from all over the world met to analyse WTO policies and their potential impacts. Amongst the most common criticisms was the WTO's alleged role in impeding national governments from granting adequate protection to the

---

[1] Because of length considerations and in order to better focus on those issues relevant for understanding the implications of WTO disciplines on domestic regulations, the authors decided to not canvass every aspect raised in the *Asbestos* case. Amongst the broad range of issues addressed in this dispute but nevertheless outside the scope of this chapter are questions relating to the panel's obligation under Art. 11 DSU (Dispute Settlement Understanding) the handling of *amicus curiae* briefs or the application of non-violation disputes for measures justified under a general exception. In order to facilitate understanding of the broader implications for internal regulatory autonomy, the authors have also finessed some technical arcania, for example while the panel and the AB (Appellate Body) conducted a separate analysis of fibres and asbestos-containing products under national treatment, we have treated the two analyses as the same because in the end the separation does not make a difference to the basic conceptual and doctrinal questions we want to address here.

[2] Marrakesh Agreement Establishing the World Trade Organization (1994) 131 ILM 1125 (hereinafter WTO Agreement).

The authors would like to thank staff of the disputing countries' delegations for making available parts of the written documentation and scientific background on the case. Robert Howse especially thanks Steve Pepa, Petros Mavroidis, Marco Bronckers, Bill Davey, Don Regan, Julie Soloway and Joseph Weiler for challenging discussions on some of these issues over the past couple of years, and Todd Carpunky, Yvan Fauchere, Gaetan Verhoessel and Robert Madelin and his team at DG Trade for more recent exchanges. We also thank Bob Hudec, Merit Janow and Gary Horlick for extremely helpful comments on an early draft (Bob has been enormously generous to us, providing extensive comments on several versions and engaging in multiple email exchanges on the key issues); we also benefited from the reactions of several of the participants at the conference at the European University Institute where the first draft was presented, especially Armin von Bogdandy, Piet Eeckhout, Joanne Scott, Graínne de Búrca and Ernst-Ulrich Petersmann. The discussion of the case on the Jean Monnet website has also been very helpful to us and we are grateful to Joseph Weiler for providing that forum for discussion. The views expressed in this chapter are the authors' personal views and not those of CIEL.

environment, or addressing consumer interests and national health and safety concerns.

Different understandings concerning the extent to which WTO rules constrain domestic regulatory autonomy have manifested themselves in recent high-profile trade controversies. In the famous *Beef Hormones* case,[3] the USA successfully challenged the EC's ban on beef injected with natural and synthetic growth hormones. The regulatory measure in question had been adopted in a response to European consumers' concerns about potential health effects of such hormones being present in foodstuffs. Similarly, in the case of genetically modified organisms (GMOs), European consumers' reluctance towards genetically modified foods triggered the European institutions to adopt detailed regulations regarding risk assessment, release authorisation, subsequent monitoring and labelling of GMOs. The WTO consistency of this regulatory framework was repeatedly the subject of controversy in the TBT Committee.[4] So far the European scheme has not been subject to dispute settlement at the WTO. Although there have been few cases where domestic regulations on health, safety or the environment have been directly challenged and found in violation of WTO law,[5] the WTO rules may already be having a chilling effect on the strengthening or development of such domestic regulatory schemes in other WTO members, thereby constraining or impeding democratic choices. If the WTO is to regain citizens' confidence, it has to prove its ability to balance the freedom of governments to pursue legitimate domestic objectives with the need to secure the benefits of trade liberalisation.

Given the economic experiences prior to the Second World War, the legal framework created by the founding fathers of the GATT[6] focused on the elimination of discriminatory practices, either explicit border measures such as tariffs and quotas or domestic regulations and policies that discriminate against imports. Thus, the fundamental constraint on domestic regulations in the original GATT was that such regulations must not discriminate either against imports or between different GATT member states [National Treatment[7] and Most-Favoured-Nation Treatment[8]

---

[3] Appellate Body Report, *European Communities – Measures Concerning Meat and Meat Products (Hormones)*, WT/DS26/AB/R and WT/DS48/AB/R, 13 February 1998 (hereinafter *Hormones*). In fact, the Appellate Body decision in this case, unlike that of the panel, was respectful of domestic regulatory autonomy, upholding the panel on very narrow grounds.

[4] Committee on Technical Barriers to Trade, established by Art. 13 of the TBT Agreement (Agreement on Technical Barriers to Trade), Annex 1 A to the WTO Agreement, Multilateral Agreements on Trade in Goods (hereinafter TBT Agreement).

[5] Most of these cases, like the *Hormones* case, *supra* n. 3, have been in the food safety area, pursuant to the WTO SPS Agreement (Agreement on Sanitary and Phytosanitary Measures), Annex 1 A to the WTO Agreement, Multilateral Agreement on Trade in Goods (hereinafter SPS Agreement). For measures which could potentially fall under both the SPS and the TBT, the latter (TBT) defers to the SPS (Art. 1.5 TBT). Given that the SPS deals predominantly with measures addressing food safety concerns, most other measures would therefore fall under TBT. (Annex A SPS establishes that the SPS covers measures to protect human, animal and plant health, from risks arising from pests and food-borne diseases.)

[6] The text of the original GATT 1947 (General Agreement on Tariffs and Trade) is now incorporated as GATT 94 into the WTO Agreement (hereinafter GATT 94).

[7] Art. III GATT. For a superb account of the evolution of the non-discrimination norm in the GATT/WTO regime, see Robert Hudec, 'GATT Constraints on National Regulation: Requiem for an "Aim and Effects" Test' (1998), 32 *The International Lawyer* 623 (hereinafter, 'Requiem').

[8] Art. I GATT.

The WTO Impact on Internal Regulations

(MFN)]. With the increasing success of the GATT in the elimination of discriminatory measures, attention eventually came to focus on non-facially discriminatory policies and regulations thought to have negative impacts on trade. Sometimes, the existence of different regulations in different countries might in itself increase the transaction costs of trade, requiring producers to adapt products to the regulatory environment in different national markets.

Also, and perhaps more importantly, protective discrimination might be hidden or structurally embedded in regulatory schemes that themselves do not explicitly contain nationality-based distinctions. For example, domestic regulations might require a particular technology on safety grounds to which domestic producers had already adapted their production, while a variety of technological approaches might in principle be possible to satisfy the regulatory concern at issue. Because of the possibility that countries might simply shift protectionism from explicit facially discriminatory measures to regulatory schemes that were covertly or structurally discriminatory, the GATT jurisprudence evolved so as to encompass protective discrimination not reflected in explicit facial classifications on the basis of national origin, and in particularly the test of 'like products' in the National Treatment obligation of the GATT, came to be interpreted in such a manner as to provide some scrutiny of non-nationality-based regulatory distinctions, to ensure that those distinctions were not merely surrogates for (obviously illegal) nationality-based ones.[9]

Deciding on a case-by-case basis which non-nationality-based regulatory classifications represent *de facto* or hidden discrimination and which represent an innocuous disparate impact on trade, unrelated to protection, is a delicate and complex exercise. Here, casting the net too broadly might transform the WTO dispute settlement organs into a routine reviewing court for ordinary domestic regulations, placing undue limits on non-protectionist regulatory processes.[10] On the other hand, a failure to consider seriously the possibility of *de facto* discrimination could undermine the integrity of disciplines on discriminatory measures generally, providing a ready means of cheating with impunity on those explicit commitments.

Such considerations resulted in the Uruguay Agreements on Sanitary and Phytosanitary Measures (SPS) and Technical Barriers to Trade (TBT). These agreements contain a range of disciplines on the regulatory *processes* that generate domestic regulations, requiring the kind of transparency, coherence and consistency in regulation that provides trading partners with assurances that protectionism is not embedded

---

[9] Panel Report, *United States – Section 337 of the Tariff Act of 1930*, BISD 36S (1990) (hereinafter *Section 337*); Panel Report, *Canada – Import, Distribution and Sale of Certain Alcoholic Drinks by Provincial Marketing Agencies*, BISD 39S (1992) (hereinafter *Canada Beer*); Panel Report, *EEC – Regime for the Importation, Sale and Distribution of Bananas*; WT/DS/27/ECU/GUA/HON/MEX/USA (hereinafter *Bananas Panel*); Appellate Body Report, *EEC – Regime for the Importation, Sale and Distribution of Bananas*, WT/DS27/AB/R, 25 September 1997 (hereinafter *Bananas AB*).

[10] Of course, in such cases there might still be a possibility to justify the measure under one of the exception provisions of Art. XX, such as Art. XX(b), which refers to measures necessary, *inter alia*, for the protection of human life and health. However, as Hudec points out, the kind of justificatory burden imposed in Art. XX assumes that a violation of the GATT has already occurred, and is designed to deal with measures, which are discriminatory, presumptively protective, and therefore which it seems entirely appropriate to expect members to have to justify in dispute settlement as in fact tailored to non-protectionist objectives. Hudec, 'Requiem', *supra* n. 7.

at some deep level in the regulatory process itself.[11] To the extent that these norms are followed, the need for case-by-case judgments under Article III should be obviated, or at least those judgments should be easier to make with legitimacy. As well, these agreements seek to reduce gratuitous regulatory diversity, requiring or encouraging (in the case of SPS) the use of international standards as inputs[12] in the domestic regulatory process, where this is consistent with the attainment of the regulatory objectives of the member state. At the same time the SPS and TBT Agreements contain certain substantive criteria or tests, related to 'inputs' or 'outputs' of the regulatory process, which on some interpretations amount to a second-guessing of democratic domestic choices about complex trade-offs between different regulatory objectives, different risks and different regulatory instruments, even in the case of facially non-discriminatory regulations, which have not been shown to be protectionist. Thus, the recent criticisms and worries that we have discussed above concerning the increasing intrusiveness of multilateral trade rules, and trade tribunals, into democratic domestic regulation.

The recent Canadian challenge to France's ban on asbestos in construction materials provides a dramatic example of how WTO rules may be invoked to challenge domestic measures aimed at addressing serious health risks. Asbestos has been long known to be a deadly carcinogen, and France's ban of the substance applied without discrimination to both domestically produced and imported asbestos. Yet Canada argued that the asbestos it exports is a 'like product' to substitute products used in construction, therefore deserving no less favourable treatment under the National Treatment standard in GATT (Article III:4). Canada also claimed that France has violated the obligation under the TBT Agreement to ensure that its regulations are the least restrictive of trade necessary to attain the legitimate regulatory objective in question, here the protection of human life and health (Article 2.2 TBT). Canada argued that used in a 'safe' manner the kind of asbestos (chrysotile) that it exports does not present health risks. However, should the complex choice of a simple ban over a regulatory scheme that attempts to control the behaviour of manufacturers and users really be second-guessed by a trade tribunal deciding at a great distance from the domestic regulatory process, and its democratic institutions?

In *Asbestos*, the panel accepted Canada's claim that asbestos and non-asbestos substitutes were 'like' products, despite the fact that the former was a proven, deadly

---

[11] At the first glance, such constraints of transparency, coherence and consistency in regulation could be viewed at posing additional limitations and therefore harming democracy. However, by ensuring openness and transparency, such provisions should actually be able to enhance democratic deliberation, at least as long as they are not applied so as unduly to delay or constrain action in response to democratic will. Therefore a balance needs to be struck between democratic requirements of public justification and democratic requirements of effective action. See generally, R. Howse, 'Democracy, Science and Free Trade: Risk Regulation on Trial at the World Trade Organization' (2000), *University of Michigan Law Review*, 2329.

[12] Thus, domestic regulations should be 'based on' international standards (SPS 3.1 or TBT 2.4), which does not mean that the outputs of domestic regulation (the substantive regulations actually adopted) must be identical to the international standards, as the Appellate Body emphasised in *Hormones, supra* n. 3, paras. 160ff. Contrast this with the incorporation by reference into WTO law of international standards for international property protection in the Berne and Paris Conventions, where the standards themselves become by incorporation WTO law, binding on WTO members. Cf. TRIPs Agreement, Art. 2 (Agreement on Trade-Related Aspects of Intellectual Property Rights, Annex 1C to the WTO Agreement [hereinafter TRIPS Agreement)].

The WTO Impact on Internal Regulations 81

carcinogen and the latter were not.[13] This resulted in a finding that France had violated Article III:4 of the GATT, in providing less favourable treatment to asbestos imported from Canada than to like substitute products. However, the panel went on to find that this violation of Article III:4 was justified under Article XX(b) of the GATT as 'necessary' for the protection of human health. With regard to Canada's TBT claim, the panel accepted a rather bizarre argument from the EC that because the French measure constituted an outright ban of asbestos it did not fall within the definition of a technical regulation in the TBT Agreement. Therefore, the panel held, the TBT Agreement did not even apply to the measure.

For those concerned with the effects of the WTO on human health and related interests, the panel ruling was hardly a victory, despite the result of upholding the French ban. The notion that health considerations should be irrelevant in determining whether products are 'like' for purposes of assessing domestic regulations appeared to speak volumes about the obtuseness of the WTO in regard to basic human interests. However, such a ruling could be understood as the logical outcome, or perhaps *reductio ad absurdum*, of the approach adopted by the Appellate Body to National Treatment in the case of internal tax measures, in cases such as *Japan – Alcohol, Canada – Periodicals* and *Chile – Alcohol*. In those cases, the Appellate Body appeared to reject the 'aims and effects' approach to Article III, which considered whether the regulatory distinction between products is based on a non-protectionist regulatory purpose (such as protection of human health). Instead, the *Asbestos* panel apparently endorsed the approach of the panel in *Japan – Alcohol*, which was in examining 'likeness', to consider only factors that were probative of a competitive relationship between the imported and domestic product in the domestic marketplace, including physical similarity, end uses and consumer tastes and habits.[14] These criteria were as a matter of jurisprudence drawn from the *Border Tax Adjustment* working party,[15] which pre-dated the establishment of the WTO. A fourth criterion was also considered, customs classification, and added to the overall *Border Tax Adjustment* approach.

On such an approach, many legitimate regulatory measures will easily fall foul of Article III, even in the absence of any protectionism. And indeed, the *Asbestos* panel elsewhere in its ruling actually made a finding that the French ban did not constitute protectionism. Thus, the panel, in developing the market-based approach to Article III apparently adopted by the Appellate Body in the Article III:2 (taxation) cases, interpreted Article III, not as guaranteeing against protectionism in internal regulations, but rather guaranteeing *market access*, subject to the ability of the defending member to provide a non-protectionist *justification* for its measure under one of the

---

[13] Panel Report, *European Communities – Measures Affecting Asbestos and Asbestos-Containing Products*, WT/DS/135/R, 18 September 2000 (hereinafter 'Panel Report').

[14] See the account of these developments in Hudec, 'Requiem', *supra* n. 7. See also Robert Howse and Donald Regan, 'The Product/Process Distinction – An Illusory Basis for Disciplining "Unilateralism" in Trade Policy' (2000), 11 *European Journal of International Law* 249, 262–8, hereinafter 'The Product/Process Distinction'; see also Marco Bronckers and Natalie McNelis, 'Rethinking the "Like Product" Definition in GATT 1994: Anti-Dumping and Environmental Protection' in Thomas Cottier and Petros Mavroidis (Eds.), *Regulatory Barriers and the Principle of Non-Discrimination in Trade Law* (Ann Arbor, MI: University of Michigan Press, 2000), 343–85, hereinafter, 'Rethinking the "Like Product" Definition'.

[15] Working Party Report, *Border Tax Adjustments*, 2 December 1970, BISD 18S/97 (hereinafter Working Party Report).

heads of Article XX. Indeed, the panel in fact pointed to the existence of Article XX as a reason for taking a market-based approach to Article III: if consideration of regulatory objectives such as health was part and parcel of Article III analysis, would not Article XX be redundant? The effect of such reasoning was to turn Article III into a positive duty on WTO members to justify all regulations that have a negative impact on market access for other WTO members, an outcome at odds with the text and structure of the GATT as it currently stands.

Upon appeal, the Appellate Body[16](AB) reversed the finding of the panel that considerations of health effects could not be taken into account in the analysis of whether two products are 'like' under Article III:4. The AB affirmed the basic purpose of Article III as the discipline of protectionist measures, not market access as such. However, the Appellate Body also accepted the appropriateness of applying market-based criteria to likeness in a case such as *Asbestos*, rather than considering regulatory purposes such as protection of health. Thus, the error of the panel was not to have applied such criteria, but to have assumed that in so doing factors such as effects on health could be excluded from the analysis. Hence, in *Asbestos*, the physical differences between products that seemed most relevant to the AB were those that resulted in differential health impacts between asbestos and substitute products. The AB also noted that consumer tastes and habits must be *analysed* as part of the evidence that is relevant to likeness, and that health effects may well be an important basis for consumers to distinguish between products as 'unlike'. Thus, the approach of the Appellate Body was to introduce the fundamental human interests at stake not through an examination of regulatory purpose, but rather by making those interests relevant to an analysis of the competitive relationship between products in the marketplace. This approach did not satisfy one member of the division of the Appellate Body deciding this case, who in a concurring opinion expressed the view that concern by his brethren to preserve an economic approach to likeness analysis had impeded a clear statement of the key human value at stake in this case – the protection of human life and health.

However, the AB made another important statement in this case – it reminded its audience that a mere finding of 'likeness' between two products does not oblige the regulating member to treat them identically in regulation. The complaining member must also demonstrate that the differences in regulation amount to 'less favourable' treatment as between *domestic* and *imported* like products, each taken as a group. In making this statement, the AB recalled the anti-protectionist purpose of Article III and suggested that 'less favourable treatment' is equivalent to protectionism. Thus, a finding of 'likeness', on market-based criteria, will not be dispositive of a finding of violation of Article III:4. In future cases, these dicta may have enormous significance – for example, in situations where the regulatory distinction is based on the process of production, even if the 'products' (for instance, turtle-friendly and turtle-unfriendly shrimp) are found to be 'like', the regulatory distinction may still survive if it does not constitute less favourable treatment of imported than domestic 'shrimp'. Thus, PPMs that apply equally to imported and domestic like 'products' will be consistent with Article III:4.

---

[16] Appellate Body Report, *European Communities – Measures Affecting Asbestos and Asbestos-Containing Products*, WT/DS135/AB/R, 12 March 2001 (hereinafter Appellate Body Report).

The WTO Impact on Internal Regulations

However, in reversing the panel on the issue of TBT applicability, the AB clearly indicated that in cases such as these, in the future, the interpretation of the TBT Agreement will be critical to the balance the WTO strikes between domestic regulatory autonomy and trade liberalisation. Understandably, the AB did not go on to complete the analysis and apply TBT in this case, because to do so it would not only have had to find additional facts, but also address itself to significant legal issues of first impression. What the AB did do, however, was to address Canada's claims that the panel's Article XX analysis was too lenient or permissive and to reject those claims even though from the perspective of judicial economy it certainly did not need even to consider Article XX (because the finding of an Article III:4 violation was reversed). Here, the AB seemed determined to make new jurisprudence, establishing an especially deferential approach to domestic regulation that addresses vital health interests.

Asbestos – The WTO Dispute

It is widely recognised that asbestos is a highly toxic material, which poses a significant threat to human health. For example, exposure to chrysotile asbestos may increase the risk for asbestosis, lung cancer,[17] mesothelioma or pneumoconiosis. These negative effects are also recognised by a recent study of the World Health Organisation (WHO).[18] However, because of its characteristic features and intrinsic properties[19] (fire-resistance), asbestos has found wide use in industrial and other commercial applications. For example, asbestos is used in brake linings and clutches or in the form of spun fibres for the production of insulating tissues or cords. Another major commercial application for asbestos is as a reinforcement material for cement, plastic or rubber. Especially before the Second World War, asbestos was widely used in many countries. Countries that have already during recent decades imported large quantities of asbestos now need to limit to the largest extent possible the negative

---

[17] Asbestos fibres have a very particular texture. The substance consists of bundles of small fibrils, one sticking to another. These fibrils separate very easily lengthways and then can form a cloud of very fine dust. This dust is often invisible but it can settle everywhere and penetrate very deep into the lungs. Extremely small fibres are particularly dangerous to health. The smaller the diameter of these fibrils, the easier it is to inhale such substance and, consequently, the higher the risk of cancer.

[18] See the WHO's International Programme on Chemical Safety (IPCS), *Environmental Health Criteria 203 – Chrysotile Asbestos* (1998) at paras. 144. This study recommends replacing asbestos by less harmful materials or technologies wherever possible. Already previously, the WHO acknowledged that there existed a link between the characteristics of asbestos and their danger to health. In 1977 the WHO classed asbestos (also chrysotile) as a category I substance, which are proven to be carcinogens. Little later, in 1986 the International Labour Organisation (ILO) followed the WHO and adopted Convention No 162, where it referred to the dangers arising from the occupational exposure to asbestos. See first written submission of the European Communities, to the WTO panel on *European Communities – Measures Concerning Asbestos and Products Containing Asbestos*, 21 May 1999 (hereinafter EC first submission) at paras. 346 and 351 ff. See also third-party written submission of the United States to the WTO panel on *European Communities – Measures Affecting Asbestos and Products Containing Asbestos* (hereinafter US written submission) at para. 8 ff.

[19] Asbestos is a mineral with exceptional physical and chemical properties. Specifically, this substance does not burn and is extremely resistant to other chemicals and to mechanical traction. So far no one has developed a natural or synthetic substitute which has all these characteristic features of asbestos fibres. See EC first submission, *supra* n. 18, paras. 343 ff.

effect on human health of the already existing amount of imported asbestos. At the same time, domestic regulators aim towards eliminating this proven and internationally recognised threat to the health of future generations.[20] In the light of these circumstances France, which previously had imported lots of asbestos, issued Decree 96–1133[21] which establishes a total ban on asbestos fibres and products containing asbestos fibres.[22] Specifically, the French Decree prohibits the manufacture, processing, import, placing on the domestic market, possession for sale, offering, sale or transfer on any ground of all varieties of asbestos fibres and any products containing asbestos fibres.[23]

Article 2 of the decree establishes an exception for existing products or material containing chrysotile asbestos. This exception is to be applied on a temporary basis, as long as there are no existing substitutes for chrysotile fibres. The use of substitute fibres is tied to two conditions. First, according to the state of art in science, such substitutes must pose smaller health risks to workers exposed to them. Secondly, the substitute has to offer all the technical safety guarantees, which were the original purpose of using asbestos. Decisions on the application of this exception are taken on a case-by-case basis, according to French administrative procedures. Because of the advances of scientific research on asbestos substitute fibres, the number of exceptions has been gradually decreasing. Also, the exceptions are applied on the assumption that, eventually, safer substitutes will be available on the market in virtually all cases, thus obviating the need to use asbestos at all in the longer term.

Already before 1998, Canada repeatedly challenged the French Decree in the TBT Committee and on 28 May 1998 Canada proceeded formally to request consultations with the European Communities.[24] According to Article 4.4 of the DSU[25] Canada

---

[20] See *ibid.*, 1.

[21] Décret No. 96–1133 du 24/12/96 relatif à l'interdiction de l'amiante, pris en application du code du travail et du code de la consommation. http://www.sante.gouv.fr/amiante/commaitre/reglementation/reglementation.htm.

[22] It is important to note that France is not the only country responding to these public health concerns arising out of the use of asbestos fibres. On the contrary, many other countries both within Europe and abroad have taken action on asbestos. Outside the European Union, such examples are Switzerland, New Zealand, the Czech Republic and Australia. Also within the European Union, several Member States have introduced national legislation to reduce the negative effects of asbestos. For example, Denmark and the UK in 1972 or Belgium, Germany, Finland and Italy, which all introduced an almost total ban on asbestos during the 1990s. Finally, since the 1980s there has also been legislative action on the European level. The most recent directive received a favourable vote on 4 May 1999. The draft version stipulates that a ban on chrysotile asbestos is to be implemented throughout the European Union by 1 January 2005 at the latest. The directive gives each Member State the freedom to choose the pace (and measures), which it deploys to achieve this harmonised position. For further information see EC first submission, *supra* n. 18, paras. 159 ff and paras. 185 ff.

[23] Note that the French decree does not apply to asbestos as a waste. Therefore there were no issues concerning the Basel Convention on the International Transport of Hazardous Waste, Basel Convention on the Control of Transboundary Movements of Hazardous Wastes and Their Disposal, 22 March 1988 (1988) 27 ILM 859.

[24] Request for Consultations by Canada, *European Communities – Measures Affecting Asbestos and Products Containing Asbestos*, WT/DS135/1, 3 June 1998.

[25] Understanding on Rules and Procedures Governing the Settlement of Disputes, Annex 2 to the WTO Agreement (hereinafter DSU).

The WTO Impact on Internal Regulations

The WTO Impact on Internal Regulations 85

alleged that the French ban severely damages Canada's economic interest, and in particular its profits from international trade in chrysotile asbestos. In Canada, asbestos is manufactured exclusively in Quebec. Partly for national unity reasons, but also because of the importance of support from Quebec to any political party in Canada that seeks to form a majority government, Quebec has frequently been the beneficiary of many industrial assistance and protective measures by the Canadian government; this trend has been exacerbated by persistently high unemployment rates in the province, which is home to many of Canada's 'sunset' or troubled industries.

Article III – National Treatment

Canada claimed that France's asbestos ban violated the National Treatment obligation in Article III:4 of the GATT, because it afforded less favourable treatment to imports of chrysotile fibres and chrysotile-cement products from Canada than to 'like products' – substitute fibres and products – some of which are of EC origin.[26] Article III:4 reads as follows: '[t]he products of the territory of any contracting party imported into the territory of any other contracting party shall be accorded treatment no less favorable than that accorded to *like products* of national origin in respect of all laws, regulations and requirements affecting their internal sale, offering for sale, purchase transportation, distribution or use . . . ' (emphasis added). It is evident that under Article III:4 discrimination is forbidden only when occurring between imports and 'like' domestic products. Consequently, the determination of what constitutes a 'like' product, in interrelationship with the interpretation of what constitutes 'less favourable treatment', provides the basis for the decision as to whether a domestic regulation is consistent with the National Treatment obligation.[27]

Despite being one of the GATT's core concepts[28] nothing in Article III or any other GATT provision provides any definition for the term 'like products'. In the 1970s, a GATT Working Party listed the basic factors which should be used when determining similarity of products, with respect to *taxation* measures; such measures are generally

---

[26] Canada, Premier exposé écrit du Canada, au Groupe Spécial, *Communautés Européennes – Mesures Concernant L'amiante et les produits en contenant*, le 26 avril 1999; Canada, first written submission to the panel in *European Communities – Measures Affecting Asbestos and Products Containing Asbestos*, paras. 280 ff. (hereinafter Canada first submission), Canada, Deuxième exposé écrit du Canada au Groupe Spécial, *Communautés Européennes – Mesures Concernant L'amiante et les produits en contenant*, 30 juin 1999, Canada, second written submission to the panel in *European Communities – Measures Affecting Asbestos and Products Containing Asbestos*, submission paras. 319ff. (hereinafter Canada second submission).

[27] Art. III basically established two types of national treatment obligations. First there are those relating to taxation (Art. III:2) and secondly, there are those relating to various other, non-tax regulations (Art. III:4). With respect to the obligations established for taxation measures, Art. III:2 again distinguishes two situations. Read together with the interpretative note to Art. III:2, one could see two different standards, one applying to like products, another applying to directly competitive or substitutable products. For the latter, difference of treatment alone would not constitute a violation; one would also need proof that internal taxes were applied 'so as to afford protection'.

[28] The notion of 'like' is used some sixteen times in the text of the GATT. Also other WTO agreements, such as the TBT or the GATS, build on the concept of 'likeness'. GATT panels have stated that this notion of 'likeness' is undoubtedly open to quite distinct interpretations. Panel Report, *United States – Measures Affecting Alcoholic and Malt Beverages*, 19 June 1992, BISD 39S/206 (hereinafter *Malt Beverages*).

supposed to be neutral with respect to consumers' choices in the marketplace, given that their purpose is to raise revenue in a manner that does not distort individual market behaviour.[29] These criteria were 'the product's end-uses in a given market; consumers' tastes and habits, which change from country to country and the product's properties, nature and quality'.[30] In the 1980s a panel on *Japanese liquor taxes*[31] added another criterion, namely uniform classification in tariff nomenclatures. Finally, two WTO panels[32] approached the question of likeness by examining whether there exists some commonality of end-uses and whether the products in question possess essentially the same physical characteristics. In recognition that where measures are being taken for non-fiscal reasons, such as environmental objectives, purely market criteria are inadequate to judge 'likeness', panels interpreting Article III:4, as opposed to Article III:2, which deals with neutral fiscal measures, developed an approach termed 'aims and effects'.[33] This test evaluated whether, on the basis of all the evidence, protectionist intent or impact was evident in the regulatory scheme and its operation.

This approach recognised that the GATT should not be used to subject to scrutiny non-protective regulatory schemes for non-commercial objectives. Its disadvantage related to the difficulties surrounding an inquiry into protectionist 'intent', largely replacing an inquiry into the meaning of 'likeness' in relation to the objective purposes and structure of the regulatory scheme, with intuitive judgements about motivation. This risked collapsing the inquiry into 'likeness' into a general judgement about protective discrimination, and thereby failing to give meaning to the ordinary meaning of the exact words in Article III:4.[34] Moreover, 'aims and effects' spilled over into the analysis of fiscal measures under Article III:2, despite the adequacy of market-based criteria to deciding the issue of likeness in the case of measures not aimed at altering market behaviour for some non-commercial purpose.[35] Finally, in the *Japanese Alcohol* case the Appellate Body upheld the panel's focus on the objective market criteria in determining likeness for purposes of applying the national

---

[29] Thus, where fiscal measures are sometimes used to affect behaviour (pollution taxes for example, where environmental standards are enforced through monetary charges or penalties attaching to the offending conduct) they are generally qualified as behavioural or Pigovian taxes, to distinguish them from typical neutral revenue-raising measures. These kinds of measures would normally not be considered as taxation measures within the meaning of Art. III:2. See Panel Report, *United States – Measures Affecting the Importation, Internal Sale and Use of Tobacco*, DS44/R, (1994) (hereinafter *US – Tobacco*). But for certain specific purposes, i.e. border tax adjustment, an earlier case, *Superfund*, had suggested that neutral fiscal measures and behavioural taxes should be treated the same. See Panel Report, *United States – Taxes on Petroleum and Certain Imported Substances*, BISD 34S, (1988) (hereinafter *Superfund*).

[30] Working Party Report, *supra* n. 15, para. 18.

[31] Panel Report, *Japan – Customs Duties, Taxes and Labelling Practices on Imported Wines and Alcoholic Beverages*, 10 November 1987, BISD 34S/83, para. 5.6. (hereinafter *Japanese Alcohol 1988*). Besides the tariff heading criterion, the other two criteria were similar properties and end-uses.

[32] Panel Report, *Japan – Taxes on Alcoholic Beverages*, 1996, WT/DS8/R, WT/DS10/R, WT/DS11/R, para. 6.22 (hereinafter *Japanese Beverages, Panel*). Similar, Panel Report, *Canada – Certain Measures Concerning Periodicals*, 1997, WT/DS31/R, para. 5.25 (hereinafter *Canada Periodicals, Panel*).

[33] See *Japanese Alcohol (1988)*, *supra* n. 31, *Canada Beer*, *supra* n. 9, and *United States – Taxation of Automobiles*, DS 31/R of 11 October 1994, unadopted (hereinafter *CAFE*).

[34] See Hudec, 'Requiem', *supra* n. 7 on the textualist critique of 'aims and effects'.

[35] *Japanese Alcohol (1988)*, *supra* n. 31.

The WTO Impact on Internal Regulations

treatment obligations with respect to neutral fiscal measures. The Appellate Body, however, did not elaborate the implications of the rejection of 'aims and effects' for Article III:4, merely stressing that the meaning of 'likeness' in different provisions of the WTO Agreements would have to be considered in each case separately.[36] However, in the later *Bananas* case, when interpreting the National Treatment provisions of the General Agreement on Trade in Services (GATS),[37] in respect to non-fiscal measures, the Appellate Body noted that in the *Japanese Alcohol* decision, it had 'rejected the "aims and effects" theory with respect to Art. III:2'.[38] In dismissing the EC argument that an absence of protective intent in the licensing schemes rendered them consistent with the National Treatment obligation of GATS, the Appellate Body did not explicitly examine the meaning of 'likeness'.[39] Based on the factual findings of the panel concerning the overwhelming discriminatory impact of the classifications in the scheme in question, the Appellate Body upheld the panel's finding of *de facto* discrimination under GATS. However, the meaning of 'likeness', as distinguished from the overall issue of whether the GATS prohibited *de facto* discrimination, was not central to the issues of law appealed in this case, and it is understandable that the decision did not develop the implications of its analysis of the issue of *de facto* discrimination for the meaning of the concept of 'likeness' under Article III:4 of the GATT, explicitly noting that in *Japan – Alcohol*, its rejection of 'aims and effects' was in respect of Article III:2. Thus, it remained an open issue how in light of the rejection of 'aims and effects' with respect to Article III:2, likeness should now be understood with respect to Article III:4 of the GATT. One reason it was appropriate that the Appellate Body not expand on this matter in the *Bananas* case was that, whatever the claims of the EC in that case about non-protectionist intent, the scheme in question was a scheme of regulation for commercial or economic purposes, not for purposes external to the management of the marketplace itself, such as environment, health and safety and so forth. Thus, this would have been an inappropriate case in which to consider the sensitive issue of how 'likeness' should be dealt with in relation to regulatory autonomy as exercised in the service of fundamental non-economic values.[40]

---

[36] Appellate Body Report, *Japan – Taxes on Alcoholic Beverages*, WT/DS8/AB/R, WT/DS10/AB/R, WT/DS11/AB/R (hereinafter *Japanese Beverages AB*) 21. In a memorable quotation, the AB specifically notes that '[t]he criteria in Border Tax Adjustments should be examined, but there can be no one precise and absolute definition of what is "like". The concept of "likeness" is a relative one that evokes the image of an accordion. The accordion of "likeness" stretches and squeezes in different places as different provisions of the WTO Agreements are applied. The width of the accordion in any one of those places must be determined by the particular provision in which the term "like" is encountered as well as by the context and the circumstances that prevail in any given case to which that provision may apply'.

[37] General Agreement on Trade in Services, Annex 1 B to the WTO Agreement (hereinafter GATS).

[38] See *Bananas AB*, *supra* n. 9, para. 241.

[39] Note that the text of Art. XVII:2 GATS reads that National Treatment might be 'either formally identical treatment or formally different treatment'. It thereby explicitly specifies that *de facto* discrimination is included in Art. XVII GATS. The above remarks of the Appellate Body are therefore strictly speaking *obiter dicta*.

[40] While preferences themselves for bananas could be understood in terms of development purposes as embodied in the Lomé Convention, the licensing schemes found to constitute *de facto* discrimination were rightly understood by the panel and Appellate Body not to be necessary and incidental to those development purposes.

In its submission in *Asbestos*, Canada alleged that asbestos and non-asbestos products were 'like',[41] because of having the same product characteristics,[42] end-uses, and falling under the same tariff classification.[43] The Europeans countered the Canadians' arguments on their own terms, claiming that the properties, nature and quality of asbestos fibres and substitute products and asbestos-containing products and substitute products are different,[44] and pointing also to differences with respect to tariff classification[45] and the end-use.

The panel, in following the market-based approach to likeness approved by the AB in *Japan – Alcohol* and subsequent cases, considered first of all the physical characteristics of asbestos and the substitute products. Although, as the EC argued, there were indisputable physical differences between asbestos fibres and the substitutes, the panel rejected these physical differences as dispositive of *un*likeness.[46] This was based on the notion that the physical differences did not matter to the functionality of the product, i.e. to its end-use in construction, etc. Having found that the products had similar physical characteristics and end-uses[47] (these two findings as noted being closely related), the panel did not find it necessary to examine consumer tastes and habits.[48] It did turn its mind to the differences in customs classification for the two products, but in light of its findings on physical characteristics and end-uses, the panel did not find the difference in customs classification to be 'decisive'.[49]

The panel categorically rejected the EC argument that in a case such as that the health risk from the product should be taken into account in the analysis of likeness and should indeed be decisive.[50] The panel suggested that were health considerations

---

[41] Note that one of the main points of controversy was which types of substances and products should be compared. Canada suggests comparing (Canadian) chrysotile and chrysotile cement on the one hand with French 'like products' such as substitute fibres (PVA fibres, cellulose and glass) and fibre cement on the other. (See Canada first submission, *supra* n. 26, paras. 295 ff, 305 ff and 310 ff.) The EC argues that the relevant comparison should be between the following products: first, domestic asbestos fibres and imported asbestos fibres (both prohibited but may be granted a temporary derogation on the same terms); secondly, domestic products containing asbestos fibres and imported products containing asbestos fibres (both prohibited but may be granted a temporary derogation on the same terms); thirdly, substitute domestic products and substitute imported products (both permitted) (see European first submission, *supra* n. 18, paras. 324 ff). The USA used a similar line of argumentation and stated that Canada failed to make the correct product comparison in order to determine whether the relevant products are like products under Art. III:4. According to the USA the relevant products to compare were the following: (1) asbestos must be compared to substitute fibres and (2) products containing asbestos must be compared to products that do not contain asbestos but which perform the same function. (See US written submission, *supra* n. 18, para. 39.)

[42] See Canada first submission, *supra* n. 26, paras. 310 and 317 ff referring to 'properties, quality and nature of the product'.

[43] For the importance of tariff headings, see first Canadian submission, *supra* n. 26, in paras. 333 ff. Note that in its first submission Canada also refers to consumer tastes and habits (para. 325), whilst in its second submission, it specifically dismisses this point and refers only to the products' end-use (paras. 329 ff), tariff heading (para. 336 ff) and properties, nature and qualities (para. 341 ff).

[44] EC first submission, *supra* n. 18, paras. 342 ff.

[45] *Ibid.*, paras. 358 ff.

[46] Panel Report, *supra* n. 13, para. 8.126.

[47] *Ibid.*, para. 8.136.

[48] *Ibid.*, para. 8.140.

[49] *Ibid.*, para. 8.143.

[50] EC first submission, *supra* n. 18, paras. 8.127 ff.

The WTO Impact on Internal Regulations

to be taken into account in determining whether products were 'like' under Article III:4, the exception with respect to health in Article XX(b) of the GATT would be rendered redundant.[51] Here, the panel appeared to be taking to the extreme the implication of the market-based approach to likeness favoured by the AB in *Japan-Alcohol* and subsequent cases. In *Japan – Alcohol*, the Appellate Body had been careful to qualify its endorsement of the market-based approach in *Border Tax Adjustment* as understood by the *panel* in *Japan – Alcohol* – it noted that the market-based criteria in *Border Tax Adjustment* were not *exhaustive* of the factors that, in a given case, might be relevant in assessing 'likeness' and it also noted that the approach to 'like products' in one legal provision of the GATT might be different from in the case of another legal provision. Thus, the door remained open to the panel in *Asbestos* to consider an additional criterion – the regulatory objective of protecting health – as relevant or indeed decisive in assessing whether the products were 'like'.

In its cross-appeal, the EC argued that the panel had erred in law in refusing to consider health effects as a separate criterion in determining whether asbestos and the substitute were 'like' products.[52]

The disposition by the Appellate Body of the EC cross-appeal on Article III:4 is, to say the least, complex. This disposition has three separate parts to it: (1) an elaboration of the general approach to the interpretation of the treaty language in Article III:4; (2) findings of error of law by the panel; (3) 'completing the analysis', where the AB goes on to apply Article III:4 correctly to the facts of the case, picking up at the point where the panel began to err in law.

In outlining the general approach to the interpretation of Article III:4, the AB places fundamental emphasis on Article III:1 as stating the general purpose that animates Article III as a whole. That principle, according to the AB, quoting its own words in *Japan – Alcohol*, 'is to avoid protectionism in the application of internal tax and regulatory measures'.[53] Thus, the meaning of 'like product' must be informed by the anti-protectionism principle of Article III:1. In order for protectionism to be possible, the regulations challenged under Article III:4 must, in the first instance, address imported and domestic products that are in a competitive relationship. Thus, the inquiry into 'likeness' in Article III:4 is about whether there is the kind of competitive relationship between the imported product and domestic products that *could* lead to a conclusion of protectionism, *if* the result of the regulatory treatment were that the imported product was treated less favourably. It is, then, not enough that there be *some* competitive relationship between the imported product and domestic products, rather the issue of likeness is one that includes the 'kind' of competitive relationship. Already here, the AB is distinguishing its approach from that of the *panel* in *Japan – Alcohol*, making it clear that what is a stake is a contextual and qualitative judgement about competitive relationships, not merely the economic analysis of cross-elasticity of demand between two groups of products. Such an assessment must be made on a case-by-case basis, informed by the general principle of anti-protectionism, which informs all of Article III.

---

[51] *Ibid.*, para. 8.130.

[52] Other Appellant's Submission by the European Communities pursuant to Rule 23 of the Working Procedures for Appellate Review, Geneva, 21 November 2000, paras. 50 ff.

[53] Appellate Body Report, *supra* n. 17, para. 97.

Once a competitive relationship has been established of the degree and kind relevant to Article III:4, then the second step of the analysis comes into play. Only where the differential treatment of the 'like' products amounts to 'less favourable treatment' of the group of imported products in relation to the group of like domestic products will there be a violation of Article III:4. In fact, the AB goes out of its way to emphasise that 'a Member may draw distinctions between products which have been found to be "like", without for this reason alone, according to the group of "like" *imported* products "less favourable treatment" than that accorded to the group of "like" *domestic* products'.[54] The AB also emphasises that less favourable treatment does not mean just *any* kind of worse treatment – 'less favourable treatment' is a concept informed by the anti-protectionist principle in Article III:1. Thus a judgement of 'less favourable treatment' implies, 'conversely', a conclusion of 'protection'.

As the AB noted, it did not need to apply the concept of 'less favourable treatment' to the facts in *Asbestos*, because it reversed the panel's ruling that the products were 'like', therefore obviating the second step of the analysis. However, this statement of the approach to less favourable treatment is a very important one. First of all, the AB has made it clear that even where *products* are in a close enough competitive relationship to be considered 'like', members of that class or group of 'like' products may still be distinguished in regulation, provided that the result is not less favourable treatment, understood as protection of domestic production. This in effect blunts, without explicitly repudiating, the product/process distinction – the much criticised idea, found in the unadopted *Tuna/Dolphin* panels, that process-based trade restrictions can never be considered as internal regulations consistent with the National Treatment standard of Article III.[55] Even if products that have different process and

---

[54] *Ibid.*, para. 100. The AB already touched on this point in the *Korea – Beef* case, para. 135, see Appellate Body Report, *Korea – Measures Affecting Imports of Fresh, Chilled and Frozen Beef*, WT/DS161/AB/R, 11 December 2000 (hereinafter *Korea – Beef* Appellate Body Report).

[55] See Howse and Regan, 'The Product/Process Distinction', *supra* n. 14. Some observers have interpreted the statement in para. 100 in a different way, namely as simply restating the proposition of the *Section 337* case, *supra* n. 9, that where there is facially discriminatory treatment of domestic and imported products, nevertheless this may still be consistent with Art. III:4 – namely where, although domestic products and imports are governed by different rules or regimes, there is nevertheless no less favourable treatment for imports. If this statement is interpreted this way however the next sentence in para. 100 appears to reverse another proposition of the *Section 337* case, i.e. that in cases where there is differential treatment of imports and domestic products, every instance of the differential treatment must result in treatment no less favourable. This is because the next sentence in para. 100 emphasises that the comparison is between the treatment of the group of like imported products and the group of like domestic products. The AB cannot be reasonably interpreted as intending to overturn such an established jurisprudential principle of the GATT, not even citing or discussing the *Section 337* (*supra* n. 9) panel here. In fact, while in *Section 337* the issue is when facially differential treatment of imports may nevertheless be 'no less favourable', in para. 100 the issue is whether a non-national-origin based regulatory distinction between like products nevertheless constitutes less favourable treatment of imports, i.e. protection. From the point of view of discerning protection in respect of origin-neutral regulatory distinctions, the fact that some imported product or other gets worse treated than some domestic product or other is not probative and may be quite misleading. This may be an innocent or purely accidental disparate impact. To determine whether an origin-neutral regulatory distinction is protective, we have to discern whether there is a connection between the design and structure of the scheme itself and less favourable treatment of imports – the issue is systemically less favourable treatment of imports, and therefore the proper framework for assessment is the structure and design of the scheme as it impacts on the treatment of the group of like imported products as a whole relative to the group of like domestic products as a whole.

The WTO Impact on Internal Regulations

production methods are considered to be 'like' under Article III:4 (which, as will be discussed below, they need not always be), regulatory distinctions may be made between them, on *any* grounds, provided the result is *non-protectionist*. Thus, for example, were all 'shrimp' considered to be 'like' regardless of whether they were turtle-friendly or not, i.e. whether or not caught in a manner that did not result in undue levels of turtle mortality, this would not *necessarily* mean that a regulation that required that all shrimp sold in the USA be turtle-friendly was inconsistent with Article III:4. One would have to consider whether the design and structure of the scheme resulted in less favourable treatment of imported shrimp as a group than domestic shrimp as a group, i.e. did the requirement result in protection of domestic production? The differential impact of such a requirement on imported shrimp *might* alter the competitive relationship between domestic and imported shrimp so as to protect domestic production if, for instance, foreign producers of shrimp faced costs of adapting their fishing practices that domestic shrimp producers did not. However, as the AB emphasises, the comparison is between the group of imports as a whole and the group of domestic products as a whole. Just because one particular foreign producer of shrimp faced a differential burden from the regulation in comparison to one particular domestic producer, a finding of 'less favourable treatment' would not be justified.

The AB's emphatic statement about the crucial second step in Article III:4 National Treatment analysis must be borne in mind in considering its approach to the first step of ascertaining whether products are 'like'; the AB admits that there is no one approach to likeness that will be appropriate in all cases, and that 'likeness' is a matter of judgement – qualitative as well as quantitative. This case-by-case approach may not seem to provide much assurance against a panel casting the net so wide, as it were, that legitimate non-protectionist regulatory distinctions are put into question. However, the *second step* of Article III:4 analysis provides a safeguard against that possibility by requiring the complaining member to establish that the regulatory distinction in question results in protection of domestic production. Thus, while, as we shall see, the AB has taken great pains to continue to distance itself from aims-and-effects analysis with respect to likeness, it has in effect brought 'aims and effects' back in at the second stage of considering whether there is 'less favourable treatment'.[56]

---

[56] This is especially evident when we recall the AB's suggestion in para. 100 of the interchangeability or of equivalence of the notion of 'less favourable treatment' with the general notion in Art. III:1 that measures not be applied so as to afford protection to domestic production. In interpreting that concept with respect to National Treatment in taxation under the second sentence of Art. III:2, into which it is explicitly incorporated by virtue of an Interpretive Note to Art. III, the AB has indicated the primary importance of examining the structure and design of the regulatory scheme in order to make a judgement on objective factors as whether the measure is protective and asserted the irrelevance of protectionist intent to that enterprise, *Japan – Alcohol* AB, supra n. 36. In the subsequent case of *Canada – Periodicals*, however, the AB did not exclude consideration of evidence such as legislative history and ministerial statements, that apparently went to protectionist intent: Appellate Body Report, *Canada – Certain Measures Concerning Periodicals*, 30 June 1997, WT/DS31/AB/R (hereinafter *Canada – Periodicals*, AB). Recently, in *Chile – Alcohol*, the AB held it was appropriate to 'relate the observable structural features of the measure with its declared purposes': Appellate Body Report, *Chile – Taxes on Alcoholic Beverages*, 13 December 1999, WT/DS87/AB/R, para. 72. These are not inconsistent rulings – an inquiry into the structure and design of the scheme may well be decisive with respect to whether it is protective, obviating the need for making sensitive judgements about intent, but this does not mean that in other cases evidence of intentional

This bring us to the general remarks of the AB concerning likeness of products in Article III:4. The AB first of all recalls the *Border Tax Adjustment* criteria, with the addition of customs classification as the fourth criterion, as one approach that has been developed to likeness under Article III.[57] However, the AB also states that the criteria in question 'are neither a treaty-mandated nor a closed list of criteria that will determine the legal characterization of products'.[58] Indeed, a panel *must* examine all the 'pertinent evidence' of likeness or unlikeness, regardless of whether that evidence goes to the kinds of 'potentially shared characteristics' identified in the *Border Tax Adjustment* criteria. This last statement is significantly stronger than the caveat in *Japan – Alcohol* that other criteria may be relevant in certain cases – it actually limits the discretion of the panel, which must weigh all the evidence in *every* case, including evidence that does not go to the potential shared characteristics identified in the *Border Tax Adjustment* criteria. At the same time, the AB notes that because the likeness inquiry is about competitive relationships between products, it is necessary for a panel always *to take into account* evidence that goes to the competitive relationship in its analysis of likeness.

It is apparent that, here, the AB is engaged in a very subtle balancing act in articulating its approach to 'likeness'. The AB makes it very clear that a panel cannot simply revert to an 'aims and effects' -type analysis as conclusive of 'likeness' or 'unlikeness'; the panel must *always* examine competitive relationships in the marketplace. At the same time, the AB goes out of its way to emphasise that there may be cases where it will be inappropriate to leave matters at that, and raises the possibility that in those cases the evidence that tips the balance may well be evidence that does *not* go into the market-based criteria articulated in *Border Tax Adjustment*. Otherwise, why make it obligatory in all cases to consider such evidence, if it exists?

Now the AB goes on to the second part of its consideration of National Treatment, the correction of the panel's errors of law. The panel erred in not considering and weighing all the evidence, and this error relates to the error of not considering *all* four of the *Border Tax Adjustment* criteria explicitly and separately. First of all, the panel focused exclusively on assumptions about end-uses of the products in coming to the conclusion that differences in physical characteristics between asbestos and the substitute products were not of a kind and degree to make these products 'unlike'. According to the AB, the analysis of physical characteristics should be made separately from an inquiry into end-uses. Physical differences between asbestos fibres and substitute products 'are "important" because the microscopic particles and filaments of chrysotile asbestos fibres are carcinogenic to humans, following inhalation'.[59] The failure of the panel to find that such differences were 'important' stemmed partly from its error of law in conflating analysis of physical

---

protection may well be relevant. Not all findings that a measure is *structurally* protective imply a cryptic judgement of protectionist animus: domestic regulators or legislators may have designed a measure without turning their minds at all to the possibility of a systematically unfavourable effect on imports. This might happen because of un- or under-representation of importer or foreign producer interests, or surrogate domestic interests, in the regulatory process – that could indicate protection at the deeper level of regulatory and political structure. However, the measures themselves may lack any direct protectionist animus. Cf. Hudec, 'Requiem', *supra* n. 7, 634.

[57] We will refer to all four criteria hereinafter as the *Border Tax Adjustment* criteria.

[58] Appellate Body Report, *supra* n. 16, para. 102.

[59] Appellate Body Report, *supra* n. 16, para. 114.

The WTO Impact on Internal Regulations

characteristics with end-uses. However, it also stemmed from the panel's error in concluding that health effects are irrelevant in analysing likeness under Article III:4. The panel took the view that, were health considerations to enter into the application of the National Treatment standard in Article III, then the health exception in Article XX would be redundant. The AB, however, considered that consideration of health effects under Article III:4 is a very different kind of inquiry from that under Article XX. Under Article III:4 the issue is how health effects impact on the competitive relationship of products in the marketplace, whereas under Article XX the issue is whether a member has a sufficient basis for adopting or enforcing a WTO-inconsistent measure on grounds of human health.[60]

In addition, the panel committed a further error when it went on to examine end-uses as a separate criterion. In concluding that the evidence of end-uses sustained a conclusion of 'likeness' between asbestos and the substitutes, the panel left matters at pointing out a small number of similar end-uses of the two products, while failing to examine evidence of a wide range of dissimilar non-overlapping functions.

More importantly still, the panel erred in failing to consider at all the evidence of consumer tastes and habits, the third criterion that it was required to consider separately. Here the AB comes closest to taking judicial notice of human health as a fundamental value: '[i]n this case especially, we are also persuaded that evidence relating to consumers' tastes and habits would establish that the health risks associated with chrysolite asbestos fibres influence consumers' behavior with respect to the different fibres at issue'.[61] While acknowledging that the initial consumers of the products are industrial users, the AB notes: '[a] manufacturer cannot, for instance, ignore the preferences of the ultimate consumer of its products. If the risks posed by a particular product are sufficiently great, the ultimate consumer may simply cease to buy that product. This would, undoubtedly, affect a manufacturer's decisions in the marketplace. Moreover, in the case of products posing risks to human health, it is likely that the manufacturer's decisions will be influenced by other factors, such as potential civil liability that might flow from marketing products posing a health risk to the ultimate consumer, or the additional costs associated with safety procedures required to use such products in the manufacturing process'.[62]

For the AB then, the test from the perspective of consumer tastes and habits is whether the products would be substitutable and in a competitive relationship in an *idealised* marketplace, one where consumers have full information, and where, at least through tort liability, negative externalities have already to some extent been internalised. As the AB emphasises, the fact of an imperfect marketplace does not mean that evidence cannot be found that is probative of how consumers *would* behave with respect to the two products in an *idealised* marketplace.[63] Indeed, to

---

[60] *Ibid.*, para. 115.
[61] *Ibid.*, para. 122.
[62] *Ibid.*, para. 122.
[63] A very similar approach is taken in Bronckers and McNelis, 'Rethinking the "Like Product" Definition', *supra* n. 15. According to Bronckers and McNelis, for physically like products to be characterised as 'unlike' on the basis of consumer tastes and habits, it would be necessary for 'consumers as a whole (rather than specific interest groups)' to distinguish between the products (at 375). We do not understand why this should be the case – competing firms in the marketplace often differentiate their products to appeal to sub-groups of consumers, and those differentiations may change competitive relationships substantially.

support the intuitions of the AB here, in the case of asbestos, the evidence of the social costs from the health risks of this substance is such that one would almost certainly expect that, in an idealised marketplace where those costs were internalised, asbestos and asbestos products would be very unlikely to be cost competitive. This sort of analysis of consumer tastes and behaviour brings into the picture the kinds of regulatory interests which had under the GATT been taken into account through the 'aims and effects' test. It is just that those interests are taken into account here by adopting not the perspective of the regulator as such, but the perspective of consumer behaviour in an idealised marketplace. However, note that part of the picture of this idealised marketplace is a liability rule that makes manufacturers responsible for the health risks posed by their products; such a rule may well be premised not only on assumptions about the efficient allocation of risk, but also on judgements about the fair, or just, distribution of risk in a society. It is thus quite possible that this particular conception of the idealised marketplace embodies a conception not only of regulation as the 'efficient' correction of market failure but also of a just allocation of liability rules and/or property rights.

The final part of the AB's discussion of National Treatment in *Asbestos* consists in completing the analysis – i.e. applying the legal interpretation of Article III:4 as corrected to the facts. Having found that the panel did not err in law in choosing to adopt the *Border Tax Adjustment* approach to likeness, the AB does not undo that choice. The AB first turns to the consideration of physical characteristics. It comes to the conclusion that asbestos and the substitutes are 'very different' physically because of the health significance of the differences. Yet the AB does not explain *why* health effects should in this instance be decisive in evaluating whether physical differences are significant enough to point to a conclusion of unlikeness. The AB might have pointed to its speculations about consumer tastes and habits. However, if the panel was wrong to conflate an inquiry into physical characteristics with an investigation of end-uses, would not the AB have made a similar error, in evaluating the significance of physical differences through the lenses of the third criterion of consumer tastes and habits? As the AB stated earlier in its examination of Article III:4, one of the questions not answered by any dictionary definition of likeness is 'from whose perspective' the significance of differences and similarities is to be evaluated. Of course, one answer is the regulator's perspective, an answer that in some form or other leads back to 'aims and effects', an outcome unacceptable to the AB. Another answer is the consumer's perspective, but that leaves it mysterious why an analysis of physical characteristics would be *logically prior* to a consideration of consumer tastes and habits, much less distinct from it.

In any case, the physical properties of the products having been determined to be 'very different', on the basis of health considerations, the AB suggests that this amounts to a preliminary or tentative finding of 'unlikeness', which Canada has a high burden to bear in reversing, through demonstrating that despite significant physical differences the products are in a sufficiently close competitive relationship, when the other factors are analysed. Here, with respect to end-uses, because there was no evidence on the record of the *extent* of non-overlapping, separate end-uses for the products relative to similar end-uses, the AB concluded that 'we cannot determine

The WTO Impact on Internal Regulations

the significance of the fact that chrysotile asbestos and PCG fibres share a small number of similar end-uses'.[64]

Two readings are possible concerning what the AB was saying here. The first reading is that it is saying that it is impossible to apply at all the second criterion of end-uses due to a defect in the factual record of the panel. If this is so, then the AB should not be completing the analysis.[65] Because on the AB's own theory of 'likeness' a panel must make a separate and thorough analysis of all four criteria if it adopts the *Border Tax Adjustment* approach. If the factual record as it stood did not permit such an analysis of the second criterion, then the AB could not, on its own terms, go on to apply adequately the *Border Tax Adjustment* approach to 'likeness'.

The alternative reading of what the AB is doing here is that it uses this criterion to present evidence of the *comparative* importance of similar as opposed to different or non-overlapping end-uses. On this reading, the AB would be holding that a member, in order to make a *prima facie* case of likeness, has to provide evidence of likeness (similar end-uses) but also evidence of unlikeness (different or non-overlapping end-uses) and show at least the preliminary plausibility that the former evidence outweighs or is more probative than the latter. On the one hand, this view of the burden of proof is consistent with the AB's view that the inquiry into likeness is *inherently* a relative or comparative inquiry, entailing an appreciation of kind and degree of similarity; thus even a *prima facie* case of likeness would need to probe degree or extent, which obviously involves comparing the evidence of likeness against all evidence, including that of unlikeness. On the other hand, it seems more intuitively plausible that in an adversarial process, where the complainant provides *some* credible evidence of likeness, it establishes a *prima facie* case, such that one would normally expect that the defending party would now have to muster equal or greater credible evidence of *un*likeness. Thus, this alternative reading raises difficult issues about the burden of proof. However, it does exonerate the AB from a straightforward error of completing the analysis on the basis of an inadequate panel factual record.

In the case of consumer tastes and habits, the third criterion, the panel held that because Canada had presented no evidence at all on consumer tastes and habits, it could not overcome the tentative or preliminary characterisation of the products as 'like' based on physical characteristics.[66] However, the reason that Canada presented no evidence, the AB noted, was its legal position that the criterion was irrelevant. Here an *error in law*, corrected only upon appeal by the AB, resulted in an inadequate factual record. Was this a reasonable basis on which to conclude that Canada had not met its burden of proof? Or should the AB instead have simply concluded that the factual record was inadequate, and refused to complete the analysis? On balance, we are of the view that the AB acted appropriately. In failing to provide evidence on consumer tastes and habits, Canada was taking an ordinary litigation risk – the risk that if the panel were to disagree with its view that this criterion was irrelevant in the circumstances, it would lose the opportunity to argue in the alternative as it were

---

[64] Appellate Body Report, *supra* n. 16, para. 137.

[65] Thus, in *Canada – Periodicals, supra* n. 56, where there was inadequate factual analysis in the panel report, the AB held that it could not go ahead and complete the analysis of 'likeness'.

[66] Appellate Body Report, *supra* n. 16, para. 139.

that consumer tastes and habits did point to a finding of likeness or at least did not detract from such a finding based on physical similarities and end-uses.

There is, arguably, a more general inconsistency between the way in which the AB completed the analysis and the overall approach to Article III:4 it elaborated in the first part of its discussion of Article III:4. In that part, it suggested that what a panel should do is to consider all the evidence of likeness on the basis of the *Border Tax Adjustment* criteria, and indeed also consider any evidence that does not go *into* the characteristics addressed by those criteria, and then make on overall judgement about whether the products are 'like' or not. However, when completing the analysis, the AB appears to privilege the investigation of physical differences as of special and prior importance, such that where that analysis points to a finding of unlikeness, the evidence on the other criteria must be virtually overwhelming to justify an overall, definitive judgement that the products are 'like'. Given that, in this case, the physical differences are significant in terms of a very fundamental human value, health, the approach does not seem unjustified. However, the AB seems to adopt it as a rule of thumb for all cases, regardless of context. Nevertheless, it is important to note the AB does not affirm the converse. That is, the AB does *not* say that, where the analysis of physical characteristics points towards *likeness*, the burden of establishing *un*likeness on the basis of *other* criteria and evidence is especially heavy. Thus, whatever the merits of the AB's prioritisation of physical characteristics, the AB is not deploying that prioritisation in such a way as to reinforce the notion that products cannot normally be unlike once it has been established that they are physically 'like'.

What then is one to make of the overall ruling of the AB with respect to Article III:4? One way of understanding this ruling is that it navigates between two 'constituencies' both of which are important to the legitimacy of the Appellate Body on the WTO rules and institutions more generally.[67] The first constituency is that of the officials (delegates, secretariat employees, etc.) who are the day-to-day guardians of the trading system – these people may be inclined to look for clear, economic guidelines in the application of trade law, and may tend to view 'market access' as the main objective of the entire system, subject to certain defined and limited 'exceptions'. The second constituency is that comprised of the groups and individuals whose interests and values are habitually given short shrift when translated into trade rules and legal interpretation by the middle-level officials. Some of these groups see the only answer to this problem as structural – a roll back of globalisation. Yet there are other groups within the second constituency, such as those who filed applications for leave to submit *amicus* briefs in *Asbestos*, who see change within the system as at least part of the solution, including more sensitive interpretations of WTO law.

The *Asbestos* ruling navigates with agility between these two constituencies. It gives to the first constituency an 'economic' framework for the application of Article III:4,

---

[67] Here we have been inspired by recent work by Joseph Weiler on the distinction between internal and external legitimacy of the WTO. See Joseph H. H. Weiler, 'The Rule of Lawyers and the Ethos of Diplomats: Reflections on the Internal and External Legitimacy of WTO Dispute Settlement', Harvard Jean Monnet Working Paper 9/00, available at www.jeanmonnetprogram.org. Assessing the first five years of AB rulings, Weiler observes that the AB has practised a legitimation strategy with 'a keen eye on balancing internal and external legitimacy' (at 16).

The WTO Impact on Internal Regulations

which is continuous with the recent jurisprudence on National Treatment in taxation. At the same time, it corrects for the narrowness of perspective of the panel, signaling that within the 'economic' framework for the analysis of likeness, broader human interests and values such as health must be taken into account. In addition, the AB has maintained two additional safety valves against interpretations of likeness under Article III:4, that threaten the legitimacy of the system by giving inadequate attention to human values and interests of a non-economic nature, in the narrow sense. The first is in the notion that the 'economic' framework is not necessarily decisive with regard to likeness in all cases, and evidence that cannot be assimilated to the characteristics important in that framework must be taken into account (even if the AB did not speculate on what such cases might be about). The second safety valve resides in the importance of establishing 'less favourable treatment', i.e. protection of domestic production, in order to prove a violation of Article III:4. To the extent that 'less favourable treatment' means treatment that is protectionist in aims and effects, this second step in Article III:4 analysis creates the kind of safe harbour for non-protectionist domestic regulations that had been the central intent behind the now repudiated 'aims and effects' test. The Member of the AB division who, in his concurring opinion, expressed the view that the AB should have stated outright that carcinogenic asbestos is not 'like' non-carcinogenic substitutes clearly, at some point, balked at this balancing act. He could not accept that the concern to preserve the 'economic' approach to 'likeness' in Article III:4 justifies the failure to make a strong and unambiguous statement that, in a case like this, health effects simply *trump* other considerations or factors that might be in play in assessing 'likeness'.

Yet, in fairness to the approach of the other two members of the division, the balance they struck is not an unprincipled compromise between interest groups. The WTO system cannot function without the support of the middle-level officials, whether delegates or Secretariat members, who oil its wheels on a daily basis. As recent events have shown, its future development can also be brought to a halt if it has no legitimacy with the broad range of interests that typically feel left out of outcomes produced by the first constituency. There is, at present, no effective political leadership to mediate these constituencies or get them to talk to one another, and the AB is arguably the only functional institution within the multilateral trading system that can articulate the outlines of an overlapping consensus. Given this predicament, the AB's approach to Article III:4 is understandable.

Some may argue that in playing this kind of role the AB has gone to the opposite extreme of its initial approach of sticking to the treaty text. However, the AB is careful to note in its ruling that the treaty text cannot resolve in any kind of straightforward positivistic way the issue of 'likeness' in Article III:4. Thus, the Appellate Body has been compelled to find a legitimate solution in the absence of an agreed approach in the treaty text itself. Under such circumstances, it has understandably resorted to techniques of adjudication described by Cass Sunstein in the US domestic context, somewhat misleading perhaps, as 'judicial minimalism'.[68] These are techniques that Sunstein argues are appropriate in cases where a court must decide a complex matter on which people feel deeply, but also on which the relevant constituencies are deeply

---

[68] C. Sunstein, *One Case at a Time: Judicial Minimalism on the Supreme Court* (Cambridge, MA: Harvard University Press, 1999).

divided on the level of principle. The court must find an outcome in the individual case before it that does not represent a choice between the ultimate values that are contested in any simple or straightforward way. It will thus craft a decision that leaves many things undecided or under-decided; which resolves issues not through reference to high general principles but to narrow factors such as burdens of proof and issues specific to the facts of the case; it will be uninclined to evolve the law in bold steps, by overtly replacing one kind of doctrinal framework with another. This kind of decision people may be able to live with, despite deep divisions among them about the general principles or norms at stake. And based on discussion about the Article III:4 analysis to date among various commentators, the AB may well have succeeded in this respect – for while the first constituency, though puzzled by certain details, sees a further development of the market-based approach,[69] the second constituency sees a greater sensitivity to basic human interests, and the legitimacy of governmental action to protect them.

Application of the TBT Agreement to the *Asbestos* Dispute

In the panel proceedings, the EC made the unusual argument that because the French measure was an outright ban it was not a technical regulation within the meaning of the TBT Agreement, and therefore the Agreement did not apply. The definition of a 'technical regulation' is 'a Document which lays down product characteristics or their related processes and production methods, including the applicable administrative provisions, with which compliance is mandatory. It may also include or deal exclusively with terminology, symbols, packaging, marking or labeling requirements as they apply to a product, process or production method'.[70] The EC argued that a measure banning a product cannot be equated with a measure that specifies the product's characteristics. The panel agreed with the EC's reasoning and held that the TBT Agreement did not apply to the measure in question. In order to characterise the measure as a straightforward ban, the panel had to accept the EC view that the part of the decree banning asbestos and the part providing for certain limited exceptions were, in essence, two separate measures. The panel's finding that TBT did not apply was also intertwined with its finding that the measure in question was a violation of Article III:4. It regarded Article XX as the appropriate context for considering whether the ban was justified on health grounds.

The Appellate Body reversed the panel's finding that the TBT Agreement did not apply. First of all, it held that the part of the decree establishing a ban and the part providing limited exceptions had to be considered as a unified whole, not two separate measures. The AB rightly observed that the exceptions would have no legal meaning unless they operated in conjunction with a general prohibition. Secondly, the AB rejected the notion that, because the decree banned asbestos as such, it did

---

[69] See certain of the comments on the ruling posted to the Jean Monnet Discussion Forum, www.jeanmonnet.org, and see the statement by several NGOs reacting to the decision: 'NGOs Welcome WTO Green Light to French Ban on Asbestos but Remain Skeptical About the WTO Dispute Settlement Process', Joint Position Statement by Greenpeace International, IBAS (International Ban Asbestos Secretariat), FIELD (Foundation for International Environmental Law and Development) and WWF (World Wide Fund for Nature, International), March 2001, www.field.org.uk.

[70] Annex I:1 TBT Agreement.

The WTO Impact on Internal Regulations 99

not describe the characteristics of a product, within the meaning of the TBT Agreement. The AB noted that the French decree did not simply ban asbestos in its natural state – it banned asbestos in products. Thus, the decree did describe a characteristic of products, namely that they be free of asbestos. As the AB clearly understood, one could hardly make the applicability of the TBT Agreement depend on semantic distinctions such as whether a member creates a list of every product and then describes a characteristic of that product as the absence of asbestos rather than simply prohibiting asbestos as a characteristic of any and all products: 'there may be perfectly sound administrative reasons for formulating a "technical regulation" in a way that does *not* expressly identify products by name, but simply makes them identifiable – for instance, through the "characteristic" that is the subject of regulation'.[71] In addition to being based on empty semantics, the EC claim that the TBT Agreement does not apply to a general ban on a toxic substance in products was at odds with one of the basic purposes of the TBT Agreement, stated in the Preamble to the Agreement, namely 'to ensure technical regulations and standards, . . . do not create unnecessary obstacles to trade'. On the EC reading of TBT, a member could undermine this objective of TBT by simply choosing the most trade restrictive instrument of all – a general ban – and thereby avoiding any scrutiny of whether its policy instrument is an 'unnecessary obstacle to trade'. By adopting the most restrictive policy instrument one avoids any inquiry about whether less restrictive alternatives might be available! The panel, at least, found the TBT Agreement non-applicable on the assumption that there would be a requirement of Article XX justification; but the EC claim was utterly egregious because the EC was also of course arguing that there was no violation of Article III:4.

Having found that the TBT Agreement did apply, the AB decided not to 'complete the analysis' given that it would have to deal with so many issues of first impression not adjudicated by the panel below, with the very real possibility that applying the relevant TBT provisions would also require a different or more extensive factual record.[72] However, the AB did provide an important clue to how it understood the relationship between the TBT Agreement and GATT, which we will explore in the section of this chapter that follows.

The Relationship Between TBT and GATT

There are several possible views concerning the relationship between TBT and GATT. One is that the TBT Agreement should be considered as a *lex specialis* to the general obligations and rights in Articles III and XX of the GATT. This would mean that, if a measure fell within the definition of a technical regulation in the TBT Agreement, its legality would be considered under that agreement, to the exclusion of Articles III and XX of GATT. A second view is that a complainant may choose to bring a claim under *either* GATT or TBT but not both. A third view is that the obligations and rights in GATT and TBT operate concurrently, and both may apply to a single dispute, provided of course the measure falls within the ambit of some provision or provisions in both agreements. This third view is basically consistent with the way in which,

[71] Appellate Body Report, *supra* n. 16, para. 70.
[72] *Ibid.*, paras. 78–83.

to date, panels and the Appellate Body have understood the relationship between GATT and other WTO treaties.[73]

Thus, it is not surprising that, in *Asbestos*, the Appellate Body should appear to endorse the third view, remarking that (for those measures that fall within its ambit) the TBT Agreement imposes obligations on members that seem to be *different* from, and *additional* to, the obligations imposed on members under GATT 1994.[74] Although the AB does not expand on why it takes this position on TBT, such a position in our estimation is structurally sound, and an appropriate understanding of both the GATT and the TBT Agreement, and their interrelationship. At first glance, both GATT Articles III/XX and the TBT Agreement appear to deal with the justification of domestic regulatory measures as related to legitimate (non-protectionist) objectives and as the least-trade-restrictive alternative reasonably available. Thus, it is tempting to conclude that, with respect to technical regulations, the TBT Agreement simply provides a more fine-tuned set of tests or criteria for achieving the same objectives as GATT Articles III/XX.

However, there are fundamental structural differences.[75] The first difference relates to the anti-protection principle, which is central to the manner in which the GATT/WTO system interacts with the domestic regulatory state. The structure represented by Articles III/XX preserves a wide field of regulatory autonomy for domestic polities (at least if correctly interpreted), by requiring that a member has to justify its public policies before the WTO tribunal (i.e. under XX) only *if* they have been found to be inconsistent with the anti-protection principle (i.e. under Article III). Thus, as the AB emphasises in *Asbestos*, even if a measure draws a regulatory distinction between products that have been determined to be 'like', there will still not be a violation of Article III:4, unless that distinction results in less favourable treatment of the group of like imported products relative to the group of like domestic products, i.e. unless the regulatory distinction results in *protection* of domestic production.[76] It is the judicious application of the anti-protection norm that, in important respects, provides assurances against the WTO Dispute Settlement Body becoming the menacing, autocratic global government that it is feared to be by many of the system's critics. In the last analysis, if the complaining member cannot prove on balance of probabilities that my internal regulation protects domestic production, the WTO dispute settlement organs do not get to second-guess my sovereign regulatory choices under Article XX.[77]

---

[73] See *Bananas panel*, paras. 7.285 ff; and *Bananas AB, supra* n. 9, paras. 217 ff; see also *Canada – Periodicals AB, supra* n. 56, 19; see also Panel Report, *Indonesia – Certain Measures Affecting the Automobile Industry*, WT/DS54/R, WT/DS55/R, WT/DS64/R, 1998 (hereinafter *Indonesian Autos*). See also Davey and Zdouc, 'The Triangle of TRIPs, GATT, and GATS' in *World Trade Forum* (Ann Arbor, MI: University of Michigan Press, 2004).

[74] Appellate Body Report, *supra* n. 16, para. 80, original emphasis.

[75] See Hudec, 'Requiem', *supra* n. 7.

[76] Appellate Body Report, *supra* n. 16, para. 100.

[77] A further hedge against this possibility is the sensitive interpretation of Art. XX, which we explore in the next section of this chapter. However, as Hudec notes, Art. XX places a substantial justificatory burden on the defending member, a burden that does not seem to sit well in the case of measures that have not been found to constitute protective discrimination, but merely have *some* kind of restrictive pact on trade: Hudec, 'Requiem', *supra* n. 7.

The WTO Impact on Internal Regulations

Now, when we turn to the TBT Agreement, we see a quite different juridical structure. First of all, the obligations in the TBT Agreement apply even to non-discriminatory technical regulations. Secondly, many of the obligations in the TBT Agreement are of a 'due process' character, ensuring transparency and integrity in the regulatory process.[78] Indeed, more generally, many features of the TBT Agreement would appear incomprehensible but for an appreciation of its overall focus on regulatory processes. For example, the TBT Agreement contains MFN and National Treatment obligations[79]; these provisions would be superfluous and inexplicable in the TBT Agreement, if that agreement were focused on the substance of regulations themselves, for already in Articles I and III:4 of the GATT there are essential identical MFN and National Treatment obligations that apply to 'laws, regulations, and requirements'. However, as is indicated in the heading of Article 2 of the TBT Agreement as a whole, the MFN and National Treatment provisions there, like the other provisions of Article 2, are with a view to ensuring certain characteristics of the regulatory *process*, namely the stages of the regulatory process concerning, respectively, the 'Preparation, Adoption, and Application' of technical regulations. Thus, where the concern about the regulatory process actually entails in the TBT Agreement some elements of judgement concerning the substance of regulations themselves, namely, whether a member's measure is the least trade restrictive available (Article 2.2), it is the *challenging member* who must prove, on the balance of probabilities, that the regulating state has *failed* to *ensure in the regulatory process* that its measure is the least restrictive of trade. This contrasts with the character of the least-restrictive means test applied under those heads of Article XX of the GATT that invoke the notion that a member's measure must be 'necessary' for a stated permissible objective, where the substance of regulations must be justified by the defendant, because protection has already been determined to exist (i.e. a violation of Article III or some other provision of the GATT, for example those dealing with discriminatory border measures, for example Article XI). It is true that this burden of proof has been somewhat modified by the notion, prominent in certain cases, that once the complainant has established a 'presumption' of violation, the burden shifts to the defending member.[80] However, there is no discovery available in WTO dispute settlement, so where the *complainant* cannot be expected in the first instance to have access to information that would normally allow it to make its claim, for instance detailed information about the internal workings of the defending member's regulatory processes, the burden may be shifted to the defendant once the complainant has gone as far as the tribunal thinks it *can* reasonably be expected to go in establishing its case on balance of probabilities, without being able to compel the production of evidence by the defendant.

Now, if TBT were to *replace* Articles III/XX of the GATT as a comprehensive legal regime in the case of technical regulations, the balance between market access and regulatory autonomy struck by the anti-protection principle would be undermined. On the one hand, the right created, in effect, by Articles III/XX to require that a member provide a justification before the dispute settlement organs for *protective*

---

[78] E.g. Art. 2.7 of the TBT Agreement establishes transparency requirements.

[79] Art. 2.1 TBT Agreement.

[80] See also Appellate Body Report, *United States – Measures Affecting Imports of Woven Wool Shirts and Blouses from India*, WT/DS33/AB/R (hereinafter *US Shirts and Blouses*).

policies would be lost – once a *prima facie* case of protective discrimination is made out, it seems unreasonable to require the complainant to show that the policies are *not* justified as the least-trade-restrictive alternative. On the other hand, there is the risk that the balance could easily be tipped the other way, if the panels and Appellate Body were to understand Article 2.2 of the TBT Agreement as playing the kind of role of strict scrutiny of substantive regulatory outcomes that Article XX plays, at least where the applicable paragraph in Article XX indicates a 'necessity' test. That is, even non-protective measures could lead to a strict standard of scrutiny under Article 2.2, thus allowing the WTO dispute settlement organs to second-guess policy outcomes for which there is not even a *prima facie* case of protective discrimination.

If these are the dangers in viewing TBT as a replacement regime for Articles III/XX, how then are we instead to apply the two regimes concurrently, while making sense of both differences and similarities in language and concepts as between the two? The answer lies in some of the complexities and sensitivities involved in applying the anti-protection principle in non-facially discriminatory measures that nevertheless have a disparate impact on trade. If a panel were only to find a violation of Article III where a protectionist intent could clearly be established behind such measures, many cases of hidden protectionism would not be caught, and this would undermine the durability of the non-discrimination norm as a reasonable balance between market access rights and regulatory autonomy (thus, the rejection of this version of 'aims and effects'). If, instead, a panel were to find violation of Article III every time there was an impact or effect on trade from a regulatory distinction not based on market criteria such as those emphasised by the panel in *Japanese Alcohol*,[81] a huge range of non-protectionist regulations would be subject to strict scrutiny under Article XX, opening up a serious threat to regulatory autonomy.

We have already explored how, through its interpretation of 'likeness' and 'less favourable treatment', the AB has attempted in *Asbestos* to provide a range of safeguards against this latter danger. However, it is clear that determining whether products are 'like' and whether there is 'less favourable treatment', i.e. protection of domestic products, entails sensitive case-by-case judgements concerning the regulatory scheme, its design, the way that distinctions are drawn within it and the relationship of those distinctions to the operation of the marketplace. Such judgements can be made with greater confidence and precision if one can have the window into the regulatory process itself that TBT disciplines should provide. One can have greater confidence that the distinctions in a regulatory scheme are in fact non-protectionist, by requiring certain things about the regulatory process that itself generates those distinctions – transparency, coherence and consistency, use of international standards as 'inputs', ensuring at each step of the process that the measures adopted are not more trade restrictive than necessary, given the kind of risk at issue (admittedly in this last case there is some substantive element, as the treaty text suggests that it is appropriate to analyse the results of the process in order to assess whether the obligation to 'ensure' has been fulfilled). If a member has fulfilled its obligations under TBT, we can have some assurance that any non-national-origin-based regulatory

---

[81] It will be recalled that the Appellate Body in *Japanese Alcohol* emphasised that criteria for likeness including these market-based criteria, but that the list was open-ended, with the relevant criteria depending on context, including presumably the regulatory context: *AB Japanese Alcohol, supra* n. 36, 21.

The WTO Impact on Internal Regulations

distinctions that have a trade impact are, nevertheless, non-protectionist. Thus, once the complainant has failed to establish a violation of TBT, it should be well-nigh impossible for it to sustain a claim that Article III:4 is violated. Similarly, a complainant who brings a claim with respect to a technical regulation under Article III, while not making any claim of a TBT violation, will risk the panel being relatively deferential to the defending member's regulatory choices. If the complainant has not sought to impugn the regulatory process itself under TBT, it cannot object to the panel affording considerable deference to non-national-origin-based regulatory distinctions in the scheme, questioned by the complainant. The implication of this is that where a regulatory scheme does not explicitly discriminate against imports, these claims will normally be brought as TBT claims. A related implication is that if, in the case of such a claim, a member happens to invoke both Article III and TBT, the panel should normally proceed in the first instance with the TBT analysis, which gives it an insight into the regulatory process. Only where the scheme provides explicit differential treatment of imports and domestic products, i.e. contains facial distinctions between products on the basis of national origin (domestic or foreign) would the panel commence with Article III:4. If, in the case of non-origin-based regulatory distinctions, there is a violation of TBT, the panel may have a view of the regulatory process that will make it more likely that an Article III:4 violation will be found, i.e. that the distinctions in question result in less favourable treatment or impacts in the sense of protection of domestic production. Of course, for reasons of judicial economy, the panel may decide, having found the measures in violation of the TBT, not to proceed to consider Article III. On the other hand, as already suggested, if the regulatory process *is* in conformity with TBT requirements, it is highly implausible that the non-national-origin regulatory distinctions generated by that process could be impugned under Article III. Of course, there will be cases where claims concerning non-facially-origin-discriminatory measures *will* be litigated under Article III, these being cases where the measure in question is not a technical regulation within the meaning of TBT (and does not fall under SPS either). However, because of the broad definition of technical regulation in the TBT Agreement, most claims that are related to regulatory schemes with non-commercial or non-fiscal purposes will not be decided under Article III.

In the case of measures that do contain facial national-origin-based distinctions, a complainant may well wish to make an Article III claim, as such measures are almost certain to constitute violations of Article III, therefore placing the onus of justification on the defendant, if indeed some purpose stated under Article XX can be invoked. (Of course, as the panel stated in the *Section 337* case, it is possible that even a scheme that discriminates facially on the basis of national origin could, in certain circumstances, nevertheless 'provide no less favourable' treatment to imports; however, such a facial distinction between domestic and imported products probably should suffice to make a *prima facie* case of 'less favourable treatment', which would then have to be rebutted by the *defendant*, who must show that while imports are treated differently there is no protection of domestic production involved in such differentiation. See the AB ruling in *Korea – Beef*, para. 157.) In the case of facial discrimination, however, the complainant may still wish to bring a TBT claim. Even if the defendant can justify its measures under Article XX, it may still be in violation of some specific provisions of the TBT Agreement. Of course, in the case of Article 2.2, if the defendant has borne the burden of proof to show that its measures are the least-trade-restrictive alternative under Article XX, it is hard to imagine how the complainant could establish a violation of Article 2.2, especially because Article 2.2 requires not that the measures be the least-trade-restrictive reasonably available, but only the least-trade-restrictive taking into account the risks that the measure address. Thus, a panel would normally consider the Article 2.2 claim *res judicata* having found that the measure is the least-trade-restrictive reasonably available for the purpose in question. This would normally suggest the logic of the panel first considering Articles III and XX of GATT before going on to adjudicate the TBT claims. Also, in order to bear the burden of proof for justification, which it is only reasonable for it to do given that one is dealing with a facially discriminatory measure, the defendant will be bringing forward a great deal of information about its regulatory scheme; this will obviate the difficulty the complainant normally faces under TBT of obtaining the information to prove a violation on a balance of probabilities without the ability to compel disclosure of evidence by the defendant, and thus in turn obviate the need to corrupt or modify burden of proof through the notion of shifting presumptions. Then, after the Article XX analysis, the panel can go on to consider any TBT claims not *res judicata* in consequence of that analysis. Of course, if the defendant is unsuccessful under Article XX, the panel may, on judicial economy grounds, decide not to proceed to the TBT claims, as the measure has already been found in violation of a WTO treaty.

The *Asbestos* Dispute and the Operative Provisions of the TBT Agreement

We have argued above that, in many respects, the TBT Agreement can be seen as a response to the delicate task of adjudicating claims about *de facto* discrimination in regulations with non-commercial or non-fiscal rationales. The TBT Agreement focuses largely on the regulatory process and its inputs, which involves necessarily *some* examination of the substantive regulatory choices of democratic polities, but avoids WTO tribunals sitting in *de novo* review of non-facially discriminatory policies, against which there is no general presumption in WTO law (unlike facially discriminatory trade restricting measures). The Preamble to the TBT Agreement reflects in a number of its provisions this view of the Agreement. Thus the Members recognise that 'no country should be prevented from taking measures necessary to ensure the quality of its exports, or for the protection of human animal or plant life or health, of the environment, or for the prevention of deceptive practices, at the levels it considers appropriate, subject to the requirement that they are not applied in a manner which would constitute a means of arbitrary or unjustifiable discrimination between countries where the same conditions prevail or a disguised restriction on international trade, and are otherwise in accordance with the provisions of this Agreement'. This provision can make sense only if nothing *per se* in the TBT Agreement prevents a member from choosing its appropriate level of protection. Otherwise, the provision would have the following, (il)logical structure: no country shall be prevented from doing x, provided it does not do x.

More generally, this crucial provision in the Preamble states the view that the provisions of the TBT Agreement represent a set of specific and limited qualifications to members' general presumed right to regulate as they see fit for the purposes

The WTO Impact on Internal Regulations

in question – or, to put it the other way round, the Agreement does not set up a general presumption against such regulations as trade barriers, which must then be scrutinised to see if they fit within certain exceptions. The provisions of the TBT Agreement must, then, not be interpreted so broadly as to nullify or fundamentally frustrate the core right to regulate as recognised in the Preamble – they merely place some conditions or qualifications on the exercise of that right.

Article 2.2 is perhaps the provision of the TBT Agreement that most clearly brings into the assessment of a member's regulatory process an element of judgement or scrutiny of its substantive regulatory outcomes. The first sentence of Article 2.2 states an obligation of members with respect to the regulatory process: they must '*ensure* that technical regulations are not prepared, adopted or applied with a view to or with the effect of creating unnecessary obstacles to international trade' (emphasis added). The second sentence indicates that this obligation to 'ensure' is to be judged against the substantive results of the regulatory process. It reads: '[f]or this purpose technical regulations shall not be more trade-restrictive than necessary to fulfil a legitimate objective, taking account of the risks non-fulfillment would create'. After stating a list of legitimate objectives that is non-exhaustive the provision closes with the following sentence: '[i]n assessing such risks relevant elements of consideration are, *inter alia*, available scientific and technical information, related processing technology or intended end-uses of products'. These various qualifications on the substantive criterion that regulations be the least-trade-restrictive necessary distinguish the TBT Agreement sharply from the strict scrutiny regime established by Art. XX of the GATT for presumptively discriminatory measures, at least with respect to measures concerned with human life and health [Art. XX (b)].[82] The qualifications remind us that the substantive criterion is with a view, not so much to justifying the measures themselves (being presumptively legitimate, they do not require a justification), but to evaluating the regulatory process that has produced the measures. Thus, the obligation to ensure the least-trade-restrictiveness of regulations is relative to the kinds of risks that would arise in the absence of the regulations. Deliberation about the choice of regulatory instrument can be a costly and time-consuming process. How far a member should be expected to go in exhausting all the regulatory alternatives to find the least-trade-restrictive alternative is logically related to the kind of risk it is dealing with. Where what is at stake is a well-established risk to human life itself (as we will argue, this is exactly the case with asbestos), a member may be expected to act rapidly, rely on the scientific *acquis* to a large extent, tending towards

---

[82] Note that not all of the heads in Art. XX require a 'necessity test' as developed by the panel in *Thai Cigarette* for Art. XX(b) which reads, 'necessary to protect human, animal or plant life or health': *Thailand – Restrictions on Importation of and Internal Taxes on Cigarettes*, BISD 34S (hereinafter *Thai Cigarette*). Other cases addressed Art. XX(g) which deals with measures 'relating to the conservation of exhaustible natural resources'. In *Reformulated Gasoline*, the Appellate Body stated for a measure to qualify as 'relating to' within the meaning of Art. XX(g), the measures had to exhibit a 'substantial relationship' with the conservation of natural resources. See Appellate Body Report in *United States – Standards for Reformulated and Conventional Gasoline*, WT/DS2, 20 May 1996 (hereinafter *Reformulated Gasoline*), 21. In *Shrimp/Turtle*, the Appellate Body stated that the US measure exhibited a 'means/ends relationship' with the legitimate policy of conserving an exhaustible and endangered species. See Appellate Body Report, *United States – Import Prohibition of Certain Shrimps and Shrimp Products*, 6 November 1998 (hereinafter *Shrimp/Turtle*) para. 135.

the more obviously effective and enforceable kinds of regulatory tools, as opposed to the more sophisticated and speculative ones. This suggests the concept of the Precautionary Principle, as articulated by the Appellate Body in *Hormones*: 'responsible, representative governments commonly act from perspectives of prudence and precaution where risks of *irreversible, e.g. life-terminating, damage to human health* are concerned'[83] (emphasis added). While, as the AB has noted in *Asbestos*, TBT obligations are 'different' from those in GATT,[84] nevertheless it is significant that in its Article XX analysis, not needing to decide the case at bar, the AB considered that the value at stake in the case of *Asbestos* 'is both vital and important in the highest degree'.[85]

In its submissions to the panel, Canada claimed that France's measure was not rationally related to the objective of protecting health and life, as well as that it is not the least trade restrictive available to fulfil the objective.[86] As the EC suggested in its reply brief, there was, however, no textual basis in Article 2.2 for separately assessing whether a measure is rationally related to its objective. In fact, Canada's arguments about the lack of rational basis for the French ban were essentially identical to its arguments that it is not the least-trade-restrictive measure available to fulfil the objective in question.

Canada's first argument was that France had acted on the basis of the historical information about the risks posed by asbestos, and this historical information did not isolate the particular kind of asbestos fibre exported by Canada, chrysotile. According to Canada the health risks that had materialised in the past are in large measure due to the use of asbestos fibres other than chrysotile, which (according to Canada) is in fact safe when used in an appropriate manner.

Given the overwhelming evidence of the serious risks to life and health posed by exposure to asbestos in general, should the TBT Agreement be interpreted as requiring that France, in order to ensure that its measure is the least restrictive of trade available, attempt to undertake new empirical work, which aims to isolate the risks posed by chrysotile, in order to determine whether France could achieve its health objective while not banning this particular form of asbestos? Here, it is important to note that Article 2.2 explicitly lists among the relevant elements of consideration in assessing risk, '*available* scientific and technical information' (emphasis added). The TBT Agreement itself appears explicitly to endorse reliance on existing, available information in the assessment of risk. Even in interpreting Article XX, which has no such explicit reference to 'available' information, the Appellate Body in *Asbestos* held that France could not be expected to adopt a less-trade-restrictive alternative that was as yet unproven in effectiveness.[87]

The *Asbestos* case is a good example of the wisdom of focusing on available information. It is true that the historical evidence of the serious risk to life and health from asbestos reflects data on exposure to many kinds of asbestos, especially those other than chrysotile. However, because the health risks from asbestos have typically

---

[83] See *Hormones* AB, *supra* n. 3, para. 124.

[84] Appellate Body Report, *supra* n. 16, para. 80.

[85] *Ibid.*, para. 172.

[86] Canada, first submission *supra* n. 26, paras. 201 ff.

[87] Appellate Body Report, *supra* n. 16, para. 174.

The WTO Impact on Internal Regulations

taken a long time after exposure to manifest themselves, to do what Canada expects would entail a strategy of waiting until there is inconvertible evidence that chrysotile also poses the health risks in question, before banning its use. It seems to amount to a nullification of a member's sovereign prerogative to protect the health and life of its citizens (which is also an *obligation* of most WTO states under international human rights law[88]), if it had to wait until a significant number of its citizens became sick or died from exposure to chrysotile in particular, before banning this substance.

In fact, chrysotile as a substance has the same basic properties as other types of asbestos. Canada's argument that it is harmless really reduces to a claim that the way in which, today, chrysotile is encased in building materials and used in accordance with safe procedures renders it harmless.[89] Here, Canada was suggesting that the EC (France) had violated Article 2.2, because it could have attained its objective merely through requiring safe use of chrysotile, a less-trade-restrictive alternative.

To what extent does Article 2.2 require a member to adopt a less-restrictive alternative regardless of the costs and feasibility of that alternative? Unlike the parallel provision in the SPS Agreement, Article 5.6, and its footnote 3, Article 2.2 does not explicitly state that least-restrictive means least-restrictive measure 'reasonable available taking into account technical and economic feasibility'. Yet such an explicit reference in Article 2.2 is not really necessary to capture the notion that regulatory costs of alternative policy alternatives should be taken into account. This is because Article 2.2 contains a much more general qualification on the notion of least-restrictive alternative – that the alternative be least restrictive 'taking into account the risks non-fulfillment would create'. As the Appellate Body clarified in *Hormones*, the notion of risk and risk assessment does not go only to the risks as they emerge under ideal or laboratory conditions, but risks that arise due to limits on the ability to control the way a product is used.[90] This finding in *Hormones* applies *a fortiori* to the conception of assessing risks under Article 2.2, where the factors to be taken into account have pointedly been left open-ended, 'available scientific and technical information' being only one among them.[91] The European Communities argue, in the *Asbestos*

---

[88] See right to life in civil and political covenants and WHO declaration on right to health.

[89] Canada first submission, *supra* n. 26, para. 73 ff: '*Effets sur la santé des principaux types d'exposition à l'amiante*', Institut National de la Santé et de la recherche Médical, Paris, éditions (INSERM: Collection Expertises Collectives, 1997).

[90] See *Hormones* AB, *supra* n. 3, para. 187, reading that risks is also 'the risk in human societies as they actually exist, in other words, the actual potential for adverse effects on human health in the real world where people live and work and die'.

[91] There are some who interpret the language 'taking into account the risks non-fulfillment would create' as imposing an additional requirement on the defending member, namely that the measure not only be the least restrictive of trade, but that it also be proportional, namely that the marginally greater risk of a less-trade-restrictive measure would need to be balanced against the decree to which the it is less trade restrictive. This is apparently the position of Hudec, 'Requiem', *supra* n. 7. However, this interpretation is inconsistent with the structure and purposes of the TBT Agreement. First of all, if a member had to live with a measure that does not fully realise its policy objective, because that measure is much less trade-restrictive than one that realises the objective fully, then a member's fundamental right to determine its appropriate level of protection would be undermined, if not gutted. A member *could* not, in effect, set a level of protection that *required* a very high level of trade restrictiveness for its full realisation. This in turn would make the least-restrictive means test in TBT much more intrusive of domestic sovereignty than the test in Art. XX(b), e.g., especially as interpreted by the AB in both *Korea – Beef* and *Asbestos* (see the discussion below at pages 321 ff). That result is obviously perverse, given that the TBT Agreement applies

case, that there are significant obstacles to ensuring that chrysotile is 'used' in such a way as to obviate serious risks to health and life. 'Safe use' as understood by Canada applies only to the installation of components containing chrysotile in the construction process. Even if perfectly enforced, such protocols would not obviate the risks to maintenance workers, much less to do-it-yourself renovators. As the EC argues, devising a regulatory scheme that would protect these potential victims through behavioural protocols would be extremely difficult, at least relative to a straightforward ban on the substance. Here, again, it is worth noting that, for purposes of Art. XX, where the treaty text itself does not have the qualifying language 'taking into account the risks non-fulfillment would create', the AB accepted, based upon the facts found by the panel, that in circumstances such as these the alternative measure of controlled use could not be viewed as achieving France's stated level of protection.[92]

Of course, almost any alternative to a ban in most cases will present some significant regulatory challenges and costs. There is a limited number of producers and suppliers of asbestos within Europe and outside. Effectively enforcing the ban would not seem to be very difficult. However, it might be objected, if less-restrictive regulatory options to an outright ban are often going to have higher regulatory costs, would not taking those costs into account under Article 2.2 render the obligation to adopt the least-trade-restrictive alternative largely meaningless? Here, however, the language 'taking into account the risks non-fulfillment will create' is very important. No risk management scheme will be so perfectly applied and enforced as to reduce risk to zero; thus, if the objective is zero risk then a ban will almost always be the least-restrictive alternative (at least assuming relatively few enforcement problems with the ban itself). Thus, at one level, Canada may be justified in suggesting that the TBT Agreement does not allow a member to set its regulations according to the principle of reducing risk to zero,[93] for if so 'the least-restrictive alternative' obligation could be reduced to something largely meaningless. However, in some cases where risk *management*, at least any available at reasonable cost, is inadequate to prevent the risk materialising, the consequences may not be particularly grave or serious. In those cases, 'taking into account the risks that non-fulfillment would create', it might be reasonable for a member to adopt the risk management scheme, despite its imperfections, because those imperfections minimally impair its ability to protect the health and lives of its citizens.[94] In other situations, however, such as that in the *Asbestos* case, where imperfect control of the risk through risk management is likely to result in consequences as serious as life-threatening cancer, not to permit an outright ban as the 'least restrictive measure' would impair the very ability of a member

---

to measures that have not yet been found to be protective, whereas Art. XX will apply in these situations only where protective discrimination, and thus a violation of Art. III:4, has already been established. Our interpretation that the language concerning taking into account the risks non-fulfilment would create provides an additional margin of appreciation to domestic regulators is, by contrast, entirely consistent with the structural differences between the two agreements, particularly the notion that many measures considered under TBT do not carry the presumption of protective discrimination, unlike Art. XX.

[92] Appellate Body Report, *supra* n. 16, para. 174.

[93] Canada, second submission, *supra* n. 26, paras. 225 ff.

[94] See the observation of the Appellate Body with respect to Art. XX in the *Korea – Beef* case, *infra* n. 99, para. 180.

The WTO Impact on Internal Regulations

to exercise its prerogative (and fulfil its international human rights obligation) to protect the right to life of its citizens. Once interests of this kind of gravity are clearly seen to be at stake, a member need not be required to adopt a less-restrictive policy instrument that provides less certain or perfect control of the risk, even by a small margin, despite the possibility that the less-restrictive instrument would be *hugely* less restrictive of trade – there is no place for balancing or proportionality analysis. This is consistent with the recognition, in the Preamble to the TBT Agreement, that the provisions of the Agreement do not nullify the basic prerogative to protect the health and life of one's citizens. This being said, a ban on asbestos, while being more restrictive of Canada's trade in asbestos than a measure that banned asbestos only where it was proven that substitutes were less safe than asbestos, might not thereby be less restrictive of trade overall. Substitute fibres are also traded products. To establish trade-restrictiveness in this instance, Canada would have to show that there are barriers to trade in the substitute products, such that any reduction in asbestos trade would not be compensated for by increased trade in substitutes.

A further claim by Canada is that the substitutes for asbestos have not been proven safe – it might turn out that the health and safety objective is actually undermined by a ban on asbestos, if the substituted substances turn out to be harmful or more harmful than chrysotile asbestos itself. In effect, Canada is saying that a less-restrictive alternative would be to require that asbestos substitutes be used only when it has been demonstrated that these are safe, or safer than asbestos itself.

The limits of *ex ante* risk prevention through prediction of risks based on testing and experimentation prior to sale in the marketplace are, in the case of many risks, quite substantial. This is obviously the case with respect to carcinogenic risks, where it may take years of exposure to a substance before cancer actually materialises. In the case of ingested substances, one means by which this problem is obviated is the exposure of laboratory animals to levels of the substance that are comparable to that which humans would have over a significant length of time. However, this is of course an imperfect substitute for actual historical epidemiological studies of human populations. Thus, regulation of carcinogenic risks generally displays a strong bias towards those risks that are already known or have materialised in actual use of the substance in the real world. Here, France has weighed the benefit of countering a massively documented risk against the cost of creating a hypothetical and unknown one (whatever risks might be created from the use of substitute fibres). Its decision reflects the heuristics of choice under uncertainty that underlie almost all risk regulation. In rejecting the version of its claim on this issue that Canada made in its Article XX submissions, the AB accepted that members have the right to act on the basis of available information concerning relative riskiness of products: 'it seems to us perfectly legitimate for a Member to seek to halt the spread of a highly risky product while allowing the use of a less risky product in its place'.[95]

This being said, France has attempted to craft its decree to take account of the possibility that substitute products may not always be less safe than asbestos – thus, there is an exception from the ban in cases where '*l'utlilisation de produit de*

---

[95] Appellate Body Report, *supra* n. 16, para. 168.

substitution ne présent pas, en l'état actuel des connaissances scientifiques, un risque moindre pour la santé des travailleurs'.[96]

Article 2.3 of the TBT Agreement states: '[t]echnical regulations shall not be maintained if the circumstances or objectives giving rise to their adoption no longer exist or if the changed circumstances or objectives can be addressed in a less trade-restrictive manner'. This provision reflects in part the realisation that, in regulating, members necessarily make use of the information available at the time they are formulating their regulations. So, if scientific information becomes available that substitute products are as risky or more so than asbestos, and it nevertheless continues to target asbestos only, France may be in violation of Article 2.3. However, the exception in the decree seems well designed to take into account possible developments in the scientific evidence concerning the relative risks posed by asbestos on the one hand and substitute fibres on the other. Taken together, Article 2.2 and 2.3 expresses a finely balanced notion of precaution: a member can base its regulations on the existing, actual evidence of risk, without waiting for a perfect or comprehensive understanding of the risks at issue; on the other hand, when, in the future, there are relevant changes in circumstances, it must revisit its regulatory choices.

Article 2.4: The Obligation to Make Use of International Standards Where Available

There is a wide range of areas where incompatible technical specifications exist merely by virtue of the historical development of individual national standards systems, and where the differences do not reflect underlying differences in values, attitudes towards risk, or policy priorities. One example that comes to the mind of any frequent traveller between North America and Europe is the size and shape of electrical plugs and phone jacks! One suspects that the persistence of such differences is due either to path dependency or protectionism, or perhaps a bit of both. Here, as is recognised in the TBT Agreement, international standardisation, in harmonising these gratuitously incompatible requirements, can play an important role in eliminating unnecessary obstacles to trade. Thus Article 2.4 of the TBT Agreement requires the use of international standards 'as a basis for' technical regulations, in cases where the use of those standards does not negatively affect the legitimate objectives that a member is seeking to achieve.

In the case of asbestos, there is widespread recognition by international organisations with standards development responsibilities in the areas of occupational health and safety (the International Labour Organisation) and health (the World Health Organisation) that asbestos exposure represents a grave health risk and that governments should take measures to eliminate such exposure. Thus ILO Convention No. 162 recommends, wherever possible, '[the] replacement of asbestos or of certain types of asbestos or products containing asbestos by other materials or products or the use of alternative technology, scientifically evaluated by the competent authority as harmless or less harmful'.[97] More specific to the kind of asbestos that Canada

---

[96] Decree No 96–1133 of 24 December 1996, Art. 2: see *supra* n. 21.

[97] ILO Convention No. 162 Art. 10 (a).

The WTO Impact on Internal Regulations

exports, the WHO communiqué states that consideration should be given to replacing chrysotile by harmless substitute materials wherever possible.

In banning the use of asbestos, except where there are no safer or technically feasible alternatives, the French decree seems to track very closely the approach to asbestos as a health risk taken by these international standards organisations. However, Canada claimed that the French ban is not consistent with international standards, because there are international standards that specify procedures for the manufacture and use of asbestos in a manner that minimises health risks.[98] However, the existence of international standards to make the risk from asbestos as small as possible is entirely compatible with the basic approach of the international standards bodies that the use of asbestos should be discontinued as soon as possible, except where technically feasible, safer alternatives do not exist. There will remain situations where asbestos is still used, either because of the need for a phase-out period of some length to allow the relevant industries to adjust their practices, find alternatives, etc. or where there are not technically available, safer alternatives. In those situations, standards to make asbestos as safe as possible will play an important role in reducing the remaining health risk.

The EC sought to counter Canada's claim, however, by the argument that the declarations of international standards bodies in this area are merely statements about the risk from asbestos and do not amount to 'standards' within the meaning of the TBT Agreement. The definition of 'standard' in Annex I to the TBT Agreement is, however, quite broad, including 'rules, guidelines, or characteristics for products or related processes and production methods', *inter alia*. It is difficult to understand how a recommendation to replace asbestos with safer materials whenever possible would not amount to a guideline for products, even if there were some question whether it could rise to the status of a 'rule', given that there is some flexibility built into the recommendations in question.

Article XX(b)

In its notice of appeal, Canada also challenged the panel's ruling that, although a violation of Article III:4, the French ban was justified under the GATT's exception for measures to 'protect human . . . life or health'. Specifically, Canada argued that the panel had committed errors of law in its interpretation of Article XX(b), developing a too deferential and permissive reading of the GATT's general exception. The Appellate Body, having found that the French ban did not violate Article III:4 GATT, could, for reasons of judicial economy, have decided not to rule on this issue. Nevertheless, it decided to address the Canadian claims, using this as an opportunity to clarify some important issues relating to Article XX(b), establishing a more deferential approach, sensitive to members' regulatory choices and domestic regulations that address vital

---

[98] Canada also claims that France is not following international standards, because the ILO Convention specifies that substitute materials must be scientifically verified as safe. However, France notes in its submission that substitute products must also be tested and their safety verified by national or international bodies: EC first submission, *supra* n. 18, paras. 249 ff, 279 ff. France does not have a unified regulatory regime it appears for testing asbestos substitutes – but nor does the ILO Convention require this; it requires only that the substitute materials themselves be subject to verification for safety, which normally occurs within the standards regime applicable to the industry in question.

health interests. In examining the panel's approach to Article XX(b), the AB adopted a two-step approach. In a first step, it addressed the question whether the French ban was indeed directed at the objectives cited in Article XX(b), notably in this case to protect human health. In a second step, it examined whether the measure at issue was 'necessary' to achieve the specific public policy goal, a level of protection against health risk. This approach is in line with previous decisions on measures falling under some of the individual subheadings of Article XX.[99]

In its first step, when analysing whether the panel was right in concluding that the French ban fell within the category of measures embraced by Article XX(b) of the GATT 1994, the AB found that 'the panel remained well within the bounds of its discretion in finding that chrysotile-cement products pose a risk to human life or health'.[100] For reaching its decision, the panel had to weigh evidence on whether the French ban was designed to *protect* health. It did this in line with *Thai Cigarette*, which had established that 'the use of the word "protection" implies the existence of a risk' and that this consequently meant that a panel had to begin its analysis 'by identifying a risk for public health'.[101] Thus, if there were no evidence that asbestos posed a risk to human health, then a ban on asbestos would not appear to be designed to protect health. In case of asbestos however, its deadly and carcinogenic characteristics are well and widely recognised, by the consulted scientists and by the relevant international bodies. This more than ample evidence on the dangers of asbestos allowed the panel to conclude that the measure was designed to protect health, and the Appellate Body upheld the panel's finding on that.[102]

However, neither the AB nor the panel said anything about *how much* evidence of health risks is needed to regard a measure as 'for the protection of health'. Arguably, this risk requirement should be *de minimis*, i.e. the minimum needed to assert with some plausibility that the measure is directed towards the goal of protecting health. With respect to asbestos, the health aspect was, as noted, obvious. In other cases, panels may have to come to grips with measures that respond to less orthodox conceptions of 'health' – for instance, conceptions that only 'organic' food products are healthy, which are not underpinned by conventional scientific understandings, but reflect more holistic views of human health as implying harmony with natural processes. Here a panel should arguably defer to measures that are taken pursuant to such appreciations of the nature of human health, where the structure and design of the scheme are consistent with it being directed towards such a conception of health, as opposed to some other policy purpose. At the same time, it would obviously

---

[99] E.g., in *Korea – Beef*, the Appellate Body had stated that '[f]or a measure, otherwise inconsistent with GATT 1994, to be justified provisionally under paragraph (d) of Art. XX, two elements must be shown. First, the measure must be one designed to "secure compliance" with laws or regulations that are not themselves inconsistent with some provisions of the GATT 1994. Second, the measure must be "necessary" to secure such compliance': (see Appellate Body Report, *Korea – Measures Affecting Imports of Fresh, Chilled and Frozen Beef*, WT/DS161/AB/R, 11 December 2000 (hereinafter *Korea – Beef* Appellate Body Report) para. 157. The Appellate Body also took a similar approach in *Shrimp/Turtle*, where it first determined that sea turtles were 'exhaustible natural resources' and then concluded that the US measure was 'related to' the goal of conserving exhaustible natural resources as required by Art. XX(g): see *Shrimp/Turtle, supra* n. 82, para. 135.

[100] Appellate Body Report, *supra* n. 16, para. 162.

[101] Panel Report, *supra* n. 13, para. 8.184.

[102] Appellate Body Report, *supra* n. 16, para. 163.

The WTO Impact on Internal Regulations

be appropriate, in considering the meaning of health, for the panel, pursuant to Article 31 of the Vienna Convention,[103] to consider definitions of the notion of health, and health risks, in international health law and policy, especially reflected in legal instruments and related policy statements of the World Health Organisation.

Having found that the French ban was a measure that protected human life or health within the meaning of Article XX(b), the panel went on to evaluate the 'necessity' of the measure. Canada appealed the panel's 'necessity' analysis on four grounds,[104] but here again the AB upheld the panel's findings, concluding that there was no 'reasonably available alternative' to the prohibition of the French import ban and, therefore, that the French measure was 'necessary to protect human health' within the meaning of Article XX(b). The AB's reasoning is interesting for a series of aspects.

First, the AB made it very clear that it is each WTO member's 'right to determine the level of protection of health that [it] consider[s] appropriate in a given situation'.[105] France had decided that it wanted to 'halt' the spread of asbestos-related health risk, and the AB accepted its goal of reducing these health risks to zero. Here, the AB rejected categorically the notion that a member's right to determine its level of protection should be subject to considerations of proportionality. Thus, a member may choose zero risk as its goal even though, if it had chosen a slightly less ambitious goal, that goal could have been achieved with a vastly less trade-restrictive policy instrument. In effect, as long as it declares its goal as zero risk, a member can be fully justified in its choice of a highly trade-restrictive instrument that achieves 100 per cent reduction in risk, even where the member could achieve a 98 or 99 per cent reduction of risk through a policy instrument that was not trade-restrictive at all. This outcome respects the hierarchy of norms reflected in Article XX – health trumps liberal trade as a value, in the presence of any genuine conflict between the two.[106] However, one must consider this finding in tandem with a related finding, in *Korea – Beef*, that a member will not easily persuade the panel that its objective is zero risk if the policy instrument it chooses is structurally incapable of achieving that objective.[107]

Another significant finding of the AB in addressing Canada's claims on appeal in *Asbestos* is that a member may single out the elimination of one kind of health risk as its objective, even if it chooses not to take regulatory action against certain other risks. Thus, France can have as an objective zero risk from asbestos, while not necessarily having such an objective with respect to the risks posed by substitute products.

---

[103] Vienna Convention on the Law of Treaties, 23 May 1969, 1155 UNTS 331, 8 ILM 679 (hereinafter Vienna Convention).

[104] Appellate Body Report, *supra* n. 16, para. 165.

[105] *Ibid.*, para. 168.

[106] One of the clearest textual indicators of such a hierarchy is the general operative clause of Art. XX, stipulating that '*Nothing* in this Agreement shall prevent' measures for the purposes indicated in the various heads of Art. XX (emphasis added).

[107] 'We think it is unlikely that Korea intended to establish a level of protection that *totally eliminates* fraud with respect to the origin of beef (domestic or foreign) sold by retailers. The total elimination of fraud would probably require a total ban of imports. Consequently we assume Korea intended to *reduce considerably* the number of cases of fraud occurring with respect to the origin of beef sold by retailers': *Korea – Beef, supra* n. 99, para. 178. As this passage indicates, and as the AB reiterates in *Asbestos*, the level of protection need not be articulated in quantitative terms.

This approach accepts that there is a wide range of social, economic and cultural factors that may affect a member's level of protection, other than the gravity of the consequences from materialisation of the risk. The fact that in banning asbestos France is permitting the use of substitute products that may also pose some risk to health does not compromise its choice of zero risk as the level of protection against *asbestos*-related health risks. If France were prevented in those circumstances from making such a choice of level of protection, this would be to compromise what the AB rightly identifies as the entirely acceptable strategy of 'seek[ing] to halt the spread of a highly risky product while allowing the use of a less risky product in place'.[108] Moreover, France could set its level of protection, and respective approaches to asbestos-containing and substitute products based on *existing* scientific evidence of the relative risks of the two. Before seeking to eliminate the risk from asbestos, it was not required to investigate exhaustively the risks from the use of substitutes.

Having thus established France's chosen level of protection, the AB went on to consider the meaning of 'necessary' in Article XX(b). Canada claimed that the ban on chrysotile asbestos was not 'necessary', because a less-trade-restrictive measure, a 'safe use' regime, was available to achieve France's chosen level of protection. In considering Canada's claim, the AB, on the one hand, approved the test in the GATT *acquis* for necessity, namely whether there is a reasonably available alternative less restrictive of trade. On the other hand, the AB referred to its judgement in *Korea – Beef*, where certain refinements were introduced to that test.

In *Korea – Beef*, the AB had observed that although one meaning of 'necessary' in ordinary language is 'indispensable', this is not the only meaning.[109] One can coherently speak of it having been necessary to do something, without the very strong implication that no other choice was available at all. However, even this less strict notion of necessity is much closer to the idea of the action being indispensable than to the idea that it merely makes a contribution to the goal or objective in question.

The AB thus bifurcates the necessity test. There are situations where the claim may be that a measure is indispensable, i.e the only available measure to achieve a member's chosen level of protection, and there are other situations in which a member may be able to justify its measure as 'necessary' within the meaning of Article XX, even if the fit is not *that* close. In these latter situations, determining whether the admittedly not indispensable measure is nevertheless 'necessary' 'involves in every case a process of weighing and balancing a series of factors which prominently include the contribution made by the compliance measure to the enforcement of the law or regulation at issue, the importance of the common interests or values protected by that law or regulation, and the accompanying impact of the law or regulation on imports or exports'.[110] Thus, the AB introduces an alternative, less strict proportionality test into those heads of Article XX, where the word 'necessary' is found. What it is crucial to understand, however, is that the AB does not introduce proportionality as an *additional* requirement where the measure is indispensable – a measure that is indispensable for achieving a member's chosen level of protection

---

[108] Appellate Body Report, *supra* n. 16, para. 168.

[109] *Korea – Beef, supra* n. 99, para. 161.

[110] *Ibid.*, para. 164.

The WTO Impact on Internal Regulations

will be 'necessary', regardless of it being vastly more trade-restrictive than the next less-trade-restrictive alternative,[111] and regardless of whether the next less-trade-restrictive alternative comes very close to achieving the member's chosen level of protection. Thus, although it is introducing balancing or proportionality analysis into Article XX, the AB is nevertheless preserving the hierarchy of norms reflected in Article XX. In fact it is introducing balancing so as to provide members with an *additional* 'margin of appreciation' in making regulatory choices to achieve the purposes stated in those provisions of Article XX that entail a necessity test.

In *Asbestos*, the AB has further refined the necessity test in Article XX. Because in *Asbestos*, France's claim, logically enough, was that no measure other than a ban could achieve its chosen level of protection, namely zero asbestos-related risk, and the AB accepted that claim, this was a case where the measure was claimed to be, and was found to be, 'indispensable'. Thus, the AB did not have to go on to engage in the kind of balancing that was discussed in *Korea – Beef*. What the AB did do however was to suggest that there may be differing levels of scrutiny applicable to the analysis of whether a measure is *indispensable*, depending on the importance of the objectives or interests it serves. Thus, it noted that a factor held to be of importance in *Korea – Beef* in conducting a proportionality analysis pursuant to the less strict branch of the necessity test might be more generally relevant to the ease with which a panel is prepared to find a measure 'necessary'. In other words, the importance of the values and interests at stake will also operate to determine the level of scrutiny when a panel is considering a claim that the measure is 'indispensable' to achieve a member's chosen level of protection.[112] Here, the AB went on to assert: 'in this case, the objective pursued by the measure is the preservation of human life and health through the elimination, or reduction of the well-known, and life-threatening, health risks posed by asbestos fibres. The value pursued is both vital and important in the highest degree'.[113]

---

[111] Here, it is important to be clear on the precise language in *Korea – Beef*, especially because the AB in para. 172 of *Asbestos* refers to balancing in *Korea – Beef* in a rather loose way that could mislead the reader into thinking it is going to go on to balance in *Asbestos*. The AB said in *Korea – Beef*: 'in sum, determination of whether a measure, *which is not "indispensable"*, may be "necessary" within the contemplation of Art. XX(d), involves in every case a process of weighing and balancing' (emphasis added).

[112] One frequent criticism of the AB rulings in *Gasoline* and *Shrimp/Turtle, supra* n. 82, which held that the language 'relating to [exhaustible natural resources]' in Art. XX(g) implied a looser fit than the necessity language in Art. XX(b), was that the AB was actually saying, apparently perversely, that it is easier to justify protecting turtles or dolphins than protecting human lives. One could see the introduction of levels of scrutiny into the analysis of whether a measure is necessary under Art. XX, with especially deferential scrutiny for measures to protect human life from deadly risks, as an indirect answer to this criticism. Of course, the criticism is not in itself very well taken – it ignores that there is additional hurdle under Art. XX(g) that does not exist under Art. XX(b), namely that the measures must be taken in conjunction with restrictions on domestic consumption or production. See *Reformulated Gasoline, supra* n. 82.

[113] An alternative interpretation of what the AB is doing here is that it is saying that there are some interests that are so vital that we simply ignore the distinction between 'indispensable' and 'necessary' in the looser sense, and simply proceed to the analysis of alternative measures, without balancing, but with a lower or relaxed level of scrutiny. The AB's observation that 'France could not reasonably be expected to employ *any* alternative measure if that measure would involve a continuation of the very risk that the decree seeks to "halt"' indicates that no balancing or proportionality analysis is being undertaken here, whether because of the importance of the interest at stake or because this is in essence a claim for indispensibility within the meaning of *Korea – Beef, supra* n. 99, para. 174.

In judging the relative importance of various objectives contained in Article XX, the AB appears to be altering, or at least supplementing, the hierarchy of norms in the treaty. The intuitive appeal of the notion that health is a vitally important objective, and our annoyance at the way in which the panel was dismissive of health under Article III:4, should not blind us to the ramifications of the interpretive move the AB is making here. One appealing view of Article XX is that it deals with the potential tension between trade liberalisation and other values, through a series of provisions that scrutinise the relation of means to ends, rather than the value of the ends pursued themselves, provided those ends fall within a discrete head of Article XX. Does the AB really have the legitimacy to say to a society that, for instance, the pursuit of religious purity or piety is a less compelling objective than the protection of human health? Does it have the *bona fides* to make a determination that the rights of people count for more than the 'rights' of animals? We would suggest that to remain consistent with its role as a treaty interpreter under Article 31 of the *Vienna Convention*, whenever the AB is hierarchising objectives within the heads of Article XX, it must do so following the hierarchies implicit or explicit in international law more generally. In defence of the Appellate Body, it had already cited a statements alluding to international health law and policy materials early in its judgement,[114] which suggested wide international recognition of the gravity of France's objective. This being said, the implications for democratic self-determination of the AB hierarchising objectives are attenuated, if only somewhat, by the fact that it is doing so in order to provide, in certain cases, a greater 'margin of appreciation' to members.

How then does this greater 'margin of appreciation' figure in the AB's rejection of the Canadian claim that 'safe use' is a reasonably available alternative measure? The AB makes several observations about this claim. The first is that 'safe use' is not a well-tested alternative, the efficacy of which is already demonstrated; this is on the basis of the scientific record before the panel. The second is that there is some actual scientific evidence that available 'safe use' procedures still leave some residual risk from asbestos. The third is that 'safe use', even if it did effectively protect against these risks in some contexts, would be particularly doubtful in other contexts, those such as do-it-yourself home renovations or the building industry, of the greatest importance to France. Here, the AB makes it clear that a member is under no obligation to attempt to achieve its level of protection using alternatives which lack certainty of effectiveness, before having recourse to a more, and indeed much more, trade-restrictive option. This clearly reverses the tendency, visible in the *Thai Cigarette* case for example, to have a member's measure fail the necessity test if there is some hypothetical less-trade-restrictive alternative available, which *may* or *might* be effective in the circumstances. In *Thai Cigarette*, the panel was considering a ban on foreign cigarettes by Thailand, which was concerned about the sophisticated techniques tobacco multinationals use to market such cigarettes to young people in particular, creating new generations of tobacco addicts. The panel determined that various kinds of regulation on the marketing and advertising activities of these multinationals were 'reasonably available' less-restrictive alternatives, despite evidence on the panel record from the World Health Organisation that it had proved impossible for developing countries, in a number of cases, to achieve their objectives

---

[114] Appellate Body Report, *supra* n. 16, para. 114.

The WTO Impact on Internal Regulations

by regulating multinationals in this manner. The corporations tended to find ways of circumventing such regulatory efforts. Applying the 'margin of appreciation' in *Asbestos* to these facts, it seems almost certain that the Article XX(b) issue would have been decided the other way by the Appellate Body, as in *Thai Cigarette* the efficacy of the suggested alternatives certainly remained to be demonstrated, especially in the context in which they would be applied.

Conclusion

In *Asbestos*, the Appellate Body of the WTO has introduced many important refinements in the interpretation and application of key provisions of the GATT that address the relationship of WTO law to internal regulation. Overall, the consequence is to provide clearer and perhaps more ample assurances to regulators that non-protectionist domestic regulations for important policy purposes will not be significantly constrained by WTO law. This should enhance what Joseph Weiler calls the 'external legitimacy' of the WTO.[115] The AB has moved in this direction however in a manner also sensitive to what Weiler terms 'internal legitimacy'. It has framed its interpretations within the evolving GATT/WTO *acquis*, and has avoided bold colours and strokes, as opposed to subtler tones and finishes. In so doing it has managed to paint a quite different picture from that characteristic of the panels in these matters, while acting with judicial caution. Perhaps, this was in part achievable because the facts of *Asbestos* raised few issues of high normative controversy – it was not a case that suggested or evoked a cultural or intellectual divide about the meaning of health or of science, or for example the appropriate limits of individual member state action to protect the environmental commons, or the balance between human rights as defined in the UN Covenants and trading rights as defined in the WTO. The AB wisely left it to others to speculate about the implications of its interpretive moves in *Asbestos* for such harder cases, giving itself ample room to craft a balance between internal and external legitimacy appropriate to the facts of those cases. At the same time, the overall direction in which it is moving is visible to all who have sharp (and unblinkered) eyes.

---

[115] Weiler, *supra* n. 67.

WILLIAM J. DAVEY

3. Reflections on the Appellate Body Decision in the *Hormones* Case and the Meaning of the SPS Agreement

One of the most important and controversial decisions of the WTO dispute settlement system in its early years was the so-called *Hormones* case, which involved claims by the United States and Canada that an EC ban on the sale and import of meat from cattle treated with growth hormones violated the WTO Agreement on the Application of Sanitary and Phytosanitary Measures (SPS Agreement).[1] In this chapter, I examine a number of the key issues in that case in light of the Appellate Body report. In particular, I will consider its rulings on several preliminary issues – the questions of burden of proof, standard of review and the precautionary principle – and then turn to its interpretation of Articles 3 and 5 of the SPS Agreement. The chapter concludes with a few observations (i) on the SPS Agreement and the extent to which it constrains governments in adopting the SPS measures of their choice and (ii) on the judicial method of the Appellate Body.

I. Preliminary Issues

The Appellate Body dealt with three important preliminary issues before turning to the substantive meaning of the obligations of Article 3 and 5 of the SPS Agreement: the question of burden of proof, the standard that should be applied by a panel in reviewing government action under the SPS Agreement and the position of the so-called precautionary principle under the SPS Agreement.

A. Burden of Proof

1. Panel Report

The panel reached two conclusions in respect of the burden-of-proof issue. First, it recalled the standard rule on burden of proof laid down by the Appellate Body in *US – Wool Shirts*: the complainant must first establish a *prima facie* case, after which the respondent has the burden to rebut the case.[2] The panel then stated

---

[1] There were two cases brought challenging the EC ban – one by the United States and one by Canada. They were considered by a single panel, which issued two, largely identical, reports. I cite the US report in this chapter. There was only one report issued on the appeal. Appellate Body Report, *EC Measures Concerning Meat and Meat Products (Hormones)*, WT/DS26 & 48/AB/R, adopted February 13, 1998, modifying Panel Report, WT/DS26/R/USA, and Panel Report, WT/DS48/R/CAN.

[2] Panel Report, paras. 8.48–8.55.

Reflections on the Appellate Body Decision in the *Hormones* Case 119

that this allocation of the burden to rebut on the EC by showing compliance with the SPS Agreement was appropriate in light of the wording of the SPS Agreement. More specifically, the panel focused on the language of Article 5.1 (it also appears in Articles 2.2, 2.3 and 5.6), which requires that "Members shall ensure...". Although the panel used this language to justify placing the burden on the EC to show that its challenged measures met the requirements of the SPS Agreement, it never suggested that this burden arose other than after the United States had established a *prima facie* case of inconsistency with the SPS Agreement. That point is underlined by the panel's concluding paragraph of the section, which states:

> We thus find that, for purposes of this dispute, the United States bears the burden of presenting a *prima facie* case of inconsistency with the SPS Agreement, after which the burden of proof shifts to the European Communities to demonstrate that its measures in dispute meet the requirements imposed by the SPS Agreement.[3]

Second, the panel analyzed the burden of proof issue separately in respect of challenges invoking Article 3 of the SPS Agreement.[4] There, it noted that there was an obligation in Article 3.1 requiring WTO Members to base their SPS measures on international standards where such standards exist. The panel viewed Article 3.3, which permits a Member to adopt a measure achieving a higher level of sanitary protection than the appropriate international standard in certain circumstances, as an exception. For the panel, if the EC invoked that exception of Article 3.3 once the US had established a *prima facie* case that there was an applicable international standard in terms of Article 3.1 and that the EC measure was not based on it, then the burden was on the EC to establish that the terms of Article 3.3 were met. The panel drew support for its ruling from Article 3.2, where it noted that there is a presumption that a measure based on an international standard conforms to the SPS Agreement, suggesting that in such a case the complainant would bear the burden of proving otherwise. The panel thought that that result implied that where a measure is not based on an international standard, it would be the respondent's burden to show that the contested measure was consistent with the SPS Agreement.

On the facts of the *Hormones* case, this meant that with respect to five of the six hormones, where the panel found that international standards existed, it put the burden of establishing compliance with Article 3.3 (and consequently with Article 5, which is referred to in Article 3.3) on the EC. With respect to the one hormone not subject to an international standard, the panel placed the initial burden of proof in respect of compliance with Article 5 on the United States.

2. Appellate Body Report

The Appellate Body categorically rejected the panel's first conclusion, accusing the panel of paying only "lip service" to the Appellate Body's decision in *US – Wool Shirts*.[5] In particular, it noted that the language that "Members shall ensure..." does not imply anything about the burden of proof in dispute settlement. It found "the

---

[3] Panel Report, para. 8.55.
[4] Panel Report, paras. 8.84–8.90.
[5] Appellate Body Report, paras. 97–102.

general interpretative ruling of the Panel to be bereft of basis in the SPS Agreement".[6] The Appellate Body's reaction is difficult to fathom. The panel report starts by quoting *Wool Shirts*, and in the language quoted above, it restates the *Wool Shirts* rule. In that part of the report dealing with the sixth hormone (the one not subject to an international standard), which is the only part of the report where the panel applied its burden of proof ruling, the Appellate Body makes no reference to the way in which the panel treated the burden of proof – which is not surprising since it followed *Wool Shirts*. Unfortunately, the issue is the first one discussed in the Appellate Body report and it set the tone for much of the rest of that report.

The Appellate Body also rejected the panel's analysis of Article 3 and the burden of proof thereunder. In its view, the sort of "general rule–exception" analysis, such as exists in respect of GATT Article III and XX, is not applicable to Article 3 of the SPS Agreement.[7] According to the Appellate Body:

> Article 3.1 of the SPS Agreement simply excludes from its scope of application the kinds of situations covered by Article 3.3 of that Agreement. . . .[8]

Interestingly, the Appellate Body does not set out the text of Article 3.1 or 3.3 at this point. An examination of the text of Article 3.1 does not inevitably lead to the Appellate Body's conclusions. The text provides:

> To harmonize sanitary and phytosanitary measures on as wide a basis as possible, Members shall base their sanitary or phytosanitary measures on international standards, guidelines or recommendation, where they exist, except as otherwise provided for in this Agreement, and in particular in paragraph 3.

The structure of the text is a straightforward statement of a general obligation followed by an "exception." One of the stated purposes of the Agreement is harmonization, which is not accomplished by national measures varying from international standards. Although there is no doubt that the Agreement provides that Members may choose a higher level of protection, it is not at all clear that their right to do so should not be viewed as an exception to the generally stated obligation. Moreover, treating Article 3.3 as an exception and placing the burden on the respondent makes sense from a practical point of view, as the complaining party will not necessarily even know what level of protection has been determined to be appropriate by the respondent.

The Appellate Body seemed to make a great deal of the burden-of-proof issue. I would argue that the issue is very often overemphasized, as it is only when the evidence on a point is in equipoise that it matters. If the preponderance of the evidence supports one side, that side wins, whether it had the burden of proof or not. This is underlined in this case, because even though the Appellate Body reversed the panel on the issue, it found that the United States met its burden in fact, even though not required to do so by the panel.[9]

---

[6] Appellate Body Report, paras. 102.
[7] Appellate Body Report, paras. 103–9.
[8] Appellate Body Report, para. 104.
[9] Appellate Body Report, note 180.

B. Standard of Review

The EC appealed generally on the grounds that the panel had failed to use the proper standard of review in assessing the EC measure. In its view, the choice was between a de novo review and a deference review, under which the panel would only verify that the required procedures had been followed. The Appellate Body noted that the SPS Agreement specified no specific standard of review, but that Article 11 of the Dispute Settlement Understanding required a panel to "make an objective assessment of the matter before it, including an objective assessment of the facts of the case and the applicability of and conformity with the relevant covered agreements."

The usefulness of the Appellate Body's conclusion is quite limited, although everyone now religiously cites Article 11 as setting out what a panel must do. In fact, Article 11 is at best only a starting point. A panel could be true to the text of Article 11 and follow either of the two polar approaches outlined by the EC. The key issue is how much deference a panel should give national authorities in making whatever determination they have made. The Appellate Body later addresses this issue indirectly in a footnote, where it recalls the principle of *in dubio mitius*.[10] The issue at hand was treaty interpretation more generally, but one can perhaps imply that if in interpreting the obligations of a treaty, a panel should defer in close cases to the least onerous obligation, then in deciding whether a party has complied with a treaty it should presumably defer to some extent to the viewpoint of the Member involved. The Appellate Body also notes later in its report that Members are free to base regulations on non-mainstream scientific opinion, a conclusion that also argues for considerable deference to be given to Members in choosing to adopt regulations. However, the Appellate Body's discussion of standard of review is not generally summarized in this report.

More relevant to the probable purpose of Article 11, the Appellate Body went on in discussing what constitutes an "objective assessment" to rule that

> The deliberate disregard of, or refusal to consider, the evidence submitted to a panel is incompatible with a panel's duty to make an objective assessment of the facts. The willful distortion or misrepresentation of the evidence put before a panel is similarly inconsistent with an objective assessment of the facts.[11]

In its evaluation of EC claims that the panel had distorted or disregarded evidence, the Appellate Body concluded that the panel incorrectly interpreted one of its experts' statements [a footnote indicated that the added breast cancer risk of zero to one in a million referred to the risk from the total estrogen load in treated meat as opposed to the actual statement by the expert (reproduced in an annex), which referred to the additional estrogen load from hormones used for growth promotion purposes in such meat].[12] It also concluded that the panel did not "represent accurately" certain unspecified statements by its experts in respect of the issue of control, which the panel had ruled was not relevant.[13] In neither case, however, did the Appellate Body find that the panel had not made an objective assessment.

---

[10] Appellate Body Report, note 154.
[11] Appellate Body Report, para. 133.
[12] Appellate Body Report, para. 138.
[13] Appellate Body Report, para. 144.

C. Precautionary Principle

One of the most interesting aspects of the *Hormones* case was the EC's decision not to invoke the precautionary principle contained in Article 5.7 of the SPS Agreement. That provision provides:

> In cases where relevant scientific evidence is insufficient, a Member may provisionally adopt sanitary or phytosanitary measures on the basis of available pertinent information.... In such circumstances, Members shall seek to obtain the additional information necessary for a more objective assessment of risk and review the [SPS] measure accordingly within a reasonable period of time.

One would have thought that if the EC were worried about whether it could meet the requirements of the SPS Agreement in respect of scientific evidence and risk assessment, then Article 5.7 would have been an obvious fall-back position.

Over the years, I have heard many explanations of why the EC chose not to invoke Article 5.7. The reasons could be called political (we have told our populations that beef from cattle treated with growth hormones is dangerous and it would undercut our credibility if we argued after all these years that we really didn't know for sure); technical legal (the hormones rule was adopted at a time when the precautionary principle was not contained in the EC Treaty and therefore the rule could not have been based on a precautionary principle); strategic legal (if we lose on the risk assessment claim, we can always implement based on Article 5.7, and defend our action in the future, whereas if we rely on it now and lose, it will be difficult to rely upon it at the implementation stage); and factual (we didn't rely on it and can't show that we did, plus we did not obtain additional information). None of these is all that convincing. From a political point of view, it is hard to see why the populace would much care about which arguments were used to defend a popular measure. The EC Treaty may not have contained a precautionary principle at the time, but it did not preclude action on such a principle, which is arguably merely a sensible government regulatory practice. The latter two are somewhat more convincing perhaps, in that the strategic argument does comport with the actual events that unfolded in the implementation period and in that the only additional information gathered by the EC after adopting the rule (principally the 1995 Commission conference) did not support the ban.

Notwithstanding its decision not to invoke Article 5.7, the EC did argue that its risk assessment could be justified by reference to the precautionary principle as part of customary international law and therefore relevant to the interpretation of the SPS Agreement. The panel's conclusion that, assuming that there were such a customary principle, it would not override the specific provisions of the SPS Agreement, was largely upheld by the Appellate Body.[14] The Appellate Body ducked the issue of whether the precautionary principle was or was not a general or customary provision of international law. It did note, however, that there could be elements of such a principle in the SPS Agreement beyond what is contained in Article 5.7 (i.e., Article 5.7 might not exhaust the precautionary principle as contained in the SPS Agreement) and that a panel should bear that in mind in determining whether there is sufficient

---

[14] Appellate Body Report, paras. 120–30.

Reflections on the Appellate Body Decision in the *Hormones* Case

scientific evidence to warrant maintenance of an SPS measure that "representative governments commonly act from perspectives of prudence and precaution where risks of irreversible, e.g., life-terminating, damage to human health are concerned."[15] This latter statement is quite important in that it underlines the Appellate Body's view, at least in this case, that panels should give some deference to a Member's decisions regarding health.

II. Article 3

As noted above, the panel viewed Article 3.1 as imposing an obligation on Members to use international standards, subject to an exception in Article 3.3 that allowed a Member to choose a higher level of protection than that embodied in the international standard, subject to complying with Article 5. This view enabled the panel to put the burden of proof on the EC with respect to Article 5 for the five hormones subject to international standards.

In its analysis, the panel concluded in the first instance that there were appropriate international standards for the five hormones and that the EC measure was not based on them. To reach that conclusion, the panel had to define the meaning of the phrase "based on." In analyzing that issue, the panel noted that Article 3.1 requires SPS measures to be "based on" existing international standards, whereas Article 3.2 provides that such measures which "conform to international standards" shall be deemed to be consistent with GATT and the SPS Agreement, and Article 3.3 allows Members to introduce measures with a "higher level of [SPS] protection than would be achieved by measures based on the relevant international standards."[16]

In defining the meaning of "based on," the panel reasoned that Article 3.3 implied that all measures based on an international standard should achieve the same level of sanitary protection, because Article 3.3's purpose was to permit under certain circumstances measures that achieved a higher level of protection:

> We find, therefore, that for a sanitary measure to be based on an international standard in accordance with Article 3.1, that measure needs to reflect the same level of sanitary protection as the standard. In this dispute a comparison thus needs to be made between the level of protection reflected in the EC measures in dispute and that reflected in the Codex standards for each of the five hormones at issue.[17]

Because the EC measure bans any hormone use and therefore any hormone residues, while the international standard permits such residues (without limit, assuming good practice in applying them), the panel reached the obvious conclusion that the EC ban was not based on the international standard.

Unfortunately for the panel, at the beginning of its analysis of Article 3, it made the statement: "However, Article 3.2, which introduces a presumption of consistency with both the SPS Agreement and GATT for sanitary measures which *conform* to international standards, equates measures *based on* international standards

---

[15] Appellate Body Report, para. 124. See text accompanying note 10 supra.
[16] Panel Report, para. 8.72.
[17] Panel Report, para. 8.73.

with measures which *conform* to such standards."[18] Although the panel never again referred to this sentence, which of course related to Article 3.2, not 3.1, the Appellate Body went ballistic:

> We read the Panel's interpretation that Article 3.2 "equates" measures "based on" international standards with measures which "conform to" such standards, as signifying that "based on" and "conform to" are identical in meaning. The Panel is thus saying that, henceforth, SPS measures of Members *must* "conform to" Codex standards, guidelines and recommendations.[19]

It then attacked this total mischaracterization of the panel's reasoning. First, it used dictionary meanings to explain why "based on" and conform to" have different meanings. Second, it noted that treaty interpreters cannot simply ignore different wordings in different paragraphs of the same provision.

Most significantly, it largely read Article 3.1 out of the SPS Agreement by announcing that

> [i]t is clear to us that harmonization of SPS measures of Members on the basis of international standards is projected in the Agreement, as a goal, yet to be realized in the future.[20]

In support of this position, the Appellate Body quoted the introductory clause of Article 3.1 ("[t]o harmonize measures on as wide a basis as possible"), the preamble to the agreement (Members "[d]esir[e] to further the use of harmonized measures between Members on the basis of international standards...") and the fact that a SPS Committee had been created in Article 12.1 "in furtherance of [the Agreement's] objectives, in particular with respect to harmonization." Amazingly, all of these would seem to support the argument that Article 3.1 was in fact mandatory and a key part of the SPS Agreement.

Nonetheless, the Appellate Body went on to cite the *in dubio mitius* rule and concluded that the language of Article 3.1: "To harmonize [SPS] measures on as wide a basis as possible, Members shall base their [SPS] measures on international standards, guidelines or recommendations, where they exist, except..." merely means that

> [u]nder Article 3.1 of the SPS Agreement, a Member may choose to establish an SPS measure that is based on the existing relevant international standard, guideline or recommendation. Such a measure may adopt some, not necessarily all, of the elements of the international standard.[21]

One wonders why, if compliance with the "obligation" of Article 3.1 is optional that Article 3.3 exists at all. The lack of any obligation under Article 3.1 suggests that Members under 3.1 would never be constrained in applying a measure that resulted in a higher level of protection than that provided by an international standard. Did

---

[18] Panel Report, para. 8.73.

[19] Appellate Body Report, para. 162. In fairness to the Appellate Body, it did not state that the panel ever said that "based on" means "conform to," but rather that the Appellate Body decided that it implied that.

[20] Appellate Body Report, para. 165.

[21] Appellate Body Report, para. 171.

Reflections on the Appellate Body Decision in the *Hormones* Case 125

the Appellate Body interpretation of Article 3.1 effectively read it and Article 3.3 out of the agreement?

As to the panel's actual reasoning as to the meaning of Article 3.1, which was based on Article 3.3, not 3.2, that "based on" as used there implied that a measure had to achieve the same level of protection as the international standard, the Appellate Body wrote:

> It appears to us that the Panel reads much more into Article 3.3 than can be reasonably supported by the actual text of Article 3.3. Moreover, the Panel's entire analysis rests on its flawed premise that "based on" as used in Article 3.1 and 3.3, means the same thing as "conform to" as used in Article 3.2 As already noted, we are compelled to reject this premise as an error in law. The correctness of the rest of the Panel's intricate interpretation and examination of the consequences of the Panel's litmus test, however, to have left for another day and another case.[22]

Thus, having demolished the straw man and eviscerated Article 3, the Appellate Body found it unnecessary to examine the panel's actual reasoning under Article 3.1.

III. Article 5.1

A. Panel Report

Article 5.1 of the SPS Agreement requires that Members shall ensure that SPS measures are "based on" a risk assessment. In its introduction to that part of its report dealing with Article 5, the panel distinguished risk assessment, which it characterized as a scientific examination, from the determination of the appropriate level of protection to be achieved by an SPS measure, an aspect of the overall process "commonly referred to **by the parties** to this dispute as an essential part of risk management." The panel then noted that Article 5.4 to 5.6 were particularly relevant to risk management.[23]

In its examination of the risk assessment part of Article 5 (Article 5.1 to 5.3), and in particular the meaning of "based on," the panel concluded that the words implied that a Member had to actually take into account a risk assessment in adopting its measure, which it concluded the EC had not done, thereby reading a so-called procedural requirement into Article 5.1.[24] On the substantive issue, the panel considered the scientific conclusions reached by the various potential risk assessment studies, the scientific conclusions reflected in the EC measures and whether the latter conclusions were in conformity with the foregoing conclusions. The panel concluded that they were not, because the studies suggested that use of hormones was safe, whereas the EC measure banned their use for the most part. It then examined several more general arguments made by the EC. With respect to the EC's argument that the studies assumed that the hormones were appropriately administered and that there were risks associated with control of use, the panel noted that the EC had provided no assessment of those risks and suggested that the

---

[22] Appellate Body Report, para. 168.
[23] Panel Report, paras. 8.91–8.97.
[24] Panel Report, paras. 8.113–8.116.

issue was really one of risk management. As to the EC's argument that its measures could be justified because it had adopted a zero-risk level of protection and the various studies did not conclude that there was no risk whatsoever from the use of hormones (for example, one concluded that there was no appreciable or no significant risk), the panel noted that it was admitted that the risks referred to by the EC were not identifiable and could not be assessed by science and that the EC measure was accordingly not based on a risk assessment in this regard.

B. Appellate Body

The Appellate Body began its analysis of Article 5.1 by rejecting the panel's reference to risk management, which it noted did not appear in the treaty text, and criticized the panel for using it "apparently... to achieve or support what appears to be a restrictive notion of risk assessment."[25] Given that the distinction had been used by the parties and is commonly employed in the field, the Appellate Body's remarks suggested some lack of understanding of SPS issues. As to the panel's use of the term, it used it in its discussion of Article 5.1 only in respect of the issue of control and not at all in its discussion of what constitutes risk assessment in general, a fact probably underlined by the Appellate Body's use of the word "apparently," highlighting once again the Appellate Body's theme that the panel was doing something devious.

The Appellate Body then turned to an examination of the notion of risk and risk assessment. In that regard, the Appellate Body noted that to the extent that the panel had purported to require a risk assessment to establish a minimum magnitude of risk, that there was no such requirement in Article 5.1. In that regard, it should be noted that the panel had clearly not done this explicitly, although the EC argued that it had done so at least implicitly. As to the notion of risk assessment, the panel had stated that this was a scientific process aimed at establishing a scientific basis for SPS measures. The Appellate Body noted that to the extent that the panel meant to exclude all matters not susceptible of quantitative analysis it was in error. Again, it is not clear that the panel meant to do so and the Appellate Body admitted the passage in the panel report at issue could be viewed as "unexceptionable."[26]

Turning to the panel's interpretation of the phrase "based on" as including a procedural requirement, the Appellate Body rejected that interpretation. It noted that the panel admitted there were no specific procedures required, which was true, but it largely ignored the panel's careful analysis of the meaning of the phrase "based on" in light of the meaning of the words and their context. Instead, the Appellate Body took the view that Members have no obligation to conduct a risk assessment. Instead, its view was that a Member simply had to be able to defend a measure as being based on a risk assessment, if challenged. Given the purpose of the SPS Agreement to promote the use of science-based SPS measures, this seems an odd conclusion, although in fairness to the Appellate Body, it is true that this requirement applied retroactively would raise problems (but that was not the main basis for the Appellate Body's ruling).[27]

---

[25] Appellate Body Report, para. 181.
[26] Appellate Body Report, para. 187.
[27] Appellate Body Report, paras. 188–91.

As to the substantive question of whether the EC measure was based on a risk assessment, the Appellate Body conceded that the panel's approach of comparing the scientific conclusions implicit in an SPS measure with the scientific conclusions yielded by the risk assessment was a useful one. It rejected the idea that the one set of conclusions had to "conform" to the other. Rather, it ruled that a risk assessment must "sufficiently warrant" or "reasonably support" the SPS measure, such that there is a "rational relationship" between them. (Whether all these phrases mean exactly the same thing is not completely clear.) In particular, it stressed that a government could legitimately choose to follow opinions on SPS measures coming from qualified and respected sources that diverged from mainstream scientific opinion (presumably those opinions would be found in a risk assessment).[28] The exact scope of the Appellate Body's definition (by itself and as compared to the panel's formulation) was not really tested in the *Hormones* case, as both the panel and the Appellate Body concluded easily that the EC measure was not based on a risk assessment. The principal point of disagreement was the extent to which issues of control should be considered in risk assessment, as opposed to risk management, and the Appellate Body rejected the panel's conclusion that the issues were a matter for risk management, but it agreed with the panel that the EC had presented no evidence of a risk assessment relating to those issues.[29]

IV. Article 5.5

Article 5.5 provides that, with the aim of ensuring consistency in the application of levels of protection in SPS measures, each Member will avoid arbitrary or unjustifiable distinctions in such levels in different situations, if such distinctions result in discrimination or a disguised restriction on international trade. The panel saw three prerequisites to establishing a violation of Article 5.5: (i) the application of different levels of protection in different situations, which (ii) were arbitrary or unjustifiable and resulted in (iii) discrimination or a disguised restriction on international trade. The Appellate Body essentially agreed.

One of the more difficult issues in applying Article 5.5 is determining when it is appropriate to compare different levels of protection. Governments clearly never have applied similar levels of health and sanitary protection across the board. For example, if toleration of cigarettes was taken as the base level of health protection, then many health-related standards would arguably be so much stricter as to be arbitrary or unjustifiable.[30] In this case, the panel viewed as comparable situations (i) the treatment of the natural and synthetic hormones for growth promotion purposes compared to the treatment of natural hormones occurring endogenously in food generally; and (ii) the treatment of the natural and synthetic hormones for growth promotion purposes in beef compared to the treatment of two non-hormone substances used for growth promotion purposes in swine. The Appellate Body rejected the first comparison, concluding that it was not appropriate to

---

[28] Appellate Body Report, para. 194.

[29] Appellate Body Report, paras. 205–8.

[30] The SPS Agreement would not apply to tobacco measures. See SPS Agreement, Annex A (definition of SPS measure).

compare the regulation of added hormones with the non-regulation of naturally occurring hormones because of the fundamental distinction that the EC did not regulate the naturally occurring hormones and could not practically do so.[31]

As to the second comparison, the panel and Appellate Body both concluded that the situations were comparable and that there was no justification for the distinction in regulation. However, on the issue of whether the distinction led to discrimination or a disguised restriction on trade, the Appellate Body reversed the panel's conclusion that it did. In reaching its conclusion, the panel had noted the Appellate Body's decision in *Japan – Alcohol Beverages*, where the Appellate Body had concluded that the extent of a tax differential could be used as a factor in deciding whether it was imposed so as to afford protection in violation of Article III:2, second sentence. For purposes of the *Hormones* case, the panel used analogous reasoning, noting the wide difference in treatment and the absence of any plausible justification – a ban on growth-promoting hormones in beef compared to no limitations on the use of growth-promoting microbiological agents in swine – despite similar cancer-causing concerns. Because the EC was not internationally competitive in beef, but was in swine, a disguised restriction on trade was found. The panel noted two additional factors – the EC's desire to reduce beef surpluses and the fact that hormones were more widely used outside the EC than inside – as supporting its conclusion.

The Appellate Body conceded that the extent of the difference in levels of protection and the lack of justification could be factors in finding that the third criteria had been met, but viewed them as less consequential in this case than had the panel. In particular, the Appellate Body seemed annoyed by the way in which the panel cited prior Appellate Body cases to support its reasoning.[32] As to the additional factors found by the panel to support its conclusion, the Appellate Body thought that there were multiple reasons for the EC rule, some of which (e.g., market harmonization) were perfectly acceptable.[33] Accordingly, it reversed the panel's conclusion that Article 5.5 had been violated.

V. Reflections on the *Hormones* Case

A. Panel–Appellate Body Relations

The *Hormones* case was the ninth panel report to come to the Appellate Body. In the prior eight cases, the Appellate Body had effectively upheld the results of the panel decisions, although it had significantly modified the basis for the results in several cases (particularly *US Gasoline* and *Canada Periodicals*). However, the tone of the Appellate Body reports made it sometimes seem that the Appellate Body was attempting to present itself as a superior, wiser decision-maker that had to lecture the not-so-bright panelists on basic principles. This drew some adverse comment from knowledgeable commentators, who viewed the criticisms as rather unfair, especially given the quality of the Appellate Body reports themselves.

---

[31] Appellate Body Report, para. 221.
[32] Appellate Body Report, para. 239.
[33] Appellate Body Report, paras. 240–46.

Reflections on the Appellate Body Decision in the *Hormones* Case   129

In the *Hormones* case, the Appellate Body at times seemed to go beyond mere criticism to impugning the integrity of the panel. For example, as noted,[34] it claimed that the panel was paying only "lip service" to the Appellate Body decisions on burden of proof in its discussion of the general burden of proof under the SPS Agreement (i.e., the rule other than that specially applicable in the panel's view to Article 3.3). Yet, when the Appellate Body reached the only part of the case where the panel had applied that particular rule on burden of proof (i.e., in respect of the sixth hormone), the Appellate Body found no problems. To take a second example, in examining the panel's view of risk and risk assessment, the Appellate Body seemed to criticize the panel not for what it had written, but rather for what the Appellate Body itself admitted did not necessarily flow from what the panel had written. Yet, instead of examining whether the panel had used the challenged statements in applying the SPS rules, which it had not, of course, the Appellate Body chose to create meanings that it admitted were not clearly in the panel report and rule them to be incorrect.[35]

One can speculate on the reasons for this behavior by the Appellate Body and, in doing so, can legitimately ask whether the Appellate Body was appropriately acting as the superior instance in a two-tier judicial system. Four possible reasons come to mind. First, for whatever reason it seems that the Appellate Body was convinced that it was created to clean up the panel process. Given that most analyses of the GATT system were rather positive,[36] it is not clear where this view came from, but it certainly existed. Second, despite this view that it had to clean up the system, the Appellate Body seemed very sensitive about the relative respect shown to panels vis-à-vis it. There seemed to be a recognition that the panel system was well-established and functioning and that the Appellate Body had to take strong action to bring it under control, to demonstrate its superiority. Third, in this specific case, it seems that the EC strategy on appeal was to claim at every turn that the panel had acted outrageously to make up its own rules and ignore the EC's carefully presented evidence. To accomplish this, the EC presented a rather distorted view of the panel decision, and seemed to succeed in setting a tone for the entire appellate process. Indeed, this seems to explain some of the instances where the Appellate Body set up straw men to knock down. Fourth, it may also be explained because of the Appellate Body's use of what might be called the book review approach to judicial review. By this I mean that the Appellate Body, particularly in its early cases, tended to focus on individual sentences in panel reports and take issue with them, rather than focus on the result and take issue with that. Put another way, in a US Supreme Court decision, the Court sets out its view of the Constitution or relevant statutes, and does not spend much time criticizing the lower court opinions. This approach inevitably gives the impression that the two judicial levels are battling one another.

In any event, over time, as the Appellate Body has seen that panels are perfectly cognizant of hierarchical nature of the system, the tone of Appellate Body reports has improved.

---

[34] See text accompanying notes 5–7 supra.
[35] Appellate Body Report, paras. 186–87.
[36] See, e.g., Robert E. Hudec, *Enforcing International Trade Law* (1993).

B. The *Hormones* Decision and the SPS Agreement

The major obligations of the SPS Agreement are Article 2, which was not discussed in detail in the *Hormones* case; Article 3 on harmonization and international standards; Article 5.1 on risk assessment; Article 5.5 on consistency of levels of protection; and Article 5.6 on least-trade-restrictive measures, which was not dealt with in the *Hormones* case.

As to Article 2, one can ask why it did not figure more prominently in the case, given it purports to lay out the basic obligations of the SPS Agreement. The Appellate Body questioned, and no more, the panel's decision to skip over Article 2 in order to treat the case under Article 5. Although it is only speculation, the panel may have been affected by its view that Article 3.3 was an exception and that its reference to Article 5 meant that the burden of proof was on the EC, thus making it easier for the panel to find the EC at fault – instead of saying that the US proved that the EC measure was not based on a risk assessment, it could conclude that the EC failed to prove that it was. As noted earlier, one can question whether the burden of proof is, or ought to be, that important in these cases, given that normally a panel will, or should, be able to reach a view on where the preponderance of evidence lies. In other words, in this case I do not think that the panel looked only at the EC evidence and concluded that it had not established that the measure was based on a risk assessment, but rather considered the arguments of both sides and concluded that it was not so based, even though the panel's ultimate conclusion was phrased so as to state that the EC had failed to carry its burden. It is perhaps easier for a panel to blame the losing party for its loss, rather than rule against it after weighing the evidence and arguments. In addition, to find a violation of Article 2 (especially 2.2) would have required the panel to make a more explicit finding on the non-existence of a scientific justification of the hormones measure.

As to Article 3, the Appellate Body decision seems to read Article 3.1 out of the agreement. Now, Members have no obligation to use international standards. In the words of the Appellate Body it is optional:

> Under Article 3.1 of the SPS Agreement, a Member may choose to establish an SPS measure that is based on the existing relevant international standard, guideline or recommendation. Such a measure may adopt some, not necessarily all, of the elements of the international standard.[37]

Given that Article 3.3, whether viewed as an exception to Article 3.1 or as a completely stand-alone provision, clearly allows Members to deviate from international standards if they wish to achieve a higher level of protection, the Appellate Body's decision has no real impact on Members who wish to go beyond international standards. It does, of course, remove any obligation for those who now do not meet international standards to raise their measures so as to meet them. Thus, bizarrely, the Appellate Body decision seems likely to lead to a reduction in the overall level of SPS protection in the world, particularly in developing countries.

As to Article 5.1, the Appellate Body's decision that a Member may adopt SPS measures without undertaking a risk assessment so long as it later can defend them

---

[37] Appellate Body Report, para. 171.

on the basis of such an assessment undermines the purpose of the SPS Agreement to promote the use of science-based measures. Of course, because governments may be required to establish that a measure is based on a risk assessment, they may deem it wise to conduct one before adopting a measure, but the Appellate Body has made it clear that no risk assessment need be undertaken in fact. This result seems a bit inconsistent with the "Members shall ensure that their SPS measures are based on an assessment of risks" language in Article 5.1, as well as other elements of Article 5, which seem to require Members to do things at the time of adopting an SPS measure. However, as noted above, perhaps this is a consequence of the fact that the SPS Agreement applies to pre-existing measures, many of which were probably adopted without consideration of factors now required to be considered by the SPS Agreement. Nonetheless, it is unfortunate that the Agreement is weakened for that can only be viewed as short-term considerations.

As to the substance of Article 5.1, the Appellate Body has given governments considerable discretion as to those upon whom they rely in their risk assessment processes [i.e., the views of "mainstream" scientists need not be followed (nor considered?)] and has required only that there be some sort of rational relationship between the risk assessment and the measure. For me, Article 5.1 was always mainly about procedure, so the fact that the Appellate Body's view of the substance of Article 5.1 is not so strict (only a rational relationship is needed) is not bothersome. It is unfortunate, however, that the Appellate Body required so little on the procedural side.

On Article 5.5, for me the difficult issue in the first place is what situations are comparable. I think that the Appellate Body was wrong in concluding that the regulation of added natural hormones cannot be compared to the non-regulation of naturally occurring hormones. In both instances, such hormones in food could be regulated, and, indeed, if hormones are dangerous, one would think that the government would regulate both categories. The fact that one group is naturally occurring does not seem so relevant. If hormones cause problems, then it makes sense to restrict foods containing them. Some people eat lots of those foods, others don't. Thus, the natural load argument doesn't make sense on an individual load basis.

That said, I do not find the rest of the Appellate Body's interpretation of Article 5.5 to be problematic. For me, this provision presents real difficulties of application. It may be possible to find comparable situations and unjustified distinctions, but it is not so clear how one is going to be able to prove that those distinctions discriminate or restrict trade. Indeed, it would seem that it would always be easier to invoke Article 2.3, which only requires the complainant to show that the measure discriminates or restricts trade. Later panel/Appellate Body decisions on Article 5.5 (i.e., *Australia Salmon*) highlight the difficulties of applying Article 5.5.

In sum, I conclude that the *Hormones* decision of the Appellate Body tends to undermine the SPS Agreement by subverting the obligation to use international standards (although because of Article 3.3, its decision simply allows justification of lower standards, but does not prevent the use of higher standards) and by finding no obligation to conduct a risk assessment prior to adopting SPS measures. The latter decision is perhaps not of great importance because, if challenged, a member will have to find a risk assessment and therefore has an incentive to conduct one in any event. Moreover, at least in advanced democracies, the risk assessment process is well-entrenched for the most part anyway.

VI. The Aftermath of the WTO *Hormones* Decision

The decision in *Hormones* was not unexpected. I have been told that the SPS Agreement was drafted with the EC hormones rules in mind and that the EC negotiators knew that those rules would be problematic under the agreement. Indeed, despite the *Hormones* decision, the EC is not currently proposing changes to the SPS Agreement.

I have often wondered if at least some services in the Commission were willing to have the hormones rules repealed. It seems odd that at the December 1995 Commission-sponsored conference on hormones, the invitees were overwhelmingly (virtually unanimously) of the view that hormone use was safe. Since at that time it seemed that the US and Canada were likely to challenge the rules, one would have thought that the EC would have invited scientists critical of hormone use. Even if that view was not the mainstream, such scientists certainly existed. Yet, if there was a thought on the part of some in 1995 that the hormone rules might be changed, the reaction to the WTO decision made it clear that repeal was not going to be politically possible, a position that has become ever more firmly entrenched in the EC with the controversies over BSE (Mad Cow), GMOs and foot-and-mouth disease.

As a result, the EC approach to implementing the WTO *Hormones* ruling has been to accept retaliatory measures imposed by the US and Canada. Those measures are more of an irritant than anything else, as the beef market in the EC is limited by strict tariff quotas. The amount involved is less than $100 million per year (nothing compared to the $4 billion involved in the *FSC* case). In the meantime, the EC has commissioned a variety of scientific analyses, which have essentially concluded that the use of one hormone should be definitively banned and that the use of the other five should be provisionally banned. New legislation to implement this result is now wending its way through the EC legislative process. Once completed, there remains the interesting question of what action the EC will take to get the US/Canadian sanctions removed, on the basis that it will then be in compliance with the SPS Agreement by having conducted a valid risk assessment and acted pursuant to the precautionary principle. Of course, the United States and Canada could concede that there has been implementation, but that seems unlikely. Because no procedures are spelled out in the WTO Dispute Settlement Understanding for dealing with a claim that sanctions should be removed because compliance has occurred, the *Hormones* case could again provoke a WTO controversy.

FRANK J. GARCIA[1]

4. The Salmon Case

Evolution of Balancing Mechanisms for Non-Trade Values in WTO

I. Introduction

The Salmon case represents an important step in the evolution of the doctrinal tools available for managing WTO disputes involving non-trade values. Joel Trachtman has termed these doctrinal tools "trade-off devices," used to guide WTO dispute settlement bodies as to how to balance and weigh the trade versus non-trade values embodied in the particular measure, and GATT/WTO provisions, at stake in a given dispute.[2] Although the Salmon case concerns the specialized WTO Agreement on the Application of Sanitary and Phytosanitary Measures (SPS Agreement),[3] it has implications for the broader development of WTO jurisprudence with respect to the place of non-trade values in the WTO regime.

The SPS Agreement sets out a road map for Members seeking to enact GATT-consistent measures addressing sanitary and phytosanitary concerns. In SPS matters, the non-trade value at stake is the protection of human, animal or plant (HAP) life or health from risks borne by imported products. The trade value at stake is the free movement of goods, because SPS measures have as their effect the prohibition or conditional entry of products deemed by the Member to pose a threat to HAP life or health.

The SPS Agreement protects Members' right to adopt necessary SPS measures (Article 2.1), but only if the SPS measure "is applied only to the extent necessary to protect human, animal or plant life or health, is based on scientific principles, and is not maintained without sufficient scientific evidence" (Article 2.2). The SPS Agreement contains numerous detailed provisions developing this basic obligation, several of these at stake in the Salmon case.[4] Essentially,the SPS Agreement sets up three basic obligations: first, an SPS measure has to be based on a risk assessment (Articles 5.1); second, an SPS measure must not result in discrimination or be a

---

[1] The author gratefully acknowledges the research assistance of Suhyun Jun and Wonhee Lee.

[2] Joel Trachtman, in his pioneering study of trade-off devices, identifies as potential trade-off devices national treatment rules, simple means-end rationality tests, necessity/least-trade-restrictive-alternative tests, proportionality, balancing and cost-benefit analysis. Joel P. Trachtman, "Trade and ... Problems, Cost-Benefit Analysis and Subsidiarity", 9 *European Journal of International Law* 32, 32 (1998).

[3] Agreement on the Application of Sanitary and Phytosanitary Measures, Dec. 15, 1993, Final Act Embodying the Results of the Uruguay Round of Multilateral Trade Negotiations, 33 *International Legal Materials* 9 (1994).

[4] The case principally involved SPS Articles 5.1, 5.5 and 5.6.

disguised restriction on trade (Article 5.5); and third, an SPS measure cannot be "more trade restrictive than required to achieve [the Member's] appropriate level" of SPS protection (Article 5.6).

Together, these three obligations can be understood as striking a particular negotiated balance between trade liberalization and the protection of HAP life or health: trade-restrictive SPS measures will be permitted if they are scientifically justified, non-discriminatory and not more trade-restrictive than necessary in view of the Member's chosen level of protection. Disputes concerning SPS measures can be seen as attempts by complaining parties to enforce that balance. Resolution of such disputes requires that WTO panels and the Appellate Body (AB) determine from the text and context of the SPS Agreement the precise parameters of that balance, and how the formal balance applies to the facts of the case.

One particular provision in the SPS Agreement, Article 5.6, introduces into SPS jurisprudence the "necessity test," long a part of GATT jurisprudence.[5] However, as will be discussed below, the SPS version of the necessity test in Article 5.6 differs in important ways from the standard necessity test found, for example, in GATT Article XX(b), which permits measures "*necessary* to protect human, animal or plant life or health." Overall, the SPS Agreement can be understood as an elaboration of Article XX(b) with respect to the specialized subject of SPS measures. However, in contrast to Article XX(b) as interpreted, the SPS necessity test as written requires consideration of the effective achievement of a Member's regulatory goals prior to invalidating its chosen measure on trade-restrictive grounds. For this reason, as I have suggested elsewhere, the SPS-version necessity test could operate in a more non-trade-value-friendly manner than the standard necessity test, taking such values into account in a manner more satisfactory to advocates of those values, and advocates of a more non-trade-sensitive WTO.[6]

The Salmon Panel is the first WTO dispute settlement body to rule on a 5.6 claim,[7] and its decision and the AB report afford the first opportunity to examine the extent to which the promise contained in the language of 5.6 is indeed borne out in its judicial application.[8] After a brief overview of the case, emphasizing those aspects most germane to the necessity test issues, I will survey the traditional GATT necessity test and the role of trade-off mechanisms more generally. I will then analyze the Salmon Panel's treatment of the SPS necessity test, and the AB's modifications of this treatment. I conclude that the AB's reaction to the Panel's approach to a Member's discretion to choose its appropriate level of protection, stakes out a strong position in respect of non-trade values in WTO, albeit in a somewhat problematic manner.

Finally, I will seek to draw broader conclusions as to the significance of this line of development for WTO "trade and" jurisprudence as a whole. Because the necessity test is employed widely throughout GATT jurisprudence, the Salmon case has the potential to influence necessity test interpretation beyond the strict SPS context.

---

[5] Other provisions employing some form of the necessity test include GATT Articles XX(a), XX(b) and XX(d); and GATS Articles XIV(a), XIV(b) and XIV(c).

[6] This, at least, is what I suggested in an earlier article touching on the subject. See Frank J. Garcia, "The Global Market and Human Rights: Trading Away the Human Rights Principle," 25 *Brooklyn Journal of International Law* 51 (1999).

[7] 5.6 was raised in the Beef Hormone case but the Panel, finding a 5.5 violation, refrained from ruling on 5.6, and the AB concurred in this application of "judicial economy."

[8] The Salmon case thus affords me an opportunity to test, in a sense, my hypothesis in the earlier article.

The Salmon Case

When one examines the AB's interpretation of the traditional necessity test in the Asbestos case, one catches a "whiff" of salmon, confirming that the Salmon case is indeed contributing to the overall task of successfully incorporating respect for non-trade values into the WTO.

II. Factual and Procedural Background and Issues in the Dispute

By virtue of Quarantine Proclamation 86A (QP86A), dated February 19, 1975, Australia prohibited the importation of dead salmon unless prior to such importation the salmon had been treated in a manner "likely to prevent the introduction of any infections or contagious disease, or disease or pest affecting persons, animals or plants." Prior to QP86A, Australia had not restricted the entry of any salmon products.

Canada sought access to Australia for five distinct uncooked ("fresh, chilled or frozen") adult salmon products: three farm-raised varieties,[9] and two ocean-caught varieties.[10] The product in dispute is uncooked, wild, adult, ocean-caught Pacific salmon. Under the authority of QP86A, Australia effectively banned the importation from Canada of uncooked ocean-caught Pacific salmon from Canada, because only heat-treated salmon could gain entry, and heat treatment would destroy the essential nature of the uncooked salmon products (other than smoked salmon, which was not at issue in the case).

Australia cited as reason the sanitary protection of local fish stocks. Aqua farming of Atlantic salmon is a major part of the Tasmanian aquaculture industry, with production at over 6000 tons in 1994–5 (valued at 63 million Australian dollars/pounds). About 40% is exported, mainly to Japan; the rest is for the domestic market. Of the domestic market share, 60% is sold fresh, the rest smoked.

On September 1, 1983, Australia's Director of Quarantine restricted the imports of uncooked salmon with the requirement, "Guidelines for the Importation of Smoked Salmon and Trout into Australia." According to the "1983 Guidelines," imports of "cold smoked" salmon were not allowed unless they were sufficiently treated to prevent the entry of disease. In December 1986 Australia further refined its heat-treatment requirements in "Conditions for the Importation of Salmonid Meat and Roe into Australia," which set up the minimum temperature requirements for heating. This was further refined in June 1988 with "Conditions for the Importation of Salmonid Meat and Roe into Australia" (the "1988 Conditions"), which again revised the oven temperatures and time for heating of salmon for importation.

In 1994, GATT consultations were held at the request of Canada. In 1995 the WTO DSU went into effect. In May 1995, Australia published a draft risk analysis (the "1995 Draft Report") to justify its restriction on Canadian salmon. The Draft Report concluded that while there was a risk of introducing exotic disease agents through the importation of uncooked salmon product from Canada and US, the risk was so small as not to merit the continued prohibition. The report therefore concluded that the importation of wild ocean-caught Pacific salmon from Canada and the US should be permitted under specified conditions. The Australian salmon industry

---

[9] Pacific and Atlantic salmon cultured on the Pacific coast, and Atlantic salmon cultured on the Atlantic coast.

[10] Ocean-caught and freshwater-caught Pacific salmon.

vigorously objected on grounds of the threat to their stocks if such diseases were to be introduced. Meanwhile, on October 5, 1995, Canada requested consultations with Australia saying that the import prohibition of fresh, chilled or frozen salmon from Canada was inconsistent with GATT 1994 and the SPS Agreement. Finally, in December of 1996 Australia issued the final risk analysis (the "1996 Final Report") in which the decision was made to maintain the measure, based on the finding of disease agents in uncooked, wild, ocean-caught Pacific salmon. No explanation for the reversal of position from the 1995 Draft Report was offered.

On April 10, 1997, the DSB established a panel by the request of Canada. The European Communities, India, Norway and the US reserved their right to participate in the Panel proceedings as third parties. The Panel consulted scientific and technical experts and met with them in early 1998, and in June of 1998 the Panel Report was sent to the Members of the WTO.

The Panel found Australia to be in violation of the SPS Agreement with respect to the measure in three basic respects:

1. Australia had maintained an SPS measure not based on a risk assessment, and therefore violated 5.1 and 2.2.
2. Australia had adopted arbitrary or unjustifiable distinctions in the levels of sanitary protection it considered appropriate in different situations, and therefore violated 5.5 and 2.3.
3. Australia had maintained a sanitary measure more trade restrictive than required to achieve its appropriate level of protection, thus violating 5.6.

Australia appealed all three findings, and in addition claimed that the Panel had "failed to interpret correctly its terms of reference with respect to the measure and the product at issue" by characterizing the challenged measure as the heat treatment requirement, instead of the import prohibition on uncooked, untreated salmon as Australia had argued. There is an interesting semantic and interpretive question at the heart of this issue: was the "measure" an import ban on uncooked salmon, or a heat-treatment requirement on smoked salmon? The Panel concluded that they were two sides of the same coin, i.e., that Australia required that uncooked salmon be heat-treated to gain entry. Australia argued that this was wrong, and that they are two separate products: uncooked salmon, which is prohibited, and smoked salmon, which must be heat-treated according to the regulations before entry.

The AB affirmed the Panel in its ultimate findings on claims 1 and 2, holding that Australia's risk assessment was flawed and the application of its measure arbitrary, though not without important modifications of the Panel's approach; and reversed the Panel on 3. In particular, the AB concluded that the Panel incorrectly characterized the measure as the heat-treatment requirement, a mistake which was to have ramifications for the Panel's entire analysis, including the subject of this chapter, the SPS 5.6 necessity test.

III. WTO Necessity Test Jurisprudence

The general scheme for consideration of non-trade values affecting GATT/WTO rules involves text-based exceptions to trade disciplines where other values are at stake, available only on the condition that additional tests or requirements are met. Such

The Salmon Case

requirements can be found in the text of the exception itself; in the introductory paragraph to the exception, or chapeau; or in the jurisprudence interpreting the exception.

Together, these requirements can be seen as "trade-off" devices, offering judicial guidance as to how panels should weigh the various interests at stake in the exercise of the exceptions. Professor Trachtman catalogues six trade-off devices: national treatment rules, simple means-end rationality tests, necessity/least-trade-restrictive alternative tests, proportionality, balancing and cost-benefit analysis.[11] The GATT/WTO treaties employ three of these mechanisms, scattered throughout various provisions: national treatment, rationality and necessity.

At one extreme, one finds the term "necessary" invoked in the national security exception of Article XXI. This provision authorizes a Member to take "any action which it considers necessary" for the protection of its "essential" security interests. Although this exception as written seems to call for application of the necessity test, this is illusory: the exception does not in fact impose such a requirement. The earlier language, authorizing a Member to take any action that "*it* considers" necessary, vests Members with the discretion to determine for themselves the necessity of action, and effectively renders the exercise of the exception non-justiciable. There is, therefore, no trade-off device, because there is no judicial evaluation to be performed. The appropriate balance has been struck legislatively, and it is one of pure discretion: national security concerns trump trade concerns, full-stop. This is one reason WTO Members have been wary of this exception.

A. Article XX

Article XX is the primary GATT provision offering policy-based exceptions to GATT disciplines. The various exceptions in Article XX range towards the other end of the spectrum from Article XXI, imposing stricter, albeit varying, levels of scrutiny and mandating some relative evaluation of trade values and competing non-trade values.

Article XX lists ten exceptions, for conflicting measures involving everything from the protection of public morals [XX(a)] to "the acquisition or distribution of products in general or local short supply" [XX(j)]. The majority of Article XX exceptions apply either a rationality test or a necessity test.[12] The basic operation of these two devices can be illustrated with reference to two exceptions of particular interest to environmentalists, and to SPS-related inquiries: Articles XX(b) and XX(g).

Article XX(b) permits measures "*necessary* to protect human, animal or plant life or health."[13] Article XX(g) permits measures "*relating to* the conservation of exhaustible natural resources. . . . " The Appellate Body has developed a two-tier approach to application of these exceptions,[14] which in practice usually involves three actual steps. First, the panel must determine if the measure comes within one of the

---

[11] Trachtman 35–6.

[12] Necessity: (a) (b) (d) and possibly (i) and (j); rationality: (c) (g) and (e).

[13] Much has been written about the Article XX(b) exception in connection with trade/environment linkage problems. See, e.g., Daniel C. Esty, *Greening the Gatt* (1994); Steve Charnovitz, "Free Trade, Fair Trade, Green Trade: Defogging the Debate", 27 *Cornell International Law of Journal* 459 (1994) (reviewing the history of trade and environmental issues).

[14] See e.g., the Shrimp Turtle AB Report, paragraphs 125 et seq.

enumerated exceptions. For exceptions like XX(b) and (g) employing a trade-off device, this first tier has two steps. First, the measure must be determined to fit within the scope of the provision, namely as a measure addressing HAP life or health, or the conservation of exhaustible natural resources, respectively. Second, the measure must satisfy the relevant trade-off device: it must "relate to," or be "necessary" with respect to, the object of the exception.

The rationality test is more onerous than no test at all, but not as strict as the necessity test. For a measure to be "related to" its object, the measure must be "primarily aimed at" accomplishing the objective;[15] there must be "a close and genuine relationship of ends and means."[16] For a measure to be necessary, this relationship is not enough: the panel must determine that there is no less-trade-restrictive alternative reasonably available. The elaboration of the word "necessary" into a less-trade-restrictive-alternative test is the work of GATT panels interpreting Article XX, starting with the Panel in *United States – Section 337 of the Tariff Act of 1930*:

> It was clear to the Panel that a contracting party cannot justify a measure inconsistent with another GATT provision as "necessary" in terms of Article XX(d) if an alternative measure which it could reasonably be expected to employ and which is not inconsistent with other GATT provisions is available to it. By the same token, in cases where a measure consistent with other GATT provisions is not reasonably available, a contracting party is bound to use, among the measures reasonably available to it, that which entails the least degree of inconsistency with other GATT provisions.[17]

Because under Article XX the burden is on the party claiming the exception, this means that it falls to the party enacting the challenged measure to persuade the panel that no other GATT-compatible or less-restrictive alternative was reasonably available to it.

Then and only then does the panel turn to the second tier, and determine if the measure meets the chapeau test, which prohibits discriminatory application of otherwise valid measures. The chapeau test is a form of balancing test, but not with respect to trade versus non-trade values. Instead, the test balances the rights and duties of states with regard to use of the exceptions, i.e., right of state to invoke exception, balanced against duty of state to respect rights of other states. The AB states the goal as finding a "line of equilibrium" between right to invoke and rights of other members. The tests are cumulative in nature: a measure must survive all three steps in order to pass muster, and it is possible for a measure to fail at the final, chapeau, level, as in the Shrimp-Turtle case.

B. Problems with the Article XX Necessity Test

The necessity test is the pre-eminent trade-off mechanism in GATT/WTO jurisprudence, appearing most frequently in Article XX and carried over into Article XIV of the GATS. As such, it is the most important test within WTO jurisprudence for determining the balance to be struck between trade and non-trade values in cases involving

---

[15] Reformulated Gasoline.
[16] Shrimp-Turtle 136.
[17] Adopted November 7, 1989, BISD 36S/345, para. 5.26.

The Salmon Case

GATT law. This is of some concern, because the standard necessity test is weak with respect to the consideration of non-trade values at stake in Article XX cases.

The language of the necessity test as found in Article XX(b) invites the substitution of the judgement of a panel of trade experts, with a built-in bias favoring trade values, in place of a legislatively determined non-trade measure, on the basis of the measure's effects on trade.[18] It would be consistent with the language of the necessity test as currently interpreted for a GATT panel to find that a measure significantly less effective in achieving the non-trade purpose would nonetheless be "reasonably available," and therefore serve as the basis for invalidating the chosen measure. This is disturbing because given that such a measure was in fact *not* chosen by the enacting state, this language would have the effect of substituting the trade panel's opinion of the rationality of alternatives for the opinion of the legislating forum.

The crux of the matter lies with the "reasonably available" component of the test as elaborated in the jurisprudence. Because the test originates in panel reports, naturally the text of Article XX itself does not give any guidance as to definition or scope of the term "reasonable" in this context. In particular, there is no clear statement regarding the need, if any, of the panel to inquire as to the *effectiveness* of an alternate measure in accomplishing the Member's non-trade goals.

To a limited extent the panel's approach to the "reasonably available" requirment in the Thai Cigarettes case invites some consideration of the effectiveness of the disputed measure in accomplishing its non-trade regulatory purpose. In discussing the necessity test, the panel there was more explicit than in the Section 337 case:

> The import restrictions imposed by Thailand could be considered to be "necessary" in terms of Article XX(b) only if there were no alternative measure consistent with the General Agreement, or less inconsistent with it, which Thailand could *reasonably be expected to employ to achieve its health policy objectives.*[19] (emphasis added)

Any less-trade-restrictive measure, which forms the basis for an invalidation of the chosen measure, must be "reasonably available" in view of the state's non-trade regulatory objectives. Joining the reasonableness language with the state's non-trade policy objectives in a single phrase is a positive step. The extent of such consideration, however, depends entirely on the interpretation of such language, and the application of the qualification, by the GATT panel.

The standard necessity test is thus structured to give preference to trade values. Measures are evaluated primarily in terms of their relative effects on trade. In other words, a measure in dispute will fail the necessity test if the panel is persuaded that an alternative measure would have imposed less restrictions on trade, provided it was *in the panel's judgement* "reasonably available." The test as written does not require that the panel investigate the effectiveness of the invalidating

---

[18] Accord Thomas J. Schoenbaum, "International Trade and Protection of the Environment: The Continuing Search for Reconciliation", 91 *American Journal of International Law* 268, 277 (1997) ("this interpretation of 'necessity' constitutes too great an infringement on the sovereign powers of states to take decisions (one hopes) by democratic means so as to solve problems and satisfy their constituents"). Trachtman concedes that in this approach the characterization of the measure to be evaluated introduces "a certain degree of outcome-determinative discretion." Trachtman, *supra* note 2, at 69. This discretion is, of course, in the hands of trade policy experts.

[19] Adopted February 20, 1990, BISD 37S/200, para. 75.

measure in realizing the non-trade value at stake, nor does it privilege the *Member's* choice of an appropriate level of non-trade protection. Not only does this trade-off mechanism fail to recognize that Members place a high priority on certain non-trade values, but it automatically privileges trade values over all other competing values.[20]

C. The SPS Necessity Test

In contrast to the Article XX necessity test, the SPS test specifically directs the panel to consider the level of protection chosen by a Member. Article 5.6 reads as follows:

> 5.6: Without prejudice to paragraph 2 of Article 3,[21] when establishing or maintaining sanitary or phytosanitary measures to achieve the appropriate level of sanitary or phytosanitary protection, Members shall ensure that such measures are **not more trade-restrictive than required** to achieve their appropriate level of sanitary or phytosanitary protection, taking into account technical and economic feasibility.

Footnote 3 to this provision adds the following important clarification:

> For purposes of paragraph 6 of Article 5, a measure is not more trade-restrictive than required unless there is another measure, reasonably available taking into account technical and economic feasibility, **that achieves the appropriate level of sanitary or phytosanitary protection and is significantly less restrictive to trade**. (emphasis added)

From the point of view of consideration of non-trade values, the language of the necessity test as found in the SPS Agreement would appear superior to that of the standard necessity test in three respects. First, the test is re-cast from a test of justification or invalidation on the basis of the availability of a less-trade-restrictive alternative; to a positive duty not to enact a measure more trade-restrictive than required to achieve a given level of sanitary or phytosanitary protection. This shift entails that the complaining party must now *prove* a violation of this duty, instead of the enacting Member needing to prove the *absence* of such a measure. Shifting the burden in this manner results in a regime that is overall more protective of Member's SPS choices.

Second, the 5.6 test presumes that the appropriate level of SPS protection is the *Member's* chosen level, not the panel's level or the level of some third-party organization. In principle, this situates the locus of decision with respect to the level of protection entirely with the Member, and gives it a non-justiciable status.

Third, the footnote specifically requires a finding that an invalidating measure would achieve the appropriate level of SPS protection, before that measure can be found to invalidate the chosen measure. This explicitly obligates the panel to

---

[20] Thomas J. Schoenbaum has argued that the current GATT/WTO interpretation of the Article XX(b) necessity test turns the provision "on its head" in a literal sense, in that "necessary" refers syntactically to the need for protection of life and health, and not to the trade effects of the measure, and is thus wrong on textual grounds. Thomas J. Schoenbaum, "International Trade and Protection of the Environment: The Continuing Search for Reconciliation", 91 *American Journal of International Law* 268, 276 (1997).

[21] SPS 3.2 establishes a presumption of necessity and WTO consistency for SPS measures based on international standards.

The Salmon Case 141

consider the effectiveness of the measure in achieving the Member's "appropriate level of protection," a significant improvement over the standard Article XX necessity test.

Based on the foregoing factors, I submit that within the WTO regime, SPS measures are a privileged class of non-trade measures, when compared to non-SPS HAP life or health measures, or other non-trade measures generally (except for national security measures). With respect to SPS measures, the SPS Agreement was drafted in the Uruguay Round to give more precise, and arguably more Member-deferential, rules for SPS matters than Article XX offers. Article XX(b) was left unchanged for the adjudication of non-SPS environmental measures.

Whether or not this enhanced level of sensitivity to the regulatory goals of Members in the SPS context is borne out in practice depends upon the interpretation afforded this language by panels and the AB. Because Salmon is the first case in which a panel has interpreted this language as the basis for a ruling, it is to the Panel report that we now turn.

IV. The Salmon Case and the Necessity Test

In its submission, Canada claimed that Australia violated Article 5.6 of the SPS Agreement by maintaining the prohibition on imports of uncooked, ocean-caught Pacific salmon, on the grounds that it was more trade-restrictive than required to achieve Australia's appropriate level of protection.

A. The Panel Report

The Salmon Panel distills Article 5.6 and its footnote into a three-part test. In order to invalidate the enacted measure, the alternative measure must

1) be "reasonably available taking into account technical and economic feasibility";
2) achieve the Member's appropriate level of SPS protection; and
3) be significantly less restrictive to trade than the contested measure.

The three elements are cumulative; in other words, a measure will be invalidated only if an alternate measure satisfies all three requirements.

The first element is not a breakthrough in necessity jurisprudence. As far back as the Section 337 case, panels were softening the rigor of the bare language of XX(b) by interpreting a requirement that the invalidating measure be "reasonably available." Article 5.6 does spell out with greater specificity what this involves: an inquiry into both the technical and economic feasibility of the alternate measure.

Similarly, the third element is familiar. It incorporates the classic less-trade-restrictive alternative language, which panels have interpreted as requiring a fact-intensive investigation of the alternative measures actually or hypothetically available to the enacting Member and their relative effects on trade.

Of these three elements, the second one is the most important from the perspective of non-trade values and Member's sovereign determinations of domestic policy. The effectiveness of the SPS necessity test in respecting these values and this discretion lies in the manner in which a Member's "appropriate" level of protection is determined. Is it solely in the discretion of the Member? Or does the Panel make its own determination as to the Member's choice of an appropriate level? What is the role of scientific evidence and the risk assessment as context for this decision? If the Panel substitutes its own judgement for that of the Member as to the appropriate level of protection, then the SPS necessity test has accomplished little over the Article XX necessity test in respecting Member sovereignty, despite the more nuanced language. Such an interpretation would effectively nullify this part of the language of the 5.6 version of the test.

The Panel had initially determined that for reasons of judicial economy it would first review the measure under SPS before considering Article XX(b), because nowhere in GATT 1994 did it contemplate that a measure found consistent with XX(b) could not also be found a violation of SPS, whereas the reverse was set out in SPS 2.4. Therefore, the Salmon Panel came to the necessity test under its SPS version in 5.6, having already determined that the measure violated SPS Article 2.2. Owing to its overall findings that the measure was inconsistent with SPS, it never reached the Article XX(b) issues.

The Panel's analysis begins with the five potential quarantine policy options identified by Australia in the 1996 Final Report, ranging from heat treatment to simple evisceration. These are

1. permit the importation of product if effectively heat-treated;
2. implement the recommendations of the Aquatic Animal Quarantine Report and allow imports of salmon but with certification and inspection requirements and only as eviscerated, filleted flesh;
3. permit the importation of retail-ready fillets, for distribution in raw form under specified conditions;
4. implement the recommendations of the 1995 Draft Report and permit the importation of headless, gilled, eviscerated product under specified conditions; and
5. permit importation of product that complies with current international standards for trade in salmon product for human consumption, namely that product be eviscerated and that no other risk-reduction measures be taken.[22]

The Panel then examined whether any of the latter four quarantine policy options met the three elements of the test under the footnote to Article 5.6, namely reasonable availability given technical and economic feasibility. The Panel excluded option 1 because it speaks of the heat-treatment requirement that the Panel considered to be the SPS measure against which the other four options are to be examined.

The Panel's work with respect to the first element of the test was relatively straightforward. Because Australia's own report described the alternatives as options "which merit consideration," the Panel found that "this implies that the 1996 Final Report put forward the four alternatives ... as technically or economically feasible policy options." The Panel therefore concluded that the first element of the test under Article 5.6 was met.[23]

---

[22] Panel Report, para. 8.168.
[23] Panel Report, para. 8.171.

The Salmon Case

143

Turning to the critical second element, i.e., whether any of these four quarantine policy options "achieves Australia's appropriate level of sanitary protection," the Panel begins with the question of how that level is to be determined. The Panel determined that ". . . the *level of* protection implied or reflected in a sanitary *measure* or regime imposed by a WTO Member can be presumed to be at least as high as the level of protection considered to be *appropriate* by that Member."[24] In other words, the Panel chose to infer the Member's chosen level of protection from the level of protection implied by the measure actually enacted. According to the Panel, Australia's "appropriate level of protection" with respect to ocean-caught Pacific salmon could therefore be presumed to be at least as high as the level of protection implied in the measure actually imposed, which in the view of the Panel was the heat-treatment requirement.

On the basis of this premise, the Panel went on to state that:

> . . . To determine whether any of the alternative measures meet Australia's appropriate level of protection, we should [. . .] examine whether these alternatives meet the level of protection currently achieved by the measure at issue.[25]

Following this reasoning and focusing its attention on the second quarantine policy option, i.e., certification, inspection, evisceration and filleting, the Panel found that there were alternative SPS measures that would meet Australia's appropriate level of protection. The Panel therefore concluded that the second element of the test under Article 5.6 was met.

On the third element, i.e., whether any of the four quarantine policy options is significantly less restrictive to trade than the SPS measure currently applied, the Panel pointed out that these four alternative quarantine policy options would allow imports of uncooked ocean-caught Pacific salmon, albeit under specific conditions, whereas the SPS measure currently applied amounts to an "outright prohibition." The Panel, therefore, concluded that the third element of the test under Article 5.6 was also met.

Having found that all three elements of the test under Article 5.6 were fulfilled, the Panel concluded its Article 5.6 analysis and determined that Australia had indeed violated the SPS necessity test, by maintaining a measure whose trade-restrictiveness was out of balance with respect to the level of protection sought by Australia.

B. Appellate Body Report

Australia filed an appeal of the Panel's report, contesting among other things the Panel's finding of inconsistency with Article 5.6. Australia did not disagree with the three-pronged legal test under Article 5.6 as set out by the Panel. Australia argued, however, that the Panel erred as a matter of law in its application of the test, particularly in the way in which it examined the second element of the test under Article 5.6, i.e., whether any of the four options achieves Australia's appropriate level of protection.

---

[24] Panel Report, para. 8.173.
[25] Panel Report, para. 8.173.

1. Characterization of the Measure in Question

The AB's review of the Panel's 5.6 rulings was colored by its earlier finding that the Panel erred in characterizing the measure in question as the heat-treatment requirement, concluding instead that the measure to be reviewed was the quarantine itself. The Panel had read the QP86A together with the 1988 Conditions to conclude that the sanitary measure in dispute was in effect a requirement that uncooked salmon be heat-treated before entry. Australia argued instead that the measure in dispute was the prohibition on entry of uncooked salmon, period. Heat-treatment was a separate measure permitting the entry of smoked salmon and other salmon products satisfying the heat-treatment requirement.

The nature of the semantic question at the heart of this issue, and the case, can be illustrated by reference to the following analogy: jurisdiction X bans the importation of oranges, and imposes a pasteurization requirement on the importation of fresh orange juice. Jurisdiction Y, an orange exporter, challenges this regime. Jurisdiction X, in Australia's position, contends that the sanitary measure in question is the prohibition on entry of oranges. Jurisdiction Y, taking Canada's and the Panel's view, contends that the sanitary measure is a requirement that oranges be admitted only as pasteurized juice.

How one resolves this semantic dispute proves to be key for the case as a whole. The reason for its importance lies in the fact that Australia had a risk assessment concerning the ban on importation, but not a risk assessment specifically on heat treatment. The Panel, in effect, read the measure to be one for which there was no risk assessment, then found an SPS violation on the basis of the absence of a risk assessment! Australia argued that this was wrong, and legal error of the first order.

The AB follows Australia's view on this critical point. Textually, QP86A "prohibits the importation into Australia of dead fish of the sub-order Salmonidae...." The AB reads this as establishing, as the measure, an import prohibition on uncooked fish. QP86A does go on to qualify this ban as follows: "unless prior to importation into Australia the fish or parts of fish have been subject to such treatment as in the opinion of the Director of Quarantine is likely to prevent the introduction of any infectious or contagious disease...." That is the language which forms the basis for the imposition of a heat-treatment requirement.

It is easy to see how the Panel could have read this as establishing a single two-part measure, "two sides of a single coin" in the Panel's phrase: an import ban on uncooked fish that is not treated according to the mandated procedures. What is fatal to the Panel's reading is that the mandated procedure, heat treatment, destroys the essential character of the original product. As the AB emphasizes:

> Fresh chilled or frozen salmon is not, and cannot be, subjected to heat treatment. As a matter of fact, heat treatment would destroy fresh, chilled or frozen salmon. As the Panel itself explicitly stated: heat treatment actually changes the nature of the product and limits its use. Heat-treated salmon can obviously no longer be consumed as fresh salmon.[26]

---

[26] AB report para. 101.

The Salmon Case

In other words, returning to the orange analogy, pasteurized orange juice is not oranges. There is no way under Australia's regime that uncooked salmon can enter *as* uncooked salmon. The Panel's interpretation strains a commonsense view of the Australian regulatory regime. In effect, the Panel reads a measure banning imports of oranges and permitting entry of pasteurized orange juice, as an SPS measure *permitting* the entry of oranges but only in the *form* of pasteurized orange juice. The better reading, and the AB's reading, is that we are dealing with in fact two measures: an import ban on oranges, and a requirement that orange juice be pasteurized before entry.

As a result of this error, the Panel's entire analysis is wrong-footed. The AB therefore had no choice but to reverse the Panel's findings on 5.1.[27]

2. SPS 5.6 and the AB Report

Turning to the Panel's finding with respect to Australia's 5.6 violation, and based on its earlier finding with respect to the nature of the measure in question, the AB agreed with Australia's first contention, namely that the Panel's 5.6 review was erroneous for the same reason that the 5.1 finding was erroneous, namely consideration of the wrong measure. Because the SPS measure at issue is not the heat-treatment requirement, but rather the import prohibition on fresh, chilled or frozen salmon, the measure to be examined under 5.6 is therefore the import prohibition. The Panel should have examined under Article 5.6 whether the import prohibition, not the heat-treatment requirement, is "not more trade-restrictive than required" to achieve Australia's appropriate level of protection.

Despite the fact that the Panel had conducted its entire analysis on the basis of the wrong measure, the AB felt it was possible to essentially conduct a de novo review of the issue of SPS 5.6 compliance on the basis of the record developed by the Panel, and proceeded to do so.

The AB began by endorsing the Panel's interpretation of Article 5.6 as establishing a three-pronged cumulative test to determine violations of Article 5.6. The AB also approved of the Panel's application of the first prong, namely its conclusion that Australia's own 1996 report established that the alternate measures are reasonably available, taking into account technical and economic feasibility.

The AB disagreed however with the Panel's approach to the key issue of establishing the Member's appropriate level of protection. Recall that the Panel had inferred this level from the level of protection reflected in the SPS measure at issue. Because in the AB's view the measure was the import prohibition, Australia's appropriate level would on the Panel's approach be a "zero-risk level" of protection. However, the AB found that in this case Australia had already determined explicitly that its appropriate level of protection was

> ... a high or "very conservative" level of sanitary protection aimed at reducing risk to "very low levels", "while not based on a zero-risk approach."[28]

---

[27] The AB did go on, however, to perform its own analysis based on the Panel's findings, concluding that the prohibition was not in fact based on an adequate risk assessment.

[28] Panel Report, para. 8.107.

In so finding, the AB relied on Australia's submissions to the Panel process. The AB therefore concluded that the *appropriate* level of protection as determined by Australia is *not* the zero-risk approach reflected in the SPS measure at issue, but somewhat lower.

How, then, should the Panel have responded to this chosen level of risk? This is the key issue of the necessity test as modified by the Article 5.6 of the SPS Agreement. While the AB established a strong pro-Member interpretation of this provision, it seems to have done so on the basis of a misreading of the Panel.

In discussing Australia's position with respect to its appropriate level of protection, the AB quoted excerpts from paragraph 8.172 of the Panel's report as follows:

> It is for Australia to decide on . . . [its appropriate level of protection], but, again, in so doing it has to act consistently with the SPS Agreement, in particular Articles 2, 5.1 to 5.3 and 5.6. Our examination under Article 5.6 is not aimed at a *de novo* review of what sanitary measure Australia should have chosen to achieve its appropriate level of protection. On the other hand, we cannot completely defer this decision to Australia and thus not give effect to Article 5.6. Our mandate under Article 11 of the DSU requires us to "make an objective assessment of the matter before [us], including an objective assessment of the facts of the case."[29]

The Panel thus seems to assert jurisdiction to review Australia's choice of an appropriate level of protection as a function of the Panel's duty to apply 5.6.

The AB disagreed with this view, and went on to clarify in the strongest possible terms that neither

> Article 11 of the DSU, [n]or any other provision of the DSU or of the *SPS Agreement*, entitles the Panel or the Appellate Body, for the purpose of applying Article 5.6 in the present case, to substitute its own reasoning about the implied level of protection for that expressed consistently by Australia. The determination of the appropriate level of protection, a notion defined in paragraph 5 of Annex A, as "the level of protection deemed appropriate by the Member establishing a sanitary . . . measure," is a *prerogative* of the Member concerned and not of a panel or of the Appellate Body.

This is certainly a strong position with respect to a Member's discretion over non-trade policy. However, it is based on a misreading of the what the Panel actually said! It is worth quoting paragraph 8.172 in full:

> 8.172 We next address the second element of Article 5.6. The alternative measure needs to achieve Australia's appropriate level of sanitary protection. We fully agree with Australia that the determination of its *level* of sanitary protection is a decision to be made by Australia, not by any other WTO Member or international organization. The SPS Agreement (in paragraph 5 of Annex A) defines this level as the level of protection "*deemed appropriate by the Member* establishing a sanitary . . . measure," *in casu*, the level deemed appropriate by Australia. However, this decision on what level of protection is appropriate has to comply with the SPS Agreement (e.g., Articles 5.4 and 5.5). *The same* applies to Australia's decision as to which sanitary *measure* will achieve Australia's *level of* protection. It is for Australia to decide on this, but, again, in so doing it has to act consistently with the SPS Agreement, in particular

---

[29] Panel Report, para. 8.172.

The Salmon Case 147

Articles 2, 5.1 to 5.3 and 5.6. Our examination under Article 5.6 is not aimed at a *de novo* review of what sanitary measure Australia should have chosen to achieve its appropriate level of protection. On the other hand, we cannot completely defer this decision to Australia and thus not give effect to Article 5.6. Our mandate under Article 11 of the DSU requires us to "make an objective assessment of the matter before [us], including an objective assessment of the facts of the case."

Read closely; the Panel is making two separate points with respect to its authority to review Member decisions. First, the Panel *affirms* that a member has the sole right to determine its appropriate level of protection, subject only to the requirements of Articles 5.4 and 5.5. That seems unexceptionable. The Panel then goes on to make a *second* point, namely that "the same" principle, namely that Member decisions must be SPS-compliant, applies to choice of *which measure* achieves *Australia's* level. This choice is subject to review under 5.6. This also seems correct. In neither case is the Panel asserting a broad right to review a Member's choice of appropriate level *as* the appropriate level – only the duty to ensure the choice of *level* is consistent with 5.4 and 5.5, in the first instance, and the duty to ensure the choice of *measure* is consistent with 5.6 in the second instance.

Instead, the AB collapses these two points and has the panel saying it "cannot completely defer" to the Member's decision as to appropriate level, when in fact the Panel says this with respect to the Member's decision as to which measure. By doing so, the AB presents the Panel as arrogating to itself the power to disregard member statements as to its appropriate level of protection and determine that from the measure enacted instead, as part of applying 5.6. The AB then seeks to correct this by clarifying that the Member has the sole prerogative to establish that level, and for the purposes of 5.6 the Panel must take that as given.

The AB then turned to the manner in which the Panel had determined what choice Australia had in fact made as to its appropriate level. The Panel inferred this from the measure Australia enacted, which in its view was the heat-treatment requirement. In the AB's judgement this approach was backwards – it is the level which determines the measure, and not vice versa.

> The words of Article 5.6, in particular the terms "*when establishing or maintaining sanitary . . . protection,*" demonstrate that the determination of the level of protection is an element in the decision-making process which logically *precedes* and is *separate* from the establishment or maintenance of the SPS measure. It is the appropriate level of protection which determines the SPS measure to be introduced or maintained, not the SPS measure introduced or maintained which determines the appropriate level of protection. To imply the appropriate level of protection from the existing SPS measure would be to assume that the measure always achieves the appropriate level of protection determined by the Member. That clearly cannot be the case.

For this reason, the AB concluded that the Panel erred in finding that for the purpose of evaluating the effectiveness of alternate measures, it should "examine whether these alternatives meet the level of protection currently achieved by the measure at issue." Instead, the Panel should have examined whether possible alternative measures met the appropriate level of protection "as determined by the Member concerned."

148   Frank J. Garcia

This position raises two issues, a textual interpretation problem and an evidentiary problem. Textually, the AB's position would seem to imply that the SPS Agreement imposed an obligation on Members to explicitly choose an appropriate level of protection as an independent requirement. The AB attempts to finesse this point by distinguishing between an implicit obligation and an explicit obligation.

> We recognize that the *SPS Agreement* does not contain an *explicit* provision which obliges WTO Members to determine the appropriate level of protection. Such an obligation is, however, implicit in several provisions of the *SPS Agreement*, in particular, in paragraph 3 of Annex B, Article 4.1[30], Article 5.4 and Article 5.6 of the *SPS Agreement*.[31] With regard to Article 5.6, for example, we note that it would clearly be impossible to examine whether alternative SPS measures achieve the appropriate level of protection if the importing Member were not required to determine its appropriate level of protection.

The distinction between implicit and explicit obligations is a perilous one, in view of the AB's restrictions on enlarging the scope of Members' obligations under the WTO agreements.

In any event, this raises the second, evidentiary point: how do you find evidence of a Member's discharge of this implicit obligation? In the Salmon case, the AB did not have to face this directly, as it concluded that it could rely on statements made by Australia in its panel submissions as to the appropriate level of protection. However, this avenue may not always be available. What counsel does the AB offer in that case?

> We believe that in cases where a Member does not determine its appropriate level of protection, or does so with insufficient precision, the appropriate level of protection may be established by panels on the basis of the level of protection reflected in the SPS measure actually applied. Otherwise, a Member's failure to comply with the implicit obligation to determine its appropriate level of protection – with sufficient precision – would allow it to escape from its obligations under this Agreement and, in particular, its obligations under Articles 5.5 and 5.6.

Unless I am misreading this, isn't this exactly what the Panel did? The AB emphatically stated that the Panel was wrong to make such an inference, and yet now it establishes this as the default approach?

I believe the root of this confusion is again with the disagreement over characterization of the measure in question. Because the Panel viewed the measure as heat-treatment, which is not a "zero-risk" but a "low-risk" level of protection, it was not misleading, and not error, to determine this level from the measure enacted or from Australia's own submissions: both established the same, low-risk level of appropriate protection. The problem arises only as a result of the AB's disagreement over the measure. If the measure is indeed the import prohibition, then the Panel's methodology would lead to a finding that Australia had chosen a "zero-risk" level of protection, contradicting Australia's own statement to the contrary. However, this

---

[30] Reasonable questions from interested Members within the meaning of paragraph 3 of Annex B can arise, in particular, with respect to the application of Article 4 of the *SPS Agreement*. Articles 4.1 and 4.2 imply, in our view, a clear obligation of the importing Member to determine its appropriate level of protection.

[31] Furthermore, it could be argued that an implicit obligation for a Member to determine the appropriate level of protection results also from Article 5.8 and Article 12.4 of the *SPS Agreement*.

conflict did not of course present itself to the Panel, because of how it characterized the measure. It is only when the measure is re-characterized as the prohibition, that the Panel's approach *appears* to lead it to disregard the party's own statements and infer a different level of protection from the enacted measure. However, this appearance is purely an artifact of the AB's own analysis, applying the Panel's method to a measure the Panel did not consider.

This would suggest that the Panel's methodology is sound after all, assuming it has correctly identified the measure. The most we can conclude from the AB's analysis here is that where a Panel does indeed face a discrepancy between the level implied in the chosen measure and a party's statements, the Panel should seriously consider choosing to rely on the Party's statements or risk reversal. This is of course problematic for other reasons, given the temptation in party submissions to offer post-hoc rationalizations.

After clarifying the appropriate legal rule, the AB found that after all it could not complete the 5.6 analysis. Because the Panel found that the 1996 Final Report did not evaluate the relative risks associated with the five options, there was no basis on which to determine if any of the alternative measures would achieve Australia's appropriate level of protection. In reversing the Panel's finding on Article 5.6, however, the AB took pains to emphasize that it was not opining as to whether Australia did or did not violate Article 5.6.

C. The Salmon Case and the SPS 5.6 Necessity Test

The Salmon case confirms that the deference accorded to Member's choice of appropriate levels of protection by language of 5.6, and the inquiry mandated by 5.6 into the effectiveness of alternate measures in reaching that level, are borne out in practice. This is important for the development of SPS law in a manner that respects the importance to Members of non-trade values in the SPS context. The AB does stake out strong pro-Member stance on discretion to choose level of protection. The fact that it seems to do so on the back of a misreading of the Panel's views is regrettable, but probably will not detract from the force of its conclusions long term.

This does not mean, however, that the AB's approach in Salmon is without problems. The AB does affirm the Panel's three-part test, which seems useful and correct. With respect to the first element, the reasonable availability of the alternate measure, the Panel's approach in relying on the Member's own risk assessment seems appropriate in cases like this one where the alternate measure is one considered by the Member. The harder case is where the alternate measure is one not considered by the Member. For such cases the Salmon Panel offers no guidance. In this sort of case, the Panel should proceed very cautiously, because the risk to Members' policy autonomy is greatest, as the Panel would be supplanting the Member's legislative judgement on the basis of its evaluation of a hypothetical.

With respect to the second element, determining the Member's appropriate level of protection, the Panel's approach in inferring this level from the enacted measure still seems viable. After all, barring cases of acknowledged regulatory failure, one could presume that a Member's enacted measure embodied a level of protection the member considered "appropriate," or else why enact it?

The AB's approach of relying on a party's statements in litigation for its appropriate level instead of its actual measures does pose some risks. The AB may be correct logically that the level determines the measure, and not in reverse, but as a practical matter this is not certain to be the case. Because there is no requirement under SPS 5.1 that the risk assessment actually had motivated the legislative decision, for example, the way is clear for post hoc rationalizations and "adoptions" of the appropriate level for tactical reasons.

Moreover, since the AB goes on to endorse the Panel's approach as the default method where a Member has not made a clear statement of choice, it is hard to understand in retrospect what all the fuss was about. Perhaps the disagreement stems from the systemic problem of the Panel's characterization of the measure, because there is only a problem when you take the Panel's approach and apply it to the AB's measure. If this is so, then imputing a level from a measure remains a sound interpretive technique.

V. Beyond Salmon: Effects of SPS 5.6 on Traditional Necessity Test Jurisprudence

Within the confines of SPS jurisprudence, the Salmon case makes important contributions to the development of the law with respect to a Member's right to establish its own level of protection for HAP life or health. In so doing, the Salmon case affirms that the SPS necessity test is more Member-protective than Article XX as interpreted to that point. However, the positive effects of the Salmon decision extend beyond SPS jurisprudence, and are already influencing the development of the traditional Article XX necessity test.

In Korea-Beef, the first major necessity test case post-Salmon, the AB is called upon to interpret the necessity test as found in XX(d). In that case, the AB elaborated a new approach to necessity determinations, at least one that was new for Article XX jurisprudence.

> In sum, determination of whether a measure, which ... may be necessary within the contemplation of Article XX(d), involves in every case a process of weighing and balancing a series of factors which prominently include "the contribution made by the compliance measure to the enforcement of the law or regulation at issue, the importance of the common interests or values protected by that law or regulation, and the accompanying impact of the law or regulation on imports or exports.[32]

This test is a radical new direction in Article XX jurisprudence, and establishes a new three-part test, or at least a test involving three components:

(1) The degree of contribution the measure makes towards achievement of the regulatory purpose,
(2) the importance of the values at stake, and
(3) the trade impact.

---

[32] Korea-Beef, para. 162.

The Salmon Case

In particular, there is a dynamic effect within the elements: the more vital the regulatory object is deemed to be, the more necessary a measure will be judged to be (and presumably the more trade restriction will be tolerated).

When one compares this to the Salmon test for 5.6, one can see similarities, in that the new Article XX test requires panels to consider the degree of contribution of the measure to a Member's non-trade purpose, which is similar to the SPS inquiry into the degree of effectiveness of the alternate measure; and to consider the importance of the values at stake, which is similar to consideration of the appropriate level of protection chosen by the member state; in addition, of course, to consideration of the measure's impact on trade.

The second element looks different, but is in fact quite similar. The point of contact with 5.6 is around the values at stake in SPS decisions versus non-SPS decisions. SPS 5.6 can be seen as reflecting a decision on the part of the WTO Members that because SPS values are so important, panels should follow a Member's decision making on values in SPS cases, rather than evaluate it independently. The focus is still on values, but the trade-off has already been made legislatively in the SPS context.

Effective contribution, values and trade impact – the same elements found at the heart of the SPS test now appear in a radical re-interpretation of traditional XX case law.

Following the Korea-Beef case, we see the AB wrestling with its new test in EC-Asbestos. It is even clearer in Asbestos that with respect to its general interpretive approach to the issues, the AB is carrying into Article XX jurisprudence concepts and approaches developed under SPS jurisprudence. For example, with respect to an argument raised by Canada in the Asbestos case that the Panel had incorrectly allowed qualitative evidence of risk, the AB noted as follows:

> As for Canada's second argument, relating to "quantification" of the risk, we consider that, as with the *SPS Agreement*, there is no requirement under Article XX(b) of the GATT 1994 to *quantify*, as such, the risk to human life or health. A risk may be evaluated either in quantitative or qualitative terms.

This seemingly casual reference to the SPS jurisprudence in an Article XX case is in fact quite remarkable.

With respect to the necessity test per se, there is also evidence of the SPS approach. In Asbestos the AB followed the same three-part analysis as in Korea-Beef: effective contribution, values, trade effects. Noting the importance of the value protected by France (human life), the AB focused the inquiry on the remaining two factors: effectiveness and trade restrictiveness.[33]

One of the clearest signs of Salmon influence is the way the AB approaches the issue of France's determination as to its appropriate level of protection from asbestos-related harms. With respect to this key issue, the AB seems to import its treatment of a Member's choice of appropriate level in the SPS context into their application of XX(b):

> We note that it is undisputed that WTO Members have the right to determine the level of protection of health that they consider appropriate in a given situation. France

---

[33] EC-Asbestos 172.

has determined, and the Panel accepted,[34] that the chosen level of health protection by France is a "halt" to the spread of *asbestos*-related health risks.

I would respectfully submit that this is far from undisputed – disputes over precisely this point are what forms the basis for Article XX cases. Within SPS one can now say as a result of the Salmon case that this is undisputed; outside of SPS and prior to Asbestos, it is only with respect to Article XXI that one could say with assurance that a Member's discretion over determining levels of regulatory protection is undisputed.

I would argue that this paragraph in fact represents a movement by the AB towards the view that when making trade-off decisions in necessity cases involving very important values such as human life or health, such determinations should be largely within the discretion of Members in Article XX contexts, in the same way that they are in SPS contexts. Confirmation for this view can be found in the way the AB decisively alters the "reasonably available" element of the traditional necessity test in Asbestos:

> In our view, France could not reasonably be expected to employ *any* alternative measure if that measure would involve a continuation of the very risk that the Decree seeks to "halt." Such an alternative measure would, in effect, prevent France from achieving its chosen level of health protection.

In so holding, the AB has now brought the two strands of the necessity test together. A measure is not "reasonably available" if it does not achieve the non-trade regulatory purpose set by the Member. This interpretation in effect reads into Article XX an SPS-style inquiry as to the effectiveness of the alternate measure, as well as an SPS-style deference to the Member's right to set its level of non-trade protection and chose effective means to accomplish it.

VI. Conclusion

The SPS necessity test has, through the AB's interpretation in Salmon, increased the likelihood that non-trade values will be respectfully considered in traditional XX cases. At a mimimum, the Salmon case has, by its influence in Korea-Beef and Asbestos, made an explicit place for consideration of such values in the case law, if not in the text itself. The main shortcoming of the AB's new approach is the possibility that the Panel will independently weigh the importance of the value pursued. This is disturbing, as this is the main issue identified as a defect in traditional XX jurisprudence. It seems that for SPS measures the political decision has been made to favor such measures, by privileging a Member's own determination of its appropriate level of protection. Perhaps this is because for SPS measures the scientific evidence and risk assessment requirements exert some check on the potential for protectionist abuse not available in standard XX cases. Nevertheless, one must wonder if the cure is worse than the disease. Is there no other way to address the risk of protectionism, say through the chapeau test, rather than to permit a trade panel to independently assess the importance of the values chosen for protection by the Member?

---

[34] *Ibid.*, para. 8.204.

JEFFREY L. DUNOFF

5. Lotus Eaters

Reflections on the *Varietals* Dispute, the SPS Agreement
and WTO Dispute Resolution

In the international arena, dramatic events often expose the law's underlying conceptual and doctrinal fault lines. The September 11 attacks (and responses), the Pinochet litigation, and the International Court of Justice's opinion on the legality of nuclear weapons amply demonstrate how extraordinary events can highlight the limits of traditional international law doctrines and principles.

Surprisingly, apparently garden-variety disputes can also reveal much about the underlying tensions in the international legal system. The *Varietals* dispute, which apparently involves nothing other than a straightforward application of the SPS Agreement, is such a case. The panel and Appellate Body reports in this dispute reveal much about the function of WTO dispute resolution and the purposes of international trade law. More importantly, like other "great" WTO cases – such as *Beef-Hormone* and *Shrimp-Turtle* – the *Varietals* dispute directs our attention to the shifting relationship between the expanding reach of international regulation and state's regulatory autonomy, and hence to some of the most important questions regarding both globalization and the status and scope of contemporary international law.

While a full defense of these claims is beyond the scope of this chapter, I will highlight several features of this understudied but remarkably rich case to outline an argument about what the *Varietals* dispute teaches us about both the current state – and our understanding – of international trade law. To do so, this chapter will proceed in six parts. Part I introduces the factual background to the *Varietals* dispute. Part II briefly reviews key provisions of the SPS Agreement. Part III discusses the panel and Appellate Body reports in the *Varietals* dispute. Part IV explores what the *Varietals* dispute reveals about the changing purpose and functions of the international trade regime. Part V examines different methods that can be used to test the arguments over whether the SPS Agreement unduly restricts states' ability to enact desirable social legislation. Finally, Part VI discusses the appropriate role of panels in food safety and other controversial disputes that pit economic against non-economic interests.

A word about the title. Writers have long used the term the "lotus eaters" to refer to a group of persons who are distracted from their quest by "narcotics" of one form or another. Sometimes the group consumes physical opiates, such as when Odysseus' crew eat lotus flowers and lose the will to continue their difficult journey home. Sometimes the opiates are psychological, as when Leopold Bloom witnesses the narcotic effect of religion on the participants in the mass at All Hallows in the Lotus

Eaters chapter of Joyce's *Ulysses*. In each case the lotus eaters are distracted from their quest and hampered in their journey.

Perhaps the ubiquity of this literary image should sensitize us to the possibility that similar "opiates" that can sedate and mislead exist in other domains. The expanding scope and detail of international trade law affords legal scholars an exceptionally broad range of research opportunities. In the past few years, many of these scholars have focused on the WTO's innovative dispute settlement system. Analysis of panel and AB reports is used to generate broad claims about the WTO system. However, Dispute Settlement Body (DSB) activity captures only a small fraction of the world of trade law and policy, and hence the reports may present a non-representative and inaccurate picture of trade law and practice. Hence, one purpose of this chapter is to raise the question of whether, in their intensive focus upon WTO dispute resolution procedures and reports, students of the trade regime may have inadvertently become lotus eaters.

I. Background to the *Varietals* Dispute

Apples are the third most valuable fruit crop grown in the United States, behind only grapes and oranges. Production has grown from an annual average of 6.5 billion pounds in 1970–75 to 10.4 billion pounds in 1990–96, with the domestic market responsible for consumption of over 5 billion pounds of apples per year. The commercial apple crop is now worth approximately $2 billion per year. U.S. farmers produce many varieties of apples, including Red Delicious (42% of the U.S. crop); Golden Delicious (14%); Granny Smith (7%); Rome (6%); McIntosh (5%); Fuji (5%) and Gala (3%). These percentages reflect important structural changes in the crop, as producers are responding to high prices for the fresh export market and changing consumer preferences for sweeter apples. As a result, varieties such as Jonathan, York, Stayman and Winesap have decreased in importance to the industry.[1]

Domestic consumption in the U.S. has remained relatively static over the last decade. Thus, domestic apple growers increasingly rely upon export markets. The U.S. is now the world's second largest fresh apple exporter, after France. U.S. growers have traditionally encountered SPS barriers to imports in a number of countries, including Japan, Mexico and South Korea.

Japan is a major producer and consumer of apples, and ranks as the world's twelfth largest apple producer. Japanese apples are known for their very high quality and prices. Japan's apple market is largely domestic; both imports and exports both account for 1 percent or less of consumption. In 1996, U.S. farmers exported $404.5 million worth of apples. However, only 0.14 percent of these exports – less than $600,000 – went to Japan.

Notwithstanding the high economic and political stakes in disputes over international trade in apples, the fact pattern giving rise to the *Varietals* dispute could hardly

---

[1] Information on international trade in apples was culled from Barry Krissoff, Linda Calvin and Denice Gray, Barriers to Trade in Global Apple Markets, Fruit and Tree Nuts Situation and Outlook (USDA Economic Research Service, August 1997); Jimmye Hillman, Nontariff Agricultural Trade Barriers Revisited, in *Understanding Technical Barriers to Agricultural Trade* 1 (David Orden & Donna Roberts, eds., 1997).

be less dramatic. Under Japan's 1950 Plant Protection Law[2] and Plant Protection Law Enforcement Regulation,[3] Japan prohibited the importation of eight agricultural products from the United States. The products – apples, cherries, peaches, walnuts, apricots, pears, plums and quince – were banned because they are potential hosts to the coddling moth, an agricultural pest that invades a number of fruit crops. Coddling moth infestation significantly reduces the commercial value of crops. This pest is not found in Japan.

Japanese law provided that this import prohibition can be lifted if the exporting country uses an alternative quarantine treatment that achieves a level of protection equivalent to the import ban. For the particular fruits and nuts at issue in this case, the U.S. used the pesticide methyl bromide, or a combination of methyl bromide fumigation and cold storage. In 1987, Japan's Ministry of Agriculture, Forestry and Fisheries developed two protocols to test the efficacy of these alternative treatments. One guideline is relevant to the initial lifting of the import ban on a product.[4] The second guideline is relevant to the approval of additional *varieties* of that same product.[5] Under this legal regime, after extensive testing, Red Delicious apples from the United States were approved for import into Japan in August 1994. However, separate and additional testing, ongoing while this dispute was being heard in WTO dispute settlement in 1998, was underway for different *varieties* of apples, including Gala, Granny Smith, Jonagold, Fuji and Braeburn apples. The United States complained that testing for each variety was lengthy (taking between two and four years to complete), costly, and unjustifiably delayed market access of U.S. products. As a legal matter, the United States argued that the requirement that each variety of a particular fruit be tested (the so-called "varietal testing requirement" or "VTR") was inconsistent with Japan's obligations under the Agreement on the Application of Sanitary and Phytosanitary Measures (the "SPS Agreement").

II. The SPS Agreement

The Agreement on the Application of Sanitary and Phytosanitary Measures (SPS Agreement) was negotiated while the Uruguay Round negotiations on the Agreement on Agriculture were underway.[6] The Agriculture Agreement was designed to reduce agricultural tariffs and subsidies, and some WTO members feared that countries might use non-tariff barriers to protect domestic agricultural sectors. That is, as traditional barriers to agricultural trade were eliminated, states might be tempted to use measures ostensibly designed to protect human, animal or plant health as an excuse to restrict trade. Such measures could, of course, negate many of the benefits otherwise derived from reducing tariffs and subsidies.

---

[2] Law No. 151 of 1950, enacted May 4, 1950, amended in 1996.

[3] Ordinance No. 73 of the Ministry of Agriculture, Forestry and Fisheries, enacted June 30, 1950.

[4] Experimental Guideline for Lifting Import Ban – Fumigation (1987).

[5] Experimental Guideline for Cultivar Comparison Test on Insect Mortality – Fumigation (1987).

[6] Sanitary and phytosanitary measures generally deal with protecting human, animal and plant life or health from risks of plant- or animal-borne pests or diseases, or additives, contaminants, toxins or disease-causing organisms in foods, beverages and foodstuffs. Examples of SPS measures include the following: (i) requiring animals and animal products to come from disease-free areas; (ii) inspection of products for microbiological contaminants; (iii) mandating a specific fumigation treatment for products; and (iv) setting maximum allowable levels of pesticide residues in food.

These concerns were not fanciful. Sanitary and phytosanitary measures are extremely common and had been proliferating in the years leading up to the Uruguay Round negotiations. For example, in 1966, only half of U.S. food imports were governed by non-tariff barriers; by the time that the Uruguay Round began in 1986, this figure had increased to nearly 90 percent.[7] Thus, exporters and exporting states had a growing interest in disciplining these measures, and this interest led to the negotiation of a new and separate WTO agreement.

While concern over the use of such measures to unjustifiably interfere with international trade existed for many years,[8] prior to the Uruguay Round, no multilateral agreement comprehensively disciplined use of SPS measures.[9] The SPS negotiations started as an attempt to elaborate on the provisions of Article XX(b) of the GATT 1947. The resulting agreement, however, extends well beyond the elaboration of existing GATT provisions, and includes a number of new obligations.

Unlike the TRIPs Agreement, which sets out specific levels of intellectual property protection that WTO members must provide, the SPS Agreement does not create specific SPS standards that governments must use. Rather, it provides general rules for governments to follow when establishing SPS measures. Like many parts of the WTO, the SPS Agreement focuses on trade facilitation through liberalization and requires national treatment, transparency and non-discrimination while providing special and differential treatment for developing countries.

As a general matter, the purpose of the SPS Agreement is to maintain a government's sovereign right to provide the level of health protection that it deems appropriate, but to ensure that these sovereign rights are not misused for protectionist purposes and do not result in unnecessary barriers to international trade. To do so, the Agreement requires that SPS measures be based upon science, and applied only to the extent necessary to protect human, animal or plant life or health. It encourages members to use international standards, guidelines and recommendations where they exist. However, members may use measures which result in higher standards if there is scientific justification. The most important SPS provisions are outlined below.

A number of provisions address the *level* of protection that states may pursue in their SPS measures, and the *means* by which states achieve these goals. In general, the agreement permits each state to choose the "level of protection" it deems appropriate "to protect human, animal or plant life or health within its territory." More specifically, Article 2 of the agreement, which sets out the parties' basic rights and obligations, affirms the "right" to take SPS measures "necessary for the protection of human, animal or plant life or health," but requires that SPS measures meet several requirements. They must (a) be "applied only to the extent necessary to protect human, animal or plant life or health," (b) be "based on scientific principles and ... not maintained without sufficient scientific evidence," (c) not "arbitrarily or unjustifiably discriminate between Members where identical or similar conditions

---

[7] A. Tutwiler, Food Safety, the Environment and Agriculture Trade: The Links, Discussion Paper, International Policy Council on Agricultural Trade (June 1991).

[8] Steve Charnovitz, Improving the Agreement on Sanitary and Phytosanitary Standards, in *Trade, Environment and the Millennium* 170, 173.

[9] To be sure, SPS measures were covered by the GATT, although these disciplines were hardly ever tested. A 1979 GATT Standards Code also proved inadequate to the perceived problems in this area, in part because only forty-six Contracting Parties adhered to this agreement.

Lotus Eaters

prevail," and (d) not "be applied in a manner which would constitute a disguised restriction on international trade."

Recognizing that states often apply different SPS measures and that regulatory heterogeneity can cause inefficiencies, Article 3 calls for the "harmonization" of SPS measures "on as wide a basis as possible." To achieve this goal, the Agreement states that "Members shall base their sanitary or phytosanitary measures on international standards, guidelines or recommendations, where they exist," and that SPS measures which conform to international standards shall be "presumed to be consistent with the relevant provisions of [the SPS] Agreement and [with] GATT 1994."

However, the agreement does not *require* the use of international standards. Rather, it provides that "Members may introduce or maintain sanitary or phytosanitary measures which result in a higher level of sanitary or phytosanitary protection than would be achieved by [international standards], if there is a scientific justification, or as a consequence of the level of sanitary or phytosanitary protection a Member determines to be appropriate."

Other SPS articles address the *justification* or *basis* for SPS measures. Article 5.1 requires each government to "ensure that their sanitary or phytosanitary measures are based on an assessment, as appropriate to the circumstances, of the risks to human, animal or plant life or health, taking into account risk assessment techniques developed by the relevant international organizations." The agreement does not specify any particular method of conducting, or any particular type of, risk assessment.[10] Instead, Articles 5.2 and 5.3 identify a number of factors that must be taken into account, including "available scientific evidence; relevant processes and production methods; relevant inspection, sampling and testing methods; prevalence of specific diseases or pests; existence of pest- or disease-free areas; relevant ecological and environmental conditions;" and relevant economic factors, such as "the potential damage in terms of loss of production or sales in the event of the entry, establishment or spread of a pest or disease; the costs of control or eradication in the territory of the importing Member; and the relative cost-effectiveness of alternative approaches to limiting risks."

There is an important provision addressing situations where adequate risk assessments do not yet exist. Article 5.7 provides that when scientific evidence is insufficient, a member country is entitled to use measures based on "available pertinent information." There are two conditions attached to this use. First, such measures must be temporary, and second, the member must seek additional evidence and must review the measure after "a reasonable period of time."

Another important SPS provision addresses the *consistency* of a state's SPS measures. Article 5.5 provides that "with the objective of achieving consistency in the application of the concept of appropriate level of sanitary or phytosanitary protection against risks to human life or health, or to animal and plant life or health, each Member shall avoid arbitrary or unjustifiable distinctions in the levels it considers to be appropriate in different situations, if such distinctions result in discrimination or a disguised restriction on international trade."

Article 7 and Annex B of the SPS Agreement concern *transparency* obligations. WTO members must publish their SPS measures promptly and have a central inquiry

---

[10] Annex A provides a general definition of risk assessment.

point where questions on SPS regulations will be answered. If an international standard does not exist and a proposed SPS measure may have a significant impact on trade, a WTO member must publish the measure at an "early stage" and notify other members through the WTO Secretariat, thus permitting other countries to become familiar with the measure and to comment on it. Except in "urgent circumstances," a member shall provide an interval between the time a new standard is proposed and when it is enacted in order to permit foreign producers time to adapt to the measure.

Finally, the SPS Agreement is explicitly related to other Uruguay Round Agreements. For example, if a measure falls within the scope of the SPS Agreement, then it is excluded from coverage under the Agreement on Technical Barriers to Trade. More importantly, disputes over the use of SPS measures are subject to the terms of the Understanding on Dispute Settlement.

III. WTO Dispute Settlement Reports in the *Varietals* Dispute

Following unsuccessful consultations with Japan over the varietal testing requirement, the United States brought the dispute into the WTO's dispute resolution system. Like the two other SPS disputes that proceeded through the WTO's dispute resolution system, the *Varietals* panel report was appealed, and the Appellate Body (AB) issued a report. Both reports are briefly reviewed and analyzed below.

A. The Panel Report

In October 1997, the U.S. requested formation of a WTO dispute settlement panel. Given the difficult scientific and technical nature of the dispute, and the number and complexity of the legal claims asserted, the panel ruled on a wide variety of legal and factual issues. The discussion below is limited to the panel's treatment of the most important legal issues that have arisen under the SPS Agreement.

(i) Scientific Basis and Risk Assessment

As noted above, Article 2.2 of the SPS Agreement requires that SPS measures be "based on scientific principles and ... not maintained without sufficient scientific evidence;" and Article 5.1 requires that they be "based on an assessment ... of the risks to ... plant life or health, taking into account risk assessment techniques developed by the relevant international organizations." The U.S. argued that, in every instance, the quarantine treatments approved for one variety of a product had always proven to be effective for all other varieties of the same product, and that there was no scientific basis upon which to require that each separate variety of a product undergo individualized testing. Japan conceded that existing treatments for coddling moths had always been found effective for additional varieties of the same product, but argued that "all this proves is the efficacy of the treatment on *tested* varieties. . . . [T]his falls short of showing absence of varietal difference within a product altogether."[11] Japan also introduced several scientific studies where certain differences associated

---

[11] Panel report, para. 8.25.

with different varieties might, according to Japan, affect the effectiveness of fumigation.[12] On the basis of these studies, Japan argued that "characteristics of a particular variety may affect fumigation efficacy and that there is not sufficient evidence to disprove that possibility."

To determine whether Japan's varietal testing requirement was "maintained without" sufficient scientific evidence, the panel had to determine whether the measure had an "objective or rational relationship" to the scientific evidence Japan submitted. To do so, the panel relied upon expert advice received from three independent scientific experts. The experts advised the panel that "there *may* be differences between varieties of the products in dispute which *may*, in turn, be relevant for quarantine purposes, i.e., which *may* affect the efficacy of [fumigation] approved for one variety of a product if applied to another variety of the same product" and that "the question whether varietal differences, if any, are significant for quarantine purposes *cannot be determined on the basis of the evidence before the Panel*."[13] The panel characterized the experts' testimony as "unanimously [stating] that – even though in theory there may be relevant varietal differences – to date there is not sufficient evidence in support of the varietal testing requirement."[14] As a result, the panel concluded that Japan's varietal testing requirement was "maintained without sufficient scientific evidence" for purposes of Article 2.2.

(ii) Provisional Measures

Article 2.2's requirement for sufficient evidence is explicitly subject to an exception in Article 5.7, which provides:

> In cases where relevant scientific evidence is insufficient, a Member may provisionally adopt...phytosanitary measures on the basis of available pertinent information, including that from the relevant international organizations as well as from...phytosanitary measure applied by other Members. In such circumstances, Members shall seek to obtain the additional information necessary for a more objective assessment of risk and review the...phytosanitary measure accordingly within a reasonable period of time.

The panel quickly disposed of the Article 5.7 issue. Japan first imposed variety-by-variety testing in 1969, and, for the products at issue in this case, in 1978. During the twenty years in which these measures were in place, Japan had not sought to obtain additional information to form a "more objective assessment of risk," nor had Japan reviewed the varietal testing requirement within a "reasonable period of time." Thus, Japan's Article 5.7 argument was rejected, and the varietal testing

---

[12] For example, Japan introduced studies where the concentration of fumigant in a test chamber, after a certain period of time, was different for different varieties of walnuts and nectarines. Panel report, para. 8.21. Japan argued that the differences in fumigant concentration reflected differences in the ability of the fruit to absorb the fumigant, which in turn "could be an indicator of differences in the efficacy of a fumigation treatment." Id. at para. 8.22.

[13] Panel report, para. 8.33 (emphasis in original).

[14] Panel report, para. 8.34. This may not be an entirely fair characterization of the experts' testimony. Dr. Ducom, for example, stated that "... the arguments are not statistically good. Scientifically, they may be good, but in practice they may be too narrow. But the answer is really difficult."

requirement deemed to be inconsistent with Article 2.2. As a result, the panel did not consider the additional U.S. argument that Japan's measure was not based upon a risk assessment.

(iii) Measures More Trade-Restrictive Than Required

The United States also argued that the varietal testing requirement was more trade-restrictive than necessary to achieve Japan's appropriate level of phytosanitary protection. Because there was no evidence that varietal differences affected the efficacy of fumigation, the United States argued that testing by product would produce the same level of protection. The panel stated that to prevail on this argument, the United States would have to show that another measure "reasonably available" would achieve the same level of phytosanitary protection and was "significantly less restrictive to trade" than the varietal testing requirement.[15]

The panel had little difficulty determining that product-by-product testing was reasonably available and significantly less restrictive to trade. However, the question whether product-by-product testing would achieve the level of sanitary protection that Japan sought was much more troubling:

> Referring to the opinions we received from the experts advising the Panel, we consider that – to date and on the basis of the evidence before the Panel – it is not possible to state with an appropriate degree of certainty that one and the same treatment would be effective for all varieties of a product. In the view of the experts advising the Panel, there is no evidence before us which establishes a causal link between divergent quarantine efficacy and the presence of varietal differences (i.e., evidence which could justify Japan's varietal testing requirement). However, at least one of the experts advising the Panel made equally clear that the U.S. alternative of one treatment for all varieties...does not, to date, have a scientific basis either.[16]

However, the panel went on to consider whether a different form of testing, focusing on the sorption level of different varieties, might be used. This test method was suggested by the experts advising the panel. The experts testified that this method of testing would be relatively easy and inexpensive to perform, would be significantly less trade-restrictive than the VTR, and would achieve Japan's level of protection. As a result, the panel held that Japan's varietal testing requirement was more trade-restrictive then necessary, and therefore inconsistent with Article 5.6 of the SPS Agreement.

For all of these reasons,[17] the panel "recommend[ed] that the Dispute Settlement Body request Japan to bring its [varietal testing measure] into conformity with its obligations under the SPS Agreement."[18] The panel report was circulated to members in October 1998 and, the following month, Japan filed its notice of appeal with the Appellate Body.

---

[15] Panel report, para. 8.72.

[16] Panel report, para. 8.83.

[17] The panel also determined that Japan's failure to publish the varietal testing requirement violated the SPS Agreement's transparency requirements. Panel report, paras. 8.105–8.116.

[18] Panel report, para. 9.3

B. The Appellate Body Report

On appeal, Japan unsuccessfully challenged the panel's determination that the VTR was inconsistent with Article 2.2's requirement that SPS measures not be "maintained without sufficient scientific evidence." Japan argued that panels should show substantial deference to regulating authorities in this context, suggesting that Article 2.2 "be interpreted in light of the precautionary principle"[19] and that Article 2.2 only be applied where "the scientific evidence is 'patently' insufficient."[20] Relying upon its *Beef-Hormone* report, the AB noted that the precautionary principle had not been written into the SPS Agreement, and that nothing in the text or the agreement limited the application of Article 2.2 in the way Japan suggested. The AB upheld the panel's finding that Article 2.2 required "a rational or objective relationship between the SPS measure and the scientific evidence."[21] The AB explained:

> Whether there is a rational relationship between an SPS measure and the scientific evidence is to be determined on a case by case basis and will depend upon the particular circumstances of the case, including the characteristics of the measure at issue and the quality and quantity of the scientific evidence.[22]

The AB rejected the panel's determination that it need not reach the question whether Japan's measure was based upon a risk assessment. The panel's finding of inconsistency under Article 2.2 concerned only the VTR with respect to apples, cherries, nectarines and walnuts. Nevertheless, the panel found that there was insufficient evidence to conclude that the VTR was inconsistent with Article 2.2 with respect to apricots, pears, plums and quince. Hence, the AB reasoned, an inquiry into the Article 5.1 risk assessment standard was necessary. Applying the definition of risk assessment used in the *Australia-Salmon* case, the AB determined that the extensive risk assessment Japan conducted was insufficient because it failed to evaluate the likelihood of the establishment of the coddling moth in Japan under the VTR.[23]

With respect to Article 5.6, which prohibits trade measures that are more trade-restrictive than necessary to achieve a member's appropriate level of protection, the AB considered cross-appeals. Before the panel, the U.S. had argued that the VTR was more trade-restrictive than necessary, as "product-by-product" testing would achieve Japan's desired level of protection. The panel had determined that there was insufficient evidence that testing by product would achieve this level of protection. Interpreting the U.S. argument as, in effect, a challenge to the panel's consideration and weighing of the evidence before it, the AB rejected the U.S. argument as outside the scope of appellate review.[24]

On the other hand, the panel had found that testing of "sorption levels" would be a less-trade-restrictive measure that would meet Japan's level of protection, and therefore found against Japan on the United States's Article 5.6 claim. Japan challenged this finding on the grounds that the experts – rather than the United States – had

---

[19] AB report, para. 81.
[20] AB report, para. 82.
[21] AB report, para. 84.
[22] AB report, para. 84.
[23] AB report, para. 113.
[24] AB report, para. 98.

suggested testing by sorption levels, and that "panels cannot find facts neither argued nor proven by the parties."[25] Doing so, Japan argued, would improperly allow a party to discharge its burden of proof through evidence and information introduced by the experts, not the party.

The AB agreed. While affirming the panel's authority to engage experts, the AB asserted that expert testimony is to be used "to help [the panel] understand and evaluate the evidence submitted and the arguments made by the parties, but not to make the case for a complaining party."[26] The AB criticized the panel for using the experts' testimony "as *the* basis" for finding the VTR to be inconsistent with Article 5.6, and concluded that the U.S. had not discharged its burden of establishing a *prima facie* case of inconsistency with Article 5.6.[27]

Finally, the AB had little difficulty rejecting Japan's challenge to the panel's finding that the VTR did not fall within the scope of Article 5.7's "exception" for provisional measures where relevant scientific information is insufficient. The AB agreed with the panel that Japan had not sought to obtain additional information, as required by Article 5.7. Moreover, Japan had not reviewed the VTR within "a reasonable period of time," as required by Article 5.7. The AB explained that "what constitutes a reasonable period of time has to be established on a case-by-case basis and depends on the specific circumstances of the case, including the difficulty of obtaining the additional information necessary for the review and the characteristics of the provisional SPS measures."[28] The AB likewise had little difficulty concluding that the panel correctly determined that Japan's failure to publish the VTR was inconsistent with Article 7's transparency requirements.

The *Varietals* dispute raises a number of factual and doctrinal puzzles. Astonishingly – given the relatively high economic and political stakes – this case was tried with virtually no evidence. Why did Japan have *no* evidence demonstrating that fumigation techniques effective on one variety would not necessarily be effective on other varieties of the same fruit? Why did the U.S. present *no* evidence demonstrating that fumigation techniques effective on one variety are effective on all other varieties of the same fruit? These failures are even more puzzling given that, according to the experts, such evidence was relatively easy to generate.[29] How is a panel to rule on this record? And how can it be that – although the undisputed evidence demonstrated that there were alternative, effective, less-trade-restrictive measures available through which Japan could achieve its desired level of phytosanitary protection – the United States lost on its argument that there were alternative, effective, less-trade-restrictive measures available?

Behind these case-specific puzzles, a number of broader systemic issues lurk. Although I cannot explore all of these issues in this chapter, I will instead outline a few of the ways that the *Varietals* dispute can shed light on three of the most

---

[25] AB report, para. 120.
[26] AB report, para. 129.
[27] AB report, para. 130 (emphasis added).
[28] AB report, para. 93.
[29] Panel report, para. 8.41.

important political and conceptual issues surrounding the WTO, in particular: (1) the purposes and goals of the SPS Agreement – and the trade regime – following the Uruguay Round, (2) the extent to which the WTO undermines the autonomy and authority of states to enact legislation on "social" issues (such as food safety, health, the environment, etc.) and (3) the appropriate role of panels (and the AB) in resolving disputes that go beyond the bounds of traditional trade law and involve trade and other important social policies (the so-called "trade and" issues).

IV. The *Varietals* Dispute, SPS Measures and the Transformation of the Trade Regime

Why did states create the international trade regime? Today, the most common answer to this question is the economic one. As summarized by Professor John Jackson, "[t]he objective [of the GATT/WTO system] is to liberalize trade that crosses national boundaries, and to pursue the benefits described in economic theory as 'comparative advantage.'"[30] The economic concept of comparative advantage teaches that, absent trade barriers, each state will specialize in the production and export of goods and services that it can produce relatively more efficiently than other nations. This specialization, in turn, increases the efficiency of international production and results in increased trade and greater aggregate welfare. All of this can best occur through open, competitive markets that accurately price goods and services, enabling the producers in each country to discover what they are comparatively good in producing.

Under this theory trade restrictions are inefficient intrusions into otherwise autonomously functioning markets, and tend to divert resources from their most highly valued uses. In particular, tariffs and other barriers transfer wealth from consumers to firms and workers in protected industries. In addition, trade barriers create "deadweight losses" – reductions in the welfare of one group that are not transferred to any other group or groups – and hence a net loss of global economic welfare. By disciplining the use of trade restrictions, the trade regime reduces these inefficiencies and permits markets to operate without state interference, promoting global economic wealth.

The SPS Agreement would appear to fit easily within this conventional model. To the extent the agreement provides a vehicle for challenging food "safety" measures that are, in fact, simply disguised protectionism, the agreement can help eliminate barriers to trade and hence enlarge aggregate welfare. However, in the trade world, things are not always as they appear.[31]

As a general matter, the *Varietals* dispute (and other SPS disputes) problematizes this conventional understanding of the trade system. Under the conventional

---

[30] John H. Jackson, World Trade Rules and Environmental Policies: Congruence or Conflict?, 49 *Washington & Lee Law Review* 1227, 1231 (1992). See also Robert E. Hudec, GATT Legal Restraints on the Use of Trade Measures Against Foreign Environmental Practices in 2 *Fair Trade and Harmonization* (Jagdish Bhagwati & Robert E. Hudec, eds., 1996) 95, 108 ("The GATT's economic goal is to promote, through liberal international trade policies, the greater effectiveness of national economies") [hereinafter Bhagwati & Hudec].

[31] Jeffrey L. Dunoff, "Trade and": Recent Developments in Trade Policy and Scholarship – and Their Surprising Political Implications, 17 *Northwestern Journal of International Law and Business* 759 (1996–97).

economic account, both the importing and the exporting state increase their social welfare when they reduce or eliminate tariffs and other barriers to trade. Unlike tariffs, an SPS measure may *enhance* social welfare in the importing country if the expected gains associated with reducing the risk and cost of a pest infestation, for example, exceed the expected loss to consumers resulting from their reduced ability to purchase foreign products. Hence, the economic model's prescription – eliminate barriers – may disserve the efficiency model's aim: increase aggregate welfare.

More specifically, it would appear that the SPS Agreement is designed to address two different types of inefficiencies. First, it appears to address the problem of disguised protectionism by requiring either the use of international standards or the use of "science" through risk assessment. Second, it appears to address the inefficiencies caused by the sheer multiplicity of national SPS standards by encouraging the use of international standards. However, once again, appearances may deceive, for there appears to be little evidence that SPS disciplines achieve either of these goals.

First, as discussed more fully below, there is little evidence that the SPS Agreement has led to an increased use of international standards. Thus, the agreement's expected result – a trend toward international harmonization of SPS measures through greater use of international standards – has not occurred. Paradoxically, the SPS Agreement may instead *decrease* the likelihood that SPS standards will be harmonized in the future. The granting of enhanced legal standing to what had previously been understood as entirely voluntary standards, the SPS Agreement will likely inhibit the future development of international standards in the food safety area. Indeed, it seems clear that the SPS Agreement had led to a greater politicalization – and reduced output – of international standard-setting activities. For example, the limited evidence available suggests that in recent years – and particularly during the first three Codex Commission sessions held after the SPS Agreement was concluded (1995, 1997 and 1999) – Codex's "work has been increasingly mired in controversy because it is now viewed as more relevant."[32] More importantly, the question of whether or not the use of international standards in the SPS context would reduce the number and/or severity of protectionist measures calls for an inquiry into these international standards. If the fear is that domestic agricultural interests can capture domestic regulatory mechanisms and produce protectionist legislation, then trade scholars should explore whether international standard-setting agencies, including particularly Codex, the IPPC and the International Office of Epizootics, are more or less subject to industry capture.

As a general theoretical matter, it is not immediately apparent whether we should expect higher or lower levels of regulatory capture at the international level.[33] However, there are reasons to be concerned that rent-seeking interests may be more likely to achieve success at the international plane. International standard-setting bodies like Codex typically provide less opportunity for public input and are less transparent than standard-setting bodies in the U.S. and at least some other states.[34]

---

[32] David Victor, The Sanitary and Phytosanitary Agreement of the World Trade Organization: An Assessment After Five Years, 32 *New York University Journal of International Law and Politics* 865, 892 (2000).

[33] For an extremely provocative discussion of this issue, see Paul B. Stephan, Accountability and International Lawmaking: Rules, Rents and Legitimacy, 17 *Northwestern Journal of International Law and Business* 681 (1996–97).

[34] See, e.g., Dueling Risk Assessments: Why the WTO and Codex Threaten U.S. Food Standards, 30 *Environmental Law* 387 (Spring 2000) (text at notes 133–35).

Lotus Eaters

For example, trade groups like the International Dairy Federation, the International Council of Grocery Manufacturers Associations, and individual corporations such as Monsanto, Kraft, General Foods, Coca-Cola and others frequently attend Codex meetings as part of the U.S. delegation. A 1993 study revealed that over 80 percent of the NGO participants on national delegations in Codex committees represented industry; in contrast, approximately 1 percent represented public interest organizations.[35]

This empirical data about participation at the international plane should not surprise. Citizens often remain "rationally ignorant" of domestic regulatory procedures; most citizens face far higher monitoring costs on the international plane than on the domestic. On the other hand, producer groups have an even greater incentive to try to "capture" an international process, such as Codex or IPPC, than they do to capture a domestic process. If an interest group can successfully obtain an international standard that disadvantages competitors, the advantages accrue on a global rather than a domestic scale. Hence, special interest groups might rationally invest more resources in efforts to capture international processes than domestic ones.[36] Moreover, many of the SPS Agreement's "checks" against enactment of domestic protectionist legislation domestically – requiring the use of science and risk assessment, that measures be no more trade restrictive than necessary, and consistency across different measures addressing similar risks, etc. – are not applied to international standards.

These concerns are not intended to serve as a proof that the level of protectionist rent seeking associated with international standards is appreciably greater than that associated with domestic lawmaking. My more limited argument is simply to suggest that there are ample theoretical grounds for concern. Moreover, while I am not aware of any full-blown empirical study of this issue, there are suggestions in the literature that international bodies, such as Codex, are subject to precisely this type of capture. David Victor, for example, has identified several "suspicious examples" of Codex standards that appear to reflect the interests of well-organized, agricultural interests, rather than the broader public interest:

> The standards for bee honey effectively barred many non-European honeys from the European market although there was little basis for doing so on grounds of food safety alone. The worldwide standard for natural mineral water, adopted in 1997, requires that natural mineral waters be bottled at the source, which favors European producers who have long done so under European law, and prohibits the use of antimicrobial agents that could make water safer. It penalizes American, Japanese, and other producers, many of whom truck or pipe their water prior to bottling and allow

---

[35] Accountable Governance in the Era of Globalization: The WTO, NAFTA, and International Harmonization of Standards, 50 *University of Kansas Law Review* 823 (2002); Dueling Risk Assessments, supra; International Trade Agreements, Regulatory Protection, and Public Accountability, 54 *Administrative Law Review* 435 (2002).

[36] See, e.g., John O. McGinnis & Mark L. Movesian, The World Trade Constitution, 114 *Harvard Law Review* 512, 556–558 (2000) (arguing that, while the WTO is a tool against rent-seeking interests, international regulatory agencies "would be particularly prone to capture by protectionist interest groups"); Peter J. Spiro, New Global Potentates: Nongovernmental Organizations and the "Unregulated" Marketplace, 18 *Cardozo Law Review* 957, 958 (1996) (noting that as "power seeps upwards [to international organizations], so too does the attention of interest groups").

166   Jeffrey L. Dunoff

(even require) anti-microbial treatments; yet there is not much justification in terms of food safety for the requirement. Piping and trucking do not intrinsically yield dirty water.[37]

In short, it is not apparent, as either a theoretical or an empirical matter, that the use of international standards is an effective tool for reducing the incidence or the effect of protectionist measures in the SPS area.

Of course, states need not use international standards and, in any event, they are frequently unavailable. In these cases, the SPS Agreement requires that SPS measures be "based on" scientific principles and "not [be] maintained without sufficient scientific evidence." Such measures must also be "based on" risk assessment methods and must be undertaken pursuant to certain risk management objectives and constraints. Hence, "science" is the key that distinguishes between those SPS measures consistent with the agreement and those in violation of the agreement. Presumably, this emphasis on "science" was attractive to trade negotiators because it purports to be a form of universal knowledge, valid across state lines, and objective in its conclusions and prescriptions. Risk assessment is similarly understood as a rational and testable methodology.

However, it is not clear that the SPS Agreement's reliance upon science in general, and risk assessment in particular, will lead to a reduction in protectionist measures. The agreement focuses upon "science," but curiously leaves this key term almost entirely undefined. However, science is not simply an objective, unbiased search for truth; "[s]ociologists of science describe science in a variety of ways: as a community, as a dialogue and as a consensus...."[38] Moreover, science does not possess a timeless or universal quality. Instead, as Jeffery Atik argues, there is "a geography of science":

> What is true and certain within one scientific community constitutes baseless conjecture in another. Science is also intrinsically historical; it is science-of-the-moment. Even relatively recent scientific belief can appear absurd when exposed to contemporary light. Early 20th century primatology reveals more about the ape-watchers than about the apes.[39]

As the beef-hormone and mad cow disputes sharply illustrate, different national scientific communities will often generate different views on the same scientific question. This observation is not offered to question the credibility or integrity of scientists, but rather to underscore the social and contingent aspects of science. Hence, the turn to science may not eliminate the cultural differences that different societies may have toward risk, but rather transfer these differences to a different stage in the decision-making process.

The focus upon science may tend to differentiate, rather than harmonize, states in yet another way. The ability to generate measures consistent with the SPS Agreement – and the ability to challenge SPS measures – require scientific capabilities and resources that are far from evenly distributed among states.[40] To the contrary,

---

[37] Victor, supra note 32, at 887–88.

[38] Jeffery Atik, Science and International Regulatory Convergence, 17 *Northwestern Journal of International Law and Business* 736, 749 (1996–97).

[39] Atik, supra, at 738.

[40] David P. Fidler, Trade and Health: The Global Spread of Infectious Diseases and International Trade, 40 *Germany Year Book of International Law* 300, 324 (1997).

Lotus Eaters 167

and not coincidentally, the "centers of scientific knowledge" – including the United States, Europe and Japan – "correspond . . . to the major players in the world trading system."[41] As a result, substantial attention has recently been devoted to enhancing developing country participation in the setting of international standards. At the Doha Ministerial, the WTO, FAO, WHO, OIE and the World Bank issued a joint statement committing themselves to help developing countries participate more fully in setting international SPS measures. The statement provided that

> We are committed to strengthen the capacity of developing countries to establish and implement science-based sanitary and phytosanitary measures, to meet the sanitary and phytosanitary requirements of trade partners and to participate fully in the work of standard-setting organizations in the establishment of international standards, guidelines and recommendations. To this end, the FAO, OIE, WHO, WTO, the World Bank and other multilateral, regional and bilateral agencies undertake technical assistance activities and investment in infrastructure, to assist developing countries in the establishment and implementation of appropriate food safety and animal and plant health measures.[42]

In September 2002, the World Bank and the WTO announced the creation of a new fund, the Standards and Trade Development Facility, to provide grants and financial support for technical assistance projects in developing countries through enhanced collaboration between the international organizations involved. Whether this facility, initially funded in the amount of $300,000, will help developing states participate more fully in international standard-setting exercises remains to be seen.

The justifications for requiring that SPS measures be based upon risk assessments is presumably similar to that requiring the use of science more generally; use of this scientific technique would help ensure that SPS measures are responsive to real, identifiable risks, and not simply mechanisms to protect uncompetitive domestic agricultural interests, or unjustified responses to "unreasonable" public concerns. A focus on risk seems to make food safety problems more tractable, because it renders problems into probabilistic and measurable terms.

Once again, however, the SPS Agreement's provisions may not be well designed to achieve the agreement's goals. Although a thorough evaluation of risk assessment is well beyond the scope of this chapter,[43] it is worth noting just a few of the problems associated with risk assessment.[44] First, there are a number of technical problems that limit the value of risk assessments. For example, "the various scientific disciplines involved in assessing risk are not sufficiently developed either to explain the mechanisms by which particular causes produce particular effects or to

---

[41] Atik, supra, at 749.

[42] A Joint Statement by the Directors-General of the Food and Agriculture Organization of the United Nations, the Office International des Epizooties, the World Health Organization, the World Trade Organization and the President of the World Bank, Participation of Developing Countries in the Development and Application of International Standards, Guidelines and Recommendations on Food Safety, Animal and Plant Health, available at http://www.wto.org/english/news_e/pres01_e/pr254_e.htm.

[43] The literature on quantitative risk assessment is enormous. For general discussion, see National Research Council, Science and Judgment in Risk Assessment (1994).

[44] For thoughtful critiques, see John S. Applegate, A Beginning and Not an End in Itself: The Role of Risk Assessment in Environmental Decision-Making, 63 *University of Cincinnati Law Review* 1643 (1995); Lee Clarke, Politics and Bias in Risk Assessment, 25 *Social Science Journal* 155, 159–60 (1988).

provide good quantitative estimates of cause-and-effect relationships."[45] Thus, in the human health field, there are often significant uncertainties associated with hazard identification, dose-response assessment and exposure assessments.

In addition to these conceptual difficulties, risk assessment is often limited by insufficient data. For example, even in the U.S., with its relatively sophisticated approach to risk assessment, the EPA has conceded that it is virtually impossible to perform any rigorous, quantitative assessments of risks other than cancer:

> While the agency attempted to provide rough qualitative rankings of cancer and non-cancer health effects, ecological risks and risks of economic damage, it found that data were simply inadequate to perform rigorous risk assessments of most existing problems and that even rough rank-orderings were virtually impossible for new activities such as biotechnology and new toxic chemicals. The study found serious conceptual difficulties in comparing risks that are fundamentally different in character (for example, comparing ecological risks to cancer risks and comparing risks of damage to developmental, immunological, reproductive, or respiratory systems). It also concluded that environmental exposure data were surprisingly poor.[46]

Given these gaps in data and understanding, regulators necessarily build a series of assumptions into their interpretations of the data, and the "models" that they use to analyze the data. Thus, risk assessment uses not only seemingly objective measurements of, for example, toxicity and exposure, "but also, less visibly, ... underlying models of causality, agency and uncertainty."[47] Hence, risk assessment is necessarily partial and selective in its treatment of causes. For example, many socioeconomic factors that tend to concentrate risk from diverse sources for minority and poor populations are often ignored in risk assessment.

Risk assessment also assumes that it is possible to capture levels of uncertainty in objective and understandable forms, but cross-cultural study of risk challenges this claim. The evidence demonstrates that even when societies use risk assessment and quantitative analysis

> they differ in how they classify and measure natural phenomena, which techniques they label as objective or reliable, how they characterize uncertainty, and what resources they apply to its reduction. Far from being a natural statement about the unknown, uncertainty about risk thus appears as the product of culturally situated forms of activity. It is a collectively endorsed recognition that there are things about our condition that we do not know; but such an admission is only possible because there are agreed-upon mechanisms for finding out more.[48]

Thus, in many different ways, the selection of models and assumptions that are the foundation of risk assessment is subject to the sorts of cultural assumptions and political pressures that the emphasis on "science" and "risk assessment" were supposed to keep out of (at least this part of) the regulatory process.

---

[45] Quoted in Percival at 483.

[46] EPA official statement.

[47] Sheila Jasanoff, Technological Risk and Cultures of Rationality, in Incorporating Science, Economics and Sociology in *Developing Sanitary and Phytosanitary Standards in International Trade* 65, 79 (2000).

[48] Id. at 80.

Lotus Eaters

Finally, it is far from clear that the SPS Agreement's other key obligation – that WTO members "avoid arbitrary or unjustifiable distinctions in the levels of protections it considers to be appropriate in different situations, if such distinctions result in discrimination or a disguised restriction on international trade" – is an effective strategy to reduce protectionist barriers to trade. This is well illustrated by the *Australia-Salmon* dispute. In that action, Canada challenged Australia's prohibitions on the import of fresh, chilled or frozen salmon. Australia argued that this ban was necessary to prevent the introduction of certain fish pathogens. Canada argued that Australia permitted the importation of other fish and fish products that could potentially introduce the same pathogens, and hence that Australia maintained inconsistent levels of protection. The Appellate Body agreed that, as Australia imposed more severe trade restrictions on products that posed a lesser threat and less severe trade restrictions on products that imposed a greater threat, it had imposed an arbitrary or unjustifiable distinction in its levels of SPS protection.

Eventually, Australia changed its regulatory regime. In part, Australia relaxed its absolute ban on the importation of Canadian salmon. However, Australia also imposed *new* trade restrictions on the other products at issue in this dispute. Thus, to come into compliance with the SPS Agreement's "consistency" requirement, Australia reduced barriers to trade in some products (salmon) and *increased* barriers to trade in other products (baitfish and ornamental fish). A WTO panel deemed these regulatory changes to be consistent with the AB's recommendation that Australia bring its measures into conformity with the SPS Agreement. Of course, if the original trade restriction was an impermissible restriction on trade, "it is difficult to imagine how the imposition of restrictions on other products (for sake of consistency) lessens this conclusion."[49] Second, it is hard to understand how the new trade barriers are justified, when they are imposed solely in effort to satisfy the agreement's consistency requirement. In other words, the agreement's consistency requirement appears to be as likely to lead to new and additional trade restrictions as it is to reduce barriers to trade.

Curiously, we are left with an agreement that seeks to reduce protectionist barriers to agricultural trade by (1) encouraging use of international standards; (2) requiring the use of "science" and "risk assessment"; and (3) requiring internal consistency across SPS measures in certain instances. However, as the discussion above suggests, it is far from clear that any of these strategies for liberalizing agricultural trade will help achieve the Agreement's goals in any systematic manner.

The economic model reviewed above is not the only explanation of why we have a trade regime. A very different model – the "embedded liberalism" model – purports to explain the international trading system as resting upon political, rather than economic, calculations.[50] Under this understanding, the GATT's drafters sought to create a multilateral, nondiscriminatory trade system. However, they were not doctrinaire

---

[49] Jeffery Atik, The Weakest Link – Demonstrating the Inconsistency of "Appropriate Levels of Protection" in Australia-Salmon (unpublished draft, on file with author).

[50] This model has been most fully explicated in the writings of John Ruggie. See generally, John Gerard Ruggie, Embedded Liberalism Revisited: Institutions and Progress in International Economic Relations, in *Progress in Postwar Economic Relations* (Emanuel Adler and Beverly Crawford, eds., 1991); John Gerard Ruggie, International Regimes, Transactions and Change: Embedded Liberalism in the Postwar Economic Order, 36 *International Organization* 379 (1982) [hereinafter Ruggie, *Embedded Liberalism*].

free traders.[51] Rather, they recognized and were responsive to the widespread public rejection of 19th century laissez-faire capitalism, and the corresponding demand for state intervention in domestic economies to protect against the dislocations associated with market economies.[52]

The embedded liberalism model understands the GATT as incorporating a series of complex compromises designed to achieve these varied ends. Thus, while the agreement was designed to lower tariffs and other trade barriers, it also includes a diverse set of exceptions and exemptions designed to protect a variety of domestic social policies.[53] For example, although quantitative restrictions were generally prohibited, they were expressly permitted for balance of payments difficulties, "explicitly including payments difficulties that resulted from domestic policies designed to secure full employment."[54] Through a series of compromises such as this, the GATT was structured in a manner that sought gains from trade, but simultaneously "promised to minimize socially disruptive adjustment costs as well as any national economic and political vulnerabilities" resulting from international specialization.[55] In short, in exchange for liberal trade policies, industrialized nations provided a variety of domestic safety nets, including unemployment compensation, severance payments and adjustment assistance.[56] Thus, "[t]he social welfare state has been the flip side of the open economy."[57]

Once again, at first glance the SPS Agreement appears to fit comfortably within the embedded liberalism model. The agreement explicitly affirms each state's ability to pick and choose its own levels of SPS protection. This seems consistent with the embedded liberalism model's emphasis that the trade regime preserve the ability of states to enact social measures as they see fit, without interference by the trade system. Again, appearances may be deceiving. The SPS Agreement can be more plausibly read as signaling the transformation of the trade regime away from the embedded liberalism compromise.

Risk is ubiquitous in our modern, technological society. It is little exaggeration to suggest that one of government's primary responsibilities is the assessment and

---

[51] As a former State Department trade policy analyst stated: "No one was committed to 'free trade'; no one expected anything like it; the term does not appear in the GATT, which simply calls for a process of liberalization with no stated objective." William Diebold, Jr., From the ITO to GATT – And Back? in *The Bretton Woods–GATT System: Retrospect and Prospect After Fifty Years* 152, 158 (Orin Kirshner, ed., 1996). See also Jacob Viner, Conflicts of Principle in Drafting a Trade Charter, 25 *Foreign Affairs* 612, 613 (1947) ("There are few free traders in the present-day world, no one pays any attention to their views, and no person in authority anywhere advocated free trade.").

[52] A contemporaneous account by the lead U.S. negotiator at the time states: "There is no hope that a multilateral trading system can be maintained in the face of widespread and protracted unemployment. Where the objectives of domestic stability and international freedom come into conflict, the former will be given priority. . . . It would be futile to insist that stability must always give way to freedom. The best that can be hoped for is a workable compromise." Claire Wilcox, *A Charter for World Trade* 131 (1949).

[53] Ruggie, *Embedded Liberalism, supra* note 50, at 396.

[54] Id. at 397.

[55] Ruggie, *Embedded Liberalism, supra* note 50, at 399.

[56] Empirical studies confirm that the nations most open to international trade generally have the highest rates of social spending. See generally Peter J. Katzenstein, *Small States in World Markets: Industrial Policy in Europe* (1985); Dani Rodrik, *Has Globalization Gone Too Far?* (1997).

[57] Dani Rodrik, Sense and Nonsense in the Globalization Debate, 107 *Foreign Policy* 19 (summer 1997).

management of risk,[58] or that problems of risk assessment and risk management have nowhere been so publicized and contentious over the last decade as in the areas of food safety. For example, chemical hazards in food-related products have been the source of several limited, but highly publicized, health crises in the last several years, such as the contamination of animal feed by dioxin in Belgium that affected food products throughout Europe. Increasingly, these type of disputes have significant trade implications. For example, during the scare over "mad cow disease" associated with British beef, France, Belgium, Germany, the Netherlands, Portugal and Sweden placed temporary bans on the import of British beef. France refused to lift its ban after the EU had declared British beef "safe," leading to proceedings at the European Court of Justice that eventually declared the French ban to be illegal. The "mad cow disease" crisis dominated EU politics for many months, and constituted what the European Commissioner for Agriculture characterized as "the biggest crisis the European Union ever had."

More recently, similar issues have arisen in the context of the regulation of genetically modified organisms (GMOs). Europeans, led by the European Commission, have adopted a significantly more rigorous approach to the regulation of GMOs than the United States, leading to U.S. complaints that the European regulations are protectionist. The international trade implications of these diverse regulatory approaches have been evident since 1996, when U.S. farmers began to export genetically modified soybeans and corn to Europe. Disputes over different approaches to the risks posed by GMOs have been extremely politicized and contentious, and it is quite possible that a dispute over GMOs will find its way into WTO dispute resolution.[59]

More recently, the U.S. and Japan have had several food-safety-related conflicts. In January 2002, Japan banned U.S. poultry imports for ninety days, in response to an outbreak of low-pathogenic avian influenza in Pennsylvania and Maine chicken farms. The United States argued that the ban was unnecessary, because the Office of International Epizootics (OIE) does not consider low-pathogenic avian influenza to be a reportable disease, meaning that countries are not required to report outbreaks of it under OIE standards. Japan lifted the ban in February. More recently, Japan banned poultry imports from Virginia for ninety days because of an outbreak of the virus in that state in late July. U.S. Department of Agriculture scientists are conducting research on the low-pathogenic virus, under the auspices of the OIE, to determine whether Japan's ninety-day bans are justified responses to the influenza outbreaks. For example, the OIE only recommends a twenty-one-day ban in the case of high-pathogenic avian influenza. Finally, the United States successfully requested formation of a WTO panel to hear its complaint about Japan's restrictions on apple imports intended to prevent the spread of fire blight. The United States argues that

---

[58] This is not only true in areas like food safety and environmental regulations. We might also understand the war on terrorism, for example, to also be in large part an exercise in risk assessment and risk management. How likely is Iraq to obtain and use weapons of mass destruction against the United States or its allies? How much security is necessary at airports and public spaces to avoid terrorist attacks? What are the risks and benefits of distributing vaccines against potential chemical and biological agents?

[59] For a thoughtful analysis of the doctrinal issues, see Robert Howse & Petros C. Mavroidis, Europe's Evolving Regulatory Strategy for GMOs – The Issue of Consistency with WTO Law: Of Kine and Brine, 24 *Fordham International Law Journal* 317 (2000).

the restrictions do not have the scientific basis required in the WTO's Agreement on the Application of Sanitary and Phytosanitary Measures.

Given different national perceptions of risk, and the highly polarized disputes associated with these different perceptions, under the embedded liberalism model one might expect special deference to domestic sensitivities in the food safety area. Conventional readings of the SPS Agreement suggest that it grants WTO members wide latitude to adopt international standards (where they exist) or to choose their own standards, so long as they do so on the basis of a risk assessment.[60]

However, we can also understand the SPS Agreement as giving states a quite different – and far more constrained – choice as they enact SPS standards. States can use internationally mandated standards, where they exist. If they don't exist – or if they exist but states elect not to use them – then states must follow an internationally mandated process when generating their own standards. That is, states can choose between international *substantive* standards, or international *process* standards. However, both forms of harmonization are deeply problematic from the perspective of the embedded liberalism model.[61]

Substantive harmonization obviously limits severely each state's autonomy to set its own standards, but in some ways the SPS Agreement's procedural requirements are even more offensive to the embedded liberalism model's sensibilities. SPS measures must be based upon scientific principles, must be based upon a risk assessment, etc. In other words, the SPS takes *one* highly particular and value-laden set of ideas regarding how to quantify and assess risk and transforms this into *the* approach to risk, universally valid across different regimes, necessarily employed across a range of safety issues regardless of a state's changed or changing economic and social circumstances, or changing public values. It would be difficult to think up an approach that is more at odds with the fundamental premises of the embedded liberalism compromise.

We are left with a puzzle. How can it be that SPS Agreement so significantly disserves the trade regime's purposes? Why do the agreement's terms fit so poorly with the goals of trade system, whether understood under the economic or the embedded liberalism model?

Perhaps I have misread the SPS Agreement. Or perhaps the economic model and the embedded liberalism model are no longer adequate explanations of the trade system. Perhaps scholars should be asking whether the new trade system serves some other purposes. However, what would these new goals be? A full answer is not possible here, but let me simply outline one suggestion. Focus for a moment on the cluster of "new" issues – including SPS measures, trade in services, intellectual property

---

[60] See, e.g., David Victor, The Sanitary and Phytosanitary Agreement of the World Trade Organization: An Assessment After Five Years, 32 *New York University Journal of International Law and Politics* 865 (2000).

[61] Harmonization is also problematic under an economic perspective. SPS measures vary widely both within and across states, because preferences and circumstances vary widely. Some states seek stringent levels of protection, whereas others readily consume riskier – and cheaper – foods. Some environments are particularly vulnerable to infestation of certain pests and hence require quarantines and other stringent measures, while other states are already infested with pests. An economic perspective would suggest that it might be difficult and counterproductive to attempt to impose uniform international standards in the face of such varied preferences and situations.

and investment – that were central to the American negotiating agenda during the Uruguay Round. Although the "new issues" are *not* identical – obviously negotiations on telecommunications or financial services differ from intellectual property rights – they do have one common or generic characteristic. Each involves not simply the move from the original GATT's focus on border barriers to behind the border barriers; in addition "trade" disciplines in each of these new areas are really about the (potential) *restructuring of the domestic regulatory and legal systems embedded in the institutional infrastructure of the economy.* The degree of intrusiveness into domestic sovereignty that this restructuring entails bears little resemblance to the shallow integration of the GATT with its focus on border barriers and its buffers to safeguard domestic policy space. It is not simply that the new WTO marks a shift from the old GATT model of *negative* regulation – what governments must not do – to *positive* regulation – or what governments must do, although this is significant enough. More dramatically, it is that – at least in the SPS context – the WTO threatens to become a re-maker of internal regulatory systems. That is, the WTO agreements require major upgrading of the institutional infrastructure in many states, including governance structures, administrative regimes, regulatory systems, legal systems, etc.[62] If this argument is descriptively accurate – and for these purposes I only advance this as a thesis worthy of serious consideration – then these new issues signal a truly radical transformation of the trading system.

V. The WTO as Straightjacket and Sin of Synecdoche

The *Varietals* dispute is a particular instantiation of the much larger debate over the reach of international trade disciplines into traditional areas of domestic regulatory authority or, more broadly, over globalization. Many international relations theorists, legal scholars and activists argue that increased international flows of money, goods, technology, people and ideas are eroding state power. More particularly, as international trade law has shifted from a focus on trade distorting policies implemented, for the most part, at the border – such as tariffs, quotas, export subsidies and the like – to a focus on "behind-the-border" barriers that touch on legitimate core interests of states – such as environmental protection and consumer safety – critics claim that the international trade system inappropriately limits government's discretion to enact and enforce desirable social legislation. As a conceptual matter, these criticisms have coalesced around the "trade and environment" debate; as a political matter, these criticisms helped fuel the street protests in Seattle and at other international economic meetings.

In the particular field of food safety and the SPS Agreement, the "straightjacket" argument cuts in two different directions. First, developing states feared that they might be forced to adopt stricter standards then they would otherwise choose. Doing so would force these states to expend resources on SPS protection that they could have (and would have preferred to) devote to other important social goals, such as

---

[62] This paragraph builds on an argument made by Sylvia Ostry. See, e.g., Sylvia Ostry, The Uruguay Round North-South Grand Bargain: Implications for Future Negotiations, in Daniel L. M. Kennedy & James Southwick (eds.), *The Political Economy of International Trade Law: Essays in Honor of Robert E. Hudec* (2001), at 285; Sylvia Ostry, [Temple paper].

economic development. These arguments about "upward harmonization" received less attention than the reverse argument about "downward harmonization." This latter argument was most often advanced by NGOs and others in developed states where SPS measures are generally higher, and where most of the NGOs who focus on food safety are located. The argument here is that SPS disciplines would allow (and encourage) other countries to question U.S. national environmental standards in the name of free trade.[63] For example, the Delaney Clause to U.S. food and drug laws[64] prohibits the marketing (and hence the import) of any food product containing any additive that has been shown to cause cancer in laboratory tests on animals. Despite the Delaney Clause's scientific linkage between animal carcinogenesis and suspicion of human carcinogenesis, some consumer and environmental advocates feared that its blanket prohibition could be attacked as scientifically unjustified, so they sounded an alarm that the SPS trade rules threaten U.S. food safety. Indeed, the "downward harmonization" argument has greater political salience and seems potentially more valid, as each of the three SPS disputes proceeded to panels and the Appellate Body has involved national SPS measures that were stronger than the relevant international standards. The argument presented in Part IV tends to support those who fear that the WTO can act as a straightjacket.

The question I wish to consider here is how we should determine whether the "WTO as straightjacket" argument is correct. What method should we apply? What counts as evidence for or against the argument? For present purposes, note the *structure* of the argument presented above, rather than its details. The form of the argument is fairly straightforward application of conventional tools of legal scholarship, including close textual readings, case-law analysis, examination of whether particular provisions of a text support the text's larger goals, and similar rhetorical moves common to legal scholarship. Thus, in form and approach (if not necessarily in conclusion), the argument above is quite similar to much of the legal scholarship addressing the "WTO as straightjacket" debate.

However, the trade regime consists of much more than a series of legal texts and panel reports. The WTO includes a Ministerial Conference, which meets at least once every two years, a General Council and Goods, Services and Intellectual Property Councils. In addition, it includes specialized committees, working groups and working parties that address individual WTO agreements and specialized topics, such as the environment and development, as well as a Secretariat with a staff of approximately 500 people. Much of the WTO's activity occurs in these bodies, yet they receive little attention in legal scholarship.

More particularly, much of the WTO's SPS-related work occurs in the SPS Committee, yet this work receives little attention from legal scholars. For example, since the SPS Agreement came into force in 1995, over one hundred specific trade concerns have been raised in the SPS Committee, ranging from restrictions on imports of hard cheeses made from non-pasteurized milk to labeling requirements on shelled eggs and the shelf life requirements for canned food products.[65] The Tanzania-EC

---

[63] See, e.g., Bruce Silverglade, The Impact of International Trade Agreements on U.S. Food Safety and Labeling Standards, 53 *Food and Drug Law Journal* 537 (1998).

[64] 21 U.S.C. §348(c)(3)(A).

[65] WHO & WTO Secretariats, WTO Agreements and Public Health 65 (2002).

fish issue provides a good illustration of how many of these issues are addressed. In early 1998, Tanzania complained to the SPS Committee that the EC was blocking fish imports from certain African states. The EC responded that it banned imports of fruit, vegetables and fish in response to a cholera outbreak in Tanzania, Kenya, Uganda and Mozambique. In June 1998, Tanzania again raised the issue, arguing that tests had not found the relevant bacteria in fresh, frozen or processed fishery products from the four states, and that the ban was having a severe effect on its economy. A WHO official stated to the SPS Committee that there was no proven risk of cholera transmission from the foods in question, and, the following month, the EC eventually agreed to resume trade in these items. Moreover, of course, the number of safety concerns are not limited to those formally discussed in the SPS Committee, as "[m]any concerns regarding food safety measures are solved bilaterally before they come to the WTO, or around the edges of the SPS Committee meetings without actually having been raised at the meeting itself."[66] Although these sorts of disputes greatly outnumber the SPS disputes that go to the WTO's formal dispute resolution process, they remain largely outside the ken of legal scholarship.

Finally and most importantly, the WTO consists of some 144 members, who are the parties that negotiate, ratify and implement the obligations set out in the various WTO agreements. These states enact hundreds of SPS measures per year, which may or may not comply with SPS Agreement disciplines. Indeed, there is reason to believe that the number of SPS measures is on the increase, as the number of notifications submitted to the WTO doubled between 1995 (220 notifications) and 1999 (438 notifications). Significantly, the number of SPS notifications increased from high-income, middle-income and low-income countries.[67]

In other words, while legal analysis tends to focus upon treaty text and panel and AB reports, these materials constitute only a small part of the trade universe. Thus legal scholarship may be guilty of the sin of synecdoche, of confusing the part with the whole.[68] Although synecdoche may be a powerful form of literary expression, it can seriously undermine the ability of legal scholarship to be policy-relevant. So when considering the "WTO as straightjacket" argument, perhaps it will be useful to focus a bit less on WTO texts and dispute resolution reports, and a bit more on *state practice.*

Of course, state practice occurs in a variety of forms and a full examination of state practice is beyond the scope of this chapter. For illustrative purposes, I will very briefly examine three levels of state practice in the SPS context. First, I'll look at executive branch interpretations of the SPS Agreement in the context of statements made in the context of domestic ratification debates. Second, I'll examine an underanalyzed type of state practice in WTO dispute resolution – the submissions of third parties who file briefs to assist the panels in their consideration of particular disputes. As detailed below, states may have incentives to make their third-party

---

[66] Id. at 65–66.

[67] John S. Wilson, The Development Challenge in Trade: Sanitary and Phytosanitary Standards 5 (statement prepared for SPS Committee, June 2000).

[68] Synecdoche is "a figure of speech in which a part is used for the whole (as *hand* for *sailor*), the whole for a part (as *the law* for *police officer*), the specific for the general (as *cutthroat* for *assassin*), the general for the specific (as *thief* for *pickpocket*), or the material for the thing from which it is made (as *steel* for *sword*)." *The American Heritage Dictionary* 1821 (Third Edition).

submissions more accurate than their statements in the context of politicized domestic ratification debates. Finally, I'll very briefly analyze state practice in the creation and implementation of SPS regulations. While this would seem to be the most important level, it receives the least attention, at least in the legal literature. Again, my goal here is not to provide an exhaustive analysis of state practice – an enormous task that I am ill-equipped to undertake – but rather to suggest that legal scholars would do well to expand their perspectives beyond the limited (albeit important) domain of WTO dispute resolution.

State Practice I – Statements in Domestic Fora

In determining the meaning of the SPS Agreement, we might look to executive branch statements made in the context of domestic ratification debates. These statements – made by the parties that negotiated the agreement to domestic law-makers in official fora – might provide useful insights into what the agreement's drafters believe the agreement to mean. A quick glance at statements made by some major trading nations suggests that the drafters did not think that the new trade disciplines included in the agreement significantly constrained state authority. To some extent, this is to be expected. Executives may reasonably believe that domestic legislators are unlikely to approve international agreements that significantly constrain their regulatory authority. On the other hand, executive branch officials have countervailing incentives not to undersell scope of trade agreement disciplines; they seek the support of export-oriented interests, who will seek constraints on other nations, and they invite more diffuse credibility problems if they misrepresent the meaning or scope of the agreement.

In the Statement of Administrative Action that accompanied the Uruguay Round Agreements Act, the Clinton administration strongly and unequivocally rejected the "WTO as straightjacket" theory in the context of the SPS Agreement:

> The [SPS] Agreement clearly does not interfere with the ability of state and local governments to maintain measures to protect human, animal or plant life or health. The Agreement... will in no way diminish or impair the Constitutional and legal rights of state and local governments to adopt, maintain, or apply measures to protect public health and the environment....
>
> The [SPS] Agreement thus explicitly affirms the right of each government to choose its levels of protection, including a "zero risk" if it so chooses. A government may establish its levels of protection by any means available under its law, including by referendum. In the end, the choice of an appropriate level of protection is a societal value judgment. The Agreement imposes no requirement to establish a scientific basis for the chosen level of protection because the choice is not a scientific judgment.... [69]

United States Trade Representative Mickey Kantor offered similar assurances as the Senate considered the Uruguay Round agreements. In a letter to the Chair of the Senate Subcommittee on Labor, Ambassador Kantor wrote that

---

[69] Uruguay Round Agreement Act Statement of Administrative Action, reprinted in U.S.C.C.A.N. 4040, 4104 (1994).

Our negotiators had strong environmental and food safety laws fully in mind in concluding the Uruguay Round agreements with our trading partners. As a result, the agreements recognize the right of each government to protect human, animal, and plant life and health, the environment, and consumers and to set the level of protection for health, the environment, and consumers – as well as the level of safety – that the government considers appropriate.

Under the WTO, most food safety laws will be covered by the "Agreement on the Application of Sanitary and Phytosanitary Measures" (S&P Agreement). The Agreement will permit us to continue to reject food imports that are not safe. Moreover, it will not require the Federal Government or States to adopt lower food safety standards. The S&P Agreement calls for food safety rules to be based on "scientific principles." That is important because many countries reject our agricultural exports on non-scientific grounds.

As a general matter, the FDA and EPA (which participated directly in the negotiations of the S&P Agreement), as well as the States, base their food safety regulations on science. Thus, meeting the basic requirement of the S&P Agreement should pose no problem for U.S. food safety rules. It is worth noting that the rule in the Agreement requiring a scientific basis applies to S&P measures. It does not apply to the level of food safety that those measures are designed to achieve. Each country and – in the case of the United States each State – is free to establish the level of protection it deems appropriate. That means, for example, that the "zero tolerance" level for carcinogens mandated by the Federal "Delaney clauses" are entirely consistent with the Uruguay Round agreements. Furthermore, a government may establish its levels of protection by any means available under its law, including by referendum.

While the S&P Agreement contains a general obligation to use international standards, it produces the ability of governments to use more stringent standards if they have a "scientific justification." The S&P Agreement makes explicit that there is a scientific justification if the government determines that the relevant international standard does not provide the level of food safety that the government determines to be appropriate. Far from undermining U.S. laws, this language serves to make clear that no "downward harmonization" is required for those laws.[70]

Officials in other states made similar claims. In Canada, for example, the SPS Agreement attracted wide public attention, and Canada's Department of Foreign Affairs and International Trade did several analyses of the SPS Agreement. Again, an executive branch represented that the agreement would not in any way threaten domestic regulations:

. . .

These provisions ensure that Canada may continue to choose its appropriate levels of sanitary and phytosanitary protection while limiting the ability of other countries to impose unjustifiable sanitary and phytosanitary restrictions on Canadian agrifood, fish and forest product exports. . . .

Canadians have long relied on scientific considerations when developing sanitary and phytosanitary regulations. Therefore, the obligation to base SPS measures on scientific principles will not affect Canada's ability to achieve its desired levels of sanitary and phytosanitary protection. . . .

---

[70] Letter from Amb. Mickey Cantor to Hon. Howard Metzenbaum, 140 Cong. Rec. S15077-01, Nov. 30, 1994.

While some international guidelines are less stringent than Canadian standards, others are more so. The Agreement on SPS will not change Canada's right to adopt and implement national sanitary and phytosanitary measures that are more stringent than international recommendations, when these are required as a consequence of the levels of protection that Canadians have chosen. Neither will it require a change to the public notification and consultation obligations that are an inherent part of Canada's existing national regulatory policy....

Requiring that SPS measures be based on an assessment of risk is consistent with current Canadian practice....

Conclusions

The new Agreement on Sanitary and Phytosanitary Measures fully protects the right of Canadians to choose the levels of sanitary and phytosanitary protection that are most appropriate for Canada. Although the Agreement on SPS does not prevent other countries from initiating a challenge against the sanitary and phytosanitary measures that Canada adopts to achieve its selected levels of protection, it clearly states that Canada retains the right to adopt and apply whatever measures are necessary to achieve the levels of protection that it has selected.[71]

Similarly, during Parliamentary debate in Australia, the Minister for Development Cooperation and Pacific Island Affairs assured legislators that the SPS Agreement would not undermine Australia's ability to enact the SPS measures it saw fit:

The agreement on the application of sanitary and phytosanitary measures – the SPS agreement – will also assist Australian exporters in ensuring that such measures are only maintained to the extent necessary to protect human, animal or plant life or health, and are scientifically justifiable.

Neither the SPS agreement nor the agreement on technical barriers to trade, the revised standards code, will alter Australia's ability to maintain more stringent measures than provided for in international standards if this is appropriate to our requirements. Australia could, however, be called upon to demonstrate that any more stringent standards do not unjustifiably restrict trade or discriminate between countries.[72]

It would be useful to survey the ratification debates of other WTO members to see if similar statements were made. If one could find that a substantial number of the governments that negotiated the SPS Agreement made similar claims about the import of the agreement's terms, this would be a powerful argument concerning the governments' understanding of the treaty they had negotiated. Of course, one would have to bear in mind that these statements were offered in (sometimes partisan) political contexts. And, if many states agreed that the agreement "does not interfere with the ability of ... governments to maintain measures to protect human, animal or plant life or health," as the U.S. claimed, one might wonder why governments took the trouble to negotiate the agreement in the first place. However, these observations do not detract from the more limited point I am trying to make, which is simply

---

[71] Full report available at http://www.dfait-maeci.gc.ca/sustain/environa/strategic/urug-en.pdf.

[72] Testimony of Minister Bilney, October 18, 1994, before the House on the second reading of the Copyright (World Trade Organization Amendments) Bill.

Lotus Eaters

that these ratification statements represent a form of state practice that might shed significant light on the parties' understandings of the obligations they undertook when entering into the SPS Agreement.

State Practice II – Third-Party Submissions in WTO Dispute Resolution

As suggested above, domestic ratification debates might not be the best place to look for a government's "true" interpretation of an international agreement. After all, executive branch officials might have a strong incentive to tell the legislative branch and its domestic constituents that an international agreement it negotiated did not restrict legislative prerogatives and its domestic freedom of action. So it might be useful to look at other forms of state practice. In particular, we might get a better sense of a government's interpretation of an agreement by looking to statements it makes in international fora. Here, governments may be constrained against making expansive arguments about a treaty's meaning out of concern that other states will adopt that argument in the future. Thus, for example, it might be useful to examine the statements made, for example, in SPS Committee meetings.

The incentive to make "accurate" statements about a treaty's meaning may be particularly strong in a legal setting. Although the WTO does not have a formal doctrine of precedent, the AB and panels do rely upon earlier reports as a form of de facto precedent.[73] Thus, all states have an interest in the outcome of any particular WTO dispute. As a named party, a government may offer certain arguments as part of a litigation strategy. However, when participating as a third party, a government may have more leeway to argue the "correct" interpretation of the SPS Agreement. Finally, government officials are well aware that in international legal settings they play a double function (dedoublement fonctionnel), and that arguments offered today can be offered in a different context tomorrow.[74] Thus, in the materials that follow, I very briefly survey the arguments made by third parties to WTO dispute resolution proceedings involving SPS issues.

In the first SPS case, the *Beef-Hormone* dispute, the United States and Canada challenged a European ban on the importation of meat produced with certain growth hormones. The proffered rationale for the ban was that the hormones might be dangerous to human health. The panel ruled against the EC, and the Appellate Body affirmed. At the panel stage, four states filed third-party submissions.

Australia argued that the EC ban was inconsistent with the SPS Agreement because it lacked a scientific justification.[75] Australia also argued that the EC had not

---

[73] Raj Bhala, The Power of the Past: Towards De Jure Stare Decisis in WTO Adjudiction (Part Three of a Trilogy), 33 *George Washington International Law Review* 873 (2001); Raj Bhala, The Precedent Setters: De Facto Stare Decisis in WTO Adjudication (Part Two of a Trilogy), 9 *Journal of Translational Law and Policy* 1 (1999); Raj Bhala, The Myth About Stare Decisis and International Trade Law (Part One of a Trilogy), 14 *American University International Law Review* 845 (1999).

[74] Georges Scelle, Le phenomene juridique de dedoublement fonctionnel, in *Rectsfragen der Internationalen Organisation* 324 (Walter Schatzel & Hans-Jurgen Schlochauer eds., 1956); Antonio Cassese, Remarks on Scelle's Theory of "Role Splitting" (Dedoublement Fonctionnel) in International Law, 1 *European Journal of International Law* 210 (1990).

[75] Panel report, para. V.3.

consistently pursued similar levels of SPS protection in comparable circumstances.[76] Australia also argued that the EC ban was imposed without an effort to minimize negative trade effects, that it was not based upon a risk assessment and that alternative and less-trade-restrictive measures were available.[77] Canada filed a third-party submission in the dispute arising out of the U.S. complaint, and argued that the EC ban was a disguised restriction on international trade, and hence GATT-inconsistent and not within the scope of GATT Article XX.[78] New Zealand argued that the ban was not based on scientific principles, nor sustained by sufficient scientific evidence. It also argued that the ban was not based upon a risk assessment. New Zealand also noted the inconsistency between the EC ban on hormone-treated beef as compared with the permission to trade other products that contained higher levels of hormone residues.

Norway argued that the EC ban was consistent with the SPS Agreement. This is the only third-party submission in any of the SPS cases to assert that the challenged measure complied with all relevant WTO obligations.

In *Australia-Salmon*, Canada challenged an Australian ban on the importation of fresh or frozen salmon in order to prevent twenty-four fishborne diseases from entering Australian waters. The panel ruled against Australia, and the Appellate Body affirmed. At the panel level, four states filed third-party submissions.

The EC emphasized that the SPS Agreement grants states broad latitude in the setting of SPS standards, yet argued that the Australian ban was inconsistent with Articles 2.3 and 5.6 of the SPS Agreement. India did not explicitly state whether the Australian ban was or was not SPS-consistent. However, the content and tone of India's submission revealed a great skepticism as to whether the Australian ban was SPS-consistent. Norway – which supported the EC's ban in *Beef-Hormone* – argued that Australia's ban was not based upon a risk assessment. Norway also argued that Australia improperly had applied different levels of protection in response to comparable risks. Finally, Norway argued that the ban was more restrictive than another readily available measure that would have produced the same level of protection. The U.S. submission argued that the ban lacked sufficient scientific justification, and that Australia improperly pursued inconsistent levels of protection against the same risks.

In the *Varietals* dispute, three states filed third-party submissions. Brazil argued that an alternative measure was available that was significantly less-trade-restrictive, and that Japan's measure was non-transparent. The EC argued that Japan's VTR lacked a scientific basis, and that the measure was applied to an extent beyond that necessary to protect plant life or health. The EC also criticized the non-transparent nature of the Japanese regulations in this area. Hungary argued that Japan lacked a sufficient scientific basis for its VTR. Hungary also argued that the measure was not based upon a risk assessment. Moreover, Hungary argued that the VTR could not be sustained under Article 5.7 as this provision does not permit SPS measures "on the basis of hypothesis, assumptions or assertions."

---

[76] Panel report, para. V.6., V.9.

[77] Panel report, para. V.8, V.10.

[78] Panel report, paras. V.11–17. Canada advanced a number of additional arguments in its dispute against the EC.

Once again, I do not pretend that I have presented a large and representative sample of state practice, and I appreciate that the statements of these third parties may not accurately reflect the views of the larger WTO membership. For present purposes, it is sufficient to note the sharp contrast between these assertions in WTO dispute resolution, detailing the various ways that the SPS measures imposed by trading partners are WTO-inconsistent, and the picture of wide discretion painted during domestic ratification debates.[79] At a minimum, we need to consider whether these assertions, generally arguing that the challenged measure is not consistent with SPS disciplines, undermine the broad claims made before domestic legislatures that the SPS Agreement will not significantly constrain the enactment of SPS measures. Do the third-party submissions, claiming that the SPS Agreement has significant bite, present a more accurate picture of state understanding of the SPS Agreement? And do these statements capture some of the ways in which the WTO agreements can act as a straightjacket, particularly given that to date the complainant has prevailed in every SPS dispute that has been decided by panels?

As the other chapters in this book demonstrate, the key holdings, the rationales offered, dicta and other features of WTO reports are analyzed in great detail, and generalizations are made and predictions offered. While much of this literature is dispute-specific, some valuable recent scholarship takes a more comprehensive and systemic approach to WTO dispute resolution, in an effort to illustrate the forest, rather than individual trees.[80] There is much to be learned from this literature, but the argument here is that we should be careful not to confuse the part with the whole. Although the three SPS disputes that proceeded to panel and Appellate Body consideration have received substantial attention, they constitute only a fraction of the SPS cases where consultations have been requested (see Appendix 1). More broadly, the disputes that come to WTO dispute resolution – in food safety as well as other areas – represent only a tiny fraction of the international trade world.

This is all intended to suggest that if one wants to understand the effect of the SPS Agreement on government actions, or to determine if the agreement is really leading to a harmonization – or a lowering – of SPS standards, examining panel and AB reports in SPS cases is the wrong place to look. Instead, we ought to focus on whether, and when, states have decided to adopt international standards; on whether, and when, states have adjusted standards to achieve comparable treatment of risk in comparable situations; and whether, and when, states have changed their internal standard-setting procedures to conform more closely to the SPS Agreement's requirements. This is a large and difficult research agenda. However, there are a few places

---

[79] I am not charging governments with bad faith in their claims that the SPS Agreement would not threaten domestic health and safety laws. The novelty of the SPS Agreement, and its provisions, necessarily limited the ability *ex ante* to predict the consequences of all the SPS discipines. The application of SPS provisions in specific fact patterns may reveal new and unanticipated interpretations. Moreover, many of the SPS provisions are stated in quite general terms, and hence their interpretation and application by dispute panels can differ substantially from predictions made during domestic ratification processes.

[80] See, e.g., Marc L. Busch & Eric Reinhardt, Bargaining in the Shadow of the Law: Early Settlement in the GATT/WTO Disputes, 24 *Fordham International Law Journal* 158 (2000); Marc L. Busch & Eric Reinhardt, Testing International Trade Law: Empirical Studies of GATT/WTO Dispute Settlement, in *The Political Economy of International Trade Law: Essays in Honor of Robert E. Hudec* (Daniel L. M. Kennedy & James D. Southwick, eds. 2001).

where it might be fruitful to start. Earlier in this chapter I discussed one dispute that was resolved in the SPS Committee, and never reached formal WTO dispute resolution. Moreover, it was a dispute where an international body, the WHO, played an important and constructive role. The suggestion here is that an inquiry into the activity in (and around) the SPS Committee would be extremely valuable. I also mentioned the hundreds of notifications that the SPS Committee receives each year. Again, these notifications provide a large and current database that could shed substantial light on the actual effect of the SPS Agreement on state behavior. Although the empirical work is yet to be done, there appears to be little evidence that the SPS Agreement has produced significant change along these dimensions in many governments' behavior.[81]

VI. A Minimalist Approach to WTO Dispute Resolution

It is a truism that there has been a dramatic shift in the focus of trade policy concerns from border barriers to barriers that exist "within the border."[82] This shift has revealed new and more subtle categories of government measures that restrict trade, including numerous health and safety and SPS measures. In part, this has led trade policy into domains that were previously considered to be purely domestic. The increasing intrusiveness of trade policy has generated a substantial political backlash and the creation of new domestic political constituencies that focus upon international trade policy.

Whereas many analysts suggest that the problem is one of distinguishing between "legitimate" health and safety regulations and those that are simply disguised protectionism, this fails to capture fully the depth and extent of the changes associated with the SPS and other Uruguay Round agreements. At a minimum, the trade regime has evolved from a system where "good" values (liberalized trade, greater aggregate welfare) conflict with "bad" values (protection of inefficient domestic industries) to a system where good values (liberalized trade) conflict with other good values (heightened consumer and food safety). In the former case, it is clear which value should win, both as a general, conceptual matter and, more often than not, in particular cases. However, when we move to disputes where the value of trade liberalization conflicts with the value of consumer safety, there is no consensus – either within or between states – over which set of values should prevail.

What should WTO panels do when faced with these sort of conflicts between trade and other values? Elsewhere, I have argued that panels should avoid determining the highly contested "trade and" issues when it is possible to do so.[83] In part, the argument grows out of the institutional politics of the WTO and the role played by

---

[81] See, e.g., David G. Victor, Risk Management and the World Trading System: Regulating International Trade Distortions Caused by National Sanitary and Phytosanitary Policies in Incorporating Science, Economics, and Sociology in Developing Sanitary and Phytosanitary Standards, in *International Trade: Proceedings of a Conference* 160–162 (2000) (arguing that international standards have had little impact in promoting international harmonization of SPS measures).

[82] See, e.g., *Fair Trade and Harmonization: Prerequisites for Free Trade? Vol. II: Legal Analysis* (Jagdish Bhagwati & Robert E. Hudec, eds., 1996).

[83] Jeffrey L. Dunoff, The Death of Trade, 10 *European Journal of International Law* 733 (1999).

WTO dispute resolution. The international trade system inevitably contains certain fundamental tensions. One, shared with other international regimes, is how to best strike a balance between pursuit of economic interests and other social interests. As the public backlash against trade liberalization suggests, the balance struck by the trade regime – and, particularly, by dispute settlement panels – has proven to be extraordinarily problematic. Another tension, also shared with other international regimes, is how to best reconcile the persistent and competing demands of principle and expediency – how to mediate the relationship between law and politics. For present purposes, I wish to reflect on this second tension.

When a domestic legislature or a WTO negotiating body confronts a fact pattern that involves a conflict among desirable values, it is both expected and appropriate for it to declare that it has weighed and struck a balance among all appropriate interests, and resolved political and policy issues through majoritarian process. However, this is not true of WTO panels. While there had long been debate over whether GATT dispute resolution should be a legalistic, rule-based system or a more flexible diplomatic mechanism,[84] the Uruguay Round Dispute Settlement Understanding ("DSU") represents an unequivocal victory for the legalists. It could not be clearer that WTO panels are not intended to be simply another forum for the resolution of politicized value conflicts. Rather, panels are to apply settled law to the facts, to resolve disputes according to pre-existing principle.[85] If panels were viewed as engaging in either policy-making or deal-making, the legitimacy of the dispute resolution system would be at risk.

This raises an unavoidable obstacle to the satisfactory resolution of many "trade and" disputes in WTO panel proceedings. These types of disputes present issues that are among the most "contested" in trade policy. To be sure, many trade issues are contested in the sense that they are subject to disagreement and dispute, but the claim here is that many "trade and" issues are "contested" in a much more fundamental way, in the sense that the fundamentals of the debate – say, the balance to be struck between trade and non-economic interests – are "up for grabs" and that those participating in these debates acknowledge the legitimacy of disagreement about these fundamental issues.[86] In this sense, the question of GATT policy towards tariffs is not contested, while that of policy regarding, say, environmental or competition issues, is highly contested.

"Trade and" issues are currently contested in a way that appears to remove them from the legal domain, and place them squarely in the political domain. WTO panels

---

[84] For a sense of the debate, see Dunoff, *Institutional Misfits, supra* note 97, at 1123–28; John H. Jackson, *World Trade and the Law of GATT* 85–88 (1989); Oliver Long, *Law and Its Limitations in the GATT Multilateral Trade System* 61–64 (1985); William J. Davey, *Dispute Settlement in the GATT,* 11 *Fordham International Law Journal* 51, 69–78 (1987).

[85] The Uruguay Round Dispute Settlement Understanding expressly provides that "recommendations and rulings of the DSB [Dispute Settlement Body] cannot add to or diminish the rights and obligations provided in the covered agreements." Understanding on Rules and Procedures Governing the Settlement of Disputes, Final Act, at Art. 3.2.

[86] For a fuller description of this concept, see Lawrence Lessig, *Fidelity and Constraint,* 65 *Fordham Law Review* 1365, 1393–96 (1997); Lawrence Lessig, *Understanding Changed Readings: Fidelity and Theory,* 47 *Stanford Law Review* 395 (1995) [hereinafter *Understanding Changed Readings*]; Lawrence Lessig, Translating Federalism: United States v. Lopez, 1995 *Supreme Court Review* 125.

can attempt to draw difficult lines in the midst of this larger political struggle; but it is precisely the contestedness of the issues that would render it almost impossible for panels to apply any nuanced test in a manner that would appear to produce consistent results. Inconsistent results in these controversial areas would invite the criticism that the outcomes are simply political. This criticism is important, because WTO dispute resolution panels, no less than other adjudicatory fora, "must act rigorously on principle, lest it undermine[] the justification for its power."[87] In other words, panels that created and applied sensitive, multifactored tests truer to the underlying values at stake in "trade and" issues would unavoidably appear political and hence undermine their institutional position. The perceived "delegalization" of WTO dispute resolution proceedings would threaten the delegitimization of these proceedings.

We can read the three SPS AB reports as being sensitive to these sort of concerns. Food safety disputes are often highly politicized, and pose many of the threats to WTO dispute resolution that "trade and" issues pose. Thus, it is interesting that in each of the SPS cases, the AB carefully limits what is decided, and often employs an analysis that is much narrower than that used by the panel.

For example, in *Beef-Hormones*, the panel held that the EC's failure to use international standards for five of the six growth hormones at issue shifted the burden of proof to the EC to justify its measures under Article 3.3 of the agreement. This holding would have greatly increased the incentive to use international standards, and raised the bar for states that wanted to use more stringent standards. However, the AB reversed the panel on this issue, and held that standards that are not based on international standards should not have a higher burden of proof.

Similarly, in *Beef-Hormones*, the panel found it necessary that a respondent demonstrate that it satisfied "minimum procedural requirement[s]" in enacting SPS measures, including that it actually took into account a risk assessment. Again, the AB reversed, on the grounds that this would require a subjective examination of what motivated the state in adopting the measure; instead the AB required that an "objective relationship" exist between the risk assessment and the SPS measure.

In both *Australia-Salmon* and the *Varietals* dispute, the panels had found a violation of Article 5.6, requiring that measures be not more trade-restrictive than necessary. In each case, the AB reversed, and did so in a way that will make it harder for future complainants to succeed on Article 5.6 claims. Similarly, in *Beef-Hormone*, the AB reversed the panel's conclusion that the EC's ban violated Article 5.5's consistency requirement.

Although each case upheld the panel's ultimate determination – that the challenged measure was inconsistent with the SPS Agreement – the AB did so in ways that deflected the force of the "WTO as straightjacket" argument, and that gave greater discretion to governments in the SPS area.

Moreover, the AB has been careful to "not decide" certain important issues in the SPS cases. The key issue here relates to the scientific justification for SPS measures. Article 2.2 requires that SPS measures be based on scientific principles and not maintained without sufficient scientific evidence. Article 5.1 requires that measures be

---

[87] Bickel, *supra* note 224, at 69.

based on a risk assessment. However, how much evidence is necessary? And what does it mean for a measure to be "based on" a risk assessment? These are the extraordinarily difficult questions upon which the SPS Agreement turns, and which give rise to concerns that the agreement unduly constrains domestic regulatory authority.

In *Beef-Hormone*, the AB said that the results of the risk assessment "must sufficiently warrant – that is to say – reasonably support" the challenged SPS measure. The AB continued:

> In most cases, responsible and representative governments tend to base their legislative and administrative measures on "mainstream" scientific opinion. In other cases, equally responsible and representative governments may act in good faith on the basis of what, at a given time, may be a divergent opinion coming from qualified and respected sources. By itself, this does not necessarily signal the absence of a reasonable relationship between the SPS measure and the risk assessment.... Determination of the presence or absence of that relationship can only be done on a case-by-case basis after account is taken of all considerations rationally bearing upon the issue of potential adverse health effects.[88]

The AB "explained" this requirement in *Varietals*:

> The ordinary meaning of "sufficient" is "of a quantity, extent or scope adequate to a certain purpose or object." From this, we can conclude that sufficiency is a relational concept.... [W]e agree with the Panel that the obligation ... that an SPS measure not be maintained without sufficient scientific evidence requires that there be a rational or objective relationship between the SPS measure and the scientific evidence. Whether there is a rational relationship between an SPS measure and the scientific evidence is to be determined on a case-by-case basis and will depend upon the particular circumstances of the case, including the characteristics of the measure at issue and the quality and quantity of scientific evidence.[89]

It is not necessary to embrace a strong version of the legal indeterminacy thesis in order to conclude that these passages resolve almost nothing. They are singularly unhelpful in giving guidance to future panels, or to states who seek to understand the bounds of the SPS Agreement so as to stay within them. Indeed, the AB's "minimalist" approach has been widely, and at times sharply, criticized.

However, the AB's minimalist approach of not deciding more than is necessary can be defended on both institutional and conceptual grounds. As an institutional matter, the AB's minimalist approach can help mitigate the legitimacy issues raised above. The conceptual defense is closely related. The underlying problem is the need – as the AB has explicitly acknowledged – to maintain the "delicate and carefully negotiated balance" between trade and food safety measures.[90] Much of the scholarship in this area privileges local autonomy and environmental/health values of economic values.[91] However, the deeper issues raised by SPS disputes (and "trade and" issues

---

[88] AB report, para. 78.
[89] Varietals AB report, paras. 19, 22.
[90] Hormones AB report, para. 177.
[91] See, e.g., Michael Trebilcock & Julie Soloway, International Trade Policy and Domestic Food Safety Regulation: The Case for Substantial Deference by the WTO Dispute Settlement Body Under the SPS Agreement, in Kennedy & Southwick, supra note 62, at 537.

186   Jeffrey L. Dunoff

more generally) are not simply questions of pitting economic against non-economic values.

There is little argument that the worldwide agricultural sector is beset by massive economic distortions enhanced, if not created, by misguided government policy. The U.S. government has engaged in massive agricultural subsidies since the time of the Great Depression, and, more recently, the EC has protected its agricultural producers via its Common Agricultural Policy. During the post-war era, developing countries, in general, went in the other direction, as they focused upon import-substituting industrialization strategies and largely ignored their agricultural sectors.[92] Add to this the fact that agriculture was largely outside the GATT system for nearly five decades, and we live in a world where "much of the world's agricultural output is produced in the wrong place."[93] As a result, much of the world's poor – who can least afford it – pay more for food. Moreover, developing countries – which often should enjoy a comparative advantage in agriculture due to low-cost labor and abundant land for cultivation – find only limited access to developed state export markets. Thus, SPS measures raise difficult distributional issues, and may undermine the very environmental and safety values that WTO critics seek to advance.

In this context, the AB's minimalist approach – deciding no more than is necessary, and often "deciding" issues in the vaguest of terms – may be politically wise. In this politically delicate area, the trade liberalizing tendencies of the WTO face sharp opposition. Indeed, the three SPS disputes vividly illustrate how resistant the international community is to disciplines in this area. In *Beef-Hormone*, the EC refused to lift its ban on hormone-treated meat, and has suffered trade sanctions as a result. In *Australia-Salmon*, Australia "complied" with the panel and AB by lowering some SPS standards and raising others. And in *Varietals*, Japan eliminated the VTR, but continues to exclude U.S. apples on the grounds that they may spread fire blight to Japan – an SPS measure that is now itself the subject of WTO dispute resolution. So the AB may be mindful that it is far from clear how much discipline in these areas the international community is prepared to accept. In this context, an insistence on principled, expansive readings of the SPS Agreement may do more harm than good. Indeed, minimalist and vague pronouncements are better then either intrusive tests – which can generate a significant political backlash – or deferential tests – which can disappoint those trade advocates who are the WTO's strongest supporters. As Daniel Farber has argued,

> Like a national legislature faced with a polarized and divisive issue, the WTO can only lose politically by embracing an explicit solution. Legislatures in such situations often resort to vagueness or open-ended delegation to administrators in the hope of seeming to take action without making enemies. This may well be the best strategy available to the WTO as well. Having established a presence in the area of food safety, the WTO may do best to avoid sticking its neck out in SPS cases.[94]

[92] G. Edward Schuh, Developing Country Interests in WTO Agricultural Policy, in *The Political Economy of International Trade Law: Essays in Honor of Robert E. Hudec* 435, 437 (Daniel L. M. Kennedy & James D. Southwick, eds., 2002).

[93] Id. at 435–36.

[94] Daniel A. Farber, The Case Against Clarity, in *The Political Economy of International Trade Law: Essays in Honor of Robert E. Hudec* 575, 580–81 (Daniel L. M. Kennedy & James D. Southwick, eds., 2002).

As Farber suggests, there is no easy answer to this highly politicized clash of values. More importantly, there can be no viable judicial resolution in this highly contested terrain.

Conclusion

The burden of this chapter has been to show that the *Varietals* dispute is less interesting for its specific facts and result than it is for the insights it provides into the structure of the SPS Agreement and the WTO more generally. It sheds light on the underlying legal structure within which WTO members find themselves enmeshed, the need to look beyond the agreement's text and WTO dispute resolution reports if we are to understand adequately the effect of the SPS Agreement, and an effective political strategy that panels and the AB might adopt in politically charged areas such as food safety. For these reasons, the *Varietals* dispute is, despite its anodyne facts and seemingly technical reports, worthy of sustained study.

Appendix 1. Disputes Referring to the SPS Agreement

Case No.	Measure	Complainant[*]	SPS art. referred to	Case status
DS3	Korea: Testing and inspection requirements	United States	2, 5	Consultations
DS5	Korea: Shelf-life regulation – frozen meat	United States	2, 5	Settlement
DS18	Australia: Import ban – salmon	Canada	2, 5	Appellate report
DS20	Korea: Shelf-life regulation – bottled water	Canada	2, 5	Settlement
DS21	Australia: Import ban – salmon	United States	2, 5	Settlement
DS26	EU: Import ban – hormone-treated beef	United States	2, 3, 5	Arbitration
DS41	Korea: Testing and inspection requirements	United States	2, 5, 8	Consultations
DS48	EU: Import ban – hormone-treated beef	Canada	2, 3, 5	Arbitration
DS76	Japan: Quarantine regulations	United States	5, 5, 8	Appellate report
DS96	India: Import quotas	EU	2, 3, 5	Settlement
DS100	US: USDA decision on poultry product safety	EU	2, 3, 4, 5, 8, Ann. C	Consultations
DS133	Slovak Republic: Transit requirements	Switzerland	5	Consultations
DS134	EU: Import duties – rice	India	2	Consultations
DS135[**]	EU: Asbestos and asbestos products	Canada	2, 3, 5	Appellate report
DS137	EU: Import restrictions – wood of conifers	Canada	2, 3, 4, 5, 6	Consultations
DS144	US: State trucking regulations	Canada	2, 3, 4, 5, 6, 13, Ann. B, C	Consultations

Case No.	Measure	Complainant[*]	SPS art. referred to	Case status
DS203	Mexico: Import restrictions – live swine	United States	2.2, 2.3, 3, 5.1, 5.6, 7, 8	Consultations
DS205	Egypt: Import restrictions – canned tuna	Thailand	2, 3, 5, Ann. B (paragraph 2, 5)	Consultations

[*] Does not include countries who subsequently requested to join consultations.

[**] The case focused exclusively on obligations under the TBT Agreement. In its request for the establishment of a panel (WT/DS/135/3), Canada claimed that the EU decree in question was inconsistent with obligations under the SPS as well as the TBT Agreement. However, Canada only pursued the claim that the EU decree was inconsistent with obligations under the TBT Agreement in its written or oral arguments before the established panel.

DONALD H. REGAN

6. Regulatory Purpose and "Like Products" in Article III:4 of the GATT (with Additional Remarks on Article III:2)

Prologue

In EC – Asbestos the Appellate Body has told us that (1) in interpreting Article III:4 of the GATT, we must take explicit account of the policy in Article III:1 that measures should not be applied "so as to afford protection to domestic production" [hereafter just "so as to afford protection"].[1] In Chile – Alcohol the Appellate Body has told us that (2) in deciding whether a measure is applied "so as to afford protection," we must consider "the purposes or objectives of a Member's legislature and government as a whole" – in other words, the regulatory purpose of the measure.[2] Chile – Alcohol was decided under Article III:2, but it involves the very same "so as to afford protection" that Asbestos says we look to in interpreting Article III:4. It follows from (1) and (2) that in interpreting Article III:4, we must consider the regulatory purpose of the measure under review.

That is the doctrinal argument for the relevance of regulatory purpose under Article III:4. In the ten years since US – Malt Beverages,[3] we have come full circle on this issue.[4] Although I think the Appellate Body is now on the right track,

---

[1] European Communities – Measures Affecting Asbestos and Asbestos-Containing Products, WT/DS135/AB/R (12 March 2001) [hereafter Asbestos or EC – Asbestos], ¶¶93, 98.

[2] Chile – Taxes on Alcoholic Beverages, WT/DS87 & DS110/AB/R (13 December 1999) [hereafter Chile – Alcohol], ¶62.

[3] United States – Measures Affecting Alcoholic and Malt Beverages, BISD 39S/206 (adopted 19 June 1992) [hereafter US – Malt Beverages].

[4] Following the lead of US – Malt Beverages, the Panel in United States – Taxation of Automobiles, DS31 (11 October 1994), originated the famous "aims and effects" language, but the report was not adopted. Thereafter the Appellate Body rejected the "aims and effects" test, and purported to reject all consideration of legislative purpose, in Japan – Taxes on Alcoholic Beverages, WT/DS8 & DS10 & DS11/AB/R (4 October 1996) [hereafter Japan – Alcohol]. Japan – Alcohol was decided under Article III:2, but in European Communities – Regime for the Importation, Sale and Distribution of Bananas, WT/DS27/AB/R (9 September 1997) [hereafter Bananas III], ¶216, the Appellate Body seemingly extended the ban on considering regulatory purpose to Article III:4, saying III:4 cases should be decided without explicit reference to the Article III:1 policy against protectionism. Chile – Alcohol commences the rehabilitation of regulatory purpose analysis, under Article III:2, second sentence, and Asbestos makes it clear that the consequences of Chile – Alcohol are much broader still. Obviously, there are complexities in the development that are beyond this footnote but that will be revealed as we proceed. This was just to explain roughly how we have "come full circle."

I am grateful to Rob Howse, Bob Hudec and Petros Mavroidis for comments on an earlier draft. Errors are of course my own.

their double volte-face on the relevance of purpose illustrates the instability of doctrine – and the Appellate Body has not yet explicitly drawn the conclusion that their holdings in Asbestos and Chile – Alcohol entail. I shall therefore argue from the text of the agreement itself that we must consider regulatory purpose in applying Article III:4.

Indeed, I shall argue for a slightly narrower proposition – that the ordinary meaning of "like products" in the context of Article III:4 directs us to consider regulatory purpose in the course of deciding when products are "like."[5] It may not be obvious that this is a narrower proposition, but it is; someone might argue that even though regulatory purpose must be considered under Article III:4, it is not properly considered as part of the "like products" inquiry. Rather, the "like products" inquiry should focus on "competitive relationship," which is one element of the general inquiry into "so as to afford protection," while regulatory purpose should be considered only in connection with a different aspect of Article III:4, the question whether foreign goods are accorded "less favorable treatment" than domestic goods. There is one puzzling paragraph in the Asbestos report that might suggest precisely this.[6] To my mind, it is much more natural, and more in line with the ordinary meaning of the words of Article III:4, to consider regulatory purpose as an aspect of "like products." However, in arguing for that, I do not mean to exclude the possibility of considering regulatory purpose under the rubric of "less favorable treatment" as well.[7]

I. The Ordinary Meaning of "Like Products" in Article III:4

I shall argue that the ordinary meaning of "like products" in the context of Article III:4 of the GATT requires us to consider the regulatory purpose of the measure under review. When the Panel in Malt Beverages considered regulatory purpose, this was not an assault on the integrity of the agreement. It was just what the agreement had always required. The argument that I now develop at length was sketched in an article on process-based measures written with Rob Howse.[8] I want to give the argument a fuller treatment and discuss some more recent cases. I also want to emphasize that the argument is separable from our position on process-based measures, which I set aside completely in this chapter.

It is commonplace that "like products" may mean different things in different provisions of the WTO agreements. The Appellate Body has confirmed in EC – Asbestos that "like" means different things even in Article III:2, first sentence, and Article III:4.[9]

---

[5] As it happens, I think the same is true of "like products" in Article III:2, first sentence, but since that is an even more controversial claim, I postpone it to section III.B below.

[6] Asbestos, ¶100, discussed in section III.A below.

[7] For further discussion, see section III.A. One advantage, from my perspective, of considering regulatory purpose as part of "less favorable treatment" is that that would allow us to uphold process-based measures that embody a non-protectionist regulatory purpose, even if the products made with the different processes are physically identical and are held on that ground to be "like" (mistakenly in my view, see Robert Howse and Donald Regan, "The Product/Process Distinction – An Illusory Basis for Disciplining 'Unilateralism' in Trade Policy," *European Journal of International Law* (2000), Vol. 11 No. 2, pp. 249–289.

[8] Id.

[9] Asbestos, ¶¶96,99.

Examining for the first time the meaning of "like products" in III:4,[10] the Asbestos Appellate Body adopts the "ordinary meaning" approach, but to my mind they only carry it through halfway. They decide correctly that competitive relationship is a necessary condition for "likeness" of products, but having found this necessary condition, they seem to treat it as necessary and sufficient, thus leaving no room for consideration of, for example, regulatory purpose.[11]

Actually, the issue of whether competitive relationship is sufficient for likeness seems to be the precise issue between the concurring Member of the Division and his two colleagues.[12] The concurring Member is willing to make a positive finding that asbestos fibers are not "like" PCG fibers, even without clear evidence on the matter of competitive relationship. In the context, this means he is treating competitive relationship as not sufficient for likeness. "It is difficult for me to imagine what evidence relating to economic competitive relationships as reflected in end-uses and consumers' tastes and habits could outweigh and set at naught the undisputed deadly nature of chrysotile asbestos fibers, compared with PCG fibers, when inhaled by humans, and thereby compel a characterization of 'likeness' of chrysotile asbestos and PCG fibers."[13] Later, "[T]he necessity or appropriateness of adopting a 'fundamentally' economic interpretation of the 'likeness' of products under Article III:4 of the GATT 1994 does not appear to me to be free from substantial doubt."[14] There is some evidence in the report, which I shall discuss in section IIIA below, that even the two "majority" members may not be quite so firmly committed to an approach based solely on competitive relationship as the report sometimes suggests, and as the concurring member fears. We should also remember that the majority members did not need to consider anything more than competitive relationship to get the right result in Asbestos itself. They might approach a different case differently. For the moment, however, I shall continue to assume that the majority members do regard competitive relationship as necessary and sufficient for "likeness." I shall pursue the ordinary meaning analysis in my own way, and then return to comment on various aspects of the Asbestos report.[15]

So, what is the ordinary meaning of "like products" in the context of Article III:4? It might seem that we need not worry about the context – that "like" has a sufficient, context-independent meaning, "physically similar." However, a moment's reflection reveals that this is inadequate. Any two objects are similar with regard to some physical properties and different with regard to others. So we need some independent criterion to tell us which properties are the ones that matter. (We also need some independent criterion to tell us what degree of similarity is required, with regard to the relevant properties, but that is a subsidiary issue.) The appeal to physical likeness

---

[10] This is what the Asbestos Appellate Body says in ¶88, deftly setting aside any possible relevance of EC – Bananas (of which more below) on the ground that in Bananas they were not called upon to address the meaning of "like products." ¶88, n.57.

[11] However, see the discussion in section III.A below of a relevant ambiguity in the Appellate Body's argument.

[12] Uniquely in the annals of the Appellate Body, there is a "concurring statement" of six paragraphs by one Member of the Division interpolated into the report, Asbestos, ¶¶149–154.

[13] Id. ¶152.

[14] Id. ¶154.

[15] See section III.A below.

Regulatory Purpose and "Like Products" in Article III:4 of the GATT 193

is seductive, for two reasons. First of all, even though we must look to something other than physical likeness for the basic specification of what matters, it remains true that whatever the ultimate ground of "likeness," as objects become more alike in their physical properties, they tend to become more alike in whatever way we are ultimately concerned with.[16] Second, if two objects are perfectly physically identical, then they must be alike in any other respects that interest us. (Remember we have set aside the objects' history for purposes of this chapter.) However, no two objects in the real world are ever identical, and small differences may matter a great deal. The difference between a useless chemical compound and a wonder drug may be a single atom. So, physical likeness, even if it is in some sense necessarily correlated with what really matters, cannot provide the ultimate criterion.[17]

We have seen that in order to have a usable conception of "likeness," we need to know which properties matter. We need an answer to the question, "Like in what respects?" In the abstract, the answer is clear: products are like if they are alike in the respects that are relevant to our purpose in making the comparison. So now the question is, what is the purpose of making the comparison? To answer that question, we must turn to the context. Article III:4 tells us that:

> The products of the territory of any contracting party imported into the territory of any other contracting party shall be accorded treatment no less favorable than that accorded to like products of national origin in respect of all laws, regulations and requirements affecting their internal sale, offering for sale, purchase, transportation, distribution or use.

This is not especially helpful. Plainly the general concern is with discrimination against foreign goods, but there are many possible understandings of discrimination, and Article III:4 gives us little help in deciding which is the relevant understanding.

Article III:1, however, which provides the context for all the further provisions of Article III, including III:4, is another matter. Article III:1 tells us very clearly that the purpose of Article III is to prevent the application of measures "so as to afford protection to domestic production," which I shall abbreviate as "so as to afford protection." To be sure, the Appellate Body seems to have told us in Bananas III that we must not look to Article III:1 in interpreting III:4, because III:4 does not explicitly refer back to III:1.[18] However, if the Bananas Appellate Body really meant to say that in interpreting III:4 we were not to consider in any way whether some measure was applied "so as to afford protection," then their prohibition cannot be honored. There is simply no way to give content to the phrase "like products" in Article III without referring to Article III:1 and the basic purpose of avoiding protectionism. We have already

---

[16] Even this claim must be taken with a grain of salt, since there is no unambiguous definition of "more alike in their physical properties." If we double one dimension of a square one unit on a side, have we made it more like a square two units on a side (because it is now like it in one dimension) or less like it (because we have turned the smaller square into a rectangle)?

[17] For similar remarks, see Robert Hudec, "'Like Product': The Differences in Meaning in GATT Articles I and III," in Thomas Cottier and Petros Mavroidis, eds., *Regulatory Barriers and the Principle of Non-Discrimination in World Trade Law* (University of Michigan Press, 2000), p. 103. Incidentally, we shall see in section III.B below that we cannot make physical likeness provide the ultimate criterion even by interpreting it very narrowly, which was the stratagem adopted by the Panel and Appellate Body in Japan – Alcohol for dealing with Article III:2, first sentence.

[18] Bananas III, ¶216.

established this with regard to Article III:4, and I shall explain in section III.B why it is true even under the narrower Article III:2, first sentence, which Bananas relies on as a controlling analogy. In any event, the Appellate Body in Asbestos, having earlier commented that Bananas did not involve the interpretation of "like products,"[19] appeals explicitly to Article III:1 and to the purpose of avoiding protectionism in interpreting III:4.[20] So either Bananas actually does allow us to look to Article III:1 in interpreting Article III:4 (I shall explain in section III.B how that might be the case), or else Asbestos implicitly revises Bananas.

We have decided that "likeness" must be interpreted in light of the purpose of avoiding protectionism. That is the only way to answer the question "like in what respects?" So, what features of products, what dimensions of likeness, does the purpose of avoiding protectionism make relevant? One set of features that we can see are relevant are features that matter to consumers. (Or more generally, to purchasers of the products, which may include manufacturers or processors using them as inputs – we shall refer to all of these as "consumers" for convenience.) Only if two products are in competition can a measure that affects them unequally operate "so as to afford protection." And products can only be in competition if they are regarded by consumers as (to some degree) substitutes. So products cannot be "like" for purposes of Article III:4 unless they are viewed by the market as substitutes.

We now have a necessary condition for likeness. We have identified some relevant features – those that matter to consumers. However, have we identified all the features that matter to likeness? Have we found a sufficient condition? To see that we have not, consider the following simple example: Milk is sold in Barataria in cardboard cartons and in non-returnable plastic jugs. Some consumers prefer their milk in cartons, some in jugs, but all are left to make their own choice. Then the Barataria legislature discovers that the plastic jugs, because they are not biodegradable, damage the local environment in a way that cardboard cartons do not. Because Barataria has a long tradition of elevated concern for the environment, the legislature adopts a regulation forbidding the sale of milk in plastic jugs. As it happens, cardboard milk cartons are made in Barataria, while the non-returnable plastic jugs are made in neighboring Titipu, so the ban on plastic jugs benefits a local industry and hurts that industry's foreign competitor. Even so, it is clear that the impetus for the ban came from environmental quarters.

It might be, of course, that the ban is unnecessary, because once the facts about environmental damage are publicized, Barataria consumers will simply avoid plastic jugs on their own, but it might not work that way. There are at least two reasons why, in the absence of regulation, even fully informed Barataria consumers might continue to treat cardboard cartons and plastic jugs as close substitutes. (1) It could be that even though many Baratarians care deeply about the environment, the milk drinkers among them happen not to. In this case the environmental harm is a pure externality, and we need the ban to correct it. Alternatively, (2) it could be that even though milk drinkers care about the environment, it is still rational for each consumer who prefers plastic jugs to buy his milk in a jug, because the environmental cost from his

---

[19] Asbestos, ¶88, n.57.
[20] Id. ¶¶93, 98.

Regulatory Purpose and "Like Products" in Article III:4 of the GATT   195

own choice to purchase a plastic jug falls mostly on others. This would be a classic prisoners' dilemma.[21]

If cardboard cartons and plastic jugs continue to be close substitutes in the market even after the environmental facts are known and publicized, and if we regard market substitutability as a sufficient condition for "likeness" of products under Article III:4, then the Barataria jug ban violates III:4.[22] However, that is not an acceptable conclusion. It should be clear that the ban is not "applied . . . so as to afford protection to domestic production" within the ordinary meaning of that phrase, and hence that the ban should not be held to violate Article III:4. The ban is simply not protectionist. To be sure, the ban burdens foreign producers disproportionately, but only because their product is disproportionately harmful to the environment. In other words, their product (plastic jugs) is not "like" the competing domestic product (cardboard cartons).

As I mentioned in the prologue, we could conceivably say that plastic jugs and cardboard cartons are "like" and then bring in regulatory purpose under the "less favorable treatment" rubric. However, if we understand that we must consider regulatory purpose somewhere, the "likeness" inquiry seems the most natural place. For a start, it should be obvious that if plastic jugs harm the environment and cardboard cartons do not, these products are not "like" in any ordinary sense. They differ in an important respect. Now we may wonder, what has regulatory purpose to do with this? The physical effects of cartons and jugs on the environment are independent of regulatory purpose – so why does the regulatory purpose matter at all? The answer, of course, is that even though the physical effects are independent of the regulatory purpose, the existence of a "harm" is not. If the effects on the environment are local, then whether the effects constitute a "harm" depends on the local evaluation of them, which is to say, on the evaluation by the Barataria regulator. So, whether plastic jugs "harm" the environment depends on the regulatory purpose; and therefore whether they are "like" cardboard cartons (which by hypothesis do no harm) depends on regulatory purpose as well.

If Barataria genuinely cares about the environment (specifically, if it genuinely disvalues the particular effects caused by jugs but not cartons), then jugs cause a harm, they are unlike cartons, and it is no Article III:4 violation to treat them differently. On the other hand, if Barataria does not genuinely care about the environmental effects of the jugs, then jugs cause no actual harm, they are "like" cartons, and the ban violates Article III:4. This last result is just as it should be: if Barataria does not genuinely care about the environmental effects of the jugs, then the supposedly "green" jug ban is a protectionist ruse. Thus does regulatory purpose determine "likeness," and ultimately whether there is protectionism and an Article III:4 violation.[23]

---

[21] There could also be a weaker sort of collective action problem: it might be that each consumer will eschew plastic jugs if, but only if, he knows enough others are doing so, in which case we may need legal intervention to provide information about the numbers.

[22] I ignore for the moment the possibility of considering regulatory purpose under the rubric of "less favorable treatment," which I mentioned in the prologue and which I will address in the next paragraph.

[23] For a very nice parallel discussion, see Frieder Roessler, *The Legal Structure, Functions & Limits of the World Trade Order* (Cameron May, 2000), pp. 122–130. This is as good a point as any to comment on an issue that may be troubling some readers: if we consider regulatory purpose under Article III rather than postponing it to Article XX, who has the burden of proof? The answer is that the complainant has the

Can it really be that the likeness of products under Article III:4 depends on the regulator's purpose? Even if someone's purpose must ground the answer to "like in what respects?," it was not the regulator who wrote Article III. True enough, but the conclusion stands. The purpose that matters most directly to the interpretation of "likeness" is of course the purpose of the drafters (and adopters) of Article III. Their purpose, as they have told us in Article III:1, was to prevent measures being applied "so as to afford protection." However, that purpose of the drafters is itself a complex one, and it is that purpose which directs our attention to the purposes of the regulatory body that adopted the measure under review.

If it still seems strange that "likeness" should ultimately depend on the purposes of someone other than the drafters of and parties to the treaty, notice that we have already encountered a much less controversial example of exactly the same phenomenon. We have already explained why products can be "like" only if they are substitutes in the market, and this requirement is by now widely recognized. Whether and to what extent they are substitutes depends precisely on consumers' purposes in buying the products. We can draw a veil over these purposes by talking about market forces and measured cross-elasticities of demand, but these forces and elasticities are merely the visible resultants of consumers' purposes. If consumers' purposes can be relevant to the likeness of products (because the ultimate purpose of the treaty provision makes them relevant), why not regulators' purposes as well (for the same reason)? It may help if we remember that regulators presumptively represent the purposes of the citizenry as a whole – people just like consumers, but a broader class. If consumers' purposes can matter to "likeness," why not the purposes of the citizenry at large?

So far my positive argument may seem to amount to little more than a bare assertion that the Barataria regulation is not protectionist. How can I be so confident that the phrase "so as to afford protection" encompasses only regulations with protectionist purpose – that it does not encompass innocently motivated regulations that have significant disparate impact on foreign products? First, there is the

burden of proof of showing protectionist purpose, since protectionist purpose is the crux of the basic violation. However, if that burden seems too heavy, we should remember the distinction between the burden of proof and the burden of going forward with the evidence. The "burden of proof" refers to the issue of who wins if, with all the evidence in, the probabilities seem equally balanced. The burden of proof of the basic Article III violation is and remains with the complainant. However, the complainant may well at some point produce enough evidence of protectionist purpose so that the defendant regulating country will lose unless they produce some evidence in response. (This is one possible meaning of a "prima facie case," although not the only one.) At this point, the defendant has the burden of going forward with the evidence – not in the sense that they have any legal duty to go forward, but in the practical sense that if they do not, they will lose. Often, I suggest, the complaining country will be able to shift the burden of going forward onto the defendant just by putting before the tribunal the text of the statute and a few basic facts about who produces what. In truth, in cases where the putative regulatory justification is one that is recognized by Article XX, it will often not make much difference whether we consider regulatory purpose under Article III or Article XX. (The burden of proof differs, but the burden of proof is usually not what decides the case. There may be other differences as well, for example in the precise way in which evidence about possible alternative measures is relevant, but such differences are not worth pursuing here.) The italicized qualification in the last sentence but two is important, because many perfectly sound regulatory policies are not recognized by Article XX. In any event, even when the differences in procedure and probable result are slight, we should apply the treaty as it is written.

Regulatory Purpose and "Like Products" in Article III:4 of the GATT   197

phrase itself – "so as to afford protection." To my ear, "so as to afford protection" has a strong purposive connotation. The reader should compare the phrase "measures applied so as to afford protection to domestic production" with a possible alternative such as "measures applied in such a way that they protect domestic production." By use of a dictionary and a grammar book one might conclude that these phrases are perfectly synonymous, but to my ear, they are very different in what they suggest about the relevance of purpose. The formulation with "so as to afford protection" has a much more purposive ring.[24]

This linguistic intuition may not seem conclusive by itself, but it is; strongly reinforced when we consider the context – not primarily the context of "so as to afford protection" in Article III:1, but the context of Article III in the GATT as whole. Why do we have Article III? We have it to prevent the use of internal restrictions to achieve goals that would otherwise be achieved by tariffs – both to preserve the value of negotiated tariff concessions, and, even where there are no concessions, as part of the project of channeling protectionism into the tariff mode so that it can be more easily negotiated down. Now, a tariff, the classic protectionist device, is both explicit in its discrimination against foreign products and purposeful. The object of the tariff is to put foreign products at a competitive disadvantage.[25] So, if the point of Article III is to prevent countries from doing by indirection what tariffs do directly, then the paradigm case of an Article III:4 violation is a regulation that discriminates against foreign products explicitly and with protectionist purpose, like the indirect subsidy measure in the classic Italian Agricultural Machinery case.[26]

In the years since Italian Agricultural Machinery, we have recognized that we cannot limit the prohibition of Article III to measures that discriminate explicitly against foreign products – that is, to origin-specific measures. Why not? Because if there were no discipline on origin-neutral measures, then carefully chosen origin-neutral measures could be used for the purpose of achieving protectionist goals. They could function as covert, or disguised, protectionism. So far so good. However, if the reason for disciplining origin-neutral measures is to prevent their use for the purpose of achieving protectionist goals, then the origin-neutral measures we want to suppress are those with protectionist purpose. That is the problem we are aiming at. The language of Article III and the function of Article III in the treaty as a whole both indicate that Article III is aimed at measures motivated by protectionist purpose. There is nothing about either the language or the treaty structure that points to any broader concern.

---

[24] It is an interesting question what native speakers think about the formulations that correspond to "so as to afford protection" in the equally authentic French and Spanish texts of the treaty. The French formulation sounds purposive to my very non-native ear. The Spanish perhaps somewhat less so?

[25] There may also be a revenue goal, but if there are import-competing producers of the same good, then the protectionist goal is manifested in the choice to raise revenue through a tariff rather than a neutral tax. If there are no import-competing producers, then the tariff might indeed be a pure revenue measure, but of course it could then equally be in the form of a neutral tax. The tariff might also be an "optimum tariff" designed to exercise collective monopsony power, but this situation is rare enough, at least in a pure form, so that the generalization in the text stands.

[26] Italian Discrimination Against Imported Agricultural Machinery, BISD 7S/60 (adopted 23 October 1958).

In response to my thesis that our concern is with protectionist purpose, it is often objected that although protectionist purpose is of course sufficient for a violation (at least in conjunction with competitive relationship), it cannot be necessary as I suggest. Two quite different claims are offered in support of this objection. The first claim is that if we require protectionist purpose for a violation, countries will be able to get away with too much covert protectionism; the dispute tribunals will be unable or unwilling to find protectionist purpose where it exists. Notice that this "objection" implicitly concedes that protectionist purpose is what we are worried about. The only dispute is about whether the inquiry into purpose should proceed directly or by indirection. What we would expect at this point is suggestions about presumptions or rules of thumb, which I am happy to incorporate into my approach,[27] or perhaps observations about the significance of particular sorts of evidence, such as evidence about possible alternative measures.[28] Instead, what we usually get is pronouncements that the issue of "so as to afford protection" must be decided "case-by-case," in the exercise of sound "judgment." This is true enough, but it provides no guidance at all in deciding any particular case. (As it happens, I think the tribunals' ability to deal with issues of purpose is already well demonstrated in practice, as I shall explain at some length in section III.B.)

The second major argument against making protectionist purpose necessary for a violation is an argument of principle that does not concede implicitly that purpose is the real crux. The argument is that even measures that have no protectionist purpose may impose costs on foreign interests that exceed the benefit to local interests. Such measures are inefficient in a standard (Kaldor-Hicks) sense. And the argument continues: if the GATT is concerned with efficiency, as it surely is at least in part, should it not forbid this sort of measure? The first point to make in response is that even if the GATT is concerned with efficiency, what Article III is concerned with is measures that are applied "so as to afford protection." I have been arguing that, in its ordinary meaning in context, that phrase refers to measures with protectionist purpose. It is perfectly plausible that the framers of the GATT (and later the WTO) meant to suppress one particular sort of inefficient measure, purposeful protectionism, which they thought the dispute mechanism could adequately identify, without aiming at another sort of inefficient measure whose identification requires a cost/benefit analysis. To my mind, the dispute tribunals are very poorly equipped to do cost/benefit analysis. It is ironic that some of the people who say dispute tribunals cannot identify purpose want to substitute an inquiry for which the tribunals are much less suited.

The second and more important point against the "Kaldor-Hicks interpretation" of Article III is that in the trade context we do not need judicial comparison of

---

[27] One very important element here is the presumption, in effect, that origin-specific regulations are illegal. For an explanation of why the language of Article III compels distinct treatment of origin-neutral and origin-specific measures, even though it does not mention the distinction explicitly, see section II.A below.

[28] Plainly, failure to use less-trade-restrictive measures that would achieve the asserted non-protectionist goal is strong evidence that the actual goal is protectionism. For fuller discussion, see Donald Regan, "Judicial Review of Member-State Regulation of Trade Within a Federal or Quasi-Federal System: Protectionism and Balancing, Da Capo," *Michigan Law Review* (August 2001), pp. 1853–1902, at 1870–1872, 1891–1892, 1899–1902.

the foreign costs and local benefits to ensure that a non-protectionist regulation is Kaldor-Hicks efficient. Rather, we can be confident that a law like the Barataria jug ban is Kaldor-Hicks efficient, or at least that it should be presumed to be so by a dispute settlement tribunal. Why? The argument is in two stages. First, a tribunal applying Article III should presume that a ban imposed by the appropriate Baratarian institution is optimal from the point of view of Baratarian interests, provided it is motivated by concern for the environment and not by protectionism. That should be relatively uncontroversial. Second, in the trade context, a law which is optimal from the point of view of the local interests will be optimal globally. This second claim may seem counterintuitive. It obviously requires an argument, which I have given elsewhere but which is too long to develop fully here.[29] All I can do here to make the claim more plausible is to suggest that the interests of foreign would-be traders are fully accounted for in the legislature's (non-protectionist, domestically optimizing) consideration of the domestic interests that want to trade with the foreigners.

By way of analogy, consider that in an unregulated failure-free market, consumers' choices in response to sellers' offers generate results that are efficient for both consumers and sellers. If a consumer decides that it is not in his interest to buy what some producer is offering, then the resulting non-purchase is efficient even though the consumer gives no thought at all to the seller's interests. For much the same reasons, if the government of Barataria correctly decides that it is not in the interests of Baratarians collectively that some good be consumed in Barataria, then the resulting non-purchases will be efficient (globally) even though the government of Barataria does not consider the foreign producers' interests. If the producers' product/price offers do not attract the consumer's custom, we will not promote efficiency by compelling a purchase. This is as true when the "consumer" is a collectivity such as Barataria as it is when the consumer is an individual, provided the collective decision is not made on protectionist grounds. If Barataria's (non-protectionist) decision is presumed to be optimal for local interests, as it should be, then in this sort of context that amounts to a presumption of global optimality as well. In sum, there is no need for dispute tribunals to worry about whether non-protectionist trade regulation is Kaldor-Hicks inefficient. Article III is right, both on grounds of judicial competence and on grounds of theory, to make protectionist purpose the central issue.[30]

I have heard a rather different suggestion about why "so as to afford protection" should be interpreted to include a concern with regulatory purpose: such an interpretation is necessary to preserve the legitimacy of the WTO institutions. Member governments would not tolerate the application of a test based solely on disparate impact, nor even one that involved serious attempts by the tribunals at cost/benefit balancing. I think this is right, but we need the earlier analysis to explain fully why it is right. Governments would not be so jealous of a "right" to pass legislation that secured small local benefits at large foreign cost, if by giving up that right they could be protected against the losses they would incur when they were on the short end. Rather, governments understand that that is not what is at issue. They understand, vaguely no doubt, that when they decide on non-protectionist grounds that some product is inappropriate for local consumption, their decision creates no inefficiency

---

[29] See Regan, supra note 28, pp. 1853–1879.
[30] Again, see id.

even though it leaves some foreign producers worse off. The decision also imposes no "harm" or "injury" to the producers it leaves worse off, no more than would an individual consumer's decision to redirect his custom. Provided the ban is non-protectionist, the foreign producers have no ground for justified complaint. So, if governments as regulators resist the idea that laws with disparate impact are ipso facto applied "so as to afford protection," they are not reneging on a commitment they made and now regret. They are merely insisting that the text of Article III be applied in accord with its ordinary meaning.

It is sometimes said that the GATT is a "commercial" or "economic" treaty, and therefore the criterion of "likeness" should be commercial or economic – hence we should consider competitive relationship, which is an economic phenomenon, but not regulatory purpose. However, it is grossly misleading to use the claim that the GATT is a "commercial" or "economic" treaty in this way. The GATT is undoubtedly a commercial or economic treaty in a loose sense, but it is not just about commerce or economics. Various Articles – Article III prominent among them – involve major limitations on Members' regulatory powers. Because those regulatory powers encompass both economic and non-economic purposes, it is implausible that the parties would have intended the scope of interference with their regulatory powers to be determined solely by "economic" criteria limited to notions like competitive relationship. The commercial aspect of the treaty justifies the inclusion of competitive relationship among the criteria of likeness, but the other aspects of the treaty make it clear we should not exclude regulatory purpose. We have seen that even to identify the "economic" phenomenon of protectionism, we must be willing to consider whether there are non-protectionist (even non-economic) regulatory purposes that explain the disparate impact on domestic and foreign products. The project of suppressing protectionism, properly understood, leaves room for the full expression of divergent national values.

Let me close this section with a nutshell reminder of the main argument: (1) The meaning of "like products" depends on the purpose of Article III. (2) The purpose of Article III is to prevent protectionism. (3) The project of preventing protectionism requires us to consider the purposes of consumers (in the guise of "competitive relationship") and the purposes of regulators – because of what protectionism is. Not every alteration in competitive conditions is a protectionist "distortion." If a measure has a disproportionate impact on foreign products because foreign products are disproportionately harmful to some public value, then there is nothing to object to. As the Malt Beverages Panel said: "[T]he purpose of Article III is not to prevent contracting parties from differentiating between different product categories for policy purposes unrelated to the protection of domestic production."[31]

---

[31] US – Malt Beverages, ¶5.25. I should mention somewhere the particular puzzle that is posed for purpose analysis by changed circumstances since the adoption of the law. Even if a regulation was adopted with an innocent purpose, it may be maintained for protectionist reasons. We could ask the question directly about the purpose of the non-repeal of the law – but often inaction has no such focused purpose as action. I have suggested elsewhere that we should deal with this problem by taking a hypothetical approach – asking whether it is reasonable to suppose that if the legislature enacted the regulation in the present, they might do so without protectionist purpose. For a fuller discussion, see Regan, supra note 28, pp. 1869–1870.

II. Objections and Answers: The Role of Article XX and the Ascertainability of Purpose

A. Article XX

A standard argument against consideration of the regulatory aim under Article III (advanced by the Panel in Japan – Alcohol, but not repeated by the Appellate Body)[32] is that such consideration would render Article XX inutile: If the measure under review is found to have a valid (non-protectionist) regulatory aim, it will not violate Article III, and there will be no need to consider whether it is excused by Article XX. If, on the other hand, the measure is found not to have a non-protectionist regulatory aim, then not only will it violate Article III, but there will be no candidate aim to consider as possibly grounding an exception under Article XX. Either way, Article XX plays no role, which violates the principle that we must not interpret a treaty in such a way as to render any provision inutile.

This argument is misguided for a number of reasons. First, even if it were true that considering the regulatory aim under Article III would leave no role for Article XX in Article III cases, it would not follow that Article XX was rendered inutile. It would still have a role to play in cases involving violations of any number of other provisions – Article II, Article XI:1, Article X, and so on – where the language does not suggest a direct concern with regulatory aim at all. The principle of efficacy requires that a treaty provision have some function; it does not require that a treaty provision should have a substantive role to play in every case to which, because of its generality, it is formally applicable.[33]

In any event, it is not true that consideration of regulatory aim under Article III renders Article XX irrelevant to all Article III cases. In particular, origin-specific measures will be treated as de jure discriminatory. They will be held to violate Article III on their face and will be remitted automatically to Article XX. Now, to the reader who has just been following along with the flow of the argument, this first mention of de jure discrimination may come as a jolt. The distinction between de jure and de facto discrimination is normally thought to be a fundamental conceptual distinction, and yet we have not hitherto bumped up against it. In retrospect, it seems that all of our discussion of the meaning of "like products" has really been about when we should find de facto discrimination. However, we never made any conscious decision to focus the inquiry that way – it just happened as we pursued the meaning of "like products." What's going on? There is another reason to pause over the de jure/de facto distinction. I have just suggested that origin-specific measures, because they are de jure, are automatically held to violate Article III and remitted to Article XX. I

---

[32] Japan – Taxes on Alcoholic Beverages, WT/DS8 & DS10 & DS11/R, ¶6.17.

[33] It has been suggested to me that perhaps an Article entitled "General Exceptions" should have some application to every prohibitory Article. This seems to read too much into a title. "General," in the context, means at most "broad, and formally universal," but not "universally efficacious in concreto." If a textual argument is required, it is worth comparing the title of Article XX, "General Exceptions," with the title of Article XXI, "Security Exceptions." If these titles are read as parallel in construction, then we see that "General" refers not to the range of other articles that may be excepted from (that is taken care of by the language "nothing in this Agreement" in both Articles XX and XXI), but rather to the nature of the considerations by which the exceptions are justified.

think this is consistent with Panel and Appellate Body practice. And yet, the text of Article III does not distinguish explicitly between origin-specific and origin-neutral measures. Indeed, the Panel in Japan – Alcohol relied on that fact when it argued that the origin-specific/origin-neutral distinction could not justify different modes of analysis.[34] Once again, what's going on?

The answer to both puzzles depends on the following observation: even though Article III does not distinguish explicitly between origin-specific and origin-neutral measures, the language and structure of Article III underwrite – I should say virtually compel – such a distinction. We have seen that in order to decide whether products that are treated differently by an origin-neutral measure are "like," we must first find some specific content for "likeness." We must decide what particular properties are relevant. It turns out that we can skip over that step when we are dealing with an origin-specific measure. The reason is that an origin-specific measure treats differently (or is potentially capable of treating differently) products that are identical in every respect except for their origin. However, products that are identical in every respect except for their origin must be "like" whatever the specific content of "likeness" in the context. If products that differed only in their origin could be "unlike," that would deprive Article III of all application; foreign products would never be "like" any local products, and it would be impossible ever to find that foreign products were treated less favorably than like local products. In sum, the language and purpose of Article III make it clear that all origin-specific measures must be held to distinguish between "like" products and thus to violate Article III (assuming the foreign products are given less favorable treatment). In contrast, we have seen that deciding whether origin-neutral measures violate Article III requires a substantive inquiry into the relevant meaning of "likeness." So, even though there is no explicit mention in Article III of a distinction between origin-specific and origin-neutral measures, the role of the "like products" concept in Article III compels such a distinction.[35]

It may seem that I still have not quite succeeded in giving Article XX a role in any Article III case. I have suggested that origin-specific measures violate Article III automatically and are therefore remitted to Article XX. How then could Article XX possibly save them? How could it ever be necessary, or even useful, to distinguish between products that are identical in every respect except for their origin? There are at least two possibilities here. The less interesting possibility for present purposes is that Article XX may in some cases justify "trade sanctions" – origin-specific measures that are adopted for the purpose of inducing the target country to change some policy of its own. I think many people are too quick to interpret genuinely regulatory measures by the importing country as trade sanctions in this sense, but trade sanctions do exist. They may even be attempts to induce a change in some policy of the target country that has no direct connection at all with the products on which the measure in question bears. Such a trade sanction might, in principle, be found to be justified under Article XX.

There is, however, a more interesting possibility, illustrated by *Maine v. Taylor*,[36] a United States Supreme Court case decided under the "dormant commerce clause."

---

[34] Japan – Taxes on Alcoholic Beverages, WT/DS8 & DS10 & DS11/R, ¶6.16.
[35] Origin-specific measures may still be rescued by Article XX, of course.
[36] 477 U.S. 131 (1986).

Regulatory Purpose and "Like Products" in Article III:4 of the GATT

Maine v. Taylor as it stands would be an Article XI case under the GATT, so I shall tweak the facts a bit (and unfortunately make them more complicated) to make it an Article III case. Certain kinds of baitfish are used by the Maine fishing industry. These baitfish are produced both in state and out of state. Some (but not all) out-of-state baitfish are infested with a parasite that is unknown in Maine baitfish. In significant concentration, the parasite would be a danger to the Maine coastal ecosystem, but in low concentrations it is not. In order to minimize the risk that infested foreign baitfish will introduce the parasite in high concentration to any coastal area, Maine adopts a law that says foreign baitfish may not be sold or used in lots larger than some specified size. The law does not apply to domestic baitfish. This is an origin-specific internal regulation affecting sale that treats foreign products less favorably than like domestic products. (Remember that not all foreign baitfish are infested with the parasite, so the Maine law does indeed disadvantage some foreign baitfish that are identical in every respect to local baitfish.) This is a violation of Article III:4, in effect just because of the origin-specificity. However, now we add a further fact: there is no non-destructive test for establishing which particular foreign fish are infested. It is therefore necessary, in order to protect Maine's ecosystem against dangerous concentrations of the parasite, to limit the sale of all foreign baitfish, including some non-infested "like" baitfish that, if the facts about each individual fish could be fully known, pose no danger at all. This ought to establish an Article XX(b) or XX(g) excuse for the Article III violation. The point, of course, is that this is a case (a relative rarity) where an origin-specific measure is necessary to achieve an "origin-neutral" (that is, non-protectionist) purpose. One function of Article XX is to rescue such cases.[37]

In parallel with its "inutility" argument, the Panel in Japan – Alcohol argued that if regulatory purpose were considered under Article III, then health measures, for example, would not be subjected to the stringent "necessity" standard prescribed by Article XX(b).[38] This of course begs the question whether all health regulations are supposed to be subjected to that stringent standard. The structure of the GATT, under which measures are considered under Article XX only if they have already been

---

[37] It might still be asked, "Why Article XX? Why not bring these considerations under Article III?" I argued above that all origin-specific measures violated Article III because they distinguished between products that were identical in all respects except their origin. We now see, from the baitfish case, that that is both true and not true. It is true in the sense that the Maine baitfish law will exclude some foreign non-infested baitfish that are in fact identical to local non-infested baitfish. It is not true in the sense that all the foreign baitfish, even the non-infested baitfish, are potentially infested – not known to be not infested and not knowably not infested – in a way that distinguish them from the local baitfish. We could say that this epistemological difference is enough to make all foreign baitfish "unlike" all local baitfish, so that the law does not violate Article III. There is a choice to be made here about the relevance of epistemological considerations to the interpretation of "likeness." My inclination, when we are confronted with an origin-specific measure, is to stick with the idea that the law excludes some identical foreign baitfish, even though we cannot identify the particular baitfish that is thus "improperly" excluded. It seems more in keeping with the general structure of Articles III and XX to say that origin specificity raises a strong presumption of illegality – both because it is rare that an origin-neutral purpose requires an origin-specific measure and because an origin-specific measure is particularly likely to be resented by the burdened foreign interests. We embody this strong presumption of illegality in our procedures by requiring that a justification for an origin-specific measure be proved under Article XX, where only certain justifications are available and the regulator bears the burden of proof. No such presumption of illegality can plausibly attach to origin-neutral measures with disparate impact.

[38] Japan – Taxes on Alcoholic Beverages, WT/DS8 & DS10 & DS11/R, ¶6.17.

found to violate some other measure, gives no reason at all to think that the stringent standards of Article XX should be read back into Article III, directly or indirectly. Article III should be applied according to the meaning of its own terms. If anything, the Japan – Alcohol Panel's approach would be likely to cause a watering down of the Article XX standards. If measures are too easily held to violate Article III and passed along indiscriminately for review under Article XX, then dispute tribunals will feel compelled to interpret XX generously to uphold innocent-seeming measures. The result will be an Article XX that allows too many exceptions, at least if it is interpreted consistently, for measures that really do violate Article III properly interpreted, or Article XI, or whatever.

In sum, the danger from giving Article XX too much to do is at least as great as the danger from giving it too little. Article XX is not supposed to do the primary work of identifying violations. Its operation is supposed to be exceptional. It is entitled "General Exceptions." Plainly what is contemplated is a normally self-sufficient inquiry under Article III (or any other prohibitory Article), which is then revised by Article XX only in rare cases. As the Appellate Body says in Asbestos, "The scope and meaning of Article III:4 should not be broadened or restricted beyond what is required by the normal customary international law rules of treaty interpretation, simply because Article XX(b) exists and may be available to justify measures inconsistent with Article III:4."[39]

Finally, it might be suggested that considering only competitive relationship under Article III, and sending on to Article XX any case in which there is a disparate impact on foreign competing products, is at least a way to avoid the difficulties of reviewing regulatory purpose. I shall argue in the next section that the difficulties of purpose review are much overstated. Nor does relying on Article XX entirely avoid purpose review, which is required in some cases by the "disguised restriction" language in the chapeau of Article XX. In addition, the arguments of the previous two paragraphs, aimed against a different suggestion for slighting Article III in favor of Article XX, weigh heavily against this suggestion as well: the suggestion does violence to the ordinary meaning of Article III; it does violence to the status of Article XX as an "exceptions" clause; and it risks watering down the standards of Article XX, with the consequence that we make too many exceptions for genuine Article III violations.

B. Identifying Regulatory Purpose

Two standard objections to a test that considers regulatory purpose are (a) that purpose is too hard to identify and (b) that tribunals are or should be reluctant to find bad purpose because of the imputation of bad faith. The first step in answering both of these objections is to clarify what we mean by the "purpose" or "aim" of a legislature or a regulatory agency. Some people say that such corporate entities do not have purposes in the way individuals do. That is true – they do not have purposes in just the same way individuals do. Even so, we would find it impossible to talk or even think about their behavior without the metaphor of purpose. The question is, what lies behind the metaphor?

---

[39] Asbestos, ¶115.

I suggest that when we talk about the "purpose" of a legislature, we are not talking about any simple aggregation of the purposes of its individual members. We are talking, rather, about the political forces that produced the particular action or action whose "purpose" we wish to identify. When I introduced the example of the Barataria plastic jug ban, I said, concerning the regulatory purpose, that "the impetus for the ban came from environmental quarters." This is the first point that eases the task of identifying purpose: we do not need to peer inside the heads of individual legislators. We only need to ascertain what political forces are responsible for the measure under review.[40]

I am not suggesting, of course, that Panels should call in political scientists as "technical experts" and turn the purpose inquiry over to them. The question for a Panel or the Appellate Body in any particular case is always about the best understanding of what went on in that case. This is a question I think Panel members and, even more, Appellate Body members can handle better than most political scientists. The evidence will always be less than a scientist would want, and its nature and quality will vary from case to case. Panelists will vary in their competence to deal with the sort of question involved – many will be highly qualified but some may not – but Appellate Body members are actually likely to be just the right sort of people to review determinations concerning purpose. They are people of wide "political" experience, whatever their precise career track. They are people who know how this aspect of the world works. That is not to say they will be infallible. Ascertaining the regulator's purpose is not always an easy task, but then, any sensible test will give rise to some hard cases. Tribunal members are actually better prepared to deal with the hard cases thrown up by a purpose test than with the hard cases under any other approach.

Nor should we forget that under the purpose test, many cases are easy. Many cases can be resolved by the merest commonsense appreciation of the content and context of the regulation. Consider the Asbestos case. The Appellate Body never allows itself to mention regulatory purpose,[41] but isn't it obvious that if regulatory purpose were openly admitted to be part of the test, they could have written a much simpler and more persuasive report? They could have said that given the established facts about the dangers of asbestos, prohibiting asbestos (even with some minor temporary exceptions) is a completely natural thing for any legislature to do, and thus when confronted with a prohibition on asbestos, they (the Appellate Body) would assume it was adopted for non-protectionist reasons, even if it had a disparate impact on foreign products, unless they were given strong evidence to the contrary. (What sort of evidence to the contrary? Well, just for example, the sort of ministerial statements about the importance of protecting local businesses that the Appellate Body considered in Canada – Periodicals.)[42] Similarly in the Barataria jug hypothetical – provided there is plausible evidence for the greater environmental costs of plastic jugs, the tribunal could say that banning plastic jugs was a fully understandable regulatory response to the problem, and once again, they would uphold the ban, even if

---

[40] For a fuller discussion of how purpose is interpreted in terms of political process, and the advantages of such an approach, see Regan, supra note 28, pp. 1882–1889.

[41] Except briefly in stating an argument of the European Communities, Asbestos, ¶86.

[42] Canada – Certain Measures Concerning Periodicals, WT/DS31/AB/R, §VI.B.3.

it had a disparate impact on foreign products, unless they were given specific reason to doubt its bona fides.

For an easy case in the other direction, consider the Mississippi wine tax invalidated in US – Malt Beverages, which gave a tax advantage to wine made with a particular grape that was grown only in the Southeastern United States and certain parts of the Mediterranean.[43] Not only did this law prefer local wines, but, as the Panel pointed out, tax distinctions based on the type of grape were unknown in other state or federal laws. Indeed, it is hard to imagine a non-protectionist regulatory purpose. Or consider Chile – Alcohol, with its strangely broken graph of tax rate versus alcohol level.[44] Or Japan – Alcohol, with its extremely disparate taxation of virtually identical products.[45]

As these cases illustrate, the tribunal can get a long way on "objective" evidence – the text, structure, and foreseeable effects of the measure under review. It is crucial to understand that saying the ultimate question is purpose does not mean the tribunal can find a violation only if some responsible official has openly declared a protectionist purpose. Objective evidence, offered by the complaining country, will often be enough to shift to the defendant country the burden of going forward with the evidence, usually by asserting a non-protectionist regulatory justification. On the other hand, if there is relevant "subjective" evidence in the form of ministerial statements, or legislative committee reports, or whatever, the tribunal should consider that too, as the Appellate Body did in Canada – Periodicals, remembering always that even such "subjective" evidence is still just evidence. The tribunal need not invalidate a measure just because one legislator, or a few, who might not be at all representative, trumpeted an illegitimate purpose to curry favor with some constituency. And of course the tribunal does not have to uphold a measure just because an innocent purpose is asserted.

In two other very interesting cases, the Appellate Body engaged in purpose review under the "discrimination or disguised restriction" language in Article 5.5 of the Agreement on the Application of Sanitary and Phytosanitary Measures [SPS Agreement]. In EC – Hormones, the Appellate Body observed that "[n]o suggestion has been made that the import prohibition of treated meat was the result of lobbying by EC domestic producers of beef,"[46] with the implication that such a suggestion would have been relevant to the proceedings. The Appellate Body also detailed sympathetically the understandable anxieties of European Communities consumers about the safety of meat. And it pointed to the felt need for some harmonized standard on hormones within the European Communities.[47] In the end, it found no protectionist purpose.[48] In Australia – Salmon, the Appellate Body was impressed by the change between the 1995 Draft Report (recommending that salmon imports be allowed) and the 1996 Final Report (recommending the ban on salmon imports), and they quote, in a context of general approval of the Panel's treatment of this point, the

---

[43]   US – Malt Beverages, ¶¶5.23–5.26.

[44]   Chile – Alcohol, WT/DS87/AB/R.

[45]   Japan – Alcohol, WT/DS8 & DS10 & DS11/AB/R.

[46]   EC Measures Concerning Meat and Meat Products (Hormones), WT/DS26/AB/R (16 January 1998) [hereafter Hormones], ¶244.

[47]   Hormones, ¶245.

[48]   Id.

Regulatory Purpose and "Like Products" in Article III:4 of the GATT   207

Panel's suggestion that the reversal might have been inspired by pressure from the local salmon industry seeking protection.[49] The Appellate Body had said earlier that the measure's not being based on a risk assessment was "a strong indication" that the measure was a "disguised restriction."[50] Of course this had not been sufficient to establish protectionist purpose in Hormones. These two cases involved serious purpose inquiry, including the consideration of a range of evidence about the political process, and to my mind they came to very plausible conclusions. Of course, Hormones and Salmon were decided under the SPS Agreement; they are not directly relevant to the question whether Article III:4 requires consideration of regulatory purpose. However, they are highly relevant to the question of the Appellate Body's competence to determine purpose where the treaty requires it.

They are also relevant, Salmon especially, to the question of the Appellate Body's willingness to actually find protectionist purpose. It is often said that tribunals will be reluctant to explicitly impute bad faith, or that they should be, but why? Tribunals must stand ready to invalidate measures. Any ground of invalidation is going to involve some kind of criticism of the regulator – if not for bad purpose, then for wanton disregard of foreign interests (in choosing unnecessarily trade-restrictive measures, for example), or for scientific ignorance. It is not apparent why criticism for protectionist purpose is the one criticism that must be avoided. How serious is the "accusation" of protectionist purpose, which is leveled not at an individual but at a legislature or a regulatory agency? It is understood that a primary reason we need international agreements to suppress protectionism is that the forces of protectionism often wield excessive influence in domestic politics, which allows them to secure measures that are damaging even to domestic welfare. The tribunal that finds bad purpose is merely saying about a particular case, "Here is an instance where the local political process went awry in just the way the whole treaty mechanism presupposes it sometimes will. The domestic forces of economic good sense need our treaty-mandated support and intervention to correct the miscarriage." What is so terrible about that?

Even if we shift our focus from the local damage done by protectionism to the violation of reciprocity – the welching on an international bargain – it is still true that the basic reason for the misdeed is not that any person, natural or legal, is evil. It is just that politics is subject to distortions. And politics is subject to distortions everywhere. If the Panels and the Appellate Body decide to start naming protectionist purpose when they see it, they will not find themselves branding just one or two countries as uniquely miscreant. Almost every WTO member, and certainly every major player, indulges in purposeful protectionism from time to time. Is it not generally understood that the Appellate Body found protectionist purpose, whether or not they said so, in Japan – Alcohol,[51] and Chile – Alcohol,[52] and Canada – Periodicals,[53] to name but a few? We should be willing to say what everyone knows, especially since doing so would allow a correct characterization of the real question in Article III cases.

---

[49]   Australia – Measures Affecting Importation of Salmon, WT/DS18/AB/R (20 October 1998), ¶V.C.3.12.
[50]   Id., ¶V.C.3.8.
[51]   See the discussion in section III.B below.
[52]   See the discussion later in this section.
[53]   See text accompanying note 42 supra.

Let us conclude this section by looking at the Appellate Body's treatment of "so as to afford protection" in Chile – Alcohol, decided under Article III:2, second sentence. The Appellate Body quotes from Japan – Alcohol, "'[I]t is not necessary for a panel to sort through the many reasons legislators and regulators often have for what they do and weigh the relative significance of those reasons to establish legislative or regulatory intent.'" Continuing on their own, "The subjective intentions inhabiting the minds of individual legislators or regulators do not bear upon the inquiry, if only because they are not accessible to treaty interpreters." But then, "It does not follow, however, that the statutory purposes or objectives – that is, the purposes or objectives of a Member's legislature and government as a whole – to the extent that they are given objective expression in the statute itself, are not pertinent. To the contrary," and here follows the famous quote from Japan – Alcohol about looking at "the design, the architecture and the revealing structure" of a measure to discern "protective application."[54] And later: "[A] measure's purposes, objectively manifested in the design, architecture, and structure of the measure, are intensely pertinent to the task of evaluating whether or not that measure is applied so as to afford protection to domestic production."[55]

So, "the purposes or objectives of a Member's legislature and government as a whole" are pertinent, to the extent they are given objective expression in the statute. This is just what I have been referring to by "regulatory purpose." To be sure, the repeated references to the purpose being given "objective expression in the statute" might suggest that the only evidence we may consult regarding the legislature's purpose is the face of the statute itself. This is belied, not only by the Appellate Body's attention to ministerial statements in Canada – Periodicals, but by their further discussion of the right way to proceed in Chile – Alcohol itself. It transpires that the Panel must consider Chile's attempt to explain away the damning appearance of the measure considered in isolation.

In the course of agreeing with Chile that its measures need not be shown to be necessary to Chile's asserted purposes, the Appellate Body says:

> It appears to us that the Panel did no more than try to relate the observable structural features of the measure with its declared purposes, a task that is unavoidable in appraising the application of the measure as protective or not of domestic production.[56]

Notice: consideration of "declared purposes" is "unavoidable." And in context it is clear that "declared purposes" means not purposes declared in the statute, but purposes declared to the Panel by Chile's lawyers. "In the present appeal, Chile's explanations concerning the structure of the New Chilean system . . . might have been helpful in understanding what prima facie appear to be anomalies in the progression of tax rates. The conclusion of protective application reached by the Panel becomes very difficult to resist, in the absence of countervailing explanations by Chile. The mere statement of the four objectives pursued by Chile does not constitute effective rebuttal on the part of Chile."[57]

---

[54] Chile – Alcohol, WT/DS87 & DS110/AB/R (13 December 1999), ¶62 (emphases in original, including emphases added by the Chile Division to the Japan quote).

[55] Id., ¶71 (emphasis in original).

[56] Id., ¶72.

[57] Id., ¶71.

Regulatory Purpose and "Like Products" in Article III:4 of the GATT

What the Appellate Body is saying is this (the principal quotation marks that follow indicate an imagined, not an actual, statement – interior quotations are actual): "We are concerned with 'the purposes or objectives of [Chile's] legislature and government as a whole.' The first place we look to ascertain that purpose is the measure itself. This measure, with its peculiar structure so strikingly linked to facts about the precise alcohol levels of domestic and foreign spirits, is powerfully suggestive of protectionist purpose – enough so that if we looked only at the statute, we would hold that it was applied 'so as to afford protection.' Even so, Chile is entitled to a chance to explain away the initial appearance. Consideration of their 'declared purposes' is 'unavoidable.' But their explanations are unpersuasive, so we find that the measure has a protectionist purpose and violates Article III:2, second sentence."

So why is Chile entitled to try to persuade the Panel that the appearance on the face of the statute is misleading? Only because the ultimate question is not about what is on the face of the statute. The ultimate question is the legislature's actual purpose. Chile must show how the measure can be understood to "objectify" an innocent purpose. If they can show that it does objectify, that is, realize, an innocent purpose, they will prevail. Note also that if they produce a persuasive innocent interpretation of a measure that seems to bear an illegal purpose on its face, they will show at the same time that there is no unique purpose "revealed or objectified in the measure itself." Or more precisely, they will show there is no unique purpose objectified in the measure itself and identifiable by reference to the measure itself. If the measure can be shown to bear more than one reasonable interpretation, then the relevant purpose for the "so as to afford protection" inquiry must be the regulator's actual purpose (or our best evidence-based judgment about the actual purpose). The Appellate Body recognizes this just by saying Chile is entitled to contest the initial interpretation of the "objective" purpose of the measure.[58]

In sum, the Appellate Body is gradually acknowledging the role of regulatory purpose. I just want to hurry them along a bit. We have evidence already that they are up to the task of reviewing purpose and that when they openly find bad purpose, the heavens do not fall.

III. EC – Asbestos and Japan – Alcohol

A. EC – Asbestos

So far I have agreed with the Appellate Body in Asbestos on a number of points: (1) Article III must be taken seriously, not just skipped through on the way to Article XX; (2) Article III:4 must be interpreted in light of Article III:1; and (3) competitive relationship between products is a necessary condition for "likeness" under III:4.

---

[58] It might seem that the Appellate Body in Korea – Taxes on Alcoholic Beverages, WT/DS75 & DS84/AB/R (18 January 1999), denied the possibility of justifying a very unequal tax scheme when it said, "[T]he reasons given by Korea as to why the tax is structured in a particular way do not call into question the conclusion that the measures are applied 'so as to afford protection to domestic production'." ¶150. This could be read as saying that attempts at explanation are irrelevant in principle. However, in context the better reading is just that Korea's attempts at explanation were so thin as to be unpersuasive. [See the Panel report, WT/DS75 & DS84/R (17 September 1998), ¶¶5.172–5.181.] And if the Korea Appellate Body in fact meant that attempts at explanation are irrelevant in principle, then Chile – Alcohol, which is both later in time and more explicit, establishes the contrary.

However, I have disagreed with their apparent finding that competitive relationship is not only a necessary condition for likeness, but also a sufficient condition. I have argued that the regulatory purpose of the measure under review must also be considered. The Appellate Body does not recognize the significance of regulatory purpose (at least not explicitly), but neither do they reject it explicitly. They simply do not mention it at all.[59] However, we shall see that regulatory purpose lurks in the background of almost all they say, and that it must be brought in to make some of their arguments complete.

Presumably one reason the Appellate Body does not mention regulatory purpose is that regulatory purpose is not one of the indicia of likeness mentioned in the Border Tax Adjustment Report.[60] The Appellate Body gives this report great prominence, with no explanation except that it has been relied on before. The Appellate Body starts its discussion of "likeness" (without at first mentioning the report) by inquiring into the ordinary meaning of the term in context. They get as far as deciding that "likeness" involves competitive relationship, with the suggestion that competitive relationship is a sufficient condition for likeness.[61] They then digress into (a) the relation between Article III:4 and Article III:2[62] and (b) the independent significance of the "no less favorable" requirement (both of which topics I shall discuss below).[63] When they return to the interpretation of "likeness," it is as if they start all over, taking as their new jumping-off point the traditional list of considerations from the Border Tax Adjustment Report.[64] After a few paragraphs of this, they reiterate that the real question is the competitive relationship between the products, whether or not we look to the report.[65] Then they devote the bulk of the remaining analysis to the proper handling of the Border Tax criteria. As Robert Hudec has observed, the Border Tax list was never put forward as more than a representative list of possible criteria that had been suggested to or in the Working Party.[66] Its canonical status should be reconsidered.

1. The Border Tax Adjustment Criteria and "Competitive Relationship"

For better or worse, the Appellate Body did rely on the Border Tax Report, so let us see how their argument goes. They begin with the first of the Border Tax criteria (as they summarize them),[67] the physical properties of the product. They point out that asbestos and PCG fibers are chemically distinct, and that they are different in physical structure. Of course there is a question about why these physical differences matter. In a sense, the reason is utterly obvious: asbestos is a carcinogen that poses

---

[59] Except, as I have noted previously, in summarizing an argument by the European Communities. EC – Asbestos, WT/DS135/AB/R (12 March 2001), ¶86.

[60] Working Party Report, Border Tax Adjustments, adopted 2 December 1970, BISD 18S/97.

[61] "Thus, a determination of 'likeness' under Article III:4 is, fundamentally, a determination about the nature and extent of a competitive relationship between and among products." Asbestos, ¶99.

[62] Id., ¶99.

[63] Id., ¶100.

[64] Id., ¶101.

[65] Id., ¶103.

[66] Hudec, supra note 17, pp. 112–113.

[67] Asbestos, ¶133.

Regulatory Purpose and "Like Products" in Article III:4 of the GATT

a severe risk to human health, while PCG fibers, so far as we know, are not. This raises a further question, however, about just how the difference in health risk makes the products "unlike" for purposes of Article III:4. To my mind, there is once again an utterly obvious answer: the severe health risk explains why a regulator would ban asbestos, even without any protectionist purpose. However, the Border Tax list does not mention regulatory purpose, and this is not the answer the Appellate Body gives.

Instead, the Appellate Body moves on to another of the Border Tax criteria, consumers' tastes and habits. These are of course the underpinning of any "competitive relationship." The Appellate Body argues that the health risk makes it implausible that there is any competitive relationship between asbestos and PCG fibers.[68] They argue in effect that with regard to the uses for which asbestos is banned, manufacturers would not buy asbestos in preference to PCG fibers even if they were allowed to, because of the health risk. There is something peculiar about this argument. If what the Appellate Body says is true, and known to the legislature, it does entail that the asbestos ban could not have been aimed at protecting domestic production of PCG fibers (which is how competitive relationship got into the discussion in the first place). It also raises the question of how the ban can serve any purpose at all. The Appellate Body's argument for why the ban is permissible seems to entail that it is pointless. Is that plausible?

Notice that there is a more standard sort of argument against the existence of a competitive relationship that raises no difficulty at all for understanding why the legislature acted. Consider a variant of our Barataria case: Barataria adopts its environmental ban on plastic milk jugs. The jug manufacturers challenge the ban on the ground that it does not apply to the domestically produced twenty-gallon metal containers that are used to deliver milk to institutional purchasers. Barataria responds by arguing, inter alia, that the twenty-gallon metal cans are not "like products" to the plastic jugs, because they are not substitutable. We can be persuaded of this claim without raising any question at all about why it is worth having a ban on plastic jugs. The argument against competitive relationship does not depend on arguing that there is no demand for plastic jugs (so long as the big cans are available) in the first place.

However, the Appellate Body's argument does involve arguing that there is no demand for asbestos (where PCG fibers can be used) in the first place. So it raises a question about why the ban is necessary. The mere fact that France had its asbestos ban suggests that their view about the shape of consumer preferences was more like Canada's view (that there was some market for banned asbestos, and some competitive relationship) than like the Appellate Body's view. It is still true, of course, that if the Appellate Body is right about the facts of consumer demand, then the law could not achieve any protectionist goal. However, this logically impeccable position seems to involve a sort of Alice-in-Wonderland view of the case.

Perhaps what the Appellate Body has in mind is the following: Fully informed and rational consumers would not buy asbestos. Therefore there would be no competitive

---

[68] Id. ¶139, relying on earlier argument in ¶¶113–123. Technically, the Appellate Body argues only that Canada has not carried its burden of proof of showing a competitive relationship, but it is plain that their attitude to what Canada needs to do is colored by their view about what is plausible.

relationship between asbestos and PCG fibers if consumers were fully informed and rational. Therefore a law that bans asbestos cannot be (or should not count as?) protecting PCG fibers. However, this is not what the Appellate Body says, and for good reason. "Rational" is a normative concept, and therefore how fully informed and rational consumers would behave is not an empirically observable economic fact (not even observable with difficulty, like cross-elasticities and actual competitive relationships given consumers as they are). Indeed, it seems all too clear that an appeal to the behavior of "rational" consumers would really be an appeal to the Appellate Body's own regulatory purpose, an appeal to their views about how consumers should behave.[69] Better in principle to rely on France's regulatory purpose than to rely on the Appellate Body's – even when the purpose, protecting health, is the same. In order to avoid relying on either France's regulatory purpose or their own, the Appellate Body must argue that there is no actual competitive relationship, because consumers as they are will not buy asbestos. Which leaves us with the problem of why France passed the law.

There is a different peculiarity in the Appellate Body's discussion of manufacturer–purchasers of asbestos.[70] The basic argument – that manufacturers will not buy asbestos because ultimate consumers will not buy products with asbestos – is doubly subject to the objection I have just raised: if consumers will not buy products with asbestos, and manufacturers therefore will not use asbestos, the need for any ban seems undercut at both levels. Aside from that, the Appellate Body also suggests that manufacturers may not buy asbestos because of possible civil liability. So why is it that domestic laws of delict that end up imposing greater liability on asbestos than on PCG fibers do not themselves violate Article III? They are certainly internal regulations that "affect" sale – that is precisely the Appellate Body's claim. Once again, it is completely obvious why such laws are GATT-legal – it is because asbestos is a powerful carcinogen. My point is just that this is not a claim about consumer preference; this is a regulatory justification. (Alternatively, one might say that the reason the liability laws are GATT-legal is that they are too general to be intended as protection for any particular product or set of products. True enough, but this argument again appeals to regulatory purpose.)

In sum, the Appellate Body's attempts to rely solely on competitive relationship, without bringing in regulatory purpose, either have an otherworldly air, or else require reference to regulatory purpose to complete them. Perhaps the Appellate Body thought WTO insiders were not yet ready for explicit appeal to regulatory purpose. However, I doubt that acknowledgment of the role of regulatory purpose can be put off much longer.

2. The Roles of Physical Properties and Competitive Relationship

The Appellate Body itself may have some ambivalence about the sufficiency of competitive relationship. If we return to the question of precisely how the physical differences between asbestos and PCG fibers, and the consequent difference in health

---

[69] The Appellate Body acknowledges in a footnote that informed consumers sometimes make choices that involve risks to their health, as with tobacco. Id., ¶122, n.103.

[70] Id., ¶122.

Regulatory Purpose and "Like Products" in Article III:4 of the GATT 213

risk, matter to the Article III analysis, we will find the report is ambiguous between the following subtly different positions:

(1) the physical differences and consequent different health risk make asbestos and PCG fibers physically unlike, and this unlikeness under one of the Border Tax categories counts in itself against a finding of overall likeness, so that even if the products were shown to be perfectly competitive, the weight of this consumer-habit-based "likeness" might not in the final analysis overbalance the independent weight of the physical-properties-based "unlikeness";[71] or

(2) the physical unlikeness and consequent difference in health risk has no weight in itself, but it makes it presumptively implausible that consumers really regard the products as substitutes, so that in the absence of strong evidence of a competitive relationship, we will find no consumer-habit-based "likeness," and Canada has not carried its burden to show likeness by positive evidence.[72]

The distinction between (1) and (2) does not matter on the facts of Asbestos as the Appellate Body sees them, which is why it can go unresolved, perhaps even unnoticed. However, the choice would matter in the Barataria jug case, or indeed in any case where the physical difference and consequent cost to some public value matters to the public at large but does not influence the particular consumers of the harmful product (whether because they just don't care, or because of the sort of collective action problem we mentioned above). In such a case, assuming the consumer indifference can be shown, (2) will lead to a finding of "likeness," and thus to the invalidation of the measure. In contrast, (1) will allow the physical and public policy difference to be counted against "likeness" even when it has no effect on consumer behavior, so the products can be found "unlike" and the measure can be upheld.

As I say, the Asbestos report is ambiguous between (1) and (2). View (2) seems the more obvious reading, and it is the reading I implicitly assumed in previous sections when I said the Appellate Body treated competitiveness as a necessary and sufficient condition of likeness. However, if the correct reading is (1), then competitiveness is not sufficient, and regulatory purpose is back in the game, even if it does not appear on the scorecard. As we said many pages ago, if we try to locate likeness or unlikeness in physical characteristics, then the question arises about which physical characteristics matter. View (2) has an implicit answer to that – the physical characteristics that matter are those, and only those, that matter to consumers. If view (1) is the proper reading, then it is not consumer preferences, or not exclusively consumer preferences, that determine which physical characteristics are relevant. So what does determine which physical characteristics are relevant? The only possible answer is "regulatory purpose." Carcinogenicity is relevant because it reveals a plausible non-protectionist regulatory purpose for distinguishing between the products. That is how it makes the products "unlike." So, if view (1) is the proper reading, regulatory purpose is even nearer the surface of the Asbestos report than our previous discussion suggested. That is the hopeful view.

---

[71] This position might be suggested by, e.g., id., ¶¶118, 121.
[72] This position is suggested by, e.g., id., ¶¶114, 115.

3. The Puzzle of ¶100

Another puzzle about the Appellate Body report in Asbestos concerns paragraph 100. The Appellate Body reminds us that even if two products are found to be like, there is still no violation of Article III:4 unless the imported products are given "less favorable treatment" than the domestic products. "[A] Member may draw distinctions between products which have been found to be 'like', without, for this reason alone, according to the group of 'like' imported products 'less favorable treatment' than that accorded to the group of 'like' domestic products."[73] The Appellate Body explicitly declines to further examine the issue of "less favorable treatment," because there was no appeal from the Panel's findings on that issue. It is therefore not clear why they raised the matter at all. The Appellate Body says it wants to avoid misunderstandings that might be brought about in future cases by the "broad scope" they give to "like products," but they do not say what misunderstandings they anticipate.

It could be that the Appellate Body was suggesting another possible route to their result in Asbestos itself. They may have been suggesting that even if asbestos and PCG fibers were held to be "like," it would still be possible to say that the group of "like" imported products (Canadian asbestos-plus-PCG fibers) was not treated less favorably than the group of "like" domestic products (French asbestos-plus-PCG fibers), because foreign and domestic products were subjected to exactly the same regulatory regime. This argument gets the right result in the case before us, and what is more, it is obviously saying something true and relevant, but it cannot be taken at face value. If it suffices to avoid a violation that foreign and domestic products are subjected to the same regulatory regime, then an origin-neutral measure could never violate Article III:4. In other words, this argument would do away entirely with de facto discrimination.

So what is the real point that the argument is making? Here is a suggestion: Asbestos is treated less favorably than PCG fibers; and asbestos is the "foreign" product; but even so, asbestos is not treated less favorably because of its foreignness. The foreign product is not treated less favorably as such. In that sense, foreign products are not treated less favorably. (And why is asbestos treated less favorably, if not because it is foreign? Plainly, because it is dangerous.) We can make the same point from the other direction: Because an origin-neutral measure subjects domestic and foreign products to the same legal regime, it presumptively accords "no less favorable treatment" to foreign products; and the presumption is not rebutted just because the measure happens to have a disparate impact on foreign products. However, the measure does accord foreign products less favorable treatment, despite its facial neutrality, if it is adopted for the purpose of disadvantaging foreign products just because they are foreign. We might say the less favorable treatment is not in the measure itself, but in its adoption. Still, there plainly is less favorable treatment when imports as such are targeted for disadvantage. Whichever direction we make the argument from, we see that we are looking to regulatory purpose to give content to "less favorable treatment," just as we earlier looked to regulatory purpose to give content to "like products." There is more than one way we

---

[73] Id., ¶100.

can bring regulatory purpose into the discussion, but one way or another it must be considered.[74]

Remember we are trying to figure out why the Appellate Body reminds us in paragraph 100 that there is no violation without "less favorable treatment." We have considered one possibility, that they are suggesting an alternate route to the result in Asbestos itself. There is another possibility worth mentioning, though it has less to do with the actual facts of Asbestos. The Appellate Body might be reminding us that we should not find a violation under an origin-neutral measure unless there is disparate impact – that is, unless foreign goods lose, or can be expected to lose, market share to domestic goods as a result of the measure. (I am not suggesting disparate impact is sufficient for an Article III violation. I am suggesting it is necessary.) Suppose, contrary to fact, that both Canada and France produce both asbestos and PCG fibers, and that Canadian PCG fibers have the same fraction of PCG sales in France that Canadian asbestos has of asbestos sales in France.[75] In these circumstances, if France passes a law disadvantaging asbestos vis-à-vis PCG fibers, that will affect sales of both asbestos and PCG fibers, but because Canada has the same share of both submarkets, there is no reason to think it will affect sales of Canadian asbestos-plus-PCG fibers any differently from the way it affects sales of French asbestos-plus-PCG fibers. There is no disparate impact; the group of foreign like products does not lose market share (nor is it disadvantaged with regard to "competitive opportunity"); there is nothing to suggest a protectionist purpose; and therefore there should be no violation.

The proposition that there is no violation in such a case seems almost too obvious to be worth asserting, but it is inconsistent with an argument advanced by the Malt Beverages Panel in striking down a New York tax that discriminated against beer from other states as well as from Canada. (They got the right result, but for the wrong reason.) The Panel suggested that there is a violation if foreign products are treated less favorably than the most favored "like" domestic product.[76] In our example from the previous paragraph, there is a violation if Canadian asbestos (or even Canadian asbestos-plus-PCG fibers) is treated less favorably than "like" French PCG fibers (ignoring the treatment of French asbestos). I have explained elsewhere why this Malt Beverages argument does violence to the text of Article III,[77] but our example reveals that it could also produce the unacceptable consequence of finding a violation of national treatment even without any disparate impact on foreign goods.[78] It happens

---

[74] It is not surprising that regulatory purpose should come in by two routes. There is one underlying question, about "so as to afford protection." If we divide that into a two-aspect question, about "less favorable treatment" of "like" foreign products, it is natural that the underlying issue can manifest itself through either aspect. The one minor difference is this: If we come to the question of regulatory purpose through the meaning of "like product," we are directed primarily to look for plausible non-protectionist purposes. In contrast, if we come to the question of regulatory purpose through the meaning of "less favorable treatment," we are directed more immediately to the question whether the actual purpose was protectionism. However, these are just opposite sides of the same coin.

[75] I ignore the fact that France is part of the European Communities. This raises some genuine questions about which producers and which markets we should look at, but those questions are peripheral to the central point.

[76] US – Malt Beverages, BISD 39S/206, ¶5.17.

[77] Howse & Regan, supra note 7, at n.22.

[78] In rejecting this argument from Malt Beverages, I cast no doubt on the result in United States – Section 337 of the Tariff Act of 1930, BISD 36S/345 (adopted 7 November 1989). The reason that product-by-product

216   Donald H. Regan

that if we analyze "like" along the lines I have been recommending, then this bad Malt Beverages argument could never actually lead to error. However, one thing the Appellate Body may be trying to do, on either interpretation of the point of paragraph 100, is to construct a "fail-safe" procedure, so that errors at one stage of the analysis can be caught and cancelled at another.[79]

B. Japan – Alcohol

In Japan – Alcohol, the Appellate Body dealt with Article III:2. Observing that Article III:2, second sentence, includes an explicit reference to Article III:1, while Article III:2, first sentence, does not, they concluded that the policy of Article III:1 (that measures not be applied "so as to afford protection") must inform the analysis under the two sentences of Article III:2 in different ways. Specifically, they said that Article III:2, first sentence, was intended as an independent and self-sufficient (partial) realization of the policy of III:1, so analysis under that sentence should proceed without explicit reference to III:1. In contrast, the analysis under III:2, second sentence, must include a step specifically adverting to the policy of III:1.[80]

I want to make four points about Japan – Alcohol, some that elaborate on things I have said elsewhere, some that are new. Here is a quick preview, to help the reader orient herself: (1) Contrary to what the Appellate Body says, Article III:2, first sentence, does not exclude direct consideration of "so as to afford protection." Indeed, at one point the Appellate Body clearly (but indirectly) acknowledge that they have considered "so as to afford protection" under III:2, first sentence. (2) Even so, the "so as to afford protection" policy of Article III:1 informs the analysis differently under the two sentences of Article III:2, as the Appellate Body says it must. There is a difference in the way the two sentences work, but the Japan – Alcohol Appellate Body misdescribes it. (3) The Appellate Body's decision that III:2, second sentence, requires specific consideration of the "so as to afford protection" issue was correct, but it was not compelled by the text of Article III in the way they claim; rather, their decision reveals an implicit understanding that dissimilar treatment of competitive products is not a sufficient ground for finding an Article III violation. (4) Indeed, the

---

or case-by-case differences in treatment mattered in that case, even if, as the United States claimed, the overall statistics showed no disadvantage to the ensemble of foreign products subjected to patent challenge, was that the randomness itself, at the product or case level, imposed uncertainty costs on investors. There is no comparable uncertainty in my asbestos hypothetical.

[79] This "fail-safe" idea was brought clearly into focus for me by conversation with Rob Howse. Notice that the existence of the "fail-safe" mechanism is not an argument for a more relaxed view about what are "like products" (and a fortiori not an argument for a more relaxed view about Article III, because Article XX waits in the wings). The point of a "fail-safe" mechanism is to have multiple safeguards against error (in this case, against inappropriate interference with innocent regulation).

There is a third possibility about Asbestos ¶100, that it is just reminding us of the standard but important point that different treatment is not necessarily less favorable treatment. At least in principle, some treatment could be different but equally favorable. This is not very plausible as an interpretation of ¶100, since this point has not even a possible application to Asbestos itself. No matter how we slice up the universe of products in Asbestos, there is never a pair of products or product groups that we could plausibly think of as being treated differently but equally favorably. (Nor does this point seem more likely to be overlooked because "like products" is given a broad scope.)

[80] Japan – Alcohol, WT/DS8 & DS10 & DS11/AB/R (4 October 1996), H.2.

Regulatory Purpose and "Like Products" in Article III:4 of the GATT

Appellate Body gives every appearance of understanding that the additional required element is protectionist purpose, even though they deny it.

Now back to the beginning. With regard to the first sentence of Article III:2, the Appellate Body says that because there is no explicit reference to Article III:1 in that sentence, the issue of "so as to afford protection" is not to be considered directly. They say that the criteria of (i) taxes on imports "in excess of" those on (ii) "like" domestic products constitute a self-sufficient (partial) realization of the policy of III:1. Now we have the perennial question, when are goods "like"? In a rather murky discussion, the Appellate Body seems to focus primarily on physical properties.[81] This could use some explanation, but I shall not object to this focus in the context. That still leaves the question, however, "Just how alike in their physical properties must products be in order to count as 'like'?"

The Appellate Body says that "likeness" must be interpreted very narrowly in Article III:2, first sentence.[82] The primary reason they suggest is that room must be left for III:2, second sentence, to have some scope. So far so good, but this tells us very little, because we do not know as yet either how broad the total scope of Article III:2 (both sentences) is to be, nor how it is to be divided between the sentences. At this point, the Appellate Body embarks on its long discussion of looking at all the evidence and exercising discretion, and it produces its famous "accordion" image.[83]

Surely it is clear that there is a second reason why "like" must be interpreted narrowly, which also helps us to see just how narrowly. If Article III:2, first sentence, is to be regarded as a self-sufficient (partial) realization of the policy of III:1, then "like" must be given a meaning that makes III:2, first sentence, work as a realization of that policy. "Like" must be given a meaning such that we are confident that any difference at all in the tax treatment of foreign and domestic products regarded as "like" does in fact reflect protectionism. So it turns out that we must consider the issue of protectionism after all, in order to assign meaning to "like," specifically in order to answer the question "how alike?" There is no alternative.

Notice I am not denying that we might in principle have a policy stated in one paragraph of a treaty or statute, and then a specific realization of that policy in another paragraph that can be applied without any reference at all to the first provision. Imagine a statute on public swimming pools that says in its first paragraph, "All public pools shall be safe for all swimmers using them," and then says in a later paragraph, "No pool for use by children under age five shall have a maximum depth greater than eighteen inches." Here the latter paragraph can be applied (at least to any ordinary case) without any attention at all to the underlying policy, but that is because "age five" and "eighteen inches" are precise terms with a clear independent content. "Like" is not similarly autonomous, not even after we have decided to concentrate on physical properties. The only way to give content to "like" in Article III:2, first sentence, is by reference to the policy of III:1. This can be done openly or covertly, but it must be done.

My claim is confirmed by a curious remark in the Appellate Body report in Japan – Alcohol. In the midst of their discussion of whether shochu and vodka are

---

[81] Id., H.1(a).
[82] Ibid.
[83] Ibid.

"like products," the Appellate Body suddenly says, in a strikingly obiter dictum, "We note that the determination of whether vodka is a 'like product' to shochu under Article III:2, first sentence, or a 'directly competitive or substitutable product' to shochu under Article III:2, second sentence, does not materially affect the outcome of this case."[84] However, the Appellate Body tells us later that an invalidation under III:2, second sentence, would require an explicit finding that the dissimilar taxation was applied "so as to afford protection."[85] So their statement that it makes no difference whether we consider the vodka/shochu pair under the first sentence of III:2 or under the second sentence entails that the Appellate Body has decided the different taxation of vodka/shochu is applied "so as to afford protection." There is nothing remarkable in the content of this decision; what is important to notice is just that the Appellate Body had made it, consciously or unconsciously. They did not in fact reach a conclusion under III:2, first sentence, without adverting to the policy of III:1.

Post-Asbestos, the Appellate Body should simply acknowledge that interpreting Article III:2, first sentence, requires consideration of the policy of III:1. We can just run the Bananas reasoning backward. In its brief treatment of Article III:4, the Bananas Appellate Body told us that because III:2, first sentence, and III:4 were alike in not referring explicitly to III:1, the relation between III:1 and those two other provisions must be the same. Bananas apparently followed Japan – Alcohol's treatment of III:2, first sentence, saying we should not look to III:1 in interpreting III:4.[86] However, now the Asbestos Appellate Body has told us, correctly, that we must look to III:1 in interpreting III:4. It follows by the Bananas major premise that we must look to III:1 in interpreting III:2, first sentence, also. So the Appellate Body can admit openly to what it is already doing.[87]

It might seem that the Dispute Settlement Body has rejected my proposal about how Article III:2, first sentence, works as recently as Argentina – Bovine Hides/Leather.[88] Argentina argued that even though the "so as to afford protection" policy of Article III:1 was not to be considered in a separate step under Article III:2, first sentence, it was nonetheless relevant in determining "likeness."[89] The Panel, whose report was adopted without appeal, said in no uncertain terms that "so as to afford protection" was not to be attended to directly in any way, shape or form – neither as a separate step nor as part of the other required steps.[90] I have already explained why I think Panels and the Appellate Body cannot abide by this general prohibition, and I have pointed out that the Japan – Alcohol Appellate Body

---

[84] Ibid.

[85] Id., H.2.

[86] EC – Bananas, WT/DS27/AB/R (9 September 1997), ¶216. For an explanation of the "apparently," see note 91 below.

[87] We could of course now deny the Bananas premise; we could say that because Article III:2 and III:4 have fundamentally different structures, there is no inference from how III:1 figures in the one to how it figures in the other. In fact, I would not argue that the Asbestos treatment of III:1 and III:4 itself entails any conclusion about III:1 and III:2, first sentence. However, the Asbestos treatment of III:1 and III:4 certainly suggests and allows the view that we should look to III:1 in interpreting III:2, first sentence, if there is independent reason to take that position, as we have seen there is.

[88] Argentina – Measures Affecting the Export of Bovine Hides and the Import of Finished Leather, WT/DS155/R (adopted 16 February 2001).

[89] Id., ¶11.133.

[90] Id., ¶11.137.

indicated it did not abide by it. Ironically, the statement of the Argentina Panel makes perfect sense in its context. The reason is that Argentina involved an origin-specific measure. In a case like Japan – Alcohol, which involves an origin-neutral measure, the reason we must appeal to "so as to afford protection," even under III:2, first sentence, is to give specific content to "like" – that is, to answer the questions "like in what respects? and to what degree?" However, we saw in section II.A that we can decide that an origin-specific measure treats foreign products differently from "like" domestic products without assigning any specific content to "like." If we do not need to give a specific content to "like" in connection with an origin-specific measure, then we do not need to consider "so as to afford protection" in any way at all – just as the Argentina Panel says. It remains true that in dealing with an origin-neutral measure such as the measure involved in Japan – Alcohol, we must somehow attend to the "so as to afford protection" policy, even under Article III:2, first sentence. If there is no separate step, then the "so as to afford protection" policy must be part of the inquiry into "likeness."

It might seem that if we look to Article III:1 when interpreting Article III:2, first sentence, then we do violence to the text in a different way, because nothing in our interpretive approach now reflects that fact that III:2, second sentence, refers back explicitly to III:1, while III:2, first sentence, does not. However, that is not true. There is still a difference in the interpretive approach to the two sentences. Under III:2, first sentence, on the approach I am suggesting, we look to the policy of III:1 as part of deciding whether products are "like." That means that once we have made the decision on likeness, and then on taxation "in excess," there is no need to consider the policy of III:1 in a separate step of the analysis. That policy has already been taken into account. In contrast, under III:2, second sentence, we can decide whether goods are "directly competitive or substitutable," and then whether they are "not similarly taxed" without considering the policy of III:1 (or at least we can come a lot closer to doing so). Hence, if the policy of III:1 is to be considered, it must be brought in a separate step of the analysis, as the Japan – Alcohol Appellate Body required. The difference between the analyses under the two sentences of III:2 lies in whether considering the policy of III:1 does or does not require a separate step.

This difference in the analysis under the two sentences of Article III:2 reflects a difference in the nature of the concepts "like" and "directly competitive or substitutable." The Appellate Body tells us that in III:2, "like" must be given a narrower meaning than "directly competitive or substitutable"; and there is no difficulty in arranging the requisite degree of likeness so that it in fact covers fewer cases. However, in a different way, "like" is essentially a broader notion than "directly competitive or substitutable." As we have pointed out, saying merely that we are concerned with the treatment of "like" products leaves completely open the dimensions of the comparison. It therefore allows us to select and focus on whatever dimensions are relevant to "so as to afford protection." (Specifically, it allows us to consider both competitive relationship and regulatory purpose.) Once we have made the decision about "likeness" in this light, the issue of "so as to afford protection" requires no further attention. In contrast, "directly competitive or substitutable" focuses on a specific dimension of comparison, the competitive relationship in the market. If this is not the only dimension relevant to "so as to afford protection" – as we have seen it is not – then we must give independent attention to the "so as to afford protection" issue, to bring in the other dimension. That is why III:2, second sentence, requires a "separate step," and III:2, first sentence, does not.[91]

There is evidence that the Appellate Body in Japan – Alcohol understood this difference between the nature of the concepts "like" and "directly competitive or substitutable," intuitively if not consciously. The Appellate Body claims that their three-stage structure of analysis under III:2, second sentence, is compelled by the text of the Article (with the Ad Note), but in truth it is not, or not in the way they say. Let us remember the language and structure. The primary text of Article III:2, second sentence, says:

> Moreover, no contracting party shall otherwise apply internal taxes or other internal charges to imported or domestic products in a manner contrary to the principles set forth in paragraph 1.

(Paragraph 1, of course, states the general principle that internal measures should not be applied "so as to afford protection.") The Note Ad Article III:2 reads:

> A tax conforming to the requirements of the first sentence of paragraph 2 would be considered to be inconsistent with the provisions of the second sentence only in cases where competition was involved between, on the one hand, the taxed product and, on the other hand, a directly competitive or substitutable product which was not similarly taxed.

The Appellate Body asserts that this structure requires the dispute tribunals to address three separate issues under III:2, second sentence – (i) whether imported and domestic products are "directly competitive or substitutable," (ii) whether the products are "not similarly taxed," and (iii) whether the measure is applied "so as to afford protection."[92] However, there is no strong textual reason why the Ad Note could not have been regarded as an independent and self-sufficient (partial) application of the policy of Article III:1 referred to in the primary text of III:2, second sentence, in exactly the same way that the Appellate Body said that III:2, first sentence, was an independent and self-sufficient (partial) application of Article III:1 itself. In other words, there is no textual reason why the Appellate Body could not have said that a violation of III:2, second sentence, required only dissimilar taxation of directly competitive or substitutable products, and no more. It would be different if the three criteria listed above ("directly competitive or substitutable," "not similarly taxed," and "so as to afford protection") were all listed side by side in one sentence, but they are divided between two places. The third criterion, "so as to afford protection," appears, by reference to III:1, in III:2, second sentence, itself. The first two criteria appear in the Ad Note. It would be very natural to regard the Ad Note as not an addition to, but an explication of, the primary sentence. The Ad Note would then bear exactly the same relation to III:2, second sentence, that the Appellate Body says

---

[91] If we look carefully, we will see that all the Appellate Body ever said about Article III:4 in Bananas was that the analysis did not require a separate step devoted to "so as to afford protection." I think saying that and only that, without explication of the role of "so as to afford protection" in the interpretation of "like products," was potentially very misleading and probably misled many readers. Still what they actually precisely said is completely consistent, both with what I am arguing here and with what they say about the relevance of III:1 to III:4 in Asbestos.

[92] Japan – Alcohol, H.2.

Regulatory Purpose and "Like Products" in Article III:4 of the GATT

Article III:2, first sentence, bears to Article III:1. If anything, the passage the Appellate Body quotes from a drafting report at the Havana Conference suggests precisely this: "The details [of Article III] have been relegated to interpretative notes so that it would be easier for members to ascertain the precise scope of their obligations under the Article."[93] This sounds more like the interpretative note is a self-sufficient spelling out of III:2, second sentence, than like it is an addition.[94]

My point is not that the Appellate Body got it wrong when they required separate consideration of "so as to afford protection" under Article III:2, second sentence. I think they got it right. My point is that they were making a choice, at least implicitly. And the best reason for making the choice they did, to require a separate step focusing on "so as to afford protection," is the point I made a moment ago: consideration of "directly competitive or substitutable" does not inevitably implicate consideration of (all relevant aspects of) "so as to afford protection" as consideration of "like" does. Furthermore, for reasons I expounded in section I, findings of "dissimilar treatment" of "competitive products" should not be regarded as sufficient grounds for finding a violation. The aspect of "so as to afford protection" that has not been considered in the course of making those findings, namely regulatory purpose, must be considered lest innocent, non-protectionist regulation or taxation be invalidated. All of this the Appellate Body may have grasped intuitively.

Did the Japan – Alcohol Appellate Body really grasp "all of this"? Did they grasp not only that we need a separate step under III:2, second sentence, to consider "so as to afford protection," but also that what is specifically required at that step is attention to regulatory purpose? I think the evidence is that they did. They considered regulatory purpose even as they claimed not to. Consider one of the most-quoted passages from the report:

> Although it is true that the aim of a measure may not be easily ascertained, nevertheless its protective application can most often be discerned from the design, the architecture, and the revealing structure of a measure. The very magnitude of the dissimilar taxation in a particular case may be evidence of such a protective application, as the Panel rightly concluded in this case.[95]

Robert Hudec says about this passage, "The quotation makes a great deal more sense if one substitutes the word 'purpose' for 'application.' "[96] I agree entirely. In addition, it is worth noting specifically the word "revealing" in the phrase "revealing structure." The clear implication is that attention to the structure will "reveal" something that is otherwise hidden. What could that be? It cannot be facial discrimination – that is too much on the surface to speak of it as being "revealed." It cannot be the actual effects of the measure – only empirical investigation of the measure in operation

---

[93] Ibid., n.52, quoting from the drafting history at the Havana Conference, E/CONF.2/C.3/59, p. 8.

[94] To be sure, treating the interpretative note as a self-sufficient spelling-out of III:2, second sentence, might not do justice to the precise logical import of the phrase "only in cases" in the Ad Note. "Only in" makes the conditions it names necessary, not sufficient. On the other hand, the use of "only in" does not deny that the named conditions are intended to be sufficient, if the general structure suggests that. I doubt the treaty drafters were always perfectly punctilious about necessary and sufficient conditions.

[95] Japan – Alcohol, H.2(c).

[96] Robert Hudec, "GATT/WTO Constraints on National Regulation: Requiem for an 'Aims and Effects' Test," *International Lawyer* (Fall 1998), Vol. 32 No. 3; pp. 619–649, at 631.

will reveal that. Surely what may be "revealed" by contemplation of the measure's design, architecture, and "revealing" structure is protectionist purpose. The use of the word "revealing" itself reveals the Appellate Body's thinking.

There is a further point about word usage. In the climactic paragraph of its report, the Appellate Body quotes and endorses the words of the Panel:

> Thus, through a combination of high import duties and differentiated internal taxes, Japan manages to "isolate" domestically produced shochu from foreign competition, be it foreign produced shochu or any other of the mentioned white and brown spirits.[97]

"Manages"? In this context, the clear connotation of "manages" is disguised purpose. The Appellate Body found that the measure was applied "so as to afford protection" because they thought it was motivated by a purpose to protect domestic production.

Summing Up

Let us quickly review our main conclusions, in reverse order:

> *III.B.* Despite its official doctrine, the Appellate Body in Japan – Alcohol did in fact think about "so as to afford protection" in connection with Article III:2, first sentence, and to all appearances they regarded protectionist purpose as the key to "so as to afford protection" in the discussion of III:2, second sentence.
>
> *III.A.* The Appellate Body in EC – Asbestos relies on arguments about competitive relationship that make sense only if we supplement them with considerations of regulatory purpose. In addition, the Appellate Body's general discussion of the role of physical likeness and competitive relationship is more ambiguous and leaves more room for consideration of regulatory purpose than is apparent on a first reading.
>
> *II.B.* In response to the claim that dispute tribunals are either incompetent or unwilling to find protectionist purpose, I pointed out that the Appellate Body already has a considerable track record of successful grappling with the issue of purpose – both in cases where they denied it or sidled around the issue (Japan – Alcohol, Korea – Alcohol, Canada – Periodicals) and in cases where they were quite open about their concern with purpose (Chile – Alcohol, EC – Hormones, Australia – Salmon). The purpose inquiry does not require us to read the minds of individual legislators. It requires an appreciation of the political forces at work in the regulating body. (The regulation itself and its foreseeable effects remain of course the primary evidence.) This is an inquiry for which the dispute tribunals are much better suited than for any other well-defined inquiry that might be suggested for deciding this range of cases.
>
> *II.A.* Considering regulatory purpose under Article III will not render Article XX inutile, nor even render it irrelevant to Article III. Origin-specific measures can be held to violate Article III on a per se basis and thus be remitted to Article XX. Although Article III does not distinguish explicitly between origin-specific and

---

[97] Japan – Alcohol, H.2(c), quoting the Panel report, ¶6.35.

origin-neutral measures, we saw that such a distinction is entailed by the structure of the "like products" issue. The real danger in this area is not that we will give Article XX too little to do, but that by finding violations of Article III too easily, we will give Article XX too much to do and weaken it unduly as a result.

I. Consideration of regulatory purpose is required by the ordinary meaning of "like products" in the context of Article III:4. "Like products" must be interpreted in light of the "so as to afford protection" policy of Article III:1, and the existence of protectionism depends on regulatory purpose. Ordinary linguistic usage confirms this; the role of Article III in the GATT as a whole confirms this; and economic theory confirms this (regulation with a non-protectionist purpose should be presumed by WTO tribunals to optimize over local interests, and in the trade context, that is enough to guarantee global efficiency).

Prologue. The Appellate Body is already logically committed by its own doctrine to considering regulatory purpose under Article III:4. It remains only for them to draw the conclusion.

DAVID PALMETER

7. The WTO Standard of Review in Health and Safety Disputes

"Standard of review" is a term widely used in the law of the United States. It is most relevant when courts are reviewing decisions of administrative agencies. Various "standards" for review are set forth in scores of federal statutes. These include the "substantial evidence," the "clearly erroneous," and the "arbitrary and capricious" tests.[1] The trade remedy statutes of the United States, dealing with the imposition of antidumping and countervailing duties, employ the substantial evidence test, i.e., whether there is substantial evidence of record to support an agency's determination.[2] These tests may apply to questions of both law and fact, questions that are not always clearly separable, particularly in an administrative law context. As a general rule, however, an agency's construction of the law it is charged with administering is entitled to judicial deference under the doctrine announced in *Chevron U.S.A. Inc. v. Natural Resources Defense Council, Inc.*[3]

US courts generally review agency decisions for conformity with the law applied by the agency. An exception is when they review the constitutionality of an agency decision, for example, for conformity to due process requirements. There would be no "*Chevron* deference" in such a case.[4] Apart from the occasional constitutional review, however, courts and agencies are dealing with the same statute.

Dispute settlement panels of the World Trade Organization often review decisions of national agencies when another WTO Member challenges those decisions. However, this review is very different from the review of an administrative agency's decision by a municipal court. When a panel reviews a national law for conformity to a WTO provision, the parallel is to a Federal Court in the United States reviewing a state law for conformity to the Constitution. A Federal Court's review of a Federal agency's decision for conformity with the statute the agency is charged with administering is one thing; a Federal Court's review of a state law for conformity with the Federal Constitution is another. WTO review of a national law resembles the latter, not the

---

[1] See generally Kenneth Culp Davis and Richard J. Pierce, Jr., 2 *Administrative Law Treatise* §§11.1–11.4 (Little, Brown, 3rd ed 1994).

[2] 19 USC 1516a(b)(1)(B)(i); the more procedural decisions are subject to the "arbitrary or capricious" test. 19 USC 1516a(b)(1) (A) and (B)(ii).

[3] 467 U.S. 837 (1984).

[4] In the trade law field, *regulations* of the Customs Service that have gone through the regular notice and comment process provided for by the Administrative Procedure Act, 5 U.S.C. §553, are entitled to *Chevron* deference. *United States v. Haggar Apparel Co.*, 526 U.S. 380 (1999). However, customs letter *rulings* that have not undergone that process do not receive deference. *United States v. Mead Corp.* 533 U.S. (2001).

The WTO Standard of Review in Health and Safety Disputes 225

former. Thus, WTO panels and the government entities whose decisions they review are not, as the saying goes, "singing from the same page" in the way that US courts and agencies typically do.

When the drafters of the *Marrakesh Agreement Establishing the World Trade Organization* and its many associated agreements explicitly addressed standard of review, they expressed far more concern over the standard that panels would employ when dealing with antidumping issues than with the standard panels would employ in any other substantive area, including health and safety. Article 17.6 of the *Antidumping Agreement* provides a detailed standard of deference to the decisions of national authorities imposing antidumping duties.[5] Article 17.6 is the only explicit standard of review provision in the entire 558 pages of the legal texts that constitute the WTO Agreements.[6]

The standard of review that applies to all other matters, including health and safety matters, is that provided in Article 11 of the WTO's *Understanding on Rules and Procedures Governing the Settlement of Disputes*, the "Dispute Settlement Understanding" or "DSU." This simply requires a panel to make an "objective assessment of the matter before it, including an objective assessment of the facts." Just what is and what is not an "objective assessment" is a question that leaves considerable room for interpretation.

Although panels must employ Article 11, they have not developed the jurisprudence of its legal content. This role has fallen to the Appellate Body as it decides claims that panels have failed to make an "objective assessment" of the matters before them. Initially, the Appellate Body clearly did not welcome these appeals, but its more recent decisions suggest that it may now be more accepting of an opportunity to give some content to the words of Article 11. Nothing in Article 11, however, permits any more or less rigorous standard of review for health and safety measures than for any other measures – assuming that a different standard is necessary. Still, it can be argued that the Appellate Body's jurisprudence is moving toward a *de facto* standard of higher deference to domestic authorities when health and safety measures are under review, albeit in the substantive provisions of the WTO Agreements, not in Article 11.

Part I of this chapter will examine the text of Article 11 of the DSU and compare it to Article 17.6 of the Antidumping Agreement. Part II will review the evolving jurisprudence of Article 11. Part III will examine the substantive Article 11 jurisprudence of the Appellate Body's reports as set out in two of its reports dealing with import bans on beef treated with growth hormones and asbestos. Part IV will conclude.

I. The Relevant Texts

Article 11 of the DSU, which is entitled "Function of Panels," specifies:

> The function of panels is to assist the DSB in discharging its responsibilities under this Understanding and the covered agreements. Accordingly, a panel should make

---

[5] The *Antidumping Agreement* is formally known as the *Agreement on Implementation of Article VI of the General Agreement on Tariffs and Trade 1994*.

[6] The English text contains 558 pages, while the French and Spanish texts are 591 and 583 pages, respectively.

an objective assessment of the matter before it, including an objective assessment of the facts of the case and the applicability of and conformity with the relevant covered agreements, and make such other findings as will assist the DSB in making the recommendations or in giving the rulings provided for in the covered agreements. Panels should consult regularly with the parties to the dispute and give them adequate opportunity to develop a mutually satisfactory solution.

The "DSB" referred to in Article 11 is, of course, the Dispute Settlement Body, which has formal responsibility for making binding recommendations and rulings based on the dispute settlement reports it adopts.[7]

The standard of review set forth in Article 17.6 of the Antidumping Agreement provides:

In examining the matter referred to in paragraph 5 [the written statement of the complaining Member and the record available to the authorities when they made the decision under review]:

(i) in its assessment of the facts of the matter, the panel shall determine whether the authorities' establishment of the facts was proper and whether their evaluation of those facts was unbiased and objective. If the establishment of the facts was proper and the evaluation was unbiased and objective, even though the panel might have reached a different conclusion, the evaluation shall not be overturned;

(ii) the panel shall interpret the relevant provisions of the Agreement in accordance with customary rules of interpretation of public international law. Where the panel finds that a relevant provision of the Agreement admits of more than one permissible interpretation, the panel shall find the authorities' measure to be in conformity with the Agreement if it rests upon one of those permissible interpretations.

While the textual contrast between Article 11 of the DSU and Article 17.6 of the Antidumping Agreement is marked, in practice they are not all that different. Article 17.6(i) deals with review by panels of the factual findings of the national authorities imposing antidumping duties. Article 17.6(ii) deals with interpretation of the text of the WTO Antidumping Agreement when examining the provisions of national laws or regulations, or their application, for conformity with WTO requirements. Article 11, by contrast, simply calls for an "objective assessment of the *matter* before [the Panel], *including* an objective assessment of the facts." The "matter," therefore, is broader than just the facts, and includes – if it does not mean – questions of law.

Article 17.6 is one of the "additional rules and procedures on dispute settlement" set forth in Appendix 2 to the DSU, and, therefore, to the extent that there is a conflict between it and Article 11, Article 17 prevails over Article 11.[8] However, the Appellate Body has held that there is no conflict.[9] Article 11 and Article 17.6(i) are essentially the same, it said, and Article 17.6(ii) simply supplements Article 11 by adding that a measure will be found in conformity with the Antidumping Agreement if it rests on a permissible interpretation of the Agreement.[10] In this it hardly can be said to

---

[7] DSU Art. 2.1.

[8] DSU Art. 1.2.

[9] *United States – Anti-Dumping Measures on Certain Hot-Rolled Steel Products from Japan*, AB-2001-2, paras. 54–62, WT/DS184/AB/R (24 July 2001) (adopted 23 August 2001).

[10] *Id.*, paras. 55, 62.

The WTO Standard of Review in Health and Safety Disputes

differ from Article 11. The Appellate Body rather pointedly noted that Article 17.6(ii) "*presupposes* that application of the rules of treaty interpretation ... could give rise to, at least, two interpretations."[11] It may well be that, in making this observation, the Appellate Body was signaling the view that the rules of treaty interpretation, as codified in Articles 31 and 32 of the *Vienna Convention on the Law of Treaties*, contemplate a single interpretation of a treaty provision, thus making Article 17(ii) largely academic. This is the conclusion reached by Steven P. Croley and John H. Jackson who observed, "Once a panel has invoked Articles 31 and 32 of the *Vienna Convention*, it presumably will have already settled on a nonambiguous, nonabsurd interpretation."[12]

It may turn out to be the case, therefore, that, in practice, there is little difference between Article 11 of the DSU and Article 17.6 of the Antidumping Agreement. At most, Article 17.6 might be said to provide "context" for Article 11, but this approach could be met with the argument that the use of different language in the Antidumping Agreement suggests that the drafters meant something different.[13] Thus, it seems more than likely that Article 17.6 will play no role – as thus far it has played no role – in the standard of review applied by panels under Article 11 to other measures, including health and safety measures.

II. Article 11's "Objective Assessment"

The first appellate challenge to a panel's decision based on an alleged failure to make an objective assessment of the facts occurred in the *Hormones* case, and the challenge was not well received.[14] "A claim that a panel disregarded or distorted the evidence submitted to it," the Appellate Body said, "is, in effect, a claim that the panel, to a greater or lesser degree, denied the party submitting the evidence fundamental fairness, or what in many jurisdictions is known as due process of law or natural justice."[15] The Appellate Body reiterated this approach in a number of subsequent cases. "An allegation that a panel has failed to conduct the 'objective assessment of the matter before it' required by Article 11 of the DSU is a very serious allegation. Such an allegation goes to the very core of the integrity of the WTO dispute settlement process itself."[16] If a panel does not "deliberately disregard," "refuse to consider," willfully distort," or "misrepresent" the evidence, and if it does not commit an "egregious error that calls into question [its] good faith," it does not act in a manner inconsistent with Article 11.[17] Complainant's "arguments ... do not disclose that the

---

[11] *Id.*, para. 59 (emphasis in original).

[12] "WTO Dispute Procedures, Standard of Review, and Deference to National Governments," 90 *American Journal of International Law* 193, 201 (1996).

[13] *United States – Imposition of Countervailing Duties on Certain Hot-Rolled Lead and Bismuth Carbon Steel Products Originating in the United Kingdom*, AB-2000-1, paras. 47, 49, WT/DS138/AB/R (10 May 2000).

[14] *EC Measures Concerning Meat and Meat Products (Hormones)*, AB-1997-2, WT/DS26/AB/R, WT/DS48/AB/R (16 January 1998) ("*AB – Hormones*").

[15] *Id.*, para. 133.

[16] *European Communities – Measures Affecting the Importation of Certain Poultry Products*, AB-1998-3, WT/DS69/AB/R, para. 133 (13 July 1998).

[17] *Australia – Measures Affecting Importation of Salmon*, AB-1998-5, WT/DS18/AB/R, para. 266 (20 October 1998).

Panel has distorted, misrepresented or disregarded evidence, or has applied a 'double standard' of proof in this case."[18] Initially, therefore, the "standard" of Article 11 did not appear to be much of a standard at all.

More recently, the tone has changed. In *Wheat Gluten*, a panel had occasion to consider the standard of review it should employ in dispute involving the imposition of safeguard measures by the United States. "[A] *de novo* review would be inappropriate," the Panel said. However, "for us to adopt a policy of total deference to the findings of national authorities could not ensure an 'objective assessment' as foreseen by Article 11 of the DSU."[19] On appeal, the Panel's decision was reversed, but with none of the harsh language so characteristic of the Appellate Body's earlier forays into Article 11. After stating that the question whether a panel's assessment of the facts was objective is, itself, a legal question, the Appellate Body stated what is virtually boilerplate in national appellate reviews: "[W]e cannot base a finding of inconsistency under Article 11 simply on the conclusion that we might have reached a different factual finding from the one the panel reached. Rather," the Appellate Body added, "we must be satisfied that the panel has exceeded the bounds of its discretion, as the trier of facts, in its appreciation of the evidence."[20] The Appellate Body then went on to note that, "we will not interfere lightly with the panel's exercise of its discretion."[21]

In the case before it, the Panel had accepted supplemental information justifying the challenged decision, information that was not contained in the decision itself. By reaching a conclusion that upheld the report in these circumstances, the Appellate Body said, "the Panel applied a standard of review which falls short of what is required by Article 11 of the DSU."[22] It then went on to give some guidance for challenging panel reports under Article 11:

> In asking us to conduct such a review, an appellant must indicate clearly the manner in which a panel has improperly exercised its discretion. Taking into account the full *ensemble* of the facts, the appellant should, at least: identify the facts on record from which the Panel should have drawn inferences; indicate the factual or legal inferences that the Panel should have drawn from those facts; and, finally, explain why the failure of the Panel to exercise its discretion by drawing these inferences amounts to an error of law under Article 11 of the DSU.[23]

III. Article 11 in Health and Safety Disputes

The *Hormones* case, the first case of any kind raising Article 11 before the Appellate Body, led to its initial "denial of fundamental fairness" interpretation. The

---

[18] *Korea – Taxes on Alcoholic Beverages*, AB-1998-7, WT/DS75/AB/R, WT/DS84/AB/R, para. 164 (18 January 1999).

[19] *United States – Definitive Safeguard Measures on Imports of Wheat Gluten from the European Communities*, para. 8.5, WT/DS166/R (31 July 2000) (adopted as modified by the Appellate Body 19 January 2001).

[20] *United States – Definitive Safeguard Measures on Imports of Wheat Gluten from the European Communities*, para. 1.51, AB-2000-10, WT/DS166/AB/R (22 December 2000) (adopted 19 January 2001).

[21] *Id.*

[22] *Id.* para. 162.

[23] *Id.* para. 175.

The WTO Standard of Review in Health and Safety Disputes

case involved a challenge by the United States and Canada to a directive of the European Communities prohibiting the use of certain growth hormones in cattle on the grounds that the hormones posed a health risk for consumers of the meat. The complainants argued that the directive was inconsistent with the EC's commitments under the WTO *Agreement on the Application of Sanitary and Phytosanitary Measures* ("SPS Agreement"). The EC appealed the generally unfavorable report of the Panel, claiming that "the panel erred in law in not according deference" to the EC decisions at issue.[24]

According to the EC's argument, panels, in "formulating the 'proper standard of review,'" have two options: (1) *de novo* review and (2) "deference," under which the Panel "should not seek to redo the investigation conducted by the national authority but instead examine whether the 'procedure' required by the relevant WTO rules had been followed."[25] The EC went on to argue that the standard set out in Article 17.6(i) of the *Antidumping Agreement* "is applicable in 'all highly complex factual situations, including the assessment of the risks to human health arising from toxins and contaminants,' and should have been applied by the Panel . . . "[26]

The argument did not impress the Appellate Body. Article 17.6(i) of the Antidumping Agreement, it held, has no relevance to disputes under the SPS Agreement.[27] To the contrary, a 1994 WTO decision provides that Article 17.6's standard of review "shall be reviewed after a period of three years with a view to considering the question of whether it is capable of general application."[28] Regardless of whether Article 17.6's standard is capable of general application, the Members of the WTO have taken no action to apply it generally. Thus, "the issue of the failure to apply an appropriate standard of review resolves itself into the issue of whether or not the Panel, in making the . . . findings . . . appealed by the European Communities, had made an 'objective assessment'" as required by Article 11.[29]

Article 11, according to the Appellate Body, "articulates with great succinctness but with sufficient clarity the appropriate standard of review for panels in respect of both the ascertainment of facts and the legal characterization of such facts under the relevant agreements."[30] The Appellate Body then succinctly and clearly proceeded to describe this succinct and clear "objective assessment" standard tautologically: "the applicable standard is neither *de novo* review as such, nor 'total deference,' but rather 'the objective assessment of the facts.'"[31]

So, an "objective assessment" is not the same as a *de novo* review or total deference, but what, precisely – in a concrete case – is it? In a later decision, the Appellate Body offered this further explanation:

> [U]nder Article 11 . . . panels must examine whether the competent authority has evaluated all relevant factors; they must assess whether the competent authority

---

[24] *AB – Hormones, supra* note 14, 110.

[25] *Id.* para. 111.

[26] *Id.* para. 113 (citation omitted).

[27] *Id.* para. 114.

[28] Footnote 79, quoting the *Decision on the Review of Article 17.6 of the Agreement on Implementation of Article VI of the General Agreement on Tariffs and Trade 1994.*

[29] *Id.* para. 118.

[30] *Id.* para. 116.

[31] *Id.* para. 117.

has examined all the pertinent facts and assessed whether an adequate explanation has been provided as to how those facts support the determination; and they must also consider whether the competent authority's explanation addresses fully the nature and complexities of the data and responds to other plausible interpretations of the data. However, panels must not conduct a *de novo* review of the evidence nor substitute their judgment for that of the competent authority.[32]

This standard sounds very close to the *Skidmore* test utilized by courts in the United States when *Chevron* deference is not applicable. Under *Skidmore*, the weight that courts will accord to agency decisions "will depend upon the thoroughness evident in its consideration, the validity of its reasoning, its consistency with earlier pronouncements, and all those factors which give it power to persuade, if lacking power to control."[33]

What does all of this mean in the WTO in practice? Apart from Article 17.6 of the *Antidumping Agreement*, panels clearly owe no deference to national authorities' interpretations of provisions of WTO agreements. That purely legal part of the "matter" before panels is decided by them *de novo*. As to purely factual questions, however, there is broad and growing case law making it clear that panels are not to conduct *de novo* review.[34] But that raises the question of how panels are to make an "objective assessment" of the facts without considering them afresh. The apparent answer is something similar to the "substantial evidence" test: If all of the witnesses say A, and the national authorities decide B, a panel most likely will find that the facts do not support the decision of the authorities. But if some witnesses say A, and others say B, panels are likely to find that the facts do provide a basis for the decision of the authorities no matter whether they decide A or B.

Hormones offers an example. One issue concerned the question of whether the hormone ban was based on an assessment of the risks involved. After evaluating the evidence presented by the EC, the Panel concluded that none of it addressed the safety of the hormones, nor did any of that evidence indicate an identifiable risk for human health. To the contrary, all of the studies referred to by the EC came to the conclusion that the hormones were safe. These conclusions were confirmed by the scientific experts advising the Panel.[35] The Panel clearly viewed this situation as one in which the evidence said A and the authorities decided B. The Appellate Body held that the Panel had not "arbitrarily ignored or manifestly distorted the evidence before it,"[36] and affirmed.[37]

---

[32] *United States – Transitional Safeguard Measure on Combed Cotton Yarn from Pakistan*, AB-2001-3, WT/DS192/AB/R, para. 74 (8 October 2001).

[33] *Skidmore v. Swift & Co.*, 323 US 134, 140 (1944).

[34] *AB – Hormones, supra* note 14, para. 117; *Wheat Gluten, supra* note 14; *United States – Safeguard Measures on Imports of Fresh, Chilled or Frozen Lamb Meat from New Zealand and Australia*, AB-2001-1, para. 106, WT/DS177/AB/R, WT/DS178/AB/R (1 May 2001); *United States – Transitional Safeguard Measure on Combed Cotton Yarn from Pakistan*, AB-2001-3, para. 69ff, WT/DS192/AB/R (8 October 2001).

[35] *EC Measures Concerning Meat and Meat Products (Hormones)*, para. 8.124, WT/DS26/R/USA (18 August 1997). The experts were selected in consultation with the parties. Two were from the EC, one each from the United States and Canada, and one from Australia. *Id.* paras. 6.1–6.10.

[36] *AB Hormones, supra* note 14, para. 145.

[37] *AB Hormones, supra* note 14, para. 235.

The WTO Standard of Review in Health and Safety Disputes

Asbestos offers a somewhat different example. In that case, Canada challenged a French ban on the use of all varieties of asbestos.[38] The Panel sustained the ban, and, in affirming the result, the Appellate Body disposed of Canada's Article 11 challenge in short order. Characterizing Canada's argument as one that simply challenged the Panel's exercise of discretion in assessing and weighing the evidence, the Appellate Body declined to second-guess the Panel, remarking that "the Panel's appreciation of the evidence remained well within the bounds of its discretion as the trier of facts."[39] Beyond this single reference to Article 11, however, the Appellate Body's *Asbestos* Report is an interesting example of a reviewing tribunal's sensitivity to disputes involving health and safety measures.

Canada had argued that France's ban was too broad, that a certain variety of asbestos – chrysotile fibres – could be used without any detectable risk.[40] Accordingly, Canada claimed, the ban on chrysotile fibres is, *inter alia*, inconsistent with the national treatment provisions of Article III:4 of GATT 1994.[41] These require WTO Members to apply their internal laws and regulations to imports in a manner "no less favourable than that accorded to *like products* of national origin."

A threshold question Article III, therefore, was whether chrysotile fibres are "like" substitute fibres. The Panel, adopting an economic or "competitive" approach to the question, agreed with Canada that chrysotile and its substitutes (such as cellulose and glass) were "like." They were competing products for many of the same uses.[42] The Panel explicitly declined to take health risk into account in evaluating likeness. Introducing the protection of health into the likeness criteria, the Panel said, would allow a Member to avoid the disciplines of Article XX where health is an explicit concern. The Panel then proceeded to find the ban justified under Article XX(b) as a measure that, even though in violation of the national treatment provisions of Article III:4, was necessary to protect human life or health, and was neither arbitrarily or unjustifiably discriminatory, nor a disguised restriction on international trade.[43]

An important similarity between *Hormones* and *Asbestos* is that in both cases, the Panel accepted the opinions of experts. In *Hormones*, as noted, the experts agreed that no studies demonstrated the risk claimed by the EC. In *Asbestos*, however, the experts disagreed with Canada's claim that chrysotile fibres posed no danger. Indeed, when Canada attempted to distinguish between chrysotile fibres and chrysotile fibres encapsulated in a cement matrix, arguing that the latter posed only a limited risk of dispersal, the experts agreed that professionals working with the product in a limited way indeed faced minimal risk.[44] But they also agreed that those who come later, such as building workers, do not have the required expertise, and are now among those most exposed to the fibres and their attendant risk.[45]

---

[38] *European Communities – Measures Affecting Asbestos and Asbestos-Containing Products*, WT/DS135/R, para. 3.8 (18 September 2000) (*"Asbestos – Panel"*).

[39] *European Communities – Measures Affecting Asbestos and Asbestos-Containing Products*, AB-2000-11, para. 177, WT/DS135/AB/R (12 March 2001) (*"Asbestos – AB"*).

[40] *Id.* para. 3.9.

[41] *Id.* para. 3.1. Canada also argued that the ban was inconsistent with the *Agreement on Technical Barriers to Trade* and with Article XI.1 of GATT 1994.

[42] *Id.* para. 8.144.

[43] *Id.* para. 8.241.

[44] *Id.* para. 8.189.

[45] *Id.* para. 8.191. The argument that asbestos imbedded in cement poses no serious risk rings particularly hollow in the wake of the destruction of the World Trade Center.

The Appellate Body affirmed the Panel's result in *Asbestos*, but with a twist. It held that the Panel's rejection of the toxicity of chrysotile fibres in its like product analysis was error. "We do not see how this highly significant physical difference *cannot* be a consideration in examining the physical properties of a product as part of a determination of 'likeness' under Article III:4 of the GATT 1994," the Appellate Body wrote.[46] "Under Article III:4," it added, "evidence relating to health risks may be relevant in assessing the *competitive relationship in the market place* between allegedly 'like' products."[47] Based on the comparative health risks, the Appellate Body concluded that chrysotile fibres and their substitutes are not "like" products for purposes of Article III:4.[48]

This did not go far enough for one Member of the division hearing the appeal. In the first public indication of non-unanimity in an Appellate Body decision, that Member concurred in the result, but added that, "It is difficult for me to imagine what evidence relating to economic competitive relationships as reflected in end-uses and consumers' tastes and habits could outweigh and set to naught the undisputed deadly nature of chrysotile asbestos fibres . . . "[49]

The distinction between the two approaches appears to be that the majority sees safety as an issue bearing upon, but not necessarily controlling, the competitive relationship; the concurring Member could not even visualize a situation in which other factors bearing upon competitiveness could override the toxicity of asbestos and make asbestos "like" anything else. Both approaches unnecessarily open a door for protectionism while doing nothing the Panel Report did not already do to sustain measures designed to protect health and safety.

The major flaw with the view of the majority is that there is absolutely no evidence of record regarding the impact of toxicity on consumer preferences. The parties did not provide evidence, one way or the other.[50] The Panel, while stating that the position of the parties did not control its consideration of the issue, concluded that investigation of consumer tastes and habits would not yield clear results.[51] It therefore declined to take a position on the issue, and decided the case on other criteria.[52]

It may be objected that "everyone knows" that asbestos is toxic, and therefore that "no one in his or her right mind" would want to be anywhere near it. The Appellate Body certainly seems to have been of that view. But it needs to be noted that asbestos was used because it served a purpose, and it certainly is possible that substitute products may not serve that purpose as well or as safely. Thus, a United States court of appeals overturned a 1989 ban on asbestos issued by the Environmental Protection Agency on grounds that EPA had not considered the overall impact of the ban, including safety.[53] "Eager to douse the dangers of asbestos," the Court said, "the agency inadvertently may increase the risk of injury Americans face."[54] Consider

---

[46] *European Communities – Measures Affecting Asbestos and Asbestos-Containing Products*, AB-2000-11, para. 114, WT/DS135/AB/R (12 March 2001).

[47] *Id.* para. 115 (emphasis in original).

[48] *Id.* para. 126.

[49] *Id.* para. 152.

[50] Asbestos – Panel, para. 8.139.

[51] *Id.*

[52] *Id.* para. 8.140.

[53] *Corrosion Proof Fittings v. Environmental Protection Agency*, 947 F.2d 1201 (5th Cir. 1991).

[54] *Id.* 1221.

The WTO Standard of Review in Health and Safety Disputes

brake linings in automobiles. Will more lives be lost in traffic accidents because a non-toxic, but perhaps less effective, product is substituted for asbestos? If so, will that number be more or less than the number of lives saved by not using asbestos?

It is clear that there are trade-offs; it is not clear that, in every instance, the best course is to avoid use of the more toxic product. It may be difficult for a Member of the Appellate Body to "imagine" such a case, but it would be better if these issues were decided on the evidence and not on the imagination.

While the Appellate Body majority clearly is correct that toxicity *could* have an impact on competitiveness, the point remains that this is not necessarily the case, and in this specific instance, there is no evidence that it did. In these circumstances, the Panel's approach seems superior to that of the Appellate Body, i.e.: (1) decide the issue of "like product" based on the available evidence regarding competitiveness; (2) in the absence of evidence as to the impact of toxicity on competitiveness, ignore toxicity for the like product analysis. This approach may lead to the conclusion of the *Asbestos* Panel – an imported product is being treated less favourably than a like domestic product. But when health and safety are the justification for the measure, the analysis does not end at "like product." This less favourable treatment is then examined under the criteria of Article XX, where health and safety may be found to justify measures otherwise inconsistent with WTO obligations.

The protectionist danger of bringing risk itself – as opposed to risk that is shown to have a competitive impact – into the like product analysis of Article III is that many non-identical, but competitive, products may offer different risks. Imported and domestic automobiles compete, although no two varieties are identical. They may well present different safety risks. One model, for example, may be safer in head-on collisions, but less safe in side-impact or rear-end collisions. It would be a fairly easy task for a government whose auto industry was stronger on one aspect of safety and weaker on the others to restrict sales (and thus, restrict imports) of autos less safe where its industry is safer, but safer where its industry is less safe, and to justify these restrictions, not on safety grounds, but as measures that do not apply to the same "like product." The argument that such "selective" concern for safety is likely to be met with the counterargument that the fact that a WTO Member elects to protect against one risk but not another is not evidence of a discriminatory intent.[55]

IV. Conclusion

The Appellate Body's *Asbestos* analysis was not, formally, a standard of review analysis. The issue was not the standard applied by the Panel to the decision of the French authorities; rather, it was a legal analysis of the national treatment provisions of Article III:4 based on the undisputed fact that chrysotile fibres are highly toxic and their substitutes are not. The Panel's factual analysis might have been "objective," in the Appellate Body's view, but it was legally incorrect.

Still, in a broader, and perhaps more practical sense, the Appellate Body's *Asbestos* opinion suggests an unspoken sympathy for what it views to be well-intentioned health and safety measures. The verbal formulae of standards of review serve the

---

[55] *Australia – Measures Affecting Importation of Salmon*, AB-1998-5, para. 152, WT/DS18/AB/R (20 October 1998) (interpreting the language of Article 5.5 of the *Agreement on the Application of Sanitary and Phytosanitary Measures* dealing with discrimination or disguised restrictions on international trade).

purpose of attempting to draw lines, but verbal formulae are inevitably unclear at some level, and open to interpretation. Most complex fact situations can be described in ways that will fit into just about any verbal formula. It really comes down, then, to the facts and how they are viewed by the tribunal. Robert E. Hudec has observed, in another context, that tribunals frequently "decide the case as best they can by making a seat-of-the-pants judgment about whether the defendant government is behaving correctly or incorrectly – a process of judgment known in some circles as the 'smell test.'"[56] The decisions of panels and the Appellate Body in disputes involving health and safety measures suggest that the "smell test" is alive and well at the WTO.

---

[56] Robert E. Hudec, "Requiem for an 'Aims and Effects' Test," 32 *The International Lawyer* 619 (1998), reprinted in Robert E. Hudec, *Essays on the Nature of International Trade Law* 359, 376 (Cameron May, 1999).

JOOST PAUWELYN

8. Expert Advice in WTO Dispute Settlement

I. Introduction

In the WTO's seven years of existence, six panels appointed scientific experts.[1] Two panels requested expert advice from other international organisations[2] and one panel appointed a linguistic expert.[3] This stands in contrast to one single resort to experts by GATT 1947 panels.[4] Very often parties to a WTO dispute also nominate experts on their delegation, be they lawyers, economists, scientists or linguists. On top of that, an increasing number of 'outsiders' or *amici curiae*, such as Non-Government Organizations (NGOs), but also industry and academics, have pressed their (expert) opinion on WTO panels. What explains this increase in expert advice before the WTO?

Firstly, WTO agreements became more technical, both in the trade/economic sense (refer, for example, to the Agreement on Customs Valuation and the Agreement on Agriculture) and the factual/scientific sense (refer to the SPS and TBT agreements). Indeed, some WTO agreements themselves set up expert bodies (such as the Permanent Group of Experts under the Subsidies Agreement and the Technical Committee on Customs Valuation under the Customs Valuation Agreement).

Secondly, certain WTO obligations adopt an explicitly economic/scientific criterion of legality, set out either in the WTO treaty itself (such as the requirement to 'base' sanitary measures on a 'risk assessment', SPS Art. 5.1) or as developed in WTO jurisprudence (such as the condition of a certain degree of 'competitive relationship', based largely on market studies, for products to be 'like' under GATT Art. III[5]). This explains why a number of WTO agreements explicitly provide for WTO panels to set up Expert Review Groups (DSU Appendix 4 and SPS Art. 11) or Technical Expert Groups (TBT Annex 2).

Thirdly, WTO dispute settlement has been 'legalised': panels have compulsory jurisdiction, panel reports are virtually automatically adopted and the legal aspects

---

[1] *EC – Hormones* (same set of experts for two panels), *US – Shrimp/Turtle* (original panel only), *Australia – Salmon* (twice: original panel and implementation panel, appointing a different set of experts), *Japan – Varietals* and *EC – Asbestos*.

[2] *India – Quantitative Restrictions* (advice from IMF on balance of payments measures) and *US – Copyright Act* (advice from WIPO on Bern Convention).

[3] *Japan – Film* case.

[4] *Thailand – Cigarettes*, requesting WHO advice.

[5] See Appellate Body report on *EC – Asbestos*.

of a dispute are subject to review by an Appellate Body. This moved away from the GATT 1947 diplomatic approach to settling disputes, where a panel often had to decide only issues of law to be applied to a 'cluster of undisputed facts'. The process now being automatic has increased the number of reluctant defendants as well as the incentive to raise procedural objections and to dispute the facts. In short, 'the lawyers have been brought in'. The bright side of this new 'litigation mode' is that the substantive legal thickening of WTO agreements has been coupled with a more sophisticated procedural WTO law, setting out rules on burden of proof, evidence, due process etc. that are, in the realm of international adjudication, quite unique in their extent of detail. Witness, for example, the increasing resort by panels and the Appellate Body to detailed working procedures and case-specific procedural rulings on issues such as jurisdiction, deadline for submission of evidence, submission of *amicus curiae* briefs, third party rights, etc. In the GATT 1947 days, all panel decisions had to wait until the final report.

Fourthly, and linked mainly to the phenomenon of *amicus curiae* briefs, the impact and stakes at play in WTO disputes are no longer limited to government-to-government trade concessions. They affect individual economic operators, including consumers and citizens at large. Hence, governments need to explain to a wide domestic audience the positions they take before a WTO panel, as well as the outcome finally obtained. This provides another incentive for 'aggressive litigation'. Moreover, domestic operators who are perhaps not fully heard by their governments want to express their (expert) opinion directly before the panel.

II. The Players

1. Scientific Experts Appointed by the Panel

Two possibilities arise in case a panel wants to appoint its own experts. Firstly, they can set up a so-called Expert Review Group pursuant to DSU Art. 13.2, for which the procedures in DSU Appendix 4 apply (these are copied, for TBT disputes, in TBT Art. 14.2 and TBT Annex 2 on Technical Expert Groups).[6] So far not a single panel has set up an expert review group. Secondly, panels can appoint individual experts. This is what all six panels which resorted to scientific experts have done so far. Each time that a party wanted to have an expert review group instead (most often this was the defendant, in particular the EC), the panel insisted on appointing individual experts. The Appellate Body has upheld this preference based on the broad language of DSU Art. 13 (referring to expert review groups as an option only), even for TBT disputes where TBT Art. 14.2 exclusively refers to technical expert groups, not to individual experts.[7]

---

[6] Also SPS Art. 11.2 explicitly refers to the possibility for a panel to establish 'an advisory technical experts group', although unlike the TBT Agreement, it does not include a copy of Appendix 4 to the DSU. The disparities among the DSU, SPS and TBT agreements in this respect (referring, for example, to 'expert review groups', 'advisory technical experts group' and 'technical expert groups', respectively) do not seem to have legal consequences. They are there because all three agreements were negotiated side by side and only brought together under one umbrella at the very end of the Uruguay Round.

[7] SPS Art. 11.2, in contrast, refers to both 'advice from experts' generally and the possibility for panels 'when it deems it appropriate' to establish an expert group.

Expert Advice in WTO Dispute Settlement

What explains this panel preference for individual experts? Firstly, expert groups must produce a 'report' (para. 6, DSU App. 4). This risks transforming the expert group into a form of 'tribunal within a tribunal'. It may tie the hands of the panel, both in the sense of the flexibility of the process of gathering advice and the end result. Individual experts allow a panel to ask specific questions to each expert, to add questions during the process, to interrogate the experts orally, etc. In terms of end result, individual experts also allow the panel to obtain the individual opinion of each expert, whereas the report of an expert group may stimulate the experts to come up with some vague and monolithic consensus position. Moreover, although the group's report is 'advisory only' (para. 6, DSU App. 4), it would be difficult for a panel to overrule any common position taken by the experts.

Secondly, an expert group is most likely to take an enormous amount of time. Appointing individual experts already makes it impossible for panels to keep within the time limits imposed by the DSU (in principle, a maximum of nine months as between the panel establishment and the circulation of the report to members, DSU Art. 12.9[8]). An expert group is likely to take even more time: firstly, because the group must come up with a report (first a draft report on which parties may comment, then a final report (para. 6, DSU App. 4); secondly, because the group has, in turn, the right to consult and seek information from 'any source they deem appropriate' (para. 4, DSU App. 4). In this context, and given the inherent uncertainty related to scientific advice, could one not expect that expert group advising panels, most often examining a high profile issue that has attracted the attention of scientists for years, would seek the advice of their peers, debate the issues for months and finally come up with a very vague and cautious report of not much value to a judicial process?

The only disadvantage linked to appointing individual experts is that it may put a heavy burden on the panel to try and find a common position or minimum common ground as between the experts. In most cases, they are not qualified to do so. The panel may achieve this common ground though by carefully drafting the questions they pose to the experts.

2. Other Expert Opinions Gathered by the Panel

DSU Art. 13 grants panels the broad right 'to seek information and technical advice from *any individual or body which it deems appropriate*' (DSU Art. 13.1) and to 'seek information *from any relevant source*' (DSU Art. 13.2). This investigative power attributed to WTO panels is thus not limited to seeking scientific advice, nor limited to seeking expert advice. With reference to DSU Art. 13, panels may, for example, 'force' the parties to a dispute to submit certain information not yet on record (if not,

---

[8] Recall that this nine-month period includes the often long lapse of time as between the establishment of a panel by the DSB and the appointment of panel members to serve on the panel as well as the time required for parties to comment on an interim report and the time needed for translation of the final report into all three official WTO languages. In practice, this leaves the panel about five months to do the actual work. The panel on *EC – Asbestos* broke all records in this respect: the DSB established the panel on 25/11/98, the panel members were selected on 29/03/99; the final report went to the parties on 25/07/00, and, after translation, it was circulated to all WTO members on 18/09/00, that is, almost two years after the panel's establishment.

panels are allowed to draw adverse inferences[9]). On the basis of Art. 13, panels have also allowed for the submission of *amicus curiae* briefs that were not requested by the panel but submitted, for example, by NGOs at their own initiative (thus interpreting the word 'seek' rather broadly). As far as expert advice is concerned, such advice may be other than scientific. It may fall within any field: technical, economic, linguistic, etc. So far not a single panel appointed economic experts though. In cases involving complex economic matters, panels should, however, not hesitate to do so.

DSU Art. 13 is not limited either in terms of the individuals or bodies that may be contacted by a panel. With reference to DSU Art. 13, panels have, for example, asked the opinion of the IMF and WIPO.[10] On that basis, WTO panels could even request the advice of WTO political organs (such as the DSB or General Council, perhaps even in order to obtain an authoritative interpretation,[11] or more technical WTO bodies such as the Textiles Monitoring Body or the Committees on Balance of Payments or Regional Trade). It could even be argued that DSU Art. 13 can be used to ask the expert opinion of other judicial bodies, such as the International Court of Justice or the International Tribunal on the Law of the Sea. With some imagination, Art. 13 could even be used by panels to ask for clarification from the Appellate Body itself.

To complete the picture of expert advice received by panels, reference could be made also to the advice they obtain from the WTO secretariat pursuant to DSU Art. 27.1 ('especially on the legal, historical and procedural aspects of the matters dealt with'). In practice, a panel is assisted by a legal officer (working either for the legal affairs division or the rules division) and a secretary (not only providing secretarial support, but also substantive input on the more technical matters of the WTO agreements involved[12]). In addition, the WTO secretariat may also provide expert legal advice to developing country parties to a dispute pursuant to DSU Art. 27.2. This advice is offered by the WTO technical cooperation division, but is limited to answering specific legal questions, not the provision of a fully fledged legal team to conduct the procedures of a case.[13]

3. Experts on the Delegation of the Parties

Crucially, experts appointed by the panel itself must be distinguished from experts sitting on the delegation of parties to the dispute. The Appellate Body made it clear that each WTO member has the sovereign right to compose its delegation as it wants.

---

[9] See the Appellate Body report on *Canada – Aircraft*.

[10] *India – Quantitative Restrictions* (advice from IMF on balance of payments measures) and *US – Copyright Act* (advice from WIPO on Bern Convention).

[11] Pursuant to Art. IX:2 of the WTO Agreement, in case, for example, two WTO rules are in a conflict that cannot be resolved by the judiciary, such as the conflict between DSU Art. 21.5 and 22.6. This would provide a powerful means to force the WTO political organs to take up their responsibility in case of certain legislative gaps (the alternative being to let the judiciary fill these gaps).

[12] Hence, in case of an SPS dispute, the secretary would come from the Agriculture division, i.e., the division that deals with the SPS Agreement.

[13] This is generally explained on the ground of the impartiality of the WTO secretariat. The Advisory Centre on WTO Law, recently set up by a number of WTO members, is supposed to fill this gap and provide lawyers to developing countries so as to plead an entire case on their behalf.

Expert Advice in WTO Dispute Settlement

Such delegation must thus not be limited to government officials. It may include also private legal counsel,[14] or independent scientific[15] or economic experts. These party-appointed experts may provide advice behind the scenes (as many law firms do), prepare independent economic or technical studies[16] and/or be present at panel hearings themselves either to present the arguments of the party concerned or to support the party's position by giving their 'independent' opinion.

It goes without saying that the opinions expressed by panel-appointed experts will carry more weight than those expressed by party experts, even if the latter are 'neutrals'. Hence, a party is better off trying to get 'its' experts appointed by the panel, rather than putting them on its own delegation. No rules or quality controls are provided in respect of whom parties to a dispute can appoint as experts. Of course, the opposing party can always 'cross-examine' party-appointed experts and disclose their incompetence or partiality.

Finally, it should be recalled that in addition to the main disputing parties, WTO disputes most often involve a large number of third parties. These third-party WTO members may also have experts on their delegation and further add to the factual record before the panel.

4. Expert Advice Before the Appellate Body

An appeal before the Appellate Body 'shall be limited to issues of law covered in the panel report and legal interpretations developed by the panel' (DSU Art. 17.6). Hence, the Appellate Body can review the law as it was declared by the panel; it cannot touch the facts as they are set out, confirmed or weighed by the panel (only wilful distortion of the facts would be seen as a legal error in the eyes of the Appellate Body[17]). The Appellate Body cannot, *a fortiori*, widen the factual record that was before the panel. It is restricted to that record. Hence, the Appellate Body cannot appoint, for example, scientific experts to enlighten its understanding of a case. It must be hoped that whatever advice the panel gathered is sufficient to clarify the minds of the Appellate Body members. The terms of DSU Art. 13 do not apply to the Appellate Body.

Still, the Appellate Body as well receives expert advice, albeit advice limited to legal issues. Firstly, the WTO has a separate Appellate Body Secretariat, composed exclusively of lawyers and administrative support staff, who provide the Appellate Body division dealing with a case with 'administrative and legal support as it requires' (pursuant to DSU Art. 17.7, normally two lawyers per case). Secondly, the parties to an appeal may, as before a panel, freely compose their delegations, so as to include, for example, private legal counsel. Thirdly, the Appellate Body confirmed that it, as well, can receive *amicus curiae* briefs. In *EC – Asbestos*, it even adopted a case-specific procedure on how such briefs must be submitted, including a procedure of application for leave to file such submissions. To obtain this leave, the essential

---

[14] See Appellate Body ruling in *EC – Bananas*.

[15] See the EC delegation in *EC – Hormones*.

[16] As is often the case in Art. III discrimination cases where, for example, the complainant commissions a market study to prove the 'likeness' or 'directly competitive or substitutable' relationship between its exports and the domestic product to which protection is allegedly afforded.

[17] *EC – Hormones*.

requirement is that the potential *amicus* explains 'why it would be desirable, in the interests of achieving a satisfactory settlement of the matter at issue, in accordance with the rights and obligations of WTO Members under the DSU and the other covered agreements, for the Appellate Body to grant the applicant leave to file a written brief in this appeal; and indicate, in particular, in what way the applicant will *make a contribution to the resolution of this dispute that is not likely to be repetitive* of what has been already submitted by a party or third party to this dispute'.[18] Once such leave has been granted, the submission itself must, however, 'set out a precise statement, *strictly limited to legal arguments*, supporting the applicant's legal position on the issues of law or legal interpretations in the Panel Report with respect to which the applicant has been granted leave to file a written brief'.[19]

In addition, in a number of cases the Appellate Body, after having reversed a panel finding, has 'completed the analysis', i.e., made a legal ruling on claims not decided by the panel in the first place. Doing so, it restricts itself though to the factual record that was before the panel and if this record is insufficiently clear it will not 'complete the analysis'.[20] In the early days of the Appellate Body discussion arose as to whether it could 'remand' a case to a panel after having reversed a panel finding. It is clear now that the Appellate Body itself may 'complete the (legal) analysis' (although it thereby takes away the 'right to appeal' of the party against whom it decides). But remand may still be useful, not for panels to make new *legal* findings, but for panels to complete the *factual* record. The Appellate Body has declared itself competent to receive *amicus curiae* briefs, even though DSU Art. 13 does not apply to it. It did so, rightly in my view, on the basis of an implicit jurisdiction adjudicators have when deciding a dispute. It could do the same when it comes to asking for factual 'advice' from panels, i.e., factual findings by panels so as to complete the factual record before the Appellate Body: the Appellate Body is not competent to expand itself the factual record, it could ask the panel to do so and on that basis 'complete the legal analysis'. The alternative is for the Appellate Body to dismiss the claim, not on the basis of it being unfounded with reference to what the *complainant* submitted to it, but because of the fact that the *panel* had not made enough factual findings. The complainant may then bring a new case, but encounter obstacles of *res judicata* (normally a new case on the same grounds can only be filed in case of 'new evidence'[21]). If the Appellate Body can receive opinions from 'outsiders' such as NGOs, why would it not be able to receive input from the very author it is reviewing, i.e., panels?

Finally, as much as panels may be able to ask the opinion of other judicial bodies, such as the International Court of Justice (ICJ) or the International Tribunal of the Sea (ITLOS), it should be possible for the Appellate Body as well to ask expert advice from its colleagues. It may be difficult to do so for the 'ego' of the Appellate Body, but it would be highly beneficial for the unity of international law (as long as the process of

---

[18] Para. 3(f), *Asbestos* procedures.

[19] Para. 7(c), *Asbestos* procedures.

[20] See the Appellate Body's refusal, in *EC – Asbestos*, to decide Canada's TBT claims after it had reversed the panel's finding that the TBT Agreement does not apply to the asbestos ban.

[21] See, for example, the revision procedure of ICJ judgements, set out in Art. 61 of the ICJ Statute, referring to 'the discovery of some fact of such a nature as to be a decisive factor, which fact was, when the judgement was given, unknown to the Court *and also to the party claiming revision*'.

Expert Advice in WTO Dispute Settlement

seeking advice remains 'advisory', i.e., as long as it does not delegate the jurisdiction that WTO members granted to the Appellate Body to another judicial body). Here again, if the Appellate Body is authorised to receive *unsolicited* briefs on legal matters from NGOs or individual law professors, why would it not be authorised to *seek* the opinion of other tribunals? It is, of course, so that whereas for *factual* issues rules on burden of proof apply, for *legal* issues the court is supposed to know the law (*jura novit curia*). Still, the fact that the Appellate Body is supposed to know the law does not mean that it cannot be advised on the matter (if not, there would be no need even for the parties to submit legal arguments).

5. Special Expert Bodies

As hinted at before, the WTO treaty itself has set up a number of expert bodies. Firstly, Art. 24 of the Subsidies agreement directs the Committee on Subsidies (a political organ on which all WTO members are represented) to establish a Permanent Group of Experts (PGE). This group is composed of five independent experts 'highly qualified in the fields of subsidies and trade relations'. The PGE has three functions: (1) it may be requested to assist a *panel* 'with regard to whether the measure in question is a prohibited subsidy' (Art. 4.5 of the Subsidies agreement); much like expert review groups, the PGE must then submit a report to the panel, but unlike expert review groups, the PGE's conclusions 'shall be accepted by the panel without modification'; (2) the *Committee* on Subsidies may seek an advisory opinion 'on the existence and nature of any subsidy'; (3) any *WTO member* may consult the PGE and the PGE may give advisory opinions 'on the nature of any subsidy proposed to be introduced or currently maintained by that member'; such advisory opinions are confidential and may not be used in dispute settlement proceedings regarding actionable subsidies. Much for the same reasons as those set out in respect of a panel's reluctance to appoint an expert review group, so far panels have never asked the assistance of the PGE.

Secondly, Art. 18.2 (as specified in Annex 2) of the Agreement on Customs Valuation establishes the Technical Committee on Customs Valuation under the auspices of the Customs Co-operation Council. Each WTO member has the right to be represented on this committee. Its functions and operation are set out in Annex 2 of the Customs Valuation Agreement. Art. 19.4 of that Agreement provides that panels 'may request the Technical Committee to carry out an examination of any question requiring technical consideration'. It must then submit a report which is like the report of expert review groups, but unlike PGE reports, *not* binding on the panel ('The panel shall take into consideration the report of the Technical Committee').

Thirdly, Art. 8 of the Textiles Agreement establishes the Textiles Monitoring Body (TMB) 'to examine all measures taken under this Agreement and their conformity therewith, and to take the actions specifically required of it by this Agreement'. The TMB consists of a chairman and ten members, discharging their function on an *ad personam* basis. The TMB does not provide expert advice to panels. Rather, it is itself a body making findings and recommendations in WTO textiles disputes. This TMB process intervenes after bilateral consultations between the parties have turned out to be unsuccessful. Before either of the parties can request a panel, they must first argue their case before the TMB. WTO panels are not bound by TMB findings. Of course, they will play an influential role in their conclusions.

6. WTO Political Organs

Finally, a few words must be said about the role considerations and decisions taken by specialised political WTO organs may play in WTO dispute settlement. Such considerations and decisions may, effectively, constitute 'expert advice' before a WTO panel. The Committees on Balance of Payments and Regional Trade, for example, (on which all WTO members are represented) are empowered to make findings in respect of the WTO conformity of, respectively, balance of payments measures and regional trade arrangements. Given that these political bodies may benefit from wider technical expertise as well as reflect the common understanding of WTO members, WTO panels would surely be inclined to take into account whatever these political bodies have decided. The Appellate Body made it clear that notwithstanding the functions of these political committees, WTO panels remain competent to review the WTO consistency of balance of payments measures and regional arrangements [and this even if such disputes involve complex technical/economic questions such as those under GATT Art. XXIV:5(a)].[22] At the same time, the Appellate Body stressed that 'panels should take into account the deliberations and conclusions of' these committees.[23] Hence, although these conclusions are not binding, like other expert advice, they would be very influential.

III. The Process

1. The Appointment of Experts

a. Who Decides that Panel Experts Are Needed?

It is for the panel to decide whether it will appoint experts. The parties may so request, but the panel is not under an obligation to accede to such request. Moreover, even if none of the parties requests the panel to appoint experts, the panel may do so at its own initiative.

In *Argentina – Footwear*, for example, Argentina asked the panel to obtain the advice from the IMF. The panel saw no need to do so and refused. On appeal, the Appellate Body noted the discretionary nature of the panel's authority to seek expert advice. What counts is whether panels have made an 'objective assessment of the matter before it' (DSU Art. 11) and in that case, the Appellate Body found, the panel did so even if it did not seek the advice from the IMF.[24] In many cases, however, it will be quite difficult for a panel to refuse a party's request to appoint experts. Not to

---

[22] See *India – Quantitative Restrictions* and *Turkey – Textiles*. See also the discussions at the DSB in the *Philippines – Autos* case, where the United States requested a panel notwithstanding the fact that the issue was being dealt with by the Committee on Trade-Related Investment Measures and the General Council. These cases not only raise the question of expert advice that can be offered by WTO political bodies. More importantly, they go to the heart of the 'institutional balance' between the WTO judiciary and the WTO legislature/executive.

[23] *India – Quantitative Restrictions*, para. 103.

[24] Note, however, that GATT Art. XV:2 does impose an obligation to consult the IMF in cases 'concerning monetary reserves, balances of payments or foreign exchange arrangements'. Advice thus obtained from the IMF must even be accepted as final. It is still an open question whether this obligation imposed on GATT Contracting Parties (now WTO members) applies also to WTO panels.

Expert Advice in WTO Dispute Settlement

do so may question the legitimacy of a panel's factual findings. To play it safe, panels will be easily convinced of a need to obtain expert advice: they are not normally technical experts themselves and have nothing to lose, except for time. The costs of the experts are borne by the WTO budget (travel and subsistence allowance plus 600 CHF per day of work), but panel members themselves are not directly affected by this budget.[25]

In contrast, in *US – Shrimp/Turtle* none of the parties requested the panel to appoint experts. Still, the panel sought expert advice. As noted before, it may do so to increase its credibility, even if it knows upfront that the expert advice may, in the end, not be used in its legal considerations. Appointing experts does give the impression that the panel takes the issue seriously and wants to obtain as much information as possible (not just the facts pre-selected by the parties). This explains why panels do not act only at the request of the parties. Moreover, from the point of view of the parties, to request that the panel appoint experts may be seen as acknowledging weakness as to the facts on which they will build their case. Indeed, to ask the panel to appoint experts at the very beginning of a panel process may somehow signal that the party in question does not think that it will, in and of itself, be able to convince the panel or to clearly explain its case.

The broad discretion bestowed on panels to decide whether or not to appoint experts is somewhat limited in the SPS Agreement. SPS Art. 11.2 states: 'In a dispute under this Agreement involving scientific or technical issues, a panel *should* seek advice from experts chosen by the panel'. The TBT Agreement does not include a similar direction. This explains why in all four SPS panels that were active to date, scientific experts were appointed. In recent SPS cases (such as the Art. 21.5 *Australia – Salmon* case and *Japan – Varietals*), the panel did not even await the first submissions of the parties but informed the parties already at the very beginning of the panel process (i.e., at the organisational meeting) that it plans to seek expert advice. It does so because of the wording of SPS Art. 11.2, but also in order to save time and get the experts appointed as soon as possible.

b. Who Can Be Appointed as Expert?

Once the panel has decided that it will appoint experts, who can be appointed? No explicit rules are provided in case the panel appoints *individual* experts (this being perhaps another reason why most panels have chosen this track). Still, the rules that are provided in Appendix 4 to the DSU for expert review *groups* (copied in Annex 2 to the TBT Agreement) have been applied by analogy. Para. 2 of Appendix 4 restricts an expert review group to 'persons of professional standing and experience in the field in question'. They shall serve in their 'individual capacities' and citizens of parties to the dispute shall not serve without the joint agreement of the parties 'except in exceptional circumstances when the panel considers that the need for specialised

---

[25] Panel members employed by the government of a WTO member are not paid. Non-governmental panel members get 600 CHF per day of work (plus travel expenses and per diem when they are in Geneva, costs that are also reimbursed to governmental panel members). The same amount is given to experts. Hence, their fee is minimal and most panel members as well as experts do it for the experience and prestige, not the money.

scientific expertise cannot be fulfilled otherwise' (para. 3). This exception may be fulfilled, for example, if the dispute raises a very country-specific disease or in case technical advice is needed on the very legislation of the defendant. Government officials of parties to the dispute shall not serve on an expert review group. This prohibition seems to be an absolute one which applies even if the exceptional circumstances referred to earlier are met.

In practice, it may be difficult for a panel to know upfront the fields of expertise that it will need during its deliberation. In *Australia – Salmon*, for example, the panel appointed experts in three fields: general risk assessment procedures, fish diseases and the procedures of the International Office for Epizootics (OIE). Still, it is crucial for a panel to appoint experts as soon as possible and to start expert procedures even before it has received the first submissions of the parties. Attached are the Working Procedures in respect of experts adopted by the panel on *Japan – Varietals*. These were adopted at the first meeting of the panel, i.e., before the panel had even received submission of the parties. In addition, new questions may arise during panel proceedings for which none of the experts that had been appointed so far have sufficient expertise. In *EC – Hormones*, for example, the EC insisted on having a cancer specialist appointed rather late in the proceedings. The panel agreed to this request. In case an expert review group had been set up, this would have been much more difficult. This flexibility offered by the appointment of individual experts may be another argument against expert groups.

Recall also that para. 4 of Appendix 4 allows, in turn, that expert review groups 'seek information and technical advice from any source they deem appropriate'. Although para. 1 stresses that expert groups 'are under the panel's authority' and that the 'terms of reference and detailed working procedures' of expert groups shall be decided by the panel, this possibility for groups to appoint their own advisers seems to go very far. It risks creating a 'tribunal within a tribunal within a tribunal'. It should be panels that appoint experts, not experts that appoint other experts.

Finally, the Rules of Conduct for the DSU that apply, for example, to panel and Appellate Body members, apply also to panel experts.[26] The guiding principle of these rules is that experts 'shall be independent and impartial, shall avoid direct or indirect conflicts of interest and shall respect the confidentiality of proceedings of bodies' (Rule II, Governing Principle). Before a panel can appoint an expert, the expert must sign a 'disclosure form', annexed to the Rules of Conduct. In the event of objections, it is the chair of the DSB who decides whether 'a material violation' of the rules occurred, in consultation with the director-general of the WTO and the chairs of the relevant WTO Councils and after having heard the expert involved as well as the disputing parties.[27]

c. How Are Experts Appointed?

No provisions were made on how experts are to be appointed. Only SPS Art. 11.2 deals with the issue indirectly, referring to 'experts chosen by the panel in consultation with

---

[26] WTO doc. WT/DSB/RC/1, dated 11 December 1996.
[27] Rule VII:5 to 10.

Expert Advice in WTO Dispute Settlement

the parties to the dispute'. In *EC – Hormones*, the parties appointed one expert each, where after the panel appointed four additional experts drawn from a list of experts provided to it by the Codex Alimentarius Commission, a list of names on which the parties had been allowed to comment. In subsequent cases, the panel has no longer allowed the parties to appoint panel experts. Instead, the panel itself appointed all experts, based on a list of names it had received from the relevant international organisation dealing substantively with the factual issues at stake. In disputes where no such organisations exist, the parties themselves were invited to suggest names on which the other parties could then comment. In cases where a panel has sought the advice of, for example, the IMF or WIPO, such advice was gathered not on an *ad personam* basis, but by sending an official panel letter to the director-general of the organisation concerned.

What is the appropriate number of experts? It would seem that an odd number is needed. Normally three should do, but this will depend on the number of disciplines involved. If there are many and widely divergent fields of expertise required, one may end up with a high number of experts (say, at least two, preferably three, for each field so that the panel does not rely on the views of just one individual). In *EC – Hormones* six experts were appointed; in *US –Shrimp/Turtle*, five; in *Australia – Salmon*, four (in the Art. 21.5 case, only three with only one of the three having served also for the original panel); in *Japan – Varietals*, three; and in *EC – Asbestos*, four. The only serious constraint that applies is, once again, time. In terms of cost, as noted before, the parties do not bear the cost because they are covered by the WTO budget, but these costs are relatively minor (travel and subsistence allowance plus 600 CHF per day of work). The trend seems nonetheless to be towards a rather low number of experts, even if different disciplines must be covered. Appointing an expert with expertise in both fields may save the WTO some money, but it risks missing out on the real experts in the field.

d. Does the Panel Get the Best Experts?

The two criteria that must be referred to in deciding whether a panel gets the best experts, following the procedures set out above, are neutrality and expertise. As Richard Posner remarked: 'The conclusions of the agreed-upon expert would be credible because of the combination of neutrality and expertise. You don't have to understand a proposition to be justified in believing it; you need only be able to repose a justified trust in the truthfulness and expertise of the person who assures you that the proposition is true'.[28] As seen above, different actors are involved in the selection process.

Firstly, the original list of names is, in most cases, provided by the international organisation working substantively on the factual issues at stake, such as the Codex Alimentarius when it comes to food safety and the OIE when it comes to animal health. Panel members are not experts themselves, so for them it is impossible to come up with such list. The fact that the list comes from an independent and substantively knowledgeable international organisation would seem like a second-best

---

[28] Richard Posner, The Law and Economics of the Expert Witness, *Journal of Economic Perspectives*, Vol 13, No. 2, 1999, 91–99, at 96.

solution (after the optimal solution of having panel members that are themselves able to select the best experts). Critics of these organisations (in particular developing countries and certain consumer protection NGOs) may point out, however, that these organisations have their own agenda and are driven mainly by export interests, in particular the interests of developed nations and those of big multinationals. Still, these organisations should normally bring together the best scientists of the world in working groups and special committees. The names on the list provided by these organisations are, moreover, not officials working for the organisation, but most often independent scientists, working for public authorities, universities or private research organisations. They are people with an international standing and if they are appointed and express bogus positions, they will be subject to peer pressure. Although the reputation costs are not as high as in domestic procedures where experts are repeat players, not to give neutral advice to a WTO panel may also ruin the reputation of an international scientist.

Secondly, an important role is played by the disputing parties themselves. They are allowed to comment on all names suggested and may object to the nomination of certain individuals. They will often be requested to rank them by preference. When they object to individuals they will be asked to give reasons. But much like what happens in the nomination process of panel members (on the suggestion of the WTO secretariat), it will be difficult for the panel to appoint someone against whom either party has explicit objections. This would run the risk of undermining the legitimacy of the panel's conclusion. Nonetheless, as with the selection of panel members, too easily accepting party objections may lead to the exclusion of the best people. The best people are normally those that have published in the field, thus expressed views in the field and hence taken position. Obviously, the party *against* whom they have taken position will then object to that individual being appointed. In the end, one may thus be able to gather consensus only around those people that have not expressed views, hence that are not normally the best experts. In terms of panel members, this may not be that bad (people with an open mind may, after all, be very good decision-makers). However, when it comes to expert advice, this may be catastrophic. There, no excuse (except for partiality) is good enough not to appoint the best people.[29]

Thirdly, the end decision in the appointment of experts lies with the panel, assisted by the WTO secretariat staff assigned to the case. The latter will often play an important role, in particular the secretary to the panel who comes from the operational division and maintains the day-to-day contact with the relevant international organisation, obtains the list of names and hears views about the names suggested from colleagues in the field. Still, in the end of the day, neither the panel members nor the WTO secretariat staff are real experts in the field, and cannot therefore ensure that the best people are selected merely by looking at a CV, a list of publications and hearsay coming from colleagues at other organisations.

---

[29] As Posner remarked (at p. 94): 'An expert witness who has a record of academic publication will be "kept honest" by the fact that any attempt to repudiate his academic work on the stand will invite devastating cross-examination'. Note, however, that the current process of appointing panel experts is still much better than relying exclusively on party-appointed experts where the risk of having so-called 'hired guns' is much greater.

Expert Advice in WTO Dispute Settlement

e. What Then Could Be Changed for the Better?

Firstly, in cases where the facts are really complex and disputed, it would be good to have a scientific expert serving on the panel itself (say, one of the three individuals normally serving on a panel). That person could play a decisive role in the appointment of experts as well as fulfil an intermediary function as between the lawyers/economists serving on the panel and the scientific experts appointed by the panel.

Secondly, one could revert to the original appointment procedures adopted in *EC–Hormones* and let the parties appoint one or two experts each. However, instead of the panel then appointing a number of additional experts, the experts appointed by the parties could themselves appoint an additional number of experts, the way party-appointed arbitrators often select the presiding member of an arbitration panel (no WTO rule directs panels to ask for a list of names of the relevant international organisation; this is a practice that developed through case law). Parties should then realise that it is in their own (long-term) interest to appoint the best experts.

2. The Gathering of Expert Advice

a. How Is the Advice Conveyed?

As noted above, an expert review group is required to submit a report, based on terms of reference to be set by the panel. It must first issue a draft report, on which the parties may comment, after which a final report will be handed out.

The practice of obtaining advice from *individual* experts shows the following: as soon as experts are appointed they obtain the entire panel record; the panel drafts questions and receives comments on these questions from the parties before they are sent out to the experts (as revised on the basis of the parties' comments); the experts are asked to provide written answers to those questions in respect of which they consider themselves competent; the parties may comment on the expert answers in writing; thereafter, an oral hearing is held with the panel, parties and experts, where the experts summarise their views, answer additional panel questions and may be examined by the parties; this hearing is normally held just before the second substantive meeting with the parties; thereafter, the panel holds its deliberations and may ask additional questions to the experts in writing (always allowing for comments by the parties); once the descriptive part of the panel report is ready, the experts are given a copy of those parts of the report in which their views are reflected so as to make sure that their views were understood correctly (in one case, *Japan – Varietals*, the panel even sent a section of its findings to the experts so as to make sure that its factual findings correctly reflected the expert views); the final panel report includes the *verbatim* transcript of the hearing with the experts as well as the panel questions to the experts with a summary of expert answers.

The publication of expert answers in the final panel report cannot be overestimated: it ensures peer pressure (if experts know that their answers will be published, they will think twice before answering) as well as the transparency of the whole expert procedure (both for governments and pressure groups). This publication is not all that obvious in WTO dispute settlement, knowing that the general principle is confidentiality of the procedures.

The process of cross-examination by the parties is not well-developed. Often, the parties will even wait to comment on the expert views until the actual substantive meeting with the panel, i.e., at a point in time where the experts can no longer respond. This should be avoided and the confrontation between experts and parties (including experts sitting on the delegation of parties) should be increased. More generally, panels should try to ensure that all the evidence submitted by the parties is also available to the experts. New evidence submitted after the consultation with the experts should not be accepted, unless the experts can also comment on it.

The experts should, in turn, submit all documentary evidence on which they base their views. This should avoid 'on the back of an envelope' calculations or purely speculative statements by experts that may easily impress panels. Experts know more than the panel (there is, in other words, an asymmetry of information); the panel wants simple and clear answers; but the expert may not always have such answers, at least not answers based on scientific research; the expert may nonetheless be tempted to make a guess, but this guess can carry a lot of weight because it is something panel members easily understand, more than intricate scientific considerations in which the nuances of a position are highlighted. Such a guess, even if it is clearly not based on objective assessments or has been demolished by scientific cross-examination, may linger on in the minds of panel members and play a crucial role. This risk materialised in *EC – Hormones*, where Dr. Lucier, after some insistence by the panel and without any empirical studies in support, expressed an opinion that there was, in his view, between zero and one in a million risk of cancer based on added hormones in beef production. This statement was taken very seriously by both panel and the Appellate Body, seemingly because it put a number on a complex factual question (albeit a very vague and low one) and this even though it was not supported by any study.

Especially for the Appellate Body it may be difficult to attribute the exact meaning and weight to expert opinions: it never meets with the experts, nor does it get an opportunity to ask questions to them.

In sum, the panel should ensure as much as possible that there is a symmetry of information as between the parties and the experts (both sides should submit all of their evidence to each other) as well as between the experts and the panel itself (this may be bolstered by appointing a scientist on the panel itself, as suggested earlier).

b. What May the Advice Cover?

Expert advice or opinions gathered by the panel itself must be distinguished from other information or facts on the panel record. Parties to a dispute rely on facts and have the burden of proving the facts they invoke. Experts on the delegation of the parties may assist the parties in doing so. Panel experts, in contrast, are allowed, even expected, to apply their expert knowledge to the facts and allegations already before the panel. They are, in other words, allowed to offer a 'personal opinion'.

Moreover, the advice offered by panel experts must, in principle, be limited to an explanation of the evidence and arguments that the parties themselves have put on the record. Panels may use DSU Art. 13 to gather further information and facts from the parties and even from *amici curiae*, confirming the inquisitorial role of panels. However, panel experts are supposed to assist the panel in understanding the factual

Expert Advice in WTO Dispute Settlement

record that is already before the panel. It is not up to panel experts to submit new evidence or to build the case of either party. Of course, much will depend on what the panel questions to the experts are, but normally the scope of these questions and answers is bound to the record put before the panel by the parties. This is a result of the adversarial character of WTO dispute settlement where the parties select the claims and defences to be examined by the panel. This adversarial character may, however, conflict with the seemingly inquisitorial function granted to panels in DSU Art. 13, bestowing upon panels the authority 'to seek information and technical advice from any individual or body which it deems appropriate'.

In *Japan – Varietals* the Appellate Body set out the limits of panel authority in obtaining expert advice. There, the United States had claimed that the varietal testing measure imposed by Japan violated SPS Art. 5.6 on the grounds that there were less-trade-restrictive alternatives available to Japan to achieve the same level of plant protection. The United States referred, in particular, to testing, not variety by variety (say, first Granny Smith apples, then Golden Delicious apples), but testing by entire product range (say, apples *tout court*). The panel rejected the United States' alternative, but on the basis of the expert advice it received, as discussed by the parties, the panel concluded nonetheless that Art. 5.6 was violated and this on the ground that testing on the basis of the sorption level of products would be a valid alternative. The Appellate Body reversed this panel finding as follows:

> Article 13 of the DSU and Article 11.2 of the *SPS Agreement* suggest that panels have a significant investigative authority. However, this authority cannot be used by a panel to rule in favour of a complaining party which has not established a *prima facie* case of inconsistency based on specific legal claims asserted by it. A panel is entitled to seek information and advice from experts and from any other relevant source it chooses ... to help it to understand and evaluate the evidence submitted and the arguments made by the parties, but not to make the case for a complaining party.
>
> In the present case, the Panel was correct to seek information and advice from experts to help it to understand and evaluate the evidence submitted and the arguments made by the United States and Japan with regard to the alleged violation of Article 5.6. The Panel erred, however, when it used that expert information and advice as the basis for a finding of inconsistency with Article 5.6, since the United States did not establish a *prima facie* case of inconsistency with Article 5.6 based on claims relating to the 'determination of sorption levels'. The United States did not even *argue* that the 'determination of sorption level' is an alternative measure which meets the three elements under Article 5.6.[30]

In *Canada – Aircraft*, the Appellate Body specified that this does not mean that a panel can only seek expert advice once the parties themselves have established a *prima facie* case.[31] It only means that expert advice may not constitute the basis of a finding of violation in respect of something which the complaining party 'had not even alleged or argued before the panel, let alone something on which [it] had submitted any evidence'.[32]

---

[30] *Japan – Varietals*, paras. 129–130.

[31] *Canada – Aircraft*, para. 192: 'A panel may, in fact, need the information sought in order to evaluate evidence already before it in the course of determining whether the claiming or responding Member, as the case may be, has established a *prima facie* case or defence'.

[32] Ibid., para. 193.

The general argument underlying the Appellate Body's approach in *Japan – Varietals* is convincing: panel experts should not make the case of either party; they are there to advise the panel. However, the specific Appellate Body finding in that case is open to criticism. Firstly, the United States *had made* a claim under SPS Art. 5.6 (albeit one based on the argument of testing by product), hence this claim *was* before the panel. What the panel did was only evaluating different arguments under this claim. The United States had submitted one factual argument, testing by product. However, on the basis of expert examination and discussions as between the parties and the experts, it became obvious that the US claim was, indeed, founded but largely on the basis of different arguments, arguments that had not been made originally by the United States, but that arose during the panel proceedings and which the United States subsequently supported. It is the Appellate Body itself which stressed the importance of distinguishing between claims and arguments in *EC – Hormones*:

> Panels are inhibited from addressing legal claims falling outside their terms of reference. However, nothing in the DSU limits the faculty of a panel to freely use arguments submitted by any of the parties – or to develop its own legal reasoning – to support its own findings and conclusions on the matter under its consideration. A panel might well be unable to carry out an objective assessment of the matter, as mandated by Article 11 of the DSU, if in its reasoning it had to restrict itself solely to arguments presented by the parties to the dispute.

In *EC – Hormones*, the issue was not that the panel had developed its own *legal* arguments. Rather, much like what Japan did in *Japan – Varietals*, the EC, on appeal, complained about the fact that the panel had found a violation under SPS Article 5.5 on the basis of a *factual* argument not made by the complainants, namely 'a supposed difference of treatment between artificially added or exogenous natural and synthetic hormones when used for growth promotion purposes compared with the naturally present endogenous hormones in untreated meat and other foods (such as mil, cabbage, broccoli or eggs)'. In *EC – Hormones*, the Appellate Body allowed the panel to come up *itself* with this additional factual argument under the complainants' claim of SPS Art. 5.5. In contrast, in *Japan – Varietals*, the Appellate Body bashed the panel for doing exactly the same in respect of a claim made by the United States under Art. 5.6 and this even if in that case the additional factual argument had not been developed by the panel itself, but by the experts advising the panel.

Indeed, if panels can obtain further factual as well as legal information on the basis of *amici curiae* briefs that it did not request in the first place, why would panels not be able to rely on facts submitted by its own experts?

Secondly, although the general reasoning that experts should advise the panel, not make the parties' case is correct, the line between the two will often be thin and difficult to control. In *Japan – Varietals*, for example, it would have been enough for the panel to explain to the United States that it would not accept the US alternative of testing by product and to ask it whether it would, in these circumstances, not explicitly adopt the alternative of testing by sorption level. If the panel had done so, the experts' argument would have become that of the complainant and all would have been acceptable to the Appellate Body. But it is quite easy to understand why the United States, in the circumstances, did *not* suggest testing by sorption as an alternative. For strategic reasons, it had to stick to its preferred alternative, testing

Expert Advice in WTO Dispute Settlement

by product; if not, it would have damaged the credibility of its factual case, namely that all varieties of the same product represent no difference in terms of plant risk.

In sum, the Appellate Body finding in *Japan – Varietals* is important as a signal that the role of experts is limited. For practical purposes, however, it will be easy for panels to continue making broad use of experts as long as they present their findings and evaluation in an appropriate way, i.e., in a way supported by either of the parties. If not, as the Appellate Body itself stated in *EC – Hormones*, not to allow panels to suggest to the parties an obvious alternative that makes scientific sense would achieve the required level of protection and allow for trade to flow, would prevent panels from making an objective assessment of the matter before it as required in DSU Art. 11 and would be against the basic purpose of WTO dispute settlement, namely to offer a positive resolution to disputes (DSU Art. 3.7).

3. The Use of Expert Advice in Coming to a Legal Conclusion

a. Expert Advice: Binding or Not?

The report of expert review groups as well as the opinions of individual experts are advisory only (para. 5 of DSU App. 4). Only advice gathered from the IMF under GATT Art. XV:2 and from the Permanent Group of Experts under Art. 4.5 of the Subsidies Agreement is binding.[33]

Of course, even if expert advice is advisory only, it will be difficult, if not impossible, for a panel to overrule a consensus position expressed by the experts. Given the asymmetry of information and knowledge between the panel and the experts, who is the panel to review the experts that it appointed? In practice, a panel will only be able to reject or downplay certain expert answers on the grounds that they are not relevant, that they are not specific enough,[34] that there is no documentary support for them or that the expert who expressed the view is not neutral or experienced enough in the field.

Especially the report of expert review groups risks being of a *de facto* binding nature. Another instance where expert advice may be *de facto* binding is when a panel decides to seek the advice from another international organisation on issues relating to the field of competence of that organisation. In *US – Copyright Act*, for example, the panel asked WIPO for 'factual information' on the negotiating history, subsequent developments and practice of certain provisions of the Bern Convention, a WIPO convention, parts of which have been explicitly incorporated into the TRIPS Agreement. It would, in that context, have been very difficult for a WTO panel to overrule the answers given by WIPO.

Expert advice is, in principle, not binding because the disputing parties have entrusted the jurisdiction to decide the case with the panel, not any other body or individual. Hence, panels may not transfer their competence to anyone else without

---

[33] In respect of GATT Art. XV:2, the Appellate Body on *India – Quantitative Restrictions* left it open as to whether *panels* (not GATT contracting parties or WTO members, the subject referred to in Art. XV:2), seeking advice under GATT Art. XV:2, would be bound by such advice. The United States answered the question in the affirmative, India in the negative.

[34] See *EC – Hormones*.

the express consent of the disputing parties. Panels may, in particular, not transfer their competence to decide the legal issues of a case. In practice, however, when panels ask questions as those put to WIPO in the *US – Copyright Act* case, the line between 'legal' and 'factual' questions may be blurred and, in effect, the advice received may well have legal value and be of a *de facto* binding nature. The same would apply in case the WTO judiciary were to ask the advice from other courts, such as the ICJ. However, as long as the panel remains in control of the adjudicating process, to ask for advice (even if it is, in effect, of a legal nature) remains a beneficial thing. It ensures that the most knowledgeable people have a word to say in the outcome of a dispute. Asking for advice only confirms the professionalism and legitimacy of the tribunal concerned and the decision it finally takes.

b. What in Case Experts Contradict Each Other?

Science is an inherently changing and uncertain field. There where under the law, in principle, only one correct legal answer exists at a given point in time, scientists may disagree on the facts, focus on different aspects of the question or express opinions with different degrees of certitude. Hence, especially if a panel asks advice from individual scientists, there is a serious risk that scientists disagree. If so, opposing experts may cancel each other out and the panel, in search of the 'one and only' legal answer, may be back at square one. How should panels then react?

In the face of opposing scientific opinions the following two elements will offer a way out:

(i) the substantive legal criterion at issue;
(ii) rules on burden of proof and standard of review.

In terms of the substantive legal requirement under examination, the issue was addressed squarely by the Appellate Body under the SPS Agreement and its requirement to 'base' a sanitary measure 'on a risk assessment' (SPS Art. 5.1). This requirement was interpreted by the Appellate Body in *EC – Hormones* to mean that 'the results of the risk assessment must sufficiently warrant – that is to say, reasonably support – the SPS measure at stake'. It added the following:

> We do not believe that a risk assessment has to come to a *monolithic conclusion* that coincides with the scientific conclusion or view implicit in the SPS measure. The risk assessment could set out both the prevailing view representing the 'mainstream' of scientific opinion, as well as the opinions of scientists taking a divergent view. Article 5.1 does not require that the risk assessment must necessarily embody only the view of a majority of the relevant scientific community. In some cases, the very existence of divergent views presented by qualified scientists who have investigated the particular issue at hand may indicate a state of scientific uncertainty. In most cases, responsible and representative governments tend to base their legislative and administrative measures on 'mainstream' scientific opinion. In other cases, equally responsible and representative governments may act in good faith on the basis of what, at a given time, *may be a divergent opinion coming from qualified and respected sources.* By itself, this does not necessarily signal the absence of a reasonable relationship between the SPS measure and the risk assessment, *especially where the risk*

Expert Advice in WTO Dispute Settlement

involved is life-threatening in character and is perceived to constitute a clear and imminent threat to public health and safety.[35]

In *Japan – Varietals*, the Appellate Body reiterated this view in respect of the requirement under SPS Art. 2.2 to only maintain health measures with 'sufficient scientific evidence', interpreted to mean that there be a 'rational or objective relationship' between the health measure, on the one hand, and the scientific evidence put forward by the member concerned, on the other.[36] It added what follows:

> Whether there is a rational relationship between an SPS measure and the scientific evidence is *to be determined on a case-by-case basis and will depend upon the particular circumstances of the case, including the characteristics of the measure at issue and the quality and quantity of the scientific evidence.*[37]

In *EC – Asbestos*, the Appellate Body confirmed its intention to uphold a measure even if it would be based only on a 'divergent opinion coming from qualified and respected sources' in respect of GATT Art. XX(b) and the exception contained therein for measures 'necessary to protect' health. It added:

> A Member is not obliged, in setting health policy, automatically to follow what, at a given time, may constitute a majority scientific opinion. Therefore, a panel need not, necessarily, reach a decision under Article XX(b) of the GATT 1994 on the basis of the 'preponderant' weight of the evidence.[38]

It further confirmed the *EC – Hormones* approach by stating that 'the more vital or important the common interests or values pursued, the easier it would be to accept as "necessary" measures designed to achieve those ends'.[39]

In sum, a WTO member may validly impose a health measure (i) even if it does so on the basis of a health risk shown only by a 'divergent' or 'minority' opinion of scientists, as long as that opinion comes from (ii) 'qualified and respected sources'. Such divergent or minority opinion will be enough in particular if (iii) the risk at stake or the value pursued is 'vital or important', i.e., 'life-threatening in character', constituting 'a clear and imminent threat to public health and safety'.

To put it differently, there is, first of all, no need to find that at least a majority of the scientific community is in favour of a proposed health measure. *A fortiori*, the fact that there are dissenting scientific opinions does not prevent a member from imposing the measure. In terms of 'quantity' of the overall scientific evidence, minority opinions may range from anything between 49% of the scientific community to close to 0%. The bigger the minority, the more likely that it is found to be sufficient.

Secondly, the minority opinion must nonetheless come from 'qualified and respected sources'. Hence, if the evidence on which the measure is based does not come from a reputable or independent source – say, a retired scientist who could

---

[35] *EC – Hormones*, para. 194, italics added.

[36] *Japan – Varietals*, para. 77.

[37] *Japan – Varietals*, paras. 73 and 84 (italics added, footnote omitted).

[38] *EC – Asbestos*, para. 178.

[39] Ibid., para. 172 [paraphrasing its earlier finding in *Korea – Beef*, para. 162, on GATT Art. XX(d)], adding that in *EC – Asbestos* 'the objective pursued by the measure is the preservation of human life and health through the elimination, or reduction, of the well-known, and life-threatening, health risks posed by asbestos fibres. The value pursued is both vital and important in the highest degree'.

well have been paid to come to certain conclusions, or evidence backed up only by scientists employed by the government imposing the measure – the measure is unlikely to pass the test.

Thirdly, in case of an alleged or perceived 'lower risk', either in terms of quantity or quality or both, the required quantum of scientific evidence increases. In other words, *a 'lower risk'*, say, animal or plant health (as opposed to human health) or 0.0001 in a million risk (versus a hundred in a million risk), will normally require *more scientific evidence.*

How these three criteria (quantity and quality of the evidence and seriousness of the risk) will interact may provide an interesting development. Would it, for example, be enough if, say, 30% of the scientific community supports the measure, but this 30% seems to be the less reputable or less credible part of the community and the risk at stake is 'only' a minor animal disease?

The above applies to what *WTO members* must come up with in terms of scientific evidence for their measures to be WTO consistent. The scientific evidence referred to is, therefore, that submitted *by the defendant party* (not that submitted by the panel's experts). Where does this leave our panel faced with opposing expert opinions (be they form the parties' experts or from the panel's experts)? The Appellate Body in *EC – Asbestos* applied the same criteria to a panel as those that it applied in *EC – Hormones* to a regulating WTO member, i.e., 'a panel need not, necessarily, reach a decision . . . on the basis of the "preponderant" weight of the evidence'. In other words, the panel as well may put aside conflicting scientific opinions and base its legal findings on minority opinions, as long as they are 'qualified and respected'. On the latter requirement, the Appellate Body noted that in case the traditional procedures for expert selection by panels (set out above) are followed and if it is made clear by the panel that experts are to answer only those questions that fall within their area of expertise, '[t]he panel was entitled to assume that the experts possessed the necessary expertise to answer the questions, or parts of questions, they chose to answer'.[40]

Hence, under most substantive legal criteria in which reference is made to scientific evidence, a solid minority opinion may suffice for a panel to find that the measure at issue is WTO consistent. In all SPS cases so far, this threshold of a solid minority opinion was *not* met. In the one GATT Art. XX(b) case, it was held that the evidence in support of the measure was overwhelming, hence largely majoritarian. The 'hard cases' are still to come.

As a fall-back solution for panels confronted with conflicting expert opinions, resort may be made to WTO rules on burden of proof. In short, it is for the member challenging the inconsistency of a measure to prove this inconsistency, hence, to prove that there is, for example, under SPS Art. 2.2 *no* 'sufficient scientific evidence'. However, as soon as that member succeeds in establishing a presumption that what it claims is true, the burden to come forward with evidence shifts to the defendant. It will then be up to that party to prove that there *is* 'sufficient scientific evidence'. In respect of exceptions, though, such as GATT Art. XX(b), it is for the defendant to prove that the measure imposed *is* 'necessary to protect' health. There, the burden of proof is shifted. This is one of the main distinguishing features between justifying

---

[40] *EC – Asbestos*, para. 180.

Expert Advice in WTO Dispute Settlement

health measures under the TBT and SPS agreements, on the one hand (burden on the complainant), and GATT Art. XX, on the other (burden on the defendant).

Finally, the standard of review to be followed by WTO panels may also offer help. This standard is 'an objective assessment of the matter before it' (DSU Art. 11; not a 'reasonableness test' or 'deferential test' nor a *de novo* review). Hence, as long as panels base their legal findings on an objective assessment of the expert advice before them, the Appellate Body will not be able to reverse the panel's treatment and weighing of expert advice. In *EC – Hormones*, the threshold has been put as high as 'egregious disregarding or distorting of evidence before the panel'.[41] If the panel refrains from such acts of bad faith, it will not be subject to review by the Appellate Body (at least not for the way it has treated expert advice).

More generally, unlike most domestic law regimes, international adjudication does not know the principle of judicial restraint in highly technical cases (where it is, in domestic law, presumed that the administration, being the expert in the field, must be given a certain margin of discretion).[42] In international law (where there is no separation of powers, but essentially states only, being one legal entity), no such distinction is made and normal rules of treaty interpretation and burden of proof apply in order to find out whether a state has breached its obligations. Still, as seen above, a degree of built-in deference can often be found in the way substantive requirements that go to the heart of state sovereignty (such as SPS obligations) have been interpreted.

IV. Conclusion

The WTO judiciary makes an increasing use of expert advice. This development must be applauded. It ensures the quality, transparency and legitimacy of WTO decisions, in particular those that cut across a number of societal values. The input of expert and other 'outside' opinions highlights the complex nature of WTO dispute settlement. It forms a process in which a large number of agents interact: the panel, the Appellate Body, the parties and third parties, party-appointed experts and panel experts, standing technical bodies and political WTO organs, *amici curiae* and other international organisations. As long as the WTO judiciary remains in control of this complex interaction, such dialogue can only be beneficial.

The injection of expert advice into the process results in four other systemic tensions: (i) the traditional government-to-government examination of disputes versus an increased input from non-governmental sources, including private economic actors; (ii) the confidentiality of the process versus the need to examine complex factual disputes in a transparent way; (iii) the adversarial nature of international adjudication versus the rather broad inquisitorial function of panels under DSU Art. 13; and (iv) the need for prompt settlement of trade disputes versus the often long period of time required to examine factually complex cases.

---

[41] *EC – Hormones*, para. 144.

[42] Note, however, that for anti-dumping disputes, Art. 17.6 of the Dumping Agreement provides for a more deferential 'reasonableness' test. In terms of policy, there is no good reason why panels ought to show more deference when examining a dumping case as opposed to when they examine a health measure. On the contrary, one would have expected that for health issues, more deference would be warranted.

The main practical suggestions in this chapter can be summarised as follows:

1. It is of capital importance that panels appoint the best experts. Expertise and neutrality are the only criteria panels can control. Objections by the parties to experts should not too easily be accepted by the panel.
2. In complex scientific cases, one of the panel members ought to be a scientist.
3. To let international organisations suggest expert names is an appropriate procedure. An alternative may be to let the parties appoint one expert each and then to ask these two experts to complete the expert group.
4. Panels should not be afraid to appoint a larger number of experts. The costs involved are low and the benefits to be drawn from having the best expert in all fields in which expertise is required are huge. Appointing economic experts should also be resorted to.
5. Appointing individual experts is likely to continue to be the preferred solution, instead of appointing expert groups, even if the WTO treaty itself focuses on expert groups.
6. For expert groups to be used, their standard working procedures ought to be changed and made more flexible.
7. In all cases where expert advice is sought, time limits in the DSU should be extended.
8. When gathering expert advice, panels must ensure a symmetry of information between the parties and the experts (both must submit all of the evidence and studies they rely on). To achieve a certain degree of symmetry of knowledge between the panel and the experts is also crucial.
9. DSU Art. 13 could be used more frequently to obtain advice from other international organisations and even other tribunals. This would provide a powerful tool against the fragmentation of international law.
10. DSU Art. 13 could even be used for panels to get advice from the Appellate Body. By analogy, the Appellate Body could exercise its power to obtain advice in the form of remanding a case to the panel for the panel to complete the factual record. This would avoid the dismissal of a case based solely on the fact that the panel record is factually insufficient for the Appellate Body to complete the analysis.
11. Panels are well-equipped to handle conflicting expert opinions: most substantive legal criteria involving scientific evidence are fulfilled as soon as a solid minority opinion can be pointed at. DSU Rules of Conduct as well as the expert selection process and way of gathering expert advice should ensure the integrity of panel experts and the high quality of expert answers. In addition, rules on burden of proof and standard of review offer a general fall-back for panels to deal with conflicting evidence.

ALAN O. SYKES

9. Domestic Regulation, Sovereignty and Scientific Evidence Requirements

A Pessimistic View

The World Trade Organization (WTO) and its predecessor the General Agreement on Tariffs and Trade (GATT) have been extraordinarily successful at liberalizing trade in the global economy. The process of liberalization has entailed a series of negotiations resulting in reciprocal commitments to reduce or eliminate tariffs, quotas and other traditional instruments of protectionism. To ensure the integrity of those commitments, it has been necessary since the inception of GATT to prohibit member nations from substituting other protectionist devices for those which they promise to forego.

Domestic regulations, in particular, can disadvantage or exclude foreign suppliers from export markets. Such regulatory obstacles to exports are known as "technical barriers to trade." A number of legal principles have evolved in the WTO system to discipline technical barriers.[1] Regulations that discriminate against foreign suppliers are the most obvious source of undesirable technical barriers, and WTO law imposes an obligation on the regulators of member nations to avoid discrimination that disfavors foreign suppliers.[2] Facially nondiscriminatory regulations that impose relatively greater compliance costs on foreign suppliers can have the same

---

[1] The subject of technical barriers and associated disputes is also the source of a rich literature on WTO law. For a few notable examples, see Robert Howse, Democracy, Science and Free Trade: Risk Regulation on Trial at the World Trade Organization, 98 *Michigan Law Review* 2329 (2000) (arguing that WTO rules on technical barriers can promote deliberative democracy); David G. Victor, The Sanitary and Phytosanitary Agreement of the World Trade Organization: An Assessment After Five Years, 32 *New York University Journal of International Law and Politics* 865 (2000) (reviewing the history of disputes in the area). The question of what role science should play within the WTO is closely related to the "standard of review" employed by WTO dispute panels in assessing the judgments of national authorities. An excellent reference on the standard of review generally is Stephen P. Croley & John H. Jackson, WTO Dispute Procedures, Standard of Review and Deference to National Governments, 90 *American Journal of International Law* 193 (1996).

[2] See GATT, Art. I and Art. III(4). The GATT Agreement is reprinted in John H. Jackson, William J. Davey & Alan O. Sykes, Documents Supplement to Legal Problems of International Economic Relations 15–78 (3d ed. West 1995) (hereafter Documents Supplement). This general nondiscrimination obligation applies more selectively in services markets, in as much as discriminatory domestic regulations are often the only sensible device for protecting domestic industries. Accordingly, nondiscrimination obligations apply only in sectors where members have agreed to them, and are subject to scheduled exceptions. See General Agreement on Trade in Services (GATS) Art. XVII. GATS is reprinted in Documents Supplement at 304–34.

I thank Jessica Romero for valuable research assistance.

effect as discriminatory regulations, however, and WTO law thus includes an array of constraints on domestic regulation that go beyond simple nondiscrimination requirements.[3]

One such constraint may be termed a "scientific evidence requirement" – a requirement that certain regulations, generally those enacted for the purpose of protecting health, safety or the environment, be based on scientific evidence. The scientific evidence may go either to the existence of a risk, or to the efficacy of the regulation in reducing the risk.

The logic of scientific evidence requirements is obvious. If a regulation that is ostensibly aimed at protecting health, safety or the environment nevertheless has the effect of restricting trade, and there is no scientific evidence of any danger to be avoided or of any reduction in risk as a result of the regulation, then the suspicion arises that the regulation is disguised protectionism. In effect, a scientific evidence requirement aids in motive review, and helps to sort regulations between those that are protectionist and those that seek to promote some legitimate, nonprotectionist regulatory objective.[4]

But scientific evidence requirements can also create hurdles for regulators who sincerely pursue objectives other than protectionism. Depending on the context, scientific evidence may be inconclusive or its conclusions highly tentative or preliminary. Convincing scientific proof of certain types of risk, particularly low level risks, may be difficult to produce. And scientists may well disagree about the existence of a risk or the efficacy of various ways to reduce it. In the face of such scientific uncertainty, scientific evidence requirements may stand in the way of honest regulatory efforts to manage risk. These concerns are not merely hypothetical. As shall be seen below, they surface clearly in WTO disputes.

The uncomfortable interface between scientific evidence requirements and conditions of scientific uncertainty poses serious challenges for the WTO system, which has always billed itself as respectful of national regulatory "sovereignty." The WTO agreements, as well as decisions pursuant to its dispute resolution process, are replete with references to the rights of each member nation to decide on the level of risk that it wishes to tolerate within its jurisdiction. This deference to national sovereignty has played an essential political role in quieting opposition to the WTO and thus in facilitating its core mission. Ideally, one might hope for an accommodation between scientific evidence requirements and "sovereignty" that allows both to be respected under WTO law.

My thesis in this chapter, however, is that such an accommodation is exceedingly difficult if not impossible: Meaningful scientific evidence requirements fundamentally conflict with regulatory sovereignty in all cases of serious scientific uncertainty. WTO law must then choose between an interpretation of scientific evidence requirements that essentially eviscerates them and defers to national judgments about "science," or an interpretation that gives them real bite at the expense of the capacity of national regulators to choose the level of risk that they will tolerate. The only middle ground lies in the rare cases where scientific uncertainty is remediable quickly at low

---

[3] See generally Alan O. Sykes, Regulatory Protectionism and the Law of International Trade, 66 *University of Chicago Law Review* 1 (1999).

[4] Id. at 17–18.

Domestic Regulation, Sovereignty and Scientific Evidence Requirements 259

cost. I further argue that "consistency" requirements cannot likely supplant scientific evidence requirements in a way that satisfactorily accommodates the tension between the desire to weed out protectionism on the one hand, and the desire to respect regulatory sovereignty on the other.

A close examination of pertinent WTO decisions to date, most importantly the decision in the "beef hormones" dispute and its unsuccessful effort to accommodate scientific evidence requirements with deference to domestic regulators, will provide the bulk of the argument. Section I provides some general background on WTO law, while Section II considers the cases.

I. Sovereignty and Scientific Evidence Requirements in WTO Law

The only substantial constraints imposed on domestic regulation by the original GATT Agreement were nondiscrimination requirements, prohibiting discrimination among trading partners (the "most-favored-nation" obligation of Article I) and between foreign suppliers and domestic suppliers (the "national treatment" obligation of Article III). These obligations were subject to exceptions, such as in the case of measures "necessary" to protect human, animal or plant health, so long as they were not "applied in a manner which would constitute arbitrary or unjustifiable discrimination between countries where the same conditions prevail, or a disguised restriction on international trade" (Article XX). Regulators were otherwise free to adopt whatever regulations they wished, even if the regulations raised the costs of foreign suppliers disproportionately and thus had the effect of insulating domestic firms from foreign competition.

The perceived inadequacy of this regime led to pressures for greater constraints on facially nondiscriminatory yet trade-distorting regulation. During the Tokyo Round of GATT negotiations in the 1970s, some of the members of the GATT agreed to a "Standards Code" that introduced a number of new disciplines. Regulations governing product characteristics became subject to a least-restrictive means requirement even if they were nondiscriminatory, and nations were required to use performance standards rather than design standards where possible (e.g., automobiles might be subject to emissions limits, but they could not be required to use a particular catalytic converter that might be more cheaply available to domestic manufacturers). Nations were encouraged to adopt international standards where appropriate to their goals. Some regulatory transparency requirements were also included, but scientific evidence requirements were not. Indeed, the code failed to address a number of important issues in the view of some signatories (among other things, it did not apply to regulations governing the way that products were produced, only to regulations governing the characteristics of the end product), and a constituency for further negotiation on the subject emerged during the Uruguay Round of the 1980s.[5]

The resulting agreements, which formed the basis for the creation of the WTO, divided technical barrier issues between an Agreement on Technical Barriers to

---

[5] For a detailed history of GATT rules in this area, and a discussion of the changes made by the WTO agreements, see Alan O. Sykes, *Products Standards for Internationally Integrated Goods Markets* 63–86 (Washington, DC: Brookings, 1995).

Trade (the TBT Agreement) and an Agreement on the Application of Sanitary and Phytosanitary Measures (the SPMs Agreement).[6] Their coverage is mutually exclusive, with the TBT Agreement applicable to all regulations not covered by the SPMs Agreement.[7] The SPMs Agreement defines SPMs, roughly, as measures by a member (a) to protect animal or plant life or health in its territory from the spread of pests or disease; (b) to protect human or animal life or health in its territory from risks arising from the presence of an additive, contaminant or disease-causing organism in a food, beverage or feedstuff; (c) to protect human life or health in its territory from risks arising from a disease-causing organism carried by an animal or plant; and (d) to prevent or limit other damage in its territory from the spread of a pest.

The substantive obligations differ between the two agreements in important ways. The TBT Agreement contains a tight prohibition on discrimination, for example,[8] while the SPMs Agreement prohibits measures that "arbitrarily or unjustifiably discriminate between Members where identical or similar conditions prevail."[9] The permissibility of limited discrimination under the SPMs Agreement is aimed at situations where the risk is greater with goods from particular sources (for example, beef from England during the mad cow scare).

By contrast, the SPMs Agreement contains significantly tighter scientific evidence requirements. The TBT Agreement merely requires that regulations "not be made more trade-restrictive than necessary to fulfill a legitimate objective," which can include "the protection of human health or safety, animal or plant life or health, or the environment. In assessing such risks, relevant elements of consideration are, *inter alia*: available scientific and technical information. . . ."[10] Seemingly, the only obligation under the TBT Agreement with respect to scientific evidence is that it be "considered."

Under the SPMs Agreement, however, "[m]embers shall ensure that any sanitary or phytosanitary measure . . . is based on scientific principles and is not maintained without sufficient scientific evidence."[11] Measures that conform to relevant international standards are presumptively in conformity with the requirements of the Agreement, and Members may only introduce or maintain measures "which result in a higher level of . . . protection than would be achieved by measures based on the relevant international standards . . . if there is a scientific justification, or as a consequence of the level of . . . protection a Member determines to be appropriate" in accordance with other provisions of the Agreement governing the assessment of risks.[12] The risk assessment provisions state that "[m]embers shall ensure that their sanitary and phytosanitary measures are based on an assessment, as appropriate to the circumstances, of the risks to human, animal or plant life or health, taking

---

[6] These agreements are modeled on similar provisions in the NAFTA. See NAFTA Chapters 7B and 9, reprinted in Documents Supplement at 546–59, 566–78.

[7] The division results from the way that negotiations were structured – technical barriers in general were entrusted to one negotiating group, but those of particular relevance to agriculture (the SPMs) were left to the agricultural negotiating group.

[8] TBT Agreement, Art. 2.1, reprinted in Documents Supplement at 150.

[9] SPMs Agreement, Art. 2.3, reprinted in Documents Supplement at 122.

[10] TBT Agreement, Art. 2.2, reprinted in Documents Supplement at 150.

[11] SPMs Agreement, Art. 2.2, reprinted in Documents Supplement at 122.

[12] SPMs Agreement, Art. 3.3, reprinted in Documents Supplement at 123.

Domestic Regulation, Sovereignty and Scientific Evidence Requirements 261

into account risk assessment techniques developed by the relevant international organizations. In the assessment of risks, Members shall take into account available scientific evidence. . . ."[13] An exception exists for cases "where relevant scientific evidence is insufficient." Then, "a Member may provisionally adopt . . . measures on the basis of available pertinent information," provided that they "shall seek to obtain the additional information necessary for a more objective assessment of risk and review the . . . measure accordingly within a reasonable period of time."[14] As indicated in the next section, these scientific evidence requirements of the SPMs Agreement have served as a basis for holding that several challenged regulations violate WTO obligations.

As the TBT and SPMs agreements created important new obligations, however, they also purported to ensure that member nations could continue to regulate to avoid risks that they do not wish to tolerate. The SPMs Agreement recites at its outset that "no Member should be prevented from adopting or enforcing measures necessary to protect human, animal or plant life or health."[15] Likewise, the TBT Agreement insists that "no country should be prevented from taking measures necessary . . . for the protection of human, animal or plant life or health, or the environment . . . at the levels it considers appropriate."[16] The evident purpose of these statements is to reassure Member nations that the WTO is not in the business of deciding which risks are acceptable and which are not. WTO law simply aims to ensure that the regulation of genuine risks is not more deleterious to trade than necessary. In this respect, both agreements promise to respect regulatory sovereignty regarding risk tolerance. The next section will suggest that the scientific evidence requirements of the SPMs Agreement, as interpreted by the WTO Appellate Body, have rendered this promise largely illusory.

II. Scientific Evidence Requirements in WTO Dispute Resolution

As noted, the role of scientific evidence requirements is much greater in situations that implicate the SPMs Agreement. Accordingly, they are the focus of attention here.

A. The SPMs Cases

The scientific evidence requirements of the SPMs Agreement have played a significant role in three reported WTO decisions to date involving European imports of beef, Australian imports of salmon, and Japanese imports of certain agricultural products. In each case, the regulation in question was held to violate WTO law.

1. European Community/Beef Hormones

The beef hormones dispute is one of the longest running trade disputes in the modern trading system. It stems from a decision by the European Union to prohibit the

---

[13] SPMs Agreement, Arts. 5.1–5.2, reprinted in Documents Supplement at 123–24.
[14] SPMs Agreement, Art. 5.7, reprinted in Documents Supplement at 124.
[15] SPMs Preamble, reprinted in Documents Supplement at 121.
[16] TBT Agreement Preamble, reprinted in Documents Supplement at 149.

administration of certain growth hormones (including estrogen, progesterone and testosterone) to cattle. Europe not only prohibited the use of these hormones domestically, but banned the importation of meat and meat products from cattle that had received these hormones abroad. These growth hormones are widely used by ranchers in the United States and Canada. After the entry into force of the agreements creating the WTO, the United States and Canada quickly brought a case alleging violations of the SPMs Agreement. A dispute panel found for the complainants on a number of grounds, some of which were reversed by the WTO Appellate Body. But the Appellate Body ultimately agreed with the panel that the European regulation violated WTO law and, in particular, the scientific evidence requirements of the SPMs Agreement. It is instructive to examine the Appellate Body's analysis in some detail.

Note first that the European regulation was nondiscriminatory, and thus beyond the reach of the basic nondiscrimination obligations that have existed since the inception of the GATT system. But it is the type of nondiscriminatory regulation that has a disparate impact on foreign trade. Meat packers in nations that permit the use of hormones cannot export to Europe unless they deal with ranchers who segregate part of their herds to be raised as hormone-free, and generate the supporting evidence of that practice necessary to satisfy European regulators. These added costs may not be worth the bother to packers who anticipate that only a modest portion of their business will involve European exports, and indeed we know that the initial impact of the hormone beef regulation was to reduce U.S. exports from about $100 million annually to zero.[17] Whether intended as a protectionist measure or not, therefore, the effect of such a regulation is to disadvantage foreign suppliers relative to domestic suppliers, and it affords a nice example of why nondiscrimination obligations alone are perceived as inadequate to address technical barriers.

But is the regulation disguised protectionism that the system should condemn? Its history suggests not. The first version of the regulation was enacted following widely publicized adverse reactions to the ingestion of beef from cattle treated with the hormone DES, reactions such as the development of breasts in young children. The European Council of Agricultural Ministers responded with a zero-risk policy, banning all growth hormones whether or not they had been shown to produce adverse reactions in humans.[18] Although there is little doubt that the regulation improved the competitive position of European beef producers and they no doubt welcomed it in part on that basis, the impetus for the measure can be traced clearly to an episode that raised bona fide concerns about the safety of growth hormones.

But the central issue before the WTO was whether the measure rested on an acceptable scientific footing, and in particular whether it was "based on" a risk assessment as required by Article 5.1 of the SPMs Agreement. In addressing this question, the WTO Appellate Body tipped its hat often to the notion that national regulators have the right to regulate low-level risks. It noted that the requirement of a risk assessment does not mean that "a certain magnitude or threshold level of risk be demonstrated" – "such a quantitative requirement finds no basis" in the

---

[17] See Alan O. Sykes, supra note 4, at 17.

[18] Id.

Domestic Regulation, Sovereignty and Scientific Evidence Requirements   263

agreement.[19] Further, "Article 5.1 does not require that the risk assessment must necessarily embody only the view of a majority of the relevant scientific community . . . responsible and representative governments may act in good faith on the basis of what, at a given time, may be a divergent opinion."[20] The requirement that a measure be "based on" a risk assessment is simply "a substantive requirement that there be a rational relationship between the measure and the risk assessment."[21]

Nevertheless, the regulation failed to pass muster. The Appellate Body pointed to studies of the safety of growth hormones done for the Codex Alimentarius, an international standard-setting body connected to the World Health Organization, which concluded that the use of the hormones in question was "safe" if they were used in accordance with good veterinary practice.[22] Hence, these scientific studies did not "rationally support" the European measure.[23]

Europe pointed to a number of studies that document a relationship between hormone ingestion and cancer, a linkage that has recently been confirmed by studies of women undergoing hormone replacement therapy, but these were deemed inadequate because "[t]he Monographs and articles and opinions of individual scientists have not evaluated the carcinogenic potential of those hormones when used specifically *for growth promotion purposes*. Moreover, they do not evaluate the specific potential for carcinogenic effects arising from the presence in "*food*," more specifically, "meat or meat products" of residues of the hormones in dispute" (emphasis in original).[24]

Europe also produced an expert witness before the dispute panel, one Dr. Lucier, who opined that the ingestion of growth hormone residues in meat would indeed cause some small number of additional cancers. He stated that of every one million women, 110,000 would contract breast cancer, of which several thousand cases likely result from the intake of exogenous estrogens from all sources. "And by my estimates one of those 110,000 would come from eating meat containing oestrogens as a growth promoter, if used as prescribed."[25] The Appellate Body might have simply noted that Dr. Lucier's opinion was not available to the European Union at the time the regulation was promulgated, and hence that the regulation could not be "based on" it. But that would have left Europe the opportunity simply to repromulgate the regulation in reliance on Dr. Lucier's analysis. Instead, the Appellate Body noted "that this opinion by Dr. Lucier does not purport to show the results of scientific studies carried out by him under his supervision focusing specifically on residues of hormones in meat from cattle fattened with such hormones. Accordingly, the single divergent opinion expressed by Dr. Lucier is not reasonably sufficient. . . ."[26]

---

[19] WTO, EC Measures Concerning Meat and Meat Products (Hormones), WT/DS26 & 48AB/R, Appellate Body Report Adopted by the Dispute Settlement Body on February 13, 1998 (hereafter "Hormones Report") ¶ 186.

[20] Id. ¶194.

[21] Id. ¶193.

[22] Id. ¶196.

[23] Id. ¶197.

[24] Id. ¶199.

[25] Id. ¶198 (note).

[26] Id. ¶199.

Europe's final line of defense was to point to the dangers of hormone abuse by cattle ranchers. Even if the Codex studies were right that hormones are "safe" when used in accordance with good veterinary practice, some ranchers might be tempted to overuse them, leaving higher and more dangerous residues. To this argument, the Appellate Body responded in essence that Europe had produced no empirical study of the risks of hormone abuse that demonstrated the magnitude or severity of the problem. Accordingly, if the justification for the regulation lay in the fear of excess residues attributable to hormone abuse, it still was not "based on" a risk assessment.[27]

2. Australia/Salmon

Australia has developed a successful salmon industry, and insists that the importation of uncooked salmon from other nations creates a risk that certain diseases of salmon prevalent elsewhere will be introduced into the Australian fish population. Accordingly, it enacted a ban on the importation of salmon from various places, including Canada. Canada brought a challenge to the ban contending, *inter alia*, that the ban was not "based on" a risk assessment.

In reviewing this claim, the Appellate Body again tipped its hat to the right of Member nations to set their own risk levels, indicating that a Member may permissibly elect a zero-risk policy.[28] But the regulation must nevertheless be based on a "risk assessment." The requirements of a "risk assessment" can be found in the definition of the term in Annex A to the SPMs Agreement. A risk assessment must

(1) *identify* the diseases whose entry, establishment or spread a Member wants to prevent within its territory, as well as the potential biological and economic consequences associated with the entry, establishment or spread of these diseases;

(2) *evaluate the likelihood* of entry, establishment or spread of these diseases, as well as the associated potential biological and economic consequences; and

(3) evaluate the likelihood of entry, establishment or spread of these diseases *according to the SPS measures which might be applied.* (emphasis in original)

In interpreting these requirements, the Appellate Body held that "it is not sufficient that a risk assessment conclude that there is a *possibility* of entry, establishment or spread of diseases and associated biological and economic consequences. A proper risk assessment of this type must evaluate the 'likelihood,' i.e., the 'probability,' of entry, establishment or spread of diseases and associated biological and economic consequences as well as the 'likelihood,' i.e., 'probability,' of entry, establishment or spread of diseases *according to the SPS measures which might be applied*" (emphasis in original).[29] "The likelihood may be expressed either quantitatively or qualitatively."[30]

---

[27] Id. ¶207.

[28] WTO, Australia – Measures Affecting the Importation of Salmon, WT/DS18, Appellate Body Report Adopted by the Dispute Settlement Body on November 6, 1998, ¶125 (hereafter "Salmon Report").

[29] Id. ¶123.

[30] Id. ¶123.

Domestic Regulation, Sovereignty and Scientific Evidence Requirements 265

Australia produced a government report that noted the possibility of twenty-four diseases being spread through imports of uncooked salmon, and offered it as the "risk assessment" on which the regulation was based. The Appellate Body found the report adequate as to the first criterion above – it identified the diseases at issue and their potential consequences. But as to the second criterion, the Appellate Body found that the report did not adequately "evaluate the likelihood" of the spread of disease through importation of salmon. It based that conclusion on the dispute panel's finding that the report contained "general and vague statements of mere possibility of adverse effects occurring; statements which constitute neither a quantitative nor a qualitative assessment of probability."[31] Likewise, the Appellate Body found the report inadequate under the third criterion because, although it identified various options for reducing the risks in question, it "does not, in any substantial way, evaluate or assess their relative effectiveness in reducing the overall disease risk."[32]

In short, even though a "zero-risk" policy is acceptable according to the Appellate Body, an adequate risk assessment must nevertheless evaluate the probability of the spread of disease, and must do so for the various alternative regulatory options as well as for the status quo ante in the absence of regulation. The probability may be assessed "qualitatively," but a conclusion that a mere "possibility" exists that disease may spread apparently falls short of a "qualitative" assessment of "probability."

3. Japan/Agricultural Products

The coddling moth is a pest that lowers the yield for a variety of fruit products, but it has not yet been detected in Japan. To prevent the introduction of the pest into Japan, the government imposes strict regulations on imported fruit, requiring that it be treated effectively with some combination of fumigation and cold storage to kill the moth at any stage of its life cycle. The United States objected to one important feature of the regulatory scheme, which in essence required an elaborate scientific investigation of the efficacy of measures to kill the moth for every individual variety of a given product (e.g., a separate study would have to be conducted for Macintosh apples and Granny Smith apples). Unless a study had been conducted for a particular variety that proved the efficacy of pest control measures to the satisfaction of Japanese regulators, that variety could not be imported into Japan.

The United States challenged the evidence on familiar grounds – that it was not "based on" a risk assessment and was maintained without sufficient scientific evidence. The Appellate Body affirmed the panel's ruling that the language in Article 2.2, prohibiting measures that are "maintained without sufficient scientific evidence," requires a rational relationship between the measure and the scientific evidence presented.[33] The dispute panel's factual determination (not appealable) that no rational relationship existed to the available scientific evidence turned heavily on the fact that Japan could not point to a single instance in which an approved method for killing the moth on one variety of fruit had not proven effective when used on another

---

[31] Id. ¶129.

[32] Id. ¶133.

[33] WTO, Japan – Measures Affecting Agricultural Products, WT/DS76/AB/R, Appellate Body Report Adopted by the Dispute Settlement Body on March 19, 1999, ¶84.

variety of the same fruit.[34] Although Japan could produce some scientific evidence of possible differences across varieties that might make treatments less effective for one variety than another, the mere possibility of a difference was not enough – the panel apparently wanted some affirmative evidence of differences in the efficacy of treatment measures across varieties to justify Japan's policy.

Japan also attempted to justify the policy as "provisional" pursuant to Article 5.7 governing conditions where "scientific evidence was insufficient." This defense failed because Japan could not show that it was engaged in an active research program "to obtain the additional information necessary for a more objective assessment" or that it had reviewed its provisional measures within a "reasonable period of time."[35]

B. Analysis and Implications

Beginning with the hormones decision, the factual propositions that underlie the Appellate Body's conclusions are surely correct. No empirical scientific analysis was presented to the WTO that specifically examined the human health risks from the ingestion of beef containing growth hormone residues, and that concluded that a risk to human health was present. Dr. Lucier's opinion did not rest on any such study that he had conducted, but was simply an extrapolation from the now well-known fact that estrogen ingestion causes an increase in the incidence of breast cancer. And no empirical scientific analysis was presented that examined the risks associated with the possible failure of ranchers to observe good veterinary practice.

Yet, one must ask what the European Union could reasonably have done to bolster the scientific case. Precisely how does one conduct a study of "the specific potential for carcinogenic effects arising from the presence in '*food*,' more specifically, 'meat or meat products' of residues of the hormones in dispute"? In theory, one might conduct cross-sectional studies comparing cancer rates in nations that permit growth hormones with rates in nations that ban them. But there are innumerable sources of external estrogens besides residues in meat, and innumerable other factors that may affect cancer rates. Can one hope to control for all these factors convincingly? And even if one could, everyone (including Europe) agrees that the marginal contribution to cancer rates from meat hormone residues is likely to be small – could one ever hope to identify such small effects at conventional statistical confidence levels?

Are animal studies the answer? Would studies of low-dose hormone administration to lab rats satisfy the Appellate Body? How could one be confident that any results from such studies carry over to humans, whichever way the result came out? And if the issue is the effect of the low residues in meat that might cause cancer at the rate of one case per million population (Dr. Lucier's estimate), how large would the population of test rats have to be for statistically convincing results to be observed?

Finally, if the concern is the risk of hormone misuse, how precisely does one study that risk? One suspects that a questionnaire to a random sample of U.S. ranchers, asking them whether they abuse growth hormones in violation of sound veterinary

---

[34] WTO, Japan – Measures Affecting Agricultural Products, WT/DS76/AB/R, Panel Report Adopted by the Dispute Settlement Body (as modified) on March 19, 1999, ¶8.42.

[35] WTO, Japan – Measures Affecting Agricultural Products, WT/DS76/AB/R, Appellate Body Report Adopted by the Dispute Settlement Body on March 19, 1999, ¶¶92–93.

Domestic Regulation, Sovereignty and Scientific Evidence Requirements 267

practice, might yield a negative response regardless of the truth. Could random samples of meat entering Europe at the border be tested for excessive residues? Would excessive residues found on occasion demonstrate an important problem of abuse? How would one determine the risks to human health of those excessive residues, any more than one could empirically assess the risks from the low-level residues associated with sound veterinary practice?

Although I am not a toxicologist, I can claim to know enough about empirical research to say that statistically convincing studies demonstrating the existence of a small health risk from hormone residues in meat are likely to be exceedingly difficult to generate. One can observe that the hormones in question are known carcinogens, and that some residue of these hormones exists in the meat. But it is likely impossible to know with any degree of statistical confidence whether these small residues, when added to the diets of people who are exposed to the same hormones from many other sources (not to mention numerous other carcinogens), do or do not cause a few more cases of cancer at the margin.

Consequently, the Appellate Body's insistence that Europe point to highly particularized studies showing a risk from hormone residues in meat likely presents an insurmountable hurdle. The effect is to make it impossible for national regulators to elect to eliminate low-level risks that are not susceptible of rigorous demonstration. That may not be bad policy, and indeed it might well be the case that Europe's ban on growth hormones would flunk any sort of careful cost-benefit analysis. But if scientific evidence requirements are construed in a way that makes it impossible to regulate risks that are not demonstrable through particularized scientific studies, they surely clash with the notion that WTO law is not meant to tell member states which risks they must tolerate and which risks they may elect to avoid.

The Australian Salmon case, in my view, is similar in this regard. While pretending to permit nations to embrace a zero-risk policy, it simultaneously holds that credible scientific opinion affirming the possibility of a risk is not enough for even a "qualitative" assessment of "probability" as required by Article 5.1. To some readers, as well as this writer, the Appellate Body's position on this issue borders on the incoherent. And whatever it is that must be done to count as an acceptable assessment of "probability," it must be done for all of the regulatory options under consideration. One again wonders exactly what it would take in the way of additional research for Australia to satisfy the Appellate Body – how can one assess the "probability" of disease spreading through imported goods if that unfortunate eventuality has (thankfully) not yet transpired? Would it suffice to demonstrate that live disease organisms reside in the carcasses of uncooked salmon (seemingly not, as that demonstration should not be a difficult one). And if that is not enough, how does one proceed to isolate the "probability" that such organisms might spread to the live fish population in Australia?

The Japanese measures at issue in the agricultural products case were similarly predicated on unproven risks, but at least that case hinted at a road map for further research. In particular, the panel decision implied that if Japan could convincingly identify one instance in which coddling moth treatment effective on one variety of fruit was ineffective on another, it might be able to justify its varietal testing requirements. And had Japan been actively engaged in research on possible varietal differences in treatment efficacy, it might have been able to justify its measures for the short term as provisional. But this decision too seems to stand for the proposition that over the long term, affirmative, convincing scientific evidence must be adduced to establish the presence of the risk in question. Bona fide concerns about possible risks are not enough.

Consider, however, the alternative. In the hormones case, the Appellate Body might have written an opinion that would permit Europe to rely on minority opinions like those of Dr. Lucier going forward, simply insisting that such an opinion be in place at the time that a regulation is enacted so that the regulation can fairly be said to have been "based on" it. An adequate "risk assessment" would exist whenever a consultant could colorably extrapolate from a known risk to suggest that a smaller risk was present though not statistically demonstrable – minimal exposure to a substance known to be dangerous in large quantity could always be regulated, for example, as might exposure to substances bearing chemical similarity to those known to be dangerous. Indeed, if experience with the American tort system teaches us anything, it is that determined parties can almost always find consultants willing to opine that risk is present, whether from Bendectin, Agent Orange, silicone breast implants, electromagnetic radiation from cell phones, or any number of other sources. An interpretation that accepts the minority opinions of consultants as "risk assessments" effectively converts scientific evidence requirements into minimal procedural hurdles that can be met easily by any determined regulators, high-minded and protectionist alike. The right of Member nations to refuse risks that they do not wish to tolerate would be preserved, but the opportunities for mischief would surely be enhanced as well.

Of course, the problem here is limited to cases of genuine scientific uncertainty. Cases surely arise in principle where the science is so clear that no doubts exist, but I suspect that these cases will rarely make it so far as to trigger a WTO dispute, and certainly that type of case is not what the WTO has seen in practice so far.

The only other class of cases in which the Appellate Body's insistence on hard supporting evidence might not intrude importantly on regulatory sovereignty are those in which scientific uncertainty can be laid to rest reasonably cheaply and quickly. A nation that eschews obvious and inexpensive opportunities for research that will confirm or deny the wisdom of its regulatory policy can hardly complain very loudly if WTO law requires those opportunities to be pursued. But again, these cases are perhaps unlikely to be the ones that provoke international disputes. It is also noteworthy that nothing in WTO treaty text or in WTO decisions to date seems to condition the stringency of the scientific evidence requirement on the technical and economic feasibility of the research program to eliminate scientific uncertainty. Technical and economic feasibility are indeed factors to be considered in deciding whether a regulatory measure represents the "least restrictive means,"[36] but WTO jurisprudence does not yet bring similar ideas to bear in judging the acceptability of a national "risk assessment."

C. Consistency Requirements as an Alternative

Before concluding, one might reasonably ask whether alternative devices exist for policing regulatory mischief that would perform reasonably well and that would

---

[36] SPMs Agreement, Art. 5.6, reprinted in Documents Supplement at 124.

Domestic Regulation, Sovereignty and Scientific Evidence Requirements 269

pose less of a threat to regulatory sovereignty than tight scientific evidence requirements. One option deserving of careful consideration in this regard is a consistency requirement, which also finds expression in WTO law. Article 5.5 of the SPMs Agreement provides that "[w]ith the objective of achieving consistency in ... sanitary and phytosanitary protection ... each Member shall avoid arbitrary or unjustifiable distinctions in the levels it considers to be appropriate for different situations, if such distinctions result in discrimination or a disguised restriction on international trade."

A nice application of this principle may be found in the Australian Salmon case, in which the Appellate Body affirmed an alternative basis for declaring that Australia's ban on salmon imports was impermissible. In particular, the evidence seemed to be quite clear that the risk to the Australian salmon population from the spread of disease was considerably greater from certain activities that Australia did not regulate at all – in particular, the importation of ornamental aquarium fish that might be released into local waters (recall the Asian carp and Northern snakehead problems in the United States presently) and the importation of live herring to use as a baitfish – than it was from the importation of uncooked salmon. Because the evidence of a greater hazard from these activities seemed compelling and Australia had no persuasive justification for ignoring these other hazards on the one hand, while regulating a lesser hazard from a product that just happened to compete with an important domestic industry on the other, the distinction was found to be arbitrary or unjustifiable and a disguised restriction.[37]

The virtue of resting the decision on the consistency issue (alone) is at first blush considerable. No longer would the WTO seemingly be telling nations that they could not regulate in the face of potentially intractable scientific uncertainty. Rather, nations would be free to regulate a hazard that was somewhat speculative, but only if they did so evenhandedly without regard to which sources of hazard were competitive irritants to domestic producers. In a circumstance like the Australian case, a weakened scientific evidence requirement would not prevent suspicious regulatory behavior from being policed.

One difficulty, of course, is that regulators will often be able to offer plausible reasons why one type of hazard is regulated and one is not. The costs of regulation may be much higher in one case than another, for example, or differences in the efficacy of regulatory options may make some types of regulation futile. If such arguments are rejected in favor of a finding of an "arbitrary and unjustifiable" distinction, the perceived intrusion on regulatory sovereignty may be no less than before.

There is also the difficult issue of which regulatory distinctions are comparable for consistency purposes. The Australian case was unusual in that one could look to the identical risk to the identical fish population from multiple sources. In the beef hormones case, by contrast, what regulations (or nonregulations) would one examine for consistency? In fact, the dispute panel examined several, including the policy of the European Union to permit certain carcinogenic medications to be used for growth promotion in piglets, and the policy of doing nothing to regulate the ingestion of naturally occurring hormones, such as those present in eggs. In the end, the Appellate Body found no violation of Article 5.5 because some of the distinctions were not arbitrary or unjustifiable (such as ignoring the hormones that

---

[37] Salmon Report ¶¶234–40.

occur naturally), and others could not be said to be a disguised restriction on trade (the medication used on piglets).[38]

A serious requirement of consistency in regulation probably could not be met by any nation – it is well known, for example, that the cost per life saved varies hugely across public safety and health regulations in the United States.[39] The only way to avoid the appearance of rampant inconsistencies will be to narrow the comparisons to regulations that appear similar in some superficial way (in the hormones case, other food regulation, other meat regulation, etc.). Alternatively, one can simply tolerate inconsistencies by recognizing that they are pervasive and rarely motivated by protectionism (as the Appellate Body essentially so found in the hormones case when it addressed the use of carcinogenic medication in piglets). Either way, one quickly becomes pessimistic about the ability of consistency requirements to step into the breach should scientific evidence requirements become more deferential.

Conclusion

The battle between the proponents of open trade and the proponents of national "sovereignty" has been central to the political fortunes of the World Trade Organization since its inception. Defenders of the system regularly insist that the tension is illusory, and that WTO rules do not intrude on proper national prerogatives. Without taking any normative position on the matter, this chapter has argued that in some contexts a serious tension indeed arises, and that the goals of open trade and respect for national sovereignty can be irreconcilably at odds to the point that one must give way. With particular regard to the scientific evidence requirements of the WTO Agreement on Sanitary and Phytosanitary Measures, the WTO Appellate Body has embarked on a course that unmistakably elevates the policing of trade-restrictive measures above the ability of national governments to address risk in the face of scientific uncertainty. There is little alternative to such a policy if scientific evidence requirements are to serve as more than window dressing.

---

[38] Hormones Report ¶246.

[39] See, e.g., Lisa Heinzerling, Regulatory Costs of Mythic Proportions, 107 *The Yale Law Journal* 1981, 2042–64 (1998); Eric Posner, Controlling Agencies with Cost-Benefit Analysis: A Positive Political Theory Perspective, 68 *University of Chicago Law Review* 1137 (2001); Richard J. Zeckhauser and W. Kip Viscusi, The Risk Management Dilemma, 545 *Annals of the American Academy of Political and Social Science* 144 (1996).

ERNST-ULRICH PETERSMANN

10. Time for a United Nations' "Global Compact" for Integrating Human Rights into the Law of Worldwide Organizations

Lessons from European Integration Law for Global Integration Law

"Everyone is entitled to a social and international order in which the rights and freedoms set forth in this Declaration can be fully realized."

Universal Declaration of Human Rights 1948, Article 28

ABSTRACT. Most people spend most of their time on their economic activities of producing goods and services and exchanging the fruits of their labor for other goods and services that are necessary for their survival and personal development. Also, international trade and investments are never ends in themselves, but *means* for increasing individual and social welfare through voluntarily agreed and mutually beneficial transactions involving the exercise of liberty rights and property rights. Even though the *economy* is no less important for citizens and their human rights than the *polity*, the interrelationships between human rights and economic welfare – notably the enormous opportunities of the international division of labor for enabling individuals to increase their personal freedom, real income and access to resources necessary for the enjoyment of human rights – are neglected by human rights doctrine. The "Global Compact," launched by UN Secretary-General Kofi Annan in 1999, calls upon business to "support and respect the protection of international human rights within their sphere of influence and make sure their own corporations are not complicit in human rights abuses." This contribution calls for a complementary "Global Compact" between the UN and UN Specialized Agencies, as well as with other worldwide *public organizations* like the World Trade Organization (WTO), so as to integrate universally recognized human rights into the law and practice of *intergovernmental organizations*, for example, by requiring them to submit annual "human rights impact statements" to UN human rights bodies and to engage in transparent dialogues about the contribution by specialized agencies to the promotion and protection of human rights. In view of the inherent tendency of liberty to destroy itself ("paradox of freedom"), human rights need legislative, administrative and judicial protection in the national and international economy no less than in the polity vis-à-vis private as well as governmental abuses of power.

Such an "integration approach" differs fundamentally from the 1945 paradigm of "specialized agencies." It takes into account the regional experiences in Europe that respect for human rights in integration law enhances not only the protection of human rights across frontiers, democratic legitimacy and *rule* of law at national and international levels of governance, but also economic and social welfare. The chapter argues that the universal recognition of human rights as "inalienable birth rights" of every human being entails "constitutional primacy" of the inalienable core of human rights vis-à-vis national and international legislative, executive

---

A first version of this chapter was submitted for the "day of general discussion" hosted by the UN Committee on Economic, Social and Cultural Rights on 7 May 2001 at the office of the UN High Commissioner for Human Rights.

and judicial activities that serve "constitutional functions" by operationalizing and balancing human rights. As in European integration law, human rights should be recognized also in global integration law as empowering citizens, as constitutionally limiting abuses of national and international regulatory powers, and as requiring governments to protect and promote human rights in all policy areas and across national frontiers. The chapter criticizes UN human rights law for neglecting economic liberties, property rights and freedom of competition because – as legal preconditions for a mutually welfare-increasing division of labor among free citizens that promote efficient use of scarce resources – economic human rights are essential for enabling individuals to acquire, possess, use and dispose of the resources necessary for enjoying human rights. A UN Action Program for integrating human rights into the law of worldwide organizations is necessary so as to render the "indivisibility" of human rights, and their instrumental functions for promoting economic and social welfare and "democratic peace," more effective. The chapter concludes with case studies on the need for integrating liberty rights and social rights into the law of the WTO so as to render human rights and also WTO law more effective.

Introduction: Time for Reconsidering the "Washington Consensus" and Strengthening Human Rights in Global Integration Law

The human rights obligations in the UN Charter and in the Universal Declaration of Human Rights (UDHR) of 1948 were negotiated at the same time as the 1944 Bretton Woods Agreements, the General Agreement on Tariffs and Trade (GATT) of 1947 and the 1948 Havana Charter for an International Trade Organization. All these agreements aimed at protecting liberty, non-discrimination, rule of law, social welfare and other human rights values through a rules-based international order and "specialized agencies" (Article 57 UN Charter) committed to the economic principle of "separation of policy instruments":

- *foreign policies* were to be coordinated in the UN so as to promote "sovereign equality of all its Members" (Article 2:1 UN Charter) and collective security;
- *liberalization of payments* and *monetary stability* were collectively pursued through the rules and assistance of the International Monetary Fund (IMF);
- GATT 1947 and the Havana Charter aimed at mutually beneficial *liberalization of international trade and investments*;
- *development aid and policies* were coordinated in the World Bank Group;
- and *social laws and policies* were promoted in the International Labor Organization (ILO) and other specialized agencies (like UNESCO and WHO).

Apart from a few exceptions (notably in ILO, UNESCO and WHO rules), human rights were not effectively integrated into the law of most worldwide organizations so as to facilitate *functional international integration* (such as liberalization of trade and payments), notwithstanding different views of governments on human rights and domestic policies (such as *communism*). In accordance with the "principles of justice" elaborated by modern legal philosophers[1] and reflected in the constitutional

---

[1] See e.g. J. Rawls, *A Theory of Justice*, revised edition 1999, Chapter II, whose conception of "justice as fairness" for defining the basic rights and liberties of free and equal citizens in a constitutional democracy gives priority to maximum equal liberty as "first principle of justice." Rawls' "principle of fair equality of opportunity" and his "difference principle" are recognized only as secondary principles necessary for socially just conditions essential for moral and rational self-development of every person. Kantian legal

Integrating Human Rights into the Law of Worldwide Organizations

law of the leading postwar hegemonic power,[2] the postwar institutions gave priority to reciprocal international *liberalization* (e.g. in the context of the IMF, GATT, WTO, WIPO and ILO) and to *wealth creation. Economic* and *social rights* and *redistribution of wealth* were perceived as primarily the responsibility of *national* governments, to be supplemented by "international benevolence."[3]

This contribution argues that there are important moral, legal, economic and political reasons why the "logic of 1945" no longer offers an appropriate paradigm for global integration and democratic peace in the 21st century. The "human rights clauses" in the European Union (EU) Treaty, in the association and cooperation agreements between the EU and more than twenty countries in Eastern Europe and the Mediterranean, and in the EU's Cotonou Agreement with seventy-seven African, Caribbean and Pacific states make "respect for human rights, democratic principles and the rule of law ... essential elements" of these agreements.[4] The Quebec Summit Declaration of April 2001 and the "Inter-American Charter of Democracy" of September 2001, adopted by more than thirty member states of the Organization of American States, likewise link the plans for a Free Trade Area of the Americas (FTAA) to the strengthening of human rights and democracy. Even though *realists* continue to dominate foreign policy-making, human rights are becoming ever more important parts of the national identity and of the foreign and security policies of states, as illustrated by the humanitarian intervention by the nineteen NATO countries in the Kosovo crisis and their invocation of NATO's mutual defense principle (Article 5) in response to the terrorist attacks in New York and Washington on 11 September 2001.[5] The now regular civil society protests at the annual conferences of the IMF, the World Bank and the WTO, and the proposals for including environmental rules and social standards into the global integration law of the WTO are further illustrations of the need to examine whether the European and American "integration paradigm" should not also become accepted at the worldwide level in order to promote consensus on a new kind of global integration law based on human rights and solidary sharing of the social adjustment costs of global integration.

---

theory also gives priority to a legal duty of states to ensure conditions of maximum law-governed freedom over moral "duties of benevolence" to provide for the needs of the citizens (cf. A. D. Rosen, *Kant's Theory of Justice*, 1993, at 217; P. Guyer, *Kant on Freedom, Law and Happiness*, 2000, at 264 *et seq.*).

[2] For instance, the Bill of Rights, which had to be appended to the US Constitution in order to secure its ratification, focuses more on "inalienable rights" to life and liberty than on social rights to secure "the general Welfare" (recognized as an objective of the US Constitution in its Preamble).

[3] On legal philosophies concerning moral and legal duties of assistance vis-à-vis "burdened societies," the "principle of just savings," a "property-owning democracy" promoting widespread ownership of economic and human capital, and on "distributive justice among peoples" see e.g. J. Rawls, *The Law of Peoples*, 1999, chapters 15 and 16. Human rights law still lacks a coherent theory on transnational economic and social human rights (e.g. to food and health protection) vis-à-vis foreign governments and international organizations. On human rights and "global justice" see R. A. Falk, *Human Rights Horizons. The Pursuit of Justice in a Globalizing World*, 2000.

[4] The quotation is from Article 9 of the Cotonou Agreement signed in June 2000 by the EU, the fifteen EU member states and seventy-seven ACP countries. On human rights in the external relations law of the EU see e.g. the contributions by Clapham, Simma, Aschenbrenner and Schulte to P. Alston/M. Bustelo/J. Heenan (eds.), *The EU and Human Rights*, 1999.

[5] See *International Herald Tribune* of 13 September 2001, at 3. See more generally e.g. D. P. Forsythe (ed.), *Human Rights and Comparative Foreign Policy*, 2000; *idem, Human Rights in International Relations*, 2000.

The needed change from international functionalism to constitutionalism does not put into question the economic efficiency arguments for "optimizing" and separating policy instruments.[6] However, European integration confirms that the collective supply of public goods (such as global division of labor) may not be politically feasible without comprehensive "package deals" including redistributive "principles of justice" and solidary responses to "market failures."[7] Less-developed countries, for instance, often perceive market competition as a "license to kill" for multinational corporations from developed countries as long as liberal trade rules are not supplemented by competition and social rules (as in the EC) promoting fair opportunities and equitable distribution of the gains from trade. In order to remain politically acceptable, global integration law (e.g. in the WTO) must pursue not only "economic efficiency" but also "democratic legitimacy" and "social justice" as defined by human rights. Citizens will rightly challenge the democratic and social legitimacy of integration law if it pursues economic welfare without regard to social human rights, for example, the *human right to education* of the 130 million children (aged from six to twelve) who do not attend primary school; the *human right to basic health care* of the twenty-five million Africans living with AIDS, or of the about 35,000 children dying each day from curable diseases; and the *human right to food and an adequate standard of living* for the 1.2 billion people living on less than a dollar a day. The new opportunities for the worldwide enjoyment of human rights created by global division of labor (such as additional economic resources, job opportunities, worldwide communication systems, access to new medicines and technologies) must be accompanied by stronger legal protection of social human rights so as to limit abuses of deregulation (e.g. by international cartels, trade in drugs and arms, trafficking in women and children), help vulnerable groups to adjust to change without violation of their human rights and put pressure on authoritarian governments to protect not only business interests but the human rights of all their citizens.

1. Legal, Economic and Political Arguments for Integrating Human Rights into the Law of Worldwide Organizations

Most of the 143 WTO member states have ratified or signed the 1966 UN Covenants on civil, political, economic, social and cultural human rights, other UN human rights covenants as well as regional and bilateral treaties on the protection of human rights. In contrast to the judicial remedies provided for in the European and Inter-American Human Rights conventions,[8] however, the worldwide human rights obligations and supervisory bodies under the six "core" UN human rights treaties (on civil,

---

[6] See e.g. W. M. Corden, *Trade Policy and Economic Welfare*, 1974; W. K. Viscusi/J. M. Vernon/J. E. Harrington, *Economics of Regulation and Anti-trust*, 2nd ed. 1997.

[7] On the need for international organizations and international aid for the provision of "global public goods" see I. Kaul/I. Grunberg/M. A. Stern (eds.), *Global Public Goods. International Cooperation in the 21st Century*, 1999.

[8] The African Charter on Human and Peoples' Rights, in force since October 1986 and now ratified by all fifty-three member states of the Organization of African Unity, does not provide for access to an African Court of human rights. The African Commission on Human and Peoples' Rights has, however, received one inter-state and several non-state complaints. In some African countries like South Africa, constitutional protection and justiciability of economic, social and cultural human rights are well established.

Integrating Human Rights into the Law of Worldwide Organizations

political, economic, social and cultural human rights; rights of the child; prohibition of torture, racial discrimination and discrimination against women) do not ensure effective protection of human rights by national and international courts.[9] The 183 multilateral treaties on labor and social standards adopted in the ILO suffer likewise from inadequate enforcement mechanisms.[10] In many countries, widespread and unnecessary poverty, health and food problems reflect a lack of effective protection of human rights through legislation, administrative procedures (e.g. in agricultural, health and labor ministries), judicial remedies and assistance by national and international organizations for the protection of human rights (e.g. to health, food and work). The more globalization renders "foreign" and "domestic affairs" inseparable, the more "realist" claims for separation of policy instruments and for "primacy of foreign policy" (including monetary policy in the IMF and trade policy in the WTO) risk undermining human rights and policy coherence at home and abroad.

From a human rights perspective, the universal recognition of human rights as part of *general international law* requires a human rights framework for *all areas* of international law and international organizations so as to render human rights more effective and promote better coherence of national and international law and policies. The state-centered tradition of treating individuals as mere objects of international law, and the contradictory behavior of governments paying lip service to human rights in UN bodies but advocating "realpolitik" without regard to human rights in "specialized" international organizations, are inconsistent with the legal primacy and constitutional functions of human rights. The universal recognition of the *indivisibility of civil, political, economic, social and cultural human rights* has contributed to increasing jurisprudence by national and international courts that economic and social rights (such as the EC Treaty guarantees of freedom of trade and non-discrimination of women) may be no less justiciable than civil and political rights.[11] Also economists, politicians and civil society groups increasingly recognize

---

[9] For critical assessments of the effectiveness of worldwide human rights treaties see e.g. P. Alston/ J. Crawford (eds.), *The Future of UN Human Rights Treaty Monitoring*, 2000. For a recent collection of international human rights treaties see e.g. *Human Rights in International Law*, Council of Europe 2000. For the political obstacles to implementing human rights in a world of "realist" power politics see e.g. D. P. Forsythe (note 5).

[10] For a recent critical assessment of the ILO supervisory and promotional systems and of other mechanisms to promote core labor standards worldwide see e.g. *International Trade and Core Labor Standards*, OECD 2000, at 43 *et seq.* In November 2000, the ILO's Governing Body concluded that the 1998 report and recommendations of the ILO's Commission of Inquiry on forced labor in Myanmar had not been implemented and therefore "sanctions" should take effect. The ILO lacks, however, powers to ensure that economic sanctions are effectively implemented.

[11] European jurisprudence (e.g. by the EC Court of Justice and the European Court on Human Rights) has long since recognized that obligations to respect, protect and fulfill economic and social human rights may be "justiciable" even if they entail not only "negative" but also "positive" obligations (e.g. to promote non-discriminatory access to education). On the particular problems of "welfare rights" (such as indeterminacy of redistributive rights, their dependence on personal responsibility), the distinction between social rights in welfare states and social human rights, and the need for constitutional safeguards against abuses of welfare institutions, see e.g. K. Arambulo, *Strengthening the Supervision of the International Covenant on Economic, Social and Cultural Rights*, 1999. Many civil and political human rights (like the right to vote) also imply not only "negative" but also "positive obligations" (e.g. to render the right effective through legislation and administrative procedures that involve economic costs).

the relevance of human rights for economic welfare, which must be defined not only in quantitative terms (e.g. as increase in real income and national production of goods and services) but also in terms of substantive freedom and real capability of citizens to have access to the resources necessary for exercising human rights. European integration offers *three important lessons* why, and how, human rights need to be integrated into the law of international organizations so as to better enable citizens to pursue their self-development, peace and prosperity across frontiers.

A. The Law of International Organizations Must Be Construed in Conformity with the Human Rights Recognized by Member States

Just as the ratification of the European Convention on Human Rights (ECHR) by all EC member states prompted the EC Court of Justice to construe EC law in conformity with the human rights guarantees of the ECHR, the law of worldwide organizations must be interpreted in conformity with universally recognized human rights law.[12] The necessary balancing of civil, political, economic, social and cultural human rights may legitimately differ from country to country in response to their different laws and procedures, resources and preferences. In worldwide organizations, governments therefore remain reluctant to incorporate "human rights clauses" into the law of specialized organizations so as to avoid conflicts between international and domestic laws. As in the EC, international courts (e.g. the WTO Appellate Body) and human rights organizations (e.g. the UN Committee on Economic, Social and Cultural Rights) should therefore take the lead – with due deference to the "margin of discretion" of democratic legislatures, and in cooperation with the growing civil society requests for more effective protection of human rights in worldwide organizations – in interpreting and progressively developing the law of specialized organizations in conformity with universally recognized human rights. The needed human rights framework for coherent national and international "multi-level governance" requires a "global compact" for incorporating human rights into the *public law* of intergovernmental organizations no less than for promoting respect for human rights in *private business practices* of international corporations. The UN should call upon all international organizations to submit annual "human rights impact statements" examining and explaining the contribution of their respective laws and practices to the promotion of human rights.

B. Human Rights Promote the Effectiveness of International Organizations

The human rights approach advocated by the UN Development Program, and its central insight that "rights make human beings better economic actors," should become accepted as a common legal framework by all international organizations.[13] Legal doctrine has long since neglected that human rights constitute not only

---

[12] As shown below, this follows both from UN human rights law as well as from the general international law rules on treaty interpretation (cf. Article 31 of the Vienna Convention on the Law of Treaties), notwithstanding the fact that the statutes of most UN Specialized Agencies (with the exception of the ILO, WHO and UNESCO) do not explicitly refer to human rights.

[13] See *Human Development Report 2000: Human Rights and Human Development*, UNDP 2000 (the quotation is from p. iii).

Integrating Human Rights into the Law of Worldwide Organizations

moral and legal rights and corresponding obligations of governments. They also serve instrumental functions for solving social problems confronting all societies,[14] such as the following:

(1) *Conflict of interest problems*: Equal human rights set incentives for transforming the Hobbesian "war of everybody against everybody else" among utility-maximizing egoists in the "state of nature" where the "wild, lawless liberty" (Kant) of individuals may depend on their physical power, into peaceful cooperation based on equal legal rights. Also in the economy, the inevitable conflicts between producer interests (e.g. in high sales prices) and consumer interests (e.g. in low prices) can be reconciled best on the basis of equal liberty rights (e.g. freedom of contract) and other human rights.

(2) *Power problems*: The history of successive "human rights revolutions" demonstrates that human rights offer "countervailing powers" enabling citizens to defend their human rights to self-government against abuses of government powers and to limit the constitutional task of governments to the "public interest" defined in terms of equal human rights.

(3) *Compliance and enforcement problems*: Most rules do not enforce themselves. There are also often no political lobbies for rule-compliance and correction of enforcement errors. Human rights (e.g. of access to courts) and corresponding obligations (e.g. for compensation for violations of human rights) set incentives for decentralized enforcement of rules by self-interested, vigilant citizens.

(4) *Value problems*: By protecting (e.g. through freedom of religion, freedom of opinion and freedom of the press) diversity of individual values and preventing majorities from imposing their value preferences on minorities, human rights promote peaceful coexistence, tolerance and scientific progress.

(5) *Scarcity problems*: Human rights (e.g. property rights, freedom of contract) set incentives for savings, investments and mutually beneficial division of labor and enable individuals to acquire, buy and sell goods and services whose supply remains scarce in relation to consumer demand.

(6) *Information problems*: Human rights (e.g. to freedom of information) not only entitle individuals to act on the basis of their own personal knowledge and to acquire and take into account the personal knowledge of others. They also protect decentralized, spontaneous information and coordination mechanisms (such as market prices) that enable individuals to take into account knowledge dispersed among billions of human beings even if individuals remain inevitably "rationally ignorant" of most of this dispersed knowledge.

As long as unnecessary poverty continues to prevent billions of human beings from enjoying human rights, the empirical evidence on the contribution of human rights to economic welfare is of particular importance for promoting the effectiveness of human rights.[15] For instance, property rights and liberty rights set incentives

---

[14] On the instrumental function of human rights for dealing with the problems of limited knowledge, conflicting interests and abuses of power see e.g. R. E. Barnett, *The Structure of Liberty. Justice and the Rule of Law*, 2000.

[15] See note 13 as well as M. Olson, *Power and Prosperity*, 2000, explaining why "almost all of the countries that have enjoyed good economic performance across generations are countries that have stable democratic governments" (p. 43), and why "individual rights are a cause of prosperity" (p. 187); R. Pipes, *Property and Freedom*, 1999, who explains prosperity as resulting from "successful struggle for rights of which the

for efficient use of resources and enable citizens to coordinate their individual investments, production, trade and consumption in a decentralized and welfare-increasing manner. By assigning liberty rights (e.g. to self-development, freedom of contract and freedom of exchange) and property rights (e.g. to acquire, possess, use and dispose of scarce resources), and by defining individual responsibility and liability rules, human rights create incentives for savings, investments, efficient use of dispersed knowledge, mutually beneficial cooperation (e.g. through agreed exchanges of property rights) and decentralized markets (e.g. for labor, capital, goods and services) aimed at satisfying consumer demand and consumer preferences. Such "economic markets" inducing investors, producers and traders to supply private goods and services demanded by consumers involve democratic "dialogues about values,"[16] which are no less important for effective enjoyment of human rights than the "political markets" for the supply of "public goods" by governments.

The centuries-old English and American common law tradition of protecting equal freedoms of traders, competitors and consumers against "unreasonable restraint of trade" and "coercion" reflect an early recognition of the historical experience that markets risk to destroy themselves (e.g. as a result of monopolization and cartel agreements) unless freedom and abuses of power are constitutionally restrained.[17] The history of competition law and constitutional law in Europe and North America confirms the economic insight that the efficiency of market mechanisms (e.g. for allocating resources in a manner coordinating supply and demand) depends, *inter alia*, on effective protection of individual freedoms (e.g. of information, production, trade, competition and freedom of association) and protection of property rights in both material and intellectual resources. If market failures adversely affect human rights, economic theory teaches that governments should correct such market imperfections through "optimal" interventions directly at the source of the problem (e.g. through labor, social and health legislation, prohibitions of cartels and environmental pollution) without preventing citizens from engaging in mutually beneficial trade.

The economic and human resources needed for the full enjoyment of human rights thus depend on making human rights an integral part of a social and sustainable market economy.[18] The successful integration of human rights into EC law and policies confirms that the economy and "specialized organizations" must not be regarded as autonomous fields unrelated to the human rights of producers, workers, investors, traders and consumers. In order to strengthen the mutual synergies between human rights and integration law also at the worldwide level, UN human rights law must

---

right to property is the most fundamental" (p. 291); World Development Report 2000/2001: Attacking Poverty, World Bank 2000; D. C. North, *Institutions, Institutional Change and Economic Performance*, 1990.

[16] Cf. W. Fikentscher, *Wirtschaftsrecht* Vol. I, 1983, at 10.

[17] On this common dilemma of market economies and democracy, and on the replacement of the rights-based common law criteria by efficiency-based economic criteria (such as absence of output and price restrictions) in modern US anti-trust law, see G. Amato, *Anti-trust and the Bounds of Power*, 1997; D. Gerber, *Law and Competition in Twentieth Century Europe. Protecting Prometheus*, 1998. More generally on the paradoxical dependence of liberty on constitutional restraints see J. Elster, *Ulysses Unbound*, 2000.

[18] See e.g. M. Robinson, Constructing an International Financial, Trade and Development Architecture: The Human Rights Dimension, in M. Mehra (ed.), *Human Rights and Economic Globalisation: Directions for the WTO*, 1999, at 187: "if we hope to see human rights flourishing, it will only be in the context of an equitable and sustainable economic order."

Integrating Human Rights into the Law of Worldwide Organizations

overcome its long-standing neglect of economic liberty rights, property rights and competition safeguards as indispensable means of promoting widespread owner-ship of economic and human capital (such as health and education) and of pre-venting small minorities from controlling the economy and polity. WTO members must likewise interpret their declared treaty objectives of "raising standards of living, ensuring full employment and a large and steadily growing volume of real income . . . , while allowing for the optimal use of the world's resources in accordance with the objective of sustainable development" (Preamble of the WTO Agreement), in con-formity with their human rights obligations.

C. Human Rights Promote Democratic Legitimacy and Self-Governance in International Organizations

At the *national level*, most of the 189 UN member states now recognize human rights and the need for constitutional rules protecting, implementing and balancing human rights. In Europe and North America, almost all countries have introduced also complementary constitutional safeguards of market economies and competi-tion laws based on the insight that equal freedoms of citizens need to be protected through institutions, procedures, substantive legal safeguards and individual rights in the *economy* no less than in the *polity* so as to prevent abuses of private and pub-lic power that were not consented to by citizens and would reduce their welfare. At the level of *worldwide organizations*, however, protection of universally recognized human rights often remains ineffective because the complementary constitutional principles needed for effectuating human rights – such as democratic participa-tion, parliamentary rule-making, transparent "deliberative democracy"[19] and judi-cial protection of rule of law – have not yet become part of the law and practices of most worldwide organizations.

The history of European integration suggests that the emergence of a human rights culture promoting democratic peace and social welfare depends on empow-ering individuals to defend not only their civil and political human rights, but also their economic and social rights through individual and democratic self-government and access to courts. Inside the EC, the judicial protection of "market freedoms" and of non-discrimination principles as fundamental individual rights[20] became an important driving force for the progressive realization of the common market and of "an area of freedom, security and justice" (Article 61 EC Treaty). The EC Court empha-sized that economic freedoms "are not absolute but must be viewed in relation to

---

[19] See e.g. H. H. Koh/R. C. Slye (eds.), *Deliberative Democracy and Human Rights*, 1999.

[20] See e.g. Case 240/83, *ADBHU*, ECR 1985 531, para. 9: "The principles of free movement of goods and freedom of competition, together with freedom of trade as a fundamental right, are general principles of Community law of which the Court ensures observance." Especially the freedom of movements of workers and other persons, access to employment and the right of establishment have been described by the EC Court as "fundamental freedoms" (Case C-55/94, *Gebhard*, ECR 1995, I 4165, para. 37) or "a fundamental right which the Treaty confers individually on each worker in the Community" (Case 22/86, *Heylens*, ECR 1987, 4097, para. 14). The ECJ avoids "human rights language" for the "market freedoms," the right to property and the freedom to pursue a trade or business in EC law.

their social function"[21] and with due regard to human rights.[22] The EC jurisprudence on social rights (e.g. "the principle of equal pay for male and female workers for equal work" in Article 141 EC Treaty) strongly contributed to the emergence of a European "social market economy" in which EC member states are required to extend social rights (e.g. to education and vocational training) to nationals of other EC member states.[23] The new treaty objective of "appropriate action to combat discrimination based on sex, racial or ethnic origin, religion or belief, disability, age or sexual orientation" (Article 13) confirms the functional interrelationships between economic and political order and human rights.

Outside Europe the withdrawal, in April 2001, of the complaints in the South African Supreme Court by thirty-nine pharmaceutical companies against government regulations facilitating access to AIDS medicaments likewise demonstrated the importance of *civil society* support and of judicial remedies for reconciling national and international economic law (e.g. on trade-related intellectual property rights) with social human rights. In UN human rights law, however, the *indivisibility of human rights* and *justiciability of economic and social rights* are not sufficiently protected so as to enable citizens, economic operators and judges to enforce and progressively develop economic and social rights in domestic and international courts (as inside the EC). An anti-market bias of UN human rights law will also reduce its operational potential as a benchmark for the law of worldwide economic organizations and for a rights-based market economy and jurisprudence, e.g. in WTO dispute settlement practice. Reconciling civil, economic and social human rights also requires us to admit that, in a world of constant change, human rights cannot be immune from adjustment pressures. Promoting individual responsibility and human capacity to adjust to inevitable change in a manner respecting human dignity remains one of the most difficult tasks of a human rights policy protecting individual liberty and global integration across frontiers.

2. Obstacles on the Way Toward a "Human Rights Culture" in Global Integration Law: Learning from European Integration

State-centered international lawyers often ignore that markets are a necessary consequence of, and an indispensable means for, effective protection of human rights. European integration confirms the insight of "functional theories" that citizen-driven market integration can set strong incentives for transforming "market freedoms" into "fundamental rights," which – if directly enforceable by producers, investors, workers, traders and consumers through courts (as in the EC) – can reinforce and extend the protection of basic human rights (e.g. to liberty, property, food and health).

---

[21] Case C-44/94, *The Queen v. Minister of Agriculture*, ECR 1995 I-3115, para. 28.

[22] Cf. L. Betten/N. Grief, *EU Law and Human Rights Law*, 1998; P. Alston *et alia* (note 4).

[23] Because of the constitutional limits of EC law, social rights were initially developed in EC law as a function of market integration rather than of the more recent EC Treaty guarantees of "citizenship of the Union" (Article 17) and of "fundamental social rights" (e.g. Article 136). On the need for integrating social rights into market integration law as a means for limiting social market failures (e.g. resulting from an unjust distribution of resources and purchasing power, inadequate opportunities of all market participants to express their "voice" and "exit") see e.g. M. Poiares Maduro, *Striking the Elusive Balance between Economic Freedom and Social Rights in the EU*, in Alston (note 4), at 459.

Integrating Human Rights into the Law of Worldwide Organizations   281

Functional "low policy integration" may also contribute more effectively to "democratic peace" than may be possible in government-centered "high policy organizations" (like the UN) whose foreign policy and security objectives often meet with political resistance on grounds of national sovereignty.

A. Market Integration Law Can Promote Human Rights

Wherever freedom and property rights are protected, individuals start producing and exchanging goods and services demanded by consumers. Enjoyment of human rights requires use of dispersed information and economic resources that can be supplied most efficiently, and most democratically, through division of labor among free citizens and liberal trade promoting economic welfare, freedom of choice and the free flow of scarce goods, services and information across frontiers.[24] The fact that most people spend most of their time on their "economic freedoms" (e.g. to produce and exchange goods and services including one's labor and ideas) illustrates that for ordinary people, unlike for many lawyers,[25] economic liberties are no less important than civil and political freedoms (e.g. to participate in the democratic supply of "public goods").

The moral "categorical imperative" and the legal human rights objective of maximizing equal liberties across frontiers corresponds with the economic objective of maximizing consumer welfare through open markets and non-discriminatory competition. Hence, there is no reason for human rights lawyers to neglect the economic dimensions of human rights problems – such as the dependence of human rights (e.g. to work, food, education, housing and health-care) on supply of scarce goods, services and job opportunities. Likewise, "economic lawyers" must not disregard the human rights dimensions of economic law, for instance that savings, investments and economic transactions depend on property rights and liberty rights (such as freedom of contract and transfers of property rights).[26] Also foreign policy-makers and economists need to reconsider their often one-sided views that economic development should be defined in purely quantitative terms (e.g. without regard to real human capability to enjoy human rights), or that the economic tasks of "specialized agencies" (like the IMF, the World Bank and the WTO) should not be "overloaded" with human rights considerations because they may be abused as pretexts for protectionist restrictions.[27]

---

[24] On the contribution of liberal trade to economic welfare and to protection of human rights (which, like any legal system, involve economic costs), and, vice versa, on the reciprocal contribution of human rights to economic welfare, see the two contributions by A. Sykes, *International Trade and Human Rights: An Economic Perspective*, and E. U. Petersmann, *Economics and Human Rights*, to the book by F. Abbott/ T. Cottier (eds.), *International Trade and Human Rights*, 2002.

[25] On the "double standard" in the jurisprudence of US courts that protect civil and political liberties through higher standards of judicial scrutiny than economic liberties, see e.g. B. H. Siegan, *Economic Liberties and the Constitution*, 1980.

[26] On the recognition of the importance of human rights for rendering environmental law and environmental protection more effective see A. Boyle/M. Anderson (eds.), *Human Rights Approaches to Environmental Protection*, 1998.

[27] See e.g. the paper on "Economic, Social and Cultural Human Rights and the International Monetary Fund," submitted by the IMF's General Counsel F. Gianviti to the UN Committee on Economic, Social and Cultural Rights at its "day of general discussion" on 7 May 2001, which emphasizes "the principle

B. Market Integration Promotes Legal and Political Integration

Free trade area agreements, customs unions and common markets were important stages in the historical formation of many federal states. The progressive evolution of the EC Treaty – from a customs union treaty focusing on economic freedoms to a modern "treaty constitution" protecting human rights and "democratic peace" far beyond the economic area – illustrates the functional interrelationships among economic, political and legal integration.

The negotiators of the 1957 Treaty establishing the European Economic Community thought that the human rights guarantees in the national constitutions of EC member states and in the European Convention on Human Rights (ECHR, 1950) were sufficient for protecting human rights in the common market. Hence, similar to GATT 1947 and the WTO Agreement, the EC Treaty of 1957 did not refer to human rights law based on the belief that mutually beneficial economic liberalization would promote, rather than endanger, the national and international human rights guarantees. Today, however, EU law has evolved into a comprehensive constitutional system for the protection of civil, political, economic and social rights of EU citizens across national frontiers. Also the objective of the EU's common foreign and security policy is defined by the EU Treaty as "to develop and consolidate democracy and the rule of law, and respect for human rights and fundamental freedoms" (Article 11). The EU has consequently insisted on including "human rights clauses" and "democracy clauses" in international agreements concluded by the EC with more than one hundred third countries. The adoption of the Charter of Fundamental Rights of the European Union in December 2000, and the proposals for incorporating this Charter into a European Constitution at the intergovernmental conference scheduled for 2004, confirm the "functional theory" underlying European integration, i.e. the view that *economic market integration* can progressively promote peaceful cooperation and rule of law beyond economic areas, thereby enabling more comprehensive and more effective protection of human rights than has been possible in traditional state-centered international law.[28]

C. Recognition of Citizens as Legal Subjects of Integration Law Promotes the Emergence of International Constitutional Law

Inside the EC and in the European Economic Area between the EC and third European countries, the treaty prohibitions of restrictions of the free movement of goods, services, persons, capital and related payments, as well as the treaty guarantees

---

of specialization that has governed the establishment of the specialized agencies and their relationships with the United Nations" (p. 44), and concludes that the UN human rights covenants "apply only to States, not to international organizations" (p. 10). These arguments, however, do not preclude the legal relevance of general international human rights law for the IMF.

[28] The number of "human rights cases" before the European Court of Human Rights far outnumbers those before the EC Court of Justice. Yet, the guarantees in the European Convention on Human Rights (ECHR) focus on civil and political rights that often do not go beyond those in national constitutions. The EC's common market freedoms and constitutional law, by contrast, go far beyond national and ECHR guarantees and have contributed to unprecedented levels of economic and social welfare, individual freedom and democratic peace of European citizens.

Integrating Human Rights into the Law of Worldwide Organizations

of non-discrimination (e.g. in Article 141), were construed by the EC Court and national courts as *individual economic freedoms* to be protected by the courts.[29] The national constitutional guarantees of "the principles of liberty, democracy, respect for human rights and fundamental freedoms, and the rule of law" were progressively recognized as "principles which are common to the Member States" and legally binding also on all EU institutions, as later acknowledged in Article 6 of the EU Treaty. In conformity with the EC Treaty requirements to comply with international law (cf. Articles 300, 307) and cooperate with other international organizations (cf. Articles 302–306), the EU Treaty now requires explicitly respect for the European Convention on Human Rights (cf. Article 6:2 EU Treaty), the 1961 European Social Charter and 1989 Community Charter of the Fundamental Social Rights of Workers (cf. Article 136 EC Treaty), and for the 1951 Geneva Convention and 1967 Protocol on the protection of refugees (cf. Article 63 EC Treaty).

The constitutional guarantees of the EU for economic liberties and complementary constitutional, competition, environmental and social safeguards have also induced numerous EU initiatives to strengthen competition, environmental and social law in *worldwide* international agreements. The strong competition law of the EC reflects the constitutional insight that – in the economy no less than in the polity – equal freedoms of citizens and open markets need to be legally protected against abuses of *public powers* as well as of *private powers*.[30] The EC Treaty prohibitions of cartel agreements (Article 81) and of abuses of market power (Article 82) are not only protected by the ECJ as *individual rights* of "market citizens." They also prompted all EC member states to enact *national* competition laws enforced by independent *national* competition authorities. Likewise, under the influence of EC competition law and of the incorporation of competition safeguards into the EC's "Europe agreements" and association agreements, also most third states in Europe have progressively introduced, since the 1980s, national competition laws protecting citizens and economic competition against abuses of private and public power.

D. Lessons for Global Integration Law?

The paradoxical fact that many developing countries remain poor notwithstanding their wealth of natural resources (e.g. more than 90% of biogenetical resources in the world) is attributed by many economists to their lack of effective human rights guarantees and of liberal trade and competition laws. The absence of effective legal and judicial protection of liberty rights and property rights inhibits investments and acts as an incentive for welfare-reducing private and governmental restrictions of trade and competition and collaboration between cartelized industries and authoritarian

---

[29] See above note 20.

[30] Also the US Supreme Court rightly emphasized that "anti-trust laws ... are the Magna Carta of free enterprise. They are as important to the preservation of economic freedom and our free enterprise system as the Bill of Rights is to the protection of our fundamental freedoms" (*United States v. Topco Assoc. Inc.*, 405 U.S. 596, 610, 1972). Yet, unlike the EC, US law does not protect economic liberties and social rights as fundamental constitutional rights of citizens, and US politicians favor a power-oriented, extraterritorial application of US anti-trust laws vis-à-vis third countries rather than worldwide competition rules as suggested by the EC.

governments.[31] The widespread abuses of private power in Africa, Asia and Latin America are no less dangerous for human rights and social welfare than abuses of public government powers. The EC proposals for complementing the liberal trade rules of the WTO by worldwide competition rules have met with increasing support notably by less-developed countries that have suffered from discriminatory cartel practices and find it politically difficult to overcome anti-competitive practices of powerful domestic industries through unilateral national legislation.[32]

Investments, production, trade and also protection of the environment depend on legal incentives and legal rights for investors, producers, traders, polluters and consumers. The EC's integration approach – notably the recognition and empowerment of citizens as legal subjects not only of human rights but also of competition law and integration law – should serve as a model also for *worldwide integration law*. The modern universal recognition of human rights as part of general international law implies that human rights have become part of the "context" for interpreting the law of worldwide organizations and must be taken into account in all rule-making and policy-making processes at national and international levels.[33] Just as the human rights guarantees and competition safeguards of the EC Treaty have reinforced the legitimacy and effectiveness of EC law and of protection of human rights throughout Europe, also UN human rights law and WTO rules offer mutually beneficial synergies for rendering human rights and the social functions and democratic legitimacy of the emerging global integration law more effective.

3. Constitutional Primacy of the Inalienable Core of Human Rights in International Law?

National and international human rights law rests on "recognition of the inherent dignity and of the equal and inalienable human rights of all members of the human family (as) the foundation of freedom, justice and peace in the world" (Preamble of the UDHR). Human dignity (e.g. in the sense of respect for the moral and rational autonomy of each individual to distinguish between good and bad and decide on one's personal goals in life) has become the common value premise of national and international human rights law.

A. Human Rights as Part of General International Law

There exist today more than one hundred multilateral and bilateral international treaties on the protection of human rights. In the UN Charter, the Universal Declaration of Human Rights (UDHR), the 1993 Vienna Declaration on Human Rights, as well as in numerous other UN instruments, all 189 UN member states have also

---

[31] See e.g. H. de Soto, *The Mystery of Capital: Why Capitalism Triumphs in the West and Fails Everywhere Else*, 2001 (e.g. describing why many natural resources in developing countries remain "dead capital" due to the lack of secure property titles and legal insecurity).

[32] Cf. E. U. Petersmann, Competition-Oriented Reforms of the WTO World Trade System, in R. Zäch (ed.), *Towards WTO Competition Rules*, 1999, 43–73.

[33] See Resolution 1998/12 on "Human rights as the primary objective of international trade, investment and finance policy and practice," adopted by the UN Sub-Commission on Prevention of Discrimination and Protection of Minorities in August 1998 and subsequently endorsed by numerous NGOs; cf. Mehra (note 18), at 123 *et seq.*

committed themselves to inalienable human rights as part of *general international law*. In addition, most states recognize human rights in their respective national constitutional laws as constitutional restraints on government powers, sometimes with explicit references to human rights as legal restraints also on the collective exercise of government powers in international organizations (see e.g. Article 23 of the German Basic Law and Article 11 EU Treaty). Human rights have thus become part also of the *general principles of law recognized by civilized nations* (Article 38 of the Statute of the International Court of Justice). As a result, international law is increasingly confronted with the "constitutional problems" addressed in the human rights jurisprudence of the EC Court of Justice: What is the essential core of human rights that must be recognized today as *erga omnes* obligations and *ius cogens*? Can governments evade their human rights obligations by exercising government powers collectively in specialized international organizations? How can the legal supremacy of international law over national law remain effective and be judicially enforced if human rights are not effectively protected in all fields of international law? Can international courts ignore the worldwide experience in all states that protection of human rights risks to remain ineffective without respect for complementary due process guarantees and other "constitutional principles" of rule of law, democratic government and judicial review? How to interpret and, in case of conflict, reconcile "state sovereignty," "popular sovereignty" and "individual sovereignty" in a manner respecting the constitutional primacy of human rights?[34]

General international law (as codified in Article 31:3 of the 1969 Vienna Convention on the Law of Treaties) requires interpreting international treaties "in their context," including "any relevant rules of international law applicable in the relations between the parties" such as universal human rights. Even though the law of, for example, the WTO does not explicitly refer to human rights, Article 3 of the WTO Dispute Settlement Understanding (DSU) requires the clarification of "existing provision of those agreements in accordance with customary rules of interpretation of public international law." Universally recognized human rights are today part of the "context" for the interpretation of the law of worldwide organizations. They may be important for interpreting not only "general exceptions" (e.g. in GATT Article XX), but also basic guarantees of freedom (e.g. in GATT Articles II–XI), non-discrimination, property rights, individual access to courts, and the "necessity" requirements for safeguard measures to protect "public interests" and human rights.

B. Has the "Inalienable Core" of Universally Recognized Human Rights Become *Ius Cogens*?

Human rights define legal principles, rights and corresponding obligations for individual and democratic self-development and are today universally recognized by all UN member states as inalienable "birth rights" of every human being that precede and constitutionally limit government powers. Human rights need to be legally concretized, mutually balanced and implemented by democratic legislation, which tends to vary from country to country. Their inalienable core, however, is

---

[34] Cf. E. U. Petersmann, International Activities of the European Union and Sovereignty of Member States, in E. Cannizzaro (ed.), *The European Union as an Actor in International Relations*, 2002.

"acknowledged" rather than "granted" by governments, as recognized in national as well as international legal practice: "Human dignity is inviolable. It must be respected and protected" (Article 1 of the Charter of Fundamental Rights of the European Union). "The German people therefore acknowledge inviolable and inalienable human rights as the basis of every community, of peace and of justice in the world" that "shall bind the legislature, the executive and the judiciary as directly applicable law" (Article 1, German Basic Law of 1949). In UN practice, the "right to development" and the corresponding government obligations are defined in terms of the realization of all human rights.[35]

The International Court of Justice (ICJ) has recognized that human rights constitute not only *individual rights* but also, in case of universally recognized human rights, *erga omnes* obligations of governments based on treaty law and general international law.[36] The universal ratification of human rights treaties (such as the UN Convention on the Rights of the Child ratified by 191 states), and the universal recognition in these treaties "of the equal and inalienable rights of all members of the human family" as set out in the UDHR,[37] reflects a worldwide *opinio iuris* on the *inalienable erga omnes* character of core human rights. This *opinio iuris* on essential and inalienable core human rights is not contradicted by the diversity of views on the precise scope, meaning and *ius cogens* nature of many specific human rights whose legal implementation may differ from country to country and from treaty to treaty. In contrast to the EC Court of Justice, which construed the common human rights guarantees of EC member states as constituting general constitutional principles limiting the regulatory powers also of the EC,[38] the ICJ has not yet specified to what extent human rights entail constitutional limits also on the UN and its Specialized Agencies. Likewise, the WTO jurisprudence has not yet clarified the impact of human rights (e.g. to human health and food) on the interpretation of, for example, the intellectual property rights guaranteed in the WTO Agreement on Trade-Related Intellectual Property Rights (TRIPS), or on the numerous WTO exceptions protecting national policy autonomy for non-trade concerns.

International legal practice confirms an increasing *opinio iuris* that membership in the UN and in the ILO entails legal obligations to respect core human rights.[39]

---

[35] See UN General Assembly Declaration 41/128 of 4 December 1986 on the "Right to Development."

[36] See e.g. the Barcelona Traction judgment (ICJ Reports 1970, 32) and the Nicaragua judgment (ICJ Reports 1986, 114).

[37] Quotation from the preamble to the 1989 UN Convention on the Right of the Child, which also confirms the universal recognition of the rights set out in the UDHR. See *Human Rights in International Law* (note 9), at 169.

[38] In *Internationale Handelsgesellschaft* (Case 11/70, ECR 1970, 1125,1134), the ECJ held that respect for human rights forms an integral part of the general principles of Community law: "the protection of such rights, whilst inspired by the constitutional traditions common to the Member States, must be ensured within the framework of the structure and objectives of the Community" (paras. 3–4).

[39] See e.g. ILO Declaration on Fundamental Principles and Rights at Work (ILO 1998, at 7), adopted by the International Labour Conference on 18 June 1998, which recognizes (in its paragraph 2) "that all Members, even if they have not ratified the Conventions in question, have an obligation, arising from the very fact of membership in the Organization, to respect, to promote and to realize, in good faith and in accordance with the Constitution, the principles concerning the fundamental rights which are subject of those Conventions, namely: (a) freedom of association and the effective recognition of the right to collective bargaining; (b) the elimination of all forms of forced or compulsory labour; (c) the

Integrating Human Rights into the Law of Worldwide Organizations

Dictatorial governments can no longer freely "contract out" of their human rights obligations by withdrawing from UN human rights covenants or ILO conventions.[40] Legal practice suggests that not only the prohibitions of genocide, slavery and apartheid, but also other core human rights must be respected even "in time of public emergency" (cf. Article 4 of the ICCPHR, Article 15 ECHR) and, since the end of the cold war, have become *erga omnes* obligations of a *ius cogens* nature.[41]

C. Constitutional Primacy of Human Rights in European Law

European integration law recognizes the legal *primacy* and constitutional functions of human rights in various ways. It was essentially due to the human rights jurisprudence of national courts in EC member states that the EC Court acknowledged, since the *Stauder case* (1969), that not only EC member states but also the EC itself must respect human rights in all EC policy areas: "respect for human rights is a condition of the lawfulness of Community acts."[42] Article 6 of the Treaty on European Union (EU) now explicitly confirms that the "Union is founded on the principles of liberty, democracy, respect for human rights and fundamental freedoms, and the rule of law, principles which are common to the Member States." Breaches of these principles can entail sanctions (Article 7) and prevent admission to the EU (Article 49 EU Treaty).

The constitutional objective of the "common foreign and security policy" of the European Union – namely "to develop and consolidate democracy and the rule of law, and respect for human rights and fundamental freedoms" (Article 11 EU Treaty) – reflects the insight that human rights apply to the exercise of all government powers, as already stated in the French Declaration of the Rights of Man and the Citizen of 1789: "The final end of every political institution is the preservation of the natural and imprescriptible rights of man. Those rights are liberty, property, security, and resistance to oppression."[43] Most policy objectives of specialized agencies (such as monetary stability, trade liberalization, health protection) can be understood as protecting liberty, property, non-discrimination and other human rights across frontiers.[44] Arguably, the universal recognition, in both national and international law, of the *inalienable character* of the essential core of human rights implies recognition of the legal primacy of their *inalienable core* vis-à-vis governmental and intergovernmental limitations that are arbitrary or "unnecessary" for protecting other human

---

effective abolition of child labour; and (d) the elimination of discrimination in respect of employment and occupation."

[40] See General Comment 5 on Article 4 of the UN Covenant on Civil and Political Rights, adopted by the Human Rights Committee on 31 July 1981 and recently revised (cf. D. Goldrick, The Human Rights Committee, 1994, at 315).

[41] For detailed references to state practice see I. Seiderman, *Hierarchy in International Law*, 2001.

[42] Opinion 2/94, European Court Reports (ECR) 1996, I-1759, para. 34.

[43] French Declaration of the Rights of Man and the Citizen (1789), section 2; cf. Finer/Bogdanor/Rudden, *Comparing Constitutions*, 1995, at 208. The constitutional theories e.g. of Kant and Rawls likewise conclude that "democratic peace by satisfaction" (as opposed to "peace by power") requires that "promotion of human rights ... should be a fixed concern of the foreign policy of all just and decent regimes" (Rawls, above note 3), at 48.

[44] On the "human rights functions" of the law of the IMF, the World Bank and GATT see E. U. Petersmann, *Constitutional Functions and Constitutional Problems of International Economic Law*, 1991, chapter VII.

rights. The explicit *necessity requirements* for limitations on freedom and on other human rights – to be found not only in national constitutions and human rights treaties but also in the safeguard clauses of worldwide and regional trade agreements (such as GATT Article XX) – must be construed in conformity with this constitutional primacy of the inalienable core of human rights.

D. Can "Specialized Organizations" Exclude Human Rights from Their Field of Specialization?

Like the negotiators of the EC Treaty in 1956/57, government representatives in specialized international organizations sometimes appear to believe that governments remain "sovereign" to exclude human rights from the law of specialized agencies and from the "covered agreements" of WTO law. Yet, the *lex posterior* and *lex specialis* rules for the relationships between successive international treaties (as laid down in Articles 30, 41 and 58 of the 1969 Vienna Convention on the Law of Treaties) cannot derogate from the *inalienable ius cogens* nature of the obligation of all national and international governments to respect the essential core of human rights (cf. Article 53 of the Vienna Convention). UN human rights law explicitly recognizes (e.g. in Article 28 of the UDHR quoted at the beginning of this chapter) that human rights entail obligations also for intergovernmental organizations. From a human rights perspective, all national and international rules, including economic liberalization agreements like the IMF and WTO agreements, derive their democratic legitimacy from protecting human dignity and inalienable human rights, which today constitutionally restrain all national and international rule-making powers.

The generously drafted "exceptions" in global and regional integration law, and the usually deferential jurisprudence of international courts (e.g. WTO dispute settlement bodies) vis-à-vis national restrictions necessary for protecting public interests,[45] confirm that, in cases of conflict, the essential core of human rights must prevail. As in EC law, the obligations of states to respect, promote and fulfill human rights must be recognized as extending also to their participation in worldwide organizations like the Bretton Woods institutions and the WTO. Neither the "progressive realization" commitment in Article 2 of the International Covenant on Economic, Social and Cultural Rights (ICESCR),[46] nor the *proviso* in its Article 24 that "(n)othing in the present Covenant shall be interpreted as *impairing* the provisions of the Charter of the United Nations and of the constitutions of the specialized agencies," can serve as pretexts for non-compliance by unwilling governments and organizations with their human rights obligations.

---

[45] See e.g. the WTO Appellate Body report of 12 March 2001 (WT/DS135/AB/R) on EC import restrictions affecting asbestos and asbestos-containing products that threaten the health of EC citizens.

[46] Cf. General Comment No. 3 on "The nature of States parties obligations (Art. 2, para. 1 of the Covenant)," adopted by the UN Committee on Economic, Social and Cultural Rights in 1990 and reproduced e.g. in A. Eide/C. Krause/A. Rosas (eds.), *Economic, Social and Cultural Rights*, 1995, at 442–445. The fact that the ICESCR formulates some rights in terms of *principles* rather than precise *rules* only indicates that some economic and social human rights, like certain civil and political rights (such as the right to vote), need to be concretized through implementing legislation and administrative or judicial decisions. On the distinction between *principles* and *rights* see e.g. R. Dworkin, *Taking Rights Seriously*, 1977, 23 *et seq.*

4. Human Rights as Constitutional Restraints on the Law and Powers of International Organizations

The "paradox of liberty," that is, that real freedom and legal constraints condition each other, applies to both national as well as international law. Article 28 of the UDHR – according to which "[e]veryone is entitled to a social and international order in which the rights and freedoms set forth in this Declaration can be fully realized" – reflects the insight that protection and promotion of human rights are often no less dependent on *intergovernmental* rules and policies (e.g. on collective security, international division of labor, prevention of terrorism) than on *national* implementing measures. Article 24 of the ICESCR confirms implicitly that human rights entail obligations not only for states but also for their collective exercise of government powers in international organizations.[47]

If human rights require international law and international institutions to be so structured as to promote and protect human rights across frontiers, how can human rights be rendered more effective in the law of worldwide organizations? The various UN Declarations on the "Right to Development" call upon international organizations to incorporate human rights into their policies and to promote participation of individuals and civil society organizations in the work of international organizations.[48] Yet, in intergovernmental organizations (like the UN) and "producer-driven" organizations (like the WTO and ILO), "top-down reforms" for strengthening human rights and democratic rule-making procedures remain slow because many diplomats and influential industries (including their worker representatives in the ILO) prefer to avoid limiting their powers and privileges in specialized agencies and benefit from continuing the classical international law approach of treating citizens as mere objects of international law that should be kept out of intergovernmental organizations.[49] Also many lawyers, economists, political scientists and ordinary citizens doubt whether the universal recognition of human rights requires the EC and worldwide organizations to evolve into human rights organizations and to supplement the international human rights guarantees by "international constitutional law."[50] Especially in the US with its long-standing reluctance to submit itself to international human rights law and its traditional focus on *civil* and *political* rather than *economic* and *social human rights*, convincing citizens, governments and courts of the need

---

[47] Article 24 states: "Nothing in the present Covenant shall be interpreted as impairing the provisions of the Charter of the United Nations and of the constitutions of the specialized agencies which define the respective responsibilities of the various organs of the United Nations and of the specialized agencies in regard to the matters dealt with in the present Covenant." By interpreting the law of intergovernmental organizations in conformity with human rights, conflicts and "impairments" can and must be avoided.

[48] See e.g. the Report of the Intergovernmental Group of Experts on the Right to Development in UN Doc. E/CN.4/1998/29 of 7 November 1997.

[49] See e.g. the special report on human rights in *The Economist* of 18 August 2001, in which the US ambassador to the UN Human Rights Commission explains the non-ratification of the ICESCR by the USA with the "concern" that this "would mean citizens could sue their governments for enforcement of rights" (p. 20).

[50] See e.g. A. von Bogdandy, The European Union as a Human Rights Organization? Human Rights and the Core of the European Union, in *Common Market Law Review* 37 (2000), 1307–1338, who argues, *inter alia*, that "human rights should not be understood as the *raison d'être* of the Union" (p. 1338), and that developing human rights from a common market perspective is often not convincing (p. 1336).

for economic and social human rights remains a political challenge that appears unlikely to be met by governments, business and courts in the US.[51]

History suggests that democratic participation in the exercise of government powers rarely comes about "top-down" without prior "bottom-up pressures" and "glorious revolutions" by citizens, parliaments and courageous judges defending human rights vis-à-vis abuses of government powers and fighting for democratic reforms of authoritarian government structures. The postwar Bretton-Woods Agreements and the UN Charter presented such hard-fought-for "revolutions" in international law designed at extending freedom, non-discrimination, rule of law and social welfare across frontiers, even though diplomats carefully avoided the politically charged language of "international constitutional law" (e.g. in contrast to the "Constitution of the ILO" of 1919).

A. Human Rights and the "Constitutional Functions" of International Guarantees of Freedom, Non-Discrimination and Rule of Law

All human rights need to be made effective and mutually balanced through national and international rule-making and rule-implementation. Reciprocal international guarantees of freedom, non-discrimination, rule of law, transparent policy-making, social safeguard measures and wealth creation through a mutually beneficial division of labor – such as those in the 1944 Bretton-Woods Agreements, the ILO Constitution, GATT 1947 and the 1994 WTO Agreement – aim at extending basic human rights values across frontiers. In this respect, they can be understood as serving "constitutional functions" for the legal protection of human rights values at home and abroad.[52] Of course, "not all international rules serve constitutional functions," and the lack of adequate constitutional safeguards in the law of international organizations facilitates "intergovernmental collusion" endangering democratic governance and human rights.[53] For example, the general exceptions and safeguard clauses in the WTO Agreement leave each government broad discretion as to how economic

---

[51] On "double standards" in US policies vis-à-vis international human rights treaties see *United States of America. Rights for All*, Amnesty International Publication 1998, at 123–135.

[52] For a detailed explanation see Petersmann (above note 44) as well as E. U. Petersmann, National Constitutions and International Economic Law, in M. Hilf/E. U. Petersmann (eds.), *National Constitutions and International Economic Law*, 1993, at 3, 47 *et seq*. The theory of the "constitutional" and "domestic policy functions" of international guarantees of freedom, non-discrimination and rule of law was developed in the 1980s (see E. U. Petersmann, Trade Policy as a Constitutional Problem. On the 'Domestic Policy Functions' of International Trade Rules, in *Swiss Review of International Economic Relations* 41 (1986), 405–439; *idem*, Constitutional Functions of Public International Economic Law, in *Restructuring the International Economic Order. The Role of Law and Lawyers, Colloquium on the Occasion of the 350th Anniversary of the University of Utrecht*, 1987, 49–75). The theory focused on the *substantive constitutional values* of the GATT 1947 guarantees of freedom, non-discrimination and rule of law, rather than on the formal primacy of "higher" international law over domestic law, or on the procedural advantages of *reciprocal pre-commitments ("hands-tying")* at the international law level designed to limit mutually harmful "beggar-thy-neighbor policies" at domestic policy levels. The theory noted "the increasing recognition of agreed principles of substantive equality and solidarity in international law" (Petersmann, note 44, at 91). Yet, in view of the "separation of policy instruments" underlying the Bretton-Woods Agreements and the cold war dissent on human rights, the theory did not challenge the "logic of 1945" and did not address the question examined in this chapter, i.e. the impact of the more recent universal recognition of human rights on the law and policies of worldwide organizations.

[53] The quotations are from the titles of various chapters in Petersmann (note 44), e.g. chapters VI and VII.5.

Integrating Human Rights into the Law of Worldwide Organizations   291

freedoms should be reconciled with other human rights subject to "necessity" and non-discrimination requirements (e.g. in GATT Article XX, GATS Article XIV, Article 8 of the TRIPS Agreement) that are similar to those in human rights law. Yet, the move from "negative integration" in GATT 1947 to "positive integration" in the WTO may endanger protection of human rights and democratic governance in areas such as health protection and intellectual property law.[54]

The focus of GATT/WTO law is neither on deregulation nor on distributive justice, but on *optimal trade regulation* through welfare-increasing *non-discriminatory internal regulation* (rather than welfare-reducing *discriminatory* border restrictions or export subsidies). GATT and WTO jurisprudence has so far hardly ever challenged the sovereign right of GATT and WTO member states to protect the human rights of their citizens through *non-discriminatory* internal or international social rules (e.g. ILO conventions, human rights treaties, environmental agreements) if procedural due-process requirements had been met (e.g. for risk-assessment procedures prior to the application of sanitary measures, consultations with exporting countries that were adversely affected by environmental regulations unilaterally adopted in importing countries).[55] Should WTO law follow the example of EU law and integrate human rights and social rules more explicitly into WTO law and jurisprudence? Or should human rights and international income redistribution be left to other "specialized agencies" like the various UN human rights bodies, the World Bank and the ILO? Is interpretation of WTO law in conformity with human rights, as required by general international law, sufficient for ensuring coherence between human rights and trade law?

B. Human Rights Require International Constitutional Law

Since the Greek republics in the 5th century BC, *constitutionalism* has emerged in a process of "trial and error" as the most important "political invention" for protecting equal liberties against abuses of power. The continuing evolution of national and international constitutionalism can be defined by *six interrelated core principles* that are recognized in the constitutional laws of most democracies: (1) rule of law; (2) limitation and separation of government powers by checks and balances; (3) democratic self-government; (4) human rights; (5) social justice; and (6) the worldwide historical experience that protection of human rights and "democratic peace" cannot remain effective without international law providing for reciprocal *international legal restraints* on abuses of foreign policy powers.[56]

---

[54] These dangers are emphasized e.g. in E. U. Petersmann, The WTO Constitution and Human Rights, *Journal of International Economic Law* (JIEL) 3 (2000), 19–25; *idem*, From 'Negative' to 'Positive' Integration in the WTO: Time for Mainstreaming Human Rights into WTO Law, in *Common Market Law Review* 37 (2000), 1363–1382.

[55] In contrast to GATT/WTO law, European Community law has gone much further in challenging and replacing national by EC social, environmental and human rights rules, cf. M. Poiares Maduro (note 23).

[56] For an explanation of this definition of "constitutionalism," and of the countless possibilities of defining and balancing these constitutional core principles in national and international law depending on the particular contexts, see E. U. Petersmann, Human Rights and International Economic Law in the 21st Century, in *Journal of International Economic Law* 4 (2001), 3–39; *idem*, How to Constitutionalize International Law and Foreign Policy for the Benefit of Civil Society?, in *Michigan Journal of International Law* 20 (1999), 1–30; *idem*, Constitutionalism and International Organizations, in *Northwestern Journal of International Law and Business* 17 (1996), 398–469.

The legal concretization of these core principles in national constitutions (e.g. in national catalogues of human rights), and increasingly also in international "treaty constitutions" (such as the EC Treaty and the ILO Constitution), and their mutual balancing through democratic legislation, legitimately differ from country to country, from organization to organization, and from policy area to policy area. There are also valid "realist" reasons why "democratic peace" may be possible only among constitutional democracies, and power politics may remain necessary to contain aggression from non-democracies where human rights are not effectively protected.[57] Yet, are there convincing arguments why "constitutionalization" of international law and international organizations may be "a step too far"?[58] Are "international constitutional law" and "cosmopolitan integration law," as explained by Kant and confirmed by European integration law, indispensable for limiting abuses of foreign policy powers and protecting equal human rights and democratic peace across frontiers?[59]

The universal recognition of human rights, and the adoption by almost all states of national constitutions and international treaties committed to the promotion of human rights, reflect the worldwide experience that human rights cannot remain effective without constitutional safeguards, democratic legislation and international law protecting freedom and rule of law across frontiers through legal restraints on abuses of power. History and constitutional theory confirm that liberty, democracy, market competition and social justice are not gifts of nature but "constitutional tasks."[60] Rule of law may be possible in a dictatorship. Effective protection of equal human rights, however, is logically and practically inconceivable without rule of law, limitation and separation of government powers, democratic self-government, social market economies identifying and satisfying consumer demand and respect

---

[57] See e.g. H. Kissinger, *Does America Need a Foreign Policy?*, 2001, according to whom "in today's world, at least four international systems are existing side by side" (at 25 *et seq*), such as "democratic peace" in relations between Western Europe and North America; "strategic rivalry" among the great powers of Asia; ideological and religious conflicts in the Middle East; and the poverty, health and civil war problems dominating politics in most of the African countries.

[58] See R. Howse/K. Nicolaidis, Legitimacy through "Higher Law"? Why Constitutionalizing the WTO is a Step Too Far, T. Cottier/P. Mavroidis (eds.), *The Role of the Judge: Experience and Lessons for the WTO*, 2003, pp. 307–348. The authors define neither their use of the term "constitutionalizing" in a precise manner nor, in their criticism of a "libertarian approach," what they mean by "the fallacy of constitutionalism." While I agree with much of their criticism (e.g. of proposals for "federal global governance"), some of their concepts remain vague (such as "top-down empowerment" in the WTO context), and the addressees of their criticism are often not identified (Howse/Nicolaidis do not refer to any of my publications listed above in footnotes 44 and 56). The authors admit that integration of human rights and environmental law into WTO law, as suggested in my publications, "could ultimately result in creating some conditions for constitutionalism in the long run." Yet, they don't refute my argument (see e.g. above note 54) that the one-sided focus of the GATS and TRIPS agreements on producer interests, and the one-sided WTO jurisprudence on environmental and health protection measures, already offer enough evidence for the need to further "constitutionalize" trade policies and WTO law (e.g. through more stringent parliamentary, judicial and civil society review at national and international levels, and more explicit references to human rights).

[59] On the need for international constitutional law in the trade policy area see e.g. chapters VIII and IX of my 1991 book (note 44), and Hilf/Petersmann (note 52), at 42 *et seq*. Specifically on the need for protecting individual rights also in the trade policy area see e.g. E. U. Petersmann, Limited Government and Unlimited Trade Policy Powers: Why Effective Judicial Review and a Liberal Constitution Depend on Individual Rights, in Hilf/Petersmann (note 52), 537–561.

[60] See e.g. F. A. Hayek, *The Constitution of Liberty*, 1960; *idem, Law, Legislation and Liberty*, 1982; W. Fikentscher, *Freiheit als Aufgabe*, 1997.

for international law.[61] Because the basic function of democratic constitutions is to protect the "rights retained by the people" (Ninth Amendment of the US Constitution) against abuses of all government powers, and most *foreign policies* become effective by taxing and restricting *domestic citizens*, constitutional restraints on *foreign policy powers* are no less necessary for the protection of human rights than restraints on domestic policy powers.[62]

How then can the "Lockean dilemma" be overcome: that most national constitutions grant governments broad discretionary foreign policy powers that can easily undermine domestic constitutional restraints (e.g. by redistributing income among domestic citizens through "voluntary" trade restrictions)? Most countries have learned through experience that *unilateral* national constitutional restraints on foreign policy powers cannot effectively deal with the "*Janus* face problem" of foreign policies, for example, the fact that foreign policy discretion to discriminate among 200 sovereign states offers governments more than 200 possibilities for discriminating among domestic citizens trading with foreign countries and for taxing and redistributing income of domestic citizens through trade restrictions. Because of the *relational nature* of most foreign policy goals (such as "democratic peace" among democracies, freedom of trade between exporting and importing countries, exchange rate stability between different currencies), foreign policy abuses can be legally limited most effectively through *reciprocal international law rules*. Such rules tend to offer also more precise substantive and procedural "benchmarks" for parliamentary, judicial and intergovernmental review of foreign policy measures than the usually vague national constitutional rules for foreign policy-making. As noted above, reciprocal international guarantees of freedom, non-discrimination and rule of law can also serve "constitutional functions" for protecting and extending human rights values across frontiers and for "constitutionalizing"[63] discretionary foreign policy powers on the basis of "higher" international law and its enforcement through national and international courts and stricter parliamentary and democratic control.

C. Human Rights as Incentives for "Decentralized Ordering" and a "Self-Enforcing Constitution" Across Frontiers: The Subsidiarity Principle

The EU "principles of liberty, democracy, respect for human rights and fundamental freedoms" (Article 6 EU Treaty) are reflected also in the explicit Treaty requirements that actions by the Community shall be "in accordance with the principle of subsidiarity" and "not go beyond what is necessary to achieve the objectives of this

---

[61] For instance, equal protection of human rights is impossible without rule of law; individual freedom requires limited government; democratic self-government cannot be maintained over time without "constitutional democracy" committed to long-term principles and human rights; abuses of power can be curtailed most effectively through divided-power systems; rule of law across frontiers is impossible without international law.

[62] For detailed explanations of these arguments see e.g. my publications quoted in note 52.

[63] On different definitions of "constitutionalization" see e.g. E. U. Petersmann, Constitutionalism and International Adjudication, in *Journal of International Law and Politics* 1999, 101–135; D. Z. Cass, The "Constitutionalization" of International Trade Law: Judicial Norm-Generation as the Engine of Constitutional Development in International Trade, in *European Journal of International Law* 12 (2001), 39–75. The methods of "constitutionalization" in EU law (such as legal supremacy with direct effect and direct applicability of EC rules) go far beyond those of worldwide international law.

Treaty" (Article 5 EC Treaty); decisions shall be "taken as openly as possible and as closely as possible to the citizen" (Article 1 EU Treaty). Similar to the historical experiences inside many federal states, the EC Treaty objective of an "internal market . . . without internal frontiers in which the free movement of goods, persons, services and capital is ensured" (Article 14) was to some extent achieved only after the empowerment of self-interested market participants to enforce access to foreign markets and freedom of competition through independent "guardians of the law" (e.g. competition authorities) and courts against governmental and private market access barriers and restraints of competition.[64] The political EC Treaty goals "to establish progressively an area of freedom, security and justice" (Article 61 EC Treaty) and a "common foreign and security policy" are likewise linked to a "basic rights strategy," as reflected in the Treaty commitment "to develop and consolidate democracy and the rule of law, and respect for human rights and fundamental freedoms" inside and outside the EC (cf. Articles 6, 11 EU Treaty).

In the context of worldwide organizations, human rights are no less important for promoting not only individual and democratic self-government and legitimacy, but also decentralized enforcement of rule of law and decentralized coordination across frontiers among billions of autonomous citizens participating in global *economic* as well as *political markets*.[65] For example:

- Human rights (e.g. to property, freedom of contract, freedom of information, freedom of opinion and association), and the market mechanisms resulting from the protection of human rights, not only empower individuals to act on the basis of their own personal knowledge and to acquire and take into account the personal and local knowledge of others of which each person is inevitably ignorant.[66] Such decentralized ordering of the actions of diverse persons with limited knowledge reduces also the need for centralized government regulation of conflicting preferences (e.g. by imposing the majorities' preferences on minorities) that might unnecessarily limit individual freedom and disrupt decentralized ordering.[67]
- Human rights enable decentralized solutions also for the "value problem" that human views about "truth" may differ, and value judgments about "the good" and "the beautiful" are not necessarily true.[68] Economic as well as political

---

[64] See the comparative study of the common market law in the USA, Switzerland, Germany and the EC in Petersmann (note 44), chapter VIII.

[65] On the gradual emancipation of the individual, and the emergence of a human right to democracy in national and international law see e.g. T. M. Franck, *The Empowered Self. Law and Society in the Age of Individualism*, 1999. On markets and democracy as organized dialogues about economic and political value judgments see e.g. Fikentscher (note 60), at 51.

[66] Cf. F. A. Hayek, The Use of Knowledge in Society, in Hayek, *Individualism and Economic Order*, 1948, 77–78; T. Sowell, *Knowledge and Decisions*, 1980.

[67] On the importance of human rights for solving this "knowledge problem" see Barnett (note 48), at 29 *et seq* who rightly emphasizes that centralized ordering – e.g. of families, companies, governmental and non-governmental organizations – "needs to take place within a decentralized framework" (at 61).

[68] On Immanuel Kant's distinction between truth (analyzed in Kant's *Critique of Pure Reason*), value judgments (analyzed in Kant's *Critique of Practical Reason*), and aesthetic judgments (analyzed in Kant's *Critique of the Human Ability to Judge*), and on decentralized methods (i.e. markets and democracy) and centralized methods (e.g. dictatorship) to overcome conflicts about value judgments, see e.g. Fikentscher (note 16), at 50–51.

Integrating Human Rights into the Law of Worldwide Organizations

markets are decentralized means for evaluating scarce resources (e.g. private and public goods and services) in a manner respecting individual freedom (e.g. of supply and demand of private goods, political votes on the collective protection of social rights) and promoting "dialogues about values" and allocation and distribution of resources in accordance with consumer demand.[69]

- By requiring respect for equal human rights and by defining core human rights as "inalienable," human rights constrain, delimit and coordinate individual freedom and other human rights, promote individual responsibility (e.g. to use resources efficiently and not to harm others), and require substantive and procedural justification of governmental restraints of human rights. Human rights require transparent government (e.g. publication of laws) and "deliberative democracy," and inform and educate people on how they can realize individual and democratic self-government and mutually beneficial cooperation across frontiers while avoiding conflicts with the independent actions of others.[70]

- Human rights justify not only individual claims and individual access to courts for the settlement of "cases and controversies" between persons who are directly affected by a dispute. They also require submission of evidence, legal reasoning and claims in terms of rights and "justice" to judges in the context of judicial procedures subject to multiple safeguards (e.g. appellate review, democratic criticism, correction by legislation).[71] Through an evolutionary common law process of adjudication and progressive national and international codification, human rights thereby promote an ever more precise definition, delimitation and evolution of civil, political, economic, social and cultural human rights across frontiers. The legal priority and judicial clarification of human rights promote continuous review and adjustment of law and "justice" to new situations like global integration.[72]

- Liberty rights, property rights and other human rights also set incentives for savings and investments (e.g. by requiring restitution or compensation in case

---

[69] Whether market competition can be said to "ensure the best possible satisfaction of demand given the scarcity of goods" (Fikentscher, note 16, at 75) depends on whether "justice" can be defined in terms of equal liberties, efficiency and avoidance of unnecessary waste of resources (cf. Petersmann, note 44, at 60–61, 86 *et seq.*), and on how social human rights (e.g. to protection against economic hardship inconsistent with human dignity) can be integrated into a "social market economy" without distortion of price mechanisms, economic efficiency and equal liberties (as required by the economic theory of optimal intervention and also by the Rawlsian theory of justice according to which "basic liberties can be restricted only for the sake of liberty" but not solely for the sake of improving the condition of those who are economically and socially least well off; cf. Rawls, note 1, at 266, 474 *et seq.*). Human rights imply, for instance, that consumers may legitimately value goods regardless of the value of work invested by producers during the production of the goods concerned.

[70] On the importance of communicating "justice" in a manner making the abstract notion of justice and its concrete requirements accessible to everyone in a society see Barnett (note 14), at 84 *et seq.*

[71] On the comparative advantages of these law-determining procedures, and their links to "justice," rule of law, as well as to the efficient use of resources, see Barnett (note 14), at 120 *et seq.*

[72] On the inevitable task of judges to decide new kinds of disputes on the basis of general *principles* rather than established *rules* that may not be adequate for dealing with unforeseen new situations, see also F. A. Hayek, 1960 (note 59), at 115 *et seq.* For a refreshing criticism of the US constitutional law tradition to focus on literary analysis and arguments over founders' intentions (rather than on the constitutional tasks and real-world consequences of alternative constitutional interpretations) see R. D. Cooter, *The Strategic Constitution*, 2000.

of takings of property rights), for reconciling conflicts among self-interested individuals (e.g. by requiring consent to rights transfers), and for decentralized "checks and balances" promoting rule of law (e.g. because of the right of self-defense by adversely affected right-holders).[73]

D. Human Rights, Common Market Rules, Competition and Trade Rules: How to Construe Liberty Rights and Their "Indivisibility"?

Human rights historically evolved in particular civil, political, economic and social contexts before the modern recognition that "all human rights are universal, indivisible and interdependent and interrelated."[74] How should human rights to liberty and equality be construed in the particular context of the law and powers of international organizations (like the EC and WTO)? European Community law, for instance, protects

- general "principles of liberty" (Article 6 EU Treaty) based on common constitutional traditions in EC member states;
- a general human "right to liberty" (Article 6) and additional specific liberty rights recognized in the Charter of Fundamental Rights of the EU[75] (e.g. in Articles 11–16);
- the "principle of an open market economy with free competition" (Articles 4, 98, 105, 157);
- general and specific guarantees of non-discrimination (e.g. in Articles 12, 13, 19, 23, 30, 39, 43, 49, 56, 90, 141 EC Treaty), some of which confer individual rights;
- a "system ensuring that competition in the internal market is not distorted" (Articles 3, g) based on directly applicable competition rules (e.g. Articles 81, 82);
- general legal principles on "a common market and an economic and monetary union" (Article 2) and on an "internal market ... without internal frontiers in which the free movement of goods, persons, services and capital is ensured" (Article 14); and
- specific treaty guarantees on "free movement of persons, goods, services and capital, and the freedom of establishment," which is also referred to in the Preamble to the Charter of Fundamental Rights of the EU.

Community law requires interpreting these various treaty provisions in a mutually coherent manner. Just as in some member countries (like Germany) the national constitutional guarantees of freedom to pursue a trade or business are construed to protect also individual rights to import and export subject to constitutional and legislative restraints, it was only logical for the EC Court of Justice to interpret the corresponding Community guarantees of "freedom to choose an occupation"

---

[73] Cf. Barnett (note 14), at 169 *et seq.*, 197 *et seq.*

[74] Vienna Declaration of the UN World Conference on Human Rights (1993), section I.5; cf. The United Nations and Human Rights 1945–1995, UN 1995, at 450.

[75] See the text published in the *Official Journal of the EC*, C 364/1–22 of 18 December 2000, and the commentary by K. Lenaerts/E. E. De Smijter, A "Bill of Rights" for the European Union, in *Common Market Law Review* 38 (2001), 273–300.

Integrating Human Rights into the Law of Worldwide Organizations

and "freedom to conduct a business"[76] in conformity with the EC Treaty's customs union principle and to recognize "freedom of trade as a fundamental right."[77] The Court likewise construes the EC's common market rules and competition rules (e.g. Articles 81:1, 82) as individual "market freedoms" that can be directly enforced by individuals through the courts.[78] In contrast, for example, to modern US anti-trust adjudication, which tends to interpret US anti-trust rules almost exclusively in the light of economic efficiency criteria and consumer welfare,[79] the inter-pretation by the EC Court of the EC's common market rules and competition rules takes into account not only economic criteria but also the contribution of the "market freedoms" and competition rules to the realization of a single inter-nal market and to the protection of individual freedom and individual access to courts.[80]

The comprehensive EC guarantees of individual economic liberties differ from the constitutional and legal traditions in countries (like England and the USA) where domestic courts accord higher standards of judicial review and protection to civil and political freedoms than to economic liberties in view of the fact that consti-tutional law and competition law have guaranteed a common market and market competition in these countries long since.[81] In other countries (like Germany), which have experienced dictatorial governments colluding with cartelized industries in suppressing the economic and political liberties of their citizens, the constitutional liberties have been construed by courts as protecting maximum equal freedoms of citizens (subject to constitutional limits and democratic legislation) in economic markets no less than in political markets.[82] EC law suggests that this comprehensive

---

[76] These fundamental rights were recognized by the EC Court on the basis of the common constitutional traditions in EC member states and are now explicitly regulated in Articles 15 and 16 of the EU Charter of Fundamental Rights (note 75) in a manner protecting legitimate expectations in rule of law (cf. Article 16: "The freedom to conduct a business in accordance with Community law and national laws and practices is recognized").

[77] See above note 20.

[78] Cf. e.g. C. A. Jones, *Private Enforcement of Anti-trust Law in the EC, UK and the USA*, 1999.

[79] See e.g. R. H. Bork, *The Anti-trust Paradox*, 1993.

[80] Cf. P. Eeckhout, Trade and Human Rights in EU Law, in F. Abbott/T. Cottier (eds.), *International Trade and Human Rights*, 2002. On the objectives of EC competition policies see C. D. Ehlermann/L. L. Laudati (eds.), *European Competition Law Annual 1997: Objectives of Competition Policy*, 1998. There is, however, today broad consensus also in the EC that competition policy should focus on economic effi-ciency and consumer welfare, and that other policy objectives (like industrial policy, protection of small and medium-sized enterprises, employment, fight against inflation, improvement of the environment) should not be pursued by competition policy, but by means of other, more effective instruments.

[81] For criticism of the US "double standard" that (since the 1930s) accords a higher degree of judicial protection to civil and political freedoms than to economic liberties see e.g. B. H. Siegan, *Economic Liberties and the Constitution*, 1980; J. A. Dorn/H. G. Manne (eds.), *Economic Liberties and the Judiciary*, 1987. J. Rawls, notwithstanding his definition of the state's first goal as protecting maximum equal liberty, likewise limits his interpretation of basic liberties to those that "are essential for the adequate development and full exercise of . . . moral personality over a complete life" (J. Rawls, *Political Liberalism*, 1996, at 293). This focus on essential civil and political liberty appears influenced by the particular context of US constitutional law where, because of the effective protection of the common market and freedom of competition through US constitutional and anti-trust law, constitutional protection of economic liberty rights may have been less necessary than e.g. in the EC.

[82] For comparative studies of national constitutional guarantees of freedom of trade see Petersmann (note 44), chapter VIII.

constitutional protection of liberty rights, in the economic area no less than in the political field, offers more protection for citizens in countries and international organizations (like the EC) that do not benefit from centuries-old constitutional guarantees of a common market and long-standing anti-trust law protecting undistorted competition (as in the USA). This is even more true if the manifold *instrumental functions of human rights* (e.g. for handling the social problems of limited knowledge, decentralized coordination, mutually beneficial division of labor, conflicts of interests, abuses of power, incentives for savings and investments, decentralized enforcement of rule of law) are taken into account. From the human rights perspective of the more than one billion people living on less than one dollar a day, the marketplace for goods (e.g. food) and services (e.g. job opportunities, education and health services) is no less important for survival and self-development than the marketplace for politics and ideas.

E. Consequences of the Indivisibility of Human Rights in European Integration Law: Lessons for Global Integration Law?

The EC Treaty clearly recognizes the European historical experience that economic, political and legal freedom cannot be separated, and that abuses of private economic power (such as the collaboration of cartelized industries with dictatorial governments in Nazi Germany) can be no less dangerous for citizens than abuses of political power. Private autonomy in law and in the economy must be protected by basic rights vis-à-vis abuses of both *political* as well as *economic power*. Thus, the EC Treaty protects "citizenship of the Union" (Article 17) by *civil rights* (such as the "right to move and reside freely within the territory of the Member States," Article 18) and *political rights* (such as the "right to vote and to stand as a candidate at municipal elections in the Member State in which he resides," Article 19) as well as *economic rights* (such as freedom of trade and competition protected by Articles 28, 29, 81 and 82) and *social rights* (such as the right to "equal pay for male and female workers for equal work or work of equal value," Article 141).[83] The EU Treaty and the EU Charter of Fundamental Rights likewise protect civil, political, economic and social human rights and fundamental rights. European integration confirms the potential synergies between human rights law and economic integration law: Inside Europe, it has become generally recognized that economic organizations (like the EC and the EEA) can pursue their objectives (e.g. of "an open market economy with free competition," Article 4 EC Treaty) more effectively if they are seen by citizens and national parliaments to support and promote human rights and social justice, and if they empower self-interested citizens to participate in democratic rule-making and to invoke and enforce the common market rules and competition rules through courts and other decentralized law-enforcement processes (e.g. through national competition authorities).

---

[83] On the interrelationships among European citizenship, nationality and the various categories of human rights, citizen rights, fundamental rights (e.g. to equal pay for male and female workers for equal work as defined in Article 141 of the EC Treaty) and other individual rights (e.g. rights dependent on residence rather than citizenship) cf. N. Reich, Union Citizenship – Metaphor or Source of Rights?, in *European Law Journal* 7 (March 2001), 4–23; M. La Torre (ed.), *European Citizenship: An Institutional Challenge*, 1998.

Integrating Human Rights into the Law of Worldwide Organizations

Articles 302–307 of the EC Treaty explicitly require the EC to cooperate with other international organizations and to respect treaties concluded by EC member states with third countries. Article 6 of the EU Treaty consequently confirms that the "Union shall respect fundamental rights, as guaranteed by the European Convention for the Protection of Human Rights and Fundamental Freedoms signed in Rome on 4 November 1950 and as they result from the constitutional traditions common to the Member States, as general principles of Community law." Agreements concluded by the EC are not only "binding on the institutions of the Community and on Member States" (Article 300:7 EC Treaty). The EC Court has recognized long since that such international agreements, and also general international law rules binding on the EC, constitute "an integral part of the Community legal system" with legal primacy over "secondary EC law" adopted by the EC institutions.[84] The EC Court therefore emphasizes that Community law must be construed in conformity with international law, and that all Community competencies must be exercised in compliance with the international legal obligations of the EC.[85] Precise and unconditional international guarantees of freedom and non-discrimination (e.g. in free-trade area agreements between the EC and third countries) were recognized by the EC Court to constitute *individual rights* whose violation by EC institutions or by member state governments may entail legal responsibilities of reparation of injury and of financial compensation of the adversely affected individuals.[86]

The jurisprudence of the European Court of Human Rights confirms the interrelationships among civil, political, economic and social human rights, for instance the importance of freedom of opinion, freedom of the press and property rights for economic competition. The Court's recognition of a larger "margin of appreciation" for governmental limitations of human rights in economic competition than in the political marketplace has remained controversial.[87] The Court has also emphasized that the human rights obligations of the more than 40 member states of the ECHR (including all fifteen EU member states) apply not only to national measures but also to *collective* rule-making in international organizations:

> Where States establish international organizations, or *mutatis mutandis* international agreements, to pursue cooperation in certain fields of activities, there may be implications for the protection of fundamental rights. It would be incompatible with the purpose and object of the Convention if Contracting States were thereby absolved from their responsibility under the Convention in relation to the field of activity covered by such attribution.[88]

---

[84] On this jurisprudence by the ECJ see e.g. D. McGoldrick, *International Relations Law of the EU*, 1997; A. Dashwood/C. Hillion (eds.), *The General Law of the EC External Relations*, 2000.

[85] See notably Case C-162/96, *Racke*, ECR 1998, I-3655.

[86] See e.g. Case 104/81, *Kupferberg*, ECR 1982, 3641; Cases C-46 and 48/93, *Brasserie du pêcheur* and *Factortame*, ECR 1996 I 1029.

[87] See e.g. the Markt Intern GMBH judgment of 20 November 1989 (Series A, no.165) and the Jacubowski judgment of 23 June 1994 (Series A no.291) of the European Court of Human Rights (reported also in D. Gomien/D. Harris/L. Zwaak, *Law and Practice of the European Convention on Human Rights and the European Social Charter*, 1996, at 288–290) in which the Court balanced the rights to freedom of expression and freedom of competition and recognized a larger margin of appreciation in economic matters even if the prohibited expressions of opinion had been factually correct. For a criticism of this jurisprudence see e.g. J. A. Frowein/W. Peukert, *EMRK Kommentar*, 2nd edition 1997, at 401.

[88] European Court of Human Rights, Third Section Decision as to the Admissibility of Application No. 43844/98 by T.I. Against the United Kingdom, 7 March 2000, at page 16 (nyr).

In *Matthews v. UK*, the European Court of Human Rights found the United Kingdom in violation of the human right to participate in free elections of the legislature even though the law that denied voting rights in Gibraltar implemented a treaty concluded among EC member states on the election of the European Parliament: "there is no difference between European and domestic legislation, and no reason why the United Kingdom should not be required to 'secure' the rights (under the ECHR) in respect of European legislation in the same way as those rights are required to be 'secured' in respect of purely domestic legislation."[89] In conformity with its consistent interpretation of the ECHR as a "living instrument" and "constitutional charter" that needs to be construed in the light of changing circumstances, the Court also admitted a complaint against all fifteen EC member states requiring the Court to find that EC member states are legally responsible for the violation of the due process guarantees of the ECHR resulting from a refusal by the EC Commission to suspend a fine imposed for infringement of EC competition rules.[90] Should, in a similar way, contracting parties of the ECHR be held legally liable for human rights violations resulting from, for example, WTO dispute settlement rulings or from their national implementation of WTO rules?

5. Indivisibility and Justiciability of Freedom and Other Human Rights in UN Law? Toward "Global Freedom"?

The 1948 Universal Declaration of Human Rights integrated civil, political, economic, social and cultural human rights in one single legal text. However, the numerous UN declarations on the indivisible and interrelated character of civil, political, economic, social and cultural human rights have so far not been translated into reality on the worldwide level of UN law. Even though the survival and personal development of billions of people depend on the international division of labor, and unnecessary poverty, food and health problems prevent billions of people from enjoying their human rights, UN human rights law and most human rights lawyers continue to focus more on protection of civil and political rights than on economic and social human rights. The UN Covenants of 1966, for example, protect "first generation" civil and political rights more effectively than "second generation" economic, social and cultural rights.[91] Only more recent UN human rights treaties dealing with specific problem areas – such as the 1979 Convention on the Elimination of all Forms of Discrimination of Women as well as the 1989 Convention on the Rights of the Child – have begun to return to a holistic human rights conception by granting equal importance to economic, social and cultural rights as to civil and political rights in their realm of protection.[92] UN law still seems far away from "making the global economy work for human rights" by embedding a strong human rights culture in the worldwide division of labor.[93]

---

[89] European Court of Human Rights, judgment of 18 February 1999 on complaint No. 24833/94; see *Europäische Grundrechtszeitschrift (EUGRZ)*, 1999, 200.

[90] See Complaint No. 56672/00 (Senator Lines v. 15 EC-States), reported in *EUGRZ*, 2000, 334.

[91] See e.g. A. Eide/C. Krause/A. Rosas (note 46), at 15–77.

[92] Cf. I. Merali/V. Oosterveld (eds.), *Giving Meaning to Economic, Social and Cultural Rights*, 2001.

[93] M. Robinson, Making the Global Economy Work for Human Rights, in G. P. Sampson (ed.), *The Role of the World Trade Organization in Global Governance*, 2001, at 209.

Human rights need to be protected, mutually balanced and reconciled not only at the national level through democratic legislation, but also across frontiers through international treaties. National and international human rights include rights to democratic participation in the exercise of government powers and rights of access to courts.[94] All legislative, executive, judicial and also foreign policy activities of governments must aim at promoting human rights: "Human rights and fundamental freedoms are the birthrights of all human beings; their protection and promotion is the first responsibility of Governments."[95] Does the collective intergovernmental rule-making in UN agencies and the WTO, often behind closed doors and without effective parliamentary control, comply with these human rights requirements of democratic rule-making maximizing human rights? Moreover, UN and European human rights law recognizes that democratic limitations on human rights are subject to constitutional requirements of legality, non-discrimination, necessity and proportionality: "In the exercise of his rights and freedoms, everyone shall be subject only to such limitations as are determined by law solely for the purpose of securing due recognition and respect for the rights and freedoms of others and of meeting the just requirements of morality, public order and the general welfare in a democratic society" (Article 29 UDHR). Are the centuries-old traditions of discriminatory border restrictions against foreign goods, foreign services and foreigners justifiable in terms of human rights notwithstanding their welfare-reducing effects?

The exercise of all human rights depends on resources (such as food, information, health and educational services). Open borders enable domestic consumers to enjoy more, better and a larger variety of goods and services at lower prices than in the domestic markets, without preventing governments from applying "optimal policy instruments" for correcting "market failures" and supplying "public goods." Because legislative, administrative and judicial protection of human rights is costly and liberal trade increases national income and consumer welfare, it is not surprising that constitutional democracies tend to have open economies, whereas non-democracies often close not only their "political markets" but also their economic markets. The manifold interrelationships between decentralized, democratic coordination among autonomous citizens in "political markets" and decentralized, rights-based coordination in "economic markets" continue to be unduly neglected by the one-sided disregard of UN human rights law for the constitutional preconditions for the proper functioning of national and international economic markets as "engines" for creating and supplying economic resources needed for enjoyment and effective protection of human rights.

The new human rights challenges resulting from the modern globalization of communications, markets and governance structures illustrate the significance of a dynamic conception of liberty, as it is reflected in the Ninth Amendment of the US Constitution: "The enumeration of certain rights in this Constitution shall not be construed to deny or disparage others retained by the people."[96] Constitutions and

---

[94] See e.g. C. Harlow, Access to Justice as a Human Right: The European Convention and the European Union, in Alston *et alia* (note 4), 187–214.

[95] Vienna Declaration (note 74), section 1.

[96] See the criticism by Hayek (note 72) that the meaning and constitutional functions of this provision were "later completely forgotten" (at 186).

human rights instruments are historical and political documents that, even though the text may focus on particular problems at a particular time (e.g. "civil" and "political liberty" rather than "economic liberty"), should be construed as protecting individuals against all arbitrary coercion. It is no coincidence in this respect that modern constitutions of European countries with historical experiences of dictatorship (notably in Germany) protect individual freedom of personal development in the *Kantian sense* of maximum equal liberty across frontiers, and grant corresponding rights of access to courts and judicial review of whether legislative or administrative restraints of individual freedom are "unnecessary," disproportionate or otherwise arbitrary.[97] Nor is it a coincidence that almost all European countries, following their negative experiences with widespread cartelization and abuses of economic power during the first half of the 20th century, have adopted national and international competition rules since the 1950s prohibiting abuses of private and public economic power and granting citizens judicially enforceable rights against restraints of competition and abuses of "market power."[98] By protecting new "transnational fundamental rights," which had previously not been recognized in national constitutions of EC member states, EC constitutional law has extended human rights across frontiers based on a dynamic conception of freedom and fundamental citizen rights.

UN law emphasizes the "indivisibility" of civil, political, economic, social and cultural human rights and the duty of states, regardless of their political, economic and cultural systems, to promote and protect all human rights and fundamental freedoms.[99] Yet, the practice of UN-specialized agencies and of the WTO is still far away from understanding and regulating economic issues as human rights issues. For example, protection of private property is not mentioned in the UN human rights covenants even though private property rights are indispensable not only for economic welfare (e.g. as legal incentives assigning responsibility for maintaining an asset, for bearing the loss for not doing so, for enabling transfers of resources and an exchange economy) but also for political freedom and the rule of law.[100]

In the jurisprudence of the EC Court of Justice and the European Court of Human Rights, economic and social rights have been recognized long since as legal and "justiciable" rights to be protected by national and international courts.[101] The entry into force in 1999 of the 1995 Protocol providing for collective complaints under the European Social Charter of 1961 confirms the increasing recognition of legal and judicial remedies for the protection also of social rights. The UN Committee on Economic, Social and Cultural Rights has consistently argued that all ICESCR rights

---

[97] See e.g. Article 2 (1) of the German Basic Law: "Every person shall have the right to free development of his personality insofar as he does not violate the rights of others or offend against the constitutional order or the moral law." Article 2 (1) has been construed by German courts to protect also individual economic freedom across frontiers (e.g. rights to import and export subject to democratic legislation); cf. Petersmann (note 44), at 336 *et seq.* Article 93 of the Basic Law protects individual access to the Federal Constitutional Court by means of direct "constitutional complaints which may be filed by any person alleging that one of his basic rights . . . has been infringed by public authority."

[98] See the books by Amato and Gerber above in note 17.

[99] Vienna Declaration (note 90), section 5.

[100] On these historical, philosophical, economic and legal links between private property and freedom see R. Pipes, *Property and Freedom*, 1999.

[101] See e.g. M. Scheinin, Economic and Social Rights as Legal Rights, in Eide *et alia* (note 46), 41–62.

Integrating Human Rights into the Law of Worldwide Organizations

constitute individual rights, and possibilities for collective rights guarantees, and corresponding state obligations to respect, protect and fulfill the rights of individuals and groups.[102] Yet, human rights are not yet effectively integrated into the law and policies of most worldwide organizations.

6. Protection of Human Rights in Economic Integration Helps Citizens to Acquire the Resources Necessary for the Enjoyment of Human Rights

Economists tend to define economic development in quantitative terms (e.g. increase in GNP and national income). The contribution of human rights to the correction of market failures (such as inadequate "voice" and "exit" opportunities in markets, "external effects," socially "unjust" distribution of income), to the reduction of transaction costs, the promotion of market competition (e.g. through freedom of association and mobility of persons), and to the protection of "substantive freedom" of consumers and of the poor have been rarely examined by economists. While the contribution of law to economic welfare has been emphasized since Adam Smith's *Inquiry into the Nature and Causes of the Wealth of Nations* (1776), the various economic theories on "law and economics," "institutional economics" and "constitutional economics" have not systematically analyzed the contribution of human rights to economic welfare. Only recently have economists suggested to define economic development in terms of real substantive freedom and "capability" of citizens to self-development.[103] A few recent economic studies offer empirical evidence that "rights make human beings better economic actors," and that economic underdevelopment (e.g. famines, lack of investments, inefficient capital markets) seems to be closely related to lack of effective protection of human rights, democracy and accountability of governments.[104]

Most lawyers likewise disregard the contribution of human rights to economic welfare. In constitutional democracies with long-standing constitutional guarantees of a common market and liberal trade (like the USA), the concept and necessity of economic and social human rights often remain controversial. Where competition is effectively protected through anti-trust law (as in the USA), competition rules are often applied on the basis of economic efficiency criteria (such as absence of price and output restrictions) rather than on the basis of equal freedoms of competitors and consumers.[105] Human rights lawyers are often averse to taking into account economics in the consideration of human rights problems, or assume that the "laws of the market" are anarchic and offer no legitimate criteria for the solution of human rights problems.

---

[102] See E. Riedel, Rights Subjected to the Complaints Procedure, paper submitted to the Workshop on the Justiciability of ESC Rights with Particular Reference to an Optional Protocol to the ICESCR at the UN High Commissioner for Human Rights, 5–6 February 2001.

[103] Cf. A. Sen, *Development as Freedom*, 1999.

[104] See the Human Development Report 2000 (above note 13) and the World Development Report 2000/2001 on "Attacking Poverty" (World Bank 2001), which defines "poverty as encompassing not only low income and consumption but also low achievement in education, health, nutrition, and other areas of human development," including "powerlessness and voicelessness" of poor people; the report emphasizes the importance of protection of property rights (e.g. p. 34) and "empowerment" of poor people through democratic processes and accountability of governments (see p. 39).

[105] See e.g. the book by Bork above note 79.

Yet, billions of individuals have to face "scarcity of resources" as their most urgent human problem (e.g. for satisfying consumer demand for food, medicines, housing, education, health services and job opportunities) and freedom of exchange as their most important "instrumental liberty" for human survival and self-development. Because the exercise of human rights depends on scarce economic resources, human beings inevitably compete for access to and allocation of such resources. Consumer-driven market prices are the only spontaneous information, allocation and coordination mechanism respecting the freedom and divergent preferences of investors, producers, traders and consumers. Division of labor, based on private property rights and equal freedoms (e.g. freedom of contract to transfer property rights), has proven to be an indispensable complement of human rights, necessary for promoting savings and investments, productive uses of scarce resources, satisfaction of consumer demand, and inducing citizens to increase the supply of goods, services and income for the enjoyment of human rights.

Economic history confirms the central insight of Adam Smith's *Inquiry into the Nature and Causes of the Wealth of Nations* (1776) that economic welfare is essentially a function of legal guarantees for economic liberty, property rights, legal security and open markets as decentralized incentives for savings, investments and division of labor. Even though many less-developed countries are rich in economic, biological and human resources, their lack of legal security and inadequate protection of property rights impede investments, savings, efficient use of resources and economic development.[106] The sad reality of unnecessary poverty and gross violations of human rights in many countries is viewed by "constitutional economics" as proof of "constitutional failures" that are due to inadequate constitutional protection of civil, political, economic and social human rights, including economic liberties, property rights, monetary and competition safeguards necessary for a mutually beneficial division of labor.[107]

The 1966 UN Covenant on Economic, Social and Cultural Rights does not protect the economic freedoms, property rights, non-discriminatory conditions of competition and rule of law necessary for a welfare-increasing division of labor satisfying consumer demand through private investments and efficient supply of goods, services and job opportunities.[108] The UN Covenant's social rights are therefore often criticized as a one-sided attempt at redistribution without adequate attention for wealth creation and without proper balance among rights and obligations.

---

[106] See e.g. de Soto (note 31), who points out that many developing countries are rich in resources that, because of inadequate protection of private property rights, remain "dead capital" that cannot be economically used.

[107] On "constitutional economics" and the need for an "economic constitution" see E. U. Petersmann (note 44), e.g. chapters III–VII, as well as D. Gerber, Constitutionalizing the Economy: German Neo-Liberalism, Competition Law and the "New" Europe, in *American Journal of Comparative Law* 42 (1994), 25–84. Numerous recent economic studies suggest "that almost all of the countries that have enjoyed good economic performance across generations are countries that have stable democratic governments." (M. Olson, note 15, at 43, 192: "The countries with the highest per-capita incomes – the developed democracies – are also the countries where individual rights are best protected.")

[108] "Economic freedoms" are mentioned only in Article 6 of the ICESCR on the right to work. Property rights were not mentioned in the Covenant because of disagreement on how to delimit private property and public interest legislation.

Integrating Human Rights into the Law of Worldwide Organizations

The EC's "treaty constitution," by contrast, protects welfare-enhancing market competition in a much more comprehensive manner in the economy no less than in the polity. Free movements of goods, services, persons, capital and related payments, non-discriminatory conditions of competition, as well as social rights, are constitutionally protected in EC law as "fundamental rights."[109] The single European market could never have been realized without private enforcement of these economic liberties by EC citizens and without their judicial protection by national courts and by the EC Court vis-à-vis governmental and private restrictions and discrimination. EC competition law and the ever more comprehensive EC guarantees of social rights and of regional adjustment assistance are indivisible components of the EC's "economic constitution" and "social market economy" without which political acceptance of the "acquis communautaire" by many less-developed, newly acceding European countries would not have been democratically feasible.[110] Indivisibility of *political* as well as *economic freedom* and responsibility, constitutional safeguards against abuses of *economic power* no less than against abuses of *political power* and social rights promoting a "social market economy" have become hallmarks of European integration law that should serve as models for worldwide integration law.

Just as European economic integration law has become reinforced by integrating human rights, the increasing calls for "mainstreaming human rights" into worldwide economic integration law (e.g. of the WTO, IMF, ILO and World Bank) offer important synergies for strengthening both human rights law and global integration law.[111] The indivisibility of civil, political, economic, social and cultural human rights requires more effective legal protection also of individual *economic liberties* as necessary precondition for *personal* and *political liberties*, stronger social rights, and a mutually welfare-increasing division of labor in which the social adjustment costs to global integration are jointly shared (e.g. through integrated IMF and World Bank assistance programs for newly acceding WTO member countries). European integration law offers important lessons for the necessary reforms of UN human rights law and of global integration law: The need for constitutional, legislative and judicial safeguards against freedom's inherent tendencies of destroying itself is a constitutional task in *all areas* of civil, political, economic, social and cultural life.

7. Human Rights Require International Competition Rules Protecting Consumer Welfare and Freedom of Choice of Citizens

Indivisibility of human rights implies that the human right to liberty must protect the right of each individual to self-determination and self-development in *all areas* of social life through constitutional restraints on power and corresponding liberty

---

[109] See above at notes 20 and 80.

[110] Cf. e.g. M. Poiares Maduro, Striking the Elusive Balance Between Economic Freedom and Social Rights in the EU, in Alston *et alia* (note 4), 449–472. On the constitutional impact of EU constitutional law on the national constitutional laws of EC members and acceding countries see A. E. Kellermann/J. W. de Zwaan/J. Czuczai (eds.), *EU Enlargement. The Constitutional Impact at EU and National Level*, 2001.

[111] See E. U. Petersmann, Human Rights, Cosmopolitan Democracy and the Law of the World Trade Organization, in Fletcher/Mistelis/Cremona (eds.), *Foundations and Perspectives of International Trade Law*, 2001, at 79–96; S. I. Skogly, *The Human Rights Obligations of the World Bank and the International Monetary Fund*, 2001.

rights of citizens provided the equal human rights of all others are respected.[112] Equal freedoms of investors, producers, traders and consumers, and their unequal resources, knowledge, capabilities and preferences, inevitably entail competition as the only decentralized information and coordination mechanism that respects individual freedom of choice and enables individuals to overcome their inevitable ignorance in an extended division of labor among billions of autonomous producers and consumers. Human rights must not ignore the historical experience and "ordo-liberal insight" that the proper functioning and perceived "justice" of economic markets depends on legal guarantees of "constitutive principles" (e.g. monetary stability, open markets, private property rights, freedom of contract, liability, respect for human rights) and "regulative principles" (e.g. policy coherence, optimal policy instruments, necessity and proportionality of government interventions) without which "market failures" and "government failures" risk distorting and discrediting competition.[113] From a human rights perspective, constitutional protection of human rights in the economy is no less important for the welfare of citizens than protection of human rights and constitutional restraints on powers in the polity.

Human rights also imply that the constitutional task of promoting non-discriminatory conditions of competition and social welfare requires not only "negative freedoms" (e.g. in the sense of absence of illegal force and unnecessary coercion). Constitutional guarantees of "positive freedoms" (in the sense of participatory and redistributive rights), of individual responsibility (e.g. for savings and investments, injury caused to others or to oneself), undistorted competition and social justice are no less necessary for promoting equal opportunities.[114] In order to remain politically and socially acceptable, market economies must offer fair opportunities *to all* (e.g. for the free development of individual capacities) and must limit, through competition law and social law, the inherent market tendencies toward self-destruction and socially unjust distribution of risks and benefits. The democratic legislation on how to balance and delimit economic freedoms (such as freedom of contract, professional and entrepreneurial freedom), property rights and social rights may legitimately differ from country to country depending on its available resources and prevailing social views. Yet, all constitutional democracies in Europe and North America recognize that neither democracies nor economies can realize their human rights objectives without institutional, procedural and substantive legal restraints on private and public power and corresponding citizen rights designed to avoid abuses that were not consented to by citizens and reduce social welfare.[115]

In the pursuit of their constitutional task of defining, delimiting, promoting, protecting and reconciling equal rights and competition across frontiers in an ever more

---

[112] On constitutions as "precommitment devices" and the need for a general "constraint theroy" see J. Elster, *Ulysses Unbound*, 2000.

[113] On ordo-liberal theories on the interrelationships between economic, political and legal order and the need for an "economic constitution" see e.g. Petersmann (note 44), chapter III; Gerber (note 17), chapter VII.

[114] On the numerous different concepts of equal freedoms, "basic capability equality" (A. Sen) and distributive justice, and on the problems of knowledge, conflicts of interests, and abuses of power confronting the implementation of concepts of social justice, see S. Darwall (ed.), *Equal Freedom*, 1995; Barnett (note 14), at 308 *et seq.*; J. Raz, *The Morality of Freedom*, 1986.

[115] On this common dilemma of democracies and market economies see Amato (note 17).

Integrating Human Rights into the Law of Worldwide Organizations

precise and more effective manner, most governments in Europe and North America have also accepted the need for international competition rules that prevent and control – for example, through competition legislation, independent competition authorities, judicial protection of individual rights and international cooperation among anti-trust authorities – "unreasonable restraints of competition" on the basis not only of equal rights, but also of economic criteria (such as prohibitions of price fixing, market-sharing and output restrictions) that offer more precise guidelines for distinguishing welfare-increasing from welfare-reducing restraints of competition. There is broad agreement among competition authorities in Europe and North America today that the direct objective of competition laws and policies should focus on economic efficiency and consumer welfare, even if their indirect long-term objectives also include protection of equal freedoms of market participants and dispersion of private and public power.[116] Other policy objectives, like protection of small enterprises and promotion of social justice, can be pursued more effectively through other policy instruments that avoid distortions of trade and competition (e.g. tax benefits and subsidies for small enterprises). The European concept of "social market economy" clearly admits that markets do not guarantee socially just results and need to be complemented by strong social rights. For example, competition, new technologies and changing consumer demand may entail "constructive destruction" (Schumpeter) and adjustment costs that may arise through no fault of producers and require a social "safety net" in order to remain democratically acceptable and protect the human rights of vulnerable groups.

8. Can a "United Nations Action Program" Succeed in Integrating Human Rights into the Law of Worldwide Organizations?

The incorporation of human rights into European integration law reflects effective protection of human rights in both the national and European economy and polity of EU member countries. UN human rights law, by contrast, has not succeeded so far to protect human rights effectively in the national and increasingly globalized economy and governance systems of all UN member states. Initiatives for integrating human rights into the law of worldwide organization are unlikely to come from specialized economic organizations like the WTO. More than fifty years after the Universal Declaration on Human Rights, it is time for a comprehensive UN program for integrating human rights in a coherent manner into the law of worldwide organizations so as to "constitutionalize" the world economy and global governance. Are the powers of the UN (e.g. under Articles 62–64 of the UN Charter) sufficient for bringing about the needed "human rights revolution"?

In contrast to the anti-market bias of earlier UN recommendations for a "New International Economic Order,"[117] the recent UN Secretary-General's report on "Globalization and its impact on the full enjoyment of all human rights"[118] is characterized

---

[116] See C. D. Ehlermann/L. L. Laudati (eds), *European Competition Law Annual: Objectives of Competition Policy*, 1998.

[117] See e.g. E. U. Petersmann, Charter of Economic Rights and Duties of States, in Bernhardt (ed.), *Encyclopedia of Public International Law* Vol.1, 1992, at 561–566.

[118] UN documents A/55/342 of 31 August 2000 and A/56/254 of 31 July 2001.

by a balanced attempt at reconciling human rights, market competition and global-ization. It emphasizes, *inter alia*,

- the worldwide opportunities of increasing the resources available for the real-ization of human rights through global division of labor provided market com-petition is accompanied by appropriate domestic policies;[119]
- the complementary functions of international guarantees of freedom and non-discrimination, for example, in IMF and WTO law and in human rights law;
- the need to correct "market failures" so as to ensure that economic growth leads to greater promotion and protection of human rights;
- the importance of human rights (such as the rights to health, food and a clean environment) for the interpretation of "public interest clauses" in the law of worldwide organizations and for the structural adjustment programs of inter-national financial institutions;
- the positive effects of new technologies (e.g. for education and the successful organization of civil society initiatives), but also their unequal distribution and certain negative effects (e.g. in terms of increased vulnerability of capital mar-kets, abuses of the Internet for spread of hate speech, etc);
- the positive contribution of human rights to a geographically more even dis-tribution of investments and financial flows, and the adverse effects of trade protectionism on development and human rights; and
- frequent links between lack of democracy and certain negative aspects of inter-national trade (such as illegal trafficking of drugs, diamonds and human beings).

The UN High Commissioner for Human Rights, whose mandate includes coor-dination of all UN human rights activities and improving their effectiveness, has likewise called for a rights-based and rules-based approach to development making the world economy and international economic institutions part of a human rights culture.[120] The "Global Compact" launched by UN Secretary-General Kofi Annan in 1999 for greater business support for human rights, core labor standards and pro-tection of the environment offers important complementary strategies for bringing the benefits of globalization and of human rights to more people worldwide. Also non-economic NGOs are increasingly involved in preparing "bottom-up reforms" of the state-centered UN system.[121]

A "Global Compact" committing all worldwide organizations to respect for human rights, rule of law, democracy and "good governance"[122] in their collective exercise

---

[119] The recent WTO report on *Trade, Income Disparity and Poverty* (by Ben-David and Winters, Special Studies No. 5, WTO 1999) offers empirical evidence that trade contributes to economic growth and promotes alleviation of poverty provided trade liberalization is complemented by appropriate domestic policies (e.g. for education, health and consumer protection) that have much larger effects on poverty alleviation than trade policy.

[120] See e.g. M. Robinson (above note 93), 209–222.

[121] Cf. the UN Secretary-General's *Millenium Report* on "We the Peoples," UN 2000, and the Progress Report by the UN High Commissioner for Human Rights on "Business and Human Rights," UNHCHR 2001.

[122] Several international organizations have committed themselves to principles of "good governance" with-out clarifying the relationship between this vague political principle and human rights, cf. e.g. *Gover-nance and Human Rights*, World Bank 1995; *Participatory Development and Good Governance*, OECD 1995.

Integrating Human Rights into the Law of Worldwide Organizations 309

of government powers would promote the overall coherence and democratic legitimacy of the UN system and create new incentives for rendering human rights more effective. Just as "European citizenship" has reinforced and enlarged civil, political, economic, social and cultural rights of EU citizens, "UN citizenship" and "good corporate citizenship" should become new legal titles for individuals and stakeholder groups for democratic participation in the UN governance systems and for greater responsiveness of the UN legal system to the needs and human rights of all people.[123] The "Global Compact" should include commitments of all international organizations to integrate human rights into their respective laws and practices and to submit annual "human rights impact statements" examining and explaining their contribution to the protection and enjoyment of human rights. Such a human rights policy could help to overcome also the widespread distrust by civil society groups vis-à-vis non-transparent rule-making in "specialized organizations." It could also assist national parliaments in exercising more effective democratic control over "multi-level governance" in international organizations.

Just as proposals for integrating human rights into European integration law were not initiated by trade politicians, it seems unrealistic to expect such initiatives from specialized worldwide economic organizations or from national trade, finance and economic ministries. In the Uruguay Round of multilateral trade negotiations, for instance, trade diplomats preferred negotiating international rules behind closed doors unobstructed by close parliamentary and democratic scrutiny; and industries lobbied one-sidedly for incorporating into the WTO "positive integration law" focusing on intellectual property rights beneficial for industries without references to social human rights. In contrast to the comprehensive obligations and forceful dispute settlement and enforcement systems of WTO law, the small WTO Secretariat and consensus-based WTO decision-making procedures remain politically weak. Obstruction by a few self-interested politicians or by non-democratic governments is often enough to prevent international organizations from referring to human rights.

As in other fields of human rights law, initiatives for protecting human rights more effectively in the economy will depend on democratic vigilance and bottom-up pressures by courageous citizens and judges defending human rights. The universal recognition of human rights promotes a progressive empowerment of individuals and of non-governmental organizations (NGOs) to insist on democratic reforms of the state-centered system of international law and international organizations. The 1966 Optional Protocol to the UN Covenant on Civil and Political Rights provides for a direct complaints procedure for individuals claiming to be victims of human rights violations. The preparations of a corresponding Optional Protocol for the International Covenant on Economic, Social and Cultural Rights (ICESCR) reflect the need, as well as the difficulties, to strengthen direct remedies for individuals in the monitoring and enforcement mechanisms of economic and social human

---

[123] Introducing "UN citizenship" as a human rights concept would, however, require far-reaching democratic reforms of the UN legal system that appear hardly feasible through amendments of the UN Charter pursuant to its Articles 108 or 109; cf. E. U. Petersmann, How to Constitutionalize the United Nations? Lessons from the "International Economic Law Revolution," in V. Götz/P. Selmer/R. Wolfrum (eds.), *Liber Amicorum* G. Jaenicke, 1998, 313–352.

rights.[124] Are non-binding UN resolutions unsuitable means for strengthening the obligation of states to protect human rights in the trade and economic policy area, including state responsibility "to ensure that private entities or individuals, including transnational corporations over which they exercise jurisdiction, do not deprive individuals of their economic, social and cultural rights"?[125]

For a globally interdependent but highly decentralized world composed of about two hundred states and several hundred intergovernmental organizations, the primacy of the UN Charter (cf. Article 103) and of UN human rights law offers a constitutional framework for the overall coherence of the policies of governments, "specialized agencies" and of the billions of producers and consumers in the global economy. While the International Labor Organization, the World Bank and the World Intellectual Property Organization have increasingly integrated human rights and individual complaints procedures into their law and practices,[126] government representatives in other worldwide organizations (like the International Monetary Fund and the WTO) remain reluctant to admit that also the *collective exercise* of their powers (e.g. in the monetary and trade policy areas) is limited by human rights and must serve the interests and democratic rights of all affected citizens. Explicit recognition of the "human rights functions" of WTO rules, even if contained only in a political declaration by WTO member states, would help to refute the claim by anti-globalization activists that "human rights offer a principle on which to base opposition to the challenges posed by economic globalization" and by WTO law.[127] Yet, without additional political initiatives by the UN Secretary-General, UN human rights bodies, domestic parliaments and other civil society representatives, the needed integration of human rights into the law of all worldwide organizations risks to make little progress.

As long as UN human rights law does not provide for effective judicial remedies at the international level, there is no reason why specialized international courts should be less capable than politicized UN bodies to protect human rights in the interpretation and application of global integration law. For example, just as the EC Court of Justice, more than thirty years ago, responded to the invocation of human rights in national courts by confirming that "fundamental human rights (are) enshrined in

---

[124] The ICESCR entered into force in 1976 and has today been ratified or acceded to by 144 states. A draft optional protocol to the ICESCR providing for a right of individuals or groups to submit communications concerning non-compliance with the covenant was elaborated by the UN Committee on Economic, Social and Cultural Rights and submitted to the UN Commission on Human Rights in 1996, but has not yet been approved by member states (cf. the Report of the High Commissioner for Human Rights in E/CN.4/2000/49 of 14 January 2000).

[125] Quotation from the 1997 "Maastricht Guidelines on Violation of Economic, Social and Cultural Rights," section 18, which continues to define state responsibility under current international law in the following terms: "States are responsible for violations of economic, social and cultural rights that result from their failure to exercise due diligence in controlling the behaviour of such non-state actors" (see Mehra, note 18, at 251–260).

[126] See e.g. IBRD, *Development and Human Rights: The Role of the World Bank*, 1998; *Human Development Report 2000*, UNDP 2000; *Intellectual Property and Human Rights*, WIPO 1999. The IMF guidelines (see e.g. *Good Governance: The IMF's Role*, 1997) and WTO reports do not explicitly refer to "human rights."

[127] For a too one-sided critique of the WTO and of "dehumanising effects of globalisation" see e.g. M. Kothari, Globalisation, Social Action and Human Rights, in Mehra (note 18), at 46.

Integrating Human Rights into the Law of Worldwide Organizations 311

the general principles of Community law and protected by the Court,"[128] WTO dispute settlement panels and WTO Appellate Body judges should acknowledge that universally recognized human rights have become part of general international law that WTO judges have to take into account in their interpretation and application of WTO rules.

9. Need for Closer Cooperation Between UN Human Rights Bodies, International Organizations, Parliaments and Non-Governmental Human Rights Groups

According to Article 18 of the UN Covenant on Economic, Social and Cultural Rights, "The Economic and Social Council may make arrangements with the specialized agencies in respect of their reporting to it on the progress made in achieving the observance of the provisions of the present Covenant falling within the scope of their activities." Human rights and their corresponding government obligations are referred to in the statutes and mandates of several international organizations, such as the human right to education to be promoted by the UN Educational, Scientific and Cultural Organization (UNESCO); the human rights to work and freedom of association to be protected by the International Labor Organization (ILO); the human right to health as the central legal objective of the World Health Organization (WHO); the human right to food as a major task of the Food and Agricultural Organization (FAO); the protection of intellectual property rights by the World Intellectual Property Organization (WIPO) and the promotion of children rights by the UN Children's Fund (UNICEF). Article 2 of the UN Covenant on Economic, Social and Cultural Rights requires the committee "to take steps, individually and through international assistance and cooperation... with a view to achieving progressively the full realization of the rights recognized in the present Covenant." More comprehensive cooperative arrangements for making the legal and supervisory activities of the UN Committee on Economic, Social and Cultural Rights and the multilateral rule-making and operational assistance by specialized international organizations mutually reinforcing are indispensable for enhancing the effectiveness of complementary international and national measures for the promotion of human rights.

In the elaboration of its so far 14 "general comments" (e.g. on the human right to health), and during its "days of general discussion," the UN Committee on Economic, Social and Cultural Rights cooperates already actively with specialized international organizations (such as WHO, IMF, World Bank, ILO, WIPO and also WTO) and non-governmental human rights groups. The Committee also submitted a declaration to the second ministerial conference of the WTO at Seattle in November 1999 reminding all states, and also the WTO, of their human rights obligations. Yet, many specialized worldwide organizations (such as IMF and WTO) lack special rules, procedures and institutions for protecting human rights in their specialized fields of activities. As a result, the "human rights functions" of economic policy objectives (such as monetary stability as a precondition for the protection of the value of property rights in money), and the "economic functions" of human rights (such as liberty rights and

---

[128] Case 29/69. *Stauder*, ECR 1969. 419, para. 7.

property rights as preconditions for a market economy), tend to be unduly neglected in specialized organizations.

The objective of integrating human rights into national and international development strategies can hardly be achieved without more political support also from parliaments and non-governmental organizations for integrating human rights into the rule-making and operational activities of specialized organizations. Human rights and the corresponding state obligations further require more effective international accountability mechanisms and judicial remedies as part of human rights law and of global integration law.

10. Human Rights and the Global Integration Law of the WTO

The numerous references in WTO law to the law of other worldwide organizations (such as the UN, the IMF and the World Bank) demonstrate the obvious fact that the WTO objective of maximizing individual and social welfare through worldwide division of labor cannot be realized without other supplementary worldwide agreements, such as the IMF rules on the promotion of stable exchange rates and on liberalization of current payments and capital flows. Can WTO law – as the most important legal and institutional framework for the worldwide liberalization of welfare-reducing discriminatory barriers to the international flow of goods, services, investments and persons – realize its ambitious goals of "global freedom," market integration, worldwide rule-making and rule of law without regard to universally recognized human rights?

The legal, political and economic arguments for interpreting WTO rules in conformity with universally recognized human rights have already been mentioned (e.g. in section 1 above). Yet, can the adjustment of WTO law to universal human rights be left to WTO judges who may be unfamiliar with human rights and the jurisprudence of human rights courts (notably those WTO panel members and Appellate Body members who are not lawyers)? How will the trade specialists in the WTO Secretariat react who have to advise and assist WTO panels in the drafting of dispute settlement reports? Will the trade diplomats in the WTO's Dispute Settlement Body adopt panel and appellate reports suggesting "new human rights interpretations" of WTO rules? How to deal with the risk of protectionist abuses of human rights arguments for justifying trade restrictions? Because the WTO perceives itself as a "member-driven organization" where multilateral rule-making will succeed in overcoming domestic protectionist pressures only with the help of political support by powerful export industries: Will economists and industries change their declared preference for "specialized organizations" and "separation of policy instruments"? Will human rights activists and UN human rights bodies support integration of human rights into the WTO? How will other worldwide organizations (like the World Bank and the IMF) react to a new "integration paradigm" linking trade liberalization and its adjustment problems to promotion of economic and social human rights and joint financial "burden sharing" (as in European integration)?

The values underlying WTO law – such as protection of legal freedom, property rights, non-discrimination, rule of law, access to courts, economic welfare and national sovereignty to pursue non-economic policy objectives that are considered more important than liberal trade – mirror corresponding human rights principles.

Integrating Human Rights into the Law of Worldwide Organizations 313

Even though WTO law nowhere explicitly refers to human rights, it serves manifold "human rights functions" across frontiers. Given the widespread bias among human rights lawyers vis-à-vis economics and WTO law, and the agnostic attitude of many trade specialists vis-à-vis human rights, it is an important task of academics to promote more dialogue and better understanding among these different communities of trade specialists and human rights advocates so as to render both human rights law and WTO law more effective in dealing with worldwide poverty, health and human rights problems.

A. Human Rights Functions of WTO Guarantees of Freedom, Non-Discrimination and Rule of Law

In contrast to most human rights treaties, the WTO guarantees of freedom, non-discrimination and rule of law go far beyond national constitutional guarantees in most countries that tend to limit economic freedom to domestic citizens and, for centuries, discriminate against foreign goods, foreign services, foreign investors and foreign consumers (e.g. by permitting export cartels). By extending equal freedoms across frontiers and subjecting discretionary foreign policy powers to additional legal and judicial restraints ratified by domestic parliaments, WTO law serves "constitutional functions" for rendering human rights and constitutional restraints more effective in the trade policy area.[129] Economic theory confirms the constitutional value of liberal trade: trade transactions are voluntarily agreed upon only if they are mutually beneficial for the seller and the buyer; and the economic gains from trade do not depend on the nationality of traders. Political theory points to additional gains from peaceful trade cooperation, such as promotion of freedom and "positive peace." Modern theories of justice justify the WTO objective of maximizing equal freedom across frontiers by the ethical "categorical imperative" (Kant) and by the rational self-interest of all individuals in equal freedom and mutually beneficial cooperation.[130] In case of potentially negative implications of liberal trade (such as trade in arms and transboundary movements of environmental waste), WTO law provides for generously drafted "exceptions" that allow unilateral national safeguard measures including governmental restrictions of freedom and property rights for the benefit of other, more important human rights (e.g. limitations of intellectual property rights so as to allow "parallel imports" of medicines at socially affordable prices; cf. Articles 6 and 8 of the TRIPS Agreement).

Constitutional theory (e.g. by Kant and Rawls) and practical experience (notably in European integration) demonstrate that national constitutions cannot effectively protect human rights and democratic peace across frontiers without complementary *international constitutional restraints* on foreign policy powers and *cosmopolitan guarantees* of human rights vis-à-vis foreign governments.[131] For example, just

---

[129] See above section 4 A., notably note 51.

[130] See e.g. J. Rawls (note 1), at 53, whose "first principle of justice" is "each person is to have an equal right to the most extensive scheme of equal basic liberties compatible with a similar scheme of liberties for others." On the interdependence among human rights, democracy, rule of law and peace see e.g. J. Symonides (ed.), *Human Rights: New Dimensions and Challenges*, UNESCO 1998.

[131] See above section 5 and Petersmann, How to Constitutionalize International Law (note 56).

as all states guarantee freedom of trade *inside* their national boundaries, effective protection of the human rights of their own citizens requires them to constitutionally protect also freedom to produce, trade and consume *across frontiers* as an indivisible part of individual liberty, as in EC law. Domestic political support for this objective can be achieved more easily through *reciprocal international agreements* rather than through *unilateral national legislation*.[132] Yet, even though WTO rules are formulated in terms of international rights and obligations of governments, they serve *human rights functions* for protecting individual liberty, non-discrimination, rule of law and welfare-increasing cooperation among domestic and foreign producers, investors, traders and consumers across frontiers.

B. The Struggle for Protecting Human Rights Across Frontiers: The Example of Liberty Rights as "Negative," "Positive" and "Institutional Guarantees"

The idea and legal recognition of "basic individual rights," "fundamental rights" and "human rights" goes back to the beginnings of written history. Precursors include the rights to asylum granted by Greek city-states; Roman citizenship rights; rights of the nobility in the Middle Ages (e.g. in the Magna Carta 1215); religious freedom protected in the constitutional charter adopted by the Dutch provincial assembly at Dordrecht in 1572; the English Habeas Corpus Act of 1679 and Bill of Rights of 1689; the French Declaration of the Rights of Man and the Citizen of 1789; and the Bill of Rights appended to the US Constitution in 1791. The particular focus of liberty rights (e.g. freedom of religion, freedom of association, freedom to demonstrate) was often shaped by historical events (such as the schism of the Christian church from the 16th century onward) and by political struggles against the rulers. Transnational protection of new "globalization rights"[133] and of non-discrimination, rule of law, democratic governance and social justice across frontiers are the human rights challenges of the 21st century.

In the history of federal states (such as the US, Switzerland and Germany) and of customs unions (such as the German Customs Union 1834–1866, the EEC Treaty), liberty rights were progressively extended across frontiers inside the federation and inside the customs union by means of *objective guarantees* of freedom of trade. The elaboration of federal *human rights catalogues* (e.g. in US, Swiss, German and EC constitutional law) and the inclusion of guarantees of human rights and democracy into international integration law (e.g. in the EU) have been politically possible only at later stages of market integration.[134] The judicial interpretation of liberty rights, and of the constitutional guarantee that no person shall be deprived of "liberty without due process of law" (Fifth and Fourteenth Amendments of the US Constitution), have changed over time both in Europe and North America.[135] In modern welfare states

---

[132] See the reasons explained in E. U. Petersmann, Why Do Governments Need the Uruguay Round Agreements, NAFTA and the EEA? In *Swiss Review of International Economic Relations* (Aussenwirtschaft) 49 (1994), 31–55.

[133] See M. D. Pendleton, A New Human Right – The Right to Globalization, in *Fordham International Law Journal* 22 (1999), 2052.

[134] For a comparative legal analysis with numerous references to the relevant legal texts see Petersmann (note 44), chapter VIII.

[135] See e.g. J. H. Garvey/T. A. Aleinikoff, *Modern Constitutional Theory: A Reader*, 3rd ed. 1994, at 618 *et seq.*

Integrating Human Rights into the Law of Worldwide Organizations 315

like Germany, for example, liberty rights are no longer interpreted only as "negative freedoms" but also as "positive rights" and "institutional guarantees" that require legislation (such as competition and social rules for a "social market economy"), enabling citizens to actively use their protected freedom and preventing abuses of power.[136] Even though "globalization of freedom" has become a new fact in many markets and communication systems, legal and human rights doctrines adjust only slowly their state-centered focus to the challenges of global integration law.[137]

a) Do Human Liberty Rights Protect Individual Freedom Across Frontiers? On Freedom of Trade and "Legal Protectionism"

National and international human rights instruments – from the US Declaration of Independence of 1776 up to the Universal Declaration of Human Rights of 1948 and the Charter of Fundamental Rights of the EU adopted in December 2000[138] – recognize not only *specific* liberty rights (cf. Article 16 EU Charter: "freedom to conduct a business in accordance with Community law and national laws"), but also unalienable *general* human rights to liberty (e.g. Article 2:1 German Basic Law, Article 6 EU Charter, Article 3 UDHR). Most human rights instruments further recognize that "human dignity is inviolable" and "must be respected and protected" (Article 1 Charter of the EU). If human dignity is interpreted in accordance with the moral "categorical imperative" as requiring maximum equal liberty for personal self-development consistent with equal human rights of all others, it is only logical to construe the general human right to liberty as applying to *all areas of personal development* that are not protected through specific human rights. Some constitutional texts explicitly provide for such general rights to maximum equal liberty subject to other constitutional restraints and democratic legislation (e.g. Article 2:1 of the German Basic Law).[139] Other constitutional systems (e.g. in the USA) achieve similar results by the constitutional requirement that governmental restrictions of freedom need a legal basis in constitutional law and democratic legislation.[140] Comparative studies of constitutional democracies confirm that in "most of the English-speaking world and most of Western Europe... there is general acceptance of a principle of maximum individual freedom consistent with equal freedoms for others" subject to democratic legislation.[141]

The Preamble to the US Constitution describes its objectives as, *inter alia*, to "promote the general welfare and secure the blessings of liberty to ourselves and our posterity." In view of the logical impossibility of enumerating all areas of individual liberty protected by the Constitution, and in order to reduce the danger of interpreting human rights catalogues as excluding liberty rights not explicitly listed, the founding fathers of the US Constitution made it explicit in the Ninth Amendment of the Constitution that "the enumeration of certain rights in the Constitution

---

[136] Cf. e.g. E. Grabitz, *Freiheit und Verfassungsrecht*, 1976.
[137] Cf. H. H. Koh, The Globalization of Freedom, in *The Yale Journal of International Law* 26 (2001), 305–312.
[138] See above note 75.
[139] See above note 97.
[140] Cf. F. L. Morrison/R. E. Hudec, Judicial Protection of Individual Rights Under the Foreign Trade Laws of the United States, in Hilf/Petersmann (above note 52), 91–133, at 92 *et seq.*
[141] C. B. Macpherson, *The Life and Times of Liberal Democracy*, 1977, at 7.

shall not be construed to deny or disparage others retained by the people." In the constitutional deliberations, other law-makers considered the Ninth Amendment as unnecessary because the constitutional principle of limited government prohibited governmental restraints of freedom that were not necessary for the protection of human rights.[142] How justified the concerns of the US founding fathers had been is illustrated by the denial by US courts of any "vested right to trade with foreign nations."[143] In European law, it has likewise been claimed[144] that the lack of any explicit legal guarantee of freedom of trade with third countries should be understood as excluding the existence of such a right, without even examining whether the "freedom to conduct a business in accordance with Community law" (now explicitly recognized in Article 16 of the EU Charter of Fundamental Rights) must not be construed in conformity with the customs union principle (Article 23 EC Treaty) to the effect that freedom to conduct a business protects also freedom to import from, and export to, third countries in conformity with EC law.

The "double standard" practiced by some courts (especially in democracies with traditionally effective constitutional safeguards of economic freedom, like England and the USA) in favor of a higher degree of judicial scrutiny in the review of governmental restraints of civil and political rights compared with economic rights, is based on grounds of constitutional separation of powers and judicial self-restraint vis-à-vis economic legislation.[145] Domestic judges tend to refrain also from reviewing compliance with WTO law and its underlying economic insight that discriminatory trade restrictions are hardly ever an optimal policy instrument for promoting consumer welfare.[146] Individual rights to maximum equal liberty in all areas of personal development are more frequent in "postwar constitutions" (e.g. the German Basic Law of 1949), "postrevolutionary" human rights instruments (like the French Declaration of Human Rights and the Rights of the Citizen of 1791) and "international constitutions" (like the EC Treaty) designed to prevent the recurrence of historical experiences of "constitutional failures" (e.g. collaboration of cartelized industries in Germany with the Nazi dictatorship). One major advantage of such broad liberty guarantees is to promote freedom and rule of law by facilitating judicial review of illegal government restrictions.[147]

---

[142] See e.g. S. Sherry, The Founders' Unwritten Constitution, in *University of Chicago Law Review* 1987, 1127 *et seq.*

[143] For a discussion of this jurisprudence see Petersmann, National Constitutions and International Economic Law (note 52), at 14–15.

[144] E.g. by S. Peers, Fundamental Right or Political Whim? WTO Law and the European Court of Justice, in G. de Burca/J. Scott (eds.), *The EU and the WTO*, 2001, 111, at 129 ("no right to trade deserves to be recognized").

[145] Cf. e.g. H. J. Abraham, *Freedom and the Court*, 5th ed. 1988, at 11–37.

[146] See note 144 above and the explanation by Corden (above note 6) why the modern economic theory of optimal interventions, and its justification of freedom of trade, have nothing to do with *laissez faire* liberalism.

[147] This is so in countries like Germany where "basic rights shall bind the legislature, the executive and the judiciary as directly enforceable law" (Article 1:3 Basic Law), and "in no case may the essential content of a basic right be encroached upon" (Article 19:2 Basic Law). For, Article 19:4 of the Basic Law guarantees recourse to a court against violations by public authority of any person's right, and the possibility of direct constitutional complaints to the Federal Constitutional Court (cf. Article 93 of the Basic Law) is frequently used by individuals requesting the Court to review whether their individual liberty protected by Article 2:1 has been unnecessarily restricted by legislative or administrative measures.

Integrating Human Rights into the Law of Worldwide Organizations   317

Do human rights end at national borders? Or do they also limit *foreign policy powers* and protect human rights across frontiers? Modern national constitutions (such as Articles 23 and 24 of the German Basic Law), European Community law and also UN human rights law (e.g. Article 28 of the UDHR) confirm that "inalienable" human rights are designed to limit all government powers, regardless of whether they are exercised unilaterally by national government institutions or collectively by international organizations. The German Law on Foreign Economic Relations of 1961, for example, explicitly recognizes that the constitutional guarantees of liberty (e.g. in Articles 2, 12 and 14 of the Basic Law) protect also freedom to import and export subject to legislative restrictions that "are to be limited as to character and extent to the minimum necessary to achieve the purpose stipulated in the empowering legislation" and "are to be formulated in such a way as to interfere as little as possible with the liberty of economic activities" (Article 1 of the German Law on Foreign Economic Relations).[148] In a judgment of 1904, the US Supreme Court likewise recognized: "No one has a vested right to trade with foreign nations, which is so broad in character as to limit and restrict the power of Congress to determine what articles ... may be imported into this country and the terms upon which a right to import may be exercised."[149]

Like most other human rights, constitutional liberty rights are subject not only to legislative restrictions aimed at balancing and reconciling different human rights. They also require legislative, executive and judicial implementing measures limiting the inherent tendencies of liberties and markets to destroy themselves (e.g. through monopolies and cartels) and enabling individuals to positively exercise their freedoms. Because, for domestic policy reasons, most governments liberalize their discriminatory border restrictions preferably through *reciprocal international agreements* (e.g. in the WTO) rather than unilaterally: Should the constitutional liberty rights of citizens be construed as conferring individual rights to free movements of goods, services, capital and persons in conformity with such international liberalization agreements ratified by domestic parliaments? Should national judges review whether discriminatory border restrictions limit individual liberty in a manner inconsistent with precise and unconditional international treaty obligations of the country concerned, or whether discriminatory border restrictions impose "unnecessary" restrictions that cannot promote equal human rights of domestic citizens?

b) Interpretation of Freedoms of Trade in International Integration Law

How should universal and regional human rights guarantees of personal liberty (e.g. in Article 3 UDHR) be construed in the particular legal context of international organizations? Do "historical," "textual" and "legalist interpretations" justify the view that such guarantees traditionally end at national borders, and their instrumental function for promoting individual and social welfare through mutually beneficial

---

[148] For a detailed discussion of the constitutional and legislative protection of "freedom of trade" in Germany see Petersmann, *National Constitutions and International Economic Law* (note 52), at 22–23.

[149] *Buttfield v. Stranahan* (1904), 192 U.S. 470, 493. For a criticism of more recent lower court decisions in the US see Petersmann (note 52), at 14–17.

cooperation across frontiers cannot justify "new interpretations"? Does the particular context of worldwide organizations (such as weak parliamentary and judicial control of collective international rule-making), and the function of human rights to protect maximum equal liberty of citizens, lend support to "contextual" and "functional interpretations" that human rights should be presumed to apply to *foreign policy powers* no less than to *domestic policy powers*, and should be construed in conformity with self-imposed intergovernmental obligations to protect freedom, non-discrimination and rule of law across frontiers?

The very idea of protecting personal self-development ("human dignity") and maximum equal liberties through human rights requires protecting also mutually beneficial *transnational* cooperation among citizens, as it has been done in the jurisprudence of the EC Court of Justice protecting free movement of goods, services, persons, capital and payments as "fundamental rights" of citizens in the EU. This legal and judicial limitation of the centuries-old tradition in nation states to discriminate against foreigners, foreign goods, foreign services and foreign investments has not only extended the fundamental rights of EC citizens across frontiers. It has also enhanced their social welfare and their potential for personal self-government and self-development. Because the "freedom to conduct a business in accordance with Community law," protected by Article 16 of the EU Charter of Fundamental Rights in accordance with the jurisprudence of the EC Court,[150] must be construed in conformity with the EC Treaty guarantees for free movement of goods, services, persons, capital and payments, it was also logical for the EC Court to recognize "freedom of trade as a fundamental right," as it had been done before by some Constitutional Courts in EC member countries.[151]

The EC Treaty's customs union principle prohibits not only discriminatory tariff and non-tariff trade barriers among EC member states (cf. Articles 28–30, 90) but also vis-à-vis third countries, as specified in the customs union rules of GATT (e.g. GATT Articles II, XI, XXIV) ratified by the EC and by all EC member states.[152] International agreements ratified by the EC, like the GATT and other WTO Agreements, are legally binding on the EC and all its member states (cf. Article 300:7) with a legal status inside the EC that is, according to the EC Court, higher than autonomous "secondary law."[153] EC law must be construed consistently with international law binding on the EC, and "the Court of Justice shall ensure that in the interpretation and application of this Treaty the law is observed" (Article 220). The EC Court should therefore guard the rule of law not only with regard to the *internal dimension* of the customs union principle (Articles 28–30, 90 EC Treaty) but also vis-à-vis its precise and unconditional *external prohibitions* of tariffs and non-tariff trade barriers because these GATT and

---

[150] For references to the ECJ jurisprudence see Eeckhout (note 80).

[151] See above note 20 and Petersmann, note 143, at 17–25.

[152] On the WTO membership of the EC and EC member states see P. L. H. Van den Bossche, The European Community and the Uruguay Round Agreements, in J. Jackson/A. Sykes (eds.), *Implementing the Uruguay Round*, 1997, at 23 *et seq.* On GATT's customs union principle as a constitutional principle explicitly incorporated into the EC Treaty see E. U. Petersmann, Constitutional Principles Governing the EEC's Commercial Policy, in M. Maresceau (ed.), *The European Community's Commercial Policy After 1992: The Legal Dimension*, 1993, 21–62.

[153] See e.g. Case C-61/94, Commission v. Germany, ECR 1996 I-3989, and note 84 for further references to the jurisprudence by the EC Court.

Integrating Human Rights into the Law of Worldwide Organizations 319

WTO obligations (e.g. in GATT Articles II, III:2, XI:1) are recognized as an "integral part of the Community legal system" with a legal rank superior to EC regulations and other "secondary law."[154] Yet, the EC Court has persistently refused to apply GATT and WTO rules and dispute settlement rulings unless EC regulations were intended to implement particular WTO obligations or made reference to specific WTO provisions.[155]

The EC Court's judicial self-restraint in ensuring the GATT – and WTO-consistency of EC regulations – undermines the rule of law and democratic legitimacy of EC law. Since the 1970s, more than thirty GATT and WTO dispute settlement reports have found the EC institutions to violate GATT and WTO guarantees of freedom of trade ratified by the EC and by all national parliaments in EC member states for the benefit of EC citizens. EC citizens and their national parliaments have never granted, either in EC law or in WTO law, a mandate to EC institutions to violate precise and unconditional WTO guarantees of freedom of trade, non-discrimination and rule of law.[156] By undermining the rule of EC law and of international law, the EC institutions undermine also their own legal and democratic legitimacy as well as the liberty rights of EC citizens to exercise their human rights across frontiers in conformity with EC law and international law binding on the EC.

The success of the EC's common market law was largely due to decentralized private and judicial enforcement of the pertinent EC rules through self-interested citizens and national and European courts. The EC's proposals for more decentralized enforcement of EC competition law by citizens and national courts are presented as a new paradigm for more democratic governance in the EU.[157] Because liberal trade and competition rules serve complementary functions for promoting individual and social welfare through "a system ensuring that competition in the internal market is not distorted" (Article 3g, EC Treaty), citizens and courts should also be more actively enlisted in the decentralized enforcement of the external customs union rules of the EC. Having recognized that the EC Treaty grants individual rights to freedom of competition and freedom of trade inside the EC, national and EC courts should protect these freedoms also in the external relations of the EC against manifestly illegal restraints of trade and competition by the EC institutions. Legal and judicial protection of such freedoms has nothing to do with "*laissez faire* liberalism" and one-sided protection of "negative liberties." Freedom of competition and freedom of trade protect also "positive liberties" of participating in a mutually beneficial division of labor. Lawyers should no longer ignore the basic insight of modern economic theory that governments should correct "market failures" through domestic

---

[154] See note 153.

[155] For recent surveys and criticism of the contradictory ECJ jurisprudence concerning the EC's GATT and WTO obligations see Peers (note 144) and G. A. Zonnekeyn, The Latest on Indirect Effect of WTO Law in the EC Legal Order, in *Journal of International Economic Law* 4 (2001), 597–608.

[156] The invocation by the EC Court (in case C-149/96, Portugal v. Council, ECR 1999 I-8395) of Article 22 of the WTO's DSU (i.e. the possibility of offering compensation by the EC so as to prevent countermeasures by third countries) cannot legally justify the refusal by the EC Court to protect the rule of law inside the EC against manifest violations of EC law and WTO law that were not democratically authorized by national parliaments.

[157] Cf. C. D. Ehlermann/I. Atanasiu (eds.), *European Competition Law Annual 2000: The Modernisation of EC Anti-trust Policy*, 2001, at xviii.

interventions directly at the source of the market distortion without restricting the gains from trade. EC lawyers defending illegal and welfare-reducing trade protectionism as "realpolitik" so as not to "disarm politicians and civil servants"[158] undermine the human rights of EC citizens to protection of maximum equal liberties, rule of law and social welfare in the EC.

C. Human Rights Criteria for Interpreting the WTO's Public Interest Clauses: The Human Right to Health and Access to Medicines

The universal recognition of human rights requires construing the numerous public interest clauses in WTO law in conformity with the human rights requirement that individual freedom and non-discrimination may be restricted only to the extent necessary for protecting other equal human rights. The non-discrimination and "necessity" requirements in the "general exceptions" of WTO law (e.g. in GATT Article XX and GATS Article XIV) reflect these human rights principles. WTO law gives clear priority to the sovereign right to restrict trade if this is necessary for the protection of human rights (e.g. to life, health, food, education, a clean and sustainable environment, and social security). The recent WTO panel and Appellate Body reports on US import restrictions of shrimp (aimed at protecting endangered species of sea turtles) confirmed that import restrictions may be justifiable under WTO law for protecting human rights values not only inside the importing country but also in other countries and in the High Seas.[159]

By prohibiting discriminatory and protectionist abuses, the "general exceptions" in WTO law aim at reconciling freedom of trade with the "human rights functions" of safeguard measures restricting liberal trade. In such legal and judicial balancing processes, human rights must guide the interpretation not only of the WTO's "exceptions" and safeguard clauses, but also the interpretation of the basic WTO guarantees of freedom, non-discrimination, property rights and rule of law, which protect the corresponding human rights guarantees of individual liberty, non-discrimination, private property and access to courts. Moreover, the right of the importing country to protect the human rights of its citizens needs to be balanced with the corresponding right of the exporting country and also with the economic insight that trade restrictions are only rarely an efficient instrument for correcting "market failures" and supplying "public goods."[160]

In past GATT and WTO practice, governments have hardly ever referred to human rights in their invocations of the "general exceptions" (e.g. in GATT Article XX) and

---

[158] Peers (note 144), at 123.

[159] See the Appellate Body report of 22 October 2001 on US Import Prohibition of Certain Shrimp and Shrimp Products, DS58/AB/RW, with references to the earlier WTO panel and Appellate Body reports.

[160] In its Resolution 1999/30 of 26 August 1999 on "Trade Liberalization and Its Impact on Human Rights," the Sub-Commission (of the UN Commission on Human Rights) on the Promotion and Protection of Human Rights declared "that sanctions and negative conditionalities which directly or indirectly affect trade are not appropriate ways of promoting the integration of human rights in international economic policy and practice." See also Resolution 1998/12 on "Human Rights as the Primary Objective of Trade, Investment and Financial Policy" adopted by the UN Sub-Commission on the Promotion and Protection of Human Rights, and Resolution 1999/30 on "Trade Liberalization and Its Impact on Human Rights" adopted by the same UN Sub-Commission in 1999.

Integrating Human Rights into the Law of Worldwide Organizations 321

other safeguard clauses in GATT and WTO law, for example, when applying measures "necessary to protect public morals" or to "protect human, animal or plant life or health."[161] There appears to be no evidence, however, that past GATT practice under Article XX has been inconsistent with human rights. GATT dispute settlement jurisprudence, for instance, has never challenged the legality of non-discriminatory, "necessary" safeguard measures under GATT Article XX. Also WTO practice seems to be consistent so far with interpreting the "general exceptions" in WTO law (e.g. Article XIV GATS, Article 8 TRIPS Agreement) in conformity with human rights (such as the rights to health, food, adequate housing and education, or the right to protection of moral and material interests resulting from scientific, literary or artistic production of which one is the author).[162] The numerous "human rights clauses" in international economic agreements concluded by the EC with third countries have likewise been used only rarely for trade restrictions as a remedy for human rights violations.[163]

General Comment No. 14 (2000) on the human right to the highest attainable standard of health (Article 12 ICESCR), adopted by the UN Committee on Economic, Social and Cultural Rights in May 2000,[164] defines the right to health as an inclusive right extending not only to timely and appropriate health-care but also to the underlying determinants of health, such as availability, accessibility and affordability of health facilities, goods and services. The legal obligations of states to respect, protect, promote and fulfill this human right requires legislative implementation, judicial protection and health policy measures that, "depending on the availability of resources, ... should facilitate access to essential health facilities, goods and services in other countries, wherever possible and provide the necessary aid when required."[165] The General Comment recognizes that trade restrictions, for example,

---

[161] For a rare exception, see the submission from Mauritius in WTO document G/AG/NG/W/36/Rev.1 of 9 November 2000, which claims that Article 20 of the Agreement on Agriculture (regarding the taking into account of "non-trade concerns") should be read in conjunction with Article 11 of the ICESCR recognizing the right of everyone to adequate food.

[162] In the negotiations for the WTO Ministerial Declaration of November 2001 on access to medicines and review of Article 27:3(b) of the TRIPS Agreement, the "Africa Group," for instance, referred explicitly to human rights as criteria for interpreting the TRIPS Agreement. The WTO Secretariat also actively contributed to the discussions leading to the report of the UN High Commissioner for Human Rights on the impact of the TRIPS Agreement on human rights (E/CN.4/Sub.2/2001/13) and to Resolution 2001/21 by the UN Sub-Commission on Human Rights on "Intellectual Property and Human Rights" (E/CN.4/Sub.2/RES/2001/21 of 16 August 2001).

[163] The EC's suspension of trade preferences for Yugoslavia in November 1991, for instance, was motivated by the military hostilities in the former Yugoslavia rather than by human rights violations. In the context of the Lomé Convention, the EC reacted to human rights violations (e.g. in Rwanda) by suspension of financial and technical assistance rather than trade restrictions. The EC's Generalized System of Tariff Preferences (GSP) offers additional preferences to developing countries that respect basic ILO guarantees (such as freedom of association and minimum age for admission to employment); temporary withdrawal of GSP benefits by the EC in response to violations of human rights have been rare (e.g. in the case of Myanmar). There is thus hardly any empirical basis for the criticism (e.g. by P. Prove, Human Rights at the WTO? in Mehra, note 18, at 32) of an alleged "bias of the WTO" because "the primary entry point for human rights concerns would be as justifications for sanctions and trade conditionalities."

[164] See UN document E/C.12/2000/4, CESCR of 4 July 2000 and on the preparatory work B. C. A. Toebes, *The Right to Health as a Human Right in International Law*, 1999.

[165] General Comment No. 14 (note 157), paragraph 39.

on individual access to essential food, drugs and health services can be inconsistent with the human right to health, and that cooperation might be required also in the WTO for the implementation of the right to health.[166]

The universalization and expanding subject matters of both human rights and intellectual property law have prompted negotiations in various UN bodies and also in the WTO on the clarification of the complex interrelationships between the TRIPS Agreement and human rights. While the need for intellectual property as incentive for research and development (e.g. of new pharmaceuticals) is no longer contested, the proper balancing between the social objectives of the TRIPS Agreement (see Articles 7 and 8), its "regulatory exceptions" (e.g. in Article 6 for "parallel imports," Article 31 for "compulsory licencing," Article 40 concerning abuses of intellectual property rights), and the appropriate scope of intellectual property protection (e.g. for genetic and other living materials, rights of indigenous peoples) raises numerous controversial questions.[167] Yet, there seems to be broad agreement that the TRIPS provisions are flexible enough to permit necessary health protection measures so as to ensure access to affordable medicines to treat AIDS and other pandemics.[168]

D. Democratic Balancing of Human Rights: Are WTO Rules Adequate?

In their continuing evolution, human rights and global integration law require constant mutual balancing and concretization aimed at maximizing human rights.[169] This human rights objective can be realized only if – similar to the bargaining inside national parliaments on the balance of private and public interests in national economic and human rights legislation – international rule-making is constitutionally restrained so as to avoid human rights being "traded away."[170] Just as views on the appropriate balancing of human rights in national legislation tend to differ depending on the interests involved, there continue to be serious doubts whether the trade-oriented TRIPS provisions appropriately balance, for example, the human rights "to benefit from the protection of the moral and material interests resulting from any scientific, literary or artistic production of which he is the author" with the right of everybody "to enjoy the benefits of scientific progress and its applications" (cf. Article 15:1 ICESCR). While national and international judges tend to exercise deference vis-à-vis legislative discretion, human rights require judges to protect the essential core of human rights against unnecessary interference by national and international rule-makers.

---

[166] See e.g. paragraphs 41, 43 and 64 of the General Comment No. 14 (note 163).

[167] See e.g. G. Dutfield, *Intellectual Property Rights, Trade and Biodiversity*, 2000.

[168] See e.g. the report of the joint WHO/WTO Workshop on Differential Pricing and Financing of Essential Drugs of 8–11 April 2001 (which notes that about 95% of the WHO list of "essential drugs" are not or no longer patented, and differential pricing and international financing of essential drugs are consistent with the TRIPS Agreement).

[169] See E. Kwakwa, Intellectual Property and Human Rights, in Abbott/Cottier (note 24).

[170] For instance, the inalienable "moral rights" of authors recognized in Article 6*bis* of the Berne Convention for the Protection of Literary and Artistic Works (1896) were not mentioned in the TRIPS Agreement. See also F. J. Garcia, The Global Market and Human Rights: Trading Away the Human Rights Principle, in *Brooklyn Journal of International Law* 1999, 51.

The high minimum standards of the TRIPS Agreement for the protection of intellectual property rights are beneficial for industries in developed countries where more than 90% of patented inventions are registered. It remains to be clarified whether the relatively vague TRIPS provisions on prevention of abuses of intellectual property rights (e.g. Articles 8, 40), on the transfer and dissemination of technology (e.g. Article 7) and on the protection of traditional knowledge, genetic resources and "farmers rights" (e.g. in Article 27) are adequate for less-developed countries, which own 90% of the world's biogenetic resources and depend on importation of technology and on more effective property rights protection of their own resources. While intellectual property protection of, for example, biotechnology may be necessary for protecting human rights (including the right to food), such protection needs to be balanced with legitimate protection of, for example, traditional knowledge owned by indigenous people, "farmers rights" and the human right to health and access to medicines at affordable prices.

The report by the UN High Commissioner on the impact of the TRIPS Agreement on human rights confirms that human rights are important "context" for the interpretation of TRIPS provisions, for instance as regards "parallel imports" of low-priced medicines, "exhaustion" of intellectual property rights, compulsory licensing and "local working" requirements for patented inventions.[171] The need for balancing human rights arises also in many other areas of WTO law and practice. The right to work, for instance, may need to be protected through social adjustment assistance (as permitted under GATT Articles XVI and XIX) if the private adjustment costs impose unjust sacrifices on workers in import-competing sectors. Human and labor rights may require governments to promote labor mobility so that unemployment caused by import competition can be compensated by new employment opportunities in the export sector. The WTO rules on non-discriminatory market access may necessitate complementary competition and social rules protecting small enterprises and vulnerable groups from abuses of market power. The WTO's safeguard clauses leave broad discretion to each WTO member country for dealing with these and other trade and adjustment problems in a manner protecting human rights with due regard to the scarcity of resources. WTO bodies must exercise deference to legitimate balancing decisions by national governments and parliaments that enjoy more democratic legitimacy for the inevitable trade-offs than distant WTO bodies focusing on trade rules.

---

[171] See the report mentioned above (note 162). Cf. also e.g. Resolution No. 2/2000 on "International Trade Law" (notably Annex I on "Exhaustion of Intellectual Property Rights and Parallel Trade") adopted by the worldwide International Law Association on 29 July 2000 (cf. ILA, Report of the 69th Conference, London 2000, 18–25), and the withdrawal, in April 2001, of the lawsuit in the South African Supreme Court by thirty-nine pharmaceutical firms against the South African government in order to enforce drug patents that would have slowed the fight against AIDS. A WTO dispute settlement panel was set up in January 2001 (cf. WT/DS199) to examine a US complaint against Brazil's industrial property law that imposes a "local working" requirement according to which a patent shall be subject to compulsory licensing if the subject matter of the patent is not worked in Brazil. Brazil justified its threat of compulsory licensing for local production of generic drugs at lower costs by health policy objectives and as a means to put pressure on US and European pharmaceutical companies to lower their prices for HIV/AIDS drugs. The US later withdrew its complaint and acknowledged the right of Brazil to take measures necessary for ensuring supply of AIDS medicaments at affordable prices to patients in Brazil.

E. Need for WTO Competition and Social Rules as Necessary Complements of Human Rights

There is broad consensus today among governments and economists that market competition may lead to "market failures" (including inadequate commercial investments for medicines needed by poor people in tropical countries) that may necessitate national competition and social rules. The widespread protectionist abuses of economic and regulatory power, such as abuses of intellectual property rights for restricting and allocating markets and for blocking competing research efforts, also require *international* competition rules in the WTO to help governments to coordinate their national competition policies and to overcome domestic protectionist pressures against effective competition rules at home. The 1997 GATS Protocol on Telecommunications, for instance, already includes detailed competition rules in view of the fact that, in many countries, telecommunication services are dominated by monopolies and distorted through subsidies and restraints of competition. The liberalization of many other services sectors (like road, rail, air and maritime transports) will likewise remain impossible without complementary limitations on monopolies and restraints of competition. Many international restraints of competition are particularly harmful for less-developed countries (e.g. in case of export cartels, international shipping and air transport cartels charging discriminatory prices on routes to developing countries). As sectoral competition rules risk being abused by special interest groups, the proposals for limiting cartel agreements, other anticompetitive business practices and abuses of intellectual property rights through worldwide WTO minimum standards for undistorted competition and transnational cooperation among competition authorities are of constitutional significance for protection of freedom, non-discrimination and mutually beneficial division of labor across frontiers.[172]

F. Need for More Democratic Rule-Making in Worldwide Organizations

Secretive and producer-driven intergovernmental rule-making procedures in specialized international organizations, including the WTO and standard-setting practices in UN Specialized Agencies (like FAO and ITU), may be inconsistent with the human rights to democratic participation in the exercise of government powers and to transparent decision-making maximizing equal human rights.[173] In order to promote more effective democratic and parliamentary control of trade policy-making, transparency and more responsible *deliberative democracy* in the trade policy area, the International Law Association has recommended the establishment of an advisory WTO parliamentary committee and of an advisory WTO civil society committee. Citizens and NGOs could thus be represented in a more balanced manner so as to make the one-sided influence of "producer interests" on trade policy-making processes more accountable vis-à-vis representatives of consumer interests and other "public interests."[174] Because more than 110 WTO member countries

---

[172] Cf. E. U. Petersmann (note 32).

[173] Cf. E. U. Petersmann, From "Negative" to "Positive" Integration (note 54).

[174] Cf. the resolution by the International Law Association mentioned in note 171.

Integrating Human Rights into the Law of Worldwide Organizations

ratified the ICESCR, and almost all of them ratified the UN Covenant on Civil and Political Rights and the UN Convention on the Rights of the Child, the time has also come for express references – in WTO Ministerial Declarations and in WTO jurisprudence – to the promotion and protection of human rights so as to enhance a more coherent constitutional discourse and more general awareness of the complementary functions of human rights and of global integration law. Such WTO references to human rights could also help other WTO bodies (such as the WTO's Trade Policy Review Mechanism) to contribute so the needed integration and "constitutionalization" of the so far fragmented human rights treaties and sectoral integration agreements.

Conclusion: Need for Multi-Level Constitutionalism Protecting Human Rights More Effectively

The universal recognition and protection of inalienable human rights at national, regional and worldwide levels requires a new human rights culture and a citizen-oriented national and international constitutional framework different from the previously prevailing state-centered conceptions and functionalism. In Europe, the emergence of "multi-level governance" has led to "multi-level constitutionalism"[175] and "divided power systems" that have succeeded in overcoming Europe's history of periodic wars and of "constitutional failures" of nation-states to protect human rights and peaceful division of labor across frontiers. Just as *within* federal states "the federal and state governments are in fact but different agents and trustees of the people, instituted with different powers, and designated for different purposes,"[176] international law and international organizations must be understood as parts of the constitutional limitations on abuses of foreign policy powers necessary for protecting human rights more effectively.[177] National constitutional law and human rights cannot achieve their objectives unless they are supplemented by *international constitutional law* and by effective protection of human rights in the economy no less than in the polity.[178]

Promotion and protection of human rights is not only the task of national and international human rights law and of specialized human rights institutions. Also the law of worldwide and regional organizations (like UN law, WTO law and EU law) serves "constitutional functions" for protecting freedom, non-discrimination, rule of law and social welfare across national frontiers. Historical experience confirms that, without such multilateral rules, national parliaments can neither effectively supervise foreign policies among 200 sovereign states nor ensure that foreign policy decisions respect human rights and rule of law not only at home but also across frontiers. European and global integration law further demonstrate that the different layers of national and international constitutional rules need to be supplemented

---

[175] Cf. I. Pernice, Multilevel Constitutionalism and the Treaty of Amsterdam: European Constitution-Making Revisited? In *Common Market Law Review* 36 (1999), 703–750.

[176] A. Hamilton, Federalist No. 46, in Hamilton et alia, *The Federalist Papers*, 1787/88.

[177] On these "constitutional functions" of international law and international organizations for the protection of human rights see Petersmann (above notes 44 and 52).

[178] See also Petersmann, Constitutionalism, International Law and "We the Citizens of the United Nations," in *Liber Amicorum H. Steinberger*, 2001.

by corresponding national and international rule-making, executive and judicial processes that must be subject to effective democratic controls and constitutional safeguards of "subsidiarity," "necessity" and "proportionality" of regulatory limitations of human rights (cf. Article 5 EC Treaty).

As described already by Kant more than 200 years ago, human rights and democracy require *national* as well as *international constitutionalism*. The democratic legitimacy of the various levels of government derives from respect for human rights and from democratic participation of citizens in the exercise of national and international government powers. Just as national citizenship and European Union citizenship are complementary (cf. Article 12 EC Treaty), citizens must become recognized also as legal subjects of international law and international organizations. Their democratic participation and more effective representation in international organizations requires far-reaching constitutional reforms of the state-centered international legal system so as to enable, for example, "UN citizens" and "WTO citizens" to invoke international guarantees of freedom before domestic courts and participate more actively in parliamentary and civil society institutions at national and international levels.

The German Constitutional Court, for example, has rightly interpreted the creation of the European Central Bank as an act that redefines the guarantee of private property in money protected by the German Constitution (Article 14) as a fundamental right.[179] From such a human rights perspective, the state-centered interpretation of the Agreement establishing the IMF as an exclusively monetary agreement on the rights and obligations of governments in the field of monetary policy, without legal relevance for the human rights obligations of governments and of UN agencies, appears too one-sided.[180] International guarantees of freedom, non-discrimination and rule of law, such as the UN guarantees of human rights and the WTO guarantees of liberal trade and property rights, should be seen as part of the domestic constitutional systems of WTO members that need be protected by domestic courts so as to safeguard human rights across frontiers. Human rights law requires that the delegation of regulatory powers to national, regional and worldwide institutions must always remain constitutionally limited. Democratic sovereignty remains, as proclaimed in the Preamble to the UN Charter, with "We the Peoples of the United Nations." The protection of human dignity and of "individual sovereignty" through human rights and global integration law remains the biggest constitutional challenge of law and governance in the 21st century at all national and international levels of the exercise of governmental and private power.

---

[179] German Constitutional Court judgment of 31 March 1998, in *Bundesverfassungsgericht* 97, 350.

[180] The presentation by the IMF legal adviser F. Gianviti, in the above-mentioned "day of general discussion" at the Office of the High Commissioner for Human Rights on 7 May 2001, of the IMF as an exclusively monetary institution – without legal mandate for promoting human rights and without legal obligations under UN human rights treaties – was rightly criticized by human rights organizations for disregarding the IMF obligations under the general human rights law (cf. Skogly, note 111, e.g. at 192 *et seq.*) as well as the "human rights functions" of IMF law (e.g. for the protection of property rights in money).

Index

AB. *See* Appellate Body
Africa, 174–175, 274, 321, 323
Agriculture Agreement (WTO), 155, 235
AIDS crisis, 280, 323
aims and effects theory
  AB and, 87, 91–92
  Article III and, 87, 102
  less favourable treatment and, 91–92
  likeness and, 87
  protectionism and, 91–92
  testing and, 87, 190
alcoholic beverages, 54, 200, 206, 207, 215. *See*
  Japan-Alcohol case; *specific cases*
amicus curiae briefs, 236, 237–238, 239, 240, 248,
  249, 250
Annan, Kofi, 308
Antidumping Agreement, 66, 225
  DSU and, 225, 226
  national authorities and, 230
  reasonableness test and, 255
  SPS Agreement and, 229
Appellate Body (AB), 5, 6–7, 30, 35, 116, 171–172,
  226–227, 234
  accordion approach and, 72
  administrative support, 239
  aims and effects, 87, 91–92. *See* aims and effects
  theory
  amicus curiae briefs and, 236, 237–238, 239, 248,
  249, 250
  appropriate role of, 163
  Article III and, 81–82, 96, 221. *See* Article III
  (GATT)
  balancing and, 50. *See* balancing
  Border Tax Adjustment and, 16, 210
  burden of proof and, 118, 129, 196,
  254–255
  Codex and, 39–40. *See* Codex Alimentarius
  Commission
  competitive relationship and, 82
  conflict and. *See* Dispute Settlement
  Understanding; *specific decisions*

consistency and, 43–44, 51. *See* consistency
  requirement
effects test and, 17
error in law and, 95
expert advice, 7, 237, 249. *See* expert advice
GATT and, 3, 16
Havana Conference, 221
health and, 82, 233–234. *See* health and safety
  measures; *specific cases*
hierarchy of objectives, 116
implicit obligation and, 148
judicial minimalism, 97
legitimation strategies, 96
less favourable treatment and, 214. *See* less
  favourable treatment
likeness and, 82, 86–87, 94. *See* like products
minimalist approach, 185, 186
national treatment and, 3. *See* national treatment
  principle
NGOs and, 240, 241
non-trade policy and,
panel decisions and, 128, 145, 205, 218–219, 249.
  See specific panels
precautionary principle, 106
protectionism and. *See* protectionism
purpose review, 206. *See specific cases*
risk and, 125, 126, 264. *See also* risk
  assessment
rule-exception analysis, 120
scientific evidence. *See* scientific evidence
Secretariat, 239
SPS and. *See* SPS Agreement
standard of review in, 226
TBT and. *See* TBT Agreement
three-stage structure, 220
WTO and, 5, 238–239
See also specific decisions, topics
apples. *See Japan-Varietals* case
Argentina-Bovine Hides/Leather case,
  218–219
Argentina-Footwear case, 242

327

Article III (GATT), 6, 86
  AB and, 81–82, 96, 221. *See also* Appellate Body; *specific decisions*
  aims and effects and, 87, 102
  Article XX and, 52, 60, 69, 81, 101, 195–196, 201, 203, 204, 209, 231. *See also* Article XX (GATT)
  balancing and, 50, 52, 53
  burden of proof and, 118, 129, 196
  competitive relationship and, 204
  conservation and, 27
  EC cross-appeal, 89
  effects test, 17
  efficacy principle, 201
  efficiency and, 198
  GATT and, 71, 190, 231
  GPA and, 3–4
  internal regulations, 56
  invalidation under, 217–218
  Kaldor-Hicks efficiency and, 198–199
  less favourable treatment and, 18–19, 89–90, 91, 214
  likeness and, 22, 96, 191, 196, 217–218
  market-based approach, 81–82. *See also* market access; protectionism
  National Treatment standard, 3, 85, 90–91, 93, 231
  natural resources and, 27
  no less favorable requirement, 210
  non-discrimination and, 21
  origin-neutral measures, 201–202
  origin-specific measures, 202
  PPM issues, 56, 58, 61. *See also* PPMs
  protectionism and, 6, 17, 82, 89–90, 194, 197, 198, 216, 220, 221, 222. *See also* protectionism
  regulatory purpose and, 190, 222–223
  scope of, 15, 55, 89
  Section 1 of, 193, 197, 216–217
  Section 2 of, 190, 216, 217–218, 219, 220, 221, 222
  Section 4 of, 190, 191–192, 193, 209, 214, 218, 223
  SPS and, 69. *See* SPS Agreement
  strict scrutiny test, 54
  subjective intent and, 15
  TBT Agreement and, 19, 71, 103. *See* TBT Agreement
Article XI (GATT), 2–3, 201
  Article XX and, 60, 204
  PPM issue, 61
  strict scrutiny test, 54
Article XX (GATT), 11, 20, 28, 52, 70–71, 111, 203, 204
  Article III and, 52, 60, 81, 195–196, 201, 203, 204, 209, 231
  Article XI and, 60, 204
  ascertainability of purpose, 201
  balancing and, 30, 51
  burden of proof and, 196

chapeau of, 26, 31, 42, 44, 45, 51, 138, 204
conflicts and, 69. *See also* DSU
conservation and, 27
consistency and, 45
discrimination and, 26, 28
disguised restriction language, 204
dispute settlement and, 5, 151–152
effet utile and, 52
efficacy and, 201
environment and, 28, 137
equivalency requirement, 42
exceptions and, 137, 204
GATT and, 44, 58, 71
general operative clause, 113
health policy and, 34, 93
human rights and, 320, 321
jurisprudence and, 11
justificatory burden, 100
less trade-restrictive alternative, 114–115
likeness and, 22, 222–223
market-based approach, 82
MFN and, 27–28
necessity and, 23. *See* necessity tests
non-discrimination and, 21
operative language of, 21
origin-neutral measures, 201–202
origin-specific measure, 203
PPM and, 58
precautionary principle, 48
primary work of, 204
proportionality test, 25
protectionism and, 20, 34, 108. *See also* protectionism
regulatory purpose, 222–223
SPS and, 6, 11, 28, 44, 45, 53, 68, 134, 140, 141, 151–152, 156. *See also* SPS Agreement
TBT Agreement and, 11, 19, 28, 106. *See also* TBT Agreement
trade liberalisation and, 116
trade-off decisions and, 152
trade sanctions and, 202
See also specific decisions, topics
asbestos. *See EC-Asbestos* case
Atik, Jeffery, 166
Australia-Salmon case, 6, 32, 135, 136, 143, 169, 179, 184, 206, 207, 264, 269
  AB and, 30
  balancing and, 133
  Canada and, 135, 180
  internal inconsistency, 43–44
  level of protection, 141–143
  necessity test and, 149, 150
  Norway and, 180
  protectionism and, 169
  QP86A and, 135
  risk assessment and, 161

Index

SPS Agreement and, 21
zero-risk policy, 267
automobiles, 64, 242

balancing, 49, 137
   Article III and, 50, 52, 53
   Article XX and, 30, 51
   Asbestos case and, 49
   Beef case and, 49, 115
   GATT and, 49
   necessity testing, 50
   non-trade values, 133
   objections to, 49
   Salmon case and, 133
Barataria case, 194–195, 205, 211
beef. *See EC-Hormones* case; *Korea-Beef* case
   decisions
beer, 54. *See* alcoholic beverages
Berne Convention, 80, 251
Biodiversity Convention, 13
Biosafety Protocol, 13
biotechnology, 323
border measures, 14, 78–79, 173
Border Tax Adjustment, 16–17, 57, 81, 92, 210
   AB and, 16, 210
   Alcohol case and, 92
   categories of, 212–213
   competitive relation and, 210
   criteria in, 89, 210, 211
   likeness and, 94
Brazil-Desiccated Coconut case, 64–65
Bretton-Woods Agreements, 272, 288, 290
BSE. *See* Mad Cow scare
burden of proof, 118, 129, 196, 254–255

Canada, 61–62, 169
   Asbestos case and, 77, 80, 84, 85, 88, 106, 111
   Hormone case and, 179
   Salmon case and, 135, 180
   TBT claims and, 239–242
Canada-Aircraft case, 249
Canada-Periodicals case, 63, 81, 91, 95, 206, 207, 208, 262
cancer, 174, 267. *See also EC-Asbestos* case
Cantor, Mickey, 176
cattle. *See EC-Hormones* case; *Korea-Beef* decisions
Charter of Fundamental Rights of the European Union, 282, 286
Chevron deference, 224, 230
Chile-Alcohol case, 81, 206, 207, 208, 209
cholera, 174–175
chrysotile. *See EC-Asbestos* case
Clinton administration, 176

Coca-Cola, 165
Codex Alimentarius Commission, 35, 36, 164, 165, 245, 263
   AB and, 36, 39–40
   meetings of, 164, 165
   NGOs and,
   Rules of Procedure, 36
   Standards of, 36, 38, 39, 165
   TBT Agreement, 39
coherence, 102
collective action problem, 195
common law tradition, 278
Community Charter of the Fundamental Social Rights of Workers, 283
comparative advantage, 163
competitive relationships, 213
   Article III and, 204
   Border Tax Adjustment and, 210
   cross-elasticity of demand, 17
   directly competitive products, 220, 239
   human rights and, 305, 324
   likeness and, 210, 222, 231–232. *See also* like products
   physical properties and, 212
   protectionism and, 200. *See also* protectionism
   toxicity and, 233
   unreasonable restraints and, 307
conflict, definition of, 65
consistency requirement, 102, 123
   AB and, 51
   GATT and, 45
   Hormone case and, 45, 184
   human rights and, 305
   scientific evidence and, 258–259, 268
   SPS and, 169
constitutionalism, 292
consumer choice, 232
   asbestos and, 212, 232
   protectionist purpose, 196
   safety and, 182
   tastes and, 232
   trade liberalization and, 182
   welfare rights and, 305
Convention of the Elimination of All Forms of Discrimination of Women (UN), 300
Convention of the Rights of the Child (UN), 300
corporations, 165, 246. *See specific corporations*
cost-benefit analysis, 23, 28–29, 137, 267
Cotonou Agreement, 273
Croley, Steven P., 227
cross-elasticity, 17
cumulative application, 63
customs classification, 92
Customs Co-operation Council, 241
Customs Valuation Agreement, 235, 241

Index

Davey, W. T., 5
de novo review, 255
deadweight losses, 163
deferential tests, 255
Delaney Clause, 174
developing countries, 238, 282–283,
   322–323
  agriculture and, 186
  conditions in, 298
  Global Compact and, 308, 309
  human rights and, 277–278, 286–287. *See* human
   rights
  liberalization and, 324
  poverty and, 277–278, 304
  scarce resources and, 303–304
  See specific countries
dioxin, 170–171
discrimination, 27–28, 90
  Article XX and, 26, 28
  GATT and, 78–79
  health policies and, 4
  against imports, 78–79
  market access and, 42
  National Treatment, 87
  non-discrimination obligation, 4, 14, 259
  protectionism and. *See* protectionism
  SPS and, 20, 21. *See also* SPS Agreement
  See specific products, decisions
Dispute Settlement Understanding (DSU), 58, 66,
   151–152, 158, 218, 225–226, 236–237, 248,
   249
  AB and. *See* Appellate Body
  amici curiae and, 236, 248, 249
  Antidumping Agreement and, 225, 226
  Appendix 2 of, 226–227
  Article 11 of, 225–226, 250
  Article 13 of, 238, 256
  expert advice and, 235, 236, 237, 243. *See also*
   expert advice
  health and safety disputes, 228
  objective assessment and, 227. *See also* scientific
   evidence
  panels and, 225–226, 235, 248, 249. *See specific*
   cases
  protectionism and, 222. *See also* protectionism
  Rules of Conduct, 244, 256
  SPS and, 229
  time limits, 237
  tribunals and, 222
  WTO and, 133, 153, 158, 224, 225, 235, 248, 249,
   285
divided-power systems, 8
Doha statement, 167
Domestic Regulation of Goods (WTO), 9
dormant commerce clause, 202–203
DSU. *See* Dispute Settlement Understanding

dubio mitius principle, 121
Dunoff, J. L., 6

EC-Asbestos case, 5, 25, 33–34, 56–57, 68, 72, 73, 151,
   190, 205, 209, 216, 239–242
  AB and, 6–7, 16, 18, 22, 24, 82
  aims and effects test, 94
  alternative measures, 16, 51
  Article III and, 80–81, 82, 83
  Article XX and, 81
  balancing and, 49
  Canada and, 77, 80, 88, 106, 111
  cancer and, 92–93
  chrysotile and, 80, 88, 106, 107, 112, 192,
   231
  composition analysis, 61–62, 83
  consumer choice, 212, 232
  EC and, 89, 107–108
  EPA and, 232–233
  evidence and, 253. *See also* scientific evidence
  France and, 30, 80–81, 84, 109–110, 211
  Hormones case and, 231
  ILO and, 110–111
  international standards and, 110
  less favourable treatment and, 102
  likeness and, 96–97, 191–192
  margin of appreciation and, 117
  period of panel, 237
  PPM regulations and, 57
  standard of review analysis, 233
  substitution and, 106, 109, 112, 192, 231
  TBT Agreement and, 98, 104
  WHO and, 83, 110–111
  WTC and, 84, 231
EC-Bananas case, 87, 192, 193, 220
EC-Hormones case, 5, 13, 22, 35, 43, 69, 78, 118–128,
   184, 206, 228–229, 230, 245, 247, 250, 251, 265
  1995 conference on, 132
  AB and, 39, 40
  Asbestos case and, 231
  Australia and, 180
  Beef decisions and, 6. *See Korea-Beef* decisions
  burden of proof and, 119
  Canada and, 179
  carcinogens and, 267
  cattle and, 262
  consistency and, 184
  EC and, 132, 184
  experts and, 244
  growth hormones, 184
  Lucier opinion, 248, 263, 266
  naturally occurring, 131
  Precautionary Principle, 46, 106
  protectionism and, 262
  risk assessment and, 107, 185
  SPS Agreement and, 20, 63, 130, 132

Index

331

United States and, 44, 119, 179
Varietals case and, 161
warning signals, 44–45
zero-risk policy, 267
EC-Sardines case, 38, 39–40, 62, 180
ECHR. *See* European Convention on Human Rights
effectiveness, principle of, 14, 63, 151–152
effects test, 17
efficiency, of markets, 163, 164
embedded liberalism model, 169, 172
    GATT and, 170
    harmonization and, 172
    SPS Agreement and, 170
end-uses, 94–95
environment, 77–78, 104, 171, 186
    Article XX and, 28, 137
    Barataria example, 195
    ecological risks, 168
    plastic jugs example, 194–195
    pollution taxes, 86
    standards and, 86, 232–233
    TBT Agreement and, 261
Environmental Protection Agency (EPA), 232–233
equal rights, 306–307
equivalence proposition, 2
estrogen, 121, 262
European Central Bank, 326
European Communities (EC) Treaty, 5, 38, 40, 47,
    62, 107–108, 261, 273, 282
    Common Agricultural Policy, 186
    common market and, 279–280
    customs union principle, 318
    GSP and, 321
    harmonization and, 38
    human rights and, 318
    ICJ and, 275, 285, 296, 302, 318–319
    integration and, 271, 274, 279–280, 282, 284
    international organizations and, 298–299
    social rights and, 279–280
    SPS Agreement and, 33
    TBT Agreement and, 38
    See also specific topics, cases
European Convention on Human Rights (ECHR),
    275, 276, 282, 283, 298–299, 300, 302
European Council of Agricultural Ministers, 262
European Economic Area, 282–283
European Social Charter, 283, 302
expert advice, 248
    AB and, 7, 249
    appointments for, 242, 247
    conflicting opinions, 231, 252, 254
    costs of, 243
    de facto binding, 251
    dispute settlement and, 235. *See also* DSU
    Hormones case and, 244
    information and, 248

legal conclusions and, 251
    minority opinions, 253–254
    neutrality of, 245
    number of experts, 245
    Permanent Group, 235, 241, 251
    review groups, 236
    scientists and, 205, 253–254. *See* scientific
        evidence
    SPS and, 243, 244–245
    TBT and, 243
    tribunal within tribunal, 237
    Varietals dispute and, 244
    WTO and, 7
    See also specific cases

fail-safe mechanism, 216
failure-free market, 199
Farber, Daniel, 186
fishing, 91, 174–175, 202–203, 269
    See also Australia-Salmon case; *EC-Sardines* case
Food and Agricultural Organization (FAO), 311
foot and mouth disease, 132
France, 61, 80
    asbestos ban. *See EC-Asbestos* case
    Canada and, 84, 85
    level of protection, 24
    National Treatment standard, 80
    regulatory purpose and, 212
Free Trade Area of the Americas (FTAA), 273
fumigation, 159

Gabcikovo-Nagymaros case, 67
Garcia, E., 5–6
GATS. *See* General Agreement on Trade in Services,
    267
GATT. *See* General Agreement on Tariffs and Trade,
    267
General Agreement on Tariffs and Trade (GATT), 1,
    33, 61, 72, 272
    AB and, 3, 16. *See* Appellate Body; *specific
        decisions*
    antiprotection principle, 100
    Article I, 27, 259
    Article II, 56, 201
    Article III. *See* Article III (GATT)
    Article VI, 72. *See also* Antidumping Agreement
    Article X, 201
    Article XI, 56
    Article XIV, 72
    Article XX. *See* Article XX (GATT)
    Article XXI, 137
    balancing test, 49
    as commercial treaty, 200
    consistency requirement, 45
    discrimination and, 14, 78, 79, 259. *See*
        discrimination

332 Index

General Agreement on Tariffs and Trade (*cont.*)
dispute resolution, 183. *See* DSU
as economic treaty, 200
efficiency and, 198
embedded liberalism model, 170
on equivalence, 42
evolution of, 14
fragmentation and, 11
free trade and, 170
incomplete contracts, 2
international standards, 40
laissez-regler aspects of, 60
legal framework of, 2, 4, 78
likeness and, 85. *See* likeness
market access rules, 55–56
MFN principle and, 12, 14, 259
national standards, 11, 13
National Treatment standard, 3, 12, 14, 79, 80
necessity and, 22, 134. *See* necessity testing
negative integration, 4–5
negative regulation model, 173
non-trade values, 136
payoffs and, 2
PPM and, 54
precautionary principle, 48
protectionism and, 9. *See* protectionism
SPS and, 60, 66, 68, 69, 74, 156. *See* SPS Agreement
Standards Code, 12, 156, 259
TBT and, 9, 60, 66, 71, 75, 99, 106. *See* TBT Agreement
Tokyo Round, 259
WTO and, 61, 74, 75, 163
See also specific articles, decisions, topics
General Agreement on Trade in Services (GATs), 1, 61, 87
National Treatment provisions, 87
necessity tests, 138
Protocol on Telecommunications, 324
General Foods, 165
Generalized System of Tariff Preferences (GSP), 321
genetic resources, 323
genetically modified organisms (GMOs), 78, 132
Geneva Convention, 283
German Constitutional Court, 326
German Law on Foreign Economic Relations, 317
Global Compact, 271
Global Integration Law, 271, 272
globalization, 96, 173, 307–308
dehumanising effects of, 310
foreign policy, 275
human rights, 272, 275, 280
integration paradigm, 273–274
international law, 275
GMOs. *See* genetically modified organisms
Great Depression, 186

green labelling requirements, 25
GSP. *See* Generalized System of Tariff Preferences
Guatemala-Cement decision, 66

HAP. *See* human, animal, or plant life or health
harmonization, 124
direction of, 174
embedded liberalism model, 172
international standards and, 120, 182
SPS measures and, 157, 172, 174
health and safety measures, 79, 104, 106, 109, 253
AB and, 233–234
constraints on, 1
discrimination and, 4
DSU and, 228
environment and, 2
HAP and, 133, 134, 138, 141
human rights and, 8, 320
liberalization and, 1
like product analysis and, 231–232, 233
risk and, 107, 231–232
trade-off decisions, 152
WTO agreement, 1
See also specific topics, organizations, decisions
Hobbes, Thomas, 277
honey, 165
hormones. *See EC-Hormones* decision; *Korea-Beef* decisions
Howse, R., 5, 191, 216
Hudec, R. E., 7, 221, 234
human, animal or plant (HAP) life or health, 133, 134, 138, 141
human rights, 271, 280, 287, 315
antimarket bias and, 280
Article XX and, 320, 321
common market and, 296
competition and, 305, 324
consumer welfare and, 305
democratic balancing of, 322
developing countries and, 277–278, 286–287
economic integration and, 303
enforcement problems, 277
European Law and, 287
health and, 8, 320
ICESCR and, 289
IJC and, 64, 238, 279, 285, 286, 318
IMF and, 326
inalienable rights and, 294
indivisibility of, 298
information problem, 277
integration and, 272, 280, 281, 284, 312
international law and, 284, 291
international organizations and, 276, 279, 289
liberty rights and, 314
medicines and, 320
multi-level constitutionalism, 325

Index

333

NGOs and, 288, 311
protectionism and, 308
rule of law and, 293
scarcity problems and, 277
subsidiarity principle,
TRIPS and, 322
UN and, 274, 280, 311
Universal Declaration, 272, 284–285, 286, 288, 300
value problem, 294
Vienna Convention and, 288
WTO and, 312, 313
Hungary, 180

ICESCR. *See* International Covenant on Economic Social and Cultural Rights
ICJ. *See* International Court of Justice
ILO. *See* International Labor Organization
IMF. *See* International Monetary Fund
in dubio mitius rule, 124
indeterminacy thesis, 185
India-Quantitative Restrictions case, 242
indispensability, 115
Indonesia-Automobiles case, 64
information problem, 277
informational asymmetry, 3
integration, 271, 272, 284
intellectual property. *See* TRIPs; WIPO
Inter-American Charter of Democracy, 273
International Bovine Meat Agreement, 13
International Court of Justice (ICJ), 64, 238, 275, 279, 285, 286, 296, 302, 318
International Covenant on Economic, Social and Cultural Rights (ICESCR), 288, 289, 309–310, 324–325
International Diary Agreement, 13, 165
international functionalism, 273–274
International Labor Organization (ILO), 108–111, 286–287, 310, 311
international law
fragmentation of, 256
globalization and, 275
human rights and, 284, 291
precautionary principle, 122
WTO and, 47
International Law Association, 324
International Monetary Fund (IMF), 238, 242, 272, 310, 326
expert review and, 251
human rights, 326
International Office for Epizootics (OIE), 35, 164, 244
EC Treaty and, 298–299
human rights and, 276, 279, 289
international organizations and, 256
United States and, 10

International Plant Protection Convention (IPPC), 35
international standards, 71, 102, 123–124
Appellate Body and, 39. *See specific cases*
asbestos and, 110. *See EC-Asbestos* case
conformity with, 34
definition of, 35
domestic regulations and, 80
GATT and, 40
harmonization and, 120, 182
national measures and, 120
protection, 32, 35
scientific evidence and, 32
SPS and, 37, 123, 164
substantive standards, 172
TBT and, 38, 39, 110
technical regulations, 110
International Tribunal on the Law of the Sea, 238
Internet, 308
Italian Agricultural Machinery case, 197

Jackson, J. H., 163, 227
Janus problem, 293
Japan-Agricultural Products case, 48, 171, 265
Japan-Alcoholic Beverages case, 44, 86, 87, 203, 206, 208, 209, 217–218
aim and effects, 81, 87
Article III and, 3, 15, 128, 216, 218
Article XX and, 203
Border Tax Adjustment and, 92
likeness and, 88, 204
market-based criteria and, 89
national treatment and, 3
origin-neutral measure and, 219
protectionism and, 89, 207, 208, 216
Japan-Varietals case, 171–172, 173, 184, 249, 265
AB and, 6, 161
background to, 154
Brazil and, 180
evidentiary basis, 162
experts and, 244, 247, 249
Hormones decision and, 161
international trade law and, 153
panel report, 158, 159
risk assessments and, 158, 185
scientific evidence and, 158, 253
SPS Agreement and, 6, 153, 249
testing requirements and, 155, 159
United States and, 160, 171–172
VTR and, 160, 161, 180, 186
judicial minimalism, 97

Kaldor-Hicks efficiency, 198–199
Kant, Immanuel, 277, 287, 294, 302, 313, 326
Kennedy Round, 11
Korea-Dairy case, 64

Korea-Taxes on Alcoholic Beverages case, 209
Korea-Various Measures on Beef decisions, 24, 25, 33, 51, 53, 72, 113, 151
    AB and, 17, 18, 22
    alternative measures, 51
    balancing test and, 49, 115
    consistency requirement, 45
    hormones. *See EC-Hormones* case
    necessity tests and, 28–29, 50, 51, 114, 115, 150
    non-fulfilment and, 28–29
    protectionism and, 103
Kosovo crisis, 273
Kraft Inc., 165

labelling, 25, 74, 78
laissez-faire capitalism, 170
least-trade-restrictive alternative, 50, 51, 137, 139
Lerner theorem, 2
less favourable treatment, 16, 17
    aims and effects analysis, 91–92
    Article III, 18–19, 89–90, 91, 214
    asbestos ban and, 102. *See EC-Asbestos* case
    like products and, 214
    protection and, 90, 97
    regulatory purpose and, 195
lex posterior principle, 65, 67
lex specialis principle, 65, 67
liability laws, 212
liberalization, 1, 134, 183, 273
    Article XX and, 116
    consumer safety and, 182
    developing countries and, 324
    health-based measures and, 1
    integration and, 272
liberty, paradox of, 289
like products, 16, 56, 102
    AB and, 82, 86–87, 94, 210
    aims and effects, 86–87, 94
    antiprotectionism and, 89–90
    Article III and, 96, 191, 196, 217–218, 219
    Article XX and, 222–223
    asbestos and. *See EC-Asbestos* case
    Border Tax Adjustment criteria, 94
    competitive relationships and, 92, 210, 222, 231–232
    cross-elasticity and, 89–90
    definition of, 72, 85–86, 87, 93, 94, 191
    economic approach to, 96–97
    end uses and, 93, 94–95
    fail-safe mechanism and, 216
    health and safety measures, 231–232, 233
    Japan-Alcohol and, 88
    jugs vs. cartons example, 195
    less favourable treatment and, 214
    market-based criteria and, 86–87, 88
    metaphor and, 87

origin-neutral measures, 202
physical characteristics and, 96, 213, 214
prima facie case of, 95
protectionism and, 86–87, 89, 217
regulatory purpose, 190, 213, 215, 223
TBT Agreement and, 72
testing and, 79
Lockean dilemma, 293
Lome Convention, 87, 321
lotus eaters, 153
Lucier opinion, 263, 266, 268

Mad Cow scare, 260
Marceau, G., 4
market access, 42, 81–82, 102, 281, 283. *See also* protectionism
Marrakesh Agreement, 9, 10, 13, 225
means-end tests, 137
medicines, 320
methyl bromide, 155
MFN. *See* most-favored-nation principle
milk, 64, 194
Mississippi wine tax, 206
Monsanto Inc., 165
most-favoured-nation principle (MFN), 14, 19, 78–79, 101, 259
multi-level governance, 8
multilateral organization (MTO), 10
multinationals, 246

national sovereignty, 258
national treatment principle, 137
    AB and, 3
    Article III and, 3
    discrimination and, 16, 87
    GATS and, 87
    GATT and, 3, 14
    protection and, 3
    rules and, 137
    taxation and, 91
    TBT Agreement and, 101
NATO, 273
natural resources, 138
necessity testing, 22
necessity testing, 151–152
    Article XX and, 23, 25, 30, 51–52, 72, 102, 105, 134, 138, 140, 150
    Article XXI and, 137
    balancing test, 50, 54
    cost-benefit analysis, 28–29
    discrimination and, 27–28
    GATS and, 138
    GATT and, 22, 134
    jurisprudence and, 150
    Korea-Beef and, 28–29, 50, 51, 150
    non-trade values, 140

Index

335

problems with, 138
protectionism and, 149
reasonably available requirement, 139
Salmon case, 149
SPS Agreement and, 25, 29, 54, 134, 140, 149, 150
syntactics and, 140
TBT Agreement and, 25, 72
trade values and, 139
two strands of, 152
Uruguay Round and, 28–29
WTO and, 23, 136
zero-risk approach, 146
negative integration contract, 2
New International Economic Order, 307
New Zealand, 180
NGO. *See* non-governmental organizations
no less favorable requirement, 210
non-governmental organizations (NGOs), 77–78, 98, 165, 174, 235, 238, 240, 241, 246, 308, 309, 311
non-trade values, 133
Norway, 180

objective assessment, 121, 206, 225, 227, 228, 229, 230, 255
Office of International Epizootics (OIE), 171, 245
OIE. *See* Office of International Epizootics
open trade, 7
origin-specific measures, 198, 215
   Article III and, 202
   Article XX and, 202, 203
   Japan-Alcohol and, 219
   likeness and, 202
   protection and, 219
Ostry, Sylvia, 173
outcome-determinative discretion, 139

Palmeter, D., 6
parasites, 203
Pauwelyn, J., 7
PCG fibers, 210, 211, 212–213
Permanent Group of Experts (PGE), 235, 241, 251
Peru, 38, 40
pests, 155, 172
Petersmann, E. U., 8
PGE. *See* Permanent Group of Experts
pharmaceuticals, 1
Philippines, 242
physical properties, 193
Pigovian taxes, 86
Plant Protection Law (Japan), 154–155
plastic jugs example, 194–195
political models, 169
pollution taxes, 86
Posner, Richard, 245
poultry imports, 171

poverty, 277–278, 303, 304
power problems, 277
PPMs. *See* process and production methods
precautionary principle, 46
   AB and, 106
   Article XX and, 48
   GATT and, 48
   Hormones decision and, 46, 106
   international law and, 122
   risk assessments and, 122
   SPS Agreement and, 46, 118, 122
   WTO and, 47
prisoners' dilemma, 195
private powers, 283
probability theory, 267
procedural requirements, 125
process and production methods (PPMs), 54, 56
   Article III and, 56, 58, 61
   Article XI and, 61
   Article XX and, 58
   Asbestos case and, 57
   developing countries and, 58–59
   distinctions based on, 56
   GATT and, 54
   SPS Agreement and, 63, 69
   TBT Agreement and, 59
   technical regulation and, 59
   territoriality and
   Tokyo Standards Code and, 58
process-based measures, 191
process standards, 172
product-by-product testing, 161
progesterone, 262
proportionality tests, 22, 25, 137
protectionism, 110, 199, 215, 232
   AB and, 206
   accusation of, 207
   agricultural products and, 12
   aims and effects analysis and, 91–92
   ALOP and, 24, 50
   antiprotection principle and, 101
   appropriate level of protection, 24, 141–143, 147
   Article III and, 6, 17, 194, 198, 216, 220, 221, 222
   Article XX and, 20, 34, 108
   barriers and, 169
   competitive relationships, 200
   consumers and, 196
   definition of, 2
   discrimination obligation, 4, 14, 259
   dispute tribunals, 222
   domestic production and, 2
   efficiency and, 198
   GATT and, 9
   goals of, 197
   HAP life and, 156
   health and safety measures and, 45

336 Index

protectionism (*cont.*)
  Hormones decision and, 262
  human rights and, 308, 315
  intent and, 91
  international standards and, 32, 35
  Japan-Alcohol and, 89, 216
  Korea-Beef and, 103
  less favourable treatment and, 90, 97
  liability laws, 212
  likeness and, 86–87, 89, 217
  market access and, 81–82
  means by which, 156
  national treatment, 3. *See* national treatment
    principle
  national values and, 200
  necessity test, 149
  non-discrimination obligation, 4, 14, 259
  optimum tariffs, 197
  origin-neutral measures, 219
  regulatory purpose and, 79, 190, 204, 208, 209,
    222, 257–258
  risk assessment and, 45, 166
  Salmon case and, 169
  scientific evidence and, 32, 166, 258
  SPS Agreement and, 31, 32, 44, 146
  tariffs and, 2–3, 78–79, 85–86, 91, 209
  Uruguay Round and, 9
  See also specific decisions, products
protest demonstrations, 77
public powers, 283
purpose, ascertainability of, 201

quarantine policies, 135, 143
Quebec Summit Declaration, 273

rationality test, 137, 138
Rawls, J., 272, 287, 295, 313
Reagan administration, 6
reasonableness test, 23, 255
redistribution, of wealth, 273
Reformulated Gasoline decision, 105
regulation, 215
  Appellate Body and, 210
  Article III and, 190, 222–223
  Article XX and, 222–223
  domestic, 257
  less favourable treatment and, 195
  like products and, 190, 213, 215, 223
  obstacles and, 257–258
  protectionism and, 79, 208, 209, 257–258
  purpose of, 79, 190, 204, 208, 209, 222, 257–258
  scientific evidence and, 257
  TBT Agreement and, 257–258
restricting trade, 258
risk assessment, 33, 113, 125, 130, 166, 167
  Appellate Body and, 125, 126, 264

  burden of proof and, 252
  causes and, 168
  cross-cultural studies, 168
  definition of, 161, 264
  health risks and, 45, 107, 231–232
  Hormones decision and, 5, 107, 185
  literature on, 167
  precautionary principle, 122
  prevention and, 109
  probability and, 267, 268
  protectionism and, 166
  safe use procedures, 116
  Safeguards Agreement, 55
  Salmon case and, 161
  scientific evidence and, 253–254
  SPMs Agreement and, 260–261, 262, 264
  SPS Agreement and, 33, 35–36, 45, 125, 260–261,
    262, 264
  TBT Agreement and, 33, 35–36, 60
  technological society and, 170–171
  terrorism and, 171
  toxicity and, 168
  Varietals dispute and, 185
  zero risk, 109, 114
Ruggie, John, 169
rule-exception analysis, 120
rule of law, 293, 313
Rwanda, 321

Sanitary and Phytosanitary Measures Agreement
  (SPS), 4–5, 9, 13, 21, 22, 41, 44, 155, 178, 206, 260
  AB and, 7–8, 46
  ALOP and, 44
  Annex A of, 31, 35, 60
  Antidumping Agreement, 229
  appropriate level in, 24, 151–152
  Article 3 of, 118, 119
  Article 4 of, 41
  Article 5.1 of, 125
  Article 5.5 of, 127
  Article 5.6 of, 250
  Article III and, 69. *See also* Article III
  Article XX and, 6, 11, 28, 44, 45, 53, 68, 134, 140,
    141, 156. *See also* Article XX
  biosafety and, 13
  burden of proof and, 118, 129, 252
  Codex standards and, 35–36
  consistency requirement, 157, 169
  discrimination and, 20, 21. *See also*
    discrimination
  disputes and, 188
  double function in, 179
  DSU and, 229. *See also* DSU
  EC and, 33
  embedded liberalism model, 170
  on equivalence, 41

Index

evidentiary problem, 148
executive branch and, 175, 176, 179
expert advice and, 243, 244–245
food safety and, 173
GATT and, 9, 66, 68, 69, 74, 133
goals of, 162–163
government action and, 118
HAP life or health, 141
harmonization and, 157, 164, 172, 174
Hormones decision and, 5, 20, 63, 130, 132
international standards, 37, 80, 123, 164
legal provisions of, 4
level of protection, 156, 168–169
Mad Cow scare and, 260
meaning of, 118
measures in, 163
national standard and, 36
necessity tests, 25, 29, 54, 134, 140, 149, 150
NGOs and, 174
non-compliance with, 70
non-discrimination obligation, 4, 14, 259
non-trade values, 140
novelty of, 181
origin of, 11
panel authority, 249
PPMs and, 63, 69. *See also* PPMs
precautionary principle, 46, 118, 122
protectionism and, 31, 32, 44, 146. *See also*
    protectionism
reasonableness and, 23
recognition and, 41
risk assessments, 33, 35–36, 43, 45, 125, 260–261,
    262, 264
scientific evidence and, 7–8, 31, 166, 260, 261
standard of review, 121
standard-setting, 35
straightjacket argument, 173
tariffs and, 164
TBT and, 73, 78. *See also* TBT Agreement
third-party submissions, 180
trade-restrictive measures, 29
transparency obligations, 157–158, 160
TRIPs and, 156
types of, 155
Uruguay Round and, 79, 155
Varietals dispute and, 6, 153
Vienna Convention and, 70
warning signals, 43
WTO and, 4, 153, 162–163, 175, 176, 260
zero-risk approach, 146
sardines. *See EC-Sardines* case
scarcity problems, 277, 303–304
Schoenbaum, T., 140
scientific evidence, 47, 166
    burden of proof and, 254–255
    consistency requirement, 258–259, 268

experts and, 253–254. *See also* expert advice
international standards, 32
opposing opinions, 252
protectionism and, 166, 258
regulation and, 257
risk assessments and, 32
sovereignty and, 257, 259
SPS Agreement and, 7–8, 31, 166, 260, 261
TBT Agreement and, 260
WTO and, 258, 259, 261
SCM provision, 15
Seattle protests, 77, 173
shrimp, 26, 91
Skidmore test, 230
smell test, 7, 234
Smith, Adam, 303, 304
social market economy, 307
socially responsible products, 58
sorption levels, 161
South Africa, 280
sovereignty, 258
    open trade and, 7
    scientific evidence and, 257, 259
    WTO and, 7, 258, 259
specialization, 170, 281
SPS. *See* Sanitary and Phytosanitary Measurement
    Agreement
standard of review, 121, 257
Standards and Trade Development Facility, 167
Standards Code, 12, 20, 259
strict scrutiny test, 54
subsidiarity principle, 35
Subsidies Agreement, 235, 241, 251
substantive standards, 172
substitutable products, 220, 239
Sunstein, Cass, 97
Sykes, A. O., 7
synecdoche, 175

Tanzania, 174–175
tariffs, 2–3, 78–79, 85–86, 91, 209. *See also*
    protectionism
Technical Barriers to Trade (TBT) Agreement, 4–5,
    9, 19, 28, 38, 53, 158
    Annex 1 of, 58, 61
    Article III and, 19, 71, 103
    Article XX and, 11, 19, 28, 29, 106
    Asbestos dispute and, 98, 104
    Biosafety Protocol, 13
    Codex Stan 94 and, 39
    consistency requirement and, 45
    developing countries and, 58–59
    disputes and, 236
    environment and, 261
    on equivalence, 42
    expert advice and, 48, 243, 260

338   **Index**

Technical Barriers to Trade (TBT) Agreement (*cont.*)
    GATT and, 9, 66, 71, 75, 99, 106
    HAP life or health and, 261
    international standards, 38, 39, 110
    July 2000 decision, 37
    least restrictive measures, 107–108
    legal provisions of, 4
    like products and, 19, 20, 72
    MFN principle and, 101
    national regulation and, 13
    National Treatment obligations, 101
    necessity tests and, 25, 72
    Operative Provisions of, 104
    origin of, 11
    PPMs and, 59
    Preamble to, 33, 104, 105, 109
    regulatory obstacles, 257–258
    risk assessments, 33, 35–36, 60
    scientific evidence and, 48, 260
    SPS Agreement and, 73
    technical regulation and, 61–62, 74, 100, 103, 110
    Uruguay Round and, 20, 79
    WTO and, 78, 260
Technical Committee on Customs Valuation, 235, 241
technical regulations
    definition of, 98, 103
    PPMs and, 59
    standards and, 62, 110. *See also specific cases*
    TBT Agreement and, 74, 100, 103
technological society, 170–171
technology transfer, 323
telecommunications
territoriality, 54
terrorism, 171
testosterone, 262
Textiles Agreement, 55, 238, 241
Thai Cigarette case, 105, 112, 116, 139
tobacco, 105, 112, 116, 139, 212
Tokyo Round, 11, 12, 20, 259
Tokyo Standards Code, 58, 59
toxicity, 99, 168, 232, 233
Trachtman, Joel, 4, 133, 139
trade and environment debate, 173
trade and issues, 163
trade contracts, 2
trade groups, 165
trade liberalization. *See* liberalization
trade-off decisions, 152
trade-off mechanisms, 133, 134, 137
Trade-Related Intellectual Property Rights (TRIPS),
    1, 2, 35, 80, 156, 251, 286–287, 321, 322, 323
transparency, 102, 157–158
treaty interpretation, 227
TRIPs. *See* Trade-Related Intellectual Property
    Rights

Türk, E., 5
tuna, 54, 90–91
Turkey-Textiles case, 5, 65
turtles, 91

UDHR. *See* Universal Declaration of Human Rights
United Nations (UN)
    Charter of,
    Committee on Economic, Social and Cultural
       Rights, 304, 309–310, 311, 321, 324–325
    Convention of the Elimination on
       Discrimination of Women, 300
    Convention of the Rights of the Child, 286, 300,
       324–325
    Covenants of 1966, 300
    FAO, 311
    Global Compact, 271
    human rights, 274–275, 280, 311. *See also* human
       rights
    specialized agencies, 324
    UDS and, 158. *See also* UDS
    UN citizenship, 309
    unemployment rates, 85
    UNESCO, 311
    UNICEF, 311
United States
    AB and, 23, 25, 26, 28
    Alcohol case and, 54, 190–191, 206. *See*
       Japan-Alcohol case
    apple imports. *See Japan-Varietals* case
    Article XX and, 51–52
    burden of proof and, 119–120
    Constitution of, 293, 301, 314–315
    Copyright Act, 251
    discrimination and, 44
    Hormones case and, 44, 119, 179. *See also*
       EC-Hormones case
    international organizations and, 10
    MTO and, 10
    poultry imports, 171
    prohibitions on, 154–155
    Shrimp decision and, 26, 34, 42, 44, 51–52, 243
    steel and, 66
    Supreme Court, 317
    Tariff Act of 1930, 138
    Universal Declaration of Human Rights (UDHR),
       272, 284–285, 300
    VTR and, 160
    Wool Shirt case, 118
Universal Declaration of Human Rights (UDHR),
    272, 284–285, 288
Uruguay Round, 10, 11, 12, 20, 61, 259–260, 309
    Agriculture Agreement, 155
    DSU and, 12, 183
    Ministerial Declaration, 9
    necessity test and, 28–29

Index

339

protectionism and, 9
SPS and, 79, 141, 155. *See also* SPS Agreement
TBT and, 20, 79. *See also* TBT Agreement
US-Gasoline case and, 23, 26, 27–28, 44, 52, 64–65, 73
US-Lamb Safeguard case, 55
US-Line Pipe case, 64
US-Malt Beverages case, 190, 215
US-Shrimp decision, 26
US-Wheat Gluten case, 228
US-Wool Shirts case, 118

Victor, David, 165
Vienna Convention, 11, 19, 41–42, 47, 70, 116, 227

warning signals, 43, 44–45
Washington Consensus, 272
wealth, redistribution of, 273
Weiler, Joseph, 96
welfare rights, 275
Weller, J., 5
wheat, 228
Wheat Gluten case, 228
WHO. *See* World Health Organization
WIPO. *See* World Intellectual Property Organization
World Bank, 310
World Health Organization (WHO), 1, 83, 110–111, 311
World Intellectual Property Organization (WIPO), 35, 251, 310, 311
World Trade Center, 231
World Trade Organization (WTO), 4, 320
    AB and, 5. *See* Appellate Body
    Advisory Centre on WTO Law, 238
    aggressive litigation, 236
    Agreement on Customs Valuation, 235
    Agriculture Agreement, 155, 235
    Annex 1A, 65, 67–68
    antiprotection principle, 100
    authority of states, 163
    Balance of Payments and Regional Trade, 242
    Biodiversity Convention, 13
    Biosafety Protocol, 13
    comparative advantage, 163
    conflicts, 65
    conflicts and, 65. *See* DSU
    criticisms of, 77–78
    delegalization of, 184
    Domestic Regulation of Goods, 9
    executive branch officials, 179
    expert advice, 7. *See* expert advice
    external legitimacy of, 5, 96
    GATT and, 60, 74, 75, 163. *See* GATT

General Council, 174
general exceptions, 290–291, 321
General Interpretative Note, 65
Global Compact, 271
guarantees of freedom, 313
human rights and, 312, 313
institutional balance in, 242
internal regulations, 77
international law, 47
Law Advisory Centre, 238
Legal Drafting Group, 10
Marrakesh Agreement, 9, 10, 13
members of, 175
minimalist approach in, 182
Ministerial Conference, 174
model of negative regulation, 173
national health policies, 1
necessity tests, 22, 23, 136
non-discrimination and, 78
non-trade values, 133, 136
official WTO languages, 237
panels and, 15, 235
Permanent Group of Experts, 241
political organs of, 242
precautionary principle, 47
public interest clauses, 320
rule of law, 313
scientific evidence, 258, 259, 261
Seattle meeting, 77–78
secondary legislation, 41
Secretariat, 174, 238, 246
sovereignty and, 7, 258, 259
SPS Agreement, 4, 37, 153, 162–163, 174, 176, 260
standard of review, 6
state practice, 175
straightjacket argument, 173, 174, 184
subsidies agreement, 241
synecdoche and, 175
TBT Agreement and, 4, 78, 260
third-party submissions, 179
Trade Policy Review Mechanism, 325
TRIPs Agreement and, 2
Vienna Convention, 41–42

Yugoslavia, 321

zero-risk policy, 148, 264
    cost-benefit analysis and, 267
    necessity tests, 146
    Salmon case and, 267
    SPS Agreement and, 146

For EU product safety concerns, contact us at Calle de José Abascal, 56–1°,
28003 Madrid, Spain or eugpsr@cambridge.org.

www.ingramcontent.com/pod-product-compliance
Ingram Content Group UK Ltd.
Pitfield, Milton Keynes, MK11 3LW, UK
UKHW020202060825
461487UK00017B/1504